D1038115

MEN IN THE AIR

Also by Brandt Aymar

Cruising Is Fun

The Complete Cruiser

Guide to Boatmanship, Seamanship,
and Safe Boat Handling

Cruising Guide

A Pictorial Treasury of the Marine
Museums of the World

The Young Male Figure

A Pictorial History of the World's Great Trials
from Socrates to Jean Harris
(with Edward Sagarin)

Laws and Trials That Created History
(with Edward Sagarin)

Also edited by Brandt Aymar

Men at Sea

Treasury of Snake Lore

The Personality of the Cat

The Deck Chair Reader

The Personality of the Bird

The Personality of the Horse

The Personality of the Dog

MEN IN THE AIR

The Best Flight Stories of All Time from Greek Mythology to the Space Age

Edited and with an Introduction
by Brandt Aymar

FOREWORD BY WALTER J. BOYNE

CROWN PUBLISHERS, INC. / NEW YORK

Published by Crown Publishers, Inc., 201 East 50th Street, New York, New York 10022

CROWN is a trademark of Crown Publishers, Inc.

Manufactured in the United States of America

For Acknowledgments see pages 553–557.

Library of Congress Cataloging-in-Publication Data

Men in the air : the best flight stories of all time from Greek mythology to the space age : an anthology of fact and fiction with a special section on Women in the air / edited and with an introduction by Brandt Aymar ; foreword by Walter J. Boyne.
p. cm.
1. Aeronautics—Miscellanea. I. Aymar, Brandt. II. Title: Women in the air.
TL546.7.M45 1989
629.13'09—dc20 89-10012
CIP

ISBN 0-517-57403-9

Design by Jake Victor Thomas

10 9 8 7 6 5 4 3 2 1

First Edition

To
John Marshall,
a fellow traveler on many wonderful flights

Contents

Mythological Flights

Interplanetary Flights: Imaginative

Human-Powered Flights

Balloons

Dirigibles

Early Manned Flights

Other Pioneer Flights

Barnstorming and Airshows

Air Battles

World War I

World War II

Vietnam

Storms

The Prop Age

The Jet Age

The Space Age

Women in the Air

Foreword

by

Walter J. Boyne

Brandt Aymar renders a double service with his fine anthology *Men in the Air.* In his introduction, he provides a wonderfully succinct history of flight keyed to his selections; the book itself offers some of the most stimulating passages ever written about air and space.

It is a tribute to his discrimination that Brandt includes not only great writers who happened to write about aviation—James A. Michener, Guy Murchie, Tom Wolfe—but, in addition, an abundant supply of that rarer commodity, great pilots who were also excellent writers. Pilots are often portrayed as resolute pragmatists, used to making decisions on the spot and forcing events to conform to needs without taking a great deal of time for reflection. Yet one has only to read the passages from Beryl Markham, Antoine de Saint-Exupéry, or Stephen Coonts to realize that pilots can also be poets.

The reason for this might be found in the ancient legend, "Flying is hours of boredom occasionally broken by moments of stark terror." There is often time for reflection in flight, when things are going well, when the weather is beautiful, when the sense of accomplishment is strong. It is then that the pilots are inspired and the seeds for future stories are sown. Then, when an engine lets go and all hell breaks loose, inspiration is tempered in a fire of anxiety that lends reality to the telling.

Men in the Air is a meaty book, one of marvelously extended scope, and it paints the true picture of the complex fabric of flying from the fragile wax wings of Daedalus to the fragile O rings of the *Challenger.* Brandt's selections successfully interweave the drama of human striving, all its tragic and comic overtones, with the unsurpassable beauty of flight. Perhaps the one common denominator in this journey from myth to Mars is the reaffirmation that the human spirit is the sole indispensable element. And this is illustrated perfectly in the section on women in the air, where we learn not only of Amelia Earhart's aerial sentiments, but also of the views of Christa McAuliffe on space.

This sense of spirit is particularly well illustrated by two very disparate groups of selections. In his "Interplanetary Flights: Imaginative," Brandt has selected authors who are able to put the reader into fantasy situations, where only the skill of the writer makes the hazards and the challenges believable. In direct contrast, in his section "Human-Powered Flights," one finds the gritty, sweaty reality of man as horsepower, a man/machine who must function perfectly to stay aloft. In both cases—imaginary and guttily true—the single element that melds the two themes together, and that really gives meaning to the whole concept of flight, is the unconquerable human essence.

This is a book for bedside reading, one to savor and to inspire dreams. Its strength and richness stems from its reflection of so many different points of view. It is fascinating to compare, for example, William Faulkner's picture of the golden age of racing in *Pylon* with that of Don Dwiggins' in *They Flew the Bendix Race.* The whole outcome of World War II in the air can be inferred by contrasting the understated but triumphant tone of Larry Forrester's *Fly for Your Life* with the sometimes strident but pessimistic air of Heinz Knöke's *I Flew for the Führer.* And the broad spectrum of flying's experience can be found by relating the exuberance of Jack Broughton's "Fifteen Sams for Geeno" with the poetry of Francis Chichester's *The Lonely Sea and the Sky.*

Like *Men at War,* the anthology of war stories put together by Ernest Hemingway many years ago, Aymar has created in *Men in the Air* both a source and a goad; reading it is wonderfully worthwhile, but it also demands that you read the entire works from which the selections were taken. I know you will enjoy it.

MEN IN THE AIR

Introduction

by Brandt Aymar

The history of man goes back thousands of years, and for all that time he dreamed that perhaps one day he would be able to fly through the sky like the birds. The history of the airplane goes back hardly a century, yet in that span of time man has seen these wildest dreams become a reality. This anthology of flight literature offers a brief glimpse into what the realization of these dreams cost him; the hopes and frustrations, the daring and daredevil, the sacrificed lives, the victories and casualties of war, the scientific breakthroughs, and the ultimate conquests of space.

It is divided into fourteen categories, covering mythological flights; imaginative flights; early flights; lighter-than-air flights; pioneering flights; barnstormings; air battles from World War I to Vietnam; flights in raging storms; prop, jet, and space flights; and the remarkable achievements of women in the air. The stories include both fiction and nonfiction and, as in the case of most anthologies, are chosen on purely personal grounds.

Greek gods and Greek heroes had no problem at all with aeronautics. When the imprisoned Daedalus and his son Icarus planned their escape from their incarceration in King Minos's tower, they constructed wings for themselves and simply flew away. Unfortunately, because the impetuous Icarus flew too high and into the sun, the wax on his wings melted so that he plunged headlong into the sea to his death. Daedalus, however, reached his destination safely—a triumph for early aviation?

Another mythological flying triumph was achieved when Perseus, with the aid of winged shoes given him by Mercury, flew to the rescue of the beautiful princess Andromeda. Chained to a rock, she fearfully awaited a cruel fate: to be devoured by a monster sea serpent. Just in time, like an eagle, Perseus swooped down and carried her away.

In a work of seventeenth-century fiction Daniel Defoe describes the building of *The Consolidator,* a mammoth craft constructed with 513 special feathers, commandeered from all parts of a prince's kingdom for the purpose of their long-awaited experiment of a voyage to the moon. Even in those days they were known as "high flyers."

In "To the Planet of the Apes" by novelist Pierre Boulle, Ulysse Mérou in the year 2500 embarks with two companions in a cosmic ship with all intention of reaching the supergigantic star Betelgeuse. "Two years after leaving our Earth we came down gently and landed without a jolt in the middle of the plateau."

From the incomparable Isaac Asimov comes *The Martian Way,* the story of the Martian extraterrestials' journey "To Saturn and Back." Their mission was to supply Mars with an adequate supply of desperately needed drinking water. From the ice rings around Saturn they dislodged a huge mountain of ice containing half a billion tons of water and brought it back to Mars. In a burst of generosity they promised the water-parched Earth shipments of ice in "million-ton lots—for a reasonable fee."

While da Vinci's designs never got off the ground, *The Mechanical Investigations of Leonardo da Vinci* during the fourteenth century laid the foundations for transforming the principles of bird flight into practical human use. Ivor B. Hart's careful study of da Vinci's manuscripts clearly shows that he was not only a real pioneer of the science of flight, but also the *first* pioneer.

In Samuel Johnson's *Rasselas* (1759), a prince fosters a flying attempt by a confident maker of wings, with disastrous results. However, Johnson predicted that as man "mounted higher, the earth's attraction, and the body's gravity, would be gradually diminished, till we shall arrive at a region where man will float in the air without any tendency to fall."

More than two hundred years later, on June 12, 1979, a remarkable success was achieved in human-powered flight when the *Gossamer Albatross* successfully crossed the English Channel, as each agonizing moment is described by Morton Grosser. Pedaling for dear life, Bryan Allen, a twenty-one-year-old California biologist, overcame exhaustion and near defeat to win the Kremer £100,000 Competition. It was the largest prize in the history of aviation.

"Up in the First Balloon" by John Lonzo Anderson opens the section on balloons and dirigibles. The famous Montgolfière brothers, Joseph and Etienne, lit the fires that sent aloft the first manned balloon over Paris on November 20, 1783.

Scarcely a year later, Vincent Lunardi describes in great detail his solo balloon flight as the first aerial voyage in England.

Early in 1785 Dr. John Jeffries, with Monsieur Blanchard, was the first to cross the English Channel in a balloon. The good doctor describes each harrowing moment from the time they left Dover until they descended in a forest outside of Calais, France.

Not only were Jules Verne's famous stories about the sea, but he told many of the sky as well. In *Five Weeks in a Balloon* his balloonists were caught up in an African equatorial storm that tossed them about unmercifully. But they did enjoy one of the grandest spectacles that Nature could offer as "The Tempest" abated.

John Wise was perhaps the country's most famous balloonist in the mid-1800s. Jack R. Hunt tells the story of "The Greatest Air Voyage Ever Made," in which Wise and three other intrepid companions took off on July 1, 1859, from St. Louis, Missouri, on board the *Atlantic,* the largest balloon in the world. The next day they landed in a tree in the township of Henderson, New York, after one of the roughest balloon trips ever made.

Guy Murchie whets your aeronautical appetite with a brief overview of major historical experiments in flying, from the eleventh century to balloon and parachute jumps during World War I, in the chapter called "Floating on Air" from his book *Song of the Sky.*

The history of dirigibles was a short one, inevitably ending in disaster. John G. Fuller conveys the concerns felt by those who had friends on the R-101 as the giant dirigible left Cardington, England, for India in October 1930. She crashed on a hill near Beauvais, France. A brief dispatch from Reuters in Paris read: "R-101 has exploded in flames. Only six saved."

Lieutenant Commander C. E. Rosendahl lived to tell the tale of "The Loss of the *Shenandoah*" in his book *Up Ship!* On September 2, 1925, the *Shenandoah* left Lakehurst, New Jersey, for a six-day "publicity" trip. Near Caldwell, Ohio, she was engulfed in a devastating squall that sent her out of control. In spite of the brave action of every crew member, the ship was literally torn apart and fell to the earth in a tangled mass.

The noted historian A. A. Hoehling gives us a superb moment-by-moment account of "The End of the *Hindenburg.*" On May 6, 1937, the mammoth dirigible arrived at Lakehurst, New Jersey, after her trip from Frankfurt, Germany. As the stunned spectators watched in horror, the greatest dirigible in the world burst into flames. The era of the Zeppelin had come to an end.

The historic demonstrations by Wilbur and Orville Wright were the first free-flights through the air in a motor-driven aeroplane. On December 17, 1903, after three test attempts, their fourth succeeded in a sustained flight of 852 feet for 59 seconds. Modern aviation was born.

Nearly six years later Louis Blériot made the first cross-channel flight on July 26, 1909. At 4:35 in the morning his plane rose from Calais on the coast of France and headed for England. Blown off his intended course to Dover, he landed on a convenient and inviting green spot on the English coast.

The rapid advance in the development of primitive aircraft is no better demonstrated than in several planes developed in 1910 by Igor I. Sikorsky. In his autobiography, *The Story of the Winged-S,* he explains his many problems with the S-2 and S-3, as he looks forward to an improved S-4 and S-5.

After the end of World War I aviators of all nations faced the challenge of who would be the first to fly across the Atlantic. Spurred on by Lord Northcliffe's £10,000-prize offer for the first nonstop transatlantic flight, innumerable teams of British aviators arrived in Newfoundland, the staging area for the planned race. One of the entrants was Captain John Alcock and Lieutenant Arthur Whitten-Brown, a pair of Royal Air Force fliers. Their plane was a converted bomber, a Vickers-Vimy biplane powered by two 350-hp Rolls-Royce engines. They took off from St. John on June 14, 1919. On the next day they landed in Clifden, Ireland, just sixteen hours, twelve minutes after leaving St. John 1,980 miles behind. For their feat, King George V knighted them.

From *We,* the personal and stirring chronicle of the world-famous transatlantic solo flight on May 20, 1927, comes Charles A. Lindbergh's own account of his flight in *The Spirit of St. Louis* from New York to Paris. As he landed at the Le Bourget airfield, "The entire field was covered with thousands of people all running toward my ship."

A few weeks later on June 5, 1927, Charles A. Levine, owner, and Clarence Chamberlain, pilot, surprised everyone, most of all Levine's wife, Grace, by simply taking off in their monoplane *Columbia* and heading for Berlin, Germany. Fuel ran out shortly before their intended destination, so they landed in a wheat field near the town of Eisleben, 110 miles short of Berlin. Richard Montague re-creates for you their exciting experiences in his *Oceans, Poles and Airmen.*

In *Skyward* Richard E. Byrd successfully reaches the North Pole in the *Josephine Ford,* a three-engine Fokker monoplane powered by 200-hp Wright air-cooled engines. "At 9:02 A.M., May 9, 1926, Greenwich civil time, our calculations showed us to be at the Pole! The dream of a lifetime had at last been realized."

The Atlantic Ocean and the North Pole having been conquered by early aviators, there remained the vast expanses of the Pacific. Nothing daunted, four Australian flyers made history with their *Flight of the Southern Cross.* Their first hop was from San Francisco, California, to Hawaii on May 21, 1928. But the longest leg was from Kauai, Hawaii, to Suva in the Fiji Islands, thence to Brisbane, Australia. In their book the authors, C. E. Kingsford-Smith and C. T. P. Ulm, vividly describe their bouts with rainstorms, blind flying, motor shimmies, even their radio's conking out. Toward the end of their flight they recall: "Above us as we emerged from the murk glittered the Southern Cross, the constellation whose name we were proud to bear on our ship."

One of America's most prominent authors, William Faulkner, devoted his famous novel *Pylon* (1935) to the subject of aviation. In his chapter called "And Tomorrow" the reporter covers the race that pilot Shumann, badly in need of the $2,000-prize money, enters. In spite of the attempts to disqualify his plane, a crate unfit to fly, he takes off and is soon in the lead. Neck and neck with his leading adversary he reaches the last pylon, and Shumann seems to be winning. Then it happened!

"The First International Aeroplane Contest" took place at Rheims, France, August 22 to 29, 1909. Glenn Curtiss had been chosen by the Aero Club of America to represent his country in the Gordon Bennett contest. His chief opponent was the noted French flyer Blériot. The day of the big race arrived (August 29) and each contestant was timed on his two runs on the twenty-kilometer course. Whoever clocked the best average time was declared the winner. Glenn Curtiss won as his friend, Mr. Bishop, cried out excitedly: "Blériot is beaten by six seconds!"

The 1947 Bendix Race was from the Metropolitan Airport, Van Nuys, California, to the Bendix home pylon in Cleveland, Ohio. It is admirably presented by Don Dwiggins in *They Flew the Bendix Race.* The winner that year was Paul Mantz in a Mustang, a North American P-51. He had won the $10,000 prize at 435 miles per hour, more than 200 miles faster than Jimmy Doolittle's speed when he won the first Bendix Race in 1931.

The popular writer and author of *Guy Gilpatric's Flying Stories* has given us "The Wing Walker" about a lady daredevil named Mary Muller. Mary and Tommy Dean were featured performers in Dean's Flying Circus. On this particular day, Labor Day, they were to perform the hazardous double aerial loop, with Mary on the wing about to transfer to the accompanying plane. As the ships bumped, Mary's arm smacked into the whirling propeller.

Man being of a warring race, it is only logical that the longest section in this anthology of flight covers air battles.

As America entered World War I, the two most famous flying aces to emerge were Eddie V. Rickenbacker for the Americans and Baron Manfred von Richthofen for Germany. In "Downing My First Hun," Eddie Rickenbacker, on April 19, 1918, finds himself over enemy lines and on the tail of a German Pfalz. "At 150 yards I pressed my triggers," then watched as the enemy plane "crashed onto the ground."

Gene Gurney, the prodigiously prolific wartime writer, has written a graphic account of "The Day They Got Richthofen." On April 21, 1918, the German "Red Baron" took off in his Fokker triplane to lead his squadron into combat. Twenty-five minutes earlier Capt. Roy Brown had lifted his British Sopworth Camel from Bertangles field. Flying with him as wingman was H. Wilfred R. May, on his first flight over their front lines. The German plane and the British were soon engaged in a dogfight. May's plane was hit by the Red Baron, but Brown managed to fire a procession of bullets along the Baron's fuselage. "A bullet struck home and Richthofen slumped forward."

Winged Victory by V. M. Yeates is one of the best British war novels to come out of the First World War. It appeared in 1934 and brilliantly conveyed the close friendship of the young pilots in a Flying Corps Squadron on the Western front. In "A Most Remarkable Escape" Tom, our RAF pilot, went into bombing action over the trenches. He was besieged by a dozen enemy planes and withering ground fire from below. He was badly wounded. His Aldis plane was smashed to bits and breaking up. Yet somehow he made it back. The total number of bullet holes his plane sustained was more than sixty, a truly remarkable escape.

Lt. Frank Luke, Jr., of the U.S. Air Service, 27th Aero Squadron, made it his specialty to attack and destroy German observer balloons. Effectively flying his Spad he scored eighteen aerial victories in seventeen days. In James C. Law's account, "They Called Him the Indestructible 'Balloon Buster,' " this American ace, on September 12, 1918, near the village of Murvaux, France, volunteered to attack an observation balloon, the most dangerous target in the air. Soon the balloon burst into flames. Two days later he made an attack on a cluster of three balloons near Boinville and claimed one, then returned the next day and destroyed a second. He was finally brought down attacking three more balloons at Murvaux. Posthumously he was awarded the Congressional Medal of Honor, the first flier to win this highest award.

It was every British pilot's wish to fly the first radically designed "Spitfires" prior to the start of World War II. In *Fly for Your Life* Larry Forrester tells how R. R. Stanford Tuck was one of a few lucky men when in December 1938 he was sent to the Vickers (Supermarine) Works at Drixford. There he was indoctrinated in the intricacies of this plane's revolutionary new concept and became one of the air force's first qualified Spitfire pilots.

A top ace of the Battle of Britain, Douglas Bader had lost both legs in a plane crash in 1931. Yet in November 1939 he was a full-fledged Spitfire pilot. Paul Brickhill narrates his inspiring story in *Reach for the Sky.* In this segment Bader took part in the "Patrol Over Dunkirk." On his return he made an awful approach to the airfield that sheered off the plane's undercart. In spite of this, the next day he was appointed Squadron Leader, his first command!

One of Ernie Pyle's most heartwarming war stories is "Miracle at Sunset." America's favorite correspondent was covering the activities of our soldiers' first big campaign in Tunisia during the North African campaign. Late one afternoon the Flying Fortresses returned from their target mission to their airbase somewhere in the desert. That is, all except one.

Novelist Len Deighton in *Goodbye, Mickey Mouse* follows a group of young American fighter pilots as they flew mission after dangerous mission from an air base in Cambridge, England, their job—to protect the huge fleets of bombers penetrating deep into Germany. In "Mustangs *vs* Messerschmitts" the escort planes were returning across the Channel after bitter action with the enemy planes. The Mustangs had taken damaging hits and were practically out of gas. Captain James Farebrother's plane was only one of two to make it back.

In *I Flew for the Führer* Heinz Knöke tells of being shot down and parachuting to where the Somme Canal meets the River Oise. It happened during the last air battle against the Americans over French territory. By means of an artful ruse, he outwitted his captors and escaped to his own German patrol.

Generally, victorious pilots of all nations avoided shooting at parachuting enemies. This practice once saved the life of Erich Hartmann, the top-scoring German pilot of all time, with 352 confirmed victories to his credit. In *The Blond Knight of Germany* authors Raymond F. Toliver and Trevor J. Constable describe many of Hartmann's conflicts with the American Mustangs during the waning years of the war. That he lived to tell his tales he attributes to his basic rule for airfighting: "The pilot who sees the other first has half the victory."

Joseph Heller's *Catch-22* is one of the best-known American novels to come out of World War II. Set in the closing months of the war, it is about an American bomber squadron on a small island off Italy. Their first bombing of Bologna being a milk run, they assigned Yossarian to fly lead bombardier with McWatt in the first formation when they went back to Bologna the next day. The mission turned out to be the exact opposite of a milk run.

Innumerable accounts have been published of the diabolical Japanese attack on Pearl Harbor. In *Day of Infamy,* Walter Lord unfolds the blow-by-blow action from the Japanese side: the Pearl Harbor approach by the carrier task force under the leadership of Admiral Nagumo, and the thundering off of the torpedo planes and dive bombers led by Commander Mitsuo Fuchida. As they reached Oahu the clouds parted. In they hurtled. Lieutenant Commander Takahashi's twenty-seven dive bombers plunged toward Ford's Island and Hickam field, Lieutenant Commander Murata's forty torpedo planes swung into position for their run at the big ships. The rest is history.

One of James A. Michener's most famous *Tales of the South Pacific* is ironically called "The Milk Run." But as it turned out, this trip to Munda was anything but. Our pilot narrator was the unlucky guy that day. "One lousy Jap hit all day on that whole strike and it had to be me who got it." His gunman was killed at once, the plane glided into the water between Wanawana and Munda, sinking in fifteen seconds. There he was, stranded in the water with nothing but a life belt, and the enemy all around trying to finish him off. How the New Zealand pilots, our F4U's, and finally the two PT boats flown directly into enemy-held Munda harbor rescued him defies the wildest imagination.

Seven Hours to Zero by Joseph L. Marx is the dramatic minute-by-minute account of the *Enola Gay's* historic flight on August 6, 1945, to bomb Hiroshima, Japan. This selection, "Dropping the Bomb Over Hiroshima," covers the actual maneuvers of the three planes (the *Enola Gay, The Great Artiste,* and *#91*) moments before the *Enola Gay* released the atom bomb, the release itself, their escape maneuvers, and their avoidance of the shock wave of the aftermath. As soon as it was all over, the usual strike report had to be sent. It was brief and to the point: primary target bombed visually with good results.

In their epic novel of the U.S. Air Force, *The Wild Blue,* Walter J. Boyne and Steven L. Thompson include an event that occurred during the Vietnam War in November 1971 at Bien Hoa Air Base. Maj. Lawrence A. White, Operations Officer, 32nd Air Transport Squadron, VNAF, had been sent over as a training officer to the Vietnamese fliers. On this occasion he was accompanying two of their pilots on a flight to Kham Loc. A report crackled over the radio that a downed American C-130 needed assistance. Major White talked with them, agreeing to attempt a rescue. The Vietnamese pilots stubbornly objected, and the commander at first refused to surrender his seat to the American so that he could pilot the plane. White pulled out his .38 pistol and hissed: "Get your ass out of that seat." "The Rescue" was a success worthy of a

Medal of Honor. Instead the Vietnamese demanded that he be court-martialed.

They called their plane *Thud,* short for F-105 Thunderchief. Thud Ridge was the name for the line of hills leading to the heart of Hanoi. *Thud Ridge* is Col. Jack Broughton's highly personal account of the USAF pilots in the Vietnam conflict. One flyer, named Geeno, was nearing the end of his tour when, as mission commander, he was chosen to lead his planes on a bombing attack on the North Vietnam Thai Nguyen railroad yard and steel complex. The target was almost inaccessible, protected as it was by Sams, Migs, and ground fire. But Geeno was not to be daunted. Diving for the target he was surrounded by six perfectly guided Sams. But the American strike was a beauty, every plane hit the target and everyone got out. Everyone, that is, except Geeno.

On December 28, 1972, pilot Jake Grafton and his bombardier Tiger Cole were scheduled for their fifth Sam-suppression mission. Their target was on the northern edge of Hanoi. Stephen Coonts, in his gripping novel *Flight of the Intruder*, takes you into the cockpit as they approached the target area and were hit by intensive ground fire. The *Intruder* shuddered from the blows. Badly hurt, the plane nevertheless managed to reach the desired position over Hanoi, and they dropped their bombs. They then headed south from the city. But with the *Intruder* in such damaged condition they were faced with two choices: nurse the plane along in an attempt to reach Laos or eject over Hanoi. But suddenly they *had* no choice as the plane erupted in flames.

If violent storms are a scourge for ships they can be no less a danger for aircraft. In 1930 Antoine de Saint-Exupéry encountered a cyclone off the Argentine coast that he graphically describes in his book *Wind, Sand and Stars.* It was, he understates, "physically, much the most brutal and overwhelming experience I ever underwent." He had taken off from the field at Trelew and was flying down to Comodoro-Rivadavia, in the Patagonian Argentine. "The sky was blue. Pure blue. Too pure . . . Not a cloud . . . I was still flying in remarkably calm air . . . And then everything round me blew up."

Francis Chichester was no stranger to the violent elements of the sea, nor to those of the air. In *The Lonely Sea and the Sky* he had just reached the shore of Australia on the way to Sydney aboard his seaplane. Suddenly the elements broke loose. Blown off course, deluded by clouds that appeared to be land, blinded by heavy rain, he finally reached a great bay where he spotted five warships at anchor. Still eighty miles from Sydney, he realized he could never make it. How welcome was the offer from the approaching launch to tow him to the *Albatross,* the only aircraft carrier in the Southern Hemisphere, and the warm hospitality of Captain Feakes of the Royal Australian Navy. Even more welcome was his satisfaction that "I had achieved my great ambition, to fly across the Tasman Sea alone."

Royal Leonard was an American pilot who held the rank of captain in the Chinese Nationalist Army in 1941. For six years he flew all over China and wrote about his experiences in *I Flew for China.* On the last day of June 1941 he was ferrying a full load of twelve passengers aboard a Douglas DC-2 of the CNAC. To evade the Japanese patrols out of Canton, they flew at night from Kweilin to Hong Kong. Arriving at their destination they found Hong Kong in the throes of a deadly typhoon. Not only was it impossible to land, but the plane was lucky to escape at all. Eventually they landed at Namyung, two hundred miles away from Hong Kong.

David Lampe, Jr., in his sensational short story "Sucked Up in a Thundercloud" tells how Derek Piggott, chief glider instructor at Lasham Airfield in England, tried for his Gold-C international achievement badge for high altitude gliding. All was going well until the glider was unexpectedly sucked into a storm cloud. Spiraling upward at an alarming rate, he passed the 25,000-foot mark. In spite of experiencing violent electric shocks, ice, and finally anoxia, Derek Piggott at last achieved the record he sought.

In his personal memoir as an air transportation pilot, *Fate Is the Hunter,* Ernest K. Gann confesses what it truly felt like to be a neophyte pilot of an early DC-2 mail-passenger plane. Their designated route was known as AM-21; its eastern terminal Newark, New Jersey, its western, Cleveland, Ohio, with many stops on the way. On this initial flight Ross, his captain and patient teacher, was appalled at the serious errors made by his copilot, yet he never showed resentment or anger. The trip was a sheer nightmare for the new pilot, but in one way it turned out to be invaluable for the humility he learned.

Among the many places visited by the adventurous Richard Halliburton in his plane dubbed *The Flying Carpet,* none was more foreboding than the flight over the Matterhorn. On a previous visit he had climbed to its summit on foot with ropes and guides. Now, piloted by Captain Stephens, they were attempting to fly over the pinnacle of the Tiger of the Alps at sixteen thousand feet. But there were four other high peaks nearby that disoriented them. Vast waves of clouds rolled below them. Each of the mountaintops seemed to shift and change appearance. Pouring over their maps helped not at all. As they climbed higher and higher, they became hopelessly confused. Where *was* the Matterhorn?

It was a toss-up whether England or America would be the first to establish a regular transatlantic flight schedule. For years British aeronautical manufacturers had been working on a solidified version of their dream ship. Now the *Emperor* was ready for a round-trip test flight from London to New York and back. In David Beaty's suspenseful novel *The Proving Flight,* the prototype plane was on its return flight "when a sudden overwhelming clatter of ice and rain broke in a great splintering mass over the nose. . . . It was as though an iceberg had disintegrated on top of them." From then on the *Emperor* was in trouble.

On October 12, 1972, a Uruguayan air force plane, chartered by an amateur rugby team, took off from Montevideo, Uruguay, bound for Santiago, Chile. It entered a cloudbank over the Andes, lost altitude in a series of downdrafts, and crashed into a mountain peak. The heart-warming and inspiring story of the survivors is told by Piers Paul Read in *Alive.* This selection encompasses the immediate shock and dismay of some of the passengers as "The Crash" seemed imminent.

The soaring first novel by Jim Shepard, *Flights,* is both comic and compassionate. Buddy Siebert, a typical thirteen-year-old, has a dream in which he imagines himself jumping into a plane parked at the Bridgeport Flight Service and flying to East Hampton on Long Island. After all, he had read *The Lore of Flight,* the Cessna manual from the public library, and had a copy of Rand McNally's maps for that area. It should be a cinch! he thinks—until he actually takes off.

It was 1943. At forty thousand feet up it is bitterly cold, seventy degrees below zero. Lieutenant Colonel W. R. Lovelace of the Army Air Force stepped out into the emptiness of the gaping bomb bays of the B-17 to execute an unprecedented parachute jump. No man had ever done this before. Martin Caidin in *The Silken Angels* describes the hell and agony he suffered during this perilous descent. Twenty years later, a parachute opening at forty thousand feet was still considered one of the most dangerous experiences any man could face.

At the end of World War II the goal of the U.S. Army Air Force was to reach the speed of sound, known as Mach 1. The plane they planned to use for this purpose was called the X-1 and was built by the Bell Aircraft Corporation. But the test pilots approached for the job were asking an outrageous sum of $150,000. Charles E. Yeager readily agreed to do it for his regular army captain's pay. In *The Right Stuff* Tom Wolfe takes you upstairs with Yeager on that 14th day of October 1947 as the X-1 goes through the "sonic wall" without so much as a bump. Instead of immediately announcing the sky-shattering news, the brass at Wright Field clamped a top-security lid on the morning's events. But soon the world would know how Charles Yeager had gone faster than any man in history.

Stranger to the Ground by Richard Bach takes you with him in the U.S. jet fighter F-84F *Thunderstreak* on a hair-raising night flight over Europe in peacetime. It is a remarkable evocation of an airman's special world, thirty thousand feet above the earth. The trip began from the runway in England and progressed to its home base at Chaumont in France. Near its destination it was no longer possible to avoid bad weather. Suddenly the tiny plane was thrown violently out of control and plunged earthward. Then from the Ground Control Approach van came reassuring approach instructions. Shortly thereafter the plane came to rest on the runway, as the group crew slid the chocks in front of the tall wheels. Now the pilot was back on the ground of his airbase in France, yet for a moment he felt himself still an alien, still a stranger to the ground.

Of the many dangers facing test pilots at the Edwards Air Force Base at Muroc Dry Lake in California, none was more hazardous than a loss of oxygen, especially when the experimental US-XP reached an altitude of eighty thousand feet. In Jon Cleary's *The Flight of Chariots* it happened to Duke Dalmead. As he began his descent he felt himself on the edge of reality. It was up to Matt Crispin, flying the chase plane, to coax him down and save his life.

What really happened to the Korean Air Lines civilian jet Flight 007, shot down on September 1, 1983, over the Soviet Union's Sakhalin Island, killing all 269 passengers and crew? Seymour M. Hersh reveals the truth in his devastating book, *The Target Is Destroyed.* Five hours and twenty-six minutes after 007's takeoff from Anchorage, Alaska, only a minute or two from the Sea of Japan, the Soviet pilot of the SU-15 was ordered to destroy the aircraft. That the Korean pilot had strayed off course and technically penetrated Soviet airspace was no humane reason to send these civilian air passengers to their deaths. "They had a right to live!"

In their book, *We Seven,* the astronauts themselves share their exciting and suspenseful experiences in space. Included is John H. Glenn, Jr.'s, orbit in the Friendship 7. We now sit in the cockpit with him as he fires three retro-rockets on schedule for his re-entry into the atmosphere. Guided and instructed each second of the way down by Texas Cap Com, then, as he comes into view, by Cape Flight, Glenn completes his momentous mission as the first American astronaut to conquer space.

After centuries of fictional moon flights, American space programs finally achieved the ultimate goal of placing a man on the moon. On July 20, 1969, Apollo 11's lunar module, *Eagle,* landed at Tranquility Base in the Sea of Tranquility. In *Footprints on the Moon* Gene Gurney tells the whole thrilling story of that world-shaking mission, from takeoff, the voyage, the twelve orbits around the moon, the undocking of *Eagle* from *Columbia,* the landing, and the incredible tasks performed by Neil Armstrong and "Buzz" Aldrin while they loped about on the lunar surface gathering rocks and soil.

In Dale Brown's riveting thriller *Flight of the Old Dog,* the unthinkable happened—the Soviet Union developed a killer laser capable of destroying America's nuclear shield. Navy Comdr. Richard Seedeck, mission commander of the *Atlantis,* was assigned the task of activating the U.S. Star Wars space station *Ice Fortress.* His task was to make operational five X-ray laser satellites. To do this he had to transfer five of them from the cargo bay of the *Atlantis* and load them into the launch cylinder on *Ice Fortress.* Assisted by Jerrod Bates, a civilian defense contractor on board the *Atlantis,* the ticklish operation began. Number one was latched into position on the *Ice Fortress.* As Seedeck was maneuvering the second X-ray satellite, a massive explosion erupted on *Ice Fortress,* as one of the projectiles detonated. Bates' voice became a scream: "Mission Control, this is *Atlantis.* We have lost *Ice Fortress.*"

In Amelia Earhart's *Last Flight* she includes a section on her Mexican flight. On April 19, 1935, she left Burbank, California, in her Vega and landed in Mexico City about thirteen hours later. For the next week President Lazaro Cardenas graciously extended his official greetings and privileges. It was on the return trip that Amelia, against the advice of Wiley Post, took the dangerous route. She cut straight across the seven hundred miles of water of the Gulf of Mexico.

Sheila Scott, the world-famous British aviatrix, was the first solo pilot to reach the true North Pole in a light aircraft. She talks of the flight in her adventure-packed autobiography, *On Top of the World.* On June 25, 1971, she took off in her Aztec plane *Mythre.* Eight hours airborne and by now unable to raise any radio contact, she was lost. The only station she managed to contact was Nord in North Greenland, way off her course. She arrived there to a very hospitable reception and a deluge of telexes. Determined to continue to the Pole, she again took off, after spending hours to fill her inside cabin fuel tanks from barrels, using hand pumps. Again she encountered ice, freezing rain, and storm clouds, but forged ahead. Her precise calculations soon told her the time was right to be at ninety North. Opening her storm window she unfurled a tiny Union Jack and, against an icy blast, let it go, exclaiming triumphantly: "We're here—I'm on Top of the World."

In her remarkable paean to flying, *On Extended Wings,* award-winning poet Diane Ackerman tells how she gained mastery over the mysteries of flight and earned her private pilot's license. This selection finds her at the airport raring to solo for the first time, and pestering Martin, her flight instructor, to let her go up. He finally agrees and she quickly grabs the keys from the rack for plane 654. From the time she takes off, she makes all the wrong maneuvers, battles with her air speeds, confuses her radio contact, forgets to hold down the plane's nose, and many other student stupidities. "How could I have messed up that badly?" she thinks. Until, on landing, she hears over the loudspeaker a voice from the Unicom: "Nice flying, Six-five-four."

On January 28, 1986, a clear day over Cape Canaveral, the space shuttle *Challenger* exploded into a fiery ball of debris, taking the lives of seven crew members, among them a teacher, Sharon Christa McAuliffe. In his dedicated book *I Touch the Future,* Robert T. Hohler captures her extraordinary enthusiasm and commitment on being chosen by NASA to be the first teacher in space. This selection covers Christa's last days, when a series of delays kept postponing the flight. Finally, in spite of icicles on the platform, the countdown got underway until at 11:38 that morning "the solid rocket boosters ignited and *Challenger* shook the Earth good-bye."

Beryl Markham became the first person to fly solo across the Atlantic from east to west. Taking off from Abingdon, England, she crash-landed in Nova Scotia, twenty-one hours and twenty-five minutes later. She recounts her nightmarish experiences in her autobiographical book *West with the Night.* In September 1936 she took off in her Vega Gull on a flight that tested all her ingenuity in coping with storms and a failing engine. Finally, past Newfoundland it spluttered and died. Luckily she had just reached shore. As the plane hit the ground, the wheels submerged and the nose of the plane was engulfed in mud.

This anthology of both fictional and actual-experience flight stories attempts to give a representative sampling of what foresighted and courageous men and women endured as they sought to conquer the air. With such a wealth of material available, this collection barely taps the mass of flying literature. So it is my sincere hope that, in addition to bringing enjoyment, reading these selections will induce you to fly off in the pursuit of many further thrilling aviation stories.

DAEDALUS AND ICARUS

by Thomas Bullfinch

The labyrinth from which Theseus escaped by means of the clew of Ariadne was built by Daedalus, a most skilful artificer. It was an edifice with numberless winding passages and turnings opening into one another, and seeming to have neither beginning nor end, like the river Maeander, which returns on itself, and flows now onward, now backward, in its course to the sea. Daedalus built the labyrinth for King Minos, but afterwards lost the favor of the king, and was shut up in a tower. He contrived to make his escape from his prison, but could not leave the island by sea, as the king kept strict watch on all the vessels, and permitted none to sail without being carefully searched. "Minos may control the land and sea," said Daedalus, "but not the regions of the air. I will try that way." So he set to work to fabricate wings for himself and his young son Icarus. He wrought feathers together, beginning with the smallest and adding larger, so as to form an increasing surface. The larger ones he secured with thread and the smaller with wax, and gave the whole a gentle curvature like the wings of a bird. Icarus, the boy, stood and looked on, sometimes running to gather up the feathers which the wind had blown away, and then handling the wax and working it over with his fingers, by his play impeding his father in his labors. When at last the work was done, the artist, waving his wings, found himself buoyed upward, and hung suspended, poising himself on the beaten air. He next equipped his son in the same manner, and taught him how to fly, as a bird tempts her young ones from the lofty nest into the air. When all was prepared for flight he said, "Icarus, my son, I charge you to keep at a moderate height, for if you fly too low the damp will clog your wings, and if too high the heat will melt them. Keep near me and you will be safe." While he gave him these instructions and fitted the wings to his shoulders, the face of the father was wet with tears, and his hands trembled. He kissed the boy, not knowing that it was for the last time. Then rising on his wings, he flew off, encouraging him to follow, and looked back from his own flight to see how his son managed his wings. As they flew the ploughman stopped his work to gaze, and the shepherd leaned on his staff and watched them, astonished at the sight, and thinking they were gods who could thus cleave the air.

They passed Samos and Delos on the left and Lebynthos on the right, when the boy, exulting in his career, began to leave the guidance of his companion and soar upward as if to reach heaven. The nearness of the blazing sun softened the wax which held the feathers together, and they came off. He fluttered with his arms, but no feathers remained to hold the air. While his mouth uttered cries to his father it was submerged in the blue waters of the sea, which thenceforth was called by his name. His father cried, "Icarus, Icarus, where are you?" At last he saw the feathers floating on the water, and bitterly lamenting his own arts, he buried the body and called the land Icaria in memory of his child. Daedalus arrived safe in Sicily, where he built a temple to Apollo, and hung up his wings, an offering to the god.

Daedalus was so proud of his achievements that he could not bear the idea of a rival. His sister had placed her son Perdix under his charge to be taught the mechanical arts. He was an apt scholar and gave striking evidences of ingenuity. Walking on the seashore he picked up the spine of a fish. Imitating it, he took a piece of iron and notched it on the edge, and thus invented the *saw.* He put two pieces of iron together, connecting them at one end with a rivet, and sharpening the other ends, and made a *pair of compasses.* Daedalus was so envious of his nephew's performances that he took an opportunity, when they were together one day on the top of a high tower, to push him off. But Minerva, who favors ingenuity, saw him falling, and arrested his fate by changing him into a bird called after his name, the Partridge. This bird does not build his nest in the trees, nor take lofty flights, but nestles in the hedges, and mindful of his fall, avoids high places.

The death of Icarus is told in the following lines by Darwin:

> ". . . with melting wax and loosened strings
> Sunk hapless Icarus on unfaithful wings;
> Headlong he rushed through the affrighted air,
> With limbs distorted and dishevelled hair;
> His scattered plumage danced upon the wave,
> And sorrowing Nereids decked his watery grave;
> O'er his pale corse their pearly sea-flowers shed,
> And strewed with crimson moss his marble bed;
> Struck in their coral towers the passing bell,
> And wide in ocean tolled his echoing knell."

PERSEUS

by Thomas Bullfinch

Perseus and Medusa

Perseus was the son of Jupiter and Danaë. His grandfather Acrisius, alarmed by an oracle which had told him that his daughter's child would be the instrument of his death, caused the mother and child to be shut up in a chest and set adrift on the sea. The chest floated toward Seriphus, where it was found by Dictys, a fisherman, who conveyed the mother and infant to Polydectes, the king of the country, by whom they were treated with kindness. When Perseus was grown up Polydectes sent him to attempt the conquest of Medusa, a terrible monster who had laid waste the country. In order to aid him in his quest Pluto lent him a magic helmet which made its wearer invisible; Mercury lent his winged shoes, and Minerva armed him with her shield, the dreaded Aegis.

Medusa was once a beautiful maiden whose hair was her chief glory, but as she dared to vie in beauty with Minerva, the goddess deprived her of her charms and changed her beautiful ringlets into hissing serpents. She became a cruel monster of so frightful an aspect that no living thing could behold her without being turned into stone. All around the cavern where she dwelt might be seen the stony figures of men and animals which had chanced to catch a glimpse of her and had been petrified with the sight.

Perseus called first upon the Graeae, and waiting a favourable opportunity when the eye was being passed from one sister to another, he seized it and would not restore it until they gave him directions for finding Medusa.

His purpose happily achieved, Perseus approached Medusa while she slept, and taking care not to look directly at her, but guided by her image reflected in the bright shield which he bore, he cut off her head.

Perseus and Atlas

After the slaughter of Medusa, Perseus, bearing with him the head of the Gorgon, flew far and wide, over land and sea. As night came on, he reached the western limit of the earth, where the sun goes down. Here he would gladly have rested till morning. It was the realm of King Atlas, whose bulk surpassed that of all other men. He was rich in flocks and herds and had no neighbour or rival to dispute his state. But his chief pride was in his gardens, whose fruit was of gold, hanging from golden branches, half hid with golden leaves. Perseus said to him, "I come as a guest. If you honour illustrious descent, I claim Jupiter for my father; if mighty deeds, I plead the conquest of the Gorgon. I seek rest and food." But Atlas remembered that an ancient prophecy had warned him that a son of Jove should one day rob him of his golden apples. So he answered, "Begone! or neither your false claims of glory nor parentage shall protect you"; and he attempted to thrust him out. Perseus, finding the giant too strong for him, said, "Since you value my friendship so little, deign to accept a present"; and turning his face away, he held up the Gorgon's head. Atlas, with all his bulk, was changed into stone. His beard and hair became forests, his arms and shoulders cliffs, his head a summit, and his bones rocks. Each part increased in bulk till he became a mountain, and (such was the pleasure of the gods) heaven with all its stars rests upon his shoulders.

Perseus and Andromeda

Perseus, continuing his flight, arrived at the country of the Ethiopians, of which Cepheus was king. Cassiopeia his queen, proud of her beauty, had dared to compare herself to the Sea-Nymphs, which roused their indignation to such a degree that they sent a prodigious sea-monster to ravage the coast. To appease the deities, Cepheus was directed by the oracle to expose his daughter Andromeda to be devoured by the monster. As Perseus looked down from his aerial height he beheld the virgin chained to a rock, and waiting the approach of the serpent. She was so pale and motionless that if it had not been for her flowing tears and her hair that moved in the breeze, he would have taken her for a marble statue. He was so startled at the sight that he almost forgot to wave his wings. As he hovered over her he said, "O virgin, undeserving of those chains, but rather of such as bind fond lovers together, tell me, I beseech you, your name, and the name of your country, and why you are thus bound." At first she was silent from modesty, and, if she could, would have hid her face with her hands; but when he repeated his questions, for fear she might be thought guilty of some fault which she dared not tell, she disclosed her name and that of her country, and her mother's pride of beauty. Before she had done speaking, a sound was heard off upon the water, and the sea-monster appeared, with his head raised above the surface, cleaving the waves with his broad breast. The virgin shrieked, the father and mother, who had now arrived at the scene, wretched both, but the mother more justly so, stood by, not able to afford protection, but only to pour forth lamentations and to embrace the victim. Then spoke Perseus: "There will be time enough for tears; this hour is all we have for rescue. My rank as the son of Jove and my renown as the slayer of the Gorgon might make me acceptable as a suitor; but I will try to win her by services rendered, if the gods will only be propitious. If she be rescued by my valour, I demand that she be my reward." The parents consent (how could they hesitate?) and promise a royal dowry with her.

And now the monster was within the range of a stone thrown by a skilful slinger, when with a sudden bound the youth soared into the air. As an eagle, when from his lofty flight he sees a serpent basking in the sun, pounces upon him and seizes him by the neck to prevent him from turning his head round and using his fangs, so the youth darted down upon the back of the monster and plunged his sword into its shoulder. Irritated by the wound, the monster raised himself into the air, then plunged into the depth; then, like a wild boar surrounded by a pack of barking dogs, turned swiftly from side to side, while the youth eluded its attacks by means of his wings. Wherever he can find a passage for his sword between the scales he makes a wound, piercing now the side, now the flank, as it slopes toward the tail. The brute spouts from his nostrils water mixed with blood. The wings of the hero are wet with it, and he dares no longer trust to them. Alighting on a rock which rose above the waves, and holding on by a projecting fragment, as the monster floated near he gave him a death-stroke. The people who had gathered on the shore shouted so that the hills re-echoed the sound. The parents, transported with joy, embraced their future son-in-law, calling him their deliverer and the saviour of their house, and the virgin, both cause and reward of the contest, descended from the rock.

THE CONSOLIDATOR

by Daniel Defoe

This great searcher into nature has, besides all this, left wonderful discoveries and experiments behind him; but I was with nothing more exceedingly diverted than with his various engines, and curious contrivances, to go to and from his own native country the moon. All our mechanic motions of bishop Wilkins, or the artificial wings of the learned Spaniard, who could have taught God Almighty how to have mended the creation, are fools to this gentleman; and because no man in China has made more voyages up into the moon than myself, I cannot but give you some account of the easiness of the passage, as well as of the country.

But above all his inventions for making this voyage, I saw none more pleasant or profitable than a certain engine formed in the shape of a chariot, on the backs of two vast bodies with extended wings, which spread about fifty yards in breadth, composed of feathers so nicely put together, that no air could pass; and as the bodies were made of lunar earth, which would bear the fire, the cavities were filled with an ambient flame, which fed on a certain spirit, deposited in a proper quantity to last out the voyage; and this fire so ordered as to move about such springs and wheels as kept the wings in a most exact and regular motion, always ascendant; thus the person being placed in this airy chariot, drinks a certain dozing draught, that throws him into a gentle slumber, and dreaming all the way, never wakes till he comes to his journey's end.

These engines are called in their country language, Dupekasses; and according to the ancient Chinese, or Tartarian, Apezolanthukanistes; in English, a Consolidator.

The composition of this engine is very admirable; for, as is before noted, it is all made up of feathers, and the quality of the feathers is no less wonderful than their composition; and therefore, I hope the reader will bear with the description for the sake of the novelty, since I assure him such things as these are not to be seen in every country.

The number of feathers are just 513; they are all of a length and breadth exactly, which is absolutely necessary to the floating figure, or else one side or any one part being wider or longer than the rest, it would interrupt the motion of the whole engine; only there is one extraordinary feather, which, as there is an odd one in the number, is placed in the centre, and is the handle, or rather rudder to the whole machine: this feather is every way larger than its fellows, it is almost as long and broad again; but above all, its quill or head is much larger, and it has, as it were, several small bushing feathers round the bottom of it, which all make but one presiding or superintendent feather, to guide, regulate, and pilot the whole body.

Nor are these common feathers, but they are picked and culled out of all parts of the lunar country, by the command of the prince; and every province sends up the best they can find, or ought to do so at least, or else they are very much to blame; for the employment they are put to being of so great use to the public, and the voyage or flight so exceeding high, it would be very ill done if, when the king sends his letters about the nation, to pick him up the best feathers they can lay their hands on, they should send weak, decayed, or half-grown feathers, and yet sometimes it happens so; and once there was such rotten feathers collected, whether it was a bad year for feathers, or whether the people that gathered them had a mind to abuse their king; but the feathers were so bad, the engine was good for nothing, but broke before it was got half way; and, by a double misfortune, this happened to be at an unlucky time, when the king himself had resolved on a voyage or flight to the moon; but being deceived by the unhappy miscarriage of the deficient feathers, he fell down from so great a height, that he struck himself against his own palace and beat his head off.

Nor had the sons of this prince much better success, though the first of them was a prince mightily beloved by his subjects; but his misfortunes chiefly proceeded from his having made use of one of the engines so very long, that the feathers were quite worn out, and good for nothing; he used to make a great many voyages and flights into the moon, and then would make his subjects give him great sums of money to come down to them again; and yet they were so fond of him, that they always complied with him, and would give him everything he asked, rather than to be without him: but they grew wiser since.

At last this prince used his engine so long, it could hold together no longer; and being obliged to write to his subjects to pick him out some new feathers, they did so; but withal sent him such strong feathers, and so stiff, that when he had placed them in their proper places, and made a very beautiful engine, it was too heavy for him to manage: he made a great many essays at it, and had it placed on the top of an old idol chapel, dedicated to an old Brahmin saint of those countries, called, Phantosteinaschap; in Latin, *Chap. de Saint Stephano;* or in English, St. Stephen's. Here the prince tried all possible contrivances, and a vast deal of money it cost him; but the feathers were so stiff, they would not work, and the fire within was so choked and smothered with its own smoke, for want of due vent and circulation, that it would not burn; so he was obliged to take it down again; and from thence he carried it to his college of Brahmin priests, and set it up in one of their public buildings: there he drew circles of ethics and politics, and fell to casting of figures and conjuring, but all would not do, the feathers could not be brought to move; and indeed I have observed, that these engines are seldom helped by art and contrivance; there is no way with them, but to have the people spoke to, to get good feathers; and they are easily placed, and perform all the several motions with the greatest ease and accuracy imaginable; but it must be all nature; anything of force distorts and dislocates them, and the whole order is spoiled; and if there be but one feather out of place, or pinched, or stands wrong, the d——l would not ride in the chariot.

The prince thus finding his labour in vain, broke the engine to pieces, and sent his subjects word what bad feathers they had sent him: but the people, who knew it was his own want of management, and that the feathers were good enough, only a little stiff at first, and with good usage would have been brought to be fit for use, took it ill, and never would send him any other as long as he lived: however, it had this good effect upon him, that he never made any more voyages to the moon as long as he reigned.

His brother succeeded him; and truly he was resolved upon a voyage to the moon, as soon as ever he came to the crown. He had met with some unkind usage from the religious lunesses of his own country; and he turned Abogratziarian, a zealous fiery sect, something like our Anti-everybody-arians in England. It is confessed some of the Brahmins of his country were very false to him, put him upon several ways of extending his power over his subjects, contrary to the customs of the people, and contrary to his own interest; and when the people expressed their dislike of it, he thought to have been supported by those clergymen; but they failed him, and made good that old English verse;

That priests of all religions are the same.

He took this so heinously, that he conceived a just hatred against those that had deceived him; and as resentments seldom keep rules, unhappily entertained prejudices against all the rest; and not finding it easy to bring all his designs to pass better, he resolved upon a voyage to the moon.

Accordingly he sends a summons to all his people, according to custom, to collect the usual quantity of feathers for that purpose; and because he would be sure not to be used as his brother and father had been, he took care to send certain cunning men, express, all over the country, to bespeak the people's care in collecting, picking, and culling them out;

these were called in their language, Tsopablesdetoo; which, being translated, may signify in English, Men of Zeal, or Booted Apostles: nor was this the only caution this prince used; for he took care, as the feathers were sent up to him, to search and examine them one by one in his own closet, to see if they were fit for his purpose; but, alas! he found himself in his brother's case exactly; and perceived that his subjects were generally disgusted at his former conduct, about Abrogratzianism, and such things, and particularly set in a flame by some of their priests, called Dullobardians, or Passive-Obedience-men, who had lately turned their tale, and their tail too, upon their own princes; and upon this, he laid aside any more thoughts of the engine, but took up a desperate and implacable resolution, viz. to fly up to the moon without it; in order to do this, an abundance of his cunning men were summoned together to assist him, strange engines contrived and methods proposed; and a great many came from all parts to furnish him with inventions and equivalent for their journey; but all were so preposterous and ridiculous, that his subjects seeing him going on to ruin himself, and by consequence them too, unanimously took arms; and if their prince had not made his escape into a foreign country, it is thought they would have secured him for a madman.

And here it is observable, that as it is in most such cases, the mad councillors of this prince, when the people begun to gather about him, fled, and every one shifted for themselves; nay, and some of them plundered him first of his jewels and treasure, and never were heard of since.

From this prince none of the kings or government of that country have ever seemed to incline to the hazardous attempt of the voyage to the moon, at least not in such a harebrained manner.

However, the engine has been very accurately rebuilt and finished; and the people are now obliged by a law, to send up new feathers every three years, to prevent the mischiefs which happened by that prince aforesaid keeping one set so long that it was dangerous to venture with them; and thus the engine is preserved fit for use.

And yet has not this engine been without its continual disasters, and often out of repair; for though the kings of the country, as has been noted, have done riding on the back of it, yet the restless courtiers and ministers of state have frequently obtained the management of it, from the too easy goodness of their masters, or the evils of the times.

To cure this, the princes frequently changed hands, turned one set of men out and put another in; but this made things still worse, for it divided the people into parties and factions in the state, and still the strife was, who should ride in this engine; and no sooner were these Skaetriders got into it, but they were for driving all the nation up to the moon: but of this by itself.

Authors differ concerning the original of these feathers, and by what most exact hand they were first appointed to this particular use; and as their original is hard to be found, so it seems a difficulty to resolve from what sort of bird these feathers are obtained: some have named one, some another; but the most learned in those climates call it by a hard word, which the printer having no letters to express, and being in that place hieroglyphical, I can translate no better than by the name of a Collective: this must be a strange bird without doubt; it has heads, claws, eyes, and teeth innumerable; and if I should go about to describe it to you, the history would be so romantic, it would spoil the credit of these more authentic relations which are yet behind.

It is sufficient, therefore, for the present, only to leave you this short abridgment of the story, as follows: this great monstrous bird, called the Collective, is very seldom seen, and indeed never but upon great revolutions, and portending terrible desolations and destructions to a country.

But he frequently sheds his feathers, and they are carefully picked up by the proprietors of those lands where they fall; for none but those proprietors may meddle with them; and they no sooner pick them up but they are sent to court, where they obtain a new name, and are called in a word equally difficult to pronounce as the other, but very like our English word Representative; and being placed in their proper rows, with the great feather in the centre, and fitted for use, they lately obtained the venerable title of the Consolidators; and the machine itself, the Consolidator; and by that name the reader is desired for the future to let it be dignified and distinguished.

I cannot, however, forbear to descant a little here on the dignity and beauty of these feathers, being such as are hardly to be seen in any part of the world, but just in these remote climates.

And first, every feather has various colours, and according to the variety of the weather, are apt to look brighter and clearer, or paler and fainter, as the sun happens to look on them with a stronger or weaker aspect. The quill or head of every feather is or ought to be full of a vigorous substance, which gives spirit, and supports the brightness and colour of the feather; and as this is more or less in quantity, the bright colour of the feather is increased, or turns languid and pale.

It is true some of those quills are exceeding empty and dry; and the humid being totally exhaled, those feathers grow very useless and insignificant in a short time.

Some again are so full of wind, and puffed up with the vapour of the climate, that there is not humid enough to condense the steam; and these are so fleet, so light, and so continually fluttering and troublesome, that they greatly serve to disturb and keep the motion unsteady.

Others, either placed too near the inward concealed fire, or the head of the quill being thin, the fire causes too great a fermentation; and the consequence of this is so fatal, that sometimes it mounts the engine up too fast, and endangers precipitation: but it is happily observed, that these ill feathers are but a very few, compared to the whole number; at the most, I never heard they were above a hundred and thirty-four of the whole number: as for the empty ones, they are not very dangerous, but a sort of good-for-nothing feathers, that will fly when the greatest number of the rest fly, or stand still when they stand still. The fluttering hot-headed feathers are the most dangerous, and frequently struggle hard to mount the engine to extravagant heights; but still the greater number of the feathers being stanch, and well fixed, as well as well furnished, they always prevail, and check the disorders the other would bring upon the motion; so that upon the whole matter, though there has sometimes been oblique motions, variations, and sometimes great wanderings out of the way, which may make the passage tedious, yet it has always been a certain and safe voyage; and no engine was ever known to miscarry or overthrow, but that one mentioned before, and that was very much owing to the precipitate methods the prince took in guiding it; and though all the fault was laid in the feathers, and they were to blame enough, yet I never heard any wise man but what blamed his discretion; and particularly, a certain great man has wrote three large tracts of those affairs, and called them, The History of the Opposition of the Feathers: wherein, though it was expected he would have cursed the engine itself and all the feathers to the devil, on the contrary, he lays equal blame on the prince, who guided the chariot with so unsteady a hand, now as much too slack, as then too hard, turning them this way and that so hastily that the feathers could not move in their proper order; and this at last put the fire in the centre quite out, and so the engine overset at once. This impartiality has done great justice to the feathers, and set things in a clearer light: but of this I shall say more, when I come to treat of the works of the learned in this lunar world.

This is hinted here only to inform the reader, that this engine is the safest passage that ever was found out; and that, saving that one time, it never miscarried; nor, if the common order of things be observed, cannot miscarry; for the good feathers are always negatives when any precipitant motion is felt, and immediately suppress it by their number; and these negative feathers are indeed the traveller's safety: the other are always upon the flutter, and upon every occasion, hey for the moon, up in the clouds presently; but these negative feathers are never for going up but when there is occasion for it; and from hence these fluttering fermented feathers were called by the ancients high-flying feathers, and the blustering things seemed proud of the name.

But to come to their general character, the feathers, speaking of them all together, are generally very comely, strong, large, beautiful things, their quills or heads well fixed, and the cavities filled with a solid substantial matter, which, though it is full of spirit, has a great deal of temperament, and full of suitable well-disposed powers to the operation for which they are designed.

These, placed, as I noted before, in an extended form like two great wings, and operated by that sublime flame, which, being concealed in proper receptacles, obtains its vent at the cavities appointed, are supplied from thence with life and motion; and as fire itself, in the opinion of some learned men, is nothing but motion, and motion tends to fire, it can no more be a wonder, if exalted in the centre of this famous engine, a whole nation should be carried up to the world in the moon.

It is true this engine is frequently assaulted with fierce winds and furious storms, which sometimes drive it a great way out of its way; and indeed, considering the length of the passage and the various regions it goes through, it would be strange if it should meet with no obstructions. These are oblique gales, and cannot be said to blow from any of the thirty-two points, but retrograde and thwart; some of these are called in their language, Pensionazima, which is as much as to say, being interpreted, a court-breeze; another sort of wind, which generally blows directly contrary to the Pensionazima, is the Clamorio, or in English, a country-gale; this is generally tempestuous, full of gusts and disgusts, squalls and sudden blasts, not without claps of thunder, and not a little flashing of heat and party fires.

There are a great many other internal blasts, which proceed from the fire within, which, sometimes not circulating right, breaks out in little gusts of wind and heat, and is apt to endanger setting fire to the feathers: and this is more or less dangerous according as among which of the feathers it happens; for some of the feathers are more apt to take fire than others, as their quills or heads are more or less full of that solid matter mentioned before.

The engine suffers frequent convulsions and disorders from these several winds; and which, if they chance to overblow very much, hinder the passage; but the negative feathers always apply temper and moderation; and this brings all to rights again.

For a body like this, what can it not do? what cannot such an extension perform in the air? and when one thing is tacked to another, and properly consolidated into one mighty consolidator, no question but whoever shall go up to the moon, will find himself so improved in this wonderful experiment, that not a man ever performed that wonderful flight, but he certainly came back again as wise as he went.

Well, gentlemen, and what if we are called high-fliers now, and a hundred names of contempt and distinction, what is this to the purpose? who would not be a high-flier, to be tacked and consolidated in an engine of such sublime elevation, and which lifts men, monarchs, members, yea, and whole nations, up into the clouds; and performs with such wondrous art, the long-expected experiment of a voyage to the moon? And thus much for the description of the Consolidator.

The first voyage I ever made to this country was in one of these engines, and I can safely affirm I never waked all the way; and now, having been as often there as most that have used that trade, it may be expected I should give some account of the country; for it appears I can give but little of the road.

Only this I understand, that when this engine, by help of these artificial wings, has raised itself up to a certain height, the wings are as useful to keep it from falling into the moon, as they were before to raise it, and keep it from falling back into this region again.

This may happen from an alteration of centres, and gravity having passed a certain line, the equipoise changes its tendency; the magnetic quality being beyond it, it inclines of course, and pursues a centre, which it finds in the lunar world, and lands us safe upon the surface.

TO THE PLANET OF THE APES

by Pierre Boulle

I am confiding this manuscript to space, not with the intention of saving myself, but to help, perhaps, to avert the appalling scourge that is menacing the human race. Lord have pity on us! . . .

As for me, Ulysse Mérou, I have set off again with my family in the spaceship. We can keep going for several years. We grow vegetables and fruit on board and have a poultry run. We lack nothing. One day perhaps we shall come across a friendly planet. This is a hope I hardly dare express. But here, faithfully reported, is the account of my adventure.

It was in the year 2500 that I embarked with two companions in the cosmic ship, with the intention of reaching the region of space where the supergigantic star Betelgeuse reigns supreme.

It was an ambitious project, the most ambitious that had ever been conceived on Earth. Betelgeuse—or Alpha Orionis, as our astronomers called it—is about three hundred light-years distant from our planet. It is remarkable for a number of things. First, its size: its diameter is three or four hundred times greater than that of our sun; in other words, if its center were placed where the sun's center lies, this monster would extend to within the orbit of Mars. Second, its brilliance: it is a star of first magnitude, the brightest in the constellation of Orion, visible on Earth to the naked eye in spite of its distance. Third, the nature of its rays: it emits red and orange lights, creating a most magnificent effect. Finally, it is a heavenly body with a variable glow: its luminosity varies with the seasons, this being caused by the alterations in its diameter. Betelgeuse is a palpitating star.

Why, after the exploration of the solar system, all the planets of which are inhabited, why was such a distant star chosen as the target for the first interstellar flight? It was the learned Professor Antelle who made this decision. The principal organizer of the enterprise, to which he devoted the whole of his enormous fortune, the leader of our expedition, he himself had conceived the spaceship and directed its construction. He told me the reason for his choice during the voyage.

"My dear Ulysse," he said, "it is not much harder, and it would scarcely take any longer, for us to reach Betelgeuse than a much closer star: Proxima Centauris, for example."

At this I saw fit to protest and draw his attention to some recently ascertained astronomical data:

"Scarcely take any longer! But Proxima Centauris is only four light-years away, whereas Betelgeuse . . ."

"Is three hundred, I'm well aware of that. But we shall take scarcely more than two years to reach it, while we should have needed almost as much time to arrive in the region of Proxima Centauris. You don't believe it because you are accustomed to mere flea hops on our planets, for which a powerful acceleration is permissible at the start because it lasts no more than a few minutes, the cruising speed to be reached being ridiculously low and not to be compared with ours. . . . It is time I gave you a few details as to how our ship works.

"Thanks to its perfected rockets, which I had the honor of designing, this craft can move at the highest speed imaginable in the universe for a material body—that is to say, the speed of light minus *epsilon.*"

"Minus *epsilon?*"

"I mean it can approach it to within an infinitesimal degree: to within a thousand-millionth, if you care to put it that way."

"Good," I said. "I can understand that."

"What you must also realize is that while we are moving at this speed, our time diverges perceptibly from time on Earth, the divergence being greater the faster we move. At this very moment, since we started this conversation, we have lived several minutes, which correspond to a passage of several months on our planet. At top speed, time will almost stand still for us, but of course we shall not be aware of this. A few seconds for you and me, a few heartbeats, will coincide with a passage of several years on Earth."

"I can understand that, too. In fact, that is the reason why we can hope to reach our destination before dying. But in that case, why a voyage of two years? Why not only a few days or a few hours?"

"I was just coming to that. Quite simply because, to reach the speed at which time almost stands still, with an acceleration acceptable to our organisms, we need about a year. A further year will be necessary to reduce our speed. Now do you understand our flight plan? Twelve months of acceleration; twelve months of reducing speed; between the two, only a few hours, during which we shall cover the main part of the journey. And at the same time you will understand why it scarcely takes any longer to travel to Betelgeuse than to Proxima Centauri. In the latter case we should have to go through the same indispensable year of acceleration, the same year of deceleration, and perhaps a few minutes instead of a few hours between the two. The overall difference is insignificant. As I'm getting on in years and will probably never be able to make another crossing, I preferred to aim at a distant point straight away, in the hope of finding a world very different from our own."

This sort of conversation occupied our leisure hours on board and at the same time made me appreciate Professor Antelle's prodigious skill all the more. There was no field he had not explored, and I was pleased to have a leader like him on such a hazardous enterprise. As he had foreseen, the voyage lasted about two years of our time, during which three and a half centuries must have elapsed on Earth. That was the only snag about aiming so far into the distance: if we came back one day we should find our planet older by seven or eight hundred years. But we did not care. I even felt that the prospect of escaping from his contemporaries was an added attraction to the professor. He often admitted he was tired of his fellow men. . . .

There was no serious incident on the flight. We had started from the Moon. Earth and its planets quickly disappeared. We had seen the sun shrink till it was nothing but an orange in the sky, then a plum, and finally a point of light without dimensions, a simple star that only the professor's skill could distinguish from the millions of other stars in the galaxy.

We thus lived without sun, but were none the worse for this, the craft being equipped with equivalent sources of light. Nor were we bored. The professor's conversation was fascinating; I learned more during those two years than I had learned in all my previous existence. I also learned all that one needed to know in order to guide the spacecraft. It was fairly easy: one merely gave instructions to some electronic devices, which made all the calculations and directly initiated the maneuvers.

Our garden provided an agreeable distraction. It occupied an important place on board. Professor Antelle, who was interested, among other subjects, in botany and agriculture, had planned to take advantage of the voyage to check certain of his theories on the growth of plants in space. A cubic compartment with sides about thirty feet long served as a plot. Thanks to some trays, the whole of its volume was put to use. The earth was regenerated by means of chemical fertilizers and, scarcely more than two months after our departure, we had the pleasure of seeing it produce all sorts of vegetables, which provided us with an abundance of healthy food. Food for the eye, too, had not been forgotten: one section was reserved for flowers, which the professor tended lovingly. This eccentric had also brought some birds, butterflies, and even a monkey, a little chimpanzee whom we had christened Hector and who amused us with his tricks.

It is certain that the learned Antelle, without being a misanthrope, was not interested at all in human beings. He would often declare that he did not expect much from them any more, and this probably explains . . .

This probably explains why he had collected in the craft—which was big enough to accommodate several families—countless vegetable species and some animals, while limiting the number of the passengers to three: himself; his disciple Arthur Levain, a young physician with a great future; and myself, Ulysse Mérou, a little-known journalist who had met the professor as a result of an interview. He had suggested taking me with him after learning that I had no family and played chess reasonably well. This was an outstanding opportunity for a young journalist. Even if my story was not to be published for eight hundred years, perhaps for that very reason it would have unusual value. I had accepted with enthusiasm.

The voyage thus occurred without a setback. The only physical inconvenience was a sensation of heaviness during the year of acceleration and the one of reducing speed. We had to get used to feeling our bodies weigh one and a half times their weight on Earth, a somewhat tiring phenomenon to begin with, but to which we soon paid no attention. Between those two periods there was a complete absence of gravity, with all the oddities accruing from this phenomenon; but that lasted only a few hours and we were none the worse for it.

And one day, after this long crossing, we had the dazzling experience of seeing the star Betelgeuse appear in the sky in a new guise.

The feeling of awe produced by such a sight cannot be described: a star, which only yesterday was a brilliant speck among the multitude of anonymous specks in the firmament, showed up more and more clearly against the black background, assumed a dimension in space, appearing first of all as a sparkling nut, then swelled in size, at the same time becoming more definite in color, so that it resembled an orange, and finally fell into place in the cosmos with the same apparent diameter as our own familiar daytime star. A new sun was born for us, a reddish sun, like ours when it sets, the attraction and warmth of which we could already feel.

Our speed was then very much reduced. We drew still closer to Betelgeuse, until its apparent diameter far exceeded that of all the heavenly bodies hitherto seen, which made a tremendous impression on us. Antelle gave some instructions to the robots and we started gravitating around the supergiant. Then the scientist took out his astronomical instruments and began his observations.

It was not long before he discovered the existence of four planets whose dimensions he rapidly determined, together with their distances from the central star. One of these, two away from Betelgeuse, was moving on a trajectory parallel to ours. It was about the same size as Earth; it possessed an atmosphere containing oxygen and nitrogen; it revolved around Betelgeuse at a distance equivalent to thirty times the space between the Sun and Earth, receiving a radiation comparable to that received by our planet, thanks to the size of the supergiant combined with its relatively low temperature.

We decided to make it our first objective. After fresh instructions were given to the robots, our craft was quickly put into orbit around it. Then, with engines switched off, we observed this new world at our leisure. The telescope revealed its oceans and continents.

The craft was not equipped for a landing, but this eventuality had been provided for. We had at our disposal three much smaller rocket machines, which we called launches. It was in one of these that we embarked, taking with us some measuring instruments and Hector, the chimpanzee, who was equipped as we were with a diving suit and had been trained in its use. As for our ship, we simply let it revolve around the planet. It was safer there than a liner lying at anchor in a harbor, and we knew it would not drift an inch from its orbit.

Landing on a planet of this kind was an easy operation with our launch. As soon as we had penetrated the thick layers of the atmosphere, Professor Antelle took some samples of the outside air and analyzed them. He found they had the same composition as the air on Earth at a similar altitude. I hardly had time to ponder on this miraculous coincidence, for the ground was approaching rapidly; we were no more than fifty miles or so above it. Since the robots carried out every maneuver, I had nothing to do but press my face to the porthole and watch this unknown world rising toward me, my brain reeling with the excitement of discovery.

The planet bore a strange resemblance to Earth. This impression became clearer every second. I could now discern the outline of the continents with my naked eye. The atmosphere was bright, slightly tinged with a pale green color verging from time to time on yellow, rather like our sky in Provence at sunset. The ocean was light blue, also with green tinges. The form of the coast line was very different from anything I had seen at home, though my feverish eye, conditioned by so many analogies, insisted wildly on discerning similarities even there. But there the resemblance ended. Nothing in the planet's topography recalled either our Old or New Worlds.

Nothing? Come now! On the contrary, the essential factor! The planet was inhabited. We flew over a town: a fairly big town, from which roads radiated, bordered with trees and with vehicles moving along them. I had time to make out the general architecture: broad streets and white houses with long straight lines.

But we were to land a long way farther off. Our flight swept us first over cultivated fields, then over a thick russet-colored forest that called to mind our equatorial jungle. We were now at a very low altitude. We caught sight of a fairly large clearing occupying the top of a plateau, the ground all around it being rather broken. Our leader decided to attempt a landing there and gave his last orders to the robots. A system of retro-rockets came into action. We hovered motionless for a moment or two above the clearing, like a gull spotting a fish.

Then, two years after leaving our Earth, we came down gently and landed without a jolt in the middle of the plateau, on green grass reminiscent of our meadows in Normandy.

TO SATURN AND BACK

by Isaac Asimov

Sankov scratched the side of his neck. "All right. In that case, I'll ask you for some advice. What can we folks on Mars do? You know Earth. You know the situation. We don't. Tell us what to do."

Digby rose and stepped to the window. He looked out upon the low domes of other buildings; red, rocky, completely desolate plain in between; a purple sky and a shrunken sun.

He said, without turning, "Do you people really like it on Mars?"

Sankov smiled. "Most of us don't exactly know any other world, Assemblyman. Seems to me Earth would be something queer and uncomfortable to them."

"But wouldn't Martians get used to it? Earth isn't hard to take after this. Wouldn't your people learn to enjoy the privilege of breathing air under an open sky? You once lived on Earth. You remember what it was like."

"I sort of remember. Still, it doesn't seem to be easy to explain. Earth is just there. It fits people and people fit it. People take Earth the way they find it. Mars is different. It's sort of raw and doesn't fit people. People got to make something out of it. They got to *build* a world, and not take what they find. Mars isn't much yet, but we're building, and when we're finished, we're going to have just what we like. It's sort of a great feeling to know you're building a world. Earth would be kind of unexciting after that."

The Assemblyman said, "Surely the ordinary Martian isn't such a philosopher that he's content to live this terribly hard life for the sake of a future that must be hundreds of generations away."

"No-o, not just like that." Sankov put his right ankle on his left knee and cradled it as he spoke. "Like I said, Martians are a lot like Earthmen, which means they're sort of human beings, and human beings don't go in for philosophy much. Just the same, there's something in living in a growing world, whether you think about it much or not.

"My father used to send me letters when I first came to Mars. He was an accountant and he just sort of stayed an accountant. Earth wasn't much different when he died from what it was when he was born. He didn't see anything happen. Every day was like every other day, and living was just a way of passing time until he died.

"On Mars, it's different. Every day there's something new—the city's bigger, the ventilation system gets another kick, the water lines from the poles get slicked up. Right now, we're planning to set up a news-film association of our own. We're going to call it Mars Press. If you haven't lived when things are growing all about you, you'll never understand how wonderful it feels.

"No, Assemblyman, Mars is hard and tough and Earth is a lot more comfortable, but seems to me if you take our boys to Earth, they'll be unhappy. They probably wouldn't be able to figure out why, most of them, but they'd feel lost; lost and useless. Seems to me lots of them would never make the adjustment."

Digby turned away from the window and the smooth, pink skin of his forehead was creased into a frown. "In that case, Commissioner, I am sorry for you. For all of you."

"Why?"

"Because I don't think there's anything your people on Mars can do. Or the people on the Moon or Venus. It won't happen now; maybe it won't happen for a year or two, or even for five years. But pretty soon you'll all have to come back to Earth, unless—"

Sankov's white eyebrows bent low over his eyes. "Well?"

"Unless you can find another source of water besides the planet Earth."

Sankov shook his head. "Don't seem likely, does it?"

"Not very."

"And except for that, seems to you there's no chance?"

"None at all."

Digby said that and left, and Sankov stared for a long time at nothing before he punched a combination of the local communiline.

After a while, Ted Long looked out at him.

Sankov said, "You were right, son. There's nothing they can do. Even the ones that mean well see no way out. How did you know?"

"Commissioner," said Long, "when you've read all you can about the Time of Troubles, particularly about the twentieth century, nothing political can come as a real surprise."

"Well, maybe. Anyway, son, Assemblyman Digby is sorry for us, quite a piece sorry, you might say, but that's all. He says we'll have to leave Mars—or else get water somewhere else. Only he thinks that we can't get water somewhere else."

"You know we can, don't you, Commissioner?"

"I know we *might,* son. It's a terrible risk."

"If I find enough volunteers, the risk is our business."

"How is it going?"

"Not bad. Some of the boys are on my side right now. I talked Mario Rioz into it, for instance, and you know he's one of the best."

"That's just it—the volunteers will be the best men we have. I hate to allow it."

"If we get back, it will be worth it."

"If! It's a big word, son."

"And a big thing we're trying to do."

"Well, I gave my word that if there was no help on Earth, I'll see that the Phobos water hole lets you have all the water you'll need. Good luck."

Half a million miles above Saturn, Mario Rioz was cradled on nothing and sleep was delicious. He came out of it slowly and for a while, alone in his suit, he counted the stars and traced lines from one to another.

At first, as the weeks flew past, it was scavenging all over again, except for the gnawing feeling that every minute meant an additional number of thousands of miles away from all humanity. That made it worse.

They had aimed high to pass out of the ecliptic while moving through the Asteroid Belt. That had used up water and had probably been unnecessary. Although tens of thousands of worldlets look as thick as vermin in two-dimensional projection upon a photographic plate, they are nevertheless scattered so thinly through the quadrillions of cubic miles that make up their conglomerate orbit that only the most ridiculous of coincidences would have brought about a collision.

Still, they passed over the Belt and someone calculated the chances of collision with a fragment of matter large enough to do damage. The value was so low, so impossibly low, that it was perhaps inevitable that the notion of the "space-float" should occur to someone.

The days were long and many, space was empty, only one man was needed at the controls at any one time. The thought was a natural.

First, it was a particularly daring one who ventured out for fifteen minutes or so. Then another who tried half an hour. Eventually, before the asteroids were entirely behind, each ship regularly had its off-watch member suspended in space at the end of a cable.

It was easy enough. The cable, one of those intended for operations at the conclusion of their journey, was magnetically attached at both ends, one to the space suit to start with. Then you clambered out the lock onto the ship's hull and attached the other end there. You paused awhile, clinging to the metal skin by the electromagnets in your boots. Then you neutralized those and made the slightest muscular effort.

Slowly, ever so slowly, you lifted from the ship and even more slowly the ship's larger mass moved an equivalently shorter distance downward. You floated incredibly, weightlessly, in solid, speckled black. When the ship had moved far enough away from you, your gauntleted hand, which kept touch upon the cable, tightened its grip slightly. Too tightly, and you would begin moving back toward the ship and it toward you. Just tightly enough, and friction would halt you. Because your motion was equivalent to that of the ship, it seemed as motionless below you as though it had been painted against an impossible background while the cable between you hung in coils that had no reason to straighten out.

It was a half-ship to your eye. One half was lit by the light of the feeble Sun, which was still too bright to look at directly without the heavy protection of the polarized space-suit visor. The other half was black on black, invisible.

Space closed in and it was like sleep. Your suit was warm, it renewed its air automatically, it had food and drink in special containers from which it could be sucked with a minimal motion of the head, it took care of wastes appropriately. Most of all, more than anything else, there was the delightful euphoria of weightlessness.

You never felt so well in your life. The days stopped being too long, they weren't long enough, and there weren't enough of them.

They had passed Jupiter's orbit at a spot some 30 degrees from its then position. For months, it was the brightest object in the sky, always excepting the glowing white pea that was the Sun. At its brightest, some of the Scavengers insisted they could make out Jupiter as a tiny sphere, one side squashed out of true by the night shadow.

Then over a period of additional months it faded, while another dot of light grew until it was brighter than Jupiter. It was Saturn, first as a dot of brilliance, then as an oval, glowing splotch.

("Why oval?" someone asked, and after a while, someone else said, "The rings, of course," and it was obvious.)

Everyone space-floated at all possible times toward the end, watching Saturn incessantly.

("Hey, you jerk, come on back in, damn it. You're on duty." "Who's on duty? I've got fifteen minutes more by my watch." "You set your watch back. Besides, I gave you twenty minutes yesterday." "You wouldn't give two minutes to your grandmother." "Come on in, damn it, or I'm coming out anyway." "All right, I'm coming. Holy howlers, what a racket over a lousy minute." But no quarrel could possibly be serious, not in space. It felt too good.)

Saturn grew until at last it rivaled and then surpassed the Sun. The rings, set at a broad angle to their trajectory of approach, swept grandly about the planet, only a small portion being eclipsed. Then, as they approached, the span of the rings grew still wider, yet narrower as the angle of approach constantly decreased.

The larger moons showed up in the surrounding sky like serene fireflies.

Mario Rioz was glad he was awake so that he could watch again.

Saturn filled half the sky, streaked with orange, the night shadow cutting it fuzzily nearly one quarter of the way in from the right. Two round little dots in the brightness were shadows of two of the moons. To the left and behind him (he could look over his left shoulder to see, and as he did so, the rest of his body inched slightly to the right to conserve angular momentum) was the white diamond of the Sun.

Most of all he liked to watch the rings. At the left, they emerged from behind Saturn, a tight, bright triple band of orange light. At the right, their beginnings were hidden in the night shadow, but showed up closer and broader. They widened as they came, like the flare of a horn, growing hazier as they approached, until, while the eye followed them, they seemed to fill the sky and lose themselves.

From the position of the Scavenger fleet just inside the outer rim of the outermost ring, the rings broke up and assumed their true identity as a phenomenal cluster of solid fragments rather than the tight, solid band of light they seemed.

Below him, or rather in the direction his feet pointed, some twenty miles away, was one of the ring fragments. It looked like a large, irregular splotch, marring the symmetry of space, three quarters in brightness and the night shadow cutting it like a knife. Other fragments were farther off, sparkling like star dust, dimmer and thicker, until, as you followed them down, they became rings once more.

The fragments were motionless, but that was only because the ships had taken up an orbit about Saturn equivalent to that of the outer edge of the rings.

The day before, Rioz reflected, he had been on that nearest fragment, working along with more than a score of others to mold it into the desired shape. Tomorrow he would be at it again.

Today—today he was space-floating.

"Mario?" The voice that broke upon his earphones was questioning.

Momentarily Rioz was flooded with annoyance. Damn it, he wasn't in the mood for company.

"Speaking," he said.

"I thought I had your ship spotted. How are you?"

"Fine. That you, Ted?"

"That's right," said Long.

"Anything wrong on the fragment?"

"Nothing. I'm out here floating."

"You?"

"It gets me, too, occasionally. Beautiful, isn't it?"

"Nice," agreed Rioz.

"You know, I've read Earth books—"

"Grounder books, you mean." Rioz yawned and found it difficult under the circumstances to use the expression with the proper amount of resentment.

"—and sometimes I read descriptions of people lying on grass," continued Long. "You know that green stuff like thin, long pieces of paper they have all over the ground down there, and they look up at the blue sky with clouds in it. Did you ever see any films of that?"

"Sure. It didn't attract me. It looked cold."

"I suppose it isn't, though. After all, Earth is quite close to the Sun, and they say their atmosphere is thick enough to hold the heat. I must admit that personally I would hate to be caught under open sky with nothing on but clothes. Still, I imagine they like it."

"Grounders are nuts!"

"They talk about the trees, big brown stalks, and the winds, air movements, you know."

"You mean drafts. They can keep that, too."

"It doesn't matter. The point is they describe it beautifully, almost passionately. Many times I've wondered, 'What's it really like? Will I ever feel it or is this something only Earthmen can possibly feel?' I've felt so often that I was missing something vital. Now I know what it must be like. It's this. Complete peace in the middle of a beauty-drenched universe."

Rioz said, "They wouldn't like it. The Grounders, I mean. They're so used to their own lousy little world they wouldn't appreciate what it's like to float and look down on Saturn." He flipped his body slightly and began swaying back and forth about his center of mass, slowly, soothingly.

Long said, "Yes, I think so too. They're slaves to their planet. Even if they come to Mars, it will only be their children that are free. There'll be starships someday; great, huge things that can carry thousands of people and maintain their self-contained equilibrium for decades, maybe centuries. Mankind will spread through the whole Galaxy. But people will have to live their lives out on ship-board until new methods of interstellar travel are developed, so it will be Martians, not planetbound Earthmen, who will colonize the Universe. That's inevitable. It's got to be. It's the Martian way."

But Rioz made no answer. He had dropped off to sleep again, rocking and swaying gently, half a million miles above Saturn.

The work shift of the ring fragment was the tail of the coin. The weightlessness, peace, and privacy of the space-float gave place to something that had neither peace nor privacy. Even the weightlessness, which continued, became more a purgatory than a paradise under the new conditions.

Try to manipulate an ordinarily non-portable heat projector. It could be lifted despite the fact that it was six feet high and wide and almost solid metal, since it weighed only a fraction of an ounce. But its inertia was exactly what it had always been, which meant that if it wasn't moved into position very slowly, it would just keep on going, taking you with it. Then you would have to hike the pseudo-grav field of your suit and come down with a jar.

Keralski had hiked the field a little too high and he came down a little too roughly, with the projector coming down with him at a dangerous angle. His crushed ankle had been the first casualty of the expedition.

Rioz was swearing fluently and nearly continuously. He continued to have the impulse to drag the back of his hand across his forehead in order to wipe away the accumulating sweat. The few times that he had succumbed to the impulse, metal had met silicone with a clash that rang loudly inside his suit, but served no useful purpose. The desiccators within the suit were sucking at maximum and, of course, recovering the water and restoring ion-exchanged liquid, containing a careful proportion of salt, into the appropriate receptacle.

Rioz yelled, "Damn it, Dick, wait till I give the word, will you?"

And Swenson's voice rang in his ears, "Well, how long am I supposed to sit here?"

"Till I say," replied Rioz.

He strengthened pseudo-grav and lifted the projector a bit. He released pseudo-grav, insuring that the projector would stay in place for minutes even if he withdrew support altogether. He kicked the cable out of the way (it stretched beyond the close "horizon" to a power source that was out of sight) and touched the release.

The material of which the fragment was composed bubbled and vanished under its touch. A section of the lip of the tremendous cavity he had already carved into its substance melted away and a roughness in its contour had disappeared.

"Try it now," called Rioz.

Swenson was in the ship that was hovering nearly over Rioz's head.

Swenson called, "All clear?"

"I told you to go ahead."

It was a feeble flicker of steam that issued from one of the ship's forward vents. The ship drifted down toward the ring fragment. Another flicker adjusted a tendency to drift sidewise. It came down straight.

A third flicker to the rear slowed it to a feather rate.

Rioz watched tensely. "Keep her coming. You'll make it. You'll make it."

The rear of the ship entered the hole, nearly filling it. The bellying walls came closer and closer to its rim. There was a grinding vibration as the ship's motion halted.

It was Swenson's turn to curse. "It doesn't fit," he said.

Rioz threw the projector groundward in a passion and went flailing up into space. The projector kicked up a white crystalline dust all about it, and when Rioz came down under pseudo-grav, he did the same.

He said, "You went in on the bias, you dumb Grounder."

"I hit it level, you dirt-eating farmer."

Backward-pointing side jets of the ship were blasting more strongly than before, and Rioz hopped to get out of the way.

The ship scraped up from the pit, then shot into space half a mile before forward jets could bring it to a halt.

Swenson said tensely, "We'll spring half a dozen plates if we do this once again. Get it right, will you?"

"I'll get it right. Don't worry about it. Just you come in right."

Rioz jumped upward and allowed himself to climb three hundred yards to get an over-all look at the cavity. The gouge marks of the ship were plain enough. They were concentrated at one point halfway down the pit. He would get that.

It began to melt outward under the blaze of the projector.

Half an hour later the ship snuggled neatly into its cavity, and Swenson, wearing his space suit, emerged to join Rioz.

Swenson said, "If you want to step in and climb out of the suit, I'll take care of the icing."

"It's all right," said Rioz. "I'd just as soon sit here and watch Saturn."

He sat down at the lip of the pit. There was a six-foot gap between it and the ship. In some places about the circle, it was two feet; in a few places, even merely a matter of inches. You couldn't expect a better fit out of handwork. The final adjustment would be made by steaming ice gently and letting it freeze into the cavity between the lip and the ship.

Saturn moved visibly across the sky, its vast bulk inching below the horizon.

Rioz said, "How many ships are left to put in place?"

Swenson said, "Last I heard, it was eleven. We're in now, so that means only ten. Seven of the ones that are placed are iced in. Two or three are dismantled."

"We're coming along fine."

"There's plenty to do yet. Don't forget the main jets at the other end. And the cables and the power lines. Sometimes I wonder if we'll make it. On the way out, it didn't bother me so much, but just now I was sitting at the controls and I was saying, 'We won't make it. We'll sit out here and starve and die with nothing but Saturn over us.' It makes me feel—"

He didn't explain how it made him feel. He just sat there.

Rioz said, "You think too damn much."

"It's different with you," said Swenson. "I keep thinking of Pete—and Dora."

"What for? She said you could go, didn't she? The Commissioner gave her that talk on patriotism and how you'd be a hero and set for life once you got back, and she said you could go. You didn't sneak out the way Adams did."

"Adams is different. That wife of his should have been shot when she was born. Some women can make hell for a guy, can't they? She didn't want him to go—but she'd probably rather he didn't come back if she can get his settlement pay."

"What's your kick, then? Dora wants you back, doesn't she?"

Swenson sighed. "I never treated her right."

"You turned over your pay, it seems to me. I wouldn't do that for any woman. Money for value received, not a cent more."

"Money isn't it. I get to thinking out here. A woman likes company. A kid needs his father. What am I doing 'way out here?"

"Getting set to go home."

"Ah-h, you don't understand."

Ted Long wandered over the ridged surface of the ring fragment with his spirits as icy as the ground he walked on. It had all seemed perfectly logical back on Mars, but that was Mars. He had worked it out carefully in his mind in perfectly reasonable steps. He could still remember exactly how it went.

It didn't take a ton of water to move a ton of ship. It was not mass equals mass, but mass times velocity equals mass times velocity. It didn't matter, in other words, whether you shot out a ton of water at a mile a second or a hundred pounds of water at twenty miles a second. You got the same final velocity out of the ship.

That meant the jet nozzles had to be made narrower and the steam hotter. But then drawbacks appeared. The narrower the nozzle, the more energy was lost in friction and turbulence. The hotter the steam, the more refractory the nozzle had to be and the shorter its life. The limit in that direction was quickly reached.

Then, since a given weight of water could move considerably more than its own weight under the narrow-nozzle conditions, it paid to be big. The bigger the water-storage space, the larger the size of the actual travel-head, even in proportion. So they started to make liners heavier and bigger. But then the larger the shell, the heavier the bracings, the more difficult the weldings, the more exacting the engineering requirements. At the moment, the limit in that direction had been reached also.

And then he had put his finger on what had seemed to him to be the basic flaw—the original unswervable conception that the fuel had to be placed *inside* the ship; the metal had to be built to encircle a million tons of water.

Why? Water did not have to be water. It could be ice, and ice could be shaped. Holes could be melted into it. Travel-heads and jets could be fitted into it. Cables could hold travel-heads and jets stiffly together under the influence of magnetic field-force grips.

Long felt the trembling of the ground he walked on. He was at the head of the fragment. A dozen ships were blasting in and out of sheaths carved in its substance, and the fragment shuddered under the continuing impact.

The ice didn't have to be quarried. It existed in proper chunks in the rings of Saturn. That's all the rings were—pieces of nearly pure ice, circling Saturn. So spectroscopy stated and so it had turned out to be. He was standing on one such piece now, over two miles long, nearly one mile thick. It was almost half a billion tons of water, all in one piece, and he was standing on it.

But now he was face to face with the realities of life. He had never told the men just how quickly he had expected to set up the fragment as a ship, but in his heart, he had imagined it would be two days. It was a week now and he didn't dare to estimate the remaining time. He no longer even had any confidence that the task was a possible one. Would they be able to control jets with enough delicacy through leads slung across two miles of ice to manipulate out of Saturn's dragging gravity?

Drinking water was low, though they could always distill more out of the ice. Still, the food stores were not in a good way either.

He paused, looked up into the sky, eyes straining. *Was* the object growing larger? He ought to measure its distance. Actually, he lacked the spirit to add that trouble to the others. His mind slid back to greater immediacies.

Morale, at least, was high. The men seemed to enjoy being out Saturnway. They were the first humans to penetrate this far, the first to pass the asteroids, the first to see Jupiter like a glowing pebble to the naked eye, the first to see Saturn—like that.

He didn't think fifty practical, case-hardened, shell-snatching Scavengers would take time to feel that sort of emotion. But they did. And they were proud.

Two men and a half-buried ship slid up the moving horizon as he walked.

He called crisply, "Hello, there!"

Rioz answered, "That you, Ted?"

"You bet. Is that Dick with you?"

"Sure. Come on, sit down. We were just getting ready to ice in and we were looking for an excuse to delay."

"I'm not," said Swenson promptly. "When will we be leaving, Ted?"

"As soon as we get through. That's no answer, is it?"

Swenson said dispiritedly, "I suppose there isn't any other answer."

Long looked up, staring at the irregular bright splotch in the sky.

Rioz followed his glance. "What's the matter?"

For a moment, Long did not reply. The sky was black otherwise and the ring fragments were an orange dust against it. Saturn was more than three fourths below the horizon and the rings were going with it. Half a mile away a ship bounded past the icy rim of the planetoid into the sky, was orange-lit by Saturn-light, and sank down again.

The ground trembled gently.

Rioz said, "Something bothering you about the Shadow?"

They called it that. It was the nearest fragment of the rings, quite close considering that they were at the outer rim of the rings, where the pieces spread themselves relatively thin. It was perhaps twenty miles off, a jagged mountain, its shape clearly visible.

"How does it look to you?" asked Long.

Rioz shrugged. "Okay, I guess. I don't see anything wrong."

"Doesn't it seem to be getting larger?"

"Why should it?"

"Well, doesn't it?" Long insisted.

Rioz and Swenson stared at it thoughtfully.

"It does look bigger," said Swenson.

"You're just putting the notion into our minds," Rioz argued. "If it were getting bigger, it would be coming closer."

"What's impossible about that?"

"These things are on stable orbits."

"They were when we came here," said Long. "There, did you feel that?"

The ground had trembled again.

Long said, "We've been blasting this thing for a week now. First, twenty-five ships landed on it, which changed its momentum right there. Not much, of course. Then we've been melting parts of it away and our ships have been blasting in and out of it—all at one end, too. In a week, we may have changed its orbit just a bit. The two fragments, this one and the Shadow, might be converging."

"It's got plenty of room to miss us in." Rioz watched it thoughtfully. "Besides, if we can't even tell for sure that it's getting bigger, how quickly can it be moving? Relative to us, I mean."

"It doesn't have to be moving quickly. Its momentum is as large as ours, so that, however gently it hits, we'll be nudged completely out of our orbit, maybe in toward Saturn, where we don't want to go. As a matter of fact, ice has a very low tensile strength, so that both planetoids might break up into gravel."

Swenson rose to his feet. "Damn it, if I can tell how a shell is moving a thousand miles away, I can tell what a mountain is doing twenty miles away." He turned toward the ship.

Long didn't stop him.

Rioz said, "There's a nervous guy."

The neighboring planetoid rose to zenith, passed overhead, began sinking. Twenty minutes later, the horizon opposite that portion behind which Saturn had disappeared burst into orange flame as its bulk began lifting again.

Rioz called into his radio, "Hey, Dick, are you dead in there?"

"I'm checking," came the muffled response.

"Is it moving?" asked Long.

"Yes."

"Toward us?"

There was a pause. Swenson's voice was a sick one. "On the nose, Ted. Intersection of orbits will take place in three days."

"You're crazy!" yelled Rioz.

"I checked four times," said Swenson.

Long thought blankly, What do we do now?

Some of the men were having trouble with the cables. They had to be laid precisely; their geometry had to be very nearly perfect for the magnetic field to attain maximum strength. In space, or even in air, it wouldn't have mattered. The cables would have lined up automatically once the juice went on.

Here it was different. A gouge had to be plowed along the planetoid's surface and into it the cable had to be laid. If it were not lined up within a few minutes of arc of the calculated direction, a torque would be applied to the entire planetoid, with consequent loss of energy, none of which could be spared. The gouges then had to be redriven, the cables shifted and iced into the new positions.

The men plodded wearily through the routine.

And then the word reached them:

"All hands to the jets!"

Scavengers could not be said to be the type that took kindly to discipline. It was a grumbling, growling, muttering group that set about disassembling the jets of the ships that yet remained intact, carrying them to the tail end of the planetoid, grubbing them into position, and stringing the leads along the surface.

It was almost twenty-four hours before one of them looked into the sky and said, "Holy jeepers!" followed by something less printable.

His neighbor looked and said, "I'll be damned!"

Once they noticed, all did. It became the most astonishing fact in the Universe.

"Look at the Shadow!"

It was spreading across the sky like an infected wound. Men looked at it, found it had doubled its size, wondered why they hadn't noticed that sooner.

Work came to a virtual halt. They besieged Ted Long.

He said, "We can't leave. We don't have the fuel to see us back to Mars and we don't have the equipment to capture another planetoid. So we've got to stay. Now the Shadow is creeping in on us because our blasting has thrown us out of orbit. We've got to change that by continuing the blasting. Since we can't blast the front end any more without endangering the ship we're building, let's try another way."

They went back to work on the jets with a furious energy that received impetus every half hour when the Shadow rose again over the horizon, bigger and more menacing than before.

Long had no assurance that it would work. Even if the jets would respond to the distant controls, even if the supply of water, which depended upon a storage chamber opening directly into the icy body of the planetoid, with built-in heat projectors steaming the propulsive fluid directly into the driving cells, were adequate, there was still no certainty that the body of the planetoid without a magnetic cable sheathing would hold together under the enormously disruptive stresses.

"Ready!" came the signal in Long's receiver.

Long called, "Ready!" and depressed the contact.

The vibration grew about him. The star field in the visiplate trembled.

In the rearview, there was a distant gleaming spume of swiftly moving ice crystals.

"It's blowing!" was the cry.

It kept on blowing. Long dared not stop. For six hours, it blew, hissing, bubbling, steaming into space; the body of the planetoid converted to vapor and hurled away.

The Shadow came closer until men did nothing but stare at the mountain in the sky, surpassing Saturn itself in spectacularity. Its every groove and valley was a plain scar upon its face. But when it passed through the planetoid's orbit, it crossed more than half a mile behind its then position.

The steam jet ceased.

Long bent in his seat and covered his eyes. He hadn't eaten in two days. He could eat now, though. Not another planetoid was close enough to interrupt them, even if it began an approach that very moment.

Back on the planetoid's surface, Swenson said, "All the time I watched that damned rock coming down, I kept saying to myself, 'This can't happen. We can't let it happen.' "

"Hell," said Rioz, "we were all nervous. Did you see Jim Davis? He was green. I was a little jumpy myself."

"That's not it. It wasn't just—dying, you know. I was thinking—I know it's funny, but I can't help it—I was thinking that Dora warned me I'd get myself killed, she'll never let me hear the last of it. Isn't that a crummy sort of attitude at a time like that?"

"Listen," said Rioz, "you wanted to get married, so you got married. Why come to me with your troubles?"

The flotilla, welded into a single unit, was returning over its mighty course from Saturn to Mars. Each day it flashed over a length of space that had taken nine days outward.

Ted Long had put the entire crew on emergency. With twenty-five ships embedded in the planetoid taken out of Saturn's rings and unable to move or maneuver independently, the co-ordination of their power sources into unified blasts was a ticklish problem. The jarring that took place on the first day of travel nearly shook them out from under their hair.

That, at least, smoothed itself out as the velocity raced upward under the steady thrust from behind. They passed the one-hundred-thousand-mile-an-hour mark late on the second day, and climbed steadily toward the million-mile mark and beyond.

Long's ship, which formed the needle point of the frozen fleet, was the only one which possessed a five-way view of space. It was an uncomfortable position under the circumstances. Long found himself watching tensely, imagining somehow that the stars would slowly begin to slip backward, to whizz past them, under the influence of the multi-ship's tremendous rate of travel.

They didn't, of course. They remained nailed to the black backdrop, their distance scorning with patient immobility any speed mere man could achieve.

The men complained bitterly after the first few days. It was not only that they were deprived of the space-float. They were burdened by much more than the ordinary pseudo-gravity field of the ships, by the effects of the fierce acceleration under which they were living. Long himself was weary to death of the relentless pressure against hydraulic cushions.

They took to shutting off the jet thrusts one hour out of every four and Long fretted.

It had been just over a year that he had last seen Mars shrinking in an observation window from this ship, which had then been an independent entity. What had happened since then? Was the colony still there?

In something like a growing panic, Long sent out radio pulses toward Mars daily, with the combined power of twenty-five ships behind it. There was no answer. He expected none. Mars and Saturn were on opposite sides of the Sun now, and until he mounted high enough above the ecliptic to get the Sun well beyond the line connecting himself and Mars, solar interference would prevent any signal from getting through.

High above the outer rim of the Asteroid Belt, they reached maximum velocity. With short spurts of power from first one side jet, then another, the huge vessel reversed itself. The composite jet in the rear began its mighty roaring once again, but now the result was deceleration.

They passed a hundred million miles over the Sun, curving down to intersect the orbit of Mars.

A week out of Mars, answering signals were heard for the first time, fragmentary, ether-torn, and incomprehensible, but they were coming from Mars. Earth and Venus were at angles sufficiently different to leave no doubt of that.

Long relaxed. There were still humans on Mars, at any rate.

Two days out of Mars, the signal was strong and clear and Sankov was at the other end.

Sankov said, "Hello, son. It's three in the morning here. Seems like people have no consideration for an old man. Dragged me right out of bed."

"I'm sorry, sir."

"Don't be. They were following orders. I'm afraid to ask, son. Anyone hurt? Maybe dead?"

"No deaths, sir. Not one."

"And—and the water? Any left?"

Long said, with an effort at nonchalance, "Enough."

"In that case, get home as fast as you can. Don't take any chances, of course."

"There's trouble, then."

"Fair to middling. When will you come down?"

"Two days. Can you hold out that long?"

"I'll hold out."

Forty hours later Mars had grown to a ruddy-orange ball that filled the ports and they were in the final planet-landing spiral.

"Slowly," Long said to himself, "slowly." Under these conditions, even the thin atmosphere of Mars could do dreadful damage if they moved through it too quickly.

Since they came in from well above the ecliptic, their spiral passed from north to south. A polar cap shot whitely below them, then the much smaller one of the summer hemisphere, the large one again, the small one, at longer and longer intervals. The planet approached closer, the landscape began to show features.

"Prepare for landing!" called Long.

Sankov did his best to look placid, which was difficult considering how closely the boys had shaved their return. But it had worked out well enough.

Until a few days ago, he had no sure knowledge that they had survived. It seemed more likely—inevitable, almost—that they were nothing but frozen corpses somewhere in the trackless stretches from Mars to Saturn, new planetoids that had once been alive.

The Committee had been dickering with him for weeks before the news had come. They had insisted on his signature to the paper for the sake of appearances. It would look like an agreement, voluntarily and mutually arrived at. But Sankov knew well that, given complete obstinacy on his part, they would act unilaterally and be damned with appearances. It seemed fairly certain that Hilder's election was secure now and they would take the chance of arousing a reaction of sympathy for Mars.

So he dragged out the negotiations, dangling before them always the possibility of surrender.

And then he heard from Long and concluded the deal quickly.

The papers had lain before him and he had made a last statement for the benefit of the reporters who were present.

He said, "Total imports of water from Earth are twenty million tons a year. This is declining as we develop our own piping system. If I sign this paper agreeing to an embargo, our industry will be paralyzed, any possibilities of expansion will halt. It looks to me as if that can't be what's in Earth's mind, can it?"

Their eyes met his and held only a hard glitter. Assemblyman Digby had already been replaced and they were unanimous against him.

The Committee Chairman impatiently pointed out, "You have said all this before."

"I know, but right now I'm kind of getting ready to sign and I want it clear in my head. Is Earth set and determined to bring us to an end here?"

"Of course not. Earth is interested in conserving its irreplaceable water supply, nothing else."

"You have one and a half quintillion tons of water on Earth."

The Committee Chairman said, "We cannot spare water."

And Sankov had signed.

That had been the final note he wanted. Earth had one and a half quintillion tons of water and could spare none of it.

Now, a day and a half later, the Committee and the reporters waited in the spaceport dome. Through thick, curving windows, they could see the bare and empty grounds of Mars Spaceport.

The Committee Chairman asked with annoyance, "How much longer do we have to wait? And, if you don't mind, what are we waiting for?"

Sankov said, "Some of our boys have been out in space, out past the asteroids."

The Committee Chairman removed a pair of spectacles and cleaned them with a snowy-white handkerchief. "And they're returning?"

"They are."

The Chairman shrugged, lifted his eyebrows in the direction of the reporters.

In the smaller room adjoining, a knot of women and children clustered about another window. Sankov stepped back a bit to cast a glance toward them. He would much rather have been with them, been part of their excitement and tension. He, like them, had waited over a year now. He, like them, had thought, over and over again, that the men must be dead.

"You see that?" said Sankov, pointing.

"Hey!" cried a reporter. "It's a ship!"

A confused shouting came from the adjoining room.

It wasn't a ship so much as a bright dot obscured by a drifting white cloud. The cloud grew larger and began to have form. It was a double streak against the sky, the lower ends billowing out and upward again. As it dropped still closer, the bright dot at the upper end took on a crudely cylindrical form.

It was rough and craggy, but where the sunlight hit, brilliant high lights bounced back.

The cylinder dropped toward the ground with the ponderous slowness characteristic of space vessels. It hung suspended on those blasting jets and settled down upon the recoil of tons of matter hurling downward like a tired man dropping into his easy chair.

And as it did so, a silence fell upon all within the dome. The women and children in one room, the politicians and reporters in the other remained frozen, heads craned incredulously upward.

The cylinder's landing flanges, extending far below the two rear jets, touched ground and sank into the pebbly morass. And then the ship was motionless and the jet action ceased.

But the silence continued in the dome. It continued for a long time.

Men came clambering down the sides of the immense vessel, inching down, down the two-mile trek to the ground, with spikes on their shoes and ice axes in their hands. They were gnats against the blinding surface.

One of the reporters croaked, "What is it?"

"That," said Sankov calmly, "happens to be a chunk of matter that spent its time scooting around Saturn as part of its rings. Our boys fitted it out with travel-head and jets and ferried it home. It just turns out the fragments in Saturn's rings are made up out of ice."

He spoke into a continuing deathlike silence. "That thing that looks like a spaceship is just a mountain of hard water. If it were standing like that on Earth, it would be melting into a puddle and maybe it would break under its own weight. Mars is colder and has less gravity, so there's no such danger.

"Of course, once we get this thing really organized, we can have water stations on the moons of Saturn and Jupiter and on the asteroids. We can scale in chunks of Saturn's rings and pick them up and send them on at the various stations. Our Scavengers are good at that sort of thing.

"We'll have all the water we need. That one chunk you see is just under a cubic mile—or about what Earth would send us in two hundred years. The boys used quite a bit of it coming back from Saturn. They made it in five weeks, they tell me, and used up about a hundred million tons! But, Lord, that didn't make any dent at all in that mountain. Are you getting all this, boys?"

He turned to the reporters. There was no doubt they were getting it.

He said, "Then get this, too. Earth is worried about its water supply. It only has one and a half quintillion tons. It can't spare us a single ton out of it. Write down that we folks on Mars are worried about Earth and don't want anything to happen to Earth people. Write down that we'll sell water to Earth. Write down that we'll let them have million-ton lots for a reasonable fee. Write down that in ten years, we figure we can sell it in cubic-mile lots. Write down that Earth can quit worrying because Mars can sell it all the water it needs and wants."

LEONARDO DA VINCI: PIONEER IN AVIATION

by Ivor B. Hart

Flight before Leonardo.—Aeronautics is a very young science. From the point of view of the achievement of "heavier-than-air" flight, it is but little more than a quarter of a century since the late Professor Langley, secretary to the Smithsonian Institution at Washington, successfully flew his *model* aeroplane for half-mile distances over the River Potomac. He called it an "aerodrome," and it measured 12 feet from tip to tip, weighed 30 lbs., and carried a steam engine and boiler weighing 7 lbs. The brothers Wright achieved the first motor-driven, *man-carrying* flight in an aeroplane for a period lasting but a portion of a minute as recently as December, 1903. Yet young as is aeronautics as a science, as an aspiration and a philosopher's dream we may claim for it the age of many centuries. Aeronautics has, in fact, a history, and although it is inevitable that we must accord to this history a much longer period of legend than obtains with most of the sciences, it is very real nevertheless.

Among those who have contributed effectively to the sum of ideas concerning flight, no figure is more striking than Leonardo da Vinci, who has this much at least in common with the science of aeronautics—that he has only recently come into his own.

Dreamers of air conquest pass before us throughout the panorama of the early history of civilisation. We see them in the winged statuary of the Egyptians and we read of them in stories of ancient Greek mythology. Ever since man has learnt to think, the challenge of the air has tantalised him. He has ever regarded as an anomaly and an incongruity that the ability to fly should be granted to birds and yet denied to him. And so we read of such legendary figures as Icarus and Perseus and Hermes, and of such entertaining but improbable stories as of Simon Magus, who, with the aid of some demon colleagues, essayed a short-lived flight and finished with a broken neck; of Abaris (as related by Diodorus of Sicily) and his flight round the world on a golden arrow (somewhat reminiscent of old Mother Shipton and of the nursery pictures of the cow jumping over the moon); and of the story of Aulus Gallius in his *Attic Nights* of

Archytas and his mechanical pigeon of wood: "To wit, it was thus suspended by balancing and was animated by an occult and enclosed aura of spirit."

Later we have the more circumstantial story of the Saracen of Constantinople who, in the presence of both the Emperor Comnenus and the Sultan of the Turks and a vast concourse of people, attempted to fly round the hippodrome at Constantinople. Wearing a long white robe braced with rods with which to catch the breeze, he took his station at the top of a tower and leaned into the wind. But "the weight of his body having more power to drag him down than the artificial wings had to sustain him, he broke his bones, and his evil plight was such that he did not long survive."

A like fate befel a similar attempt in the year 1065 by Oliver Malmesbury. Then there is Roger Bacon's classical thirteenth-century prophecy that—

> an instrument may be made to fly withal if one sit in the midst of the instrument, and do turn an engine, by which the wings, being artifically composed, may beat the air after the manner of a flying bird. . . .

In the fifteenth century we come to records concerning the famous astronomer Regiomontanus. We are told of him that in his workshop at Nurenburg was an automaton in "perpetual" motion, and that he made an artificial "fly" which, "taking its flight from his hand, would fly round the room," and at last, as if weary, would return to his master's hand, and that he fabricated an eagle which, on the Emperor's approach to the city, he sent out, high in the air, a great way to meet him, and that it kept him company to the gates of the city. Shorn of all the inevitable additions of credulous narrators the probability is that Regiomontanus, who was of a mechanical turn of mind, fashioned a clockwork contrivance which, more by luck possibly than by design, acted as a glider when released. Finally, there are records of experiments by an obscure contemporary of Leonardo, one Giovanni Baptista Danti, who essayed a flight at Perugia towards the close of the fifteenth century by means of a contrivance of wings which worked "with a horrible hissing sound." It was perhaps an imitation of one of the machines which Leonardo himself designed.

Da Vinci and His Problem of Flight.—Leonardo da Vinci was born in 1452 and died in 1519. It is therefore obvious from what we have said that in attempting to tackle seriously the problem of flight he owed next to nothing either to his contemporaries or to those who lived before his day. Careful study of his manuscripts make it clear to all fair-minded students that, in the truest sense of the term, da Vinci was not only a real pioneer of the science of flight, but was also the first pioneer. With all his many interests and activities, he yet gave, at intervals during thirty years of his life, a close consideration to the problem. It fascinated and held him. His ambition appears to have been to achieve a flight from the summit of Monte Ceceri (the name of a bird), situated a little to the north and east of Fiesole. No doubt the name appealed to the artist in him as being peculiarly appropriate.

> From the mountain which bears the name of the great bird, the famous bird will take its flight, and will fill the world with its great fame,

he writes; and again,

> The great bird [he frequently refers to his conception of a flying machine as a bird] will take its first flight on the back of the great bird, and filling the world with stupor and all writings with renown and bringing glory to the nest where it was born.

These are extravagant words which carry their own significance as to the frame of mind of him who penned them, but, coming as they do from one whom we know to have been imbued with the scientific spirit, they have an added importance. It is not surprising, therefore, that we meet with his discussions on flight both as early as the year 1488, during his residence at Milan, and as late as 1514, whilst at Rome. His main contribution to the subject, the note-book *Sul Volo degli Uccelli (On the Flight of Birds),* was written at Florence in 1505.

There were certain fundamental ideas which clearly guided da Vinci through the whole course of his investigations. Of these the most important was the time-old view that the imitation of the bird was the right line to adopt, and that its study would reveal the true secrets of flight.

> A bird [writes he] is an instrument working according to mathematical law, an instrument which it is within the capacity of man to reproduce with all its movements, though not with a corresponding degree of strength, for it is deficient in the power of maintaining equilibrium. We may therefore say that such an instrument constructed by man is lacking in nothing except the life of the bird, and this life must needs be supplied from that of man.

He had no illusions as to the comparison between a bird using its own living members and accessories and a man using wings and accessories which have no life in themselves:

> The life which resides in the birds' members will, without doubt, better conform to their needs than will that of man which is separated from them, and especially in the almost imperceptible movements which preserve equilibrium. But since we see that the bird is equipped for many obvious varieties of movements, we are able from this experience to deduce that the most rudimentary of understanding and that he will to a great extent be able to provide

> against the destruction of that instrument of which he has himself become the living principle and the propeller.

Another fundamentally sound principle laid down by Leonardo should also be noted, namely, the need for study of the medium in which flight is carried out.

> To attain to the true science of the movement of birds in the air it is necessary to give first the science of the winds, which we will establish by means of the movements of water. This science will be a degree [means] of arriving at the knowledge of the winged creatures in the air and in the wind.

Was da Vinci attempting the impossible? He lived centuries before the days of mechanical power. The problem before him was, therefore, the attachment to the human frame of contrivances to be worked by muscular energy only, in conjunction with such natural assistance as could be derived with understanding from air currents. The history of flight before the days of steam, oil and gas engines includes many similar attempts after Leonardo's times, all unsuccessful, and even up to very recent years we should perhaps have dismissed the idea as incapable of achievement. The time has now come to abandon this attitude. That which Leonardo sought to achieve over 400 years ago, and for which many an intrepid adventurer has since laid down his life, has to some extent been accomplished.

To-day aeroplane flights in machines without mechanical power, on the glider principle, have been successfully carried out. One of the consequences of the Treaty of Versailles was that Germany was forbidden to build aeroplanes fitted with engines. German inventors were thus driven to the old problem of pre-engine days, and with that superior knowledge of the principles of flight which was of necessity denied to Leonardo da Vinci, they have been the pioneers in the finding of a solution. This solution is not of the type for which da Vinci worked. There is no attachment to the human frame of a scheme of mechanical wings to be operated by muscular energy. It has been rather a case of a modern type of aeroplane without an engine, deriving its power from a stiffening breeze, and operated by a man, and capable of both manoeuvre and control. To this extent the problem that Leonardo set himself has actually been solved.

It is important to notice that throughout Leonardo faces his problem in a true scientific spirit. He looks to those beings who do fly, he studies them carefully, their physiology, their anatomy, the medium in which they exist; he studies their movements through a vast variety of conditions. To every effect which he observes he looks for a cause, and to that cause he applies modifying conditions. He seeks and makes deductions, always with a view to obtaining control.

There are two very interesting contributions to the general subject of air conquest for which we are indebted to da Vinci. They are not only important in themselves, but serve also to show another aspect of the real man of science in the object of our study. The first of these is Leonardo's invention of the parachute. In the *Codex Atlanticus* we read:

> An object offers as much resistance to the air as the air does to the object. [Note here a fifteenth century statement of the law of reactions.]You may see that the beating of its wings against the air supports a heavy eagle in the highest and rarest atmosphere, close to the sphere of elemental fire. Again you may see the air in motion over the sea fill the swelling sails and drive heavily-laden ships. From these instances and the reasons given, a man with wings large enough and duly connected might learn to overcome the resistance of the air, and by conquering it, succeed in subjugating it and rising above it.

Here, clearly, we have the principle of the parachute, and Leonardo includes in his manuscript the figure here shown together with the accompanying explanation:

> If a man have a tent roof of calked linen 12 braccia broad [roughly a bracci equals a yard] and twelve braccia high, he will be able to let himself fall from any great height without danger to himself.

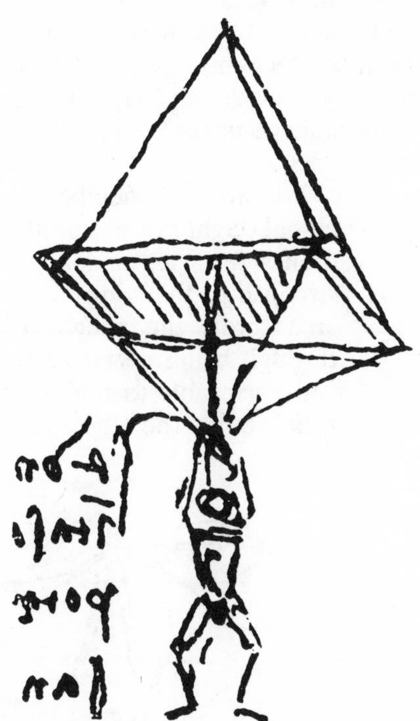

There is evidence that nearly a century *(c.* 1595) after da Vinci's invention, and probably as a direct result of it, Veranzio, a Venetian, modified the original design, using a sort of square sail extended by four rods of equal size and having four cords attached at the corners. Nevertheless, the first real descent in a parachute was not made till 1783, when Lenormand carried out a successful experiment from an observatory at Montpellier.

The other contribution is da Vinci's virtual discovery of the "lighter-than-air" principle. Leonardo was aware of the now familiar principle of the decreasing density of the atmosphere with altitude. "The air," he remarks, "has greater density when nearer to water and greater rarity when nearer to the cold region, and midway between these it is purer." Further, he knew of the principle of the fire balloon. Vasari tells us that he made figures of thin wax of strange shapes and filled them with warm air, causing them to "fly" through the air to the great surprise of onlookers. Why then was Leonardo not diverted to the study of balloons and aerostatics? So much simpler in basic theory is this than the sister study of aerodynamics that as soon as hydrogen was discovered the science of ballooning monopolised the whole attention of students of aeronautics, to the detriment of heavier-than-air design. Having regard to da Vinci's intellect, his practical bent and his opportunities, he could undoubtedly have made the fire balloon and the parachute the starting point of a very successful venture in the field of aerostatics. But this had no appeal for him. In a balloon there is neither life nor control. In the "bird" of da Vinci's imagination there was both, and with this goal clear in his mind there was no room for diversion. We have here a clear instance of the influence of scientific purpose. One less imbued with the true scientific spirit would have lost sight of the original problem in the joy of a new discovery off the beaten track. That this was not so with Leonardo is a fact which must affect our estimate of his scientific worth.

Leonardo da Vinci's Flying Machines.—We come finally to da Vinci's notes on flying machines. We have seen the general nature of our philosopher's observations and experiments and of the arguments and principles he brought to bear upon them. How did he apply these to the design of suitable mechanism wherewith to achieve for mankind his ambition of mastery over the air? He lay down very specifically a principle for general guidance in the design of wings.

> You are to remember [wrote he] that your bird [*i.e.,* flying machine] ought not to imitate anything but the bat because the membranes form an armour or liaison to the armour, that is to say, strength to the wings. And if you imitate the wings of the feathered birds, the wings are more powerful in bone and nerve, through being pervious; that is to say, the feathers are disunited and permeable to the air. But the bat is aided by the membrane which binds the whole and is not pervious.

This was sound advice and finds its final expression in modern aviation design. It is but a small step from the impervious membrane of a bat's wing to the doped fabric of an aeroplane wing. Yet how far did Leonardo follow this advice himself? Here was a line of attack on his practical problem which, in the light of modern developments, would appear to have contained the germs of some possible success. Yet in fact he appears to have neglected it, and it is disappointing that the sketches and notes in his manuscripts show Leonardo to be occupied chiefly with the idea of the substitution of "jointed" oars for wings. An almost isolated exception occurs in one note-book in which we meet with a sketch of an artificial wing, obviously modelled after the wing of a bat. Against the shaded

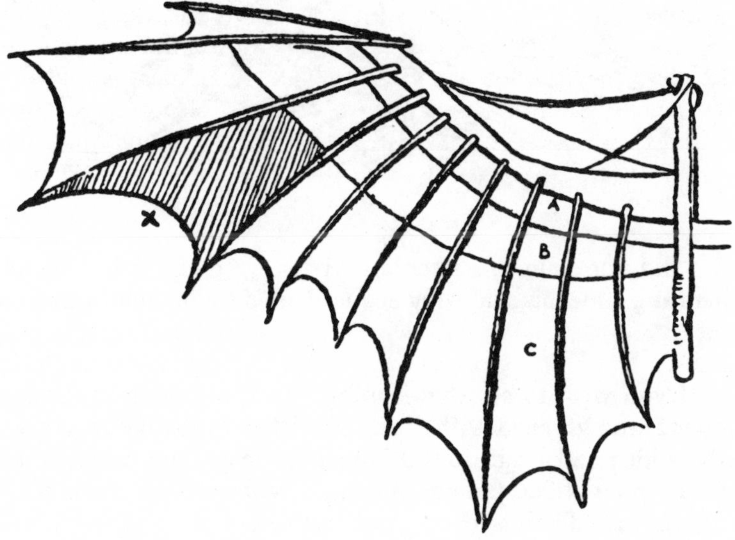

portion *X* he writes: "Make the meshes of this fibre of 1/8 in. width." Further details of construction are given with reference to the letters *A, B* and *C* in the diagram as follows:

> *A* will be of blades of deal, which has threads (?) and is light. *B* will be of fustian, on which will be glued the feathers, so as not to be easily pervious to the air. *C* should be of starched light silk, and in order to test it, you may make it of thin pasteboard.

Presumably Leonardo abandoned this type of wing as impracticable. Possibly he may have concluded that the wind resistance created by such an expanse of wing surface was far too much for the muscular energy of the human frame to cope with, but if this had been the case, one would have supposed the scientific alternative would have been to have reduced the area of surface accordingly. It seems probable that Leonardo attempted some experiments with a mechanical wing, and if so it is difficult to believe that the relationship between wing surface and wind

resistance did not claim his attention. Thus we meet with a sketch of a man operating a mechanical wing accompanied by the following explanatory note:

> If you wish to see the true test of the wings, take some pasteboard strengthened with fibre, and fitted with cane ribs, a wing of the width and length of 20 braccia at least, and fix it on a board (sheet-pile) of 200 pounds weight; it will produce, as shown in the figure, an effective force. And if the board of 200 lbs. is lifted before the wing falls, the test is good, but see to it also that the force be prompt (to act) and if the above-mentioned effect is not obtained, lose no more time on it.

We conclude from Leonardo's note-books—and these are almost our sole materials for judgment—not only that he either abandoned or neglected the idea of a "bat's wing" surface, but also that he came to no settled conclusions as to the use of a "jointed oar." Regarding it from the modern point of view, it is obvious that the air displacement created by the movement of a form of "oar" through the air must of necessity be utterly inadequate for the generation of a sufficient force to support a human being plus mechanical attachments. Consequently one need not be surprised at the variety, the vagueness, and the incompleteness of design displayed in many sketches and notes in Manuscript B. and in the *Sul Volo degli Uccelli.* They reflect the artist and the visionary vainly striving to link up with the engineer and the scientist. Da Vinci's scientific intuition was wonderful. His "sensing" of laws of nature was one of the most remarkable traits in his personality, and it carried him far—certainly far beyond his contemporaries. But there are serious limitations to this type of personality. Between the sensing of a law and an exact knowledge of its comprehension and its consequences lies a wide gulf of mathematical expression and equipment, and in this gulf it was inevitable that Leonardo would grope and flounder with little chance of success.

As a consequence the flying machines of Leonardo da Vinci are mainly of artistic and historic interest. This figure shows a typical example of a da Vinci wing—the left half only of the "machine." The following note accompanies the sketch:

> *a b c* arranges that in rising the part *m n* is promptly raised; *d e f* arranges that in descending *m n* is promptly lowered, and the wing (thus) fulfils its purpose; *r t* lowers the wing with the foot, that is to say, by extending the legs; *v s* raises the wing by the hand and the turn.

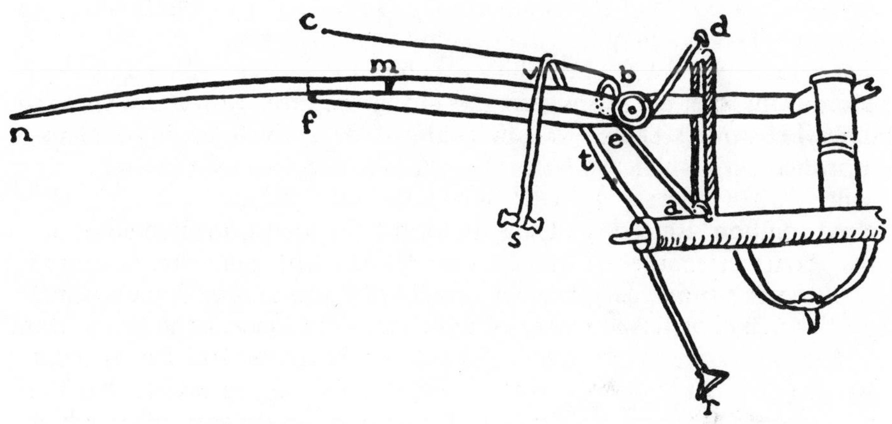

The next figure [top of following page] shows one of da Vinci's flying machines. The aviator is lying on a plank in front of which is a sort of pole. Fixed to this pole we see a rounded iron shank, and the jointed "oars" or wings are attached to this shank. The wings are operated by the feet by means of stirrups *c* and *d,* the right foot lowering the wing and the left raising it. The design is difficult to follow, but that Leonardo intended it seriously is evidenced by the following interesting paragraph: "You will experiment with this instrument on a lake, and you will carry engirdled a long wine skin, so that in falling you will come to no harm."

Other designs show double systems of oars, and he frequently favours the use of two ladders at the base of the machine to represent the feet of the "bird" and to serve the purpose of climbing into his instrument.

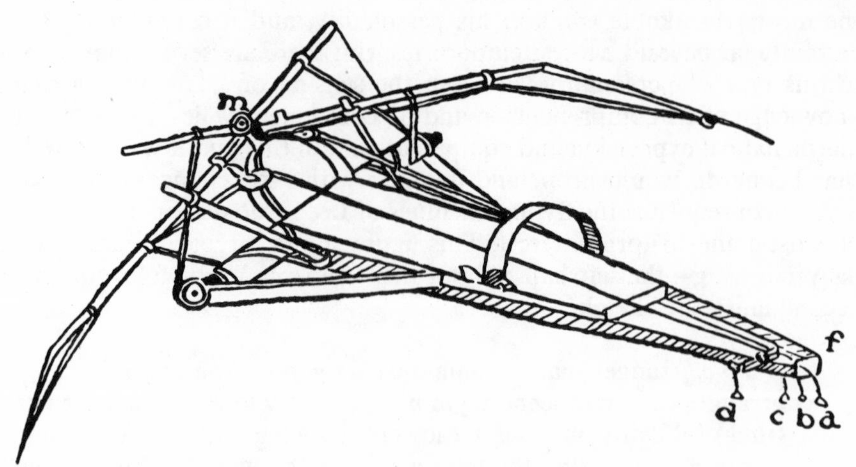

There is, however, one further design which calls for comment, since it constitutes a very real contribution to the science of aviation. It shows, in fact, that da Vinci may fairly lay claim to the invention of the helicopter; that is to say, to a type of machine capable of vertical movement upwards and downwards, and of hovering in any given position for any required time. Leonardo's sketch is now outlined. It consists of a mechanism furnished with a helical wheel. This wheel is actuated by a twisted spring which, when released so as to unwind itself, sets the helical wheel in rapid rotation. Referring to this instrument, Leonardo comments,

> I say that if this instrument made with a helix is well made, that is to say, of flaxen linen, of which one has closed the pores with starch, and is turned with great speed, the said helix is able to make a screw in the air, and to climb high. Take the example of a wide and thin ruler and directed violently into the air; you will see that your arm will be guided by the line of the edge of the said board. . . . One is able to make a little model of this of cardboard, whose axis should be of thin steel wire, twisted with force; on freeing this, it causes the helix to turn.

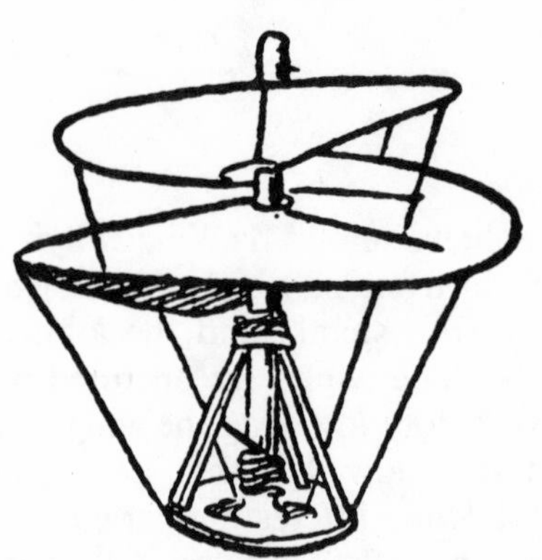

Here, then, beyond doubt, and for the first time in history, we have the principle of the helicopter.

What are we to conclude from all these activities? We have reviewed at some length the full scope of Leonardo da Vinci's researches and investigations in the field of aviation, and it is impossible to withhold our admiration for their breadth and their thoroughness. That he failed to achieve flight in no wise detracts from the value of his work. It is doubtful indeed if he ever even made the attempt himself. Jerome Cardan, the mathematician, whose father was a contemporary of Leonardo, who knew him and his work, tells us in his *de Subtilitate* that "Leonardo da Vinci also attempted to fly, but misfortune befel him from it. He was a great painter." This appears to be the only reference to an actual attempt. Nevertheless, Leonardo's work in aviation was real enough, and having regard to the limitations imposed upon him by the knowledge of his days, it was *scientific.*

A DISSERTATION ON THE ART OF FLYING

by Samuel Johnson

Among the artists that had been allured into the happy valley, to labour for the accommodation and pleasure of its inhabitants, was a man eminent for his knowledge of the mechanick powers, who had contrived many engines both of use and recreation.

This artist was sometimes visited by Rasselas, who was pleased with every kind of knowledge, imagining that the time would come when all his acquisitions should be of use to him in the open world. He came one day to amuse himself in his usual manner, and found the master busy in building a sailing chariot: he saw that the design was practicable upon a level surface, and with expressions of great esteem solicited its completion. The workman was pleased to find himself so much regarded by the prince, and resolved to gain yet higher honours. "Sir," said he, "you have seen but a small part of what the mechanick sciences can perform. I have been long of opinion, that, instead of the tardy conveyance of ships and chariots, man might use the swifter migration of wings; that the fields of air are open to knowledge, and that only ignorance and idleness need crawl upon the ground."

This hint rekindled the prince's desire of passing the mountains; having seen what the mechanist had already performed, he was willing to fancy that he could do more; yet resolved to enquire further before he suffered hope to afflict him by disappointment. "I am afraid," said he to the artist, "that your imagination prevails over your skill, and that you now tell me rather what you wish than what you know. Every animal has his element assigned him; the birds have the air, and man and beasts the earth." "So," replied the mechanist, "fishes have the water, in which yet beasts can swim by nature, and men by art. He that can swim needs not despair to fly: to swim is to fly in a grosser fluid, and to fly is to swim in a subtler. We are only to proportion our power of resistance to the different density of the matter through which we are to pass. You will be necessarily upborn by the air, if you can renew any impulse upon it, faster than the air can recede from the pressure."

"But the exercise of swimming," said the prince, "is very laborious; the strongest limbs are soon wearied; I am afraid the act of flying will be yet more violent, and wings will be of no great use, unless we can fly further than we can swim."

"The labour of rising from the ground," said the artist, "will be great, as we see it in the heavier domestick fowls; but, as we mount higher, the earth's attraction, and the body's gravity, will be gradually diminished, till we shall arrive at a region where the man will float in the air without any tendency to fall: no care will then be necessary, but to move forwards, which the gentlest impulse will effect. You, Sir, whose curiosity is so extensive, will easily conceive with what pleasure a philosopher, furnished with wings, and hovering in the sky, would see the earth, and all its inhabitants, rolling beneath him, and presenting to him successively, by its diurnal motion, all the countries within the same parallel. How must it amuse the pendent spectator to see the moving scene of land and ocean, cities and desarts! To survey with equal security the marts of trade, and the fields of battle; mountains infested by barbarians, and fruitful regions gladdened by plenty, and lulled by peace! How easily shall we then trace the Nile through all his passage; pass over to distant regions, and examine the face of nature from one extremity of the earth to the other!"

"All this," said the prince, "is much to be desired, but I am afraid that no man will be able to breathe in these regions of speculation and tranquility. I have been told, that respiration is difficult upon lofty mountains, yet from these precipices, though so high as to produce great tenuity of the air, it is very easy to fall: therefore I suspect, that from any height, where life can be supported, there may be danger of too quick descent."

"Nothing," replied the artist, "will ever be attempted, if all possible objections must be first overcome. If you will favour my project I will try the first flight at my own hazard. I have considered the structure of all volant animals, and find the folding continuity of the bat's wings most easily accommodated to the human form. Upon this model I shall begin my task tomorrow, and in a year expect to tower into the air beyond the malice or persuit of man. But I will work only on this condition, that the art shall not be divulged, and that you shall not require me to make wings for any but ourselves."

"Why," said Rasselas, "should you envy others so great an advantage? All skill ought to be exerted for universal good; every man has owed much to others, and ought to repay the kindness that he has received."

"If men were all virtuous," returned the artist, "I should with great alacrity teach them all to fly. But what would be the security of the good, if the bad could at pleasure invade them from the sky? Against an army sailing through the clouds neither walls, nor mountains, nor seas, could afford any security. A flight of northern savages might hover in the wind, and light at once with irresistible violence upon the capital of a fruitful region that was rolling under them. Even this valley, the retreat of princes, the abode of happiness, might be violated by the sudden descent of some of the naked nations that swarm on the coast of the southern sea."

The prince promised secrecy, and waited for the performance, not wholly hopeless of success. He visited the work from time to time, observed its progress, and remarked many ingenious contrivances to facilitate motion, and unite levity with strength. The artist was every day more certain that he should leave vultures and eagles behind him, and the contagion of his confidence seized upon the prince.

In a year the wings were finished, and, on a morning appointed, the maker appeared furnished for flight on a little promontory: he waved his pinions a while to gather air, then leaped from his stand, and in an instant dropped into the lake. His wings, which were of no use in the air, sustained him in the water, and the prince drew him to land, half dead with terrour and vexation. The prince was not much afflicted by this disaster, having suffered himself to hope for a happier event, only because he had no other means of escape in view.

SAMUEL JOHNSON—*Rasselas,* 1759

HUMAN-POWERED FLIGHT ACROSS THE ENGLISH CHANNEL

by Morton Grosser

When the *Gossamer Albatross* lifted off the pad, the spectators behind it were cheering wildly. Bryan could not hear the applause. He had been concentrating so hard on the airplane and on keeping his mind clear and unfragmented that he had even forgotten about the water. The last time he remembered seeing it, it had been just below the level of the concrete. Now, as he cleared the edge of the pad, it was 20 feet (6 metres) below him—it was like flying off a cliff. "What a rush!" he called into the microphone.

The plane was heading east by north as it took off, and once airborne Bryan began a sweeping right turn that would line him up with the waiting escorts. A few moments later the *Albatross* was soaring silently over the four idling Zodiacs like the great white bird it was named for. Jim Burke remembers his heart beating fast as the plane crossed above him, and he gunned the throttle of his outboard to fall in behind the right wingtip. "Altitude fifteen," Bryan reported.

"Roger, let's see if you can bring it down to ten," Sam answered. "Looks beautiful . . . Let's go for it."

The two big project boats waited out in deep water with the press fleet and an R.N.L.I. *Waveney*-class lifeboat from Folkestone, their engines rumbling in neutral. Paul had set up his project control on the *Lady Ellen Elizabeth,* crewed by John Ward, John Groat, and Frank Booton. With him were his sons Parker and Tyler and two official observers, David Faulkner Bryant and Ron Moulton. For Moulton, the dream was still persisting. As the *Gossamer Albatross* curved gracefully toward them, growing steadily larger, he could not convince himself that the scene was real. Tyler stood at the stern, sighting across his thumbs on a ruler marked to correspond with the *Albatross*'s wingspan seen at a distance of 1500 feet (457 metres). "Let's go!" he called, and the Moonraker's diesels opened up with a roar, accelerating the boat to 10 knots in a trough of white foam.

To starboard, the *Tartan Gem* followed the *Lady Ellen*'s course of 135°. Beside its 3-man crew, the *Gem* carried Don Billet, Jack Conmy, Dr. Ingrid Dodd, Don Monroe, Joe Thompson Sr., and Joe Thompson Jr. The other members of the film crew, Louis Prézelin and Tony Zapata, were in the fourth Zodiac with Tom Horton, Larry McNay, and Ted Ancona driving. The cameramen were ecstatic, and the temptation for the press boats to get a little closer, a little ahead of the plane, was already beginning to set in. In the right Zodiac with Jim Burke, Sam Durán, and Bill Watson, Otis Imboden exclaimed to himself after one shot, "That's a cover!"

"How're you feeling, Bryan?" Sam transmitted.

"Stabilized out very nicely, no problem." His legs pumping methodically at 80 rpm, Bryan was beginning to realize all the implications of the flight. ". . . So many things that we were doing for the first time. Flying over water, flying with all the boats out there . . . it struck me, what an audacious thing we were doing." Although most of us had pushed that thought to the back of our minds, it had occurred to everyone on the team at various times, and as a result the *Albatross* carried a number of private good luck totems. All of them were featherweight, since even a rabbit's foot seems heavy on a human-powered aircraft.

Under the starboard canard tip was the badge of the Kent Gliding Club, where several of the team members had qualified. On the fuselage, in addition to the three big oval Du Pont logos and the airplane's name on the upper fuselage fairings, there was a small "USA" badge on the right front, the badge of R.A.F. Manston symmetrically opposite it, a 10-pence airmail stamp on the left rear, and on the right side, Bryan's octagonal green "Nothing to Declare" sticker, brought back from a day trip to France.

"Control to *Albatross*. Stay . . . somewhat low, so you don't wear yourself out. Clear." Bryan followed this well-meant advice, dropping down to 10 feet, and almost immediately reported difficulty: "Getting some odd turbulence there for a sec." Steve Elliott, driving the smallest Mark III Zodiac with Kirk Giboney and Taras Kiceniuk, speeded up a bit to cover the left side more closely. "Bryan, this is Taras. What's your flying speed?"

"Flying speed presently is six and three-quarters [on the arbitrary scale of the airspeed instrument], altitude is ten feet."

"Roger. Experiment for minimum power speed, and fly just a hair faster. Over."

"Check."

Fifteen minutes into the flight, most of the problems that were to dog the rest of it had begun to show up. The first one was depth perception. Even though he had an altimeter, Bryan was uneasy when he found that he could look right through the surface of the water, without being able to determine where it was. The second one was turbulence. At 05:06 Sam asked Bryan if it felt any different flying over water. "Yeah, there's a pretty definite interlinking between the water and the air. A smooth sort of bumpiness, but it's bumpy all the time." The third one was cockpit ventilation. Despite a 50-percent-reflectivity Mylar panel on the port side of the fuselage, the cabin interior had already started to warm up, and condensed moisture was beginning to fog the windows. Bryan reported that the airflow improved somewhat when he opened the rear adjustable vent. The fourth problem was interference by the press boats. They had been given diagrams and a patient explanation showing them why it was vital to the safety of the airplane that they stay behind and away from it. For some of them, it was clearly a waste of breath.

05:07: For the Zodiacs it was like formation flying. Dave Saks was driving the center Mark V, carrying Blaine Rawdon and Joe Mastropaolo (first and second rescue divers), and Sterling Stoll. As the press boats converged from both sides, Sterling asked Sam to move his Zodiac further out to the right to keep traffic away. Sam complied, and a moment later the first irritation could be heard in his voice: "Taras, check that boat out in front, get him outa there."

The *Lady Ellen Elizabeth* was maintaining contact with both the project boats and the shore radios. From the St. Margaret's Bay Radar Station, where Dick Woodward and Dave McNay had driven after the takeoff, a crisp and attractive female voice informed MacCready that H.M. Coast Guard was tracking the *Albatross* flotilla on radar. Judy and Marshall MacCready had meanwhile raced pell-mell to the ferry terminal in Folkestone, and just made it aboard the Sealink *Horsa,* bound for Boulogne. When the ship's purser asked Judy for their tickets, she explained why she hadn't had time to buy any and offered to do so then. The officer excused himself, and a few moments later returned with an invitation from the captain for Judy and Marshall to come up to the bridge. "The tickets . . . ?" she asked.

"Just you go along and don't worry about them, ma'am, we'll sell you some in a bit."

Twenty minutes later the 5000-ton, 19-knot *Horsa* was following a course parallel with the *Gossamer Albatross,* and Judy and Marshall were watching the plane through the captain's binoculars. Not many of the *Horsa*'s other passengers could have realized how hard Bryan Allen was working. At 25 minutes into the flight his answers to radio calls were beginning to be punctuated by puffs for breath. "Bryan, what would you estimate it is, powerwise?" Sam asked.

"Hard to say, about point two eight [0.28 horsepower]."

"Roger. Oh, we're about three miles out now."

They were actually somewhat farther than that, but Bryan sensed that the flight was going slower than planned, and that he was beginning to fall behind. He looked over his left shoulder and was disheartened to find that he could still see the cliffs of Dover. The *Albatross* veered 30° off course, and he vowed not to look back again.

From the Zodiacs the *Horsa* seemed gigantic, even at the safe distance it maintained. There was enough mist to keep the project boats' visibility down to a few miles, but on the radar screens at Cap Gris-Nez, the Channel already looked like a busy thoroughfare. On an ordinary day about a thousand ships pass through the 22.3-mile (36-kilometre)-wide slot of ocean between the Warren and Cap Gris-Nez. Although the average ferry passenger sees the Channel as only an empty expanse of water, to the coast guards and the mariners navigating it, it is as cluttered as a city street with traffic lanes, buoys, lights, and obstacles. It is also cluttered with the wrecks of ships whose pilots have ignored or fallen afoul of those hazards.

On the big radar screens at Cap Gris-Nez the *Albatross* flotilla appeared as a cluster of luminous orange dots, a small amber Pleiades moving slowly—painfully slowly—across the main traffic lanes of *La Manche.* Every few times the scan cursor swept around the tube face, larger, brighter, and faster pips would appear at the top and bottom of the screen headed up- or down-Channel, at right angles to the *Albatross*'s course. As each ship came within range, it was called on the Coast Guard VHF frequency and warned in English, French, or German that a human-powered aircraft and its attendant boats were crossing the Channel at a speed of about 8 knots. Each ship also received the latest position we had plotted for the airplane and was asked to avoid interfering with its course if possible. Most of them were courteous and cooperative.

Up to this point the flight had progressed smoothly, almost monotonously, with Bryan turning the propeller at about 100 rpm and maintaining an altitude of 8 to 10 feet. His control motions were smooth and minimal, and he only varied from his normal position to sip some water or adjust his helmet or microphone. At 05:30 Sam asked for an altitude check, and received no answer. "Bryan, this is Sam. How're you feeling?" Still no answer. "Bryan, I'm not really getting you at all. Can you nod your head if you can hear me . . . Roger, okay." Allen could still receive the project radio transmissions, but he couldn't answer. At the time he thought that the perspiration running down his hands had short-circuited the press-to-talk button, but since there was no static or variation, he later concluded that one of the two fine wires to the button must have broken during a control motion.

By 05:52 Bryan had pedaled 9.6 miles (15.5 kilometres), and was abeam of the Varne lightship. Half of his water was gone, and the flight was about 22 percent behind Paul's original schedule. The flotilla had veered slightly north of the theoretically shortest flight path of 138° magnetic corrected to avoid a southbound ship track, and the 3- to 4-knot easterly wind that we had recorded at Cap Gris-Nez was also blowing in mid-Channel. The water, which had been relatively smooth for the beginning of the flight, now began to show ripples of turbulence and a short swell.

At that point Bryan dipped lower, partly because of perception problems, and partly to try to find smoother air. The flying effort went up immediately: "Altitude three feet," Taras cautioned. Allen realized that he was in a trap, because it takes much more power to pump the plane up to a higher altitude than to maintain it at a constant height. "Altitude! Two feet," from Taras and Sam simultaneously. "Bryan, this is Sam. Watch your altitude." Bryan nodded, but couldn't seem to get much above three feet; it was as if the air-water boundary layer were holding the plane down. At that point Paul MacCready's estimate of the flight's chance for success sank from 16 percent to zero.

One hour and seventeen minutes: "Altitude two feet!" Taras cried. "Bryan, this is Sam, on your right. Did you say you were tired?" Even though the media crews couldn't hear the radio transmissions they sensed that something was wrong. All courtesy went by the board as what Jim Burke now began calling the "press jackals" came roaring in, tossing the Zodiacs in their wakes. "Watch your altitude," Sam warned again, and then, "Taras, get that boat out of there. Get that boat *out of there!"* Steve and Jim gunned their engines to head off the press boats, but the wakes of the larger craft spread into the flight path. Taras sounded angry and alarmed, "Altitude three feet . . . Altitude two feet! ALTITUDE ONE FOOT! . . . Altitude two feet."

"That's better," Sam called.

The airplane stabilized a little higher, but the swells seemed to lick upward at the *Albatross*'s fuselage, and Bryan's control motions were more extreme. Sam pulled up close to the plane and Bryan was able to get across to him that his hand was tired. "Okay, Bryan, this is Sam. If it gets to the point that you really want to ditch it, or something like that, raise your right hand up over your head and we can move into position." Bryan acknowledged that. "Another thing, what we could do, if you want, we could give you a tow . . ."

"Altitude one foot. Altitude four feet," Taras reported. The lower Bryan flew, the higher Taras's voice went. Paul radioed to Sam that if Bryan needed a tow, they should be sure that he got it in time, and that they should turn the plane into the wind (to the left), and then slowly curve around toward England. While Paul was talking, the flotilla was being orbited in what Ron Moulton described as "curious fashion" by a small warship. This was the *Lyre,* a French ex-minesweeper converted to a patrol boat, and one of the two problem ships of the flight. We had called her repeatedly, asking her to report her position, and to please avoid the *Albatross* flotilla, but without any response. A commandant of the French Coast Guard eventually convinced her to reply and bear off.

Bryan meanwhile kept plugging ahead, but it was obvious that he was having trouble. His altitude dropped to one foot repeatedly over the wave crests. Still, he refused to quit. Paul advised Sam and Bryan that "There's another one and a half hours of flight time required to . . . reach France." Bryan's receiver was noisy, and all he heard was "One and a half . . . to reach France." His heart sank: "One and a half *what?* Hours? How can I do *that?* Never mind the headwinds, just pedal," he told himself, hoping that the message would reach down into his muscles. Pedal and fly. By 06:25 Paul could encourage Bryan with a milestone: "Control to airplane. We're just about two-thirds of the distance from England . . . to . . . France . . . meaning that it's only about an hour to go. Clear." Sam asked Bryan to nod if he got a good copy. Bryan did, and Sam had hardly gotten, "Excellent, great, thank you," out before the *Albatross* dropped to one foot again. Kirk Giboney, the first back-up pilot, came in over Taras's radio, "Get it up, Bryan, get it up!" Bryan tried, but realized that he was close to exhaustion. "It's no use . . . I'll have to ditch or take a tow from one of the Zodiacs," he thought. At 06:26 he raised his right hand, the signal to scrub the flight.

"OKAY, OKAY, WE'RE COMING IN!" Sam called. Bill Watson readied the modified fishing rod that carried the tow line. The catch ring was under the airplane's fuselage, near the front wheel. Bryan put out a tremendous burst of power and climbed to 15 feet (4.5 metres) so Sam's boat could get underneath the plane. Jim gunned the engine, and began what developed into an inadvertent and frustrating marine ballet between the *Albatross* and the Zodiac. Although the boat could match the airplane's speed perfectly, matching its lateral motion in the wave chop was almost impossible; the two craft veered sideways past each other again and again, while Bill stood up and tried to snag the fuselage, and Jim lay down in the bottom of the boat to avoid being hit by the plane's propeller. After the third unsuccessful try Bill suddenly realized that Bryan was intentionally trying to avoid him; each time he reached up with the rod, Bryan would pull the airplane out of reach. After four minutes of this, the other boats were baffled. "Sam, can you give us a status report?" Sterling asked. By that time Sam's crew had heard over the drone of the outboard Bryan saying ". . . try it up here for a while."

"I had accepted the inevitable—I had to give up. Then, when I did climb up to ten or fifteen feet I found the air much smoother, and thought, All right! We can keep going!"

"Bryan's tryin' it up a little higher, to see if it's less turbulent. He didn't want us to hook him in . . . at this time," Sam reported to the other boats.

At 06:38 Allen's water supply ran out, and a few moments later Sam noticed Bryan tapping the altimeter. He realized that something must be wrong with it; in fact the batteries were dead. For Bryan, this was one more burden; near the limits of his physical capability, he was learning a lesson that all seaplane pilots know by heart. "I couldn't really judge my altitude from the wave or ripple size. I could look out to the side and estimate my altitude from the angle to the various boats, but that angle would change as they would get closer or farther away. There just wasn't a reliable reference point I could depend on. There's also something slightly hypnotic about flying over water, especially when you're flying close to it. It's a very smooth rolling surface. I would become hypnotized by whatever that was, ripple size or something. Then I would hear 'One foot!' in my earphones."

Despite their self-discipline, the crew's fatigue and edginess was beginning to show through. At 06:40 several of them saw a large dark shadow in the distance and thought, *France!* Unfortunately, it was not France, but the bulk carrier *Jacob Russ,* and it had been preoccupying the radar crew and the French Coast Guard for the past half hour.

All supertankers and large bulk carriers transiting the Channel are subject to special traffic controls. They are required to use assigned lanes, to report their position frequently, and to carry pilots for longer times than smaller ships. The *Jacob Russ* was one of these monsters, 922 feet (281 metres) long by 140 feet (42.6 metres) beam (the Wright brothers' first successful engine-powered flight could have been made *across* the deck of this ship). She was registered in Hamburg, and had a deadweight tonnage of 137,644—more than one and a quarter million times the weight of the *Gossamer Albatross.* She was northbound in the Channel, and when her Dutch captain was first informed about the *Albatross,* he wanted no part of it. He made it clear in truculent terms that he refused to change speed or course, and that the flotilla would have to look out for itself. A few moments later he was notified by the Calais Pilot Board that he was expected to take aboard a pilot for the next section of the Channel passage. This precipitated a verbal battle that made our problem seem trivial, and tied up both Channel 6 and Channel 10 (the main intership and Coast Guard radio frequencies) for the next half hour.

Meanwhile the *Lady Ellen Elizabeth* was still leading the *Albatross* fleet on a bearing that was both north of the ideal line, and a collision course with the *Jacob Russ* as well. The British and French coast guards gave us special permission to use Channel 16, the emergency frequency, to call Paul and warn him to veer south in order to avoid the ship. Sam relayed the decision to the plane: "Bryan, what we're gonna do, is probably go behind this thing . . . It's probably gonna be a good mile ahead of us or so, we'll be behind him before we reach him." Bryan could only nod and pedal. At 06:49 the lead boat had reached the *Jacob Russ*'s track and found that the turbulence in its wake was no worse than what they were already experiencing. Paul called that to Bryan and told him that there was less than one-quarter of the flight remaining. Two minutes later the batteries for the *Albatross*'s speedometer ran out. Like the altimeter batteries, they had lasted almost exactly the two hours predicted; it was just that two hours wasn't long enough.

Allen was now flying without his crucial water supply, without a radio transmitter, and without instruments, in a cockpit that was getting increasingly fogged with moisture despite the vents. "One foot!" Sterling called. "ALTITUDE ONE FOOT, GET IT UP!" Taras trebled. Bryan put out another burst of energy and dragged it up to five feet. At that moment he grimly recalled that one of the Kremer Channel Prize rules was that the altitude of the plane must not exceed 50 metres. No problem there, he thought.

06:57: Sam, quietly, without an exclamation point: "Bryan, I think I can see land." For Bryan it is like a vision of Atlantis. There are still more than three miles to go, and he knows that he is fading rapidly. At two hours and ten minutes, he gets a stab of pain in his right calf, the first cramp. He shifts most of the pedaling load to the left leg, and the cramped calf eases, to be replaced by another one in the left thigh. He knows from experience that without water and rest they are not going to go away.

Slowly, the coast of France begins to materialize out of the haze. The camera Zodiac has already pulled ahead to land, and Sam reports that he can see the lighthouse at Cap Gris-Nez. At the CROSSMA station the French Coast Guards have changed shifts. The new detail, Christian Chaudru, Arnaud Souplet, and Olivier Tresca, are still helping the bleary-eyed *Albatross* crew to warn ships away until the flotilla crosses the inshore traffic zone boundary, when the newsmen begin to appear. Willem Van Loon of Du Pont Netherlands arrives to lend a hand, as does Jean Louf with the Maschelein brothers, who have driven all night from Belgium to be here for the landing.

Will there be a landing? Carrying red smoke flares and spotlights we race down to the beach at the foot of the cliff. The tide is near neap, and there is a large expanse of wet brown sand exposed. As we reach the water's edge the camera Zodiac beaches in the surf, and Louis and Tony jump ashore, cradling their movie cameras. With binoculars, one can just make out the plane, floating like a spectral creature in the white haze. It seems to be standing still, both to us and to Bryan: "I can make out the French coast, but it seems to come no closer . . ." "C'MON, BRYAN, C'MON UP, C'MON!! . . . YOU'RE MUSHING!" "All right! Altitude two . . . Time of flight two hours and twenty-four minutes."

For the fourth time during the flight Bryan thinks, "Well, this is it. I've done the best I could . . . and I haven't made it." And for the fourth time, some voice inside him answered, "No, doggone it, I've still got a little bit left and I'm gonna keep going." The plane's airspeed was now about 12 miles (19.3 kilometres) per hour, against a headwind of half that. To everyone—pilot, boats, beach crew—it was like slow motion, as if the plane were suspended in some lucent gel instead of air. "Only one and a quarter miles to go!" Paul transmitted. Privately, he raised his estimate of success from zero to 20 percent. "Like a Kremer length," Sam answered. Bryan, listening, thought, "Less distance than for the original Kremer Prize . . . no headwinds or turbulence then, no thirst, no cramps . . ."

Still, he pedaled inexorably closer. When he was within 1 mile (1.6 kilometres) of shore the water became too shallow for the bigger boats to maneuver; at 07:30 the *Lady Ellen Elizabeth* turned sharp left, and the flight director's Zodiac took over the lead. "Heading straight into the sun, Bryan. Watch your altitude," Sam warned. As soon as he said it he flashed on Icarus, and Bryan, in the mute body of the *Albatross,* did the same thing. He was too tired not to smile. Now the plane was clearly visible and beautiful from the shore. We were *willing* him to reach land; it was a physical sensation that you could feel in your chest. "I talk to myself and sense that my friends are talking too: Don't give up hope now, you *can* do it."

On the beach we are dazedly aiming our spotlights at the plane in what is almost full daylight. At 07:31 I set off the first smoke grenade. It is disheartening; the brilliant red plume streams out nearly horizontal from my raised arm, straight toward the *Albatross:* pure headwind. "Okay, Bryan," Sam calls, "you should be able to see some red smoke over there." Bryan looks, and once again the altitude drops to two feet. A moment later the French television networks send up a small red helium blimp to lift their transmission antenna. It makes an ideal aiming point for the boats, but Bryan is almost too exhausted to care. Both his left and right thighs and his right calf are cramping now. "One foot! Don't head for those rocks." Sam's tone is more plaintive than commanding.

The rocks were like the final test in a classical ordeal. The massive wedge of gray-black stone pointed seaward, blocking the south end of the beach below Cap Gris-Nez. At that surreal moment it seemed that it must have been placed there only a few minutes before, when we weren't looking, to foil the flight at the last moment. The southbound tide was running at more than three knots, and the point deflected the stream out toward the slowly approaching boats. Jim Burke had to angle his Zodiac at 30° to the tide to maintain course, and behind him Bryan kept drifting to the right, south, below the rocks. A press boat, sensing his distress, moved close in to starboard, too close, and its outriggers nearly took off the *Albatross*'s right wingtip. "Stick with us, Bryan; don't go to the right. Watch your altitude," came Sam's reassuring voice. "C'mon, Bryan, *hang on,"* Sterling called.

For a moment Bryan considers crashing on the rocks; it would still be land. Then he changes his mind, and decides to fly around them, against the wind, and try to save the plane. "One hundred yards. I am flying on reserves I never knew I had." We light the second smoke flare to show the wind direction. The *Albatross* suddenly yaws seaward, away from the beach, and Bryan bears down on the controls. The canard tilts all the way over, straining at the anti-yaw cords; at a hundred feet from the beach Allen has the hideous thought that he has blown it, is going to crash in the waves at the last minute instead of making it to land.

It is Janet's job to catch the ground handling line when the *Albatross* lands and stabilize the plane. She is running down the beach toward it, waving her scarf, screaming at the top of her lungs, "COME ON, BRYAN!!" For an agonizing moment the canard remains tilted over, and then the plane responds. Everything holds. Suddenly it is past the rocks, floating toward us, growing bigger and more familiar every second. A crowd of newsmen and spectators is running alongside it; it is strangely quiet; we can hear the sound of their footsteps on the sand. Janet is running the other way, toward the plane, fixated on the starboard wing line. Bryan stops pedaling, and the *Gossamer Albatross* hovers in the air for a few seconds, as if it is loath to land. Then it slowly settles to the ground, and Janet catches the wing cord and balances it against the wind. It is 07:40, Greenwich Mean Time. The flight is over.

On the *Lady Ellen Elizabeth,* Paul can still not allow himself to believe that the flight is successful. Parker MacCready, over the boat radio, wistfully: "Sam, did he make it to the land?" There is no answer from shore, and then they can see that the *Albatross*'s propeller is stopped, and that the plane is stationary and upright. "Bryan, from Control, *Congratulations! Wonderful!*" Paul calls. "Project boats and airplane, from Control. We just sighted a large shark in the water, right here, so, glad Bryan made it all the way."

Bryan, too, is glad. The flight has taken 2 hours and 49 minutes, exactly one minute less than the absolute endurance limit of 170 minutes that Joe Mastropaolo had predicted five days earlier. The great circle distance was 22.2583 statute miles (35.8212 kilometres), but Paul has calculated that the *Albatross* flew more than 35 miles (56.3 kilometres) through the air to cover that distance.

A few seconds after the plane lands the right side of the cockpit is mobbed by newsmen, all converging on the point where the flying wires are attached at the bottom of the fuselage. Cameras held overhead, strobes flashing, microphones thrust forward like prehensile auditory organs, the media have arrived. Between the crowd's treading on the wires and a shift in wind, the plane begins to tilt over to starboard, and dozens of willing but unschooled hands grab for the port wing line, trying to pull it down against the *Albatross*'s nearly infinite roll moment. "Turn it *into the wind,*" we shout, to no avail. More and more hands pull on the line, until the spar, able to survive the English Channel, but not the hands of would-be helpers, gives up and breaks inboard of the left wing joint. Bryan has punched a hole through the Mylar on the right side of the fuselage; as Sterling cuts the door open with a sheath knife Bryan looks up at the broken wing and murmurs, "That's a bit of a drag."

"Where's Ingrid? Where's Ingrid?" Jack Conmy, so excited he can hardly bear it, fights his way through the crowd to find Dr. Dodd holding Bryan's arm, right where she's supposed to be. (Conmy refused to empty his water-filled boots for hours, and finally used them to baptize the floor of the bar at the Hotel Normandy in Wissant. His telegram announcing the successful flight to his cohorts at Du Pont headquarters in Wilmington began, "Oh, Ye of little faith . . .") Ingrid finds Bryan in remarkably good condition: He can walk, he can smile, and he can drink, first champagne, and then, more importantly, water.

As soon as he is out of the cockpit, team members are hugging him, Sam, Blaine, Bill, Taras, Janet, Lin Burke. He is given a shy kiss by an American lady who lives nearby, and a nosegay of flowers by the Lady Mayor of Wissant. A crocodile of little French schoolchildren right out of *Madeline* stands watching solemnly. It is an altogether appropriate greeting.

Meanwhile, on the *Lady Ellen* John Ward has opened a bottle of champagne, and Sterling has radioed to say that Jim Burke is on his way out to pick up Paul. A few minutes later they are on the beach, once again soaking wet, and Paul hobbles over to Bryan on his damp cast and gives him a giant, grinning bear hug. His immortal words? "Well done, take the rest of the day off!"

UP IN THE FIRST BALLOON

by John Lonzo Anderson

"This little voyage," wrote an enthusiastic man of that day, "will remain forever famous in the history of human audacity."

But it can remain famous only if we are reminded of it now and then. This is to remind you.

"Audacity" is certainly the right word. Just imagine trusting yourself to a flimsy contraption made entirely of paper, cloth, ropes, and a little wood, flying through the sky at the mercy of any wind that cares to come along; and with a roaring fire leaping inside the thing, threatening at any moment to burn it down on top of you and out from under you! Would you do it? Especially if no one had ever done it before?

November 20, 1783. All is ready and the weather at last is right. The word spreads early in the morning. This is the day.

All the great and near-great of Paris hurry into their *voitures* and stream out into the country to the Château de la Muette, where the *Enfants de France,* little son and daughter of the King, live with their governess, the beautiful Madame la Duchesse de Polignac.

The duchess, with the help of the Duc de Chartres, brother of the King, has made all arrangements. Launching platform and poles have been set up in the huge gardens of the château. Pilâtre de Rozier, sick with disappointment, is nevertheless loyally on hand to do his part.

As the fire is built and the inflation begins, the young Marquis d'Arlandes, slightly pale with excitement, stands ready to climb onto the gallery.

Etienne and the Duc de Chartres approach him.

"Monsieur le Marquis," says Etienne, "I venture to suggest that you take a companion on this voyage."

D'Arlandes hesitates. He is naturally jealous of his honor and pride.

"I suggest," continues Etienne, "that you take along Monsieur Pilâtre de Rozier."

"But . . ." says d'Arlandes, "His Majesty . . ."

"I will answer to His Majesty," puts in the duke.

"You will need Pilâtre," urges Etienne. "He is experienced in handling the aerostat. Also, it is quite possible that it will take two men to keep the fire going strongly enough. And finally there is the question of balance. If you are alone, the weight on your side will decrease as you use up fuel, and the machine will tilt over."

D'Arlandes bows politely. "As you say," he says. "I welcome the company of Monsieur Pilâtre."

Pilâtre is told. He embraces d'Arlandes gratefully.

D'Arlandes climbs aboard, takes his place at the porthole, surrounded by piles of fuel and pails of water, with sponges. The sand ballast is removed from the side opposite him and is replaced by Pilâtre and more fuel and water. A porthole is cut for Pilâtre.

Etienne wants to make a captive test before the *montgolfière* is released. The fire is increased, the aerostat rises on its ropes. The balance is perfect. But as has so often happened before, a sudden wind comes up. The *Réveillon III,* held by the ropes, swoops and crashes into the leafless tree-tops. Large holes are torn in the bag. Pilâtre builds up the fire and lifts the machine free; but it has to be taken down and repaired.

The women in the crowd volunteer to patch it. Duchesses and marchionesses, nursemaids and seamstresses roll up their sleeves and go to work with large upholstery needles. In an hour and a half the *Réveillon III* is ready for action again.

D'Arlandes is in his place. Pilâtre is talking with friends.

The Duc de Chartres says: "What's the matter, Pilâtre? Aren't you going?"

Pilâtre glares at him. "I *beg* your pardon!" he says stiffly, and hops aboard.

This time there is no nonsense of ropes. The aerostat is quickly inflated and released, rises with a breath-taking sweep.

The crowd gasps, its own breath taken away. Then, awe-struck, it is quiet, as if at a funeral. Fear for the two travelers is in every face.

The voyagers can be heard, quite clearly, shouting to each other as they leap across the sky. The crowd is astounded.

Swiftly the *montgolfière* rises until it is above the few white clouds that are drifting in the blue sky. The wind is taking it straight toward Paris. Over the Isle of Swans it passes, over the Invalides. The smoke which pours from its base clings close about it, sometimes almost hides it from view.

The people of Paris are in the streets, on the roof-tops. Many are on their knees, praying. There are no cries of joy, only silence, as they stare open-mouthed upward and listen in awe to the voices from the sky.

Bundled up in an invalid's chair on the balcony of his home on the Passy hillside sits Benjamin Franklin, old and unwell, watching the magnificent *Réveillon* through a telescope. He turns to his nurse and says: "Only a few months ago the idea of witches riding through the air upon a broomstick and that of philosophers upon a bag of smoke would have appeared equally impossible and ridiculous!"

Up above, Pilâtre and d'Arlandes are experiencing sensations never before felt by man.

At the zooming take-off they gasp with the crowd, but for a better reason. The speed of the climb seems terrific.

As the earth drops away and they catch their breath they notice the silence of the crowd.

"They're worried about us," says d'Arlandes.

Pilâtre, who can't see him unless they are both at their portholes, yells: "Did you say something?"

"I say they're worried about us," shouts d'Arlandes. "Let's wave and reassure them."

He waves his handkerchief; but Pilâtre, knowing what will happen if the fire slackens, is getting down to business.

D'Arlandes stands absorbed in the view, amazed at the total and unexpected silence of the upper air. He has forgotten that he is supposed to work his way on this voyage.

"Hey!" yells Pilâtre. "You aren't doing anything and we're hardly rising at all any more!"

"Oops!" says d'Arlandes. "Pardon!" and he gets busy feeding his side of the fire and stirring it with his iron poker. Clouds of red sparks swirl inside the great dome, die out, and slither down the inside walls.

The aerostat rises some more. The wind is carrying it toward Paris.

Both men are constantly coughing and choking from the overflow of smoke that billows from the base of the *Réveillon.* No matter what they do, the smoke hovers close about them, stinging their eyes and throats. It can't blow away and they can't leave it behind, for the *montgolfière* travels exactly with the speed of whatever wind it rides.

It's impossible to escape the smoke even by going up or down. If they descend, it blasts up in their faces; if they rise, the smoke is rising, too, even faster.

D'Arlandes takes time to look around. Things appear so different from up here, it's difficult to tell where you are.

Pilâtre is peering down through the inside of the aerostat, past the furnace. "Here's the river," he shouts, "and we're going down! All right, my friend, how about some fire?"

They don't know it, but they are in the down-draft caused by rivers, which fliers of the future will come to know so well. The draft is sucking them toward the earth and along the path of the river, at right angles to their former course.

Frantically they work at the fire. The fresh straw doesn't catch fast enough. The Isle of Swans in the river just below seems to draw them like a magnet. With their pitchforks they loosen the straw and lift it a little. Suddenly the fire blazes up with a roar. The aerostat bounds upward.

The Isle of Swans is past. They are over the placid water, gliding smoothly upstream.

"Ah," shouts Pilâtre, "that's better!"

In a couple of seconds they hear plainly from below: "Ah, that's better!" in the same voice.

"Hear the echo from the water!" says Pilâtre.

"From the water," says the river.

Pilâtre laughs. "Too bad you haven't got your flute, Monsieur. You could play a duet with yourself—while you're resting!"

D'Arlandes takes the gibe like a man, grins, and feeds the fire.

"Say!" exclaims Pilâtre. "That gives me an idea!" He sings the first line of *"Malbrouck s'en va-t-en guerre,"* and when it comes back up from the river he tries hastily to harmonize with it, singing tenor.

The effect is very comical. D'Arlandes howls with glee and tries it himself.

Suddenly there is a cracking sound from the dome. D'Arlandes peers up inside, but can see nothing for the smoke.

Now there is a jolt, as if the *Réveillon* had been hit over the head with a great club.

"What are you doing?" yells d'Arlandes. "Dancing?"

"I'm not dancing," says Pilâtre.

"Good," says d'Arlandes. "Then it must be a new current of air to take us away from the river—I hope!"

But the course still clings to the river.

"We're getting out of balance," says Pilâtre. "You'll have to use more of your fuel."

D'Arlandes works hard for a while. He gets the fire so hot that the *montgolfière* is able to wrench itself free of the river draft. Now the wind is carrying it across the city.

There is a sound like that of a rope breaking. D'Arlandes peers up inside the dome again. Through the smoke he sees daylight. There are several large holes in the fabric.

"We've got to make a landing!" shouts d'Arlandes.

"Why?"

"Look!"

Pilâtre sees. He grabs a sponge out of a pail of water; so does d'Arlandes; and they manage to reach most of the holes and stop the fire that is eating away at them. Pushing against the fabric along the gallery they find that the terrific heat has charred it. It is coming loose from the framework.

"We've got to land!" repeats d'Arlandes.

"Can't," says Pilâtre grimly. "We're over Paris."

While they doused the scorching holes the aerostat has been losing altitude fast. The fire has to be built up, even at the risk of burning more holes. They build it up.

"We can get across Paris," says Pilâtre. "We *must!*"

They test the main brace-ropes. They are tight. Only a few of them have broken. But the holes beyond their reach are getting bigger. Because of the coating of alum they aren't blazing; just charring away round the edges.

From now on it's a fight between keeping the fire hot enough to hold up the aerostat in spite of the holes and yet not so hot as to set the thing on fire, alum, sponges, and all.

Both men are black as coal-miners with soot. The heat and smoke make white furrows of perspiration and tears on their faces. Pilâtre has taken off his coat. D'Arlandes, more fastidious, keeps his on.

The roof-tops are too near for comfort. Just ahead, the towers of Saint-Sulpice threaten to spike the aerostat.

"Never mind the holes! We've got to build up the fire!"

But just in time a new current of air spins them off to the south. They miss the towers, but they are descending fast, much too soon. Over there is the edge of the city.

"Let her burn! We've got to get across the boulevard!"

The fire roars hotter. The holes spread wider; smoke and bits of charred fabric pour out through them. But the *Réveillon III* is still in the air.

A few hundred yards more; beyond the boulevard there is plenty of open space.

They work feverishly, now at the fire, now with the sponges.

The boulevard is crossed.

"Pied à terre!" yells d'Arlandes.

They stop feeding the fire. They are sliding toward the earth. They almost scrape a windmill. Ahead the Butte-aux-Cailles, Quail Hill, is rising to meet them.

When the gallery touches the hill Pilâtre is on the side away from the wind. The dome tilts above him, spills out its heat, and collapses on top of him. D'Arlandes leaps off and runs round to help him, but Pilâtre crawls out unhurt from under the heap.

Together they haul at the fabric, trying to pull it off the smoldering heater. People are streaming across the fields from the boulevard. They lend a hand. They rescue most of the fabric and beat out the fire. But Pilâtre's coat has been burned up.

The police arrive and form a cordon to keep back the swelling crowd.

It is cold, and Pilâtre, soaked with perspiration, is freezing without his coat. A laborer in the crowd insists on giving him his. It is big enough for two Pilâtres.

The Duc de Chartres arrives on horseback. He has galloped all the way through Paris in pursuit of the *Réveillon.* He embraces the two voyagers. He arranges to have the aerostat packed up and taken to Réveillon's.

Then he hauls the heroes off, d'Arlandes looking like a dandified chimneysweep and Pilâtre like a second-class ragpicker, to join Etienne and collect with him the triumph of the greatest day of their lives.

THE FIRST AERIAL VOYAGE IN ENGLAND

by Vincent Lunardi

At five minutes after two, the last gun was fired, the cords divided, and the Balloon rose, the company returning my signals of adieu with the most unfeigned acclamations and applauses. The effect was, that of a miracle, on the multitudes which surrounded the place; and they passed from incredulity and menace, into the most extravagant expressions of approbation and joy.

At the height of twenty yards, the Balloon was a little depressed by the wind, which had a fine effect; it held me over the ground for a few seconds, and seemed to pause majestically before its departure.

On discharging a part of the ballast, it ascended to the height of two hundred yards. As a multitude lay before me of a hundred and fifty thousand people, who had not seen my ascent from the ground, I had recourse to every stratagem to let them know I was in the gallery, and they literally rent the air with their acclamations and applause. In these stratagems I devoted my flag, and worked with my oars, one of which was immediately broken, and fell from me, a pidgeon too escaped, which, with a dog, and cat, were the only companions of my excursion.

When the thermometer had fallen from 68° to 61° I perceived a great difference in the temperature of the air. I became very cold, and found it necessary to take a few glasses of wine. I likewise eat the leg of a chicken, but my bread and other provisions had been rendered useless by being mixed with the sand, which I carried as ballast.

When the thermometer was at fifty, the effect of the atmosphere, and the combination of circumstances around, produced a calm delight, which is inexpressible, and which no situation on earth could give. The stillness, extent, and magnificence of the scene, rendered it highly awful. My horizon seemed a perfect circle; the terminating line several hundred miles in circumference. This I conjectured from the view of London; the extreme points of which, formed an angle of only a few degrees. It was so reduced on the great scale before me, that I can find no simile to convey an idea of it. I could distinguish Saint Paul's and other churches, from the houses. I saw the streets as lines, all animated with beings, whom I knew to be men and women, but which I should otherwise have had a difficulty in describing. It was an enormous beehive, but the industry of it was suspended. All the moving mass seemed to have no object but myself, and the transition from the suspicion, and perhaps contempt of the preceding hour, to the affectionate transport, admiration and glory of the present moment, was not without its effect on my mind. I recollected the puns on my name, and was glad to find myself calm. I had soared from the apprehensions and anxieties of the Artillery Ground, and felt as if I had left behind me all the cares and passions that molest mankind.

Indeed, the whole scene before me filled the mind with a sublime pleasure, of which I never had a conception. The critics *imagine,* for they seldom speak from experience, that terror is an ingredient in every sublime sensation. It was not possible for me to be on earth, in a situation so free from apprehension. I had not the slightest sense of motion from the Machine. I knew not whether it went swiftly or slowly, whether it ascended or descended, whether it was agitated or tranquil, but by the appearance or disappearance of objects on the earth. I moved to different parts of the gallery. I adjusted the furniture, and apparatus. I uncorked my bottle, eat, drank, and wrote, just as in my study. The height had not the effect, which a much lesser degree of it has near the earth, that of producing giddiness. The broom-sticks of the witches, Ariostos's flying-horse, and even Milton's sun-beam, conveying the angel to the earth, have all ideas of effort, difficulty, and restraint, which do not affect a voyage in the Balloon.

Thus tranquil, and thus situated, how shall I describe to you a view, such as the ancients supposed Jupiter to have of the earth; and to copy which there are no terms in any language. The gradual diminution of objects, and the masses of light and shade are intelligible in oblique and common prospects. But here every thing wore a new appearance, and had a new effect. The face of the country had a mild and permanent verdure, to which Italy is a stranger. The variety of cultivation, and the accuracy with which property is divided, give the idea, ever present to a stranger in England, of good civil laws and an equitable administration: the rivulets meandering; the Thames glistning with the rays of the sun; the immense district beneath me spotted with cities, towns, villages and houses, pouring out their inhabitants to hail my appearance: you will allow me some merit at not having been exceedingly intoxicated with my situation.

To prolong the enjoyment of it, and to try the effect of my only oar, I kept myself in the same parallel respecting the earth, for nearly half an hour. But the exercise having fatigued, and the experiment having satisfied me, I laid aside the oar, and again had recourse to my bottle; this I emptied to the health of my friends and benefactors in the lower world. All my affections were alive, in a manner not easily to be conceived; and you may be assured that the sentiment which seemed to me most congenial to that happy situation was gratitude and friendship. I will not refer to any softer passion. I sat down and wrote four pages of desultory observations, and pinning them to a napkin, committed them to the mild winds of the region, to be conveyed to my honoured friend and patron, Prince Caramanico.

During this business I had ascended rapidly; for, on hearing the report of a gun, which was fired in the Artillery Ground, I was induced to examine the thermometer, and found it had fallen to 32°. The Balloon was so much inflated as to assume the form of an oblong spheroid, the shortest diameter of which was in a line with me; though I had ascended with it in the shape of an inverted cone, and wanting nearly one third of its full complement of air. Having no valve, I could only open the neck of the Balloon; thinking it barely possible that the strong rarefaction might force out some of the inflammable air. The condensed vapour around its neck was frozen, though I found no inconvenience from the cold. The earth, at this point, appeared like a boundless plain, whose surface had variegated shades, but on which no object could be accurately distinguished.

I then had recourse to the utmost use of my single oar: by hard and persevering labour I brought myself within three hundred yards of the earth; and moving horizontally, spoke through my trumpet to some country people, from whom I heard a confused noise in reply.

At half after three o'clock, I descended in a corn field, on the common of North Mimms, where I landed the cat. The poor animal had been sensibly affected by the cold, during the greatest part of the voyage. Here I might have terminated my excursion with satisfaction and honour to myself; for though I was not destitute of ambition, to be the first to ascend the English atmosphere, my great object was to ascertain the effect of oars, acting vertically on the air. I had lost one of my oars; but by the use of the other I had brought myself down, and was perfectly convinced my invention would answer. This, though a single, was an important object, and my satisfaction was very great in having proved its utility. The fatigues and anxiety I had endured, might have induced me to be content with what I had done, and the people about me were very ready to assist at my disembarkation; but my affections were afloat, and in unison with the whole country, whose transport and admiration seemed boundless. I bid them therefore keep clear, and I would gratify them by ascending directly in their view.

My general course to this place, was something more than one point to the westward of the north. A gentleman on horseback approached me, but I could not speak to him, being intent on my re-ascension, which I effected, after moving horizontally about forty yards. As I ascended, one of the ballustrades of the gallery gave way; but the circumstance excited no apprehension of danger. I threw out the remainder of my ballast and provisions, and again resumed my pen. My ascension was so rapid, that before I had written half a page, the thermometer had fallen to 29°. The drops of water that adhered to the neck of the balloon were become like chrystals. At this point of elevation, which was the highest I attained, I finished my letter, and fastening it with a cork-screw to my handkerchief, threw it down. I likewise threw down the plates, knives and forks, the little sand that remained, and an empty bottle, which took some time in disappearing. I now wrote the last of my dispatches from the clouds, which I fixed to a leathern belt, and sent towards the earth. It was visible to me on its passage, for several minutes; but I was myself insensible of motion from the Machine itself, during the whole voyage. The earth appeared as before, like an extensive plain, with the same variagated surface; but the objects rather less distinguishable. The clouds to the eastward rolled beneath me, in masses immensely larger than the waves of the ocean. I therefore did not mistake them for the sea. Contrasted with the effects of the sun on the earth and water beneath, they gave a grandeur to the whole scene which no fancy can describe. I again betook myself to my oar, in order to descend; and by the hard labour of fifteen or twenty minutes I accomplished my design, when my strength was nearly exhausted. My principal care was to avoid a violent concussion at landing, and in this my good fortune was my friend.

At twenty minutes past four I descended in a spacious meadow, in the parish of Stondon, near Ware, in Hertfordshire. Some labourers were at work in it. I requested their assistance; they exclaimed, they would have nothing to do with one who came in the Devil's house, or on the Devil's horse (I could not distinguish which of the phrases they used) and no intreaties could prevail on them to approach me. I at last owed my deliverance to the spirit and generosity of a female. A young woman, who was likewise in the field, took hold of a cord which I had thrown out, and calling to the men, they even denied that assistance to her request which they had refused to mine. A crowd of people from the neighbourhood soon assembled, who very obligingly assisted me to disembark. General Smith was the first gentleman who overtook me—I am much indebted to his politeness—he kindly assisted in securing the Balloon, having followed me on horseback, from London; as did several other gentlemen, amongst whom were Mr. Crane, Capt. Connor, and Mr. Wright. The inflammable air was let out by an incision, and produced a most offensive stench, which is said to have affected the atmosphere of the neighbourhood. The apparatus was committed to the care of Mr. Hollingsworth, who obligingly offered his service. I then proceeded with General Smith, and several other gentlemen to the Bull Inn at Ware. On my arrival, I had the honour to be introduced to William Baker, Esq., Member for Hertford in the last parliament. This gentleman conducted me to his seat at Bayford Bury, and entertained me with a kind of hospitality and politeness, which I shall ever remember with gratitude; and which has impressed on my mind a proper idea of that frank liberality and sincere beneficence, which are the characteristics of English Gentlemen.

The general course of the second part of my voyage, by which I was led into Hertfordshire, was three points to the eastward of the north from the Artillery Ground, and about four points to the eastward of the north from the place where I first descended.

This is the general account of my excursion. I shall take a few days to recover my strength, and whatever particulars occur to me I shall send you.

I am, with great regard,

Your much obliged,

And humble servant,

London, Sept. 24, 1784 VINCENT LUNARDI.

THE FIRST BALLOON CROSSING OF THE ENGLISH CHANNEL

by Dr. John Jeffries

Having agreed with M. Blanchard (in consideration of my engaging to furnish him with all the materials and labour to fill the Balloon, and to pay all the expences of transporting them) that I should accompany him in his intended Aerial Voyage from Dover into France, we left London for that purpose, December the 17th, 1784; having previously shipped for Dover the Balloon and Car, with materials and apparatus for filling the Balloon.

From the necessary time taken up in repairing and adjusting our apparatus, &c, and after that was completed, from a series of intemperate and tempestuous weather, we never had a possibility of making our attempt until the seventh of January, 1785, when, after having encountered, almost from the hour of my arrival at Dover, a variety of discouragements and oppositions to the accomplishing my design, the weather being more favourable, we determined to proceed, by filling the Balloon, and attempt our enterprize.

The whole of the week, but more especially the preceding day, the weather had been very tempestuous, with strong winds and rain from the Eastward and Northward, which changed in the course of the evening to North, and became very severely cold.

The morning was remarkably fine, clear, and serene, but with intense frost. The wind, as far as it could be ascertained, appeared to be about North North-West, or North-West by North; but of that kind which the pilots said did not extend far from the shore; and that the wind usually prevailed in such weather and seasons, and *probably did then prevail,* on the French coast, equally *from that land,* and *in a direct contrary course from what it then appeared to be at Dover;* as at this time there was not wind enough to determine any thing by boats or shipping. I was somewhat embarrassed at this idea *from professional men.*

However, observing very light scudding clouds above, which appeared to take a proper direction for our Voyage; and noticing, at the same time, that smoke from the Castle did the same, we determined to proceed accordingly; when having raised a paper kite, and launching a paper Mongolfier, and a small gas Balloon, each of which took, as far as we could trace them, a course favourable to our Voyage, we began to entertain more confidence of success.

The Balloon being filled a little before one o'clock, we suffered it to rise, so as to be disengaged from the apparatus, &c. for filling it, and to be drawn down again just at the edge of the Cliff, where we attached the wings or oars, with the moulinet and governail, to the Car:——And exactly at one o'clock (having in the Car with us, three sacks of sand ballast, of ten pounds each; a large parcel of pamphlets, two cork jackets, a few extra clothes of M. Blanchard; a number of inflated bladders, with two small anchors or grapnels, with cords affixed, to assist our landing) we rose slowly and majestically from the Cliff, which being at the time of our ascent from it almost covered with a beautiful assembly from the city, neighbouring towns and villages, with carriages, horses, &c. together with the extensive Beach of Dover, crowded with a great concourse of people, with numbers of boats, &c. assembled near the shore, under the Cliffs, afforded us, at our first arising from them, a most beautiful and picturesque view indeed.

On this experiment I did not take with me any other philosophical instrument, but my Barometer and Mariner's Compass.

At the instant before we rose from the Cliff, the mercury in the Barometer was at 29 inches, seven-tenths; and the wind appeared to be about North North-West, though so much of a calm, as to make the sea appear like a fine sheet of glass.

At a quarter past one o'clock we appeared to have risen considerably, but yet to have made very little progress, and that rather to the Eastward. The weather continued delightful, and we began to have a most enchanting prospect of the distant country back of Dover, &c. enjoying in our view a great many towns and villages; among which I could distinguish the venerable City of Canterbury; but as a counterpart to this pleasing scene, we began to have a very extensive and formidable view of the Breakers, (I judge around the Goodwin Sands) and which we unfortunately seemed to be approaching.

The mercury in the Barometer had now fallen to 27 inches, three-tenths, and we passed over several vessels of different kinds, which saluted us with their colours, as we passed them; and we began to overlook and have an extensive view of the coast of France; which enchanting views of England and France being alternately presented to us by the rotary and semicircular motion of the Balloon and Car (a circumstance mentioned in our former experiment) greatly increased the beauty and variety of our situaion.

At half past one o'clock, the Balloon seemed to be distended to its utmost extent, and thereby (as in our former experiment) drew up the Car close to it; on which occasion, recollecting the importance of a sufficiency of inflammable air, to the completion of our Voyage, and that it was not possible to determine exactly, how much of it might escape if we opened the valve, we *only untwisted the two tubes at the bottom of the Balloon,* by which it had been filled with the gas, and cast them over the sides of the Car; and in a minute or two we had the pleasure to see them become distended through their whole length, beginning at the ends attached to the Balloon. We also had the farther satisfaction to observe, that by this method, no more of the gas or inflammable air would escape, than was absolutely necessary to relieve the Balloon, and to prevent it from bursting. This period we employed in attaching the bladders we had taken with us, to the circular hoop between our Car and the Balloon.

At 50 minutes after one, (having, I judge, been too inattentive to the state of the tubes on the outside of the Car) I found we were descending fast. We immediately took in the tubes within the Car, and secured them, and cast out one sack of ballast; but the mercury in the Barometer still rising, we cast out half another sack; on which we began to rise, and the mercury again to fall in the Barometer.

We appeared at this time to be about one-third of the way from the English towards the French coast.

We now began to lose all distinct view of the Castle of Dover. At two o'clock we attached two small slings to the circle over us, towards each end of the Car, and a third in the middle of it, a little lower than the other two, to rest our feet upon; the three being designed to favour our beaver, like retreat upwards, in case we were forced down into the water.

We now found that we were descending again; on which occasion we were obliged to cast out the remaining sack and an half of ballast, sacks and all; notwithstanding which, not finding that we rose, we cast out a parcel of the pamphlets, and in a minute or two found, that we rose again; and now appeared to be about mid-way between the English and French coasts.

At about a quarter after two o'clock, I found that we were again descending; this induced us to cast out, by small parcels, all the remaining pamphlets; notwithstanding which, I could barely discover that we rose again.

We had not now any thing left to cast away as ballast in future, excepting the wings, apparatus, and ornaments of the Car, with our cloaths, and a few little articles; but as a counterpart to such a situation, we here had a most enchanting and alluring view of the French coast, from Blackness and Cape Blanez to Calais, and on to Gravelines, &c.

At about half past two I found we were again descending very rapidly, the lower pole of the Balloon next us having collapsed very much, so that the Balloon did not appear to be three-fourths distended with gas. We immediately threw out all the little things we had with us, such as biscuits, apples, &c. and after that one of our oars or wings; but still descending, we cast away the other wing, and then the governail; having likewise had the precaution, for fear of accidents, while the Balloon was filling, partly to loosen and make it go easy, I now succeeded in attempting to reach without the Car, and unscrewing the moulinet, with all its apparatus; I likewise cast that into the sea. —Notwithstanding all which, the Balloon not rising, we cut away all the lining and ornaments, both within, and on the outside of the Car, and in like manner threw them into the sea; after which, we cast away the only bottle we had taken with us, which in its descent appeared to force out a considerable steam like smoke, with a hissing or rushing noise; and when it struck the water, we very sensibly (the instant before we heard the sound) felt the force of the shock on our Car; it appearing to have fallen directly perpendicular to us, although we had passed a considerable way during its descent.

As we did not yet ascend, we were obliged, though very unwillingly, to throw away our anchors and cords; but still approaching the sea, we began to *strip ourselves,* and cast away our cloathing, M. Blanchard first throwing away his *extra coat,* with his surtout; after which I cast away my *only coat;* and then M. Blanchard his other coat and trowsers: We then put on and adjusted our cork-jackets, and prepared for the event.

We appeared at this time to be about three quarters of the distance towards the French shore, and we were now fallen so low, as to be beneath the plane of the French Cliffs. We were then preparing to get up into our slings, when I found the mercury in the Barometer again falling, and looking around, soon observed that we were rising, and that the pleasing view of France was enlarging and opening to us every moment, as we ascended, so as to overlook the high grounds.

I judged that we were at this time about four or five miles from the shore, and appeared to approach it fast. We soon had a fine view of Calais, and a great number of other towns, villages, villas, &c.

We now ascended to a much greater height than at any former period of our Voyage, and exactly at three o'clock we passed over the high grounds between Cape Blanez and Blackness; thus forming in our ascending entrée a most magnificent arch; at which time, nothing can exceed the beautiful appearance of the villages, fields, roads, villas, &c. under us, after having been just two hours over the sea.

The mercury in the Barometer had now fallen to 23 inches, three-tenths; at which time a packet of letters, cast out by M. Blanchard, was several minutes in reaching the surface of the earth, and afforded an amusing scene to us, in observing it during its descent; it appearing, in its progress, to pass along over inclosures, houses, roads, &c. as if running after us; and finally settled in a field, in a straight line perpendicular to us.

From this circumstance of the manner of the descent of the packet, I am led to suspect, that my idea of taking the balls with me, to assist (by their descent) the Compass in determining our course, was a mistaken one; and to apprehend that I should not have derived from them that assistance which I fought.

The weather still continued fine, and very clear; the rays of the sun, though almost horizontal, shining very bright; but from the height which we were now at, and from the loss of our cloaths, we were almost benumbed with cold.

By our velocity, the wind seemed now to be considerably increased; and from our course I judge it must have been more westerly than before, as we appeared to be approaching fast to the grounds covered with water on our left, above, and a little to the right of Calais; but in a few minutes, I perceived that we had again changed our course, which was now towards the South-West, and that we were gradually descending; to favour which, we untied our slings, and took off our cork-jackets, (being the only things we had then left, excepting the Barometer) to cast away as ballast occasionally.

We now found ourselves approaching towards a forest, which appearing to be more extensive than it was probable we should be able to pass entirely over, we cast away one cork-jacket, and soon after it the other, which almost immediately checked, and altered the angle of our descent. We had now approached so near to the tops of the trees of the forest, as to discover that they were very large and rough, and that we were descending with great velocity towards them; from which circumstances, and from the direction of our course at this time, fearing that the Car might be forced into some of the trees, so violently as to separate it from the cords that connected it with the net which covered the Balloon, I felt the necessity of casting away something, to alter our course; happily (it almost instantly occurred to me, that probably we might be able to supply it from within ourselves), from the recollection that we had drank much at breakfast, and not having had any evacuation; and from the severe cold, little or no perspiration had taken place, that probably an extra quantity had been secreted by the kidneys, which we might now avail ourselves of by discharging. I instantly proposed my idea to M. Blanchard, and the event fully justified my expectation; and taking down from the circle over our Car two of the bladders, for reservoirs, we were enabled to obtain, I verily believe, between five and six pounds of urine; which circumstance, however trivial or ludicrous it may seem, I have reason to believe, was of *real utility* to us, *in our then situation;* for by casting it away, as we were approaching some trees of the forest higher than the rest, it so altered our course that, instead of being forced hard against, or into them (as at that instant appeared probable that we should be), we passed along near them in such a manner, as enabled me to catch hold of the topmost branches of one of them, and thereby arrest the farther progress of the Balloon, which, almost the instant the Car touched the trees, so as to take off a part of its weight, was disposed to ascend again; and in that position continued for a considerable time, waving over our heads, making a very pretty appearance above the woods, until, having for some time held the valve open, a sufficiency of gas had escaped, to dispose the Car to settle on the branches, when, by disengaging, and pushing it from one to another, we found a sufficient space between the trees to admit us to descend tranquilly to the surface of the ground, a little before four o'clock, it having been about half after three when I first stopped the progress of the Balloon over the forest; which I have since been informed, is called the *Forest of Guines,* not far from *Ardres,* and near the spot celebrated for the famous interview between Henry the Eighth, King of England, and Francis the First, King of France.

We instantly set about emptying the Balloon, and used every other exertion to acquire some warmth, and recover the use of our limbs, which were much cramped and stiffened from cold, and the situation we had been confined to in our Car.

In a short time many persons made their way to us in the Forest, from whom we received every kind of civility and assistance; particularly, in immediately sparing from themselves cloathing for us, &c.

We were likewise soon honoured with invitations from the neighbouring Gentlemen, &c. particularly from the Viscount Desandrouin, to visit him, and take some refreshment; after which, we were by them politely furnished with carriages, &c. to convey us to Calais, where, notwithstanding it was past midnight, and the gates had long been shut, the Guards had received orders to open them to us: Accordingly we were admitted, and even found the Commandant fitting up to receive us, which he did with great cordiality.

THE TEMPEST

by Jules Verne

"See," said Joe, "what comes of playing the sons of the moon without her leave! She came near serving us an ugly trick. But say, master, did you damage your credit as a physician?"

"Yes, indeed," chimed in the sportsman. "What kind of a dignitary was this Sultan of Kazeh?"

"An old half-dead sot," replied the doctor, "whose loss will not be very severely felt. But the moral of all this is that honors are fleeting, and we must not take too great a fancy to them."

"So much the worse!" rejoined Joe. "I liked the thing—to be worshipped!—Play the god as you like! Why, what would any one ask more than that? By-the-way, the moon did come up, too, and all red, as if she was in a rage."

While the three friends went on chatting of this and other things, and Joe examined the luminary of night from an entirely novel point of view, the heavens became covered with heavy clouds to the northward, and the lowering masses assumed a most sinister and threatening look. Quite a smart breeze, found about three hundred feet from the earth, drove the balloon toward the north-northeast; and above it the blue vault was clear; but the atmosphere felt close and dull.

The aëronauts found themselves, at about eight in the evening, in thirty-two degrees forty minutes east longitude, and four degrees seventeen minutes latitude. The atmospheric currents, under the influence of a tempest not far off, were driving them at the rate of from thirty to thirty-five miles an hour; the undulating and fertile plains of Mfuto were passing swiftly beneath them. The spectacle was one worthy of admiration—and admire it they did.

"We are now right in the country of the Moon," said Dr. Ferguson; "for it has retained the name that antiquity gave it, undoubtedly, because the moon has been worshipped there in all ages. It is, really, a superb country."

"It would be hard to find more splendid vegetation."

"If we found the like of it around London it would not be natural, but it would be very pleasant," put in Joe. "Why is it that such savage countries get all these fine things?"

"And who knows," said the doctor, "that this country may not, one day, become the centre of civilization? The races of the future may repair hither, when Europe shall have become exhausted in the effort to feed her inhabitants."

"Do you think so, really?" asked Kennedy.

"Undoubtedly, my dear Dick. Just note the progress of events: consider the migrations of races, and you will arrive at the same conclusion assuredly. Asia was the first nurse of the world, was she not? For about four thousand years she travailed, she grew pregnant, she produced, and then, when stones began to cover the soil where the golden harvests sung by Homer had flourished, her children abandoned her exhausted and barren bosom. You next see them precipitating themselves upon young and vigorous Europe, which has nourished them for the last two thousand years. But already her fertility is beginning to die out; her productive powers are diminishing every day. Those new diseases that annually attack the products of the soil, those defective crops, those insufficient resources, are all signs of a vitality that is rapidly wearing out and of an approaching exhaustion. Thus, we already see the millions rushing to the luxuriant bosom of America, as a source of help, not inexhaustible indeed, but not yet exhausted. In its turn, that new continent will grow old; its virgin forests will fall before the axe of industry, and its soil will become weak through having too fully produced what had been demanded of it. Where two harvests bloomed every year, hardly one will be gathered from a soil completely drained of its strength. Then, Africa will be there to offer to new races the treasures that for centuries have been accumulating in her breast. Those climates now so fatal to strangers will be purified by cultivation and by drainage of the soil, and those scattered water supplies will be gathered into one common bed to form an artery of navigation. Then this country over which we are now passing, more fertile, richer, and fuller of vitality than the rest, will become some grand realm where more astonishing discoveries than steam and electricity will be brought to light."

"Ah! sir," said Joe, "I'd like to see all that."

"You got up too early in the morning, my boy!"

"Besides," said Kennedy, "that may prove to be a very dull period when industry will swallow up every thing for its own profit. By dint of inventing machinery, men will end in being eaten up by it! I have always fancied that the end of the earth will be when some enormous boiler, heated to three thousand millions of atmospheric pressure, shall explode and blow up our Globe!"

"And I add that the Americans," said Joe, "will not have been the last to work at the machine!"

"In fact," assented the doctor, "they are great boilermakers! But, without allowing ourselves to be carried away by such speculations, let us rest content with enjoying the beauties of this country of the Moon, since we have been permitted to see it."

The sun, darting his last rays beneath the masses of heaped-up cloud, adorned with a crest of gold the slightest inequalities of the ground below; gigantic trees, arborescent bushes, mosses on the even surface—all had their share of this luminous effulgence. The soil, slightly undulating, here and there rose into little conical hills; there were no mountains visible on the horizon; immense brambly palisades, impenetrable hedges of thorny jungle, separated the clearings dotted with numerous villages, and immense euphorbiae surrounded them with natural fortifications, interlacing their trunks with the coral-shaped branches of the shrubbery and undergrowth.

Ere long, the Malagazeri, the chief tributary of Lake Taganayika, was seen winding between heavy thickets of verdure, offering an asylum to many water-courses that spring from the torrents formed in the season of freshets, or from ponds hollowed in the clayey soil. To observers looking from a height, it was a chain of waterfalls thrown across the whole western face of the country.

Animals with huge humps were feeding in the luxuriant prairies, and were half hidden, sometimes, in the tall grass; spreading forests in bloom redolent of spicy perfumes presented themselves to the gaze like immense bouquets; but, in these bouquets, lions, leopards, hyenas, and tigers, were then crouching for shelter from the last hot rays of the setting sun. From time to time, an elephant made the tall tops of the undergrowth sway to and fro, and you could hear the crackling of huge branches as his ponderous ivory tusks broke them in his way.

"What a sporting country!" exclaimed Dick, unable longer to restrain his enthusiasm; "why, a single ball fired at random into those forests would bring down game worthy of it. Suppose we just try it once!"

"No, my dear Dick; the night is close at hand—a threatening night with a tempest in the background—and the storms are awful in this country, where the heated soil is like one vast electric battery."

"You are right, sir," said Joe, "the heat has got to be enough to choke one, and the breeze has died away. One can feel that something's coming."

"The atmosphere is saturated with electricity," replied the doctor; "every living creature is sensible that this state of the air portends a struggle of the elements, and I confess that I never before was so full of the fluid myself."

"Well, then," suggested Dick, "would it not be advisable to alight?"

"On the contrary, Dick, I'd rather go up, only that I am afraid of being carried out of my course by these counter-currents contending in the atmosphere."

"Have you any idea, then, of abandoning the route that we have followed since we left the coast?"

"If I can manage to do so," replied the doctor, "I will turn more directly northward, by from seven to eight degrees; I shall then endeavor to ascend toward the presumed latitudes of the sources of the Nile; perhaps we may discover some traces of Captain Speke's expedition or of M. de Heuglin's caravan. Unless I am mistaken, we are at thirty-two degrees forty minutes east longitude, and I should like to ascend directly north of the equator."

"Look there!" exclaimed Kennedy, suddenly, "see those hippopotami sliding out of the pools—those masses of blood-colored flesh—and those crocodiles snuffing the air aloud!"

"They're choking!" ejaculated Joe. "Ah! what a fine way to travel this is; and how one can snap his fingers at all that vermin!—Doctor! Mr. Kennedy! see those packs of wild animals hurrying along close together. There are fully two hundred. Those are wolves."

"No! Joe, not wolves, but wild dogs; a famous breed that does not hesitate to attack the lion himself. They are the worst customers a traveller could meet, for they would instantly tear him to pieces."

"Well, it isn't Joe that'll undertake to muzzle them!" responded that amiable youth. "After all, though, if that's the nature of the beast, me mustn't be too hard on them for it!"

Silence gradually settled down under the influence of the impending storm: the thickened air actually seemed no longer adapted to the transmission of sound; the atmosphere appeared *muffled,* and, like a room hung with tapestry, lost all its sonorous reverberation. The "rover bird" so-called, the coroneted crane, the red and blue jays, the mocking-bird, the flycatcher, disappeared among the foliage of the immense trees, and all nature revealed symptoms of some approaching catastrophe.

At nine o'clock the *Victoria* hung motionless over Mséné, an extensive group of villages scarcely distinguishable in the gloom. Once in a while, the reflection of a wandering ray of light in the dull water disclosed a succession of ditches regularly arranged, and, by one last gleam, the eye could make out the calm and sombre forms of palm-trees, sycamores, and gigantic euphorbiae.

"I am stifling!" said the Scot, inhaling, with all the power of his lungs, as much as possible of the rarefied air. "We are not moving an inch! Let us descend!"

"But the tempest!" said the doctor, with much uneasiness.

"If you are afraid of being carried away by the wind, it seems to me that there is no other course to pursue."

"Perhaps the storm won't burst to-night," said Joe; "the clouds are very high."

"That is just the thing that makes me hesitate about going beyond them; we should have to rise still higher, lose sight of the earth, and not know all night whether we were moving forward or not, or in what direction we were going."

"Make up your mind, dear doctor, for time presses!"

"It's a pity that the wind has fallen," said Joe, again; "it would have carried us clear of the storm."

"It is, indeed, a pity, my friends," rejoined the doctor. "The clouds are dangerous for us; they contain opposing currents which might catch us in their eddies, and lightnings that might set on fire. Again, those perils avoided, the force of the tempest might hurl us to the ground, were we to cast our anchor in the tree-tops."

"Then what shall we do?"

"Well, we must try to get the balloon into a medium zone of the atmosphere, and there keep her suspended between the perils of the heavens and those of the earth. We have enough water for the cylinder, and our two hundred pounds of ballast are untouched. In case of emergency I can use them."

"We will keep watch with you," said the hunter.

"No, my friends, put the provisions under shelter, and lie down; I will rouse you, if it becomes necessary."

"But, master, wouldn't you do well to take some rest yourself, as there's no danger close on us just now?" insisted poor Joe.

"No, thank you, my good fellow, I prefer to keep awake. We are not moving, and should circumstances not change, we'll find ourselves to-morrow in exactly the same place."

"Good-night, then, sir!"

"Good-night, if you can only find it so!"

Kennedy and Joe stretched themselves out under their blankets, and the doctor remained alone in the immensity of space.

However, the huge dome of clouds visibly descended, and the darkness became profound. The black vault closed in upon the earth as if to crush it in its embrace.

All at once a violent, rapid, incisive flash of lightning pierced the gloom, and the rent it made had not closed ere a frightful clap of thunder shook the celestial depths.

"Up! up! turn out!" shouted Ferguson.

The two sleepers, aroused by the terrible concussion, were at the doctor's orders in a moment.

"Shall we descend?" said Kennedy.

"No! the balloon could not stand it. Let us go up before those clouds dissolve in water, and the wind is let loose!" and, so saying, the doctor actively stirred up the flame of the cylinder, and turned it on the spirals of the serpentine siphon.

The tempests of the tropics develop with a rapidity equalled only by their violence. A second flash of lightning rent the darkness, and was followed by a score of others in quick succession. The sky was crossed and dotted, like the zebra's hide, with electric sparks, which danced and flickered beneath the great drops of rain.

"We have delayed too long," exclaimed the doctor; "we must now pass through a zone of fire, with our balloon filled as it is with inflammable gas!"

"But let us descend, then! let us descend!" urged Kennedy.

"The risk of being struck would be just about even, and we should soon be torn to pieces by the branches of the trees!"

"We are going up, doctor!"

"Quicker, quicker still!"

In this part of Africa, during the equatorial storms, it is not rare to count from thirty to thirty-five flashes of lightning per minute. The sky is literally on fire, and the crashes of thunder are continuous.

The wind burst forth with frightful violence in this burning atmosphere; it twisted the blazing clouds; one might have compared it to the breath of some gigantic bellows, fanning all this conflagration.

Dr. Ferguson kept his cylinder at full heat, and the balloon dilated and went up, while Kennedy, on his knees, held together the curtains of the awning. The balloon whirled round wildly enough to make their heads turn, and the aëronauts got some very alarming jolts, indeed, as their machine swung and swayed in all directions. Huge cavities would form in the silk of the balloon as the wind fiercely bent it in, and the stuff fairly cracked like a pistol as it flew back from the pressure. A sort of hail, preceded by a rumbling noise, hissed through the air and rattled on the covering of the *Victoria.* The latter, however, continued to ascend, while the lightning described tangents to the convexity of her circumference; but she bore on, right through the midst of the fire.

"God protect us!" said Dr. Ferguson, solemnly, "we are in His hands; He alone can save us—but let us be ready for every event, even for fire—our fall could not be very rapid."

The doctor's voice could scarcely be heard by his companions; but they could see his countenance calm as ever even amid the flashing of the lightnings; he was watching the phenomena of phosphorescence produced by the fires of St. Elmo, that were now skipping to and fro along the network of the balloon.

The latter whirled and swung, but steadily ascended, and, ere the hour was over, it had passed the stormy belt. The electric display was going on below it like a vast crown of artificial fireworks suspended from the car.

Then they enjoyed one of the grandest spectacles that Nature can offer to the gaze of man. Below them, the tempest; above them, the starry firmament, tranquil, mute, impassible, with the moon projecting her peaceful rays over these angry clouds.

Dr. Ferguson consulted the barometer; it announced twelve thousand feet of elevation. It was then eleven o'clock at night.

"Thank Heaven, all danger is past; all we have to do now, is, to keep ourselves at this height," said the doctor.

"It was frightful!" remarked Kennedy.

"Oh!" said Joe, "it gives a little variety to the trip, and I'm not sorry to have seen a storm from a trifling distance up in the air. It's a fine sight!"

THE GREATEST AIR VOYAGE EVER MADE

by Jack R. Hunt, USNR

It was dusk on July 1, 1859, as four excited men in St. Louis, Missouri, boarded the *Atlantic,* the largest balloon in the world. Thousands of paying spectators were clamoring for its release. Most of them had been there throughout the hot, sultry day. They were afraid the flight might be postponed.

The sight of such an anxious crowd was no new experience for the pilot of the big balloon. John Wise had been only twenty-seven in 1835, when he made his first ascent from the corner of Ninth and Green Streets in Philadelphia, Pennsylvania. He had then been just a country boy with a yen to fly. His first balloon was homemade from plans which he drew after studying the atmosphere, hydrostatics, and pneumatics. He had planned on making a single flight to experience the thrill of being in the air; however, once he tasted success, he devoted his life to aeronautics. He had risen a mile aloft over Philadelphia! That was thirty-four years and two hundred and thirty flights ago. This flight was for much higher stakes.

Eventually the crowd broke through the police lines and, converging upon John Wise, demanded to know whether his intentions were honorable, or whether this was another hoax to take their money and cancel the flight as often had been done at county fairs. The intrepid aeronaut and director in chief of the Transatlantic Balloon Company paused long enough to address them.

"Ladies and Gentlemen! I have never been a party to a balloon ascension that did not come off as scheduled. On more than one occasion, I ascended in an unsafe balloon—at great personal risk, rather than disappoint my admirers. Ladies and gentlemen, the field of aeronautics has become a science. I assure you, we will ascend in very short order."

Pointing toward a much smaller balloon a short distance away, he continued, "A well-known local aeronaut has offered to act as our guide on this historic event. He will take yonder balloon and lead us upward into that great river of air that sweeps ever eastward. Ladies and gentlemen, I give you Mr. Robert Brooks."

Mr. Brooks bowed, climbed into the basket of his one-man balloon, and with a wave of his hat ascended.

Back at the large balloon, John Wise was almost ready for the launching. The *Atlantic* was a huge, beautiful machine believed to be capable of crossing the Atlantic—hence its name. John Lamountane, one of the crew, had been in charge of its construction. It was fifty feet in diameter and sixty perpendicular, and was made of lacquered silk covered by a woven hemp net. At the bottom of the net was an iron load ring, below which was suspended a wicker basket. A special lifeboat, capable of carrying a thousand pounds, was suspended fifteen feet below the basket. The boat was encased in a heavy canvas jacket which acted as a sling and protective cover. A rope ladder enabled the crew to climb between boat and basket.

This flight, St. Louis to New York, was a test to prove the airworthiness of the balloon and demonstrate a theory advanced by Wise that a river of air flowed west to east and might serve as an avenue of travel around the world. Wise had often noted at various altitudes that the air flowed east, and he kept notes regarding his observations. In May 1842 he wrote in a log of one of his flights, "It is established now beyond a doubt in my mind *that a current from west to east in the atmosphere is constantly in motion* within the height of twelve thousand feet above the ocean. Nearly all of my trips are strong proof of this."

This particular flight would end in New York and, after preparation, the flight across the Atlantic would begin from there. St. Louis had erected an arena on the city common and had allowed the promoters of the flight to charge admission to defray expenses, a common practice of that time.

Plans for the transatlantic flight called for a two-man crew with enough ballast to complete the journey. Since this leg of the flight to Europe would not be as long as the North Atlantic crossing, Wise decided that a larger crew could be taken and some ballast dispensed with. The crew, therefore, was to consist of himself, John Lamountane, O. A. Gager, promoter of the venture, and a last minute addition, a reporter named Hyde from the St. Louis *Republican,* who proposed that he should go along to write a description of the flight. The American Express Company also asked Wise to carry a few sacks of mail to dignitaries on the East coast. These, too, were accepted and a few more ballast bags were left behind.

As Brooks, in the pilot balloon, drifted out of sight eastward, Wise boarded the wicker basket where he could control the valve cord. Below, in the lifeboat, the other three made themselves comfortable. Supplies consisted of a bucket of lemonade, a lunch basket with a well-cooked turkey, and a valise of champagne. The mail sacks and ballast bags were stowed in the lifeboat. At 6:45 P.M. the anchor lines were cut and, as thousands cheered, the adventurous quartet drifted majestically skyward. Wise decided to capture the thrill of the moment for posterity. He took out his notebook and wrote:

"The city of St. Louis, covering a large area, appears to be gradually contracting its lines and has finally hid itself under a mantle of smoke. We gaze upon the fading outlines of the country with sentimental yearnings as we recur to the parting farewell of the kind friends we left behind, while at the same time our hearts are filled with joy upon the prospects of a glorious voyage to our good friends in the East, to whom has already been announced the fact of our coming."

The first night of the voyage was uneventful. The crew took turns standing watch. At first it was easy to spot towns by the lights but, as the night wore on, there were fewer and fewer lights. The man on watch amused himself by shouting to the world below. The shouting would cause the dogs to bark. Whenever the balloon was over a village, hundreds of dogs could be heard barking at once. Often this commotion would cause lights to come on and angry voices could be heard cussing the dogs.

The night had been clear and cold in the upper air. As dawn broke, Lake Erie was seen to the east. Smoke rising from farmhouse chimneys suggested the thought of hot coffee to the flyers and it was decided to drop in on some farm family for breakfast. Gas was valved to start the descent but as the crew neared the ground they became aware that they were traveling at a surprising rate of speed. A line dropped over the side tangled with some trees and momentarily stopped the lifeboat with such force that the occupants were almost thrown out. A hurried consultation resulted and the idea of a hot breakfast was abandoned. Ballast was dumped and the balloon rose back into the calm upper air.

Exactly twelve hours after takeoff, the *Atlantic* crossed the shoreline of Lake Erie near Toledo. Clouds were forming to the south and the surface of the lake was very rough. The balloon was drifting at a ground speed of better than sixty miles per hour. The remainder of the morning was spent uneventfully as the balloon passed over several boats and traveled the two hundred and fifty miles to Niagara Falls. In an endeavor to shift course more to the south, ballast was jettisoned. The balloon rose to ten thousand feet. From that altitude, the Niagara River looked like a silver cord linking Lakes Erie and Ontario. Clouds seemed to be manufactured in the falls and to take up an orderly line of march toward the east, expanding as they traveled along beneath the balloonists.

By now, a feeling of apprehension gripped Wise, who had become aware of the significance of the clouds closing in on them and of the ever-increasing velocity of the wind. He was facing a storm with a crew of novices. Hyde was on his first ride. Gager made but one previous ascension. Lamountane had completed a mere half dozen flights and was really being groomed as a crew member because of his experience in seamanship which might stand them in good stead if they were forced down during the ocean flight. As the city of Rochester came into view, Gager looked up to the wicker basket and asked, "Professor, what keeps you so quiet?"

Startled, Wise replied, "Do you not see anything extraordinary down there?"

"Why, yes," answered Gager, "the wind is very strong. I could even hear the limbs of the trees crack as if they were splitting from the trunks, but," he hesitated, "I was thinking we might make a landing near Rochester, drop off Hyde and myself to take the mail down to New York while you and Lamountane continue the journey as long as you care to."

"All very well considered, my friend, but do you realize we are traveling better than ninety miles an hour?"

Hyde and Lamountane had also become aware of the situation below, although they could not completely grasp the gravity of it. Now that everyone was concerned about their predicament, a consultation was called to decide on a course of action. In spite of Wise's warning, the first suggestion was to attempt a landing. However, before much could be said, the balloon began settling. When they had descended far enough to see the trees bending and hear the wind as they sped madly along, the problems of a landing became quite evident. The crew in the lifeboat were fairly hypnotized by the destruction below.

Lamountane broke in. "Professor, what can we do?"

"Throw everything overboard!"

The mail sacks were quickly jettisoned and shortly the balloon was rising again and the occupants could momentarily relax. As this crisis passed, Hyde, who until now had contributed very little to the discussion, worriedly asked, "Is there great danger?"

"Yes," replied Wise. "I see no earthly chance unless we land in the water."

He called Gager up into the basket and the two debated hurriedly. "The wisest plan is to swamp the balloon in the lake, if we can intercept a boat," confided the pilot.

Gager, without a thought for the loss of the money invested in the venture, said: "Whatever you say, but do we stand a chance of being picked up in those mountainous waves down there?"

The two looked over the side at this point and saw they were again falling. Wise threw over the valise of champagne with which he had planned to celebrate their arrival in New York. The only ballast left in the basket now was a grapnel on a rope and a small hatchet.

Wise looked into the boat below and saw Hyde scribbling on a pad. He wondered if it were notes for a story, or the reporter's last will and testament. Lamountane was exploring the boat for any form of ballast. Wise told them to climb up into the basket so they could cut the boat loose and thus remain in the air a little longer. Hyde immediately climbed up but Lamountane elected to stay below and asked for the hatchet. He intended cutting out the double bottom of the boat to use for piecemeal ballast. The hatchet was passed down and Lamountane began in earnest to tear the boat apart. A few sticks had been tossed overboard when the boat smashed into the water with a huge splash. When the spray died down, Lamountane's hat could be seen floating on the crest of a wave. Wise shouted, "Lamountane's gone!"

But the words had barely left his lips when he heard a voice sing out, "No I'm not, it's only my hat!"

The sailor was lying in the bottom of the boat with his arms wound around one of the cross seats. He resumed his hacking as the lifeboat bounced along on the crest of the waves. Finally, the double bottom was gone and the airship gained a few hundred feet altitude. Lamountane joined the others in the wicker basket.

The storm clouds were now thick and black around the balloon. The lake was surging and foaming like a thing gone mad. Wise suddenly pointed. "I think I see a steamer out there! Will we swamp the balloon?"

A unanimous "No!" was the response.

Lamountane complained of being sick and unable to swim. Hyde said, "If we are to die, let's die on the land—if we can reach it."

Gager expressed the same sentiment.

It was evident that they had all forgotten how rough the land had looked before and they were now hoping against hope for a miracle to happen. Minutes seemed like ages as everyone watched for something other than clouds and spray. Suddenly, something could be seen up ahead. It was a steamer, the passenger ship *Young America,* and it was crossing directly in their path.

Wise resurrected the idea of landing on the water and of being picked up by the ship. He recalled a similar incident on Lake Erie. He had become lost and was rescued by a brig after landing in the water. When he again put it to the rest of the hapless crew, they were still solidly against it. Wise now calculated the group had traveled over one hundred miles across the lake and should be making landfall within a half-hour. The rest of the crew seemed to gain solace from this report. At 1:35 P.M. Hyde declared that he saw land, but that it looked like a million miles off.

"Too near for our comfort," was the aeronaut's retort.

Wise now reasoned that he might be able to swamp the balloon in the water just before it reached the shore. He cautioned them all to hang on tight, and busied himself with the valve cord. Wise claimed it was a turn of fate. Other aeronauts say he misjudged the rate of descent. Whatever the cause, before he could bring the gasbag down to water level, it bounced with a violent crash upon the shore. Instantly, he threw out the grapnel and with the others, held on for dear life.

The balloon rebounded and shot up over the treetops. The grapnel caught in a tree but it was like a fishhook anchoring a battleship. In another moment the balloon went dragging along through the treetops like a mad elephant through a jungle. The thing that saved the occupants was the large iron ring Mr. Wise had installed above the basket to distribute the load of the car and the lifeboat along the net. The balloon went careening over the countryside at a terrific rate and it seemed unbelievable that anyone could survive this dashing and crashing process. Eventually the basket lodged in the side of a high tree, the balloon split with a loud bang and then, like a dying whale, collapsed.

There they were, the boat still fastened by three ropes, hanging at a sixty-degree angle. The men examined themselves to learn if there were serious injuries. Much to their surprise, no one was hurt. Ignominiously they climbed down the inclined deck of the boat and dropped to the ground.

Several people had watched the drama and had come running to where the flight ended. After expressing their sentiments about anyone who would venture forth in such a contraption, they told the travelers that they were near the town of Henderson, New York, twelve hundred miles from St. Louis—as the crow flies; but they hastened to add that this was not a fit day for a crow to be flying.

John Wise walked to a small stump, wearily sat down, pulled his notebook from his pocket and dutifully wrote.

"July 2, 1859, two thirty-five P.M., landed in a tree on the place of Truman Whitney, in the township of Henderson, in the county of Jefferson, in the State of New York. Thus ended the *Greatest Air Voyage Ever Made.*"

FLOATING ON AIR

by Guy Murchie

The sky has not been easy to explore. Even as I look out my round window at 11,000 feet, I realize that the lower air is about eight hundred times lighter than the water that is the lightest medium below it. Yet many times it has been invaded by beings heavier than itself. For again and again has life risen up from the gentle earth and the sea to dare to fly. And five times it has amply succeeded.

After the very early passive launchings of pollen and spores and tufted seeds came the winged insects nearly a billion years ago in the earth's first active conquest of the air. Second, the ancient pterodactyls and other flying reptiles. Third, the birds. Fourth, the bats. Fifth, man.

Although man's great victory has come largely in my own half lifetime, it is already complete enough to be accepted casually by many professional flyers. I personally find it hard to share their carefree forgetfulness of the meaning of flight. Perhaps it is from having spent so many years entirely on the ground between flying jobs that the sky still slaps me fresh in the face at every take-off.

It hit me especially hard one night while climbing over San Francisco Bay into the vast moonlit Pacific Ocean of the air with a load of human blood for Korea. I sensed anew then the boldness of this upper world of the future that we are just managing to peek at through its slightly opened door.

Casual as they are, the flying men of today have a rashness of spirit that I feel in my every bone as I slant upward over the sparkling cable-car hills of the gold-rush city. Of course the men of last century were bold too in their way, but they were dealing with the homely things they knew: marlin spikes and axes and muzzle-loading guns, cross-trees and whales and the great waves of the ancient deep. Today the instruments we use and invent are so strange their strangeness alone is frightening, and the very waves of our ocean have scarce begun to be understood.

It is plain that life on earth has suddenly quickened. One generation has leapt off a horse's back and through the sonic wall. Life moves naturally upward in a spiral, but here the spiral is bent strangely, before continuing its accelerating, buoyant course. It is the way of things important to life. It is irregular, not entirely predictable, but continuing: the motion of air under wings that hold up airplanes and birds, the flow of blood, the breath of consciousness, the growth of stars, even the prophetic revelations of God.

It was the Persian poet, Firdausi, in the eleventh century who wrote of an early human attempt at flying by the eccentric Shah Kai Kaoos who built himself a unique craft shaped like a four-poster bed. Being better versed in falconry than mechanics, Kai Kaoos harnessed four eagles for motive power, one at each corner. To get his engines to lift he placed raw meat above them on the tops of the sharpened posts. Firdausi reported that the Shah managed to get this contraption off the ground but had trouble synchronizing his motors and soon had to make a forced landing in the desert from which he was rescued only with the greatest difficulty.

The medieval windmill was another precursor of human flight, providing a close model of the modern four-bladed, square-edged propeller—almost as prenatal human growth reviews human evolution.

The idea of using hot air or gas as a lifting agent seems to have come to many persons during the last four centuries. Leonardo da Vinci is credited with having once made some wafer-thin figures of wax which he filled with hot air and launched into the sky on the occasion of Pope Leo X's coronation.

The Jesuit, Francisco de Lana, designed an aerial sailing ship in 1670 with four copper vacuum spheres to lift it. His theory of buoyancy was remarkably advanced but perhaps he realized that his vacuum spheres could not be both thin enough for lightness and thick enough to withstand the inward pressure of the air, for he never tried to build it.

A few years later in 1709, however, another Jesuit, Bartholomeu de Gusmão, actually sent up a small hot-air balloon and designed a large airship on the hot-air principal which might well have carried him aloft had he had faith or fortune enough to execute his ideas.

In those days the feminine principle of passive, rotund, floating flight was even less understood than the bird-inspired masculine concept of active, flapping flight—yet it was destined to come to glorious fulfillment both soon and suddenly in 1783. That was the famous year when two French brothers in the paper-making craft noticed how a fire wafts pieces of paper upward on its hot clouds of smoke, and they tried filling a paper bag full of the same kind of smoke to see if it would rise too.

It did. Even better than they had expected! And so Joseph and Etienne Montgolfier got started in ballooning. They looked up Priestley's famous treatise on air, and made bigger and bigger bags of hot smoke until on June 5 of that year, feeling confident at last that they had hold of a real discovery, they put on a public ascension before a thousand spectators in the market place of their home town of Annonay, near Lyons.

This first full-size balloon was made of linen and paper, 105 feet in circumference and buttoned together in gores. The Montgolfiers built a fire of straw and wool under it, filling it quickly with thick yellow smoke. Then they cut the cords and it rose impressively for several thousand feet, landing ten minutes later about a mile and a half away.

This demonstration by the Montgolfiers made a tremendous sensation and within a week was the talk of all Europe. The Paris Academy straightaway commissioned its physicist, J. A. C. Charles, to investigate. Professor Charles may have assumed that the balloon's inventors utilized Cavendish's recent discovery of hydrogen, then popularly known as "inflammable air," for he quickly designed his own idea of a hydrogen balloon and had one made thirteen feet in diameter which he set up on the Champ de Mars before a crowd composed largely of "philosophers, officials, students, and loiterers" on August 27. Although it rained that day, the balloon rose on schedule and disappeared into the low clouds. A wag among the open-mouthed spectators just then turned to the aged American ambassador standing near him and asked "Of what use is a balloon, Mr. Franklin?"

Replied the inventor of the lightning rod, "Of what use, sir, is a newborn baby?"

An hour later some peasants near Gonesse saw a strange globe miraculously descend from the clouds and bounce upon a field. Frightened but fascinated, they gathered around the mysterious buoyant object. When one jabbed it with his pitchfork it hissed forth a dangerous smell, so the others all joined in killing the evil creature with spades and scythes. When nothing remained but shreds, the corpse was dragged off tied to the tail of a horse.

Meanwhile the Montgolfier brothers had come to Paris to demonstrate their hot-air balloon to the Academy. They built a new and fancy one with colorful decorations and pictures on it, which ascended successfully on September 12. By this time people were talking about human travel by balloon, but no one had yet volunteered to try it, so on September 19 the Montgolfiers sent up a large balloon carrying a sheep, cock, and duck to see if life could survive way up there in the unknown.

After the barnyard delegation landed safely a new balloon was built for human passengers and the king wanted to send up two criminals for the first flight, but Pilâtre de Rozier, curator of the Royal Museum of Natural History, persuaded His Majesty that the privilege of being the first human to fly was too rare an honor to waste on a convict, so he and the Marquis d'Arlandes were given the chance. During November they cautiously experimented in the new balloon while it was tethered and at last on November 21 were cut loose on the world's first free human flight!

This momentous event went off smoothly and the balloon rose some 500 feet and drifted five miles over the Bois de Boulogne in plain sight of hundreds of cheering people.

From this date ballooning was accepted throughout the Western world, and Professor Charles completed the first hydrogen balloon of almost modern form in time to take off on December 1 from the Tuileries with a fellow balloon maker named Roberts. This remarkable craft, launched in 1783, still the birth year of ballooning, was complete with rubberized fabric, a net to support the basket, top valve, ballast, and a barometric altimeter. Charles flew all the way to Nesle that time, twenty-seven miles.

Only a year later a balloon crossed the English Channel from Dover to the forest of Guînes in France. Jean-Pierre Blanchard was the first, and among the greatest, of aerial showmen. A "petulant little fellow" around five feet two inches tall and "well suited for vapourish regions," he made the first ascents in America and in many European countries, and was determined to be the first man to fly the channel. Not having much money, however, he persuaded an American physician, Dr. John Jeffries, to finance the trip. But he tried desperately to prevent the doctor from accompanying him and diluting the glory. He pretended the balloon was not big enough to support them both and secretly wore a lead-lined belt to prove it.

His unpleasant argument with Jeffries was patched up only at the last moment by the Governor of Dover Castle as the two men took off from the white cliffs on January 7, 1785. Their interesting cargo included a barometer (for reading height), a compass, anchors, flags, cork life jackets, thirty pounds of ballast, a packet of pamphlets, a bottle of brandy, biscuits, apples, and the latest in aerial navigation equipment: a large rudder, two big silk-covered sky oars, and Blanchard's famous "moulinet"—a hand-operated revolving fan, which was the first big step upward in the windmill's evolution into the propeller.

They got away safely on a fine northwesterly breeze, but the crossing proved a hair-raising adventure. Evidently the sky was full of cumulus clouds with strong updrafts beneath them and downdrafts between, for the balloon kept rising and falling with bewildering inconsistency until the two men were at their wits' end. One can imagine what the uncontrolled Blanchard muttered to his companion every time the balloon started downward toward the sea. As the balloon moved with the air rather than through it, the rudder was entirely useless, and the oars and moulinet were ridiculously unwieldy and ineffective under the great sluggish hulk of the hydrogen bag.

They had not reached halfway before all the ballast was gone and they had to jettison the anchors, the rudder, oars, moulinet, even the brandy, in order to stay in the air. Just off the French coast the situation looked so desperate that both men, after relieving themselves, started removing their clothes and the panicky Blanchard had just tossed overboard his trousers with a dramatic gesture when an unexpected updraft raised the balloon so high that he nearly froze before they finally descended into the trees twelve miles beyond the coast. The car of the balloon can be seen today in the Calais Museum.

The original Montgolfière or hot-air balloon was within two years almost entirely supplanted by the superior Charlière or hydrogen balloon and ballooning became a widely practiced sport. To what lengths impetuous Frenchmen carried ballooning in the decades that followed cannot be better illustrated than by the duel fought on May 3, 1808, when two emotional gentlemen of Paris blazed away at each other with blunderbusses while drifting in balloons half a mile above the Tuileries Gardens.

Probably the biggest part in history played by balloons was during the siege of Paris in 1870–71 when sixty-six of them evacuated about a hundred important persons, nine tons of mail, and four hundred homing pigeons from the city. At first the balloons took off by day but when a few were nearly shot down by Prussian bullets and shells, night departures became more common. Fifty-nine of these balloons actually succeeded in landing in friendly territory, five fell into enemy hands, and the remaining two were presumed lost at sea. The zeppelins of World War I later also evolved from balloons but balloons have since then, despite their increasing use in meteorology and air-raid defense, faded in importance relative to the airplane.

Before the epic story of the airplane, however, we must take up another earlier invention that developed almost simultaneously with the balloon: the parachute, a natural vehicle of passive flight.

So natural is the parachute in fact that not only have seeds and spores resorted to its principle but many animals have adopted either it or its companion principle of gliding, obviously the prelude to active flight.

The insects were earth's first real flyers, most of them—especially the very small ones—using the parachute idea about as much as the wing to stay aloft. Their very minuteness has made that inevitable for the same reason that the surface of any small object is greater in proportion to its weight (more parachutelike) than that of a larger object of similar shape and material.

You can figure this out mathematically on the basis of simple dimensions. As surface has only two dimensions and weight (like volume) three, so the relationship between surface and weight is proportionately as the square to the cube. Thus a creature loses more weight than surface as he becomes smaller, and it is its *relatively* great surface that gives the little ant enough air resistance to parachute safely any distance. Large beetles can do fairly well in parachuting too. Even a mouse can drop from an airplane without much risk of injury. A rat, however, is usually knocked out. A dog is killed. A man is broken. A horse splashes. An elephant disintegrates.

For this reason specialization in the form of a parachute is unnecessary to any animal smaller than a mouse. But many animals only a little bigger have adopted them in varying degrees from the Malayan umbrella lizard or draco, with his gorgeously colored folding parasol made of fine membrane stretched over actual ribs, to the Bornean glider snakes which can suck their bellies against their backbones and float from tree to tree like ribbons on the wind.

The first human to design a parachute seems to have been the versatile Leonardo about A.D. 1500, but the only actual use for parachutes after his time was in the popular "umbrella dance" often put on by court entertainers who amused their royal patrons with tremendous leaps made possible by big umbrellas attached to their belts.

It was not until the birth year of the balloon, 1783, that the real parachute became an independently proven possibility. In that year Sebastian Lenormand made himself the first full-fledged parachute and jumped with it from the tower of Montpellier Observatory in France. He landed safely but seems to have regarded his apparatus as nothing more than a new means of escaping from fires in tall buildings.

Showman J. P. Blanchard was the first person to use a parachute in a drop from a balloon. In 1785 he released one from several thousand feet up containing a dog in the basket beneath it. The dog barked on the way down and landed unharmed.

Blanchard still felt uneasy about trying the parachute himself but finally did so eight years later. His primitive parachute either was too small for his weight or swayed very violently for Blanchard hit the ground so hard he broke his leg.

The real father of the parachute is generally considered to be André Jacques Garnerin, who had plenty of time to design parachutes while serving a prison sentence in Budapest. Shortly after his release he made his first drop over Paris in 1797, followed by many more descents in other parts of France and England. His 'chutes oscillated so violently that he would get actively seasick on the way down and usually arrived in no condition to appreciate the raucous enthusiasm of the cheering crowds who wanted to carry him triumphantly on their shoulders.

Garnerin's parachutes were like huge beach umbrellas with a basket hanging below similar to a balloon's car. They were made of canvas about the same size as modern parachutes but inevitably heavier and they must have hit the ground much harder.

The first life saved by parachute was that of a Polish aeronaut named Jordaki Kuparento whose poorly made hot air balloon caught fire over Warsaw in 1808. Luckily he had a parachute aboard, got it opened up in time, and managed to drop to safety.

A few years later Garnerin's niece, Eliza Garnerin, was the first woman parachutist. But there was still a lot of basic experimenting to be done before the parachute would achieve its present perfection, and one of the wide-eyed young spectators of Garnerin's first descent in London, Robert Cocking, was the first to be killed in an attempt to improve on it.

Parachutes first came into common use by German aviators during the last few months of World War I while the Allied flyers still considered them too bulky and heavy to be worthwhile except in the case of observation balloons which often were shot down several times daily.

But just after the war the seat-pack type of 'chute was generally adopted for its efficiency, weighing only eighteen pounds and replacing the seat cushion so that it carried the aviator instead of the aviator carrying it. More than 1500 experimental jumps were made at the end of the war in perfecting this invention, while literally millions of descents have been made since then in working out the exact parachute procedures used today.

The parachute schools now teach students such long-proven lessons as the headlong dive from open cockpit planes for getting one's head and shoulders away fast. And that after you jump it's important to wait before pulling your ripcord until you have lost your forward speed—especially if you jumped out of a plane traveling several hundred miles an hour, which may well be enough to tear your parachute apart or jerk the harness clean off you. Contrary to what you might think, your speed through the air just after jumping is almost certainly decreasing rather than increasing—for at least several seconds—and the faster your plane was moving the more certainly this is true.

The modern manuals explain that you should not dive with your knees drawn up because that makes you somersault, and when you pull the ripcord while somersaulting, the lift webs are apt to yank up between your knees, causing you to descend hanging upside down and probably painfully. A British pamphlet says, "a very good view of the ground is at once obtained but the position is extremely uncomfortable, definitely undignified, and you may even lose things out of your pockets."

The American Naval Manual thoughtfully adds: "If one of those things in your pocket happens to be your address book, you'll bewilder the farmer who picks it up and also leave yourself with nothing to do at night but go to the movies. That's hard on your eyes."

Some think that the opening of a parachute after falling for a mile or so must be a terrific jerk but the modern 'chutes have built-in shock absorbers to make your whole ride more comfortable. The silk or nylon canopy is woven loosely enough so that some of the air flows right through it and the remaining trapped air has just enough resistance to slow you up like an automobile with brakes applied, which is much gentler than hitting a stone wall.

The serious swaying that bothered Garnerin and Blanchard so much is virtually impossible in a modern 'chute, and even if you should find yourself swinging a little you can easily eliminate it by pulling on the shroud lines, spilling air out of one side or the other of your canopy. You can change your angle and speed of descent that way too, thus controlling to an important degree where you are going to land.

You should of course have a fair amount of time to work on your landing on the way down. Once it opens, your parachute slows your falling speed to about twenty feet a second—depending on your weight and the density of the air.

The manuals advise jumping from above 1000 feet, and consider it very dangerous to bail out from less than 250 feet. However, a few lucky lads have gotten away with it under desperate circumstances at around 100 feet, which can be taken as the absolute limit below which it's a better bet to stick with your falling aircraft even if it's full of dynamite and heading for a cliff.

In general the higher you are when you jump the better your chances—that is, up to 20,000 feet or so, depending on the conditions of weather and air. Jumps have been made from much higher without ill effects, but above 30,000 feet the shortage of oxygen becomes a problem of first importance. Special oxygen masks and even heated pressure suits are now being used in stratospheric parachuting.

THE LAST FLIGHT OF THE R-101

by John G. Fuller

The concern for their friends on the R-101 didn't fade when Major Villiers and Aleen arrived back at their Hertfordshire home. Aleen tried hard to shake off her feeling of depression. She was unsuccessful. Villiers was still troubled about why "Brancks," as he called him, had never come back down to say goodbye. He tried to concentrate on completing his report for the Imperial Conference, "An Approach to Civil Aviation." He had a hard time doing it. He was thinking of the R-101 leaving the mast. Why had they had to drop so much ballast? It could obviously mean only one thing—the whole ship was heavy, especially at the bow. He had watched the R-101 leave the tower many times before. They never had had to sacrifice such a large amount of the precious ballast.

The technical section of the report he was working on was too difficult to handle that evening. There were too many disturbing feelings both Aleen and he were experiencing. Villiers was not a technical man. He preferred the subject matter of policy and planning, which he had no trouble in grasping. He finally gave up, and he and Aleen went to bed early.

Both were staunch members of the Church of England, and both of them prayed for a safe voyage for the ship. Villiers' grandfather had been the Bishop of Carlyle. His wife's father had held the same post. Religion was a natural and integral part of their lives, and they carried it into their everyday living. Villiers was convinced that he would never have gotten through the First World War without it, so many times did he come close to death. They both believed in the utter reality of the spirit. They saw no conflict between the ideas of the Christian Spiritualists and the conventional theology of the church.

Villiers' own psychic experiences were few. He would on occasion get an overwhelming sense of the presence of a loved one who had died, and sometimes feel they were in communication with him. Although his rational mind could not explain such incidences, he accepted them as part of a greater picture beyond the senses. He never believed in going to a medium, although he had on one occasion. The experience indicated to him that there had to be some validity in the psychic. His father had "come through." He was described in detail by the medium, along with a number of verifiable facts. His father had also identified himself by describing the crooked finger he had had since birth. In Villiers' mind, there was no possible way for the medium to know this or any other of the multiple, intimate facts revealed about his father, long since dead at the time of the session. But he felt uneasy about the experience, almost as if he were intruding. He never went back.

For the most part, Villiers was a realist and a man of action. At the age of forty-four, he played golf and tennis vigorously, and never lost his interest in cricket. He lived a disciplined life, a hangover from his long and active years in the military. His performance in the service, which had won him his D.S.O., the Croix de Guerre and the Legion of Honor, provided enough discipline to last him a lifetime.

Aleen and the Major drifted off into an uneasy sleep. Around midnight, Aleen woke him up. She was terrified. She had had one of the most vivid dreams she had ever experienced. She saw the R-101 clearly, moving across the sky. Then without warning, it went crashing to the ground.

They both attributed the nightmare to their deep anxiety, and finally dozed off again to sleep.

As the R-101 headed toward its first checkpoint over London, a lavish dinner was being prepared on board. There was an ample supply of champagne. The rains had come now, with gusty winds and a vengeance. They had gone barely 35 miles, over the village of Hitchin, when the vessel began pitching and rolling heavily. It seemed to have trouble gaining altitude, and it kept dipping unpredictably. In the smoking room, sitting on the wicker lounge, Squadron Leader Rope took notice of it. He was the technical assistant to Richmond, the designer. Beside him was Henry Leech, the foreman engineer from the base at Cardington.

"I never knew her to roll so much," Rope said to Leech. "She feels more like a seagoing ship than an aircraft."

Rope didn't seem too worried about it. It was the first time that the R-101 had been flying in any kind of substantial rough weather, and perhaps it was to be expected. In the control car, the concern centered on the dropping of all that water ballast so early in the trip. Four tons, out of nine-and-a-half, had had to be sacrificed, all of it from the bow tanks. The only emergency ballast left in the forward part of the ship was half a ton. It could not be dumped automatically in an emergency. A man would have to be sent scurrying up forward to release it by hand, to lighten the load and try to get the ship level. With the changes in pressure on the gas bags at different altitudes, this could be critical.

They were still over Hitchin, when Arthur Bell, the gondola engineer in the aft-engine power egg, reported that his engine had suddenly stopped. W. R. Gent, the supervising engineer for the flight, scampered down the precarious ladder to the gondola, and joined Bell.

"It's the main oil pressure, sir," Bell told him.

Henry Leech joined them in moments. Jammed into the narrow cabin, the three began working. The rain was heavy, beating on the window. The ship was still pitching and rolling heavily. It was hard to keep their balance.

Down below the ship, in Hitchin, the countryside was drenched in rain, and the trees and bushes were bending in the wind. Shane Leslie, a well-known author of the twenties, and his wife were having dinner at West End Farm, their Hertfordshire cottage. Suddenly, they heard their two servants scream. They rushed out to the garden terrace. Over a field of mushrooms, they saw the red and green running lights of the R-101. The giant hull was barely visible in the lowering clouds and rain. But it was there, and it seemed to be aiming straight for their cottage.

It was low, so low that Mrs. Leslie felt that it couldn't possibly miss scraping their roof. She thought: "This is the end of our cottage." The Leslies and the servants scattered. They were absolutely certain the ship was coming down on them. They watched, their field and garden faintly illuminated by the lights of the saloon cabins. Their farm was on a hill, a sudden rise of about 600 feet above sea level. The ship seemed to barely clear the trees along their driveway. She was dipping, then rising, as if she was straining to get higher. They went back in the house and checked the clock in their living room. It was 8:15 in the evening.

The huge skin of the vessel, the envelope, was now sodden with water, adding weight to the ship, making it harder to control. As the engineers worked on the aft engine, the wireless room sent a message back to the Cardington base:

> OVER LONDON. ALL WELL. MODERATE RAIN. BASE OF LOW CLOUDS 1500 FEET. WIND 240 DEGREES. 25 M. P. H. COURSE NOW SET FOR PARIS. INTEND TO PROCEED VIA PARIS, TOURS, TOULOUSE AND NARBONNE.

There was no mention of the broken-down engine, nor of the inordinate pitching and rolling. No change in altitude was noted. All seemed well, according to the message at least.

Shortly after eight o'clock, the Meteorological Office at Cardington had wirelessed a message to the R-101. It was not good news:

> NEXT TWELVE HOURS FLIGHT SE ENGLAND, CHANNEL, NORTHERN FRANCE, WIND AT 2000 FEET FROM ABOUT 240 DEGREES 40 TO 50 MILES AN HOUR. CLOUDY LOCAL RAIN.

This was serious. The early forecasts had predicted winds in the neighborhood of 20 to 30 miles an hour. To face a possible 50-mile-an-hour wind would put the heavily loaded R-101 to a flying test she had never experienced, over a terrain where cross-currents and vertical drafts would be sure to occur. No other British airship had met such a velocity over land before.

Below, in London, the spectators gathered, in spite of the chilling rain and the wind. The ship seemed unusually low. Her nose was well down, her tail up. The crowds could even see people in the cabins, in spite of the clouds and darkness.

Major Scott was immediately presented with the storm warning, while the ship was still over London. It was hard to tell where the responsibility for decisions actually lay. The passengers and officers aboard were top-heavy with rank and brass. Irwin was technically in charge of the flight, but Major Scott had many more hours of command experience. Colmore was the overall boss of the project, but not the flight. Lord Thomson and Sir Sefton could, if they wanted to, probably overrule everyone with their authoritative weight.

In this case, it was Scott who probably made the decision not to turn back. He was a resolute and fearless commander, too much so, some of his fellow officers thought. He had headed the R-100 into the teeth of a storm on the Montreal flight, and some of the crew thought they were lucky to survive. The fact was that the R-101 now kept going, heading toward France, toward the center of a rising storm.

With four of the five engines still operating well, the R-101 crossed over the lights of Hastings, site of the historic battle, and out over the darkness of the Channel. It was shortly after 9:30. The alternate routing over Deal, toward Dunkirk, had not been chosen this time. The rain was increasing, as well as the wind. There was no question that its velocity had been underestimated. Over the Channel, the concern would not be too great. It was when they reached the rolling terrain of France that concern would grow. The turbulence and the gusts would be bound to increase.

But the message from the ship was not discouraging:

> AT 2135 GMT CROSSING COAST IN VICINITY OF HASTINGS. IT IS RAINING HARD AND THERE IS A STRONG SOUTHWESTERLY WIND. ENGINES RUNNING WELL AT CRUISING SPEED, GIVING 54.2 KNOTS. CLOUD BASE IS AT 1500 FEET. . . . SHIP IS BEHAVING WELL GENERALLY AND WE HAVE ALREADY BEGUN TO RECOVER WATER BALLAST.

The rain water was doing its part of the job, flowing in through the openings at the top of the envelope to replenish part of the ballast lost at the start. There was no mention of the non-operational aft engine, nor of concern for the storms ahead.

Over the Channel, the three cramped engineers were still working furiously on the recalcitrant aft engine. They were not making any obvious headway, and the ship was dragging several tons of useless weight because of it. Leech paused in his work long enough to glance out the window, and was rather startled at the low altitude of the ship. He could clearly see the whitecaps through the darkness. He estimated that the ship was only 700 or 800 feet above them. Engineer Cook, in the port midship engine, could also distinctly see the choppy white waves. He looked out several times. The ship would dip and get lower, then rise again. It was common for an airship to plunge up and down in squally weather. He found it hard to believe the control car was allowing the ship to dip so low.

Electrician Disley joined the wireless operator for a moment, in the wireless room immediately adjoining the control cabin. It was around ten o'clock now, and the ship was still over the sloppy waters of the Channel. Nearby, Navigator Johnston was dropping calcium flares to check the drift. As they landed in the water, he could check the crabbing movement of the ship, as the wind pushed it out of its course.

Looking into the control car, Disley was surprised to see First Officer Atherstone suddenly grab the elevator wheel from the height coxswain. The altimeter, if it was correct, showed that they had dipped to 900 feet. But there was always a problem with the barometric altimeter. A reading could sometimes indicate an altitude considerably higher than the ship actually was. Atherstone spun the wheel at the port side of the control car hard. Then he handed the wheel back to the coxswain.

"Do not let her go below 1,000 feet," he warned.

It was an unusual procedure. Atherstone must have been seriously concerned to take the wheel himself.

No word was heard back in Cardington from the R-101 until 11:36 P.M., when a new wireless message arrived:

> CROSSING FRENCH COAST AT POINTE DE ST. QUENTIN. WIND 245 TRUE 35 MPH.

Back at Cardington, there was surprise. The Channel crossing had taken roughly two hours. The distance from Hastings to the French port was approximately 60 miles. The previous wireless reports from the R-101 didn't add up. She should have traveled considerably farther if the earlier reports had been correct. It was confusing.

The watch had changed at eleven o'clock. The fresh crew would stay on duty until 2 A.M., when the alternate shift would come on. By eleven, the stubborn aft engine was fixed. It would help increase power against the increasing winds. By midnight, the ship settled down to the routine details of the flight. At eighteen minutes after midnight, another wireless message was sent to Cardington. The ship would soon be out of range, and would depend on Croydon, Le Bourget in Paris, and Valenciennes for its cross-bearings and communication.

The midnight message read:

> 2400 GMT 15 MILES SW OF ABBEVILLE. AVERAGE SPEED 33 KNOTS. WIND 35 MPH. ALTIMETER HEIGHT 1500 FEET. WEATHER INTERMITTENT RAIN. CLOUD NIMBUS AT 500 FEET.

After the official information had been dispatched, a more relaxed report came over, heartening the observers at Cardington:

> AFTER AN EXCELLENT SUPPER OUR DISTINGUISHED PASSENGERS SMOKED A FINAL CIGAR, AND HAVING SIGHTED THE FRENCH COAST HAVE NOW GONE TO BED TO REST AFTER THE EXCITEMENT OF THEIR LEAVE-TAKING. ALL ESSENTIAL SERVICES ARE FUNCTIONING SATISFACTORILY. THE CREW HAVE SETTLED DOWN TO A WATCH-KEEPING ROUTINE.

It was a comfortable picture now. The lights in the lavishly decorated saloon were turned low. The equally opulent smoking room was dimmed, but was available to anyone who was restless or who wanted to find a fellow insomniac in the early morning hours to share a nightcap or the excitement of traveling in the clouds in such luxury. The passengers, with perhaps a touch too much of champagne, enough anyway to relax in the comfortable bunks in their staterooms. The officer of the watch in the darkened control cabin, monitoring the altimeter, the compass, the pitch and roll indicators, the engine room telegraph pedestals standing by if needed. The engineers in their egg-shaped gondolas, shaken by noise and vibration, but watching with satisfaction the performance of their engines. The riggers on watch on the keel catwalk, more than the length of two football fields, roaming it in silence as the engines purred smoothly beneath the ship.

There would be those annoying and sometimes frightening pitches, yaws and dips. There would also be the likelihood of the storms getting worse, of the gas bags surging and swaying against the struts and girders, of the thin and questionable skin of the envelope that had never faced a 50-mile wind beating against it under cruising power. These were imponderables. They clouded the comfortable portrait of a luxury liner of the air moving like a magic carpet over the villages of France.

At 1:18 A.M., the airship sent a radio message to Croydon: "Thanks for valuable assistance. Will not require you further tonight." Croydon was not dismissed so easily: "Am remaining on watch," they wirelessed back.

The R-101 passed over the Poix aerodrome, about 30 miles from the French coast, on the way to Paris, at around one in the morning. The wind was fiercer now, and the rains lashed at it with greater fury.

M. Maillet, manager of the Poix airfield, heard the engines and peered through the thick rain and mist to look for it. Finally he saw something —a strip of white lights in a row. He could barely make out the hull of the ship. She was moving slowly, along the railway line.

She appeared to be struggling hard against the wind. He was convinced she was low, very low, too low. The ship could not be at more than 300 feet, maybe less. As a veteran observer of aircraft, he did not like what he saw. He gauged by her direction that she was heading toward Beauvais, the next town to the south, on the Paris route. He felt troubled. She was less than half her length from the ground.

At Le Bourget, the historic field where Lindbergh had landed the *Spirit of St. Louis,* the wireless operator was keeping close touch with the R-101. The signal was loud and clear. Leech and Gent, the two senior engineers, had made their way to the smoking room to relax after the tension in getting the aft engine going again. It wasn't long before Captain Irwin joined them. He was pleased with their repair job, and told them so. After a short respite, he left. Tired, Gent said that he was going to head for his stateroom, while Leech decided to take another look at all the engines.

It was a long tour of duty. He had to scramble from transverse frame #4, all the way back to #11. He would have to walk in the swinging, pitching ship nearly 400 feet each way, climb down the ladders to the engines, and climb up again into the hull after each engine inspection. He did it. It took the better part of an hour, but all was well with the engines, and he was relieved. He went back to the smoking room, too tense to sleep. It was empty. He poured a drink, and sprawled out on the settee to have another cigarette. Sleep was hard to come by.

In the control car, there seemed to be trouble with the altimeter. Some of the crew felt they were always nearer the ground than the altimeter showed. Ever since the Channel, in fact.

Shortly after quarter of two, the wireless man at Le Bourget joined up with a station at Valenciennes, and sent the R-101 a clear position fix. They figured the ship to be one kilometer from Beauvais, give or take a fraction. The operator in the wireless room of the R-101 sent back a simple, cheery message: "Thank you. Good night."

They were over Beauvais when the watch was changed at 2 A.M. The change was made calmly enough. Nobody seemed concerned. Engine man Binks made his way along the keel catwalk. He had had a hard time waking up after a restless sleep, and had stopped and poured himself a mug of hot chocolate, as a wake-me-up. He moved through the transverse frames from #8 to #11, and climbed down into the aft-engine car about three or four minutes late. He was relieving his friend Bell, who greeted him in mock anger for being late.

The two chatted a minute, over the roar of the engine, about its performance. There had been no trouble since the oil pressure failed back over Hitchin, some six hours before.

Engineer Alfred Cook climbed down the ladder to the midship engine on the port side to take over from engineer Blake promptly on schedule. Blake was tired. After a quick exchange of greetings, he went up the ladder and headed for his crew quarters.

In the same manner, engineer Savory took over the starboard midship engine from his crew-mate Hastings. He checked over the operation of the engine, which seemed in good order.

Electrician Disley was sound asleep in his bunk, near the main electrical switchboard. He was lying with his head toward the bow of the ship, and he suddenly found himself sliding backwards on his bunk. Then he felt the ship come out of the dive, and was considerably relieved. It had been a steep one.

Leech was still alone in the smoking room at this time, at about five after two. He was about to have another sip of his drink, when he found himself sliding down the settee, toward the forward bulkhead, and came to a stop against it. At the same moment, a siphon and several highball glasses on a table near him slid to the floor. Then the table itself skidded down the floor toward the bulkhead. He leaned over, picked the unbroken glassware up and put it back on the table.

In the village of Beauvais, Louis Petit and his wife were getting ready to go to bed. They ran a general store in the town, and had just finished up a rather busy Saturday night. The hour was later than usual for them. As M. Petit began to undress, he heard a noise that sounded like thunder. He quickly ran out on the street. He looked up. He saw what he described as a lit-up village in disguise. It was low, very low. It looked as if it might impale itself on the church steeple.

He knew that the "Zepp," as he called it, was due to pass over the town, but he immediately realized that the ship was in trouble. The hull was moving broadside, not forward. It was sliding sideways, out of control. It was being whipped by the wind and the rain. His wife was now beside him, and they looked on in horror. Then the lights suddenly disappeared in the sky. Seconds later, they were on again. Then off. Then on and off.

Each time they did this, the ship seemed to be getting lower. Monsieur and Madame Petit stood transfixed, hardly daring to think about what was going to happen next.

George Darling, a British racehorse owner visiting his friend Marcel Debeaupuis near Beauvais in the village of Allone, had gone to bed. But he had not yet gone to sleep. He heard the motors of the R-101 coming nearer. He looked out the window. Through the rain the ship could be seen low above the rolling hills near Beauvais. There was a howling gale outside now, and he wondered how any aircraft could survive. The strip of lights along the hull blinked off and on. Then he saw the ship plunging up and down like a dolphin. There was no question in his mind that it was in trouble.

He called to Debeaupuis, who had also been roused from sleep. They watched together, both in suspense and uncertainty.

It was nearly five minutes after two. On board the R-101, there was no sign of any restless passengers wandering through the passageways. In the passenger cabins, Lord Thomson, Sir Sefton and the other visitors were sleeping soundly. In the pantry, someone in the crew was having a snack of tinned corned beef and some cold peas. He was surrounded by tins of biscuits and sardines.

Over Beauvais, the ship seemed to circle, like a dog looking for a comfortable place to lie down. It seemed to be skimming dangerously low, over both fields and houses. By now, it seemed that half the town, in various stages of undress, had come out to the streets. Some felt that it actually had brushed against the spire of the cathedral and the side of a factory building nearby. It looked like a drunken, reeling monster with its crabwise motion.

Out on the soaked, undulating fields and orchards near Beauvais, Alfred Roubaille was breaking the local laws by setting snares for rabbits. He was working along a wooded area, near a hummock of land. It was called Therain Wood. It was a lonely spot, nearer Allone than Beauvais. He wasn't altogether comfortable about his illegal hunting, but there was Sunday dinner to think about, and times were not that good for him and his family.

Roubaille heard the sound of the engines too, over the rush of the wind near Therain Wood. He looked up from his snares and saw it. It was brightly illuminated. It was moving very slowly, but it was coming directly toward him. He had trouble believing what he was seeing. The great hull of the ship seemed to be sinking in front of him. It was still moving forward, but its nose was pointed down. He was frozen in horror.

Binks was still chatting with Bell in the after-engine car. They were talking of oil pressure, engine cooling and the rpm's of the Diesel. There seemed to be no problem any more. Quite suddenly, they felt the nose of the ship sink down. The dive must have lasted nearly half a minute. Then the craft leveled off again. In moments, there was another dive. As it happened, the engine room telegraph rang, and the indicator moved to SLOW. Bell grabbed the throttle, and pulled it back.

Alfred Cook, in the port midship engine cab, had barely time to get adjusted to the noise of the motor before he noticed the ship diving, and the engine telegraph ringing to SLOW. He immediately cut the throttle back, but as he did, the ship went into another, steeper dive. He looked out the gondola window. The ground was coming up to meet him.

Savory, in his engine cabin on the starboard midship car, felt only one dive. But it was a steep one. He was standing with his back to the starting engine, looking aft. Suddenly, he was thrown back against it. He had no idea what was going on.

Right after Henry Leech had picked up the siphon and the highball glasses in the smoking room, he felt the nose of the ship take another dive. It didn't seem to him to be as sharp as the first. Then he heard the engine room telegraph ring. All along he had felt that the ship had been pitching dangerously. He still suspected that something was wrong with the altimeter. He was glad his wife had given him that sprig of white heather. He needed it for luck. But he still had confidence in the ship, in spite of the pitching that had bothered him over the past half hour.

Electrician Disley's crew quarters were above and slightly astern of the control car, almost amidship. He had no way of seeing outside, but he could sense that the R-101 was struggling against the storm. He was not too disturbed. He, too, heard the engine room telegraph ring out, and he knew that the sudden change in the engines would have a strong effect on the generators. If a wire broke, there was the danger of fire. The switchboard was close to his left hand. He instinctively reached for it. There were two main switches. He grabbed one of them and tripped it.

Up in the control car, the height coxswain was spinning the wheel to a full "up" position. They were dumping ballast now—including precious fuel oil. Rigger Church was ordered up to the forepeak to dump the manual ballast tanks there. The ship was badly out of trim, and the forward tanks could not be released from the control car. As he was approaching the tanks, he clearly heard the crack of fractured girder or strut. He had never heard anything like it before.

From his position at the edge of the woodland, at the foot of the gentle hill, poacher Alfred Rabouille was still staring upward, as if hypnotized. The gargantuan airship was coming almost directly at him. She was getting closer, closer to the earth. Her nose suddenly dipped again.

On the ship, electrician Disley saw Chief Coxswain Hunt flash by, going aft, along the passage way. He called out one simple sentence: "We're down, lads!"

Roubaille saw it happen, not more than a hundred yards away. The forward part of the ship crunched into the top of the hummock. There was a tremendous explosion. Roubaille was knocked off his feet. He picked himself up. There were two more explosions. Then the whole ship seemed to burst into flames. The midship section collapsed, telescoped like an accordion, as if the ship had broken her back.

He heard people in the ship. They were screaming for help. A blast of heat struck him, burned his eyes. The whole sky lit up. He was seized with uncontrollable terror. He could not look at nor listen to the scene he saw. All reason left him. He completely lost his head. He ran as hard as he could to get away from the nightmare.

Binks and Bell, in the after-engine gondola, felt their car strike the ground, then skid along it as the bottom caved in. An explosion followed, and they were surrounded by fire. Soon the eggshell cabin was engulfed by the flame around it. They grabbed greasy engine-wiping rags, held them over their heads and around their faces to insulate themselves from the heat. They were certain they were goners.

Suddenly a cascade of water came down on their gondola from the burning hull above. Ballast, it would have to be. It splashed through on them, making a pocket clear of flames. They soaked their clothes in it, smashed their way out of the car somehow, found themselves among the bushes on the ground.

All that Savory could remember was that he heard the sound of things breaking, and a rumbling and crashing noise that was terrifying. His engine was still running at cruising speed; he had received no signal to reduce it. There was a vivid flash bolting in through the open door of his engine car. It blinded him, dazed him, scorched his face. He remembers little after that—except that a local villager grabbed him, led him away from the burning wreckage.

Electrician Disley never got to pull that second switch. It is doubtful if it would have helped prevent the huge fire and explosion of the hydrogen. A hot cylinder of a ruptured engine pushed up against the hull would do it. Or a spark from a backfire. Or a piston shot into the side. Or any of the electrical wires. The explosion, given the conditions of the crash, was not only probable; it was certain.

The whole ship was impossible for Disley to describe. It was roaring like a furnace. He felt himself drop down to the base of the envelope. There was just the thin fabric to hold him. He kicked and punched at it. It broke, and he dropped to the ground. He looked up to see if he could help anyone else. It was hopeless. The entire length of the hull was now burning. A villager found him, wandering near the wreck.

Engineer Cook succeeded in stopping his engine, just before he felt the crash. He looked out of his gondola window, and saw the main body of the ship strike the ground. It seemed to slide along, and then come to an abrupt stop. The explosion took place almost immediately. He found himself caught in the canvas of the envelope. He clawed at it with teeth and nails, broke out of it at last, fell to the wet grass below.

In the forepeak of the bow section, rigger Church never reached the release valve on the ballast tank. Oddly enough, the crash wasn't too severe, even in his forward position. But he found himself tangled in blazing canvas and twisted duraluminum girders. He fought his way out with his blistered hands, dazed and scorched. He heard a voice yelling from a gondola. He staggered away from the wreckage, then collapsed into the arms of a rescuer.

In the smoking room, Leech felt the ship crunch into the hill. The shock was surprisingly mild. Suddenly, there was darkness. Then, there was the brilliant flash of a flame. The entire ceiling telescoped down on the top of the settee. It left only four feet of height in the room. He crawled toward a partition in the wall, ripped it away with his hands.

George Darling and his friend Debeaupuis were in their car almost at the moment the ship crashed. They threw on boots and coats over their pajamas, gunned the car over the short distance to the hill. They jumped out, raced across a beetroot field toward the burning ship. The flames were lighting up the sky for miles around, coming mostly from the bow and mid-section of the ship.

They found Bell and Binks near the tail section. Leech joined them in moments. Except for some surface burns, they seemed to be all right. They were even calm. But Leech was insistent. He wanted to go back in to save his burning pals. Along the sides of the ship, they could see some of them, clawing at the windows, screaming, fighting to get out, until the victims fell back into the cabin helplessly.

Darling and Leech somehow got into the tail section. They made their way forward. They saw some bodies piled up. The heat was that of a furnace. They were forced back.

Another Englishman, James Bunting, was driving back to the Dover ferry. It was a miserable night to drive. Between Allone and Beauvais, the rain let up a moment, and he got out to wipe off his windshield. He heard a noise that sounded as if a large Diesel lorry were coming down the road toward him. Instead, it was the R-101. It looked like a floating railway carriage to him.

Then he heard the explosion. The flames were orange and blue, like a gas fire, he noted. He ran across the field with some other motorists who had stopped behind him. A quarter of a mile from the ship, it became unbelievably hot. He could hear screaming from the distance. Then a crewman staggered toward him. His clothes were on fire. Bunting grabbed him, rolled him in the grass.

Across the field, the framework of the airship was illuminated by the flames. It looked like a grasshopper in silhouette. The gendarmes and the 51st French Infantry began arriving, in lorries, ambulances and horse-drawn carts. The cavalry arrived, too, carrying bedsheets hastily mustered from the households of Beauvais. They would be urgently needed to wrap the corpses in.

News of the crash reached London and Cardington piecemeal. Sometime around four in the morning, someone in the Air Ministry was awakened by a call from Leech. He was not badly injured. He said they had crashed on top of a hill at a few minutes after two in the morning, that the ship had burst into flames, that only six of the crew and none of the officers or passengers had been saved. He didn't know the names of the other survivors, but knew that Binks and Savory were injured.

News from the wire services was scattered. Just before five in the morning, Reuters reported:

AN EXPLOSION OCCURRED ABOARD THE R-101 AT TWO-THIRTY THIS MORNING WHILE SHE WAS A FEW MILES FROM BEAUVAIS.

By five-thirty, a Reuters dispatch from Paris read:

ALARM HAS BEEN CAUSED HERE BY AN UNCONFIRMED REPORT THAT THE AIRSHIP HAS BLOWN UP.

The final brief dispatch was at least clear:

R-101 HAS EXPLODED IN FLAMES ONLY SIX SAVED.

Whitehall and Downing Street officials were awakened in their homes in the small hours of the morning. They made their way into London from country homes. Prime Minister Ramsay MacDonald went first to the Air Ministry, where he was briefed, then on to his office at 10 Downing Street.

The news traveled fast, once the tragedy was confirmed. Milkmen, delivering in the dark hours of the morning, woke their customers to tell them. In Cardington, there was total shock and despair. The prime population of the community had been wiped out.

When first light came, the rain and the wind had not let up. In the grey light, the twisted metal still sizzled and sputtered in the smoking ruins. Police and soldiers formed a cordon around the wreckage and stretchers were laid out beside the orchard. On them were laid the sheet-covered bodies. None were recognizable. They were literally roasted, their hands clenched, some with their arms raised as if to protect themselves against the fire. There were watches and rings on some. Nearly all of the watches were stopped at 2:05.

To some, the wreckage from a distance looked like a half-built railway station. To others, the smouldering skeleton looked like a beached whale. Strips of fabric still fluttered in the wind. The flat surface of the elevators at the tail still held their canvas. The tail towered over 60 feet above the ground, and there was an RAF flag still intact, luffing in the breeze. A British officer eventually claimed it.

The control car was jammed up into the hull, a hopeless tangle trapping the bodies of the officers of the watch.

Leech, Disley, Binks, Bell, Savory and Cook were the only survivors, except for Rigger Church and a rigger named Radcliffe, each of whom died shortly afterward. The rescuers tried to keep what possessions there were, close to the unrecognizable bodies they seemed to come from. There were some photos that miraculously escaped, a compass, sets of keys, a leather belt with a white buckle, scissors, cigarettes and occasionally a ring on a blackened finger.

When the coffins arrived, each was numbered, and each had a box attached with the same number, so that the belongings could be checked by bereaved relatives, and they would not have to look inside the coffins to see the disfigured remains of their loved ones. The official count of the dead came to 48, after the two who were fatally injured died. The actual number could only be clearly determined by counting the number of skulls. All would be buried in unmarked coffins in a common grave. There were so few who could be identified, even with the help of the possessions found on some. Among the belongings raked out of the ruins, however, was one that could be unmistakably identified. It was a rimless monocle.

No command officer of the ship survived the holocaust. The control car was almost unrecognizable. What went on in those last minutes in that car seemed as if it would be buried forever in the minds of those handling the ship in those short but critical moments of crisis. Only Irwin, Scott, Atherstone, Colmore, or Johnston could provide even a clue to the total background and picture of what brought the tragedy about. And they were dead. As the legend went, dead men could tell no tales. Or could they?

THE LOSS OF THE *SHENANDOAH*

by C. E. Rosendahl

The general interest of the country in our Navy and its aircraft, and in our own first American airship product the *Shenandoah,* in particular, led to the planning of an extended flight of that ship into the middle west as both the Atlantic and Pacific seaboards had already seen the ship. At the Ford Airport at Dearborn, Michigan, there had been erected the first private mooring mast in the United States, and the Navy had been requested to test it out. Such an overland flight would also provide the training of personnel in cross-country flying which might be necessary in shifting our forces to the localities where most needed. In view of the well-known frequency of thunderstorms and kindred disturbances in the Mississippi Valley region during the summer, the flight was planned for early September when they would be on the decrease. Likewise, the large number of fairs and similar gatherings in vogue at that time of year, offered a splendid opportunity for display of the ship to the maximum number of our mid-west population. Accordingly the first leg of the *Shenandoah's* mid-western flight was from Lakehurst to Scott Field, near St. Louis, to land and service at the Army's lighter-than-air base there. Thence the course led by circuitous route to Minneapolis and to Detroit (Ford Airport), and then back to Lakehurst. In laying down the route on charts in preparation, Lieutenant Commander Hancock and I for some strange reason decided not to lay down the return path until we should start back. We came back by totally unexpected routes.

And so, on the afternoon of 2 September 1925, the *Shenandoah* cast off from the Lakehurst mast, fully groomed for a cruise of some five to six days. Probably because of excellent weather and the convenient hour, there was an unusually large gathering of friends and relatives at the foot of the mast as the "Daughter of the Stars" slipped her moorings and quietly slid off westward. Very quickly the forty-three of us on board fell into regular routine. At an economical airspeed of 38 knots, Philadelphia, Lancaster and the Susquehanna drew astern. Our route lay via York, Chambersburg, Bedford, Somerset, Connellsville; by shortly after midnight we had crossed the Alleghanies very smoothly at an altitude of 3800 feet, with everything in the ship functioning quite normally.

From Wheeling our course was set for Zanesville, Ohio, and our altitude decreased to 2500 feet. At midnight, Lieutenant-Commander Hancock with whom I alternated in watches of four hours on and four hours off, relieved me of the navigator's watch and eagerly I sought my bunk up in the keel. Having been called at 3:30 A.M. for my next watch, I was soon back in the control car. As was customary, all the lights in the car except the dim ones over the instrument boards were extinguished; these and the phosphorescent glow of radium dials were all that disturbed the darkness. The elevatorman was engaged in his duty of keeping the ship at the designated altitude; the rudderman was keeping the ship to her compass course; the radioman was busy with the flow of messages to and from the ship, a number of them being messages of greeting and welcome. At the windows, Captain Lansdowne and several of the officers were watching the weather. We were then over Byesville, Ohio, making very little ground speed, with all five engines running, and had just decreased our altitude to 2100 feet by altimeter. To the northward and eastward a severe electrical display and heavy clouds stood out vividly several miles distant. I was told we had changed course during the midwatch to avoid a thunderstorm. Other portions of the sky were now clear. Often on previous occasions the ship had been in strong winds that had materially reduced her speed over the ground, but now even with three of the engines speeded up and the other two at cruising speed, we made no gain and our drift increased. Captain Lansdowne was a thorough student of flying weather and although we had passed all evident danger, he remained on the bridge. The weather map on our departure had been considered a reasonably safe one as the disturbance centered near the Great Lakes should normally move on northeastward out of our path, and there were no indications of serious trouble along our course.

The dull moon ahead was setting with a weakening glow. During my drift observations out the window, there appeared on the starboard bow a thin dark streaky cloud just apparent in the dull moonlight. Lieutenant Anderson, the aerologist, seated at another window saw it at about the same time. Almost immediately the Captain came over to view this formation that was either coming towards us or building up rapidly. About this same instant, Chief Rigger Allen at the elevators reported the ship rising. He was told to check her. This he could not do. "She's rising at two meters per second and I can't check her, sir," he reported. The engines were speeded up. The inclination of the ship driving downward against the rising air current was considerable. With my flashlight I read it several times at 18 degrees. "Don't exceed that angle," ordered the Captain. "We don't want to go into a stall." Meanwhile at the beginning of the rise, the Captain had ordered the course changed somewhat to the left, i.e., to the southward. We then realized that we had run into a forming line squall—a line marked by the streaky roll cloud where winds of different temperatures and from different directions clash sharply and set up turmoil and vertical air currents both up and down. But even at this stage we felt no immediate concern for the safety of the ship as airships had plowed through storms before; though of course no one particularly relished being in any storm.

From 2100 feet to 4000 our involuntary rise continued and there seemed to check. But it was only momentarily, for again the upward rush took charge in spite of our driving down against it, and at a greater rate than ever before. "I've got the flippers hard down and she won't check," reported Allen. "Don't worry," replied the Captain, for he knew Allen at the wheel was one of our very best. Joffray at the rudders, another experienced and fully reliable man, called out "Hard over, sir, and she won't take it," for the Captain had ordered further changes of course to the south. The ship was now rolling and felt like a raft being tossed about in a mountainous sea.

As an airship rises into the rarer, less dense atmosphere, where the external pressure diminishes, the helium within the ship expands and swells out the cells. At a point called "pressure height," the cells become 100% full and any further ascent and consequent diminution of external pressure would result in accumulating a gas pressure within the cells, which if unrelieved might eventually crush the surrounding structure and burst the cells. To guard against this danger, the cells are fitted with automatic valves set to open at a safe pressure and discharge their helium into the air. In the second phase of the rise, we knew we were near our "pressure height." Taking into consideration the known rate of rise and the consequent discharge of helium that the automatic valves could accommodate, the Captain decided to assist the automatics by use of another set called "maneuvering" valves actuated by hand controls from the car. For five full minutes I timed the hand valving as Lieutenant Houghton swung on the control wheel and held these valves open. We were now glad to get rid of some of the helium that otherwise was so precious.

Up in the keel passageway, the off-watch section of the crew asleep in their bunks needed no general alarm to arouse them. Trained instinct plainly told them the unusual motion of the ship meant we were in difficulty. Quietly in that practically dark labyrinth they slipped into their clothes and began to help their shipmates on watch. The clanging of engine telegraphs told the engineers more speed was wanted. Elusive flashlight beams punctuated the darkness as the men rushed about their duties. "Anti-knock dope" had to be injected into the fuel for maximum engine speeds at that altitude. Reserve radiator water and spare lubricating oil must be quickly available. The deck force, patrolling throughout the keel, watched that the control wires did not jam; they rushed to each gas cell valve to see that it was operating. Jackknife in one hand, they felt the bulging cells with the other, ready to slash the fabric and help release the pressure should it exceed what their trained touch told them was safe. Keel officers wended their way from stem to stern directing and inspecting. For not by any means are all the necessary thought and action demanded by such an occasion—or at any time—concentrated in the control car alone. Like the unseen bunker trimmers below decks or the powder crews in the magazines of a man-of-war, the men up inside the keel of an airship have very vital duties to perform.

Chief Radioman Schnitzer, entirely unperturbed, came into the control space wearing his headphones and asked me for our latest position in order that he might reply to a message requesting it. "Our position hasn't changed appreciably since the last report," I told him, "and besides there's too much going on right now to figure it out for you." With a calm "aye, aye, sir," he stepped into the radio compartment and closed the door—for the last time.

Our release of helium had undoubtedly been effective. For brief moments more our rise continued and then came to a stop. We were now about to meet the inevitable down currents of the squall—the rush of air downward like a waterfall, carrying everything with it. Considerable buoyancy had been lost by valving helium and consequently the ship was sure to be quite "heavy." Such heaviness would accelerate our rate of fall. Dropping a compensating amount of ballast before we gathered much downward momentum would help us keep the ship under control; simultaneously several hands reached for the ballast toggles in the control car. Tons of water gushed from the openings along the bottom. And then came the expected fall of the ship. From about 6200 feet we shot down at a terrific rate of over 1400 feet per minute for perhaps over two minutes. My eardrums felt ready to burst!

Suddenly and abruptly our descent was checked by being caught in an upward current, this one more violent than that in the first rise. And of course, another downward rush had to be anticipated. Our water ballast gone, other weights must be ready to dump overboard to check the next fall. There were of course spare parts and other equipment that could be dispensed with. Up in the keel, in each nest of three aluminum gasoline tanks, the middle one holding some 700 lbs. was arranged as a "slip tank" to be cut adrift to fall through the cover if needed as emergency ballast. These tanks had no distant control and had to be released at their positions in the keel. Already the captain had sent messages up there to stand by to drop such tanks when the word was passed. Already eager men stood by patiently, pliers in hand. It was by the dropping of these very slip tanks that we might prevent the possible plunging of the ship into the ground. During our rapid ascent #2 engine had burned up from loss of oil; shortly thereafter #1 went out from loss of circulating water and rang up "stop." With only three engines remaining in operation, our ballast and helium greatly reduced, our trip was surely cut short, but who cared now about the trip? The thing was now to save the ship! Our salvation lay in the slip tanks!

Another message to the keel certainly wouldn't hurt; and so the Captain calmly sent me up there to check and see that the preparations were actually ready for the momentous order. It was more than momentous to me—it saved my life! To get up into the keel, one had to go up a ladder through a narrow conning tower-like trunk. Just as I stepped upon the rungs of the ladder, the ship took a very sudden upward inclination that seemed to me very much like the beginning of a loop in an airplane. The angle was greater than any I'd ever experienced before in an airship. The control car was not an integral part of the hull for having once contained an engine, it was suspended below the ship by wooden struts and wires. As I climbed up the ladder, I heard the snapping of struts. The flashlight in my hip pocket caught on the edge of the trunk, tearing off pocket with a "lucky" piece, keys and all other contents. The control car then seemed to lag behind the sharp upward thrust of the bow. However, little did one think the car would leave the ship as the suspension wires could be expected to hold it to the hull. The snapping of the struts, I thought, must have been due to the very severe and sharp rolling. Working my way up into the keel, I started aft intending to go amidships where the greatest number of fuel tanks were to be found and where the keel officer and other personnel would surely be standing by.

I had gone but a short distance along the keel when there was a terrific clashing, metallic din and a combination of noises easy to remember, more than difficult to forget. The bottom panel of the outer cover and several of the transverse structural members of the flat keel were cut loose along one side, as the control wires from aft carrying the free control car like a plummet, tore along the bottom before they pulled out completely. The keel walkway, thus left unsupported along one side, effectively impeded passage except by laboriously crawling around amidst wires and through the structure outboard of the keel. And whether it occurred simultaneously I cannot say; but my next recollection is that of standing there looking aft, faced with the unbelievable vision of the rest of the ship floating rapidly away from me and downward into the dull gray light of the breaking dawn. It was preceded and accompanied by that unmistakable "cry" of metal under severe stress—this time really distress. It was as though a thousand small metal pieces had been thrown in a heap and violently tramped on; as though a thousand panes of glass had been hurled from on high to pavement beneath.

At once I realized that the dropping away of the stern portion was partly due to the rapid rise of my own part of the ship. Glancing forward I could see the gaping open wound in the keel where the control car had been. Very shortly I heard a crash, more of a thud; it must have been the control car! It was too awful to contemplate—my shipmates who must have been in it; my own close call a matter of but seconds. I still saw the after portion of the ship settling to the ground and then suddenly arrested in its downward path as it struck. Could any one survive that crash? It seemed like an awful dream; a nightmare from which I'd probably be aroused shortly to go on watch.

But it was no dream. Lightened by the several thousand pounds of the lost control car, without the weight of any engines, and with all its gas cells intact, the bow section of about 200 feet in length, shot upward rapidly, almost out of sight of the ground, possibly to 10,000 feet. Twice we were in heavy rain. The spinning in a horizontal plane made it necessary to hold on tight. Dizziness—even seasickness—seemed inevitable if this kept up. My first impulse was that of fright at being alone; I could no doubt slash the cells to release helium and bring the bow down to earth, but with no one to help handle ballast, I'd probably hit hard and get gloriously and inextricably tangled up in wires and structure on crashing. Imagine my relief, when upon shouting, I got replies from both directions. Aft of me, nearer to the jagged open break were Chief Machinist Halliburton and Machinist's Mate Shevlowitz. Forward of me but out of sight, Lieutenant Roland Mayer answered up telling me that Colonel Hall, Lieutenant Anderson and Aviation Chief Rigger McCarthy also were there near him. What a great piece of luck! From that moment on we knew we could get down fairly safely anyhow. Our portion of the ship was hardly of the conventional balloon shape, but the simple principles of free-ballooning were nevertheless in effect. Mayer and I carried on a conversation and laid out a plan of campaign. His crew forward had access to a valve control wire to one of the cells; there was still some water ballast in one bag; the landing ropes and mooring wires looked all right. In my group, we still had some fuel tanks and other weights to use as ballast and could release gas by climbing up to slash cells.

Colonel Hall and Lieutenant Anderson had left the control car just after my departure. So close was Anderson's escape that, as the control car tore away, he suddenly found himself, saturated with gasoline from a nearby tank, astride the 12-in. catwalk in the dangling keel holding on to wires and structure, directly over the area vacated by the car, with now only the open sky beneath him. As soon as possible, Mayer lowered him a line and gingerly passing it under one arm at the same time, "Andy" got himself safely into the bowline. Then those above hauled him up to safety.

Completing our organization, we decided to descend and try for a landing. All this time our derelict hulk was describing a circle some ten to twelve miles in radius about the fallen remainder of the ship. By concerted valving of helium and dumping of gasoline or other ballast, we kept our descent under control. On the first try for a landing, the wind was still carrying us over the ground at about 25 miles per hour—too high for landing a balloon like ours in safety. There was no reason to get hurt now in a rough landing even though probably no one before ever longed so wholeheartedly to set foot on firm ground as we did. So we decided to stay in the air and resist the lure of the ground. But before we could begin to rise again, a giant tree in a clump along a hillside stuck its towering head up into our privacy, ripping a gash in the cover for almost the full length. As soon as we gained altitude after this impact, we called the roll. McCarthy was missing, knocked out of his perch by the inquisitive tree. Badly injured he was found later. Surgical skill and strong willpower in due time restored him to further airship duty.

Continuing our queer journey until we saw that the surface wind had moderated extensively, we prepared for the landing, this time safe and successful. Trail ropes and mooring wires were dropped out as for a usual landing. By valving carefully we regulated our descent. A few men on the ground following this queer apparition breathlessly, had no time to grab our lines as strange voices from the sky called out for them to do. Perhaps they thought we were performers from the county fair nearby. But our course was a favorable one, for right ahead we were sure to fetch up on a hillside after passing between a barn and a house. Valving effectively now, we continued on down. Those of us who were able crawled high up in the structure and slashed gas cells to make sure we'd stay on the ground. Gradually we settled, open end leading, and made contact with good old terra firma so gently that not even an egg would have been cracked. Those in the very nose, which touched first due to drag of the ropes, stepped out and made fast to fences, post and trees with the ship's lines and wires. Then they threw us a ship's heaving line and I crawled up and made it fast to a secure part of the structure, the jagged open end of which, as it lay on the hillside, was still some twenty feet up in the air. Slowly, Halliburton, Shevlowitz and I, unscratched and unscathed, let ourselves down the line hand over hand to the welcome lap of mother earth. Only a little over an hour previous, our proud *Shenandoah* had been an intact live creature; now she lay there crushed. To prevent the bow section from tearing away in the rising wind and sun, I called for pistols and sorrowfully we shot holes through the tops of the cells to release their helium back to nature whence it came.

And now let us trace the fortunes of the other portion of the storm-torn *Shenandoah.* In the terrific conflict of currents in the turmoil of the squall, at about one-third of her length (some 200 feet) from the bow, the ship had collapsed on top and opened up on the bottom, soon tearing apart into two sections. It was as though the ship had been held up at each end and then struck on top with a giant's hammer and twisted by the snout at the same time. The control car, deprived of struts and suspensions, at first remained connected by control cables leading along the bottom to the rudders and elevators. As the bottom of the ship opened up, the control cables had either to stretch to the new distance or to pull out. Actually, a sheave bracket over the car where the cables turned to pass down into the car, pulled out starting the disintegration of the structure above. Whipping aft on the end of the control cables like a pendulum bob, the now free control car swung, and, as the cables tore out of the ship, plunged precipitately to the ground. With it, Lieutenant Commander Lansdowne, Lieutenant Commander Hancock, Lieutenant Lawrence, Lieutenant Houghton, Chief Rigger Allen, Rigger Joffray, Chief Radioman Schnitzer and Machinist's Mate Moore, met their fate.

As the two main portions of the ship separated, no doubt the jagged edges at the break tore the forward gas cell of the stern section, deflating it rapidly during the fall. Led by Lieutenant Bauch, ever calm and alert, the men in that after portion threw overboard tools, spare parts, lubricating oil, fuel tanks, personal effects and whatever they could lay their hands on. By so doing they effectively checked their rate of descent so successfully that even though a few of them were precipitated through the cover as they landed, their lives were spared. To their own efforts, calm thinking and quick correct action they owe their survival. But as they neared the surface, the deflating section near the jagged break collapsed, hurling to the ground the two engine cars attached to it. Three loyal men, sticking to their posts, went down in those cars: Aviation Chief Machinist's Mate Broome and Aviation Machinist's Mates 1st Class Mazzuco and Spratley. The Chief Engineer, Lieutenant Edgar W. Sheppard, and his leading petty officers, Aviation Chief Machinist's Mates J. W. Cullinan and B. B. O'Sullivan, for the whole period of uncertainty previous to the break had been dashing about from engine to engine, doing everything humanly possible to keep the power plants going during our moments of distress. They were unfortunate enough to be at just that spot when the bottom opened up. Cullinan and O'Sullivan must have been hurled through the opening. Sheppard and Shevlowitz (the latter saved with the bow section) were perilously near the sharp break. As Sheppard struggled to hold on, Shevlowitz tried to help him. "Never mind me—look out for yourself" were Sheppard's last words, for in a flash before Shevlowitz could reach him, the wires and structure to which Sheppard clung pulled out free.

The entire absence of fire in the presence of so much volatile gasoline was a remarkable feature of this disaster. The mechanics in the engine cars were 100% on the job and snapped off their ignition switches before crashing. The 29 survivors out of 43 in the ship's company must be attributed to helium. Had the inflation medium been hydrogen (as in the British R-101) it is most probable that there would have been no survivors.

Freed of the collapsed section, the remainder of the stern picked up and dragged on a bit. Then spinning 180°, it left the rear car sitting on the ground alone, and came to rest. Lieutenant Bauch, thrown through the cover as he landed, at once stationed lookouts to follow the forward section in which eight of us were still ballooning. Ship's Cook Hahn, a survivor of the stern section, reaching the nearest telephone sent a message to Lakehurst giving the names of the survivors and dead of whom he was cognizant, and stating that one portion of the ship was still afloat. His message was an efficient statement of fact and ventured no conjectures. But how many hopes of anxious relatives and friends must have been inspired by his report of that queer spectacle still drifting in the heavens! Bauch then mustered his survivors and dispatched two petty officers to the bow section as he saw us come to earth some twelve miles away. At once Bauch apportioned the tasks to the other survivors there with him, of slashing the remaining cells in their wreckage, picking up valuable parts, and with leaden hearts, began the most sorrowful task of all of caring for our fallen shipmates.

The lists compiled by Bauch and brought by Chief Rigger Allely reached me within an hour of my landing and were a great help in reaching definite conclusions as to survivors and missing. The Captain and the Executive Officer were both on the casualty list, leaving me the senior survivor. Filling the lists with those of my own knowledge, I rushed to a telephone to inform the Navy Department. By coincidence, at that very moment, Bauch was trying to telephone a message from another point and the operator connected me with him. With our combined information, I telephoned a message to the telegraph office. Very soon I set up headquarters at the station at Caldwell, Ohio, and from then on the wires were kept hot. Through the radio and the press the whole country soon had the sad news.

During the period of uncertainty preceding the breaking up of the ship, there came to my attention only the highest type of discipline, bravery, attention to duty, calculated and efficient action, but above all, even in despair, only cool, calm, giving and acknowledging of orders. At no time while I was in the control car during the period preceding the break-up was there a single word spoken out of the conversational tone. This was particularly true in the case of Captain Lansdowne. Although the gravity of the situation was most apparent, his order to me to go up into the keel to check the readiness of the fuel tanks was given in an absolutely calm, self-possessed manner. Lieutenant Houghton, the officer on the deck, was particularly keen to observe every incident and assisted the Captain with advice and efficient response to every order given him. Lieutenant Commander Hancock, although he had been relieved of the watch, had voluntarily remained continuously in the control car since his relief, and assisted the Captain throughout our period of difficulties. Lieutenant Lawrence, also off watch, sensed the dangerous position of the ship and came down into the control car a few minutes before the break to render what assistance he could. Allen, Joffray, Schnitzer and Moore, the enlisted men in the control car, also remained calmly at their stations and perished traditionally at their posts of duty. Lieutenant Sheppard's unselfish bravery in his unparalleled predicament was outstandingly heroic.

After reaching Caldwell, numerous important decisions faced me. I could picture the anxious relatives back in Jersey. Some of the families there would surely never believe the dispatches until confirmed by personal appearances of their loved ones. Others would have to be told the sad details and assisted in their plans for the future. The first important duty after the dispatch of all available information and the request for official aid, seemed to be to get the survivors home. That afternoon, after a chance to clean up, 24 survivors were entrained for Lakehurst. Five of us remained there with the fourteen of our shipmates who were no longer mindful of the toil and strife—and the future.

Although the *Shenandoah's* personnel contained a high proportion of most reliable, efficient and trustworthy men, I was particularly fortunate in having such splendid examples as Lieutenant Bauch, Lieutenant Mayer, Aviation Chief Machinist's Mate William A. Russell, and Aviation Chief Rigger Arthur E. Carlson remain with me at Caldwell. Their tasks were far from pleasant, but all of them are particularly gifted by nature to do things with their hands as well as their heads. The highest compliment I can pay them is to state that I can conceive of no emergency whatsoever that might ever confront me, no moment of despair however dark in which I should not be more than satisfied to have their services and presence available to me.

The Navy Department, in quick response to my dispatches, soon had every sort of help on the way to us. Lieutenant Commander Wiley flew in from Detroit where he had been awaiting the *Shenandoah's* arrival. Army officers stationed nearby were soon on hand to help. Captain Steele, Commander Klein, Lieutenant Stewart, arrived the next day from Lakehurst. Navy recruiting station personnel in the vicinity including Lieutenant Morris and three medical officers, Lieutenants Minnick, Moore and Shaddy, soon reached us and took over many of our sad burdens. All of them received letters of commendation for their valuable help.

Although I had made efforts to get accurate photographs of the wreckage immediately upon its landing, none of them materialized, or else some one has concealed those pictures taken then. Practically every photograph of the wreck that you have seen was taken hours after the wind had beaten the wreckage into tangled masses and after souvenir hunters had done immeasurably more. But there are 29 of us who have earlier mental photographs that are forever indelible.

THE END OF THE *HINDENBURG*

by A. A. Hoehling

The Reederei, preparing a short news bulletin to this effect, notified the Deutsche Nachtrichtenbüro, the official government news agency. And, curiously enough, one of the first to pick up the happy DNB tidings was the *Graf Zeppelin,* sailing homeward and now west of the Canary Islands. Captain Hans von Schiller smiled when his radio operator handed him the brief dispatch, but he was not surprised. After all, as any airshipman well knew, the *Hindenburg* was the greatest airship ever built. Why shouldn't it have landed?

The *Hindenburg* swept in at a height of 590 feet over the south fence of the airfield, well under the overcast, traveling at a brisk 73 knots. At last, Herb Morrison, the announcer from WLS, was able to start his recording.

"Here it comes, ladies and gentlemen," he spoke in clear, dry Midwestern accent, "and what a sight it is, a thrilling one, a marvelous sight. It is coming down out of the sky pointed toward us, and towards the mooring mast. The mighty diesel motors roar, the propellers biting into the air and throwing it back into gale-like whirlpools. Now and then the propellers are caught in the rays of sun, their highly polished surfaces reflect. . . . No one wonders that this great floating palace can travel through the air at such a speed with these powerful motors behind it. The sun is striking the windows of the observation deck on the eastward side and sparkling like glittering jewels on the background of black velvet. . . ."

"This great floating palace" made itself heard as well as seen and, certainly, felt.

"When the airship next appeared," C. B. Allen tapped out his story for the nearing deadline of the New York *Herald Tribune,* "it was from the west where the sky was clearing, and it came close to the field at a low altitude, 500 or 1000 feet. It was apparent that she was going to try for a landing but before doing so Captain Pruss made one trip over the field and those standing on the ground heard his sonic altimeter as he established the ship's definite height from the ground. Cdr. Charles E. Rosendahl, commandant of the Naval Air Station, was standing at the mooring mast which the *Hindenburg* was to use and called attention to the 'beep-beep' noise made by the sonic altimeter."

She continued on a north-northeast course past the hangar and crossed the far boundary of the airfield before commencing a long, slow sweep westward. It was almost weigh-off time—that is, the airship itself had to be balanced, like some monster set of scales, so it would approach the mast on an even keel. At least, if it were to approach nose-down, that condition should be effected through the proper angle of the ship's elevator controls, not through an imbalance or uncontrollable whim of an untrimmed Zeppelin.

As the *Hindenburg* passed the western boundary of the field and turned southward to parallel the fence, gas was valved from the rear cells. She was indicating lightness in this segment, most likely due to runoff of the rain water and drying of the fabric. The engines were put on "Idle Ahead." Gradually, she mushed down to 490 feet over the scrubby, drab-green pine trees. She was so low that the passengers could see the soldiers from Fort Dix pacing along the fences, Springfield rifles over their shoulders.

When she hove once more into clear view of those at the landing circle, she became an especially joyous sight to the hungry sailors, who received no bonus for this duty, not even the dollar an hour, parsimonious as it was, that the Reederei paid the Lakehurst civilians.

"The final few minutes it would take to complete the job of securing the ship at its mooring had become an ambrosia," observed the naval linesman Vincent Sheridan, a lighter-than-air veteran, "lifting our spirits after a dismal soggy day during which we had waited while one landing after another had been canceled because of weather, for we knew that shortly we could change from our wet clothing, enjoy our supper and pursue whatever sailors pursue after hitting the beach. . . ."

The photographers and reporters were also glad the long wait was over. Cameras were trained on the nose of the airship as she hovered over the southwest corner of the station. She would have to come nearer, however, for clear pictures. From this journalistic group, of course, two members remained absent: the newsreel man enjoying the movie at Lakewood, the reporter in the New York bar. The latter had just been tipped off by a contact in Lakehurst that the dirigible was over the field. This meant, after another drink, it would be time to dial the city desk and start paraphrasing von Meister's press release for his "eyewitness" arrival story.

Between 7:12 and 7:20 P.M. the *Hindenburg* moved slowly eastward, crossing the air station boundary once more, weighing off. It was determined that she was now light in the nose and gas was valved from two forward cells for fifteen seconds in an effort to correct this imbalance. The engines were placed on "Idle Astern."

As she was coaxed down to 360 feet, she continued to drift forward, even though her huge propellers were still backing up. Over the rifle range, the two forward cells were valved again. Finally, it seemed that the big airship was in trim and ready to land. She approached the living quarters and the officers' club of the air station, commencing to turn back eastward and then south to attain the mooring circle. At this juncture, however, Sauter reported through his telephone:

"Ein Tausend kilo-schwer!"

In other words, from the way she was riding in the stern the experienced airship engineer estimated the *Hindenburg* was about a ton tail-heavy—not excessive for a Zeppelin which grossed nearly 250 tons. The remedy was simple. In three different releases, 1000 kilograms of water ballast were dumped from the stern tanks.

If this man-caused shower splashed any spectators, they probably wouldn't have noticed; they were so wet already this early evening.

The command, which considered the *Hindenburg* still slightly tail-heavy, ordered six additional men to landing positions in the nose of the dirigible. This brought to twelve the crewmen now stationed far forward. There were hand grips and wooden platforms available for this number, which therefore could not be considered unusually great.

This final trimming operation had the desired effect. As Bauer observed, she was now "level as a board." In apparent balance, the dirigible could be maneuvered as desired. Pruss ordered the elevators in down position. At the same time, noting the effects of a sudden wind shift to the southwest with an estimated strength of 8 knots, he ordered rudder hard to port to compensate, thus keeping her nose into the wind. He watched the ground crew changing position accordingly in order to receive the big Zeppelin.

Experienced airship traveler Adelt, aware of the turn, remarked to his wife Gertrude, "Lehmann must be in a hurry to get down." However, weary of riding out the storm as both Pruss and Lehmann undoubtedly were, the losing of altitude and the final tight turn were not "based on desperation," as Vincent Sheridan and other line handlers were inclined to believe. The ship was almost twelve hours behind schedule. It was time to land.

All the spectators noticed the turn as she descended. Stephen Schofield, the undergarment salesman, had perhaps the most unusual impression of the condition of the airship: "The forward half of the dirigible was a glistening silver color. The stern half was a very dull gray color. . . . There must have been superheat in that section."

At 7:21, at a height of 200 feet, the forward starboard handling line was dropped out of the nose of the ship, immediately followed by the port line. Both Pruss in the *Führergondel* and Lieutenant Tyler on the ground observed "a cloud of dust" fly from each rope coil as it smacked onto the sandy ground, indicating the ropes were dry. As a matter of fact, Bill Springfield, the Acme photographer, attested to the same phenomenon: dust rising from the saturated sandy soil of Lakehurst.

In the next moment, the line handlers had hold of the ropes and were connecting them to the larger guy lines which had been held in readiness. These in turn would be fastened to capstans for stronger and more positive control.

The sight was not only a thrilling one to Rosendahl, drenched and tired, but also a harbinger of great relief after a day of uncertainty, delay and consummate worry.

"There in imposing, majestic silence," he recalled, "the vast silvery hulk of the *Hindenburg* hung motionless like a framed, populated cloud. Everything within and without the ship was proceeding in an entirely normal manner. In only a few minutes more the ship would reach the ground and her mooring mast safely and smoothly."

While cameramen recorded the endless fascination of a giant airship coming out of the skies to its mooring, and many of the waiting throng inched closer in the hopes of glimpsing those whom they were greeting, others were ready to leave for Lakehurst to return with the *Hindenburg* this same evening.

At Newark Airport, John J. Bergen, of Glen Ridge, New Jersey, telephoned the air station to ascertain if it was time to fly there. He planned to attend the coronation and, ultimately, continue to Switzerland to join his vacationing wife and two children. Bergen, a Navy pilot in the World War, received his long-distance phone connection to Lakehurst with surprising speed and, as it happened, found himself talking with an old friend, Lieutenant M. F. Flaherty, who had the operations watch.

"The ship's overhead," came the familiar voice of Flaherty, who apparently was looking out of a window. "She's just coming down. There go the ropes out to the ground crew. Sure, come on down. Commander Rosendahl will be glad to have you!"

Bergen looked at his watch as he left the phone booth. It was nearly 7:25 P.M. He picked up his hand luggage and hurried toward the gate and the small aircraft he had chartered for the short hop.

In the Hotel Pennsylvania, Rolf Anders, son of the Dresden tea merchant, waited for the telephone call which would inform him that his father Ernst had landed in Lakehurst and would soon be on his way to New York. In Chicago, the family of J. Burtis Dolan, the perfume executive, thrilled and surprised at the receipt of his radiogram, listened for the presumably imminent ringing of the hall telephone.

While along the wet macadam road curving into Lakehurst drove Hilgard Pannes from Plandome, Long Island, eager to welcome his mother and father, Mr. and Mrs. John Pannes. Hilgard, who had sailed around the world two years previously, had left his home on Woodland Drive with some trepidation; his grandmother, Mrs. Hilda Pannes, eighty-seven and sick, was momentarily alone.

In the town of Lakehurst, Reichelderfer and his family were among the few remaining at home. The population was distributed between the air station and the open streets where they could observe the fat, elongated hull of the *Hindenburg* maneuvering just over the pine tops. He was ready to lock his suitcase, while his young son Bruce, unable to restrain his curiosity further, wandered onto the front porch and listened to the throaty rasp of four Mercedes-Benz diesels.

On the field, the landing party almost had their unwieldy, massive charge lassoed, but not quite. The wind, capricious as ever, about 7:24 P.M. smacked her port side, causing a marked drift to the right. This in turn made the linesmen hold tight onto the port ropes until taut. They had to dig their heels deeper and deeper into the wet sand to maintain their balance against the vast buoyancy of the airship.

Newsreelmen and newspaper photographers trained their cameras on the ground crew. It was not an uncommon occurrence for line handlers to be jerked upward by the Navy's airships, perilous acrobatics which in the past had made spectacular action pictures. There was, this day of uncertain winds, the possibility that the *Hindenburg* might unexpectedly lunge skyward.

In the passenger compartment, Otto Clemens, pointing his camera downward, was also photographing the line handlers.

Atop the mast, Lieutenant R. W. Antrim noticed something peculiar: what he thought to be a portion of the fabric behind the after port engine "very loose and fluttering." However, even at his 75-foot elevation, Antrim, who was booked this night on the return flight of the *Hindenburg,* was still more than 100 feet below the underside of the airship and about five times that distance from the nose, out of which the steel mooring cable had not yet begun to unwind.

As a matter of fact, correspondent Alice Hager saw much the same manifestation. She thought of it as a "rippling."

Bosun Fred Tobin glanced at something which seemed to him even more peculiar: "The lower rudder was hard left, the upper rudder seemed to be amidships or possibly three to four degrees right." He mentioned this apparent discrepancy to two of the men standing beside him.

While Francis Hyland, the line handler in No. 1 position directly under the airship's tail, continued to gawk upward for the signature he had scrawled on the lower fin the past autumn, the ship like a huge cloud came down lower and lower. He was momentarily startled by what he took to be a backfire: flame spurting out of the after port side engine as it was reversed to aid the ground crew holding the weight and tidelike surge of the airship.

And W. W. Groves, the Yale & Towne engineer, was noticing something he thought interesting: a small spark "like static electricity" dancing somewhere overhead and underneath the hovering airship, not far from the tail. He opened his mouth to comment to a companion standing beside him.

But Groves never formed his words. The time, 7:25 P.M., had arrived.

Two of the four crewmen in the lower fin of the airship just happened to be staring upwards at Gas Cell No. 4, which was the only cell the full rear panel of which they could see plainly. With no warning, lightning-fast, the fire appeared towards the middle of this hydrogen-filled cell, less than fifty feet ahead of and above the witnesses.

"Blitzlicht!" the thought flashed through Sauter's mind. It was like a flashbulb suddenly going off, it appeared to the chief engineer, or the quick snapping on of a flashlight. The initial diameter of the brilliant

flare was remarkably well defined: no more than three feet, located towards the cell's center, just where the main or axial catwalk tunneled through the cell.

To Lau, the flash—accompanied only by a low "pop" like the noise attending the lighting of a gas burner on a stove—was initially of the same dimensions as observed by the chief engineer, red, blue and yellow in color, but more exactly centered around the catwalk and the two maneuvering valves located there.

Kollmer heard the "pop" as "the firing of a gun, a small gun or rifle," though he was looking at the ground at that split second and did not see the first flare. Freund, standing on a small ladder leading out of the fin and onto the catwalks, had straightened out the tangled rope and was in the act of lowering it when he heard "a muffled detonation, a whoom!" At once he was "surrounded by fire . . . a living hell." Thus, the nearest man to the explosion, he had been too close for the perspective which had been afforded Sauter and Lau.

As the chief engineer shouted, "Stay down!" Lau, transfixed, watched "aluminum parts and fabric parts thrown up!" In the next fraction of a second the entire gas cell "disappeared by the heat."

Because of the great length of the *Hindenburg,* the spectators on the ground, shocked and horrified beyond capacity for understanding or in many cases even adequate expression, actually saw the initial pluming of the hydrogen fire before those in the passenger compartment or even the *Führergondel* were aware that anything had happened. There were minor variations in the way the incipient holocaust registered on the individual witnesses.

Rosendahl saw "a small burst of flame" just forward of the upper vertical fin, and he realized "at once" that "that spelled the doom of the ship."

Mrs. Rosendahl, standing in the imperfect shelter of the mast, started screaming, thinking the dirigible was going to plummet onto her husband, who was much closer to it than she was.

Vincent Sheridan, the line handler, noted, "The first and only inkling we needed that the ship was gone was a sudden lighting of an otherwise gloomy afternoon . . . a sudden glow." Near him, someone shouted, "Run for your lives!"

Von Meister observed "the reflection of very strong light on the entering edge of the upper fin; a fraction of a second later or practically simultaneously there was a burst of flame out of the port side of the ship. . . ."

Madeline Lupton, the perennial sight-seer, detected "a faint pink glow in the lower center of the ship . . . like some thick silvery fish with a rosy glow in the abdomen. . . . It began small and pale and spread redder and larger. . . ."

Mrs. W. R. van Meter, of Upper Darby, Pennsylvania, had a similar impression. "The stern lighted up sort of like a Japanese lantern," then "flames inside, swirling around and lighted up the covering of the bag so that I could see the framework of the ship through the covering." She was joined in the lantern simile by George Ream, aeronautical inspector with the Bureau of Air Commerce, aware too of a small fire atop the airship "like a kerosene lamp wick which had been trimmed unevenly making the flame jagged."

Albert E. Reitzel, assistant solicitor with the Department of Commerce, at Lakehurst on immigration matters, saw a "puff-like flame, about 50 feet forward of the vertical fin, which impressed me as being the size of a house door."

Gage Mace, assistant operations manager for American Airlines, watched "a shower of sparks which shot up apparently from the top of the bag and to rear, just forward of the vertical fin followed instantly by a column of yellowish flame." At least two spectators from Lakehurst believed the ship's stern portion to be, at first, glowing "a golden pink like sunrise," then the flame funneled upward like "fire up a chimney."

Henry Roberts, the radio editor of *Aero Digest,* observed "a yellow flash," followed by a "bright explosion," which sounded "like a firecracker." And Mrs. Leif Neandross, just arrived from Ridgefield, to meet Otto Clemens, also watched in horror the airship "light up all inside." The parents of Peter Belin turned back to their car in despair, while Mrs. George Lutfy was praying that her "dear father," Philip Mangone, would "die at once and not suffer."

Now, as the fire gained instant headway and plumed upward in one mushrooming, boiling cloud, brilliant as "a million magnesium flares," Herb Morrison, from his calm description of what had commenced as a routine landing, shouted hysterically into the microphone of his recorder:

". . . It's burst into flames . . . get this Charlie, get this Charlie. . . . Get out of the way, please, oh my, this is terrible, oh my, get out of the way, please! It is burning, bursting into flames and is falling on the mooring mast and all the folks we . . . this is one of the worst catastrophes in the world! . . . Oh, it's four or five hundred feet into the sky, it's a terrific sight. . . . Oh, the humanity and all the passengers!"

Murray Becker, switching film in his Speed Graphic as fast as he could focus and click the shutter for one picture, summed up his rapid impression: "A moment of spectacular madness." And Bill Springfield of Acme, taking photographs with equal rapidity, made the mental description: "A small light inside the ship near the tail assembly, a ball of fire exploding in a cloud of orange colored flames."

The newsreelmen, perched atop their cars, impeded by the heavy equipment, held their ground, even those in line of the airship's estimated fall to earth, and let the suddenly priceless 35-mm celluloid whir through the camera sprockets. Never had lens and sensitive film captured such a scene.

Across the highway from the air station, in Lakehurst, Lieutenant Reichelderfer put his suitcase down, hearing a resounding explosion. His boy Bruce shouted from the porch: "There's a big fire and smoke coming up from the field!"

Reichelderfer knew at once that he would not be flying to Germany tonight. At Point Pleasant, fifteen miles distant, a "muffled, booming whoosh!" was distinctly heard.

Mechanics such as Jonny Doerflein, Adolf Fischer, Raphael Schaedler and German Zettel or the engineer Eugen Schauble, in the relative isolation of their diesel gondolas, were aware first of no more than "a shaking." Schauble thought, "A rope is broken."

George Hirschfeld, on the promenade deck, was also aware of a shaking, as was Luftwaffe Lieutenant Hinkelbein. But Leonhard Adelt's first awareness was more typical of other passengers. Momentarily, "a remarkable stillness" had taken possession of their surroundings, next, the spectators on the ground "visibly stiffened." The transition was so rapid that Otto Clemens did not even know that he had just photographed the reflection of the fire on the wet earth and some linesmen actually commencing to run.

In the next fraction of a second, Adelt heard "a light dull detonation, from above, no louder than the sound of a beer bottle being opened," followed by "a delicate rose glow as though the sun were about to rise."

Standing beside Hinkelbein in the dining saloon, Margaret Mather read the message of disaster in the face of the young pilot, "a look of incredulous consternation."

In the writing lounge, Colonel Nelson Morris first heard a report, "not loud, just as a regular service rifle would sound."

"There was a blinding light," according to Spah, the acrobat, "then an explosion. The steward tried to calm the passengers, assure us all that everything was all right. Before the steward could walk three steps the stern of the ship sank."

Passengers began to tumble one atop the other, "a mass of shrieking, crying people!"

Margaret Mather, her poet's eyes not deserting her even in this instant of fiery apocalypse, noted the arrival of fire, "long tongues of flame, bright red and very beautiful," while "my companions were leaping up and down amid the flames. The lurching of the ship threw them repeatedly against the furniture and the railing. . . ."

As Margaret wrapped her heavy wool coat closer to shield herself, especially her eyes, a man—the same one who had exclaimed *"Mein Gott!"* at the departure from Frankfurt—detached himself from the rest of the maddened, leaping human beings and hurled himself against a railing "with a loud, terrible cry:

" 'Es ist das Ende!' "

Farther forward, in the radio cabin, Herbert Dowe heard "some tearing in the ship," and then through his little window observed "a flame as if somebody made a photographic exposure with a flashlight."

Aside from the twelve in the nose of the Zeppelin, the occupants of the

Führergondel were among the last on board to be aware of the mortal wound so unexpectedly and mysteriously sustained by the ship being controlled from their forward position. Captain Wittemann, at first but vaguely disturbed, felt the initial shock transmitted the airship's sixth-of-a-mile length, spending itself like an ocean wave rolling onto a beach. He turned to a quizzical Captain Pruss and asked:

"Is a rope broken?"

"No," Pruss replied, matter-of-factly. Sammt, in turn, looked questioningly at Pruss, then at Lehmann, himself conscious of "a heavy push."

In the next second Wittemann heard the cry "Fire!" and he did not have to ask again what was the trouble. At the rudder, Schoenherr commenced to groan, "Oh, oh, oh!" in a weird lament of despair.

Now Wittemann saw the red glare. Zabel believed he heard the fire bell ringing above Schoenherr's continuing moan, "Oh, oh, oh . . . !"

Ziegler, with odd detachment, remarked to himself what a strange yellow color the air beneath the ship had turned. Then this former merchant marine officer set about looking for the log book. Wittemann ran back and forth, from one side to the other of the control car, looking out at the reddening world just beyond the windows.

Bauer was now aware the tail had burned away and the *Hindenburg* was therefore a flaming derelict, still aloft but out of control, and he knew she would crash in a matter of seconds. He suspected water ballast must have fallen loose from the effect of the fire itself. However, when he tried to dump more water manually, there was no response from the control cables.

In the tail, the four men trapped there agreed, it was "extremely bright," but none of them was conscious of heat. The blistering inferno of hydrogen, after devouring Cell 4 in one molten gulp, blasted at Cells 3 and 5 and then tore on like an incandescent tornado through the 803 feet of the *Hindenburg,* roaring toward the bow.

The men knew the ship was plummeting. As it did so, they were showered by pieces of burning fabric and dripping aluminum. For no understandable reason, all four were missed by most of the searing downpour as they hung to their disintegrating roost. They shielded their faces —and waited.

One gondola, housing the port stern engine, broke loose and hurtled to the ground with the impact of a huge, dud aerial bomb. The other gondolas clung to the flaming, rapidly sinking airship.

In the passenger compartment, Steward Nunnenmacher "fell to the floor between the legs of a lady. I lifted myself on the window railing and I saw several people on the window, but I couldn't reach that window. Who opened the window I do not know, and somebody of the passengers sat on the window frame. Then I saw Mr. Kubis, the chief steward, and I called to him, 'Mr. Kubis, jump out!'

"Mr. Kubis said, 'No, I cannot, it is too high yet . . . !' "

Margaret Mather was thinking it was "like a scene from a medieval picture of hell."

Clemens thought it was time to get out. Standing at a window beside John Pannes, he shouted to the travel official, "Kick hard with me, Mr. Pannes, and we can jump through this opening!"

"You go," replied Pannes, "I must find Mrs. Pannes first." And he vanished toward a sea of flames cascading into the compartment.

Peter Belin and Joseph Spah, however, had jumped, giving little thought to the height. Spah hit so hard he bounced. George Willens, the Detroit executive who was taking movie films, was close by the spot where the acrobat landed.

"How on earth did you do it?" he asked in awe.

"I don't know," Spah replied, out of breath. "Whew, am I lucky!" Then Willens watched him dash off, presumably in search of his family.

Peter Belin, exclaiming, "I lost my watch!" started, perhaps reflexively, back toward the blazing airship. He was at once restrained by sailors and other line handlers. By Rosendahl's appraisal, there was "a progressive burning" of the dirigible. He noted: "As the stern burned, the ship, having lost buoyancy in that portion, assumed a stern-down attitude and as the fire progressed forward, the ship of course settled to the ground at what we would consider a moderate rate of descent. . . ."

This "progressive" destruction was accompanied by several distinct, heavy explosions as two or three cells apparently ignited simultaneously. The stricken Zeppelin cracked in the middle as she neared the ground, her forward portion reached skyward at an acute angle and flames poured from her nose like fire out of a volcano—a monstrous torch in the fading twilight.

The sounds themselves were the sounds of terror. Henry Roberts, the editor, heard the bow emitting "a deep, low hiss as it burned, against a background of screams."

In this most forward section, Joseph Leibrecht, an electrician, who had first been aware of a "swishing" sound, hung onto his overhead hand grips with strength born of paralyzing fear. As he rode the falling, mortally stricken airship down, he observed a terrible sight: the other eleven men in the nose of the ship falling in rapid succession back into the raging crucible which had been the interior of the *Hindenburg.*

"There was fire everywhere," wrote Alice Rogers Hager, the reporter, "rushing, sweeping its way through the pitiful, crumpling wreckage. It was not possible that anything should be alive in that inferno. Yet, men leaped out. . . ."

Even for an experienced news reporter such as Herb Morrison, the wild, blistering spectacle was too much, and he half-sobbed, "I can't talk, ladies and gentlemen. . . . I have got to stop for a minute, for it's the worst thing I have ever witnessed!"

"We all seemed to get the message at the same instant," thought Vincent Sheridan, "for we all started to evacuate en masse. Burdened as we were by wet clothing and hampered by the sodden sandy terrain we were less than 20 feet ahead of the flaming mass as it followed us and hit the ground at our heels."

Corpulent Detective Arthur Johnson, not so agile, fell three times in attempting to flee the flaming wreckage from the skies, and then was knocked over by an automobile. Durable, nonetheless, he kept running and reached a telephone to give the New Jersey State Police what was probably the first bulletin out of Lakehurst of the catastrophe.

"Ambulances, doctors, nurses . . . !" he shouted breathlessly into the mouthpiece.

W. J. Barnard, a student at the Navy Aerological School and member of the line handling party, chose a route of escape toward the mooring mast, "which could have proven disastrous, but was made because that was the direction I was facing at the time, and the falling debris and bodies seemed to be on the sides." Relatively distant as he was from the fire, all the hair on the back of his head and neck, where the protection of his white cap left off, was neatly singed off.

"Spellbound by this most unexpected tragedy," Rosendahl watched the flames moving along the fabric of the big hull, like a flash fire in a field of dry corn stalks, "greedily devouring the illustrious name 'HINDENBURG' letter by letter."

At about this moment, the husky bosun of the linesmen, "Bull" Tobin, roared: "Navy men, stand fast! We've got to get those people out of there!" Navy and civilians both, the line handlers, who had scurried out of the path of the plummeting, burning airship, turned and started back towards the conflagration, even as figures emerged miraculously free from the flames and ran possibly faster than human beings had ever run before.

As they raced away, the Navy men passed them, hurrying into the flames, suddenly unconcerned about the mortal peril in their paths. They "dove into the flames like dogs after rabbits," it appeared to Gill Robb Wilson, New Jersey State Aviation Commissioner.

People escaped in various ways once the airship was down. Mrs. Doehner simply threw her small boys out of a window. Nelson Morris, breaking burning metal rods like twigs which obstructed his path, walked out. Even then it occurred to him it was "the most remarkable thing that I know in my life," since he was scarcely singed.

"Suddenly I heard a loud cry, 'Come out, lady!' " noted Margaret Mather. "I looked and we were on the ground. Two or three men were peering in, beckoning and calling to us. I got up incredulous and instinctively groped with my feet for my handbag, which had been jerked from me when I fell. . . ."

Even now, at this moment of unexpected salvation, Margaret recognized a wild, netherworld beauty in the scene, the flames "flying all around, like birds, lighting on my arms, so I would have to brush them off."

Mrs. Marie Kleeman, going to visit her daughter and son-in-law in Andover, Massachusetts, landed with starkly contrasting savoir-faire. The debarkation stairs, burned from their fittings, fell into place on the ground. She walked off the *Hindenburg* just as in normal debarkation. Elsa Ernst, just as elderly, slid down a rope.

In the *Führergondel* Captain Lehmann issued his only command of the journey: "Everybody out!" Believing it to be "high time to get out too," Wittemann recalled the ensuing escape:

"I was in the middle of the control room behind Captain Lehmann and I saw Captain Lehmann step out of the ship through a small window in the front of the starboard side. I immediately followed him but I could not emerge as quickly because the window construction from the top had already collapsed, so that I was hindered in getting out.

"I saw, when I was still engaged in emerging, Captain Lehmann, Captain Pruss and Captain Sammt run away towards starboard. I was intent on following them and then I saw that behind them the flames and the framework crashed through to the ground. Thus their escape was cut off. There was no use to run into the fire because it was clear to me that I would burn there, and that I had to look for another avenue of escape. I went back to the neighborhood of the control car. . . . I dropped down in the neighborhood of the control car to the ground and waited. I was hardly bothered by the fire in the position. I did not feel any excessive heat.

"And I noticed that the wind was drifting the flames and the smoke towards starboard, and then I saw a clear opening shortly after on the port side, and with a quick decision I ran there and without difficulty through a short streak of fire that came through. I went back once again towards the control car and it had become not dangerous at that time, to see whether anybody had been left in the car. I could not see anybody, and went back out of the framework."

Remarkably unscathed were two crewmen in particular, Dorrflein, the mechanic, and Werner Franz, a fourteen-year-old cabin boy, drenched by the ship's own water tanks. Kubis, Ziegler, Zabel, Bauer and Wittemann also emerged with few or no burns, but they returned to the flaming wreckage in an endeavor to save anyone who might still be trapped inside. Even Sauter, Kollmer, Lau and Freund appeared from the wholly consumed tail section relatively unscathed.

Pruss, who had made good his first escape, returned in an effort to aid Speck, the radio officer, who was having difficulty in extricating himself from the flaming debris of the control car. In so doing, the captain of the *Hindenburg* was seriously hurt. Lehmann, too, emerged in critical condition, muttering, *"Das versteh ich nicht, das versteh ich nicht . . . !"*

He could not understand.

To his friend Leonhard Adelt, not so severely burned and now inquiring almost accusingly, "What was it?" he mumbled *"Blitzschlag!"* The captain, while being assisted toward the air station dispensary, had a subsequent idea it might have been a lightning bolt.

Wittemann, as soon as he was certain he could be of no more assistance, ran to Rosendahl, with an insistent request:

"I must speak with you, as soon as possible—in private."

. . . the *Hindenburg* was down, its hydrogen consumed, only its fuel oil sending billowing clouds of smoke skyward, looking for all the world, according to Albert Reitzel, "like the vast skeleton of a fish stripped of its flesh and enveloped in flames along its lower part." It had happened in 32 seconds.

While many of the throng which had been on the field converged towards the glowing, smoking wreckage, others, sick at heart, started away. Margaret Mather's sister-in-law and her niece, for example, assumed there were no survivors. Stunned beyond capacity for coherent speech or even demonstrative grief, the two women drove off towards Washington Crossing, New Jersey, where they could rest at a friend's house. Mrs. Ira Crawford was crying so that she could hardly drive Verna back along Range Road the few minutes to Cedar Avenue.

When Verna and her mother arrived home they found their neighbor Allen Hagaman's daughter Sarah just leaving. There was a look on fifteen-year-old Sarah's face that would come back to haunt Verna, and she hardly had to explain in words. For Allen, whom Verna remembered hurrying but a few minutes ago down the road, eating his ham sandwich, had been under the gondola which crashed onto the field.

Now Verna began to sob, even as her mother. She cried so that when she walked into the living room she didn't even hear the record, which she had forgotten to turn off, whining over and over, "The Dipsy Doodle. . . ."

Nor, indeed, did either of them pay heed to the wail of fire trucks, ambulances and police cars converging on this piny swath of habitation from every direction. Others were starting out from as far away as Philadelphia, Cape May and Asbury Park.

It was, as the man standing beside Margaret Mather had cried, *"das Ende!"* The *Hindenburg,* a twisted, hotly smouldering skeleton, lay near muddy, obscure Paint Branch creek, 4381 miles from Frankfurt, 77 hours in time. Here in tortured death reposed the alpha and omega of the super-airship, the dream of giant luxury liners of the sky.

The era of the Zeppelin had passed in 32 seconds in the wet New Jersey twilight. All at once the rigid, hydrogen-filled airship was extinct. It had passed even as the dinosaur.

FIRST SUCCESS FOR THE WRIGHT BROTHERS

by Wilbur and Orville Wright

Wilbur Wright to his family

Kitty Hawk, December 14, 1903

We gave machine first trial today with only partial success. The wind was only about 5 miles an hour, so we anticipated difficulty in getting speed enough on our short track (60 ft.) to lift. We took to the hill and after tossing for first whack, which I won, got ready for the start. The wind was a little to one side and the track was not exactly straight down hill, which caused the start to be more difficult than it would otherwise have been. However, the real trouble was an error in judgment in turning up too suddenly after leaving the track, and as the machine had barely speed enough for support already, this slowed it down so much that before I could correct the error, the machine began to come down, though turned up at a big angle.

Toward the end it began to speed up again but it was too late, and it stuck the ground while moving a little to one side, due to wind and a rather bad start. A few sticks in the front rudder were broken, which will take a day or two to repair probably. It was a nice easy landing for the operator. The machinery all worked in entirely satisfactory manner, and seems reliable. The power is ample, and but for a trifling error due to lack of experience with this machine and this method of starting, the machine would undoubtedly have flown beautifully.

There is now no question of final success. The strength of the machine is all right, the trouble in the front rudder being easily remedied. We anticipate no further trouble in landings. Will probably have made another trial before you receive this unless weather is unfavorable.

On December 15, Orville Wright sent a telegram to his father:

"Misjudgment at start reduced flight to hundred and twelve. Power and control ample. Rudder only injured. Success assured. Keep quiet."

From Orville Wright's Diary

Thursday, December 17, 1903

When we got up, a wind of between 20 and 25 miles was blowing from the north. We got the machine out early and put out the signal for the men at the station. Before we were quite ready, John T. Daniels, W. S. Dough, A. D. Etheridge, W. C. Brinkley of Manteo, and Johnny Moore of Nag's Head arrived. After running the engine and propellers a few minutes to get them in working order, I got on the machine at 10.35 for the first trial. The wind according to our anemometer at this time was blowing a little over 20 miles (corrected) 27 miles according to the Government anemometer at Kitty Hawk. On slipping the rope the machine started off increasing in speed to probably 7 or 8 miles. The machine lifted from the truck just as it was entering on the fourth rail. Mr. Daniels took a picture just as it left the trucks.

I found the control of the front rudder quite difficult on account of its being balanced too near the center and thus had a tendency to turn itself when started so that the rudder was turned too far on one side and then too far on the other. As a result the machine would rise suddenly to about 10 feet and then as suddenly, on turning the rudder, dart for the ground. A sudden dart when out about 100 feet from the end of the track ended the flight. Time about 12 seconds (not known exactly as watch was not promptly stopped). The flight lever for throwing off the engine was broken, and the skid under the rudder cracked.

After repairs, at 20 minutes after 11 o'clock Will made the second trial. The course was about like mine, up and down but a little longer . . . over the ground though about the same in time. Distance not measured but about 175 feet. Wind speed not quite so strong.

With the aid of the station men present, we picked the machine up and carried it back to the starting ways. At about 20 minutes till 12 o'clock I made the third trial. When out about the same distance as Will's, I met with a strong gust from the left which raised the left wing and sidled the machine off to the right in a lively manner. I immediately turned the rudder to bring the machine down and then worked the end control. Much to our surprise, on reaching the ground the left wing struck first, showing the lateral control of this machine much more effective than on any of our former ones. At the time of its sidling it had raised to a height of probably 12 to 14 feet.

At just 12 o'clock Will started on the fourth and last trip. The machine started off with its ups and downs as it had before, but by the time he had gone three or four hundred feet he had it under much better control, and was traveling on a fairly even course. It proceeded in this manner till it reached a small hummock out about 800 feet from the starting ways, when it began its pitching again and suddenly darted into the ground. The front rudder frame was badly broken up, but the main frame suffered none at all. The distance over the ground was 852 feet in 59 seconds. The engine turns was 1071, but this included several seconds while on the starting ways and probably about a half second after landing. The jar of landing had set the watch on the machine back, so that we have no exact record for the 1071 turns. Will took a picture of my third flight just before the gust struck the machine. The machine left the ways successfully at every trial, and the track was never caught by the truck as we had feared.

After removing the front rudder, we carried the machine back to camp. We set the machine down a few feet west of the building, and while standing about discussing the last flight, a sudden gust of wind struck the machine and started to turn it over. All rushed to stop it. Will, who was near the end, ran to the front, but too late to do any good. Mr. Daniels and myself seized spars at the rear, but to no purpose. The machine gradually turned over on us.

Mr. Daniels, having had no experience in handling a machine of this kind, hung on to it from the inside, and as a result he was knocked down and turned over and over with it as it went. His escape was miraculous, as he was in with the engine and chains. The engine legs were all broken off, the chain guides badly bent, a number of uprights, and nearly all the rear ends of the ribs were broken. One spar only was broken.

THE FIRST CROSS-CHANNEL FLIGHT

by Louis Blériot

At 4.30 we could see all round. Daylight had come. M. le Blanc endeavoured to see the coast of England, but could not. A light breeze from the S.W. was blowing. The air was clear. Everything was prepared. I was dressed as I am at this moment, a "khaki" jacket lined with wool for warmth over my tweed clothes and beneath my engineer's suit of blue overalls. My close-fitting cap was fastened over my head and ears. I had neither eaten nor drunk anything since I rose. My thoughts were only upon the flight and my determination to accomplish it this morning. 4.35! *Tout est prêt!* Le Blanc gives the signal and in an instant I am in the air, my engine making 1,200 revolutions—almost its highest speed—in order that I may get quickly over the telegraph wires along the edge of the cliff. As soon as I am over the cliff, I reduce my speed. There is now no need to force my engine.

I begin my flight, steady and sure, towards the Coast of England. I have no apprehensions, no sensations, *pas du tout.* The *Escopette* has seen me. She is driving ahead at full speed. She makes perhaps 42 kilometres (about 26 miles) an hour. What matters? I am making at least 68 kilometres (42½ miles). Rapidly I overtake her, travelling at a height of 80 metres (about 250 feet). The moment is supreme, yet I surprise myself by feeling no exultation. Below me is the sea, the surface disturbed by the wind, which is now freshening. The motion of the waves beneath me is not pleasant. I drive on. 10 minutes have gone. I have passed the destroyer, and I turn my head to see whether I am proceeding in the right direction. I am amazed. There is nothing to be seen, neither the torpedo-destroyer, nor France, nor England. I am alone, I can see nothing at all—*rien du tout!* For 10 minutes I am lost. It is a strange position to be alone, unguided, without compass, in the air over the middle of the Channel. I touch nothing. My hands and feet rest lightly on the levers. I let the aeroplane take its own course. I care not whither it goes. For 10 minutes I continue, neither rising nor falling, nor turning. And then, 20 minutes after I have left the French coast, I see the green cliffs of Dover, the Castle, and away to the west the spot where I had intended to land. What can I do? It is evident that the wind has taken me out of my course. I am almost at St. Margaret's Bay, and going in the direction of the Goodwin Sands.

Now it is time to attend to the steering. I press the lever with my foot and turn easily toward the west, reversing the direction in which I am travelling. Now indeed, I am in difficulties, for the wind here by the cliffs is much stronger, and my speed is reduced as I fight against it. Yet my beautiful aeroplane responds. Still steadily I fly westwards, hoping to cross the harbour and reach the Shakespeare cliff. Again the wind blows. I see an opening in the cliff. Although I am confident that I can continue for an hour and a half, that I might indeed return to Calais, I cannot resist the opportunity to make a landing upon this green spot. Once more I turn my aeroplane, and, describing a half-circle, I enter the opening and find myself again over dry land. Avoiding the red buildings on my right, I attempt a landing; but the wind catches me and whirls me round two or three times. At once I stop my motor, and instantly the machine falls straight upon the land from a height of 20 metres (65 feet). In two or three seconds I am safe upon your shore. Soldiers in khaki run up, and a policeman. Two of my compatriots are on the spot. They kiss my cheeks. The conclusion of my flight overwhelms me.

LOUIS BLÉRIOT—*Daily Mail,* 26th July 1909

THE FIRST FLIGHTS OF IGOR I. SIKORSKY

by Igor I. Sikorsky

In the morning of the next day, June 3, 1910, on the way to the field, we made plans for the first test of the S-2. The cloudiness and very light wind appeared favorable. The S-2 was wheeled out of the hangar, I checked the controls, climbed into the seat behind the motor, and shouted,

"Contact."

The engine was quickly started. While three men held the plane, I gradually opened the throttle, and a few moments later the good sound of the motors, the propeller blast, and the smell of burned castor oil told me that it was time to try.

I gave the signal, and the plane was released. The S-2 had a much better acceleration. From the very first moment I could feel that the stronger propeller blast made the control more effective and the tail went up at once. I had no tachometer, not a single instrument, in the S-2. A few seconds later, feeling that the speed was already well in excess of what the previous plane could ever do, I gradually started to move the stick back. A moment later, I was in the air. All my attention was concentrated on the controls. Having never before been in the air, even as a passenger, I had to learn quickly the necessary movements which were familiar in imagination but not yet in reality. By delicately pushing or pulling the stick I could hold the plane at two to four feet of altitude for a time, which appeared quite long to me, as well as to the witnesses of this first flight.

Finally, the plane, for some reason, settled down. Feeling that the wheels were again on firm ground, I cut the ignition. A few moments later, the men who witnessed this flight crowded around the ship far more excited than I was myself. This was the first time that any person then present on the field had seen a flying machine in the air and their excitement and enthusiasm were perhaps far in excess of what this very modest performance deserved. The flight was about 200 yards long at an altitude of two to four feet, and lasted about twelve seconds. I made no more tests that day. With reverence, and almost with tenderness, my boys put the S-2 back in the hangar.

Seriously feeling the lack of instruction in my piloting, as well as in design, I tried at least not to lose any data that would be useful. Therefore, this flight was followed by a discussion during which, with the help of the witnesses, a reasonable picture was evolved of how the plane took off, how it behaved in flight, and so forth, to check my own impressions.

The next day I rolled the plane out with much more confidence and decided to fly higher and farther; if possible, across the whole field. I took off and continued to hold the stick slightly back. To my delight, the plane arose in the air to some six or eight feet. Next, however, to my surprise, the ship started to settle down and landed rather heavily although without damage. I repeated this attempt a few times, but to my disappointment, the results were no better. The plane would take off every time, but then it would settle down no matter what I did with the controls. I tried to push the stick, and this would only cause it to descend more quickly. It would usually reach no more than six to ten feet of altitude so that the duration of each of these hops was even shorter than that of the first flight. Apparently there was still not enough power, or, possibly, something else was wrong.

A few days later I decided to have the S-2 held for a longer time after starting the engine and to adjust it for maximum power. With the tail up and the wings nearly horizontal, I ran the plane longer than usual, permitting it to gain all the speed it could. Then I pulled the stick back. The rise was quicker and much higher than ever before. My assistants said later that it was very high, as high as a four story building. Then again it started to come down and continued to lose altitude in spite of everything I tried to do with the elevator. With its motor working, the plane landed in a normal position but very heavily. The landing gear collapsed and the S-2 turned over, breaking the propeller and suffering other damages. In spite of that, I felt quite happy and even proud. I was delighted with the "high" flight, and even the slight crash was a normal event in aviation at that time. I decided not only to repair, but also to improve the plane.

During the next three weeks the plane was repaired, the fabric covering tightened and improved and a few other refinements were incorporated. On June 29th, it was again ready for flight. I took off as usual, climbed to ten or fifteen feet, and tried to hold the plane at that height. To my great satisfaction, it did not settle down but obeyed the controls and continued to fly nicely. Gently, I tried the elevator and ailerons. The plane responded well. For the first time I stayed in the air as long as I wanted to, and finally landed on the other end of the field. The flight was repeated. Again it was nice and smooth about one-half minute long from one end of the field to the other. This was finally real flying, and it made me extremely happy. The size and shape of the field prevented my making a circle in the air within its limits. To circle, it was necessary to take off, fly across a wide ravine some twenty-five feet deep, with a swamp at the bottom, continue the turn over reasonably smooth land, and, finally, after crossing a small river, return again to the point of departure.

On the afternoon of the next day, I took off with the S-2, having in mind a flight which would bring me back to the point of departure. The little plane climbed easily to about twenty-five feet. I crossed the field, flying a straight line and approaching the boundary, and started to turn toward the ravine. The smoke of burning castor oil and even drops of it were thrown by the propeller blast on my hands and face. The little plane was smoothly sailing through the air, gradually gaining altitude and giving the most delightful feeling of flying. I crossed the border of the ravine and was then some sixty or eighty feet high over the swamp. Instead of the rush of the ground under the plane which was so familiar during previous runs and low flying, I now saw the ground far below moving slowly, and I had the wonderful feeling of flying, floating in the air. My joy, however, was of short duration. Being busy with my first turn in the air and with the new sensation, I did not notice soon enough that the swamp below had started to move up toward the plane. Instinctively, I pulled the stick. The ship's descent was slowed for a moment, but then it became much worse, and the next moment the S-2 crashed on the opposite slope of the ravine. I climbed out from the débris of the plane with only scratches and bruises, but the S-2, including the engine, was a complete wreck.

There was not even any question of repairing it. The loss of the plane and engine was a hard blow, and we were further distressed because we could not find out the reasons for the trouble. Before I took off, some of the people present went to the end of the field to get a good view of the plane in flight. They saw the whole event at close range, and their observations were in complete accord with my own impressions. It was certain that the plane was in normal position at all times and the motor worked well until the very moment of the crash.

The exact reason for that disheartening crash was not clearly established and understood until a year later. The S-2, with the 25 horsepower engine and a home-made propeller, had barely enough power to stay in the air, and flew only a few miles above its minimum speed. There was not a single instrument on board. In fact, speed indicators for aviation were not yet in use. Therefore, I had no way of determining the loss of speed except by feeling and experience, and of that I did not have much because my total time in the air was then not over eight minutes. The S-2 had just about enough power to maintain horizontal flight. The turn required a little more power, but the chief trouble was created by a sort of air pocket, which existed frequently above the cool swamp in the ravine. Later on, I crossed it many times with more powerful and efficient machines, and while I could often feel the down pull, I would pay no attention to it. But for the little S-2, it was enough to cause a loss of altitude. By pulling the stick I made matters worse, stalled, as we call it now, and came down abruptly.

During its whole career, the S-2 spent some eight minutes in the air. The longest flight, lasting forty-nine seconds, was the last one. Yet these few minutes in the air represented almost the only reliable source of practical information with respect to design, construction, and piloting that were at my disposal. I learned many important things during these short hops, mostly of a few seconds each. Many fundamental perceptions, such as take-off, action of the controls in the air, and in landing, which only two months previous I had tried to imagine, now became reasonably clear facts which I could understand. But, together with the beginning of actual experience and knowledge, came the realization of the great difficulties of pioneering in aviation. Reflections of that sort, as well as many others, occupied my mind while I took a few days' rest after that significant flight, and "landing."

The S-2 was down and out. For the sake of economy, I removed the bolts, turnbuckles and cables which represented nearly all that could be salvaged. The helicopter was disassembled and placed in permanent storage. The little 15 horsepower motor was sold and the 25 horsepower engine was damaged beyond repair.

The new program of work was, nevertheless, quickly decided upon, and during the month of July, I made a design, prepared drawings, and soon afterward started the construction of the next plane. This ship, to be known as the S-3, was in general similar to the previous one, but it was larger, was designed to have a 40 horsepower motor and boasted various improvements which were the result of the experience gained with the S-2. The ailerons were larger and of better design, and the control cables were tighter, since the looser cables on the first two planes had not given the quick response which was so necessary. The wings were more accurately constructed, and were also better covered.

In August I made a short trip abroad, visiting Paris, and obtained a 40 horsepower Anzani motor. About three more months of hard work, and late in November, 1910, the S-3 was completed, transported to the field and assembled.

Early the next month I made the first flight, again crossing the field from one end to the other. The plane was obviously superior to the previous one. The take-off, control, and other characteristics were much improved, and there was a good excess of power.

Winter was early that year and the small river and the few lakes situated around the field were frozen solid. During the second week of December, I made several more flights on the S-3, gradually gaining familiarity and confidence with the controls. All these hops from one end of the field to the other lasted about half a minute. The plane would climb easily to some forty feet and would clearly have gone higher but I could not push the plane up and land within the limits of the field. During these few days I made in all twelve "hops," and then decided to try again a real flight, a complete circle in the air landing near the place of departure.

On Monday, December 13th, commencing the thirteenth flight in the S-3, I took off from the usual spot and gradually climbing, left the field at some eighty to one hundred feet altitude. I carefully started a right hand turn. The plane obeyed the controls and stayed in the air excellently.

From time to time I made small movements with the control levers in order to check the responsiveness of the ship. Glancing around, I noticed that the field had already been left behind and that the snow-covered ground was farther below than I had ever seen it before. My joy, however, was again of short duration. At first I suspected, and then saw for certain, that the engine was gradually losing power. Next, I realized that the plane was already unable to hold the altitude and was coming down. My piloting in this emergency was not so bad. Pushing the stick, I prevented the plane from losing more speed and finally made a somewhat rough landing which, however, the plane was strong enough to stand. Unfortunately, it happened to come down on the surface of one of the ponds. The ice was strong enough to hold a man, but, under the impact of the plane, it broke and the S-3, badly damaged by the broken ice, turned over and sank nose down. The pond was about four feet deep in this place, and the trailing edges of the wings and the broken tail stayed above the surface, while the motor lodged about two feet below. Sitting behind the motor, I was completely submerged in the water, but managed to crawl out without much difficulty from the wrecked ship. Pushing aside the floating cakes, I reached the edge of the solid ice, climbed on it, and waited there a few minutes for the arrival of my men. They confirmed my observations, saying that the engine apparently lost revolutions. On that calm winter day they could hear the motor plainly, and were able to recognize the loss of power from the sound. Someone even said that it appeared similar to the noise of the engine when run with retarded spark.

To find the cause of the trouble was very important, and feeling that I could not get any more wet than I already was, I went back to the plane. I could not see the engine, which was about two feet below the water, but by inspecting the rear part I located the distributor and found it shifted all the way to the retarded position. Therefore, the cause of the crash was at least definitely established. I went home while my men got the plane out of the water and brought it back to the hangar. The mechanic informed me later in the evening that the motor was all right, and the plane although seriously damaged, could be repaired.

The whole flying career of the S-3 lasted a little over a week and consisted of thirteen flights of a total duration of about seven minutes. The last flight was fifty-nine seconds. Whatever I might decide to do next, it was clear that flying would again be interrupted for several months, and plenty of hard work, and expense would ensue before the next attempt became possible.

December 13 was followed by a few days of rather gloomy reflections. It was exactly two years before that I had started active work in aviation. Expenses already represented a heavy tax on the modest fortune of my father, which consisted of the savings of a life time as a practicing physician, and of my sister, who had organized and was managing a private school for feeble-minded children. None of the money that I had spent was easily earned. But I never heard a word of complaint, and was at that time not even informed of the criticisms and warnings that some family friends considered it their "duty" to give my father about my "obviously hopeless" attempts. Moral and financial support and encouragement from my father and the rest of the family I most certainly had, yet I realized well the full meaning of the extra mortgage on the house which had been discussed in order that my work could continue.

The two years of work did considerable harm to my studies in the Institute. I was already far behind almost every student of my year. The liberal faculty was willing to grant me the maximum extension that was legally possible, but there was a time limit when a certain minimum of examinations had to be passed. While I had learned much during the two years of aviation work, yet these studies were in a different direction from the program of the Institute. Besides, I had learned by then quite well that success in pioneering work requires one hundred per cent of one's time and energy. Even ninety per cent would not do. So it was necessary to make a choice. I could resume normal studies in the Institute, which practically assured me a diploma and a reasonable career. In that case it would be possible eventually to take up again work in aviation, but the chance of leadership would be lost.

At that time reliable information and aeronautical science were practically non-existent and the pioneer designer and pilot had only his own meager experience, practical judgment and imagination to supply the necessary data on which to build his machine. When the plane was ready, and no one could tell whether or not it was any good, the designer had to become a pilot and, having no instructor to explain or give advice, he had to seek flying knowledge by studying the birds, by playing with models, and again by relying on imagination. After a crash it was sometimes difficult to know whether the machine was bad or the pilot had made a mistake, or whether it was something else. In order to win against such considerable odds, it was necessary to invest every bit of energy and time. Not eight hours a day, but often sixteen hours of intense and extreme effort were needed, and even so the results were anything but certain.

My own ideas and feelings about aviation had already changed. At the beginning, the work of design and construction was fun, while the flights in my own machine were anticipated as delightful thrills. Now the construction of the planes became serious work. Still more so was the flying. I had learned by theory and practice that a minor deficiency in the plane or a slight error in piloting, or finally one of several unknown causes, the existence of which I had reason to suspect after the event of June 30th, could result in a crash. This was a source of real worry, but not because of any fear of personal danger. I believed in my ability to get safely out of such accidents, but every serious crash would mean an interruption of flying for several months, heavy expenses, and would reduce the chances of final success. Therefore, the impressions of the flights, particularly of the latest ones, were quite different from my early illusions. All attention during these flights was concentrated in watching the motor, operating the controls while learning to do so, and watching for the landing. The thrill and happy sensations could be experienced after the landing, by memory and by looking at photographs.

Departures from my original ideas of the early period were considerable. I had a feeling that I had started my aviation work not two but some twelve years before. And the same was to a certain degree true with respect to results. Experience, direct information and the training of my intuition, however, had all gained to an extent greater than the short period of two years. By intuition I mean the ability to arrive at a reasonable solution of a problem when data for a solution by ordinary methods is not available. This was the way most of the design problems, not only in aerodynamics, but even in stress, were solved. While for instance, the structural analysis of a wing would be itself a simple engineering problem, yet to approach it in a normal way one would need to have information about the center of pressure, distribution of lift between the upper and lower wings, forces of air gusts, and other details. Since all this was not available, it was necessary to rely chiefly on "guess." In this respect, apparently real progress had been made. I remembered the difficulties with which we were confronted at the early period, many of which now appeared easy and simple. I had a feeling that I had begun to learn to develop the ability which is so important for pioneering and inventive work, namely the ability to distinguish between the valuable and the worthless products of imagination. The first may be considered as intuitive imagination, while the latter may be called day-dreaming and lead to failure and possibly tragedy.

Finally, in order to view the situation from another angle, I tried to picture what would happen if I were really to desert pioneer flying and prepare myself for a career and a more conventional job. Then I realized that this would mean failure and loss, personal and otherwise. For myself, it would mean preferring a comfortable job to a real chance to work, and possibly leadership in a most interesting line of modern engineering which had captured my whole heart and soul. Moreover, quitting now would waste all the confidence and support which I had received from my family. So as a result of these and other thoughts, a decision was reached not to slow down the work but to push it ahead as vigorously as possible, even if it meant sacrificing my diploma at the Polytechnic Institute. Once the decision was made, my doubts and worries disappeared, at least for a while.

During the latter part of December, a program of future activity was prepared and the work resumed. I wanted to use as many parts of the S-3 as possible, including the engine, and to produce the S-4 plane, introducing certain improvements. Besides that, I decided to build another airplane, the S-5, with a heavier, more reliable engine, larger wing area, different control arrangements, and various other changes, which had been suggested by careful study and an analysis of previous planes. The program called for both planes to be ready for flight early in the spring.

ALCOCK AND BROWN FLY THE ATLANTIC

by Lowell Thomas and Lowell Thomas, Jr.

After Blériot's conquest of the English Channel, it was inevitable that the next major challenge for aviators of all nations would be a non-stop flight across the Atlantic. At first, the coming of World War I interfered with this, although as early as 1913 Lord Northcliffe and the London *Daily Mail* had offered £10,000 for a first non-stop aerial crossing in either direction. The flight had to be made in less than 72 hours, with the takeoff and landing points somewhere in the United States, Canada, or Newfoundland on one side, and the British Isles on the other.

When the First World War ended in 1918, commercial flying was still in its infancy, and the public, generally speaking, had a suspicion of airplanes whose job, first and foremost, had been to spread death and destruction throughout the four years of conflict. Thousands of wartime pilots found themselves with nothing to do, and many turned to other professions despite all the flying experience they had acquired during the war. Still, some were determined to pursue flying careers no matter what the odds, and their ambitions received quite a boost in the very month of the Armistice when Lord Northcliffe and the *Daily Mail* renewed that £10,000 prize offer for a first non-stop transatlantic flight.

By the spring of 1919, the island of Newfoundland off the coast of Canada had become the busiest aviation center in the world. Airplanes were being crated in by freighter from England, landing fields and hangars were under construction, and aviators, mechanics, and navigators were arriving on every steamer. The intense preparations for flights across the English Channel in 1909 had been leisurely compared with the feverish activity that now gripped Newfoundland, the staging area for a far more spectacular and dangerous race.

At least four teams of British aviators had arrived by the middle of May and more were expected with each passing day. Two private fliers, Harry Hawker, an Australian, and Kenneth MacKenzie-Grieve, had pitched their camp at Mount Pearl Farm where they were running their Sopwith biplane through a series of tests. Captain Fred P. Raynham and his navigator, C. W. F. Morgan, were preparing their Martinsyde biplane on a landing strip at nearby Quidi Vidi, while at Harbor Grace, a third team, headed by Vice Admiral Mark Kerr, was assembling a huge four-engine Handley-Page biplane. With the bases located within a 100-mile radius of each other, there was an air of competition, and all this was heightened by a growing international corps of newsmen who were sending out daily dispatches on the flight preparations. Naturally the Newfoundlanders were watching all these developments with intense interest and amazement.

Soon the Americans were in the running too, although their plans did not call for a non-stop flight to the British Isles, and therefore they would be ineligible for the *Daily Mail* prize. The United States Navy had decided to demonstrate the range and power of its new Curtiss Flying Boats by sending three of these planes on a flight from Newfoundland to the Azores, thence to Portugal and on to Plymouth, England. Even if only one of them made it to the Azores, America could claim the honor of first flying the Atlantic, although it would be over a shorter distance than the route from Newfoundland to the British Isles.

The Navy planes made their base at Trepassey, Newfoundland, and American warships were assigned areas all the way across the ocean to the Azores as standby vessels for refueling and rescue duties. Moving swiftly to get into the air ahead of the British, all three American planes, the NC-1 NC-3, and NC-4, took off from Trepassey late on the afternoon of May 16. First, the unlucky NC-1 was forced down in the Atlantic within 200 miles of the Azores and the crew was rescued. Then, the hapless NC-3 lost its bearings in a fog, came down at sea, and was missing for 52 hours. But it taxied through rough seas for 205 miles while riding out a gale and finally arrived safely in the Azores. Meanwhile, the NC-4 under Lieutenant Commander Albert C. Read with a crew of four, including pilots Walter Hinton and E. F. Stone, did manage to fly all the way to the Azores, covering the 1380-mile distance in about 15 hours. Then several days later, the NC-4 continued on to Portugal and arrived in England near the end of May, completing the entire journey from Newfoundland in about two weeks.

So the NC-4 became the first heavier-than-air craft to cross the Atlantic and its crew won much temporary fame for the achievement. However, this still left unclaimed the *Daily Mail*'s prize for a non-stop flight between North America and the British Isles in less than 72 hours. Moreover, flying the Atlantic without rescue ships deployed along the way remained a far bigger challenge in the eyes of a watching world.

On May 16, the day the American planes had taken off from Trepassey, the British aviators on Newfoundland were straining at the leash. And when the word came through that Commander Read and the NC-4 had reached the Azores, Hawker and Grieve made a final inspection of their Sopwith, then roared out across the Atlantic heading for Ireland. Less than an hour later, Raynham and Morgan, not to be left behind, sent their Martinsyde down the runway at Quidi Vidi, but failed to get off the ground. In their haste to follow their rivals, they tried to take off in a cross wind and their plane crashed into a ravine, injuring Morgan so seriously that he had to give up flying.

For the next several hours, Hawker and Grieve flew on toward Ireland, but loose solder in the radiator clogged the water-circulation system, forcing the plane down into the ocean a thousand miles east of Newfoundland. They were missing and given up for lost for the next seven days until the news came through that a Danish freighter had rescued them at sea, and a highly excited British public gave them a heroes' welcome when they reached London. Harry Hawker went on to become famous in aviation as one of the founders of Hawker Siddeley Aviation, Ltd.

Two British flying teams had failed in their attempts to cross the ocean while Admiral Kerr was still assembling his Handley-Page biplane at Harbor Grace, hopeful of getting away on his own flight by early June. But he was facing the threat of stiff competition from a pair of Royal Air Force fliers who had entered the race: their names—Captain John Alcock and Lieutenant Arthur Whitten-Brown. They had arrived at St. John's on May 13, but their airplane was stored in crates on board another vessel which wasn't due for another two weeks.

Who were these new entries? Some four months before, Arthur Whitten-Brown, a thirty-three-year-old World War I veteran born in Glasgow of American parents, had been looking for a job. He also had hopes of soon marrying Kathleen Kennedy, the beautiful red-haired daughter of a major in the British Ministry of Munitions. But the all-important question of a job had to be settled first.

During his early years, Brown attended school in England and, even though he possessed American citizenship, he had joined the British Army to fight the Germans. As a lieutenant, he led his men in battles at Ypres and along the Somme, then transferred to the Royal Flying Corps as an observer. Twice shot down, on the second time he was taken prisoner and spent fourteen months in a German POW camp before being repatriated.

During the war years Brown had made an intensive study of aerial navigation and after the Armistice he began making the rounds of aircraft firms that were showing an interest in transatlantic flying. One afternoon he visited the Vickers plant at Weybridge near London, and the superintendent, Maxwell Muller, listened quietly as Brown stated his qualifications. Then Muller asked:

"You are a navigator. But can you navigate a plane across the Atlantic?"

"Yes," Brown replied, apparently without misgivings.

"Then we have a job for you," Muller continued. "The *Daily Mail,* as you know, is offering a prize of £10,000 for the first plane to fly the Atlantic non-stop. We want our plane to be the first to do it, and Vickers doesn't care about the money. The men who fly the plane can have that. We have the pilot, and we have the plane, so come along and meet both."

A few moments later Brown was shaking hands with Captain John Alcock, a twenty-six-year-old British pilot who had come out of the war with seven enemy planes to his credit and a Distinguished Service Cross among his decorations. From the point of view of personality, the two were a study in contrasts, but they developed a liking for each other almost immediately. Brown, the Scottish-American, was slight of build, dark-haired, rather quiet and reserved. Alcock was sturdy, round-faced and blond, with a ready wit, a dry humor, and very British.

In fact, Alcock was a pioneer of British aviation, and had received his flying certificate at the age of twenty when he became an instructor in aerobatics. During the war he had flown bombing missions against the Turks, including one daring raid on Constantinople. Like Brown, he too had been taken prisoner after he was forced to ditch his plane in the Aegean off Gallipoli.

Together, Alcock and Brown looked over their transatlantic plane—a Vickers-Vimy biplane powered by two 350-hp Rolls-Royce engines. A converted bomber, it had been earmarked for raids on Berlin and had a cruising speed of about 90 miles per hour with a range of some 2400 miles. Considerable work remained before it would be ready for the flight, but by early May final tests were completed and the disassembled plane was placed in crates for the voyage to Newfoundland. The two fliers, aware of the hazards of their mission, put their personal affairs in order and Arthur Whitten-Brown told an understanding Kathleen Kennedy their marriage would have to be postponed until after the flight.

When they arrived at St. John's, Alcock and Brown took up residence at the Cochrane Hotel, the bustling headquarters of transatlantic aviators during that hectic spring of 1919. With their plane still en route from England, they spent the next few days trying to find a suitable landing strip, a task that wasn't so easy. Newfoundland was in the midst of a real estate boom, brought on by all this sudden demand for aerodromes, and property owners were asking sky-high prices for land that had even the remotest appearance of being level. Every day for a week, Alcock and Brown drove for miles over seemingly endless bad roads in an effort to find a suitable field, but it was a desperate search. The aerodrome at Mount Pearl Farm, recently vacated by Hawker and Grieve, would have been perfect, but the owner wanted $3000 rent until June 15 and $250 a day after that. Another likely area was found near Harbor Grace, but here Alcock was confronted with a demand for $25,000 when he approached the owner. The Newfoundlanders obviously were determined to make hay while they had the chance.

The Vickers-Vimy arrived and the tedious job of assembly began at Quidi Vidi where Captain Raynham generously offered the use of his aerodrome facilities, even though the runway there would not be long enough to permit the Vimy to take off with a full load of gasoline. Still looking for a landing field, Alcock and Brown divided their time between the plane and a search of the countryside until one afternoon their luck took a new turn. The owner of a large meadow near a place called Monday's Pool made them a reasonable offer. They promptly leased the land, and hired a labor force of thirty men who brought along picks and shovels to level the hillocks and remove the rocks and boulders. The work was completed on June 9 and Alcock flew the Vimy over from Quidi Vidi with a light load of gasoline.

For the next four days, Alcock and Brown virtually lived with their meteorological officers, but each day the weather reports were unfavorable, with high winds, fog, and rain continuing out over the North Atlantic. Coupled with their irritation over the delay was a growing apprehension that Admiral Kerr and his Handley-Page crew were almost ready to take off. But regardless of the weather, Alcock and Brown finally decided to wait no longer.

Early on the morning of Saturday, June 14, they showed up at the aerodrome in their electrically heated flying suits and, together with their mechanics, they began filling the tanks with a full complement of 870 gallons of gasoline and 40 gallons of oil. Their personal luggage was stored in a compartment near the single open cockpit. For food they took aboard sandwiches, chocolate, malted milk, and a thermos of coffee, along with a few small bottles of brandy and ale. Fitted into the area around the cockpit was a mail bag with three hundred private letters, and also their mascots, "Twinkletoes" and "Lucky Jim," two stuffed black cats which Kathleen Kennedy had given them before they left England.

At 4 A.M., they were again told that weather conditions were something less than perfect.

"Strong westerly wind. Conditions otherwise fairly favorable."

A few hours later, a cross wind was blowing from the west and the two fliers decided to wait a little longer in the hope that it would die down. But the morning hours gave way to the afternoon with the wind still blowing as furiously as ever.

Convinced that he could get the plane off the ground without a crash, Alcock made his decision. First, he asked the Vickers manager on the field for permission to take off, then he motioned Brown on board. Standing together in the cockpit, both fliers turned to say goodbye to their mechanics and a crowd of Newfoundlanders who had come down from St. John's to see them off.

Navigator Brown announced:

"Our objective is the Irish coast. We shall aim at the center of our target."

And Alcock, the blithe spirit, added:

"Yes, we shall hang our hats on the aerials of Clifden Wireless Station as we go by. So long."

At 4:10 P.M., the chocks were removed from the wheels—and the mechanics, hanging on the wings and tail, "let go" as Alcock gave both engines full throttle and the Vimy started across the turf. The two fliers were seated side by side in the cockpit as they headed over the slightly inclined runway into the westerly wind.

The plane lurched and lumbered forward for 300 yards before the wheels left the ground, and it was none too soon. A line of hills and treetops lay ahead, and gale-force winds were bedeviling Alcock's efforts to gain altitude as the Vimy slowly climbed to 800 feet and over the trees. With his machine now well under control, Alcock headed over the fishing fleet in Concepcion Bay and then on beyond Signal Hill to the open Atlantic.

It was at St. John's in 1901 that Signor Guglielmo Marconi received the first wireless signal ever sent across the Atlantic. And now, eighteen years later, the Marconi Station was flashing the news of the takeoff to every ship in the North Atlantic, asking them to be on the lookout and give the plane's position if sighted. Brown would be counting on this information to aid the navigation, and the moment the Vimy left the coastline he unstrung the wireless aerial to tap a message to the Marconi operator:

"All well and started."

Gradually, Alcock nosed the Vimy upward until they were at 3000 feet, while far beneath them the gray waters of the Atlantic were rolling and tossing in a gale-force wind. But the westerly wind which had been a problem on the takeoff, was now their friend, boosting them along at more than a hundred miles an hour. With both engines running smoothly and the getaway a success, Brown decided to run the wireless apparatus through a few tests, just to make sure it was working properly.

"Say, Jack," he said over the telephone, "I'm going to send St. John's a few words of greeting."

"Tell them we'll be across in sixteen hours," answered Alcock, "if this wind keeps us in its lap."

Brown began tapping out the Vimy's own call letters, D.K.G., but as he worked the key, the spark grew weaker and weaker until there was no flashing blue light at all. It was a difficult problem, for the wireless generator received its energy from a small, wind-driven propeller located under the forward fuselage and it couldn't be seen from the cockpit.

Brown told his companion about the trouble and, holding tightly to the struts, he climbed out on the wing for a close look at the four-bladed wireless propeller, despite Alcock's emphatic warning against taking such a risk. With the wind screaming around him, Brown crouched on the lower wing, and peering underneath the yellow fuselage, he saw a propeller with only one blade—the other three were gone, probably sheared away by the severe rocking of the plane on the takeoff. For the rest of the flight, their wireless would be out of commission and beyond hope of repair. They would have no way of sending or receiving messages, no way of getting their bearings from ships at sea, and all through the tense hours that lay ahead, they would be completely isolated from the world.

Throughout the early evening hours they flew between layers of clouds above and below, with the ocean completely shut off from view. Then, shortly after 7 P.M., more trouble. The starboard motor began coughing and stuttering so badly that both fliers were thoroughly alarmed as they leaned out to look at the motor. A large chunk of the exhaust pipe had split away, and, as they watched, it changed from red- to white-hot, then gradually crumpled as it grew softer in the intense heat. Three cylinders of the starboard engine were throwing their exhaust fumes straight into the air without benefit of the usual outlet, but throttling down the starboard motor was out of the question, and the exhaust problem was with them to stay.

Brown had brought along a small bubble sextant and was relying entirely on this for directional navigation. It was still evening, and he was taking sights on the stars and moon when suddenly the Vimy plowed into a thick bank of fog. Shouting into the intercom, he told Alcock to go higher, and when they reached 12,000 feet the stars once again were there to guide them.

The hours passed monotonously, and soon it was well past midnight with the moon still shining brightly above them, coloring the clouds with tinges of silver, gold, and red. Below, they could see the Vimy's shadow moving across the layer of clouds that covered the ocean. Twice during the night they polished off a quick sandwich along with a few shots of brandy, and they fought constantly to ignore the drone of the motors which almost lulled them to sleep.

Just as the sun was beginning to rise, the plane ran into another wall of fog, and they had the sensation of flying inside a bottle of milk. With nothing but the white mist around them, they lost their sense of balance and a glance at the instrument panel showed the plane was not on an even keel, and might even be flying upside down. Even worse, it was plunging rapidly through the clouds with the altimeter dropping to 2000—1000—then 500 feet. And the tension was growing in the cockpit.

If the cloud layer reached all the way down to the ocean, Alcock would be unable to see the horizon in time to counteract the spin and avoid a crash. Preparing for the worst, Brown loosened his safety belt and they were less than a hundred feet from the water when, in a moment of flashing light, the plane shot out of the cloud vapor into the clear atmosphere.

But the ocean did not appear below them!

The plane was tilted at an angle, and the line of the horizon seemed to be standing vertically to their view. But Alcock quickly regained his visual equilibrium, and the Vimy responded to the controls. At full throttle, he swung the plane back on a level course even though they were flying a mere 50 feet over the ocean. The danger was past, but they were lucky to be out of that one.

For the next three hours, the Vimy moved in and out of a procession of clouds that enveloped the plane time and again, only to give way to patches of blue. But the clouds soon massed into a black wall and a driving rain began lashing the fuselage. Minutes later it turned to snow, and then to a heavy sleet. Trying to rise above the storm, they reached 9000 feet when Brown saw the glass face of the gasoline overflow gauge clotted with snow and ice. To guard against carburetor trouble, they had to read this gauge at any given moment, and clearing away the ice and snow would be no simple task. It was fixed to one of the center struts and Brown decided that, once more, it was up to him to climb out of the cockpit.

Holding on to a cross-bracing wire to keep the wind from blasting him off the side, he knelt on the wing and managed to reach up and wipe the sleet from the gauge. Time and again, Brown repeated the performance as the storm continued, and he implored Alcock to keep the plane on a level keel while he was out there on the fuselage.

They kept themselves warm by huddling as far down in the open cockpit as possible, while Alcock took the plane higher and higher, hoping to get above the sleet. And it was 6 A.M. when Brown saw the sun glinting through a gap in the clouds. Even though the horizon was shrouded in fog, he was able to get a reading that showed they were nearing the Irish coast and he scribbled Alcock a message:

"Better go lower; the air will be warmer and we may spot a steamer."

Once again, Alcock was feeling his way down through the clouds, knowing that at any moment the wheels might strike the surface of the sea. Then, the plane suddenly emerged from the cloud bank, and both engines responded as Alcock opened full throttle again. But there was no sign of a ship on the cold, gray ocean below as they roared on toward what they hoped would be the emerald coasts of Ireland.

It was exactly 8:15 A.M., and Brown had just finished screwing on the lid of the thermos flask when Alcock grabbed his shoulder, and pointed. There, looming through the mist, were two tiny specks of land—and Brown put both his charts and the thermos away. His navigation duties were over. They had spotted two islands off the Irish coast, and a moment later the mainland came clearly into view.

Still uncertain of their exact location, they crossed the coastline looking for a railway to follow. But when the masts of the Clifden Wireless Station pierced the sky ahead, they knew they were on the beam. It was time for a decision, and Brown asked a crucial question:

"Shall we land at London, or Clifden?"

Alcock was quick to answer, for he feared that Admiral Kerr and his Handley-Page might even then be roaring up somewhere behind them, anxious to beat them to the prize.

"I think we'd better make it Clifden," he said. "All we have to do to win is reach the British Isles, and it'll lengthen our flying time if we go on to London."

As they circled the wireless aerials of Clifden looking for a spot to land, Alcock saw what appeared to be a level stretch of ground. He brought the Vimy in for a perfect landing and it rolled for a hundred feet or so when—without warning—up it went on its nose.

Despite the benign appearance of their landing site, they had come down in an Irish bog. Brown was uninjured, but the soil of Ireland had risen up to give Alcock a black eye and a pair of badly bruised lips. Even so, as he climbed out of the wreckage a grin spread around his swollen mouth, and with a wink toward the Vimy he managed to say:

"She's a pretty fair old boat, eh what?"

The following morning the New York *Times* told the story in its page one headline:

> ALCOCK AND BROWN FLY ACROSS THE ATLANTIC; MAKE 1,980 MILES IN 16 HOURS, 12 MINUTES; SOMETIMES UPSIDE DOWN IN DENSE, ICY FOG

King George V soon issued the orders making them Sir John Alcock and Sir Arthur Whitten-Brown, and Lord Northcliffe wrote the check for £10,000, shares of which the two fliers generously gave their mechanics.

Brown married his fiancée, Kathleen Kennedy, and he lived to the age of sixty-two. Sir John Alcock, however, was tragically killed in a plane crash in France only six months later.

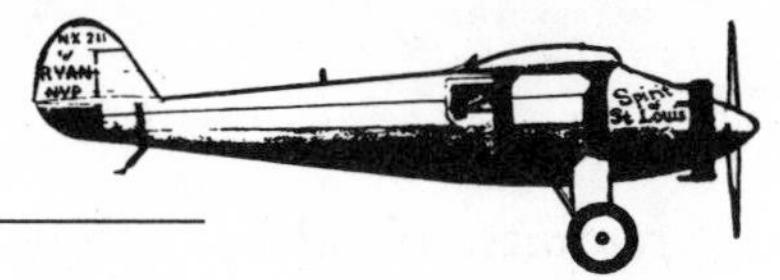

NEW YORK TO PARIS

by Charles A. Lindbergh

At New York we checked over the plane, engine and instruments, which required several short flights over the field.

When the plane was completely inspected and ready for the trans-Atlantic flight, there were dense fogs reported along the coast and over Nova Scotia and Newfoundland, in addition to a storm area over the North Atlantic.

On the morning of May 19th, a light rain was falling and the sky was overcast. Weather reports from land stations and ships along the great circle course were unfavorable and there was apparently no prospect of taking off for Paris for several days at least. In the morning I visited the Wright plant at Paterson, New Jersey, and had planned to attend a theatre performance in New York that evening. But at about six o'clock I received a special report from the New York Weather Bureau. A high pressure area was over the entire North Atlantic and the low pressure over Nova Scotia and Newfoundland was receding. It was apparent that the prospects of the fog clearing up were as good as I might expect for some time to come. The North Atlantic should be clear with only local storms on the coast of Europe. The moon had just passed full and the percentage of days with fog over Newfoundland and the Grand Banks was increasing so that there seemed to be no advantage in waiting longer.

We went to Curtiss Field as quickly as possible and made arrangements for the barograph to be sealed and installed, and for the plane to be serviced and checked.

We decided partially to fill the fuel tanks in the hangar before towing the ship on a truck to Roosevelt Field, which adjoins Curtiss on the east, where the servicing would be completed.

I left the responsibility for conditioning the plane in the hands of the men on the field while I went into the hotel for about two and one-half hours of rest; but at the hotel there were several more details which had to be completed and I was unable to get any sleep that night.

I returned to the field before daybreak on the morning of the twentieth. A light rain was falling which continued until almost dawn; consequently we did not move the ship to Roosevelt Field until much later than we had planned, and the take-off was delayed from daybreak until nearly eight o'clock.

At dawn the shower had passed, although the sky was overcast, and occasionally there would be some slight precipitation. The tail of the plane was lashed to a truck and escorted by a number of motorcycle police. The slow trip from Curtiss to Roosevelt was begun.

The ship was placed at the extreme west end of the field heading along the east and west runway, and the final fueling commenced.

About 7:40 A.M. the motor was started and at 7:52 I took off on the flight for Paris.

The field was a little soft due to the rain during the night and the heavily loaded plane gathered speed very slowly. After passing the half-way mark, however, it was apparent that I would be able to clear the obstructions at the end. I passed over a tractor by about fifteen feet and a telephone line by about twenty, with a fair reserve of flying speed. I believe that the ship would have taken off from a hard field with at least five hundred pounds more weight.

I turned slightly to the right to avoid some high trees on a hill directly ahead, but by the time I had gone a few hundred yards I had sufficient altitude to clear all obstructions and throttled the engine down to 1750 R.P.M. I took up a compass course at once and soon reached Long Island Sound where the Curtiss Oriole with its photographer, which had been escorting me, turned back.

The haze soon cleared and from Cape Cod through the southern half of Nova Scotia the weather and visibility were excellent. I was flying very low, sometimes as close as ten feet from the trees and water.

On the three hundred mile stretch of water between Cape Cod and Nova Scotia I passed within view of numerous fishing vessels.

The northern part of Nova Scotia contained a number of storm areas and several times I flew through cloudbursts.

As I neared the northern coast, snow appeared in patches on the ground and far to the eastward the coastline was covered with fog.

For many miles between Nova Scotia and Newfoundland the ocean was covered with caked ice but as I approached the coast the ice disappeared entirely and I saw several ships in this area.

I had taken up a course for St. Johns, which is south of the great Circle from New York to Paris, so that there would be no question of the fact that I had passed Newfoundland in case I was forced down in the north Atlantic.

I passed over numerous icebergs after leaving St. Johns, but saw no ships except near the coast.

Darkness set in about 8:15 New York time and a thin, low fog formed through which the white bergs showed up with surprising clearness. This fog became thicker and increased in height until within two hours I was just skimming the top of storm clouds at about ten thousand feet. Even at this altitude there was a thick haze through which only the stars directly overhead could be seen.

There was no moon and it was very dark. The tops of some of the storm clouds were several thousand feet above me and at one time, when I attempted to fly through one of the larger clouds, sleet started to collect on the plane and I was forced to turn around and get back into clear air immediately and then fly around any clouds which I could not get over.

The moon appeared on the horizon after about two hours of darkness; then the flying was much less complicated.

Dawn came at about 1 A.M. New York time and the temperature had risen until there was practically no remaining danger of sleet.

Shortly after sunrise the clouds became more broken although some of them were far above me and it was often necessary to fly through them, navigating by instruments only.

As the sun became higher, holes appeared in the fog. Through one the open water was visible, and I dropped down until less than a hundred feet above the waves. There was a strong wind blowing from the northwest and the ocean was covered with white caps.

After a few miles of fairly clear weather the ceiling lowered to zero and for nearly two hours I flew entirely blind through the fog at an altitude of about 1500 feet. Then the fog raised and the water was visible again.

On several more occasions it was necessary to fly by instrument for short periods; then the fog broke up into patches. These patches took on forms of every description. Numerous shorelines appeared, with trees perfectly outlined against the horizon. In fact, the mirages were so natural that, had I not been in mid-Atlantic and known that no land existed along my route, I would have taken them to be actual islands.

As the fog cleared I dropped down closer to the water, sometimes flying within ten feet of the waves and seldom higher than two hundred.

There is a cushion of air close to the ground or water through which a plane flies with less effort than when at a higher altitude, and for hours at a time I took advantage of this factor.

Also, it was less difficult to determine the wind drift near the water. During the entire flight the wind was strong enough to produce white caps on the waves. When one of these formed, the foam would be blown off, showing the wind's direction and approximate velocity. This foam remained on the water long enough for me to obtain a general idea of my drift.

During the day I saw a number of porpoises and a few birds but no ships, although I understand that two different boats reported me passing over.

The first indication of my approach to the European Coast was a small fishing boat which I first noticed a few miles ahead and slightly to the south of my course. There were several of these fishing boats grouped within a few miles of each other.

I flew over the first boat without seeing any signs of life. As I circled over the second, however, a man's face appeared, looking out of the cabin window.

I have carried on short conversations with people on the ground by flying low with throttled engine, shouting a question, and receiving the answer by some signal. When I saw this fisherman I decided to try to get him to point towards land. I had no sooner made the decision than the futility of the effort became apparent. In all likelihood he could not speak English, and even if he could he would undoubtedly be far too astounded to answer. However, I circled again and closing the throttle as the plane passed within a few feet of the boat I shouted, "Which way is Ireland?" Of course the attempt was useless, and I continued on my course.

Less than an hour later a rugged and semi-mountainous coastline appeared to the northeast. I was flying less than two hundred feet from the water when I sighted it. The shore was fairly distinct and not over ten or fifteen miles away. A light haze coupled with numerous local storm areas had prevented my seeing it from a long distance.

The coastline came down from the north, curved over towards the east. I had very little doubt that it was the southwestern end of Ireland but in order to make sure I changed my course towards the nearest point of land.

I located Cape Valentia and Dingle Bay, then resumed my compass course towards Paris.

After leaving Ireland I passed a number of steamers and was seldom out of sight of a ship.

In a little over two hours the coast of England appeared. My course passed over Southern England and a little south of Plymouth; then across the English Channel, striking France over Cherbourg.

The English farms were very impressive from the air in contrast to ours in America. They appeared extremely small and unusually neat and tidy with their stone and hedge fences.

I was flying at about a fifteen hundred foot altitude over England and as I crossed the Channel and passed over Cherbourg, France, I had probably seen more of that part of Europe than many native Europeans. The visibility was good and the country could be seen for miles around.

People who have taken their first flight often remark that no one knows what the locality he lives in is like until he has seen it from above. Countries take on different characteristics from the air.

The sun went down shortly after passing Cherbourg and soon the beacons along the Paris-London airway became visible.

I first saw the lights of Paris a little before ten P.M., or five P.M. New York time, and a few minutes later I was circling the Eiffel Tower at an altitude of about four thousand feet.

The lights of Le Bourget were plainly visible, but appeared to be very close to Paris. I had understood that the field was farther from the city, so continued out to the northeast into the country for four or five miles to make sure that there was not another field farther out which might be Le Bourget. Then I returned and spiralled down closer to the lights. Presently I could make out long lines of hangars, and the roads appeared to be jammed with cars.

I flew low over the field once, then circled around into the wind and landed.

After the plane stopped rolling I turned it around and started to taxi back to the lights. The entire field ahead, however, was covered with thousands of people all running towards my ship. When the first few arrived, I attempted to get them to hold the rest of the crowd back, away from the plane, but apparently no one could understand, or would have been able to conform to my request if he had.

I cut the switch to keep the propeller from killing someone, and attempted to organize an impromptu guard for the plane. The impossibility of any immediate organization became apparent, and when parts of the ship began to crack from the pressure of the multitude I decided to climb out of the cockpit in order to draw the crowd away.

Speaking was impossible; no words could be heard in the uproar and nobody apparently cared to hear any. I started to climb out of the cockpit, but as soon as one foot appeared through the door I was dragged the rest of the way without assistance on my part.

For nearly half an hour I was unable to touch the ground, during which time I was ardently carried around in what seemed to be a very small area, and in every position it is possible to be in. Every one had the best of intentions but no one seemed to know just what they were.

The French military flyers very resourcefully took the situation in hand. A number of them mingled with the crowd; then, at a given signal, they placed my helmet on an American correspondent and cried: "Here is Lindbergh." That helmet on an American was sufficient evidence. The correspondent immediately became the center of attraction, and while he was being taken protestingly to the Reception Committee via a rather devious route, I managed to get inside one of the hangars.

Meanwhile a second group of soldiers and police had surrounded the plane and soon placed it out of danger in another hangar.

The French ability to handle an unusual situation with speed and capability was remarkably demonstrated that night at Le Bourget.

Ambassador Herrick extended me an invitation to remain at his Embassy while I was in Paris, which I gladly accepted. But grateful as I was at the time, it did not take me long to realize that a kind Providence had placed me in Ambassador Herrick's hands. The ensuing days found me in situations that I had certainly never expected to be in and in which I relied on Ambassador Herrick's sympathetic aid.

These situations were brought about by the whole-hearted welcome to me—an American—that touched me beyond any point that any words can express. I left France with a debt of gratitude which, though I cannot repay it, I shall always remember. If the French people had been acclaiming their own gallant airmen, Nungesser and Coli, who were lost only after fearlessly departing in the face of conditions insurmountably greater than those that confronted me, their enthusiastic welcome and graciousness could not have been greater.

In Belgium as well, I was received with a warmth which reflected more than simply a passing curiosity in a trans-Atlantic flight, but which was rather a demonstration by the people of their interest in a new means of transportation which eventually would bring still closer together the new world and the old. Their welcome, too, will be a cherished memory for all time.

In England, I experienced one final unforgettable demonstration of friendship for an American. That spontaneous wonderful reception during my brief visit seemed typical of what I had always heard of the good sportsmanship of the English.

My words to all those friends in Europe are inadequate, but my feelings of appreciation are boundless.

When I was contemplating the flight to Paris I looked forward to making a short tour of Europe with especial regard to the various airports and aeronautical activities.

After I arrived, however, the necessity for returning to America in the near future became apparent and, after a consultation with Ambassador Houghton, who informed me that President Coolidge was sending the cruiser *Memphis* to Cherbourg for my return journey to America, I flew the "Spirit of St. Louis" to Gosport early one morning. There it was dismantled and crated, through the courtesy of the Royal Air Force which also placed a Woodcock pursuit plane at my disposal.

I returned to London in the Woodcock and a few days later flew to Paris in another R.A.F. machine of the same type.

I remained overnight in Paris, and early the next morning flew a French Breguet to Cherbourg where the cruiser *Memphis* was waiting.

Admiral Burrage met me at the dock, and after going aboard the *Memphis* I became acquainted with Captain Lackey and the officers of the ship. During the trip across they extended every courtesy and did everything within their power to make the voyage a pleasant one.

A description of my welcome back to the United States would, in itself, be sufficient to fill a larger volume than this. I am not an author by profession, and my pen could never express the gratitude which I feel towards the American people.

The voyage up the Potomac and to the Monument Grounds in Washington; up the Hudson River and along Broadway; over the Mississippi and to St. Louis—to do justice to these occasions would require a far greater writer than myself.

Washington, New York, and finally St. Louis and home. Each of these cities has left me with an impression that I shall never forget, and a debt of gratitude which I can never repay.

COLUMBIA LANDS IN GERMANY

by Richard Montague

Rumors were spreading that the *Columbia* was about to start for Germany, which Levine denied, but shortly after midnight on June 4 [1927] Chamberlin announced that he would take off in a few hours. He refused to name his destination, but at the hangar he received a radiogram from Lincoln Eyre, Berlin correspondent of the *New York Times,* saying that all Germany was awaiting the *Columbia's* arrival. Chamberlin grinned. "Well, we'll be glad to drop in on them on the way back," he said, leaving reporters with the impression that he hoped to fly even farther. He did say he would keep the plane in the air as long as the engine functioned and the gasoline supply held out.

This time he gave the Nassau County cops the takeoff notice they wanted so that they wouldn't thwart the project. In fact, a squad of motorcycle police escorted the *Columbia* as she was towed tail first to Roosevelt Field. The police also kept a small crowd at bay while mechanics loaded the main gas tank with 390 gallons and put aboard fifty-five additional gallons in 5-gallon cans.

Who, if anybody, was going along with Chamberlin? When reporters asked the airman, he only smiled. Nobody paid much attention to a black limousine that rolled up near the starting area at the west end of the runway. In it were Mr. and Mrs. Levine, but they had come, it was assumed, just to see the *Columbia* take off.

Levine, in a pin-striped blue business suit and without a hat for his balding head, got out of the car with a roll of charts. He walked over to the plane and thrust the charts through the window. "Are you going?" somebody asked him. Levine merely looked at the questioner. Somebody also inquired who was going to be the navigator. "He's not here yet," Levine replied. A few minutes later he disappeared in the crowd.

Harold Kinkaid asked that the engine be started. Kinkaid, known generally as "Doc," was a Wright engine man who had accompanied Byrd to Spitsbergen and tuned up Lindbergh's engine. Now he listened with an expert ear to the roar of another Whirlwind. "Never heard a motor sound better," he said. A mechanic shut it off.

Another mechanic discovered that the main gas tank would hold ten more gallons. These were poured in to make the total gasoline load 455 gallons, five more than Lindbergh had carried. Then Carisi, who had worked on the plane devotedly for months, started the engine again. Although he had often declared that he was not "one of those emotional wops," he was so overcome by the apparent certainty that the *Columbia* was really going at last that he climbed up to the window and planted a resounding kiss on Chamberlin's cheek.

Chamberlin idled the engine for a few minutes and then opened it up. The roar resounded down the field and the plane trembled and strained against the wheel chocks. Chamberlin throttled it down again, looked at a knot of persons behind the ropes and nodded. And suddenly out of the crowd darted Levine. Keeping his head down and looking at nobody, he ran around the plane to the other side, opened the door and climbed in. Quickly he closed the door and slumped down in the seat next to Chamberlin, keeping his gaze averted from his wife.

Grace Levine was once known as "the Belle of Williamsburg," having won two beauty contests in that section of Brooklyn. She had been a good wife to Levine, had borne him two children and stood by him in the face of criticism and ridicule. She and her husband had discussed recent rumors that he might fly to Europe with Chamberlin, and together they had laughed at the absurdity. Once she had said she would burn the plane if he tried to fly across the ocean in it.

Now she turned to some friends who had come with her to see the takeoff. "What's all this foolishness of Charles getting into the plane?" she asked. Nobody knew. She became frightened and started to get out of the car.

Carisi ran up to reassure her. "It's all right," he said. "It's only a test run." And indeed, for a while it seemed to be only that. When the wheel chocks were removed Chamberlin gunned the plane down the runway for several hundred yards. Then, to avoid hitting some people whom the police hadn't kept back far enough, he turned off the course and returned to the starting area near Curtiss Field. He handled the heavily laden craft as if she were a highly maneuverable fighter plane.

Carisi sprinted over to the machine and stood beside the window, one foot on a wheel. "What are you doing, Mr. Levine?" he yelled. "Your wife is going out of her mind! She has got the idea that you are going to Europe in the plane!"

But Grace Levine was now smiling happily. Her husband wasn't going to fly, after all. She laughed at her former nervousness. How foolish she had been! She was still laughing when Chamberlin opened up the engine again. The propeller blast blew Carisi away and the *Columbia* started to roll.

Now the monoplane was roaring over the same path Lindbergh had taken, a runway that was dry instead of soggy. With six inches more wingspread—forty-six and a half feet—and a load some 500 pounds heavier than the Ryan had had, the *Columbia* took off in 2,000 feet, less than half the distance her rival had used.

It was a beautiful Saturday morning. The sun was a glowing red ball and the light clouds above it were edged with gold. But Grace Levine was sobbing hysterically as the small plane climbed into the air shortly after six o'clock. "He isn't really going!" she cried. "He isn't really going!" And then, as the plane became a dot and disappeared, she began to weep bitterly.

The faithful Carisi came over and put his arms around her. "He'll make it," he told her. "You should be proud of him. He's a brave boy."

Only a few people besides Chamberlin had known that Levine was planning to go. Bellanca had suspected and opposed the project because he felt that Chamberlin needed a competent navigator. Still another who had had an inkling of Levine's intention was Samuel Hartman, his attorney.

Hartman told reporters later that Levine had sat up most of the night before the takeoff writing notes to his wife and his lawyer and making a will disposing of an estate of $5,000,000. The note to Hartman said: "Well, I'm off. Bet you'll be surprised, but don't worry. We will make it. Will cable you first moment I can and wish you would sail over to join me when I dine with Mussolini. Have arranged to have you continue checking out the monthly allowance checks should anything happen, but I am sure I'll be back soon enough."

The monthly allowance checks, Hartman explained, referred to various charities and needy individuals. They amounted, he estimated, to $30,000 a year. He didn't name the recipients. The statement that they existed startled many persons who had been exposed to Levine.

This tale, and the courage Levine was showing in attempting a transatlantic flight, caused many to wonder if he wasn't a good fellow, after all. There was talk that whatever his faults, he had vindicated himself. Now that he was at least temporarily famous, people wanted to believe in his essential nobility, an attribute they had already accorded Lindbergh and which on lesser occasions Americans bestow on baseball players, prize fighters and football stars.

The *Columbia*'s takeoff made big headlines both in the United States and Europe, although the plane's destination was uncertain. The two most likely objectives seemed to be Berlin or Rome, though there was also speculation about Warsaw, Vienna and Prague.

The German capital prepared for a welcome that would outdo Paris' greeting of Lindbergh. High government officials, it was said, would meet the gallant fliers at Tempelhof Airport, where three thousand police would keep the immense crowd from storming the plane. The Berlin field, as well as airports at Cologne, Hamburg and Bremen, would be kept lighted through the night. And Lufthansa, the German air trust, would have planes flying along the western border to meet the *Columbia* and escort her in.

Newspapers ran off extras about the flight, and hotels set up information bureaus to provide excited guests with the latest news on the plane's progress. Attention centered on Chamberlin rather than on Levine, who was then known to few Europeans. It was considered a happy omen that the last two syllables of the pilot's name spelled the name of the city toward which the Bellanca seemed to be headed.

But Rome saw itself, not Berlin, as the fliers' goal. After all, for a plane designed by an Italian, what could be a more appropriate destination than the Eternal City? Italian newspaper presses whirled out extra after extra. But even these weren't enough. Crowds collected in front of the newspaper offices demanding even later intelligence about the machine that was supposedly speeding toward them.

Aboard the plane all was not entirely well. After the first hundred miles Chamberlin noticed that the earth inductor compass was misbehaving. He was attempting to follow a great-circle course modified, in accordance with last-minute weather forecasts, by Goldsborough and Balchen. Setting the indicator to match his course, he tried to keep the pointer at zero, but it wouldn't stay put. At Newport, Rhode Island, they were four or five miles off course, and when they reached what appeared to be Cape Cod the needle began swinging from side to side in a meaningless and maddening dance. Moreover, there seemed to be an extra hook on the arm of land below that didn't appear on their chart. They couldn't be sure they were really over the Cape.

Chamberlin circled about, hoping that the aberrant compass would return to normal. They had flown about 200 miles and had 3,400 to go. Should they rely on their $50 magnetic compass to guide them? Or should they return to Roosevelt Field and have the $1,000 earth inductor adjusted? They talked it over and decided to go on.

Chamberlin kept circling until he got a bearing on what he thought was the tip of Cape Cod and had oriented himself with the help of the sun. Then, steering by the magnetic compass, which was jiggling from the engine vibrations, he headed out over the water toward Nova Scotia. The air was smooth and they went along a few hundred feet over the ocean, sighting several sailing yachts and fishing smacks and waving to their crews. But a northeast wind was rising and slowed them down.

In two hours, Chamberlin figured, they ought to hit Yarmouth. But the second hour passed with only blue water below. A third hour faded into the past. What if the magnetic compass had failed too and was prompting them to fly in circles on a crazy course that would end in a splash and a hiss and a silence?

The main gas tank was shaped like an upright piano and the eleven 5-gallon cans were strapped on its ledge. Levine now emptied the first of these into the tank. Each can was fitted with a petcock and the tank had a rubber hose connection, so the operation was simple. When a can was emptied, Levine threw it overboard to clear the space on the tank shelf and give access to the rear of the cabin.

Finally, to their relief they sighted Nova Scotia. Their magnetic compass was doing its stuff, after all. Chamberlin took the new bearing his charts called for and pointed the *Columbia*'s nose toward Newfoundland. The wind had now veered from dead ahead to quartering from the east and southeast. To counteract its thrust and to keep the plane on course, Chamberlin had to crab sideways into the wind. As the plane flew on, her position in relation to the magnetic pole varied, but Goldsborough and

Balchen had taken this into account on the charts. Chamberlin followed the magnetic bearings they had given, compensating for his estimated wind drift.

Soon he let Levine take the stick and reached for the food Mrs. Chamberlin had prepared. There were ten chicken sandwiches on toasted rye bread, two vacuum bottles of chicken soup, a vacuum bottle of coffee and half a dozen oranges. The hot soup tasted fine, Chamberlin reported later. But he took only a bite or two from a sandwich.

By the time they reached Halifax the wind was blowing across their course from the south, necessitating more crabbing and slowing their progress eastward by about 30 miles an hour. They were now two hours behind schedule because of the head and quartering winds, but the air currents were at last shifting in their favor and starting to push the plane along. And since the magnetic compass seemed to be working satisfactorily, things began to look up.

Chamberlin climbed to 2,000 feet to let the plane take advantage of the tailwind, and headed for Trepassey, Newfoundland. He had decided to go slightly south of the great-circle route to avoid a storm area shown on the weather map. By the time they reached Trepassey, Levine had emptied and thrown out the last of the 5-gallon cans and the way to the rear of the cabin was open. Chamberlin let his companion take over the plane again and went back to put on his cold-weather clothing—heavy woolen drawers to be pulled over trousers and a woolen shirt with parka hood. Then he stretched out on the gas-tank ledge to get a little rest before the coming night over the ocean. But he couldn't sleep.

Some 2,500 feet below them stretched the last of Newfoundland they would see—rough, desolate country blotched with swamps and wasteland. After a while they sighted the ocean and, a few miles offshore, what seemed to be the white sail of a fishing boat. The red sun was sliding down behind the world to the west and its last rays picked out the white triangle and turned it a luminous pink. It was like a great jewel risen from the blue of the sea. Then they saw it was an iceberg. Chamberlin took a final bearing and headed east across the Atlantic. Levine grinned. "Europe next stop," he said. "Well, here goes nothing."

They flew on toward the night which was creeping over the northern sea. Soon they were looking down on a scatter of icebergs. While admiring their beauty, Chamberlin used them to check the drift of the plane until they faded like ghosts into the darkness.

The air was now so calm that the remarkably stable plane was flying itself without the touch of human hand or foot. Chamberlin had attached a spring to the rudder bar which he had devised to compensate for propeller torque, and left the controls alone for as much as two hundred miles at a stretch.

Presently they were soaring above clouds. And then, through a rift, they saw the lights of a ship three or four thousand feet down. Levine blinked a flashlight but there was no answering signal. The incident depressed them. They wanted to be sighted and reported often; it would reassure their wives and facilitate a search if they had to come down at sea. But after an hour or two, when they were flying at 3,000 feet, they saw the lights of another ship. And this one instantly answered Levine's flashlight blinkings. Immensely cheered, they flew on. Only later did they learn that no report from either vessel was ever received on shore.

Soon clouds blanketed the world below and then the gray mass started up toward them. The Bellanca climbed until she could climb no more. With her still-heavy load of gasoline she couldn't struggle higher than 15,000 feet, and the cloud bank ahead of her loomed three or four thousand feet higher. The short northern night was fading ahead of them and giving way to a slow dawn. In this meager light the plane entered the gray mist. The temperature was one degree below freezing. A thin layer of ice began to form on the cabin windshield and on the leading edges of the wings.

Wing ice was a terror to the fliers of those days, since they had no equipment to melt it or break it up. And many a plane crashed because the thin film changed the contours and destroyed the lifting effectiveness of wings, as well as adding to the load the machine was carrying. So Chamberlin cut the throttle and headed down through the blankness, hoping for a space between the underside of the cloud bank and the sea. He also hoped that the altimeter would continue to work—a faulty reading could plunge them into the waves.

Ten thousand feet. Six thousand. Three thousand. Two. Still nothing visible below but gray. One thousand. Chamberlin flattened out a little. He would ease her down to a hundred feet but no farther. Then he would pull up and fly on and perhaps leave the mist behind.

He had been revving up the engine at intervals to keep the spark plugs free of oil so that the Whirlwind would run smoothly when he needed it. And suddenly he did need it. Below 800 feet the gray ghostly stuff thinned, and whitecaps appeared. There was enough light now to see that it was raining.

Apparently this was the storm area shown on Dr. Kimball's weather map. They could run out of it, he had said, by turning south. Chamberlin banked to the right, but for an hour the rain continued to beat against the windshield. Then they emerged into beautiful clear weather.

The ocean had a brown appearance and the air was so warm that both men discarded their heavy clothing. Chamberlin decided they were over the Gulf Stream and coursing the steamer lanes to Europe. He set a new great-circle course for Land's End on the southwest coast of England.

Their watches were still running on New York time, five hours behind London's, so when the sun appeared out of the sea they did some quick figuring. This sunrise was two and a half hours earlier than the June 5 sunrise would be in New York. Hurrah! They must be halfway across the ocean.

The wind was still behind them and the Bellanca was moving toward Europe at a speed which was probably around 120 miles an hour. The magnetic compass, as far as they could tell from the position of the sun, was still giving accurate guidance. They celebrated with a Sunday breakfast of oranges, chicken soup and coffee.

They were flying at an altitude between 2,000 and 3,000 feet now, so that the tailwind could do its best for them. About nine o'clock they sighted a Scandinavian tramp, though they couldn't make out her name. Chamberlin came down to 300 feet, but the name was still only a jumble of letters to the fliers. They circled the ship and the crew waved. They felt sure that the ship would report them—and learned later that she didn't. After a couple of hours they sighted another tramp, and again couldn't make out the name. Again they thought that she would report them; they were wrong this time too.

But at four-thirty that afternoon they got one of the big thrills of the trip. The liner *Mauretania* appeared so suddenly and so close that it seemed as if she had sprung out of the sea. She had come over the horizon under the plane's nose at 25 knots or so, and the Bellanca, with a quartering 25-mile wind behind her, was doing 120 miles an hour or better. The big Cunarder, with her four red funnels, white superstructure and black hull, and with flags flying and decks lined with passengers, was a glorious sight. Chamberlin pointed the plane down toward her and flashed by at the height of her top deck. Then he banked sharply and came up on the opposite side.

Throttling the plane, which was now slowed further by the wind, he kept just abreast of the liner, while her wildly excited passengers tossed hats, books and umbrellas into the air. They had read about the *Columbia*'s progress in the ship's news bulletins and could readily identify her from the Department of Commerce experimental license numbers on her wings—NX 237—and the number 140 on her fuselage, given her for the national air races a year earlier.

As they flew along abreast of the liner, Levine noticed a group of officers on the bridge. He leaned out the window and made motions with his hands as if he were punching a telegraph key. The officers stopped waving and nodded and the *Mauretania* did what was asked, giving the United States the first news that the plane was nearing Europe.

Levine leafed through a copy of the *New York Times* which they had aboard. On the marine page he read that the liner had left Southampton at noon the day before. Then he looked again at the chart, which showed the lanes that transatlantic liners were using that month. From these data he and Chamberlin calculated they were 400 or 500 miles west of Land's End (actually the distance was about 350) and pretty well on course.

Then Chamberlin opened the throttle, pulled ahead of the liner, banked and came back right over the ship and along her wake. This invisible air path would lead him to Land's End. He had to crab into the wind to stay with it. The maneuver gave him what he needed—both the compass heading and the correction to compensate for the wind.

The *Mauretania*'s passengers were still waving when the *Columbia* was a speck in the sky. They had had another unforeseen excitation earlier the same afternoon: the Cunarder had passed the U.S. Navy cruiser *Memphis,* which was bringing Lindbergh home. Now her passengers had seen two more heroes in the making.

Half an hour after leaving the *Mauretania,* Chamberlin sighted the *Memphis.* But she was about ten miles to the south and he turned down Levine's suggestion that they fly over and "jazz her up" a bit. The afternoon was waning and so was the perfect weather. A haze dead ahead was thickening, low-hanging clouds had appeared and flashes of lightning heralded rain squalls. Before sunset they saw the *Transylvania* and circled over the liner. Thereafter they passed a tanker but didn't come down to identify her. And then, through the haze, they saw the low cliffs of Land's End, lit by the long rays of the setting sun.

The wind behind them had strengthened, and while their air path over the sea was smooth, it became turbulent as they circled above the coast, checking its outlines against their charts. Dusk was moving in over the green countryside. With a black, stormy night in prospect there was a great temptation to land on the hospitable Cornish shore.

Now the clouds were becoming thick. Chamberlin climbed above them and headed eastward. Through a rift in the rack he saw Plymouth and got another bearing: they were about five hour's flying time from Berlin. However, the clouds were rising higher and Chamberlin realized that he was very tired, that he might not be able to find the German capital, that if he did find it he might have trouble landing in the dark. He headed in the direction of Berlin but decided that even if he reached it he would stay aloft until dawn. There was plenty of gas to last through the short night.

The Bellanca had climbed to 15,000 feet. Now, with the cloud mass still rising straight ahead, she had to go higher. Chamberlin nursed her up to 18,000, then 20,000 feet. Still the cloud barrier towered above them.

Should they try to fly through it? Up ahead they might hit a mountain while their altimeter showed they still had plenty of altitude. The only thing to do, Chamberlin felt, was to fly along the western edge of the cloud range and kill time until it became light enough for him to see if it extended all the way down to the earth. So he flew north for fifteen minutes, then turned and cruised south for another fifteen, repeating the turnabout over and over. Several times he felt sure he was flying over the North Sea, for great black canyons in the cloud range indicated the presence of water far below. The moon had slipped down beneath the sea of clouds but a glittering spangle of stars provided both welcome company and golden gauges to steer by.

Chamberlin was nearing exhaustion. The thin air was making the plane hard to handle; he had to work the controls almost continually to keep her level. And insufficient oxygen, added to nearly forty hours of sleeplessness, was making him light-headed. Dawn paled the east again and Chamberlin realized that he would pass out soon unless he got some rest. They were still flying at 20,000 feet or higher, with the cloud floor visible below them. Surely Levine could handle the ship for a while.

"See what you can do with her," Chamberlin told his companion and eased himself onto the gas-tank shelf. Levine managed to keep the plane level for about ten minutes; then, either by losing altitude or by following a box canyon in the clouds, he got into the bewildering mist. As inexperienced pilots sometimes do, he tried so hard to keep the Bellanca horizontal that he pulled the nose up too far and the plane stalled. Unable to rise higher, she pointed the left wing toward the earth and went into a deadly spiral. Since Levine could see nothing but mist, he had no idea what was happening.

But Chamberlin, half asleep, sensed disaster. He slid off the tank and into his seat. The Bellanca's wings had started to shiver. The rudder was flapping violently back and forth, shaking the rear end of the plane as if it would tear it off, at the same time whipping the rudder bar to and fro so viciously that Chamberlin didn't dare try to stop it all at once.

The second memorable event of the trip affected the two men in different ways. Chamberlin was badly scared but Levine enjoyed the situation. He had taken his hand off the quivering stick and his feet off the jerking rudder bar and was sitting there chuckling at the antics of the plane. She was behaving, he said later, like a bucking bronco.

These antics, the rush of air and the instruments told Chamberlin that they were plunging toward the sea at terrifying speed. The altimeter needle was racing past hundred-foot marks as if they represented inches. The needle on the airspeed indicator was jammed against the pin which marked 160 miles an hour, the most the instrument was capable of showing.

Chamberlin knew that if he tried to pull out too suddenly he probably would rip the wings off the plane, and if he pushed too hard against the rudder bar it would break the control cables. He set about the latter task gingerly, pushing at the bar with increasing strength as it neared the end of its swing. Gradually he tamed the berserk bar and was able to steer out of the spiral. Then he slowly flattened the dive until the plane lost her dangerous speed.

By this time the altimeter showed 4,000 feet. They had dropped more than three miles. Heading east, they were still in the gray mist. All they could see through the windshield was the blue spurts from the Whirlwind's exhaust pipes. The flames turned the haze into an eerie blue blur.

Chamberlin figured they were now flying over Germany. He thought they must be somewhere near the Harz Mountains, and although he knew these were several thousand feet high, he decided to go lower to try to find some landmark shown on their chart. They slid down below 1,000 feet before they came out of the gray to find themselves flying in rain over a river. Soon they saw the glare of blast furnaces. Chamberlin thought they must be over Essen. Levine disagreed. He said the lights below were those of Bremerhaven. As proof, he added that he had been in Bremerhaven once.

They flew around in the rain, looking for a name on a factory roof. From the air the scene looked like the traditional concept of hell. Flames flared up from the blast furnaces, painting the low clouds a lurid red. Almost as soon as the fire gushed up, the rain-filled gusts slapped it down and spread it over the ground. Even if they had wanted to land in the area it would have been well-nigh impossible in that storm. Not until the next day did they find out that the city was Dortmund.

Soon they saw white flares being fired into the air not far away. They headed toward them and saw a flying field. On it, in the growing light, they spotted a few men. Chamberlin idled the engine, came down to about twenty feet, stuck his hand out the window and yelled downward at the top of his voice, *"Nach Berlin? Nach Berlin?"* He swept over their heads and banked around to see if they had understood him. All of them pointed in about the same direction. Chamberlin headed that way.

It was just after four-thirty and the fuel was getting low. They were pointing eastward from Dortmund on a course that would take them south of the German capital. But both men thought they were heading for Berlin and Chamberlin held the course until the gasoline gauge neared zero. He wanted to land near some village while he still had enough fuel left to use the engine in landing. But Levine wanted to go on until the last drop was used, so Chamberlin told him to go to the rear of the cabin and act as ballast, for with empty tanks the Bellanca was nose-heavy. A few minutes later the faithful engine coughed and stopped. Chamberlin brought the plane into the wind and came down in a pretty, dead-stick landing. Shortly before six o'clock the Bellanca rolled to a smooth stop in a small wheat field near the town of Eisleben, birthplace of Martin Luther.

They had been in the air for almost forty-three hours and were still 110 miles short of Berlin, but their straight-line distance from Roosevelt Field was 3,905 miles, 295 miles longer than Lindbergh's. Actually their zigzag course had taken them well over 4,000 miles. Indeed, Chamberlin estimated later that in the last ten hours of their journey they had moved eastward only 300 miles, though they must have flown 1,000 miles in that time.

They had come down safely, however, and there was plenty of reason to be thankful. In the sudden silence they heard the singing of birds. They got out of the plane and stretched their stiff limbs.

FIRST TO THE NORTH POLE

by Richard Evelyn Byrd

With a total load of nearly 10,000 pounds we raced down the runway. The rough snow ahead loomed dangerously near but we never reached it. We were off for our great adventure!

Beneath us were our shipmates—every one anxious to go along, but unselfishly wild with delight that we were at last off—running in our wake, waving their arms, and throwing their hats in the air. As long as I live I can never forget that sight, or those splendid fellows. They had given us our great chance.

For months previous to this hour, utmost attention had been paid to every detail that would assure our margin of safety in case of accident, and to the perfection of our scientific results in the case of success.

We had a short-wave radio set operated by a hand dynamo, should we be forced down on the ice. A handmade sledge presented to us by Amundsen was stowed in the fuselage, on which to carry our food and clothing should we be compelled to walk to Greenland. We had food for ten weeks. Our main staple, pemmican, consisting of chopped-up dried meat, fat, sugar and raisins, was supplemented by chocolate, pilot-bread, tea, malted milk, powdered chocolate, butter, sugar and cream cheese, all of which form a highly concentrated diet.

Other articles of equipment were a rubber boat for crossing open leads if forced down, reindeer-skin, polar-bear and seal fur clothes, boots and gloves, primus stove, rifle, pistol, shotgun and ammunition; tent, knives, ax, medical kit and smoke bombs—all as compact as humanly possible.

If we should come down on the ice the reason it would take us so long to get back, if we got back at all, was that we could not return Spitzbergen way on account of the strong tides. We would have to march Etah way and would have to kill enough seal, polar-bear and musk-ox to last through the Arctic nights.

The first stage of our navigation was the simple one of dead reckoning, or following the well-known landmarks in the vicinity of Kings Bay, which we had just left. We climbed to 2,000 feet to get a good view of the coast and the magnificent snow-covered mountains inland. Within an hour of taking the air we passed the rugged and glacier-laden land and crossed the edge of the polar ice pack. It was much nearer to the land than we had expected. Over to the east was a point where the ice field was very near the land.

We looked ahead at the sea ice gleaming in the rays of the midnight sun—a fascinating scene whose lure had drawn famous men into its clutches, never to return. It was with a feeling of exhilaration that we felt that for the first time in history two mites of men could gaze upon its charms, and discover its secrets, out of reach of those sharp claws.

Perhaps! There was still that "perhaps," for if we should have a forced landing disaster might easily follow.

It was only natural for Bennett and me to wonder whether or not we would ever get back to this small island we were leaving, for all the airmen explorers who had preceded us in attempts to reach the Pole by aviation had met with disaster or near disaster.

Though it was important to hit the Pole from the standpoint of achievement, it was more important to do so from that of our lives, so that we could get back to Spitzbergen, a target none too big. We could not fly back to land from an unknown position. We must put every possible second of time and our best concentration on the job of navigating and of flying a straight course—our very lives depended on it.

As there are no landmarks on the ice, Polar Sea navigation by aircraft is similar to that on the ocean, where there is nothing but sun and stars and moon from which to determine one's position. The altitude above the sea horizon of one of these celestial bodies is taken with the sextant. Then, by mathematical calculations, requiring an hour or so to work out, the ship is located somewhere on an imaginary line. The Polar Sea horizon, however, cannot always be depended upon, due to roughness of the ice. Therefore we had a specially designed instrument that would enable us to take the altitude without the horizon. I used the same instrument that we had developed for the 1919 trans-Atlantic flight.

Again, should the navigator of a fast airplane take an hour to get his line of position, by the time he plotted it on his chart he would be a hundred miles or so away from the point at which he took the sight. He must therefore have quick means of making his astronomical calculations.

We were familiar with one means of calculation which takes advantage of some interesting astronomical conditions existing at the North Pole. It is a graphical method that does away largely with mathematical calculations, so that the entire operation of taking the altitude of the sun and laying down the line of position could be done in a very few minutes.

This method was taught me by G. W. Littlebales of the Navy Hydrographic Office and was first discovered by Arthur Hinks of the Royal Geographic Society.

So much for the locating of position in the Polar Sea by astronomy, which must be done by the navigator to check up and correct the course steered by the pilot. The compass is generally off the true course a greater or less degree, on account of faulty steering, currents, wind, etc.

Our chief concern was to steer as nearly due north as possible. This could not be done with the ordinarily dependable magnetic compass, which points only in the general direction of the North Magnetic Pole, lying on Boothia Peninsula, Canada, more than a thousand miles south of the North Geographical Pole.

If the compass pointed exactly toward the Magnetic Pole the magnetic bearing of the North Geographical Pole could be calculated mathematically for any place on the Polar Sea. But as there is generally some local condition affecting the needle, the variation of the compass from true north can be found only by actual trial.

Since this trial could not have been made over unknown regions, the true directions the compass needle would point along our route were not known. Also, since the directive force of the earth's magnetism is small in the Far North, there is a tendency of the needle toward sluggishness in indicating a change in direction of the plane, and toward undue swinging after it has once started to move.

Nor would the famous gyroscopic compass work up there, as when nearing the Pole its axis would have a tendency to point straight up in the air.

There was only one thing to do—to depend upon the sun. For this we used a sun-compass. The same type instrument that had been invented and constructed for our 1925 expedition by Albert H. Bumstead, chief cartographer of the National Geographic Society. I do not hesitate to say that without it we could not have reached the Pole; it is even doubtful if we could have hit Spitzbergen on our return flight.

Of course, the sun was necessary for the use of this compass. Its principle is a kind of a reversal of that of the sundial. In the latter, the direction of north is known and the shadow of the sun gives the time of day. With the sun-compass, the time of day is known, and the shadow of the sun, when it bisects the hand of the 24-hour clock, indicates the direction after the instrument has been set.

Then there was the influence of the wind that had to be allowed for. An airplane, in effect, is a part of the wind, just as a ship in a current floats with the speed of the current. If, for example, a thirty-mile-an-hour wind is blowing at right angles to the course, the plane will be taken 30 miles an hour to one side of its course. This is called "drift" and can be compensated for by an instrument called the drift-indicator, which we had also developed for the first trans-Atlantic flight.

We used the drift-indicator through the trapdoor in the plane, and had so arranged the cabin that there was plenty of room for navigating. There was also a fair-sized chartboard.

As exact Greenwich time was necessary, we carried two chronometers that I had kept in my room for weeks. I knew their error to within a second. There seems to be a tendency for chronometers to slow up when exposed to the cold. With this in mind we had taken their cold-weather error.

As we sped along over the white field below I spent the busiest and most concentrated moments of my life. Though we had confidence in our instruments and methods, we were trying them for the first time over the

Polar Sea. First, we obtained north and south bearings on a mountain range on Spitzbergen which we could see for a long distance out over the ice. These checked fairly well with the sun-compass. But I had absolute confidence in the sun-compass.

We could see mountains astern gleaming in the sun at least a hundred miles behind us. That was our last link with civilization. The unknown lay ahead.

Bennett and I took turns piloting. At first Bennett was steering, and for some unaccountable reason the plane veered from the course time and time again, to the right. He could glance back where I was working, through a door leading to the two pilots' seats. Every minute or two he would look at me, to be checked if necessary, on the course by the sun-compass. If he happened to be off the course I would wave him to the right or left until he got on it again. Once every three minutes while I was navigating I checked the wind drift and ground speed, so that in case of a change in wind I could detect it immediately and allow for it.

We had three sets of gloves which I constantly changed to fit the job in hand, and sometimes removed entirely for short periods to write or figure on the chart. I froze my face and one of my hands in taking sights with the instruments from the trapdoors. But I noticed these frostbites at once and was more careful thereafter in the future. Ordinarily a frostbite need not be dangerous if detected in time and if the blood is rubbed back immediately into the affected parts. We also carried leather helmets that would cover the whole face when necessary to use them.

We carried two sun-compasses. One was fixed to a trapdoor in the top of the navigator's cabin; the other was movable, so that when the great wing obscured the sun from the compass on the trapdoor, the second could be used inside the cabin, through the open windows.

Every now and then I took sextant sights of the sun to see where the lines of position would cross our line of flight. I was very thankful at those moments that the Navy requires such thorough navigation training, and that I had made air navigation my hobby.

Finally, when I felt certain we were on our course, I turned my attention to the great ice pack, which I had wondered about ever since I was a youngster at school. We were flying at about 2,000 feet, and I could see at least 50 miles in every direction. There was no sign of land. If there had been any within 100 miles' radius we would have seen its mountain peaks, so good was the visibility.

The ice pack beneath was criss-crossed with pressure ridges, but here and there were stretches that appeared long and smooth enough to land on. However, from 2,000 feet pack ice is extraordinarily deceptive.

The pressure ridges that looked so insignificant from the plane varied from a few feet to 50 or 60 feet in height, while the average thickness of the ice was about 40 feet. A flash of sympathy came over me for the brave men who had in years past struggled northward over that cruel mass.

We passed leads of water recently opened by the movement of the ice, and so dangerous to the foot traveler, who never knows when the ice will open up beneath and swallow him into the black depths of the Polar Sea.

I now turned my mind to wind conditions, for I knew they were a matter of interest to all those contemplating the feasibility of a polar airway. We found them good. There were no bumps in the air. This was as we had anticipated, for the flatness of the ice and the Arctic temperature was not conducive to air currents, such as are sometimes found over land. Had we struck an Arctic gale, I cannot say what the result would have been as far as air roughness is concerned. Of course we still had the advantage of spring and 24-hour daylight.

It was time now to relieve Bennett again at the wheel, not only that he might stretch his legs, but so that he could pour gasoline into the tanks from the five-gallon tins stowed all over the cabin. Empty cans were thrown overboard to get rid of the weight, small though it was.

Frequently I was able to check myself on the course by holding the sun-compass in one hand and steering with the other.

I had time now leisurely to examine the ice pack and eagerly sought signs of life, a polar-bear, a seal, or birds flying, but could see none.

On one occasion, as I turned to look over the side, my arm struck some object in my left breast pocket. It was filled with good-luck pieces!

I am not superstitious, I believe. No explorer, however, can go off without such articles. Among my trinkets was a religious medal put there by a friend. It belonged to his fiancée and he firmly believed it would get me through. There was also a tiny horseshoe made by a famous blacksmith. Attached to the pocket was a little coin taken by Peary, pinned to his shirt, on his trip to the North Pole.

When Bennett had finished pouring and figuring the gasoline consumption, he took the wheel again. I went back to the incessant navigating. So much did I sight down on the dazzling snow that I had a slight attack of snow blindness. But I need not have suffered, as I had brought along the proper kind of amber goggles.

Twice during the next two hours I relieved Bennett at the wheel. When I took it the fourth time, he smiled as he went aft. "I would rather have Floyd with me," I thought, "than any other man in the world."

We were now getting into areas never before viewed by mortal eye. The feelings of an explorer superseded the aviator's. I became conscious of that extraordinary exhilaration which comes from looking into virgin territory. At that moment I felt repaid for all our toil.

At the end of this unknown area lay our goal, somewhere beyond the shimmering horizon. We were opening unexplored regions at the rate of nearly 10,000 square miles an hour, and were experiencing the incomparable satisfaction of searching for new land. Once, for a moment, I mistook a distant, vague, low-lying cloud formation for the white peaks of a far-away land.

I had a momentary sensation of great triumph. If I could explain the feeling I had at this time, the much-asked question would be answered: "What is this Arctic craze so many men get?"

The sun was still shining brightly. Surely fate was good to us, for without the sun our quest of the Pole would have been hopeless.

To the right, somewhere, the rays of the midnight sun shone down on the scenes of Nansen's heroic struggles to reach the goal that we were approaching with the ease of an eagle at the rate of nearly 100 miles an hour. To our left, lay Peary's oft-traveled trail.

When I went back to my navigating, I compared the magnetic compass with the sun-compass and found that the westerly error in the former had nearly doubled since reaching the edge of the ice pack, where it had been eleven degrees westerly.

When our calculations showed us to be about an hour from the Pole, I noticed through the cabin window a bad leak in the oil tank of the starboard motor. Bennett confirmed my fears. He wrote: "That motor will stop."

Bennett then suggested that we try a landing to fix the leak. But I had seen too many expeditions fail by landing. We decided to keep on for the Pole. We would be in no worse fix should we come down near the Pole than we would be if we had a forced landing where we were.

When I took to the wheel again I kept my eyes glued on that oil leak and the oil-pressure indicator. Should the pressure drop, we would lose the motor immediately. It fascinated me. There was no doubt in my mind that the oil pressure would drop any moment. But the prize was actually in sight. We could not turn back.

At 9.02 A.M., May 9, 1926, Greenwich civil time, our calculations showed us to be at the Pole! The dream of a lifetime had at last been realized.

THE FLIGHT OF THE *SOUTHERN CROSS*

by C. E. Kingsford-Smith and C. T. P. Ulm

We had much more drinking water on this hop. That was a necessary precaution, because in the last six hours' flying before we landed at Wheeler Field, there was a parching drought aboard the *Southern Cross.* We had drunk all the water during the night, and early hours, and did a rigorous thirst after sunrise.

On this occasion we determined that if possible we would not again suffer the pangs of drought. Our food was practically all in the form of sandwiches. Nothing else was so easily handled in the confined space in which we lived. We have never eaten so many sandwiches in our lives, and when we left Kauai we brought with us whole regiments of them, thanks to the kindness of Mr. and Mrs. Faye, our hosts at Kauai. So far as was possible, we planned to defeat thirst and hunger on the long hop.

From 7 A.M. to 8 A.M. we bowled along at a ground speed of 81 knots. Our altitude was still only 500 feet. We were figuratively hugging the sea as long as we could to save that vital gasoline. But it was apparent that our best-laid plans in this respect would very shortly "gang agley."

Visibility was still good, our oil pressures and temperatures were perfect, but far ahead the horizon was blotted out by low drifting clouds. It was growing duller. The sun was obscured by murk. There seemed to be water in the air. Rain apparently was blowing up many miles ahead.

Again we had just breakfasted on sandwiches and coffee, and were feeling in excellent humor, when we were suddenly jolted out of our comfortable frame of mind once more. Warner sent through a note. We had lost the radio beacon. Its signals had faded away at 8.15, and we were only three hours out. We had expected that its friendly buzz would have accompanied us for seven hours.

This, however, was not the worst news.

We had just a little more than an hour's flying without the radio beacon, when Warner reported that our radio equipment was completely out of action. We were then flying towards what looked like a barrier of rain in the far distance. Our altitude was only 550 feet, and our air speed was 77 knots.

Between 8 and 10 o'clock the rosy promise that seemed to have been held out at sunrise had changed for the worse. A stern tussle with rainstorms looked inevitable in an hour or so, and we found ourselves again cut off from the world. The radio beacon had failed us, our own instrument had decided to declare a strike, and for the second time in five hours' flying we found ourselves in that isolated world whose limits were set by the front windshields and the exhaust pipes. And this time it was a more dismal world than the first occasion when we had been isolated from the radio voice of the world. There was no sun awakening a flash and sparkle from the sea. The innocuous cumulus packs had given place to wicked-looking rain clouds that seemed to be charged with all the evaporated waters of the globe.

We missed the chats with the world. With every mile the loss of the radio words became greater. Our sense of loneliness increased. We felt in the miserable position that a man must feel who suddenly has lost the use of his voice. Our radio voice was silent, the radio voices of the two continents were also silent, and there we were plunging into gloom actual and temperamental. The actual gloom came down on us like a damp blanket. The ship was slipping along splendidly at a ground speed of 90 knots, when the wind began to freshen. Its sudden puffs turned to tugs and slaps and punches. Ahead, great dark clouds tumbled in a headlong rush. The wind whipped up from ten to twenty miles an hour. The sun was blotted out. At 11.40 A.M. we plunged into the squall, still voiceless.

Right ahead the nimbus clouds dissolved in a curtain of rain. The fringe of it splashed us before we flew round the main deluge. From that moment began a wild aerial jazzing out of the way of rain. The storms that had been lurking ahead for the previous three hours flung themselves across our path. Like ominous gray curtains that trailed their fringes across the surface of the sea, rainstorms charged at us from every direction, driven before a fresh wind. Ulm swung the ship out of the way of one storm, and Smith steered her clear of a second. But the dark curtains closed in—beset us from every side, and merged into a great belt of swishing water.

It was a cheerless hour. Visibility shrunk from seven or eight miles to one, then to half or less. Just when a dim and dismal path seemed to be opening out before us through these walls of water, the wind chopped round and closed the murky corridor. Kingsford-Smith set the nose of the *Southern Cross* down one of these watery corridors in a dash between the merging squalls. He got through, and we earned a slight respite from the battering by the wind. But it was only a passing lull.

The rainstorms surged in round us again. We were 600 feet up, and as we had been flying for only six and a half hours, our petrol load was still tremendous. To fly low in such atrocious conditions, heavily overloaded, was an experience that did not at all add any to the peace of mind.

To dodge around the fringes of the storm and to climb through the murk were the kind of maneuvers that were going to mop up our gasoline at a disconcerting rate. To fly low overloaded in the face of the savage chopping gusts with visibility shrinking to a few hundred feet was to flirt a little too dangerously with risk. We were indeed on the horns of a dilemma. We were forced to decide on a policy, as we had not the faintest idea how long this battering by the storms might continue. That policy was to climb, to risk a heavier petrol consumption, and hope for the best. So we opened up the motors to 1,775 revolutions, and plowed up through rain and storm and a jolting nasty wind which blew in sudden gusts.

Visibility shrunk at an incredible rate; the rain became thicker, and at 11.50 A.M. we were flying blind and climbing to get out of the deluge. The plane bumped heavily in the tearing gusts, and we got out of it at 1,000 feet, only to be faced with another menacing black curtain of water. Our spell of blind flying through slashing rain was not a long one, but the ship bucked and lurched heavily as the wind seemed to chop in three directions at the same moment. Visibility opened up to about 200 feet again just before noon, when we began to glide down to 600 feet to get under a rainstorm that was massing up ready to burst on us in full fury. Just as suddenly as we had to fight these squalls, we tore through into moderately clear air once more. We were, of course, plugging along at 76 knots all the time.

Noon (12.30 Honolulu time) saw us just through the barrier of squalls. Lyon took a sight with the Sextant to get our latitudinal position. We were then seven hours from Kauai. Kingsford-Smith had flown 4½ hours, and Ulm 2½ hours. There had been a long silence from Jim Warner in the navigating cabin, and it was clear that we were still without our radio voice or ears. Yet we had the utmost faith in the ability of Jim. If the radio equipment could be readjusted, Jim was the man to fix it.

In the thrill of sidestepping, or rather side-sliding, out of the path of storms, we had forgotten the atmospheric conditions. It dawned on us as we emerged from the tumult of rain, that it was oppressively hot in the cockpit. The heavy water-laden air, the passage into a definite tropical zone, and the waves of heat from the motors, caused us to perspire. As we took our coats off, we swept past a cloud bank abeam that was just dissolving into a rainstorm that looked more wicked than those through which we had passed.

At 12.45 (Honolulu time) we had flown 630 miles in just seven hours, at an average ground speed of 90 miles an hour. Lyon, after his observations, then passed through our position as being "Latitude by observation, 12 deg. 47 min.; by dead reckoning, 12 deg. 58 min.; Longitude 163 deg. 13."

Rainstorms came sweeping up at us endlessly, lashing the plane, beating a lively tattoo on the windshield, and making us fly through a murky soaked world that seemed to have no boundaries. Conrad's skipper preferred to plow through a China Sea typhoon rather than run up his coal bill. Like him, we became misers of petrol. We resolved to keep flying at 600 feet, because if we went higher, we would burn more fuel. When we plunged into a heavy rainstorm at 12.50 there was only one bright spot in a most cheerless prospect. The motors were fighting the storms with such stubbornness that our ground speed was maintained in a most satisfactory way. Kingsford-Smith flew seven minutes blind through the new storm. The rain poured in rivulets from our windshield, and though it was high noon, and a tropic noon at that, we tore through a wall of water where visibility ceased to exist.

Already in seven hours we had experienced more blind flying on this stage of our flight than on the 27½ hours between Oakland and Honolulu.

What is blind flying? Most long distance airmen know, but to the average man in the street the term may be rather vague.

If you have ever tried to drive a motor car along a bush road on a pitch black night without a headlight or a rear light, or even a match, you will gain some slight idea of the meaning of blind flying. But even then, with that nightmare experience, you would not have lived through all the thrilling uncertainty of flying a plane in a dim opaque world of nothingness. That is because in a car you could only go forwards or backwards.

In a plane there are any number of movements that have to be regulated. It not only goes forward, but may climb or drop or bank or sidestep, or drift.

How do you know when a plane is banking, when all round you is inky blackness? How can you tell its drift sideways? You can do none of these things without the proper instruments, and without the blindest, the most implicit faith in them. In blind flying when a plane charges through lashing rain in a black void, there is a contest between your senses and your instruments.

Your senses may lead you to believe that the ship is climbing or descending. They may tell you that the plane is banking steeply. And it is possible for the senses to be quite inaccurate.

It seems revolutionary to oppose the dictum of the senses in such a matter as this. Yet in blind flying, if the instruments show that the plane is banking when your senses indicate that it is thrashing its way forward on an even horizontal wing, the instruments are correct, and not your senses. It is not easy to allow the mind to become as elastic as this. The process is in the same category as that which a dentist demands of a patient when he asks him not to sit rigid against the forceps, but to relax. To relax the mind in such a way as to doubt your own senses is no joke. Yet that is what blind flying demands during every minute when visibility is definitely cut out.

Your whole world is reduced to an instrument board illuminated by an electric torch. Over the edge of the windshields of the cockpit there is nothing but blank grayness. At the sides there is nothing but blank grayness. Behind you there is nothing but blank grayness. Unlike the darkened car on the darkened road, however, there is nothing to hit if the altitude is correct.

If the altitude was not carefully adjusted and watched, however, with us there was the ghastly possibility of hitting the surface of the ocean. That was where our altimeter played its important part. It told us constantly how far from the sea we were when we were plunging through that soupy grayness. Without those instruments it would have been impossible to fly blind for an hour without disaster.

At 1.22 P.M., when we came out of our third spell of blind flying, on the new stage of the flight, Warner had good news for us to relieve the gloom that is apt to settle on one in those patches of blank grayness. Both radio transmitters were working normally again. Once more we had our link with the world, and to speak figuratively, we had "come back to life."

A little later we again dashed into heavy cloud banks. We climbed, and once more had to sidestep two savage bursts of rain that came tearing at us. The cloud curtains thickened; the rain lashed us with greater fury, and again we were in that dim opaque world flying blind. The windshields began to leak, and water started to trickle in on us. Then our real personal discomfort commenced. Water splashed into the cockpit and soaked our feet and legs. In less than half an hour we were very damp and a little disgruntled. For an hour we flew low against oblique sheets of stinging rain.

There was one vast difference between this leg of the flight and the trip to Honolulu. That crushing monotony of calm sea and cloud beauty did not linger with us. We were about ten hours out, and there had not been a continuous half hour of monotony. Things seemed to happen in a steady sequence. There was the losing of the radio beacon, the capriciousness of our own radio instrument, the supposed gas leak, the opening lively rounds with the rainsqualls, and the sudden transitions from murk to blind flying. We had plunged on through the driving rain for about another hour, and we were beginning to believe that the rush of incident was about to ease, when there was another scare and a few moments of anxiety. We were just changing over at the controls, working them on an hourly duty roster.

Kingsford-Smith had taken over the controls, when there was a sudden tremulous cough in the starboard engine. It was not a bad spluttering cough, but just sufficient to break that wonderful harmonious chorus that the motors had played for us now over 3,000 miles of ocean.

We thought hard for a few seconds. Then came a note from Lyon to ask about the motor. Our ears were so attuned to the steady thunder of the three motors that in the navigating cabin Lyon and Warner had also instantly detected the unusual highpitched bark of the starboard engine.

What was wrong? We were nearly a thousand miles out over a stretch of ocean that could not possibly have looked more inhospitable or forbidding.

Were the motors going to let us down after the wonderful comradeship they had shown us since we left the Golden Gate? We were secure in the fact that at least all three motors would not—to use the boxing term—"throw up the sponge" at the same moment, or even in the same hour.

It would have been extremely bad luck for one of them to have refused duty, but it would not have been altogether desperate.

Yet that cough sounded menacing. For 3,000 miles across the great sweep of ocean that we had covered, our ears had become sensitized to the slightest irregularity in the beat of those motors. We were constantly on the alert, listening, so to speak, like an Indian with his ear to the ground, with the essential difference that our ears were very far from ground of any kind. Mile after mile one could not dull this tense ear strain for the possible cough or splutter of one of the engines. It was only a natural inclination, as the motors were to be either our salvation or our destruction.

Yet, though only one of the motors had coughed suddenly in the midst of that cheerless rain-soaked afternoon, and we looked at the bright side even of possible trouble with the starboard engine, insofar as the outcome was concerned, the prospect of tinkering with a misbehaving motor out there over strange sea, and in the midst of savage gusts, was not the least reassuring.

The cough ceased as quickly as it began. We were all ears.

Was it only a passing irregularity? But no. It came again, definite and unmistakable. There was a splutter and a sort of kick. Nothing could be left to chance. We could not charge on through the rain disregarding that motor, and possibly laying the foundation of disaster. We started out to investigate. We did not for a moment believe that the cough was caused by a fault in the motor itself. The first theory that ran through our minds was that a defect had developed in the gasoline feed line. An inspection by Ulm discovered no visible trouble in the gas lines. It was possible, however, that rain had percolated into the carburetor stoves, and that this had led the starboard motor to dance a little.

At any rate, the revolutions of the starboard motor were normal at 1,600, and the oil pressure and temperature were right. Intermittently, for about eight minutes, came this discordant note in the roar of that engine. Then the coughs stopped abruptly. The roar, steady and rhythmic, swelled out as before. Ulm entered in the log probably one of the most historic jottings that the book contained. It read: "Starboard engine has quit shimmying."

At the moment, that entry was as pleasing to us as if he had to put down on paper that Fiji was in sight. Our altitude was 550 feet, and our speed 77 knots. All was well with the world. Yet the temporary irregularity of the engine had caused us to train our ears with greater concentration, for a possible renewal of the "shimmying." That, too, was but a natural result of the scare. The rain seemed to get a little lighter, and at 4.22 P.M. we had been eleven hours in the air for the day. Our estimate was that we had averaged 100 or more statute miles hourly. Lyon worked up the longitudinal position, and in a note that he passed through he told us that at 4 P.M. (*Southern Cross* time) and 4.25 (Honolulu time) we were in Latitude 7° 27′ N. and 167° 30′ W. Longitude. We had covered 1,026 nautical miles at an average hourly speed of 106.55 miles.

We had now broken free from the wet cloud banks, the rain had stopped, and although a thick haze lay along the horizon ahead, it looked as if we would have a clear night with good flying conditions. We felt that we certainly deserved such a night, as from before noon the rain had made our lives miserable.

We plotted our probable progress, based on the favorable outlook that the checking of our longitudinal position had given us. Given favorable conditions, we believed that we would pass over the Islands of the Phoenix Group that night. It was then 6.10 P.M., and dry, all except our feet and legs, where the water had cascaded on us from the windshields.

Again our forecast of a fine night went astray. When you are bowling along at a ground speed of 85 knots, you sometimes overlook the fact that great sweeps of sea are being left behind rapidly, and that while the weather indications may look promising at one point, two hours' flying further on may bring you into the foulest of weather.

It was so with us. As the daylight began to wane fast, we started to climb for our night flying. This was our settled policy, as it was safe at a good altitude, and, in addition, it was the means of prolonging the day. High up there we had the advantage of the rays of the sun as it slid under the horizon, even though darkness may have fallen completely at the ground or sea level.

The clearness that had appeared ahead was now no more. New mountain peaks of cloud heaped up on the southwestern horizon. They were thick and dark. We climbed steadily at 69 knots. We expected that we would get above the menacing peaks at 5,000 feet, but we had not pulled up to more than 1,200 feet when rain burst on us once again from the foothills in this vast range of cloud. We opened up the motors to 1,700 revolutions, so that we could climb more rapidly, and at the moment had to swing right off our course to fly round a wall of rain of tropical violence that charged right at us.

We began to fly in circles always steadily upwards. This was the sort of thing that always reawakened those qualms about the terrific drain on our gasoline. We probably in our mental state on this occasion exaggerated the thirst of those motors when they began to haul the heavy load aloft, because it was one of the longest and most strenuous climbs of the whole flight.

There was always, too, the feeling that while we were seeking to soar over these cloud pinnacles we were getting nowhere. Progress was cut down to a few miles. It was a breathless race between the *Southern Cross* and the clouds. First we gained, then they puffed up beneath the plane. Rain battered at the windshields, and the wind seemed to stand off like a boxer and punch us. We had been battling upwards in this way for about ten minutes, when the flexible lead of the exhaust pipe carried away off the center motor. No damage was done, and we did not worry unduly over the incident. As long as nothing more vital fell off we were quite at ease in mind. As we climbed the rain grew worse. It slashed and tore against the windshields. The clouds seemed to get blacker and thicker the further we struggled aloft, and for the fourth time since we left Barking Sands we were flying blind.

In the midst of that cloud bank it was as black as the blackest night, yet the altimeter told us that we were climbing at the rate of 250 feet a minute, and at 6.20 P.M. we had mounted to nearly 2,000 feet. We burst out of the first prison house of clouds, and found ourselves above the lower ranges of them. We could see about us again, and the dying sun lit up the tumbling cloud masses in a picture as striking as those that we had seen just before we reached Honolulu. But there was a difference. It lay in the fact that there was nothing kindly in these great cloud valleys down which we looked from the sides of the cockpit. They were the color of heavy coal smoke, and inspired a certain amount of awe. And the rain was dogging us for every mile. It often blotted out everything, and our damp feet and legs grew more damp as it tumbled in rivulets over the windshield.

We were forcibly reminded of the 2,500 miles of rain through which we had battled on our 7,500 miles flight round the Australian continent. The rivulets coming over the windshields turned to rushing cascades, and we got sodden from the knees down. At 5,000 feet, and after a sudden swing almost at right angles to our course, we shook off the clinging rain clouds, but there were still higher mountains of cloud before us, and the haulage was heavy on the three roaring motors.

From this point, a little after 7 o'clock in the evening, it became a tense race between the *Southern Cross* and the clouds to reach 10,000 feet. Only such an altitude we felt would carry us into clearer flying conditions. At 7.15 P.M. we had reached 7,500 feet, but there was none of the sunset glory that had enlivened our lot a little on the previous hop. Inky blackness, rain, and capricious winds made up the cheerless outlook for the night. So it was with the greatest fervor with which anything was ever penned that Ulm included in the log the sentence "we see a rotten night ahead." Clouds completely surrounded us, and we passed through another of those frequent periods when we were unable to take our bearings. It rained hard in bursts, and we kept flying in circles.

But after a long and grim fight we won that race. At 8,000 feet we had beaten the uprush of the cloud banks. We looked down into a world of tumbled vapor, ranging away in ragged fringes on every side. Yet the struggle up there through the cloud masses was well worth the reward that awaited us when we scaled them.

Above us as we emerged from the murk, glittered the Southern Cross, the constellation whose name we were proud to bear on our ship. It winked out a genial welcome to us after the stress of the battle far below. It glimmered on the port bow like a shower of diamonds in a vault of the deepest blue. There were other stars there too, of course, but we hardly saw them. The Southern Cross was to us the symbol of success. It seemed to hang there beckoning its namesake with the three droning motors. It looked good. We were still far from our goal, the sea swept by, the tangled cloud wreaths far below looked just as relentless, yet the sight of the Southern Cross seemed to give us the impression that the worst was over, that we would win our way through to Suva.

AND TOMORROW

by William Faulkner

"All right," the reporter said. "Let's go." They walked again; it was about a mile; presently the road ran beside the field beyond which they could see the buildings—the detached office, the shop, the hangar with a broad legend above the open doors: ORD-ATKINSON AIRCRAFT CORPORATION—all of pale brick, as neat as and apparently contemporaneous with Ord's new house. Sitting on the ground a little back from the road they watched two mechanics wheel out the red-and-white monoplane with which Ord had set his record and start it and warm it, and then they saw Ord himself come out of the office, get into the racer, taxi to the end of the field and turn and takeoff straight over their heads, already travelling a hundred feet ahead of his own sound. "It's forty miles over to Feinman from here," the reporter said. "He flies it in ten minutes. Come on. You let me do the talking. Jesus," he cried, in a kind of light amazed exultation, "I never told a lie in my life that anybody believed; maybe this is what I have been needing all the time!" When they reached the hangar the doors were now closed to a crack just large enough for a man to enter. Shumann entered, already looking about, until he found the aeroplane—a lowwing monoplane with a big nose and a tubular fuselage ending in a curiously flattened tailgroup which gave it the appearance of having been drawn lightly and steadily through a huge lightlyclosed gloved fist. "There it is," the reporter said.

"Yair," Shumann said. "I see. . . . Yes," he thought, looking quietly at the queer empennage, the blunt short cylindrical body; "I guess Ord wasn't so surprised, at that." Then he heard the reporter speaking to someone and he turned and saw a squat man with a shrewd Cajun face above a scrupulously clean coverall.

"This is Mr. Shumann," the reporter said, saying in a tone of bright amazement: "You mean Matt never told you? We have bought that ship." Shumann did not wait. For a moment he watched Marchand, the note in both hands, looking at it with that baffled immobility behind which the mind flicks and darts like a terrier inside a fence.

"Yair," Shumann thought, without grimness, "he can't pass five thousand dollars anymore than I could. Not without warning, anyway." He went on to the aeroplane, though once or twice he looked back and saw Marchand and the reporter, the Cajun still emanating that stubborn and slowly crystallising bewilderment while the reporter talked, flapped, before him with an illusion of being held together only by the clothes he wore; once he even heard the reporter:

"Sure, you could telephone to Feinman and catch him. But for God's sake dont let anybody overhear how Matt stuck us for five thousand bucks for the damn crate. He promised he wouldn't tell." But there was no telephoning done apparently, because almost at once (or so it seemed to Shumann) the reporter and Marchand were beside him, the reporter quiet now, watching him with that bright attention.

"Let's get it out where we can look at it," Shumann said. They rolled it out onto the apron, where it squatted again, seemed to. It had none of the waspwaisted trimness of the ones at the airport. It was blunt, a little thickbodied, almost sluggish looking; its lightness when moved by hand seemed curiously paradoxical. For a good minute the reporter and Marchand watched Shumann stand looking at it with thoughtful gravity. "All right," he said at last. "Let's wind her up." Now the reporter spoke, leaning lightly and slightly just off balance like a ragged penstaff dropped pointfirst into the composition apron:

"Listen. You said last night maybe it was the distribution of the weight; you said how maybe if we could shift the weight somehow while it was in the air that maybe you could find . . ." Later (almost as soon as Shumann was out of sight the reporter and Marchand were in Marchand's car on the road to the village, where the reporter hired a cab, scrambling into it even before he had asked the price and yelling out of his gaunt and glare-fixed face, "Hell, no! Not New Valois! Feinman Airport!") he lived and relived the blind timeless period during which he lay on his stomach in the barrel, clutching the two bodymembers, with nothing to see but Shumann's feet on the rudderpedals and the movement of the aileron balancerod and nothing to feel but terrific motion—not speed and not progress—just blind furious motion like a sealed force trying to explode the monococque barrel in which he lay from the waist down on his stomach, leaving him clinging to the bodymembers in space. He was still thinking, "Jesus, maybe we are going to die and all it is is a taste like sour hot salt in your mouth," even while looking out the car window at the speeding marsh and swamp through which they skirted the city, thinking with a fierce and triumphant conviction of immortality, "We flew it! We flew it!"

Now the airport; the forty miles accomplished before he knew it, what with his skull still cloudy with the light tagends of velocity and speed like the drifting feathers from a shot bird so that he had never become conscious of the sheer inertia of dimension, space, distance, through which he had had to travel. He was thrusting the five dollar bill at the driver before the car began to turn into the plaza and he was out of it before it had stopped, running toward the hangar, probably not even aware that the first race was in progress. Wildfaced, gaunt and sunkeneyed from lack of sleep and from strain, his clothes ballooning about him, he ran into the hangar and on to where Jiggs stood at the workbench with a new bottle of polish and a new tin of paste open before him, shining the boots, working now with tedious and intent concern at the scar on the instep of the right one. "Did he—" the reporter cried.

"Yair, he landed it, all right," Jiggs said. "He used all the field, though. Jesus, I thought for a while he was going to run out of airport before he even cut the gun; when he stopped you couldn't have dropped a match between the prop and the seawall. They are all upstairs now, holding the caucus."

"It'll qualify itself!" the reporter cried. "I told him that. I may not know airplanes but I know sewage board Jews!"

"Yair," Jiggs said. "Anyway, he wont have to make but two landings with it. And he's already made one of them."

"Two?" the reporter cried; now he glared at Jiggs with more than exultation: with ecstasy. "He's already made two! We made one before he left Ord's!"

"We?" Jiggs said. With the boot and the rag poised he blinked painfully at the reporter with the one good hot bright eye. "We?"

"Yair; him and me! He said how it was the weight—that maybe if we could just shift the weight somehow while it was in the air—and he said 'Are you afraid?' and I said 'Hell yes. But not if you aint, because Matt gave me an hour once, or maybe if I had had more than an hour I wouldn't have been.' So Marchand helped us take the seat out and we rigged another one so there would be room under it for me and I slid back into the fuselage because it aint got any crossbracing, it's mon—mon—"

"Monococque," Jiggs said. "Jesus Christ, do you mean—"

"Yair. And him and Marchand rigged the seat again and he showed me where to hold on and I could just see his heels and that was all; I couldn't tell; yair, after a while I knew we were flying but I couldn't tell forward nor backward or anything because, Jesus, I just had one hour with Matt and then he cut the gun and then I could hear him—Jesus, we might have been standing on the ground—he said quiet, 'Now slide back. Easy. But hold tight.' And then I was hanging just by my hands; I wasn't even touching the floor of it at all. Jesus, I was thinking 'Well, here it is then; it will be tough about that race this afternoon'; I didn't even know we were on the ground again until I found out it was him and Marchand lifting the seat out and Marchand saying 'Goddamn. Goddamn. Goddamn' and him looking at me and the bastard crate standing there quiet as one of them photographs on Grandlieu Street, and then he says, 'Would you go up again?' and I said 'Yes. You want to go now?' and he said, 'Let's get her on over to the field and qualify.' "

"Sweet Jesus Christ," Jiggs said.

"Yair," the reporter cried. "It was just weight distribution: him and

Marchand rigged up a truck inner tube full of sand on a pulley so he can— And put the seat back and even if they see the end of the cable they wouldn't— Because the only ship in it that can beat him is Ord's and the purse aint but two thousand and Ord don't need it, he is only in it so New Valois folks can see him fly the Ninety-Two once, and he aint going to beat that fifteen-thousand-dollar ship to death just to—"

"Here; here," Jiggs said. "You're going to blow all to pieces in a minute. Smoke a cigarette; aint you got some?" The reporter fumbled the cigarettes out at last, though it was Jiggs who took two from the pack and struck the match while the reporter stooped to it, trembling. The dazed spent wild look was still on his face but he was quieter now.

"So they were all out to meet him, were they?"

"Jesus, did they," Jiggs said. "And Ord out in front; he recognised the ship as soon as it come in sight; Jesus, I bet he recognised it before Roger even recognised the airport, and by the time he landed you would have thought he was Lindbergh. And him sitting there in the cockpit and looking at them and Ord hollering at him and then they all come back up the apron like Roger was a kidnapper or something and went into the administration building and a minute later the microphone begun to holler for the inspector, what's his—"

"Sales," the reporter said. "It's licensed; they can't stop him."

"Sales can ground it, though," Jiggs said.

"Yair." The reporter was already turning, moving. "But Sales aint nothing but a Federal officer; Feinman is a Jew and on the sewage board."

"What's that got to do with it?"

"What?" the reporter cried, glaring, gaunt, apparently having already rushed on and out of his precarious body so that only the shell glared back at Jiggs. "What? What's he holding this meet for? What did he— Do you think maybe he built this airport just for a smooth place for airplanes to land on?" He went on, not running yet but fast. As he hurried up the apron the aeroplanes overtook and passed him, banked around the field pylon and faded on; he did not even look at them. Then suddenly he saw her, leading the little boy by the hand, emerge from the crowd about the gate to intercept him, wearing now a clean linen dress under the trenchcoat, and a hat, the brown hat of the first evening. He stopped. His hand went into his pocket and into his face came the expression bright, quiet, almost smiling, as she walked fast up to him, staring at him with pale and urgent intensity.

"What is it?" she said. "What is this you have got him into?" He looked down at her with that expression, not yearning nor despair, but profound tragic and serene like in the eyes of bird dogs.

"It's all right," he said. "My signature is on the note too. It will hold. I am going in right now to testify; that's all that's holding them; that's all that Ord has to—" He drew out the nickel and gave it to the boy.

"What?" she said. "Note? Note? The ship, you idiot!"

"Oh." He smiled down at her. "The ship. We flew it, tested it over there. We made a field hop before we—"

"We?"

"Yes. I went with him. I laid on the floor in the tail, so we could find out where the weight ought to be to pass the burble. That's all it was. We have a sandbag rigged now on a cable so he can let it slide back. It's all right."

"All right?" she said. "Good God, what can you know about it? Did he say it was all right?"

"Yes. He said last night he could land it. I knew he could. And now he wont need to make but one more. . . ." She stared at him, the eyes pale cold and urgent, at the face worn, dreamy, and peaceful in the soft bright sun; again the aeroplanes came in and snored on and away. Then he was interrupted; it was the amplifier; all the amplifiers up and down the apron began to call his name, telling the stands, the field, the land and lake and air, that he was wanted in the superintendent's office at once. "There it is," he said. "Yair. I knew that the note would be the only thing that Ord could . . . That was why I signed it too. And dont you worry; all I need to do is walk in and say 'Yes, that's my signature.' And dont you worry. He can fly it. He can fly anything. I used to think that Matt Ord was the best pilot alive, but now I—"

The amplifier began to repeat itself. It faced him; it seemed to stare straight at him while it roared his name deliberately as though he had to be summoned not out of the living world of population but evoked, peremptory and repetitive, out of the air itself. The one in the rotunda was just beginning again when he entered; the sound followed him through the door and across the anteroom, though beyond that it did not reach—not into the board room of yesterday where now Ord and Shumann alone occupied the hard chairs. They had been ushered in a half hour ago and sat down facing the men behind the table; Shumann saw Feinman for the first time, sitting not in the center but at one end of the table where the announcer had sat yesterday, his suit, double-breasted still, tan instead of gray beneath the bright splash of the carnation. He alone wore his hat; it appeared to be the smallest object about him; from beneath it his dark smooth face began at once to droop into folds of flesh which, constricted for the instant by his collar, swelled and rolled again beneath the tight creases of his coat. On the table one hand bearing a gold-clamped ruby held a burning cigar. He did not even glance at Shumann and Ord; he was looking at Sales, the inspector . . . a square bald man with a blunt face which ordinarily would be quite pleasant, though not now . . . who was saying:

"Because I can ground it. I can forbid it to fly."

"You mean, you can forbid anybody to fly it, dont you?" Feinman said.

"Put it that way if you want to," Sales said.

"Let's say, put it that way for the record," another voice said—a young man, sleek, in horn rim glasses, sitting just back of Feinman. He was Feinman's secretary; he spoke now with a kind of silken insolence, like the pampered intelligent hateridden eunuchmountebank of an eastern despot: "Colonel Feinman is, even before a public servant, a lawyer."

"Yes; lawyer," Feinman said. "Maybe country lawyer to Washington. Let me get this straight. You're a government agent. All right. We have had our crops regimented and our fisheries regimented and even our money in the bank regimented. All right. I still dont see how they did it but they did, and so we are used to that. If he was trying to make his living out of the ground and Washington come in and regimented him, all right. We might not understand it any more than he did, but we would say all right. And if he was trying to make his living out of the river and the government come in and regimented him, we would say all right too. But do you mean to tell me that Washington can come in and regiment a man that's trying to make his living out of the air? Is there a crop reduction in the air too?" They—the others about the table (three of them were reporters)—laughed. They laughed with a kind of sudden and loud relief, as though they had been waiting all the time to find out just how they were supposed to listen, and now they knew. Only Sales and Shumann and Ord did not laugh; then they noticed that the secretary was not laughing either and that he was already speaking, seeming to slide his silken voice into the laughter and stop it as abruptly as a cocaine needle in a nerve:

"Yes. Colonel Feinman is lawyer enough (perhaps Mr. Sales will add, country enough) to ask even a government official to show cause. As the colonel understands it, this airplane bears a license which Mr. Sales approved himself. Is that true, Mr. Sales?" For a moment Sales did not answer. He just looked at the secretary grimly.

"Because I dont believe it is safe to fly," he said. "That's the cause."

"Ah," the secretary said. "For a moment I almost expected Mr. Sales to tell us that it would not fly; that it had perhaps walked over here from Blaisedell. Then all we would need to say would be 'Good; we will not make it fly; we will just let it walk around the pylons during the race this afternoon—' " Now they did laugh, the three reporters scribbling furiously. But it was not for the secretary: it was for Feinman. The secretary seemed to know this; while he waited for it to subside his unsmiling insolent contempt touched them all face by face. Then he spoke to Sales again. "You admit that it is licensed, that you approved it yourself—meaning, I take it, that it is registered at Washington as being fit and capable of discharging the function of an airplane, which is to fly. Yet you later state that you will not permit it to fly because it is not capable of discharging the function for which you yourself admit having approved it—in simple language for us lawyers, that it cannot fly. Yet Mr. Ord has just told us that he flew it in your presence. And Mr—" he glanced down; the pause was less than pause— "Shumann states that he flew it once at Blaisedell before witnesses, and we know that he flew it here because we saw him. We all know that Mr. Ord is one of the best (we New Valoisians believe *the* best) pilots in the world, but dont you think it barely possible, barely I say, that the man who has flown it twice where Mr. Ord has flown it but once . . . Wouldn't this almost lead one to think that Mr. Ord has some other motive for not wanting this airplane to compete in this race—"

"Yair," Feinman said. He turned to look at Ord. "What's the matter? Aint this airport good enough for your ships? Or aint this race important enough for you? Or do you just think he might beat you? Aint you going to use the airplane you broke the record in? Then what are you afraid of?" Ord glared from face to face about the table, then at Feinman again.

"Why do you want this ship in there this afternoon? What is it? I'd lend him the money, if that's all it is."

"Why?" Feinman said. "Aint we promised these folks out there—" he made a jerking sweep with the cigar— "a series of races? Aint they paying their money in here to see them? And aint it the more airplanes they will have to look at the better they will think they got for the money? And why should he want to borrow money from you when he can maybe earn it at his job where he wont have to pay it back or even the interest? Now, let's settle this business." He turned to Sales. "The ship is licensed, aint it?" After a moment Sales said,

"Yes." Feinman turned to Ord.

"And it will fly, wont it?" Ord looked at him for a long moment too.

"Yes," he said. Now Feinman turned to Shumann.

"Is it dangerous to fly?" he said.

"They all are," Shumann said.

"Well, are you afraid to fly it?" Shumann looked at him. "Do you expect it to fall with you this afternoon?"

"If I did I wouldn't take it up," Shumann said. Suddenly Ord rose; he was looking at Sales.

"Mac," he said, "this aint getting anywhere. I will ground the ship myself." He turned to Shumann. "Listen, Roger—"

"On what grounds, Mr. Ord?" the secretary said.

"Because it belongs to me. Is that grounds enough for you?"

"When an authorised agent of your corporation has accepted a legal monetary equivalent for it and surrendered the machine?"

"But they are not good for the note. I know that. I was a damn stickstraddler myself until I got a break. Why, damn it, one of the names on it is admitted to not be signed by the owner of it. And listen: yair; I dont even know whether Shumann did the actual signing; whoever signed it signed it before I saw it or even before Marchand saw it. See?" He glared at the secretary, who looked at him in turn with his veiled contemptuous glance.

"I see," the secretary said pleasantly. "I was waiting for you to bring that up. You seem to have forgotten that the note has a third signer." Ord stared at him for a minute.

"But he aint good for it either," he said.

"Possibly not, alone. But Mr. Shumann tells us that his father is and that his father will honor this signature. So by your own token, the question seems to resolve to whether or not Mr. Shumann did or did not sign his and his father's name to the note. And we seem to have a witness to that. It is not exactly legal, I grant you. But this other signer is known to some of us here; you know him yourself, you tell us, to be a person of unassailable veracity. We will have him in." Then it was that the amplifiers began to call the reporter's name; he entered; he came forward while they watched him. The secretary extended the note toward him. ("Jesus," the reporter thought, "they must have sent a ship over for Marchand.")

"Will you examine this?" the secretary said.

"I know it," the reporter said.

"Will you state whether or not you and Mr. Shumann signed it in each other's presence and in good faith?" The reporter looked about, at the faces behind the table, at Shumann sitting with his head bent a little and at Ord halfrisen, glaring at him. After a moment Shumann turned his head and looked quietly at him.

"Yes," the reporter said. "We signed it."

"There you are," Feinman said. He rose. "That's all. Shumann has possession; if Ord wants anymore to be stubborn about it we will just let him run to town and see if he can get back with a writ of replevin before time for the race."

"But he can't enter it!" Ord said. "It aint qualified." Feinman paused long enough to look at Ord for a second with impersonal inscrutability.

"Speaking for the citizens of Franciana who donated the ground and for the citizens of New Valois that built the airport the race is going to be run on, I will waive qualification."

"You can't waive the A.A.A.," Ord said. "You can't make it official if he wins the whole damn meet."

"Then he will not need to rush back to town to pawn a silver cup," Feinman said. He went out; the others rose from the table and followed. After a moment Ord turned quietly to Shumann.

"Come on," he said. "We'd better check her over."

The reporter did not see them again. He followed them through the rotunda, through the amplifier's voice and through the throng at the gates, or so he thought because his policecard had passed him before he remembered that they would have had to go around to reach the apron. But he could see the aeroplane with a crowd standing around it. The woman had forgotten too that Shumann and Ord would have to go around and through the hangar; she emerged again from the crowd beneath the bandstand. "So they did it," she said. "They let him."

"Yes. It was all right. Like I told you."

"They did it," she said, staring at him yet speaking as though in amazed soliloquy. "Yes. You fixed it."

"Yes. I knew that's all it would be. I wasn't worried. And dont you . . ." She didn't move for a moment; there was nothing of distraction especially; he just seemed to hang substanceless in the long peaceful backwash of waiting, saying quietly out of the dreamy smiling, "Yair.

Ord talking about how he would be disqualified for the cup, the prize, like that would stop him, like that was what . . ." not even aware that it was only the shell of her speaking quietly back to him, asking him if he would mind the boy.

"Since you seem to be caught up for the time."

"Yair," he said. "Of course." Then she was gone, the white dress and the trenchcoat lost in the crowd—the ones with ribbon badges and the ones in dungarees—which streamed suddenly down the apron toward the darkhorse, the sensation. As he stood so, holding the little boy by one damp sticky hand, the Frenchman Despleins passed again down the runway which parallelled the stands, on one wheel; the reporter watched him takeoff and half roll, climbing upside down. Now he heard the voice; he had not heard it since it called his own name despite the fact that it had never ceased, perhaps because of the fact:

". . . oh oh oh mister, dont, dont! Oh, mister! Please get up high enough so your parachute can try to open! Now, now; now, now. . . . Oh, Mac! Oh, Mr. Sales! Make him stop!" The reporter looked down at the boy.

"I bet you a dime you haven't spent that nickel," he said.

"Naw," the boy said. "I aint had a chance to. She wouldn't let me."

"Well, my goodness!" the reporter said. "I owe you twenty cents then, dont I? Come—" He paused, turning; it was the photographer, the man whom he had called Jug, laden again with the enigmatic and faintly macabre utensils of his calling so that he resembled vaguely a trained dog belonging to a country doctor.

"Where in hell you been?" the photographer said. "Hagood told me to find you at ten oclock."

"Here I am," the reporter said. "We're just going inside to spend twenty cents. Want to come?" Now the Frenchman came up the runway about twenty feet high and on his back, his head and face beneath the cockpitrim motionless and alert like that of a roach or a rat immobile behind a crack in a wainscoat, his neat short beard unstirred by any wind as though cast in one piece of bronze.

"Yair," the photographer said; perhaps it was the bilious aspect of an inverted world seen through a hooded lense or emerging in grimacing and attitudinal miniature from stinking trays in a celibate and stygian cell lighted by a red lamp: "and have that guy come down on his whiskers and me not here to get it?"

"All right," the reporter said. "Stay and get it." He turned to go on.

"Yair; but Hagood told me—" the photographer said. The reporter turned back.

"All right," he said. "But hurry up."

"Hurry up what?"

"Snap me. You can show it to Hagood when you go in." He and the boy went on; he did not walk back into the voice, he had never walked out of it:

". . . an in-ver-ted spin, folks; he's going into it still upside down—oh oh oh oh.—" The reporter stooped suddenly and lifted the boy to his shoulder.

"We can make better time," he said. "We will want to get back in a few minutes." They passed through the gate, among the gaped and upturned faces which choked the gangway. "That's it," he thought quietly, with that faint quiet grimace almost like smiling; "they aint human. It aint adultery; you can't anymore imagine two of them making love than you can two of them airplanes back in the corner of the hangar, coupled." With one hand he supported the boy on his shoulder, feeling through the harsh khaki the young brief living flesh. "Yair; cut him and it's cylinder oil; dissect him and it aint bones: it's little rockerarms and connecting rods. . . ." The restaurant was crowded; they did not wait to eat the icecream there on a plate; with one cone in his hand and one in the boy's and the two chocolate bars in his pocket they were working back through the crowded gangway when the bomb went off and then the voice:

". . . fourth event: unlimited free-for-all, Vaughn Trophy race, prize two thousand dollars. You will not only have a chance to see Matt Ord in his famous Ninety-Two Ord-Atkinson Special in which he set a new land plane speed record, but as a surprise entry through the courtesy of the American Aeronautical Association and the Feinman Airport Commission, Roger Shumann, who yesterday nosed over in a forced landing, in a special rebuilt job that Matt Ord rebuilt himself. Two horses from the same stable, folks, and two pilots both of whom are so good that it is a pleasure to give the citizens of New Valois and Franciana the chance to see them pitted against each other. . . ." He and the boy watched the takeoff, then they went on. Presently he found her—the brown hat and the coat—and he came up and stood a little behind her steadying the boy on his shoulder and carrying the second melting cone in his other hand as the four aeroplanes came in on the first lap—the red-and-white monoplane in front and two more side by side and some distance back, so that at first he did not even see Shumann. Then he saw him, higher than the others and well outside, though the voice now was not from the amplifier but from a mechanic:

"Jesus, look at Shumann! It must be fast: he's flying twice as far as the rest of them—or maybe Ord aint trying.—Why in hell dont he bring it on in?" Then the voice was drowned in the roar, the snarl, as the aeroplanes turned the field pylon and, followed by the turning heads along the apron as if the faces were geared to the sound, diminished singly out and over the lake again, Shumann still quite wide, making a turn that was almost a skid yet holding his position. They converged toward the second pylon, the lake one; in slightly irregular order and tiny now with distance and with Shumann still cautiously high and outside, they wafted lightly upward and around the pylon. Now the reporter could hear the mechanic again: "He's coming in now, watch him. Jesus, he's second—he's diving in— Jesus, he's going to be right behind Ord on this pylon; maybe he was just feeling it out—" The noise was faint now and disseminated; the drowsy afternoon was domed with it and the four machines seemed to hover like dragonflies silently in vacuum, in various distance-softened shades of pastel against the ineffable blue, with now a quality trivial, random, almost like notes of music—a harp, say—as the sun glinted and lost them. The reporter leaned down to the woman who was not yet aware of his presence, crying,

"Watch him! Oh, can he fly! Can he fly! And Ord aint going to beat the Ninety-Two to— Second money Thursday, and if Ord aint going to— Oh, watch him! Watch him!" She turned: the jaw, the pale eyes, the voice which he did not even listen to:

"Yes. The money will be fine." Then he even stopped looking at her, staring down the runway as the four aeroplanes, now in two distinct pairs, came in toward the field, increasing fast. The mechanic was talking again:

"He's in! Jesus, he's going to try Ord here! And look at Ord giving him room—" The two in front began to bank at the same time, side by side, the droning roar drawing down and in as though sucked down out of the sky by them in place of being produced by them. The reporter's mouth was still open; he knew that by the needling of nerves in his sore jaw. Later he was to remember seeing the icecream cone crush in his fist and begin to ooze between his fingers as he let the little boy slide to the ground and took his hand. Not now though; now the two aeroplanes, side by side and Shumann outside and above, banked into the pylon as though bolted together, when the reporter suddenly saw something like a light scattering of burnt paper or feathers floating in the air above the pylontip. He was watching this, his mouth still open, when a voice somewhere said, "Ahhhhhhh!" and he saw Shumann now shooting almost straight upward and then a whole wastebasketful of the light trash blew out of the aeroplane.

They said later about the apron that he used the last of his control before the fuselage broke to zoom out of the path of the two aeroplanes behind while he looked down at the closepeopled land and the empty lake, and made a choice before the tailgroup came completely free. But most of them were busy saying how his wife took it, how she did not scream or faint (she was standing quite near the microphone, near enough for it to have caught the scream) but instead just stood there and watched the fuselage break in two and said, "Oh damn you, Roger! Oh damn you! damn you!" and turning, snatched the little boy's hand and ran toward the seawall, the little boy dangling vainly on his short legs between her and the reporter who, holding the little boy's other hand, ran at his loose lightlyclattering gallop like a scarecrow in a gale, after the bright plain shape of love. Perhaps it was the added weight because she turned, still running, and gave him a single pale cold terrible look, crying,

"God damn you to hell! Get away from me!"

THE FIRST INTERNATIONAL AEROPLANE CONTEST

by Glenn Curtiss and Augustus Post

Prior to the first flights in New York City I had formulated plans for an improved machine, designed for greater speed and equipped with a more powerful motor. I wanted to take part in the first contest for the Gordon Bennett Aviation cup at Rheims, France, August 22 to 29, 1909. This was the first International Aviation Meet held, and much was expected of the French machines of the monoplane type. Great was my gratification, therefore, when I received word from the Aero Club of America, through Mr. Cortlandt Field Bishop, who was then president, that I had been chosen to represent America at Rheims.

Without allowing my plans to become known to the public I began at once to build an eight-cylinder, V-shaped, fifty horse-power motor. This was practically double the horse-power I had been using. Work on the motor was pushed day and night at Hammondsport, as I had not an hour to spare. I had kept pretty close watch on everything that had been printed about the preparations of the Frenchmen for the Gordon Bennett race and although it was reported that Blériot, in his own monoplane, and Hubert Latham, in an Antoinette monoplane, had flown as fast as sixty miles an hour, I still felt confident. The speed of aeroplanes is so often exaggerated in press accounts that I did not believe all I read about Blériot's and Latham's trial flights.

The motor was finished, but there was no time to put it in the new machine and try it out before sailing. It was, therefore, given a short run on the block, or testing-frame, hurriedly packed, and the entire equipment rushed to New York barely in time to catch the steamer for France.

The time was so short between the arrival of our steamer and the opening of the meet that in order to get to Rheims in time to qualify, we had to take the aeroplane with us on the train as personal baggage. Thanks to the kindness of the French railway officials, who realised our situation, and evidently had imbibed some of the prevailing aviation enthusiasm, we arrived at Rheims in quick time. In those early days of aviation there was not the keen partisanship for monoplane or biplane that one finds everywhere to-day; nor was there the strong popular feeling in France in favor of the monoplane that exists today. An aeroplane was simply an aeroplane at that time, and interesting as such, but naturally all Frenchmen favored their compatriots who were entered in the race, particularly Blériot, who had just earned world-wide fame by his flight across the English channel. The Frenchmen, as well as Europeans in general, fully expected Blériot to win with his fast monoplane.

My own personal hopes lay in my motor. Judge of my surprise, therefore, upon arriving at Rheims, to learn that Blériot, who had probably heard through newspaper reports that I was bringing over an eight-cylinder motor, had himself installed an eight-cylinder motor of eighty horsepower in one of his light monoplanes. When I learned this, I believed my chances were very slim indeed, if in fact they had not entirely disappeared. The monoplane is generally believed to be faster than the biplane with equal power. I had just one aeroplane and one motor; if I smashed either of these it would be all over with America's chances in the first International Cup Race. I had not the reserve equipment to bring out a new machine as fast as one was smashed, as Blériot and other Frenchmen had. Incidentally, there were many of them smashed during the big meet on the Plain of Bethany. At one time, while flying, I saw as many as twelve machines strewn about the field, some wrecked and some disabled and being hauled slowly back to the hangars, by hand or by horses. For obvious reasons, therefore, I kept out of the duration contests and other events, flying only in such events as were for speed, and of a distance not to exceed twenty kilometers, which was the course for the Gordon Bennett contest in 1909.

It is hard enough for any one to map out a course of action and stick to it, particularly in the face of the desires of one's friends; but it is doubly hard for an aviator to stay on the ground waiting for just the right time to get into the air. It was particularly hard for me to keep out of many events at Rheims held from day to day, especially as there were many patriotic Americans there who would have liked to see America's only representative take part in everything on the programme. I was urged by many of these to go out and contest the Frenchmen for the rich prizes offered and it was hard to refuse to do this. These good friends did not realise the situation. America's chances could not be imperilled for the sake of gratifying one's curiosity, or national pride. On top of the urgings of my American friends to go out and fly and take chances of having a whole machine when the day for the Gordon Bennett should arrive, I was penalised for not starting in the speed race, the Prix de la Vitesse, the penalty being one-twentieth of the time made when I should start in this event. However, I made a number of trial flights and ten official ones, during the meet, without mishap, except a sprained ankle. This was the result of running through growing grain at the time of landing and being thrown out of the machine. I was also fortunate in being the only aviator who took part in this first big meet to land at the hangar after each flight.

During this period of waiting, and making explanations to enthusiastic Americans who could not understand why I did not fly all the time, my mechanician, "Tod" Shriver, attracted a tremendous amount of attention from the throngs that visited the hangars because he worked in his shirt sleeves. They thought "Tod" picturesque because he did not wear the

French workman's blouse. Shriver used to say that if he were picturesque in shirt sleeves there were about fifty million perfectly good Americans across the Atlantic who formed probably the most picturesque crowd on earth.

In the try-outs it became evident to the Frenchmen that my aeroplane was very fast and it was conceded that the race for the Gordon Bennett Cup would lie between Blériot and myself, barring accidents. After a carefully timed trial circuit of the course, which, much to my surprise, I made in a few seconds less than M. Blériot's time, and that, too, with my motor throttled down slightly, I gained more confidence. I removed the large gasoline tank from my machine and put on a smaller one in order to lessen the weight and the head-resistance. I then selected the best of my three propellers, which, by the way, were objects of curiosity to the French aviators, who were familiar only with the metal blades used on the Antoinette machine, and the Chauvière, which was being used by M. Blériot. M. Chauvière was kind enough to make a propeller especially fitted to my aeroplane, notwithstanding the fact that a better propeller on my machine would lessen the chances of the French flyers for the cup. However, I decided later to use my own propeller, and did use it—and won.

August 29 dawned clear and hot. It was agreed at a meeting of the Committee, at which all the contestants were present, that each contestant should be allowed to make one trial flight over the course and that he might choose his own time for making it, between the hours of ten o'clock in the morning and six o'clock in the evening. The other starters were Blériot, Lefebre, and Latham for France, and Cockburn for England. As I have already stated, Blériot was the favourite because of his trip across the English channel and because of his records made in flights at various places prior to the Rheims meet.

As conditions were apparently good, I decided to make my trial flight shortly after ten o'clock. The machine was brought out, the engine given a preliminary run, and at half past ten I was in the air. Everything had looked good from the ground, but after the first turn of the course I began to pitch violently. This was caused by the heat waves rising and falling as the cooler air rushed in. The up and down motion was not at all pleasant and I confess that I eased off on the throttle several times on the first circuit. I had not then become accustomed to the feeling an aviator gets when the machine takes a sudden drop. On the second round I got my nerve back and pulled the throttle wide open and kept it open. This accounts for the fact that the second lap was made in faster time than the first. The two circuits were made safely and I crossed the finish line in seven minutes, fifty-five seconds, a new record for the course.

Now was my chance! I felt that the time to make the start for the Cup was then, in spite of the boiling air conditions, which I had found existed all over the course and made flying difficult if not actually dangerous. We hurriedly refilled the gasoline tank, sent official notice to the judges, carefully tested the wiring of the machine by lifting it at the corners, spun the propeller, and the official trial was on. I climbed as high as I thought I might without protest, before crossing the starting line—probably five hundred feet—so that I might take advantage of a gradual descent throughout the race, and thus gain additional speed. The sun was hot and the air rough, but I had resolved to keep the throttle wide open. I cut the corner as close as I dared and banked the machine high on the turns. I remember I caused great commotion among a big flock of birds which did not seem to be able to get out of the wash of my propeller. In front of the tribunes the machine flew steadily, but when I got around on the back stretch, as we would call it, I found remarkable air conditions. There was no wind, but the air seemed fairly to boil. The machine pitched considerably, and when I passed above the "graveyard," where so many machines had gone down and were smashed during the previous days of the meet, the air seemed literally to drop from under me. It was so bad at one spot that I made up my mind that if I got over it safely I would avoid that particular spot thereafter.

Finally, however, I finished the twenty kilometers in safety and crossed the line in fifteen minutes, fifty seconds, having averaged forty-six and one-half miles an hour. When the time was announced there was great enthusiasm among the Americans present, and every one rushed over to offer congratulations. Some of them thought that I would surely be the winner, but of this I was by no means certain. I had great respect for Blériot's ability, and besides, Latham and his Antoinette might be able to make better speed than they had thus far shown. In a contest of this sort it is never safe to cheer until all the returns are in. I confess that I felt a good deal like a prisoner awaiting the decision of a jury. I had done my best, and had got the limit of speed out of the machine; still I felt that if I could do it all over again I would be able to improve on the time. Meantime Cockburn, for England, had made a start but had come down and run into a haystack. He was only able to finish the course in twenty minutes, forty-seven and three-fifth seconds. This put him out of the contest.

Latham made his trial during the afternoon but his speed was five or six miles an hour slower than my record. The other contestants were flying about thirty-five miles an hour, and were, therefore, not really serious factors in the race.

It was all up to M. Blériot. All day long he tinkered and tested, first with one machine and then another; trying different propellers and making changes here and there. It was not until late in the afternoon that he brought out his big machine, Number 22, equipped with an eight-cylinder water-cooled motor, mounted beneath the planes, and driving by chain a four-bladed propeller, geared to run at a speed somewhat less than that of the engine. He started off at what seemed to be a terrific burst of speed. It looked to me just then as if he must be going twice as fast as my machine had flown; but it must be remembered that I was very anxious to have him go slow. The fear that he was beating me was father to the belief.

As soon as Blériot was off Mr. Cortlandt Field Bishop and Mr. David Wolfe Bishop, his brother, took me in their automobile over to the judges' stand. Blériot made the first lap in faster time than I had made it, and our hearts sank. Then and there I resolved that if we lost the cup I would build a faster aeroplane and come back next year to win it.

Again Blériot dashed past the stand and it seemed to me that he was going even faster than the first time. Great was my surprise, therefore, when, as he landed, there was no outburst of cheers from the great crowd. I had expected a scene of wild enthusiasm, but there was nothing of the sort. I sat in Mr. Bishop's automobile a short distance from the judges' stand, wondering why there was no shouting, when I was startled by a shout of joy from my friend, Mr. Bishop, who had gone over to the judges' stand.

"You win! You win!" he cried, all excitement as he ran toward the automobile. "Blériot is beaten by six seconds!"

A few moments later, just at half past five o'clock, the Stars and Stripes were slowly hoisted to the top of the flagpole and we stood uncovered while the flag went up. There was scarcely a response from the crowded grand stands; no true Frenchman had the heart to cheer. A good, hearty cheer requires more than mere politeness. But every American there made enough noise for ten ordinary people, so that numbers really counted for very little in the deep feeling of satisfaction at the result of the first great contest in the history of aviation. Mr. Andrew D. White, accompanied by Mrs. Roosevelt and Miss Ethel Roosevelt, came over to our car and congratulated me. Quentin Roosevelt, who had been in a state of excitement throughout the day, declared it "bully," while his brother Archie wanted to be shown all about the working of the machine. M. Blériot himself, good sportsman that he is, was among the first to extend congratulations to America and to me personally.

There was a reason beyond the mere patriotism why the Americans felt so happy over the result; it meant that the next international race would be held in the United States, and that the best foreign machines would have to come across the ocean to make a try for the cup the following year.

In commenting upon the result the Paris Edition of the New York *Herald* said that the race had rehabilitated the biplane; that while the lightness and bird-like lines of the monoplane had appealed to the crowd as the ideal representation of artificial flight, "the American aviator proved that the biplane not only possessed qualities of carrying weight and undoubtedly of superior stability, but that, if need be, it can develop speed equal to, if not superior to, its smaller rival."

Offers of engagements to fly in Germany and Italy came pouring in. To accept these meant a good deal of money in prizes, for it had been proven that I had the fastest aeroplane in the world. I accepted some of them, as I had learned that the conditions for flying at the big meets in Europe were almost ideal and that there was a tremendous amount of interest everywhere, among all classes. A big meet was organized at Brescia, Italy, and I went there from Rheims. Here I carried my first passenger, the celebrated Italian poet and author, Gabriele D'Annunzio. He was wildly enthusiastic over his experience, and upon being brought back to earth said with all the emotion of his people: "Until now I have never really lived! Life on earth is a creeping, crawling business. It is in the air that one feels the glory of being a man and of conquering the elements. There is the exquisite smoothness of motion and the joy of gliding through space— It is wonderful! Can I not express it in poetry? I might try."

And he did express it in poetry, a beautiful work published sometime later.

After winning the Grand Prize at Brescia and taking a wonderful motor trip over the Alps with Mr. Bishop, I hurried home to America to look after my business affairs, about which I had not had time even to think during the Rheims and Brescia meets.

Note by Augustus Post

Delegations of enthusiastic friends met Mr. Curtiss in New York, among them members of the Aero Club of America and other representative organisations. There followed a series of luncheons and dinners which seemed without end. Among all these the luncheon given by the Aero Club of America at the Lawyers' Club was notable because every one present showed such a warm interest in the success of American aeronautics, and such a firm determination not only to keep the trophy in this country, but to defend it the next year in an aviation meet that should be even greater than that with which Rheims had led the way.

But the real celebration took place in the little village of Hammondsport, the place where Mr. Curtiss was born and reared, and where he knew every man, woman, and child. The men in the factory and all his other warm friends got together and decided that there must be something out of the ordinary when he got back to town. They planned a procession all the way from Bath to Hammondsport, a distance of ten miles, with fireworks along the route. But a heavy rain came on just in time to spoil the fireworks plan, so they engaged a special train and this passed through a glow of red fire all the way home from Bath. At the Hammondsport station there was a carriage to draw him up the hill to his home, and fifty men furnished the motive power. There were arches with "Welcome" in electric lights, banners, fireworks, and speeches. Through the pouring rain there was a continuous procession of his friends and acquaintances—townspeople who had always given him their loyal support and the men from the shop who had made his success possible.

It was after eleven o'clock when the crowd dispersed—an almost unholy hour for Hammondsport. —AUGUSTUS POST.

THE GREAT SKY DUEL

by Don Dwiggins

The way Paul Mantz figured it, nobody could beat his Mustang racer, NX-1202, unless somebody came along with as good a ship, equal flying skill and a little better luck, so he bet $10,000 he'd win the 1947 Bendix Race.

Of the thirteen war surplus starters at Metropolitan Airport, Van Nuys, six were Mustangs, three were P-38 Lightnings, the others a Corsair, a Kingcobra, a Thunderbolt and an Invader. Mantz was not particularly worried about the other Mustangs; the plane to keep an eye on was Glenn H. McCarthy's stripped-down Lightning, the *Flying Shamrock.*

McCarthy, a Texas oil millionaire, had spent $100,000 on the *Shamrock,* named after a hotel he owned in Houston. The pilot was Jim Ruble, a former U.S.A.A.F. captain. Sporting a huge green shamrock on its nose, the Lightning was stripped, clipped and waxed, fitted with a near-flush canopy and four streamlined drop tanks. McCarthy claimed she was a full 100 miles per hour faster than the military version.

Two weeks before the race, McCarthy lit up a cigar, cleared his throat and told reporters: "Gentlemen, I sure hope you don't think I'm bragging, but I've got five hundred thousand dollars that says Ruble wins the Bendix!"

In Los Angeles, aviation writer Marvin Miles hurried out to Lockheed Air Terminal, where Paul Mantz based his Honeymoon Express airline, and told him of McCarthy's bet.

"Oh, what a sucker!" Mantz yelled. He scribbled a telegram:

"WILL PUT $10,000 IN ESCROW IN LOS ANGELES BANK AGAINST YOUR SAME AMOUNT IN ESCROW IN BANK AS WAGER MY P-51 WILL BEAT YOUR P-38 IN BENDIX. IS IT A DEAL?"

A wire came back immediately: "YES. MC CARTHY."

Mantz asked Miriam Johnson, his secretary, how much cash he had in the bank. "About two thousand dollars, Paul," she said.

"Aviation is always a feast or a famine, and this was a famine," Mantz later said. "I went to John Masterson, producer of the Art Linkletter show, and borrowed another five thousand. Then I called Carl Squier at Lockheed and told him I was a little short and needed three thousand. In ten minutes I had the money."

Interest in the Bendix Race, spurred by the McCarthy-Mantz side bet, was enhanced with William P. ("Bill") Odom, famous round-the-world flyer, entering the lineup with his P-47 Thunderbolt. And there was a sleeper in the race—Joe De Bona's Mustang, the *Magic City*. Like Mantz's record-breaking wet-wing job, De Bona's was surgically clean, firecracker hot. His backers, actor Jimmy Stewart and producer Robert Riskin, had given him a blank check to beat Mantz.

In picking De Bona for their pilot, Stewart and Riskin made a wise choice. De Bona, president of the Beverly Hills Lions Club and a prominent real-estate man, was more than a weekend society flyer. A veteran of the Air Transport Command, he had flown thousands of hours ferrying B-17's to Europe, and had once piloted a P-38 across the Pacific Ocean.

In the spring of 1943 Lieutenant De Bona had showed typical courage when he crashed behind the green curtain of Brazil's forbidding Amazon country after both engines quit during a ferry flight. He brought the transport down in a tiny clearing, slithered into a swamp. Already a veteran of jungle survival in Guadalcanal, he strung an antenna wire over a tree and hopefully transmitted his position to an air base 125 miles away, then settled down to wait. Later he told about his experiences:

"I didn't dare go far from the plane, for I would have been lost in ten minutes in that forest. Once I started to climb a tree to look over the countryside, but I came down in a hurry when I met a snake gazing at me through the branches.

"The days were blazing hot, with occasional squalls of drenching rain. I could do nothing but sit them out under what little shelter my plane could give me. At six o'clock, night came down with equatorial suddenness. Then swamp mosquitoes came on duty, buzzing about me until dawn. I slept or tried to sleep on the tail of my ship, using my rubber raft as a mattress and my parachute as a mosquito net. It was stifling hot, and jungle ants swarmed over me twenty-four hours a day."

Contracting fever, De Bona lay waiting for death, unsure whether his radio message had been heard. He ate his emergency rations, but had no water except what he could collect from the rainfall. Search planes found him fourteen days later and parachuted a canteen to him. It landed in a river infested with deadly piranha. Finally a native search party reached him on foot and led him out to a skiff in which he returned to the air base "somewhere in Brazil."

Besides Mantz, Ruble, Odom and De Bona, the most favored entries in the 1947 Bendix Race included Edmund P. ("Ebby") Lunken, Bruce A.

Gimbel, William F. Eddy, and Tommy Mayson—all flying Mustangs. Both Eddy and Mayson had participated in the Bendix Race of the previous year. Lunken, from Cincinnati, was an unknown. Gimbel was flying Jackie Cochran's P-51; she was staying with her husband, Floyd Odlum, at the Mayo Clinic.

The balance of the lineup included Marine Corps Reserve pilot F. P. Whitton, with his Corsair; Joseph Kinkella, of Kingman, Arizona, with a Bell Kingcobra; William P. Lear, Jr., back again with his P-38, the Reynolds *Little Bombshell,* sponsored by a ballpoint-pen maker; and two women: ex-Wasp Jane Page, with a P-38, and Dianna Cyrus with her Douglas A-26 Invader, the *Huntress.*

The day of the race came. First to take off was Jane Page's silver P-38, flagged into the air at 4:36 A.M., long before dawn, so she could reach Cleveland in time to enter a women's feature race there. Uneventfully, the others began the long flight eastward until, under a brilliant sun, Ruble took the flag, wheeled into position and gunned his P-38 down the runway. The *Shamrock* virtually staggered under its big fuel load.

Crouched on the wing of his red Mustang, Mantz watched Ruble with a critical eye. This was the ship he had to beat to win the $10,000 bet with McCarthy. He admired the way Ruble lifted the Shamrock from the runway. Then, unexpectedly, Ruble ran into trouble. Mantz saw something break away and fall to the ground—the port tip tank. Tumbling end over end it crashed beside the runway in a shower of sparks, igniting its volatile high-octane fuel in a blazing pyre.

Ruble kept going. He still had ample fuel to reach Cleveland nonstop if nothing else happened. He climbed steeply into the morning sun, a glint of white, and disappeared. Ruble knew this was a firewall race, a duel that called for full throttle all the way, straining his two engines to their utmost. However, the strain proved to be too much—while crossing northern Arizona under high blower, riding a tail wind that boosted his ground speed to well above 500 miles per hour, Ruble heard the screech of metal, then an explosion. A turbo supercharger blew up. Smoke and flames poured from under the cowling.

Ruble was through. There was no time to attempt a forced landing. He had to get out. Jettisoning the small canopy, he thought momentarily of the tail boom waiting to break his back. But without hesitation he released his belt, placed his feet firmly on the seat and, straining every muscle in his body, shoved upward to clear the boom. The slipstream struck him with full force, tumbling him backward. He missed the tail boom by inches, stabilized his fall and yanked the parachute D-ring. His parachute blossomed overhead, and as he swung gently earthward, into an Indian reservation near the Grand Canyon, he saw the *Shamrock* crash and explode. Ruble was picked up by an Indian on horseback. He made his way back to civilization at five miles an hour.

All Paul Mantz had to do now to win the $10,000 bet was to reach Cleveland, but he was out to win the Bendix Race. Joe De Bona's Mustang, not Ruble's P-38, was now his adversary. It was going to be Mantz's toughest race. He knew this from the way De Bona handled his ship on takeoff . . . professional, smooth, decisive, a bullet boring down the 6,000-foot runway, flashing through a vertical turn to begin an arrow-straight flight to the finish line.

Lunken, Gimbel and Eddy followed in their P-51's, then Tommy Mayson got into trouble. A gasoline truck backed into a wingtip of his plane and loosened the sealant inside. Mayson knew that if Larry Therkelsen, the starter, spotted the leak he was through. He engaged Therkelsen in conversation while a friend crawled under the wing with a rag, pretending to wipe dust off.

"You look okay," Therkelsen said finally. "You're next off."

Mayson jumped into the cockpit and became airborne quickly, but more trouble was ahead. "I was making good time, when my prop control arm to the propeller governor broke, and the spring-loaded governor dropped back to 2,200 rpms instead of the 3,000 rpms which I needed to race at high altitude. Mantz had set that up, and this was one of his ships. My plane not only slowed up but I also had to drop down to a lower altitude on account of weather. I finished fifth, in the pack."

As Mayson taxied to the parking ramp after crossing the finish line, his Packard engine quit, he was out of gas.

One by one the other entrants were eliminated as Mantz and De Bona settled down to their long sky duel. Odom's P-47 Thunderbolt again had failed to start. His ship, the *Reynolds Bombshell,* began leaking fuel badly, and unlike Tommy Mayson he couldn't hide it. Joseph Kinkella's Kingcobra got as far as Pueblo, Colorado, where fuel line trouble forced him to land. And Dianna Cyrus, at the controls of her A-26 Invader bomber, the *Huntress,* became lost.

Considered one of America's great women pilots, Dianna Cyrus was a heroic girl whose life had held much tragedy. Her husband, a World War II pilot, had been killed on a combat mission in an A-20 Havoc attack bomber, in 1945. After his death she and her sister, Dorro Converse, set out to execute a series of record speed runs.

Dianna had been taught to fly in 1943 by her late husband, Capt. John V. Cyrus. It was her dream to carry on in the world of the sky they both loved. In July 1947, the month before the Bendix Race, she and Dorro had flown the *Huntress* from Burbank to Denver for an intercity speed record of 2 hours 19 minutes 20 seconds. It was the first of what she hoped would be a glittering string of victories that her husband would have been proud of.

Now, in the Bendix sprint, a combination of unexpected weather, a faulty compass, and the pressure of the race turned the *Huntress* far off course to the north. Wandering over the countryside of Michigan, Dianna made her decision. She could not hope to win the Bendix Race. So land. Down below, she spotted a crop duster's tiny field, near Saginaw. She made an expert short-field landing, remembering what had been drilled into her mind by Capt. Cyrus: "Don't push your luck. When things go wrong, find an alternate plan. Make your decision on the basis of what the facts are, not what you wish they were."

Dianna faced facts the next year, while flying cargo for Eagle Air Freight out of Burbank. Her copilot was handsome Robert Bixby. She fell in love and married him. From the day of their honeymoon flight, delivering fresh-cut flowers to Eastern markets, the Flying Bixbys seemed headed for the happiness that had escaped her. Now her home was in the sky. She planned an exciting round-the-world flight to break Bill Odom's record of 73 hours 5 minutes 11 seconds.

Dianna originally had intended to make the world flight alone, but now it would become a second honeymoon. In their ship, a converted Mosquito bomber, the *Huntress II,* the Bixbys began their aerial odyssey at San Francisco early in 1950, flying to Newark, then across the Atlantic to Paris, and on to Cairo and Karachi. There engine trouble ended their attempt to beat Odom's record. They completed the world flight leisurely.

In 1954 Dianna, now a mother of two children, once more made plans to circle the globe in record time in the *Huntress II,* alone. Months passed, during which she and Bob flew regularly over the rugged mountains of Baja California, hauling cargos of produce. Always dreaming of the global record flight, she took off from Long Beach Airport one day in January 1955, flying a converted A-20 bomber. Bob followed in a DC-3, a second ship of their Bixby Airborne Products line.

At the tip of Baja California, ominous weather moved in to obscure the field at Los Planes ranch, their southern terminus. Her husband heard Dianna's voice crackle over the radio. He was over Santa Rosalia, in clear skies. Dianna had just passed Carmen Island. Only the peaks of the mountains protruded above the overcast there.

His mouth cottony, Bob Bixby prayed that her skill would get her through. She would be low on fuel, unable to fly back.

"I'm letting down, Bob," she called again. "I'm over water."

Helplessly, her husband acknowledged, then said quietly, "Take it easy, honey."

He thought of the advice Capt. Cyrus had given her, "don't push your luck . . . make your decision on the basis of what the facts are . . ."

Dianna, he knew, would do that. She was committed. She let down through the overcast, and died, decapitated by a roll of barbed wire torn loose from the cargo bay. Ironically, it happened ten years to the day after Capt. Cyrus had been killed—and in the same type of aircraft.

Paul Mantz had been Dianna Cyrus's technical advisor in the 1947 Bendix Race, as he had been for Amelia Earhart before the war. Now, boring steadily through the substratosphere in his powerful Mustang—the same one that carried him to victory in the 1946 Bendix Race—he was making far better time. A tail wind urged him from check point to check point with unexpected speed; his estimates fell behind. This would be his best race, but where was De Bona? He had taken off ahead of De Bona and the same providential winds no doubt were helping the ex-ATC pilot over the course to Cleveland.

The hours passed, the sun dropped behind. It was going to be a great day. Pleasant thoughts crowded his mind. Ten thousand dollars in his pocket already, if he just crossed the finish line. Another ten thousand if he won. Poor McCarthy—the three-leafed symbol of luck hadn't worked. Racing takes more than luck. It takes everything you've got. Paul was giving it everything he had.

Crouched inside the little cockpit, Mantz flew with the skill that had cheated death many times as a Hollywood stunt flyer. He bored on eastward, across the Mississippi, over fields of corn spreading like patchwork over Indiana, diving fast now, into Ohio, along the lakeshore, and there it was, Cleveland, the Bendix home pylon. Mantz thundered across the line in 4 hours 26 minutes 57.4 seconds, a good quarter of an hour faster than the year before. He landed, tired, and waited for De Bona.

Joe De Bona was not long in coming; like a meteor he dived out of the west to hurtle across the finish line so close to Mantz's time that the crowd of thousands in the grandstands began a rhythmic chant, some for Mantz, some for De Bona. Finally the official timers handed the results to Bendix's new president, Malcolm P. Ferguson. De Bona had flown the race in 4 hours 28 minutes 15 seconds, just one minute 17.6 seconds behind Mantz. He'd lost by a bare two miles an hour.

Mantz, like Frank Fuller now a two-time Bendix Race winner, grinned and slapped De Bona's back. They were friendly enemies. They would race again the next year.

The balance of the 1947 race was anticlimactic—Lunken finished third, after a five-hour flight. Gimbel came in fourth, Eddy fifth, Mayson sixth, Whitton seventh, Lear eighth, and Jane Page ninth.

Having swept all the first six places, the Mustang was still unbeatable.

THE WING WALKER

by Guy Gilpatric

One of the boys phoned me at my mother's that you were asking where I was and how you wanted me to come back here and take charge of the motor assembly in the factory. Well, I drove down this morning to tell you I'll be glad to take the job.

I'm through with flying, though. I never want to get near a plane again. You know how I used to have the itch, kind of. I bet most of the boys here in the shop have got it yet. These birds who come to work on motorcycles every morning doing ninety with their cutouts open and wearing flying helmets and goggles and all that stuff—why, they're just trying to kid themselves that they're pilots. I used to try it, too. No more, though! I wouldn't go over to the field this afternoon to see the best flying show ever put on the books.

It's not cold feet, exactly. That crash I had didn't really get my nerve. But on Labor Day . . .

Well, I'll tell you about what I was doing all last summer, and then you'll understand me better when I come to the part about Labor Day.

You'll probably remember about a year ago, when I was working here, we got the order from the Air Mail for those V3X engines and you sent me over to the field to install them. Well, in the hangar next to the Air Mail was a little fellow named Tommy Dean. He used to come in and chew the sock with me, and a couple of times I went over to his place and he showed me an old Canadian Jenny he had, all painted red. He used to carry passengers with it on Sundays at five dollars a throw. Two or three times, when he was having trouble with his old teapot of an engine, I helped him out and fixed her up so she'd run like new. And he took me up for a couple of rides, and it made me crazier to learn to fly than ever.

One day he told me he'd got some money somewheres and was going to start a flying circus. He wanted to know if I would go to work for him and come on the road for the season.

Well, I always wanted to get outside again ever since the war, and I was glad to work for Tommy. He was one fine boy. He said he'd teach me to fly and that listened best of all. That's why I quit my job here in the shop and went over to Tommy's place.

He bought two new machines—that is, they were surplus army ships that had been in the crates ever since '18, but had got pretty lousy in the meanwhile. We put new fabric on the wings and fixed them up where they needed fixing, and they really weren't such bad ships at that. Well, we decided we ought to have a wing walker with the flying circus—you know, one of these nuts that do acrobatic stuff while the plane is in the air—so we stiffened up the ribs along the leading edge and fixed up the wing skids so's an acrobat could hang on 'em. Then we rigged the running gear so we could put on a trapeze, put foot stirrups on top of the center section and all the usual stuff. Betweentimes, Tommy was giving me dual control in the air on the old Canuck JN, and I was taking to it like a duck takes to water.

After three or four hours in the air with Tommy, he let me take her up solo. And after a few weeks alone, I had her eating out of my hand, doing loops and all. Flying really ain't hard, and it really ain't thrilling—except at times. But it makes up for it then!—Jesus H. Christ, I'll say it does!

Well, Tommy advertised in *The Billboard* and got hold of a fellow to manage us, a guy named Holtz. He was a pretty good manager, too. He got in touch with two or three wing walkers, and they came down to the field and did their stuff for a tryout.

Well, one of them was pretty good—he was one of these iron-jaw birds, and his specialty was hanging by his teeth from the fifteen-foot trapeze on the running gear. It was some stunt, all right. But Tommy caught him hitting the bottle once or twice over in the corner of the hangar before they went up, and Tommy didn't have any use for guys that needed Dutch courage. So he told this bird we didn't want him. Edwards, his name was—Dare-Devil Edwards. Maybe you read about him getting killed out on the Coast somewheres, doing his stuff for the movies.

Well, when none of these birds measured up, Tommy said the booking agent had spoken to him about some girl acrobat that had been with Corticelli's Combined Three-Ringed Circuses, who wanted to break into the air game; and what a knockout it would be to have a lady dare-devil and all that. Well, neither Tommy nor I was anxious about having a woman around, but we figured Holtz was right when he said what an attraction she'd be. So Tommy says all right, go ahead and trot her out.

So that Sunday out she came.

Now, of course, I know what you're thinking when I talk about a lady wing walker. You're thinking about some tough old battle-ax with bleached hair and maybe a gold tooth showing and a build on her like a riveter. But this one was nothing like that.

Her name was Mary Muller, and she was no beauty nor anything like that either. But the first time I saw her, she made me think of a school teacher when I was a kid in school that I was in love with. She was pretty plain, but awful nice, and I guess maybe three or four years older than Tommy or me.

She said she hardly knew anything about heavier-than-air work. She'd done a season making triple parachute drops off an old smoke-bag balloon. She said she had a couple of ribs caved in one time when the 'chute swung her into some telephone wires. Most of the time she'd been with a circus doing trapeze and tight-wire stuff over the net. But she'd quit the circus this year, and I found out later it was because some man had been bothering her.

That was the funny thing about Mary Muller, and maybe you've known women who were the same way. I told you she wasn't pretty and I know all she wanted was to be left alone. But she was always being bothered by men. She just couldn't help it, and there's lots of guys that are always on the prod, and so poor Mary used to have a tough time keeping clear of them. Believe me, she was so nice that I was sorry for her, and besides that I liked her a whole lot myself.

Well, that first day when she came down to the field, Tommy took her in the air and did some spins and falling leafs and things, and when they landed she said it was the greatest stuff in the world. She said the old balloons and the circus trapeze stuff wasn't in it! I remember she was so happy about it that she looked younger than she was, and yes, she really did look kind of pretty. All lighted up, like.

And I remember that Tommy was more polite when he helped her out than he ever was with paid passengers. Passengers always made him sore, somehow; he was awful highstrung, and they always say such damn fool things.

We took her over to the hangar and asked her to show us some of her acrobatic stuff. We rigged up a trapeze over a roof beam and she put on a suit of old oily flying overalls and went to it. Well, I'm here to state she was good. She did giant swings and double cuts and all that stuff, and I've paid half a buck many a time to see a whole lot worse in vaudeville. And finally, just to show us what she had, she chinned herself ten times with one hand—and here I am a big husky bird sticking out my chest because I can do it four!

And mind you, she wasn't all lumps and knotty muscles, either—just sort of slim and womanly. Womanly. I guess that was what she was most of all—womanly. All the time you saw her and talked to her and thought about her, that was the thing you remembered most. I guess that had been the cause of her troubles, too.

Well, anyway, after we'd seen her work, there in the hangar, we talked it over and agreed that she was O.K. We could feel just from meeting her that she had the nerve, and she sure had shown us that she had the stuff. So Tommy hired her for a hundred per and five percent, and started to work her out in the air.

He took her up for a couple of more rides, just to get her used to it better.—Doing his stuff of course, because you might as well set on the ground as do straight flying. Then he had her climb out of the seat onto the wing and stay there hanging to a strut while he did some vertical banks and Immelmans.

Finally, when she'd got pretty good, I took the other ship up close to them, with a photographer in the back seat. We took some pictures of her hanging by one hand from a wing skid at three thousand feet and standing on her head on top of the plane. These pictures were for Holtz to send around to booking agents and such to book dates with, and for the Sunday newspapers. I have a set of those pictures in my grip and sometime I'll show 'em to you. We took 'em from maybe only twenty feet away, and I want you to tell me what kind of an expression you see on Tommy's face as he watches that girl do her stuff. I know he used to be all sweaty around the eyes when he came down and took his goggles off, poor kid.

Well, we booked as "Dean's Flying Circus, Featuring Mademoiselle Marie Mallaire, the Vamp of Cloudland." Tommy raised an awful holler about the vamp stuff, but Holtz said he knew his job. I guess he did, all right, because he got us booked to some pretty good money—mostly country and state fairs, with some conventions and things like the Elks and Shriners and the Legion.

But, say, I wish I could tell you this story right. I can go on this way giving you the facts, but it's not half the story without your knowing Mary. She was aces up. She was some woman! You shouldn't think about her like a sweetheart or a wife or a mother or a sister, but a *woman.* I hope you can get me, because I can't exactly say what I'm trying to say. It's funny . . .

I want to tell you it was some sight to see that woman work, after we'd all practiced up. Tommy would take her up a thousand or fifteen hundred feet, with her in the back seat and him in front. Then she'd stand up and climb onto the top wing, all dressed in her white flying suit. And she'd stand up there, leaning against the rushing wind and balancing herself with her hands above her head. Then she'd climb down onto the bottom wing and walk out to the tip, swinging herself along from the wires to the struts, the same as a trolley-car conductor goes along the running board of an open car. When she got out to the tip she'd reach around underneath and grab hold of the wing skid and swing down and hang by one hand—waving the other and throwing kisses with it. And finally she'd come back and climb down between the wheels on the running gear, cast loose the rope ladder and climb down it, swinging around beneath the plane like a big white pendulum.

Finally we all got so good that I used to jockey over underneath Tommy's plane, when she was on the ladder, and she'd change over to my ship. Then I'd take her once around the field and she'd transfer back to Tommy. It was some stunt! Believe me, all three of us were nervous when we did it, but there was big money in it and that was what we were out for.

Then Mary said why didn't we put on a parachute jump, too. So we got her a 'chute—a safety-pack, like the air-mail pilots use. When she got through with her wing walking and changing planes, she'd climb to the back seat in Tommy's ship, snap the spring hook of the 'chute onto the big steel ring on her harness, and then Tommy would start a loop, stall the ship when it was upside down, and she'd fall out head first—like it was accidental.

Boy, that was some thriller, all right, seeing her fall like a stone for a hundred feet—and then see the big white 'chute bust open like a cloud, and her come floating down on it!

That girl could handle a 'chute, too! A lot of people will tell you you can't steer a 'chute, but you can. You just pull on the shroud lines on the side you want to go toward, and it folds in a little on that side and you sort of side slip in that direction. Of course you don't want to pull them too much, or the 'chute will fold in and spill all the air out of it. And then God help you!

Well, we worked up all this stuff, and believe me we could put on a swell forty-minute show. We flew our first date on Decoration Day over in Pennsylvania. Everybody said we had all the other flying circuses lashed to the mast. From there we worked over across into Ohio and out that way for a couple or three months, filling maybe a date a week.

Of course, at some places we had three- and four-day dates. Somebody on the fair committee, or whatever it was, always gave us a car to use, and we had a fine time. I had two other guys to help me with the planes. Tommy was a white man and said I was an aviator now and not to bother with mechanicking any more, except to make sure everything was O.K. We were making big money—I know my share of it ran over a hundred a week and, naturally, I was pulling down the smallest end of it.

We had pretty good weather on the average. We struck a couple of mean days, of course, and some small fields with trees and wires and things to fly out of. But on the whole we couldn't kick. Tommy and I flew the ships from place to place, carrying the mechanics. Holtz and Mary would go in the train, shipping the tools and spares and things by express.

I never had such a fine time in my life as I did those summer months. We were all mighty happy. Believe me, I made up my mind that outdoors was the place for me. I remember how I used to love the smell of those fairs and carnivals—there's something about them you can't smell anywhere else. It's a mixture of the peanuts and the popcorn and the hot dogs cooking, and the green grass that's been trampled on, and the wet dust where they've been sprinkling the track. Then there's the smell of the country people in their best clothes, and the funny *laundry* kind of smell from the little kids in their stiff starched dresses.

Mary was enjoying herself, too. Only once did I see her troubled, and the guy that caused it got hurt. He was a bird that had known Mary in some circus she'd been in, and he was running a razzle-dazzle or a Ferris wheel or something at the Clyde City Centennial where we were flying. I noticed she was kind of worried when she came out to the grounds every day we were at Clyde City.

Once I happened to see her looking at this bird who was standing in the crowd. He was looking at her. We were just rolling the ships into the tent after the flight, so in a minute or so I moseyed over through the crowd and asked him to step to one side with me for a minute. Well, he looked toward Mary again and came along with me around behind some booths and things. Then I asked him what the hell he meant by it.

He says, "Now listen here, friend, all this is none of your business. Miss Muller's a friend of mine I knew way back three years ago, so mind your own business."

So I says, "Well, listen here, friend, I'm making it my business, and I'm telling you to lay off."

And he says, "Well, listen here, friend, if you think I'm trying to get fresh with Miss Muller, you got me wrong. I asked her to marry me three or four times, and I meant it. And I'm going to ask her again, because that's how much I think of her."

So I says, "Well, listen here, friend, if there's any asking to be done, Tommy Dean's the boy to do it."

Somehow, just at that very moment, it seemed that I realized Tommy was in love with her and she with him. It's funny how you can be looking right at something for a long time and then suddenly see it as you have never seen it before. Just as if somebody switched a searchlight on it.

"Tommy Dean?" says this bird, looking up sudden and spitting on the grass in a tough way. "Well, I don't know what prior claims this Tommy Dean has got. Who's Tommy Dean, anyway? And who are you? I guess you're just a God damned butt-in, if you ask me."

He made a swipe at me, and so I lit into him and beat him pretty thorough. I was kind of sorry afterward because he hadn't seemed such a bad bird. I guess he was serious about Mary, all right. Anyway, the date was over that afternoon, so we didn't see him again and I didn't say anything about it to Mary. I think she must have guessed a little what happened, because that night at supper in the hotel she asked me how I skinned my knuckles so bad.

I got red and said, "Oh, nothing." She looked at me a minute and lay her hand on my arm very soft, and smiled. Her blue eyes were awful soft, too. Gee, but she was some woman!

Now that I realized Tommy loved her, I could see it more and more all the time. And I could see that she was just the same way about him. There were times, when she looked at him, when her face really became sort of beautiful. So one day I said to him, "Tommy, we know each other pretty well, now, and I hope you'll excuse what I'm going to say. Why don't you speak to Mary?"

He looked at me kind of queer, and swallowed.

"Speak to Mary?—What about?"

So I took him by the arm and I had to swallow once or twice too. But I said right out: "Tommy, you love Mary and she loves you. She's the finest woman in the world, and that's the kind you've got coming to you. Why don't you get married?"

Well, he didn't say anything for a few minutes. Then he led me over to a wing crate in the back of the tent and made me sit down beside him. "Eddy," he said, quiet like, "I didn't know anybody knew I loved Mary and I never was sure she cared about me. I hoped it, sure—but how do you know it?"

So I told him that I couldn't tell exactly why, except that she was so—well, so darned *womanly* whenever she looked at him or talked about him. I couldn't explain it exactly, but he understood what I meant. He just sat there clasping and unclasping his hands so hard that the knuckles got all white.

Finally he said, "Well, Eddy, I'll ask her to marry me when we finish the season—but good Lord, it would get my nerve to ask her now and then have to watch her doing her stuff and hang by one hand and go plunging down in that 'chute! It's bad enough now, knowing I love her and seeing her do it. And maybe—maybe it's as bad for her. But as long as we haven't really *spoken* about it to each other, it ain't quite the same. But just a word or so, and then somehow that one little bit of whatever it is that keeps us going would break and be gone. When she'd smile at me from out there on the wing tip, and when I'd turn around and watch her hook onto her 'chute before I start the loop—why, we'd both know what each other was thinking and it would get our nerve. No, Eddy, I'll wait till we finish the season. I'd never let her finish it, only I know she'd never quit now." He looked at me kind of eager. "You don't think we could make her quit if we asked her to, do you, Eddy?"

Well, I knew she wouldn't, she was that game, and I told him so. We sat there on the crate for maybe an hour or so with neither of us saying much. Then the crowd started coming around the tent and the band was playing and the trotting races started, and pretty soon it was time for us to fly.

We went up and did our stuff. Once she smiled at me way up there in the air when she swung onto my plane from the rope ladder. Even with her helmet and goggles and oil all over her face from the engine, she looked beautiful! It was just one of those little minutes when she looked that way, because mostly, like I told you, she looked kind of plain.

Tommy kept his ship wing and wing with mine all the time I had her aboard and he never took his eyes off her. Then we swung over the infield of the track and Tommy came over me with the ladder dragging into us and his wheels almost touching my head. She grabbed it and climbed into his ship again. Then I did a wing-over and a barrel roll, and went down in a spin, leaving them the air for the parachute jump which was the big stunt. This was the way we always worked it.

Well, I landed and sat in my machine looking up, and Holtz yelled through his megaphone about "A-viay-tor-r Dean and Madam-o-zell Mal-laire will now perform the hazardous doub-bul a-eerial loop!"

The band always stopped playing at this point, and it was always awful quiet except for the buzz of Tommy's motor way up there in the blue sky with all the crowd necking up.

Then Tommy pulled up into a slow loop, stalled at the top upside down, and out she fell like a stone.

It was a hell of a sight—on the level, it was! Holtz always made it worse by screaming, "My God, she's falling!" Then the 'chute always flared open, and you could hear the people breathe, and the band would bust into "The Star-Spangled Banner." Mary'd come floating down with Tommy circling around her, and the show was over.

I remember that afternoon Tommy was sweatier than usual around the eyes when he took his goggles off. He asked me for a cigarette as soon as he got out of the ship, which he didn't usually do. He was always sort of scornful about fliers needing a smoke as soon as they landed.

When they brought Mary around the track in a car, bowing and throwing kisses to the hicks in the stand, he took both hands to help her out. It seemed to me he made a half move, as if he wanted to put his arms around her. His face was different than usual, and for a second or so when he had her by the hand, I saw that same strange kind of beautiful look on hers.

That night, after Mary had gone to bed, he had Holtz and me come up to his room in the hotel. The three of us went over the dates we had booked ahead. He canceled all but the best ones. He said we'd had a good season and made money, and he wasn't going to have us strain our luck and work our heads off on cheap barnstorming. It was almost fall now, and pretty near the close of the season—after we'd played the big state fairs.

Well, I was sorry to see that he was getting jumpy. I knew that was what was the matter. And I was sorry because I figured that what I'd said to him that afternoon was the reason. But at that, we'd be wise to lay off a little. The toughest bird in the world gets pretty tired flying out of small fields in all kinds of weather, doing the stuff we were doing, and knowing that the crowds all the time were hoping some of us would get killed. Isn't that what the crowd comes to see?

Well, we had a good date booked for Labor Day at a big fair they were having at Pine Falls. We got down there three days ahead and got the ships in fine shape. It was hotter than hell's hinges down there, and inside our big tent it was like a Turkish bath. Mary and Tommy went over to the lake every day for a swim. I went over one afternoon, too. You bet Mary made those hicks take notice when she did swan dives and back dives off a thirty-foot tower they had on the pier. It scared Tommy to watch her, but he didn't trust himself to say anything.

We were to fly at four o'clock Labor Day afternoon. It was terrible hot. There were big white thunder clouds all around, but they looked tight, as if they had skins on 'em. You could tell it wasn't going to rain till away late in the evening. There wasn't a breath of wind. You could see the heat waves dancing on the roof of the grandstand and on the track like over the top of a stove. It meant rotten flying, with a lot of nasty bumpy air from the hot air currents and the cloud shadows. I'd rather fly in a snowstorm than in heat, any time.

Well, they had their trotting races and their running races and flivver races. The bands played and the people went shrieking around on the "Ocean Wave Roller Coaster," and the dizzy dips and all that stuff. You could hear the barkers yelling—then it all stopped quiet while they announced us.

We took the planes across into the infield and ran the engines a little. I took off first. Well, I got the rottenest bumping from that air I ever had. They were mean kind of kicks and surges, so that the controls wouldn't answer. You'd yank the ailerons or the elevator, and the stick would just flop around loose in your hand, as if the control cables had busted. And it was hard air to climb in—I bet it took me five minutes to get up a thousand feet, where I did some loops and vertical banks and things.

Well, when I got through doing my stuff, I looked over the side and saw Tommy had already taken off. He was getting bumped around same as I was. I waited till he came up out of the warm air to where it was a little cooler and steadier, then I dove over and flew along close to him. He shook his head and grinned and pointed down, and I knew he meant how rotten the air was. Even up where we were now it was pretty rough, and we didn't dare fly too close for fear we might bump into each other.

Well, we did some stuff together—loops side by side and so on—and then we went down to six hundred for Mary to do her wing walking. We usually went lower, but today it was too rough. I remember her smiling over the edge of the cockpit at me as she rubbed resin into her gloves and shoes so's she wouldn't slip.

Then she climbed out onto the wing and went to it. Every time the plane hit a bump or fell into a hole, I could see Tommy fighting the controls for all he was worth to keep the ship steady for fear Mary would get jolted off. And believe me, there was a couple of times when she had to stop her stuff for a minute and hang on with both hands. Then she'd laugh and wave to Tommy or maybe over at me, and start in her stunts again. Gee, but she was some woman!

Well, it came time for her to do the transfer. We were getting bumped around so bad that I hoped Tommy wouldn't let her try it. But he started to climb his ship up to smoother air and so I stuck along with him. We took a long, straight climb that brought us outside the fair grounds and over the town, and it was rows and rows of little bungalows, all exactly alike, with a little garage out behind them.

When we got high enough, we turned around and headed back, and Mary climbed down onto the running gear and let out the rope ladder. Of course Tommy couldn't see her because his lower wing was in the way, but I waved at her and she nodded back. Then she slid off the axle and started down the ladder so's to be on the bottom rung ready to transfer to my plane when we got over the grandstand.

Well, I was watching her from maybe forty feet away, when all of a sudden I got a bump that threw me right into my safety belt, and half a second later Tommy's plane got it too. Then . . . I don't know exactly how it happened. I guess that when their ship got bumped, the ladder with Mary on it sort of whipped around. And Mary's left arm went right into the propeller. It hit her just above the elbow.

There she was, with her arm hanging limp and kind of twisted, and the whole side of her white suit getting red—and her clinging there dazed, not knowing exactly what had happened. I'll tell you I damned near went crazy hoping she wouldn't let go.

Tommy must have felt the jar when the prop hit her arm. I guess the blade must have split and vibrated, because he throttled his engine and started down on a flat glide. Well, he couldn't see what had happened, and he was leaning over one side, then the other, trying to see Mary. Then I saw him put his hand up to his goggles, quick, and wipe 'em off. I guess it was some of Mary's blood blown back on them by the propeller. He looked at his hand and held it toward me and waved it around, and I could see he was yelling and frantic—but, of course, I couldn't hear him on account of the motor.

I was trying to figure out some way to get close enough to catch Mary if she fainted, knowing all the time there wasn't a chance in a million to do it. And all this time we were getting lower and lower, because Tommy didn't dare open up his engine.

Well, finally Mary started groping up the ladder, using only one hand. Slowly, slowly, she crawled onto the bottom wing, and God knows how she ever did it. Tommy let go of the controls and leaned way out, grabbed her and finally dragged her up into the back seat.

All this time his ship was sagging and diving down, because nobody was flying it. And I hung along as close as I dared. When he got her into the hind cockpit, he climbed forward and grabbed the control again. We were way down low over town and getting bumped around frightful by the hot air.

It seemed a year before we got near that fair ground. Just as we were about to head down to land, a terrible thing happened. Tommy's propeller broke, and before he could grab the switch and shut off the power, the engine raced itself loose and busted up out of the motor bed. A couple of pieces of the metal cowl tore off and flew back and caught in the wires. Well, I guess the gas line broke, or maybe the hind end of the engine stove in the tank—anyhow, in a second Tommy's ship was all ablaze in the front cockpit where he was. Well, for a second I felt sick and raving mad, because I was so close and could almost touch him and not able to do a thing.

He scrambled up out of the seat with his hands over his mouth and his clothes all on fire, and he sprawled back over the cowl to where Mary was lying. I saw him sort of lift her up and snap the parachute hook into her harness and then drop her overboard out of the ship.

And all through the fuselage of his plane the flames were roaring like a blow torch, and a trail of black smoke and bits of burning fabric fluttered behind.

Tommy climbed out on the left wing as far as he could, but the damned thing went into a tail spin and I guess he had breathed in some flames. Anyway, he must have known that he was through. There's hardly a chance with fire in the air. I followed him down as close as I could, and it was pretty near a straight dive, and suddenly we shot down past Mary swinging around on her parachute, and I thanked God she was safe. The jerk of the 'chute snapping open must have brought her to, because I saw her face in a flash as we went down past her, and, well—she saw what was happening to Tommy.

Tommy's plane hit over by the edge of the infield. I couldn't bear to watch the last part of the fall. I knew he was gone. But I looked up and I saw Mary about three hundred feet up, and I remember there was a big patch of red on the 'chute from where she'd bled on it in the machine. I guess she'd seen Tommy crash into the ground, because just as I looked up, she was reaching up into the shrouds with her one good hand and pulling them and swaying the 'chute with her body.

I turned sick when I saw what she was trying to do. I was hollering "No! No!" like in a nightmare. In a second or so, she had folded up one side of the 'chute clear under, and it all lost its shape and folded up like a rag. She came falling straight down.

As she went by me with that big silk 'chute streaming straight up behind her, I couldn't see the blood on it any more. It looked all white, exactly like a bride's veil. It was beautiful—and oh, Christ Almighty, it was awful!

There were people rushing all over the field like ants. There was such a crowd all over it that I couldn't land. Tommy's plane was blazing so nobody could get near it. But I was pretty near crazy, so I took a chance and landed in the back stretch of the track. I guess I hit a tree or something, because I remember an awful crash. Then I remember running across the field toward that big fat column of black smoke floating straight up.

I fought my way through the crowd and got in to where the two of them were laying. They had fallen within a few feet of each other and for a half a second, I saw them. I was just covering my face with my hands when that Ferris wheel guy I'd had the fight with at Clyde City came running up. We just held on to each other and cried like babies.

Then some state police came galloping up on horses and Holtz, the manager, came and put me in an ambulance. I remember wondering what was stabbing me in the lungs every time I breathed.

After that I don't remember much for a couple of weeks. Then I went to visit my mother and rested up most of the winter. Finally I got so I could sleep again and now I am okay.

The only thing is, when I take this job, I don't want to do any installation work on the planes at the field. I have got a bellyful of planes, even when they're on the ground. I want to work right here in the factory.

World War I
DOWNING MY FIRST HUN
by Eddie V. Rickenbacker

It will be noticed that my preparation for combat fighting in the air was a gradual one. As I look back upon it now, it seems that I had the rare good fortune to experience almost every variety of danger that can beset the war pilot before I ever fired a shot at an enemy from an aeroplane.

This good fortune is rare, it appears to me. Many a better man than myself has leaped into his stride and begun accumulating victories from his very first flight over the lines. It was a brilliant start for him and his successes brought him instant renown. But he had been living on the cream at the start and was unused to the skim-milk of aviation. One day the cream gave out and the first dose of skim-milk terminated his career.

So despite the weeks and weeks of disappointment that attended my early fighting career, I appreciated even then the enormous benefit that I would reap later from these experiences. I can now most solemnly affirm that had I won my first victory during my first trips over the lines I believe I would never have survived a dozen combats. Every disappointment that came to me brought with it an enduring lesson that repaid me eventually tenfold. If any one of my antagonists had been through the same school of disappointments that had so annoyed me it is probable that he, instead of me, would now be telling his friends back home about his series of victories over the enemy.

April in France is much like April anywhere else. Rains and cloudy weather appear suddenly out of a clear sky and flying becomes out of the question or very precarious at best. On the 29th of April, 1918, we rose at six o'clock and stuck our heads out of doors as usual for a hasty survey of a dismal sky. For the past three or four days it had rained steadily. No patrols had gone out from our aerodrome. If they had gone they would not have found any enemy aircraft about, for none had been sighted from the lines along our sector.

About noon the sun suddenly broke through and our hopes began to rise. I was slated for a patrol that afternoon and from three o'clock on I waited about the hangars watching the steadily clearing sky. Captain Hall and I were to stand on alert until six o'clock that night at the aerodrome. Precisely at five o'clock Captain Hall received a telephone call from the French headquarters at Beaumont stating that an enemy two-seater machine had just crossed our lines and was flying south over their heads.

Captain Hall and I had been walking about the field with our flying clothes on and our machines were standing side by side with their noses pointing into the wind. Within the minute we had jumped into our seats and our mechanics were twirling the propellers. Just then the telephone sergeant came running out to us and told Captain Hall to hold his flight until the Major was ready. He was to accompany us and would be on the field in two minutes.

While the sergeant was delivering the message I was scanning the northern heavens and there I suddenly picked up a tiny speck against the clouds above the Forêt de la Reine, which I was convinced must be the enemy plane we were after. The Major was not yet in sight. Our motors were smoothly turning over and everything was ready.

Pointing out the distant speck to Jimmy Hall, I begged him to give the word to go before we lost sight of our easy victim. If we waited for the Major we might be too late.

To my great joy Captain Hall acquiesced and immediately ordered the boys to pull away the blocks from our wheels. His motor roared as he opened up his throttle and in a twinkling both our machines were running rapidly over the surface of the field. Almost side by side we arose and climbing swiftly, soared away in a straight line after our distant Boche.

In five minutes we were above our observation balloon line which stretches along some two miles or so behind the front. I was on Jimmy's right wing and off to my right in the direction of Pont-à-Mousson I could still distinguish our unsuspecting quarry. Try as I might I could not induce the Captain to turn in that direction, though I dipped my wings, darted away from him and tried in every way to attract his attention to the target which was so conspicuous to me. He stupidly continued on straight north.

I determined to sever relations with him and take on the Boche alone, since he evidently was generous enough to give me a clear field. Accordingly I swerved swiftly away from Captain Hall and within five minutes overhauled the enemy and adroitly maneuvered myself into an ideal position just under his sheltering tail. It was a large three-seater machine and a brace of guns poked their noses out to the rear over my head. With fingers closing on my triggers I prepared for a dash upwards and quickly pulled back my stick. Up I zoomed until my sights began to travel along the length of the fusilage overhead. Suddenly they rested on a curiously familiar looking device. It was the French circular cocard painted brightly under each wing! Up to this time I had not even thought of looking for its nationality, so certain had I been that this must be the Boche machine that had been sighted by the French headquarters.

Completely disgusted with myself, I viraged abruptly away from my latest blunder, finding some little satisfaction in witnessing the startled surprise of the three Frenchmen aboard the craft, who had not become aware of my proximity until they saw me flash past them. At any rate I had stalked them successfully and might have easily downed them if they had been Boches. But as it was, it would be a trifle difficult to face Jimmy Hall again and explain to him why I had left him alone to get myself five miles away under the tail of a perfectly harmless ally three-seater. I looked about to discover Jimmy's whereabouts.

There he was cavorting about amidst a thick barrage of black shell-bursts across the German lines. He was half-way to St. Mihiel and a mile or two inside Hun territory. Evidently he was waiting for me to discover my mistake and then overtake him, for he was having a delightful time with the Archy gunners, doing loops, barrels, side-slips and spins immediately over their heads to show them his contempt for them, while he waited for his comrade. Finally he came out of the Archy area with a long graceful dive and swinging up alongside my machine he wiggled his wings as though he were laughing at me and then suddenly he set a course back towards Pont-à-Mousson.

Whether or not he knew all along that a German craft was in that region I could not tell. But when he began to change his direction and curve up into the sun I followed close behind him knowing that there was a good reason for this maneuver. I looked earnestly about me in every direction.

Yes! There was a scout coming towards us from north of Pont-à-Mousson. It was at about our altitude. I knew it was a Hun the moment I saw it, for it had the familiar lines of their new Pfalz. Moreover, my confidence in James Norman Hall was such that I knew he couldn't make a mistake. And he was still climbing into the sun, carefully keeping his position between its glare and the oncoming fighting plane. I clung as closely to Hall as I could. The Hun was steadily approaching us, unconscious of his danger, for we were full in the sun.

With the first downward dive of Jimmy's machine I was by his side. We had at least a thousand feet advantage over the enemy and we were two to one numerically. He might outdive our machines, for the Pfalz is a famous diver, while our faster climbing Nieuports had a droll little habit of shedding their fabric when plunged too furiously through the air. The Boche hadn't a chance to outfly us. His only salvation would be in a dive towards his own lines.

These thoughts passed through my mind in a flash and I instantly determined upon my tactics. While Hall went in for his attack I would keep my altitude and get a position the other side of the Pfalz, to cut off his retreat.

No sooner had I altered my line of flight than the German pilot saw me leave the sun's rays. Hall was already half-way to him when he stuck up his nose and began furiously climbing to the upper ceiling. I let him pass me and found myself on the other side just as Hall began firing. I doubt if the Boche had seen Hall's Nieuport at all.

Surprised by discovering this new antagonist, Hall, ahead of him, the Pfalz immediately abandoned all idea of a battle and banking around to the right started for home, just as I had expected him to do. In a trice I was on his tail. Down, down we sped with throttles both full open. Hall was coming on somewhere in my rear. The Boche had no heart for evolutions or maneuvers. He was running like a scared rabbit, as I had run from Campbell. I was gaining upon him every instant and had my sights trained dead upon his seat before I fired my first shot.

At 150 yards I pressed my triggers. The tracer bullets cut a streak of living fire into the rear of the Pfalz tail. Raising the nose of my aeroplane slightly the fiery streak lifted itself like the stream of water pouring from a garden hose. Gradually it settled into the pilot's seat. The swerving of the Pfalz course indicated that its rudder no longer was held by a directing hand. At 2000 feet above the enemy's lines I pulled up my headlong dive and watched the enemy machine continuing on its course. Curving slightly to the left the Pfalz circled a little to the south and the next minute crashed onto the ground just at the edge of the woods a mile inside their own lines. I had brought down my first enemy aeroplane and had not been subjected to a single shot!

Hall was immediately beside me. He was evidently as pleased as I was over our success, for he danced his machine about in incredible maneuvers. And then I realized that old friend Archy was back on the job. We were not two miles away from the German anti-aircraft batteries and they put a furious bombardment of shrapnel all about us. I was quite ready to call it a day and go home, but Captain Hall deliberately returned to the barrage and entered it with me at his heels. Machine-guns and rifle fire from the trenches greeted us and I do not mind admitting that I got out quickly the way I came in without any unnecessary delay, but Hall continued to do stunts over their heads for ten minutes, surpassing all the acrobatics that the enraged Boches had ever seen even over their own peaceful aerodromes.

Jimmy exhausted his spirits at about the time the Huns had exhausted all their available ammunition and we started blithely for home. Swooping down to our field side by side, we made a quick landing and taxied our victorious machines up to the hangars. Then jumping out we ran to each other, extending glad hands for our first exchange of congratulations. And then we noticed that the squadron pilots and mechanics were streaming across the aerodrome towards us from all directions. They had heard the news while we were still dodging shrapnel and were hastening out to welcome our return. The French had telephoned in a confirmation of my first victory, before I had had time to reach home. Not a single bullet hole had punctured any part of my machine.

There is a peculiar gratification in receiving congratulations from one's squadron for a victory in the air. It is worth more to a pilot than the applause of the whole outside world. It means that one has won the confidence of men who share the misgivings, the aspirations, the trials and the dangers of aeroplane fighting. And with each victory comes a renewal and re-cementing of ties that bind together these brothers-in-arms. No closer fraternity exists in the world than that of the air-fighters in this great war. And I have yet to find one single individual who has attained conspicuous success in bringing down enemy aeroplanes who can be said to be spoiled either by his successes or by the generous congratulations of his comrades. If he were capable of being spoiled he would not have had the character to have won continuous victories, for the smallest amount of vanity is fatal in aeroplane fighting. Self-distrust rather is the quality to which many a pilot owes his protracted existence.

It was with a very humble gratitude then that I received the warm congratulations of Lufbery, whom I had always revered for his seventeen victories—of Doug Campbell and Alan Winslow who had brought down the first machines that were credited to the American Squadrons, and of many others of 94 Squadron who had seen far more service in the battle areas than had I. I was glad to be at last included in the proud roll of victors of this squadron. These pals of mine were to see old 94 lead all American Squadrons in the number of successes over the Huns.

The following day I was notified that General Gerard, the Commanding Officer of the Sixth French Army, had offered to decorate Captain Hall and myself in the name of the French Government for our victory of the day before. We were then operating in conjunction with this branch of the French Army. The Croix de Guerre with palm was to be accorded each of us, provided such an order met the approval of our own government. But at that time officers in the American Army could not accept decorations from a foreign Government, so the ceremony of presentation was denied us. Both Captain Hall and myself had been included, as such was the French rule where two pilots participated in a victory.

The truth was that in the tense excitement of this first victory, I was quite blind to the fact that I was shooting deadly bullets at another aviator; and if I had been by myself, there is no doubt in my own mind but that I should have made a blunder again in some particular which would have reversed the situation. Captain Hall's presence, if not his actual bullets, had won the victory and had given me that wonderful feeling of self-confidence which made it possible for me subsequently to return to battle without him and handle similar situations successfully.

THE DAY THEY GOT RICHTHOFEN

by Gene Gurney

The spring rains had finally stopped and the faint light of dawn poked through the scattering clouds. In the distance the cannonading at the front continued. Capt. Roy Brown of the Royal Air Force slowly rose from his bunk, walked to the window and studied the clearing skies. It was April 21, 1918, and today he would again do battle with the enemy.

Donning his flying togs he walked wearily toward the Officers' Mess for breakfast. He had been in combat for 18 continuous months, and had shot down 12 enemy aircraft. War, then, was not new to this aviator, but at 24 years of age he felt very old, very tired. Each day the pains in his stomach became more intense. "Nervous stomach" they called it: war killing and the constant tension of aerial combat were the harassment of his easy good nature and soft manner. He longed to return to his Canadian home, but he had a job to do and he knew he must stay to finish it. He was a good pilot, a superior marksman, and a leader his men could rely upon.

He forced himself to eat his breakfast, washing it down with the military ration of milk and brandy, a combination which, unknown to Roy Brown, did great damage to his weary stomach. A few of his men had openly noted that Roy was looking thinner, but Roy kept to himself the pain that was sapping his strength. He had to hang on for just a while longer.

Twenty-four miles away, on the other side of the bursting shells, the rattling machine guns and the maze of muddy, rain-soaked trenches, another airman rose from his bed to greet the slowly dawning day. Manfred, Baron von Richthofen, leader of the famous German *Jagdstaffel*—the "Flying Circus"—viewed the clearing skies with anxiety and good cheer. For weeks the spring rains had grounded the flyers, and although it had let up sufficiently the evening before to allow the German ace to down two more Allied planes to bring his total to 80 kills, he still viewed happily the prospect of a bright, clear day. Today, he felt, there would be new glory.

Richthofen was tall, straight, and dashingly handsome in his always correct uniform. His flying prowess was famous throughout the world. He was the Red Knight of the German Empire, and the living symbol of the glory of the Fatherland.

He had slept well that night. The freshness of the dawn and the distant pounding of the guns at the front sent the thrill and excitement of the hunt and the kill surging through his veins. Breakfast was served to him in his room and he ate a regal meal.

The son of a Prussian military man, the young, 25-year-old German ace had made history in his meteoric rise to fame. It was only yesterday that, having reached the fantastic tally of 80 victims for his deadly guns, he had been personally decorated by Kaiser Wilhelm. He was soon to be given the title of *Rittmeister,* Commander in Chief. Not only had he personally destroyed fourscore Allied aircraft, but his brilliant leadership and ingenious aerial tactics had been responsible for the death of hundreds more of the enemy.

Among his many stratagems was the plan he devised to move his squadron quickly from one area at the front to another by loading his planes on railroad flatcars.

Seeing his brightly colored aircraft rolling down the rails on top of the flatcars, the Germans, reminded of a traveling circus, had adopted the nicknames, "Flying Circus" and "Tango Circus," for Richthofen's squadron. His own plane was painted a bright red, the only ship in the German Air Corps to have that distinctive color. The Allies referred to him as the Red Baron.

Richthofen was a remarkable hunter as well as the world's leading combat flyer. The hunt and the kill were always moments of great joy and personal triumph for the baron. He killed in the forest for sport and in the air for glory. For each enemy plane he shot down he ordered an engraved silver loving cup. He piled up his victories so rapidly that the silversmith was still a dozen cups behind when he lost his most valued customer.

The secret of the baron's amazing success was, to no small extent, his ability to single out the inexperienced flyers, pounce upon them and send them crashing to earth. Among his 80 confirmed victories were included 69 green, young lieutenants and five sergeant-pilots. His 80th victim, Second Lt. D. E. Lewis, who lived to tell the story, later wrote of his experience:

"On the evening of April 20, twelve of us left the airdrome on an offensive patrol. . . . The day had been a stormy one, with intermittent squalls, and there were still heavy clouds in the sky when we reached the German lines.

"I was attacking a bright blue machine, which was on a level with me, and was just about to finish this adversary off when I heard the rat-tat-tat of machine guns coming from behind me and saw the splintering of struts above my head.

"I left my man and wheeled quickly to find that I was face to face with the renowned Richthofen. . . . The baron always flew a bright red machine, that is how I knew it was he.

"I twisted and turned in the endeavor to avoid his line of fire, but he was too experienced a fighter, and only once did I manage to have him at a disadvantage, and then only for a few seconds, but in these few ticks of the clock I shot a number of bullets into his machine and thought I would have the honor of bringing him down, but in a trice our positions were reversed and he had set my emergency petrol tank alight, and I was hurtling earthward in flames.

"I hit the ground . . . at a speed of 60 mph, was thrown clear of my machine and except for minor burns, was unhurt."

Richthofen pulled his spotlessly clean flying togs over his blue silk pajamas and walked briskly from his quarters. The three-winged Fokker airplanes were lined up in flawless rows. Called Tripes, the German fighter planes of the Flying Circus had scored impressively against the Allied airmen. Richthofen's own ship, a special gift from the manufacturer, Anthony Fokker, was in perfect condition. Its bright red color stood out even among the other brightly painted ships of the squadron.

At the airplane an orderly handed the Red Baron sealed papers. He tore open the seal and read the contents. They were his battle orders for the day: their mission was to destroy all Allied reconnaissance planes in the sector. The army was preparing for a big push, and the enemy must be denied the valuable information that the darting reconnaissance ships could provide. None must get through!

The baron stuffed the orders in his tunic, and went to the briefing room to see that his men were made aware of their mission for that day.

Just before 10:00 he was back at his plane. From behind the hangar came running his pet hunting dog, Moritz. The large dog made a dash to jump on the bottom wing of the baron's airplane. Richthofen smiled, leaned over and patted the happy animal. One of the mechanics watching this little incident approached the famous ace.

"I beg your pardon, sir," said the man, "but may I take a picture of you and your dog beside the plane? I would be very proud to own such a picture."

The baron nodded.

"Oh, no, sir," cried another mechanic, his face paled with fright, "you mustn't allow a picture. It will bring you bad luck!"

The baron scowled at the man. "Silly superstition," he said, waving to indicate that he was ready for the picture to be taken.

The superstition to which he had referred was one that had existed among the German flyers since Richthofen's good friend, the great German ace, Oswald Boelcke, had allowed himself to be photographed just prior to taking off on what turned out to be his last mission.

The picture was snapped: the last picture ever made of Baron Manfred von Richthofen.

He climbed aboard his Fokker triplane, signaled his squadron, and easing the throttle forward bounced down the soggy field and felt the rush of the wind lift him into the clear blue sky. The time was 10:26.

Twenty-five minutes earlier, from the Bertangles field, Capt. Roy Brown had similarly eased forward the throttle of his cherry-nosed Sopwith Camel. Just prior to takeoff, after briefing his men on the mission that day, he had watched the ground crew roll his airship out of the repair tent and into position on the wet flying field. His stomach still ached and it was without enthusiasm that he signaled his flight of five planes for takeoff and roared across the field into the air. Climbing eastward, 15 Camels headed toward the front—three flights of five with Maj. Charles Butler commanding the lead flight, and Capt. Roy Brown leading the flight on the right. They climbed steadily to 15,000 feet and there leveled out for their scouting back and forth across the enemy lines. They had no oxygen equipment, and at that extreme altitude the exhaust fumes in the open cockpit were causing Brown to suffer severe nausea. He tightened his safety belt and tried to ignore the volcano boiling inside him.

From the German airfield at Douai, Richthofen, leading 15 planes of *Staffel* 5 and *Staffel* 11—his other squadron—had taken off and joined the formation. The ground crews watched the join-up and the long, steady climb to altitude. The Germans leveled off at 17,000 feet and headed westward to seek out the enemy's reconnaissance planes. The deadly squadron of multi-colored hawks soared along the front awaiting their prey.

They did not have to wait long.

Below, two lumbering British RE-8's came chugging along, reconnoitering the German entrenchments in the French village of Hamel. The Red Baron signaled for four Tripes to go down and get them. The Fokker triwinged pursuit planes peeled off with an easy grace and swooped earthward for the unwary scouts.

The baron smiled. Hunting would be good today. When the conditions were just exactly right, he himself would scream down for added glory. He was a superb pilot, but he took no unnecessary chances. He could well afford to wait until the conditions were perfect. But unknown to him there was now less than a half a mile separating him from Capt. Roy Brown and death.

Suddenly the pain in Roy Brown's stomach seemed to relax and his mind snapped clear of the fog that the pain had forced upon it. In that same instant he noted that his flight and the flight on his left had become separated from Maj. Butler's lead flight. He made a three-sixty—a complete circle—but could not spot the other formation. The leader of the left flight looked over at him, and Capt. Brown made a T signal with his hands, advising the other flight to join in behind him. Thus, regrouped, he turned his airmen in toward the front lines.

As he turned he caught in the corner of his eye the flicker of a motion. Looking down he spotted the two RE-8's turning, too late, to escape the German hawks that were screaming down upon them from above. In that same instant he saw several thousand feet above his own group, a bright red Fokker and the distinctive colors of the Flying Circus.

For an instant Brown hesitated, as he eyed the enemy far out and above. He paused, but for a second, for the two RE-8's were in trouble.

He signaled his men for a "dive and cover" tactic, and eight cherry-nosed Camels plunged into a 200-mph descent with two ships remaining aloft as cover. The wind whistled through the struts and around the open cockpit. Brown pressed the throttle to the firewall, but he could see that his flight was not going to arrive in time to meet the onrushing Germans.

The two British scouts twisted and turned to avoid the German pursuits, but it appeared that the Germans would arrive well ahead of the racing R.A.F. fighters.

Watching from below, the Australian antiaircraft batteries were not unmindful of the drama that was taking place above them. The "Archies" threw up a murderous barrage at the four incoming Tripes. The Germans heeled over quickly to dodge the sudden volley from below, and in that priceless moment of time the British scouts were able to make a quick, last-minute break for the safety of their own lines.

From above Richthofen watched gloomily the unsuccessful attack below. His orders were that no British reconnaissance ships were to return to their bases with information. He held up his arm and signaling his men, he sent down his entire outfit—Fokkers and Albatroses—to crush the stubborn enemy.

Flying with Capt. Roy Brown, as a wingman for one of the veteran pilots of Brown's command, was Lt. Wilfred R. May. This was May's first flight over the front lines, and Brown had made clear his orders: "Stay out of the dogfights"; "Combat only a stray or inexperienced or wounded plane"; "Concentrate more on formation flying than visual scouting." Brown had been most emphatic in his order. More young flyers on their first mission were lost in air collisions with brother planes than in combat. Lt. May, like all new pilots, had much to learn, and Brown wanted him to take his lessons in easy stages, lest there be but a single lesson.

Lt. May was in the flight behind Brown when they streaked down upon the enemy.

Meanwhile the four Fokkers had been so anxious to flame the two British scouts that without noticing they had slid past their own lines and into Allied territory. Brown noticed their frantic efforts to reach the British planes, and he realized that today the enemy was not interested in the usual air duel, but was out for a purpose: to stop Allied aerial intelligence. Something big must be in the wind.

Looking around for the two RE-8's, he saw them returning once again to the German lines. The Fokkers banked in toward the scouts. Brown and his flight had now made the distance into position to meet the enemy fighters, and immediately engaged them. The Fokkers turned with the Camels and tried to get by them to the safety of their own lines. Outnumbered, the Germans were cut off in enemy territory. The whine of the engines and the chatter of machine guns filled the morning air.

Lt. May, falling back from the fight, dropped lower and lower. A single Fokker shook loose and, slipping toward the deck, scooted for safety. May saw the enemy. The temptation was too great and the setup too perfect. His orders said that he could do combat with a single ship. Down he went toward the German. He held forward pressure on the stick in a steady dive to a converging point just ahead of the enemy plane. The Tripe came into his sights. May squeezed his trigger. One short burst. The plane exploded in a ball of flame and spun crazily toward the earth. His first kill.

Brown had instructed him: "If you get your first kill, hard-rudder and fire-wall it for home, and that is an order!" Lt. May, elated at his victory, racked his plane upon a wing and horsed back on the stick, bending around toward home. He opened full throttle and scurried across the treetops for his home field.

The big dogfight continued with renewed fury with the arrival of the main body of the German fighters. The air was filled with twisting, turning, diving planes. Lt. F. J. W. Mellersh pegged a blue-tailed triplane. Mackensie flamed a red-tailed Fokker and Taylor snuggled up behind another tri-winged enemy and laced it with a fatal flurry of lead. A German scored on Mackensie who, fighting his half-shot-away controls, headed down toward the British lines. Planes were going down all over. In the mad tangle of the battle there was no way to tell which side held the advantage.

Capt. Roy Brown had two Fokkers on his tail firing lethal bursts at him. He headed for the deck, slipping and skidding as he went. He bottomed-out just above the trees, and the two ships pressed in. Horsing back on the stick, he felt his plane fall over on a wing and begin to spin. The Germans did not care to follow. Kicking opposite rudder and pepping his stick forward he broke the spin just above the trees and leveled out.

At that instant he caught sight of Lt. May heading for home. To his right he saw the unmistakable bright red Tripe of the Allies' most feared enemy. His heart jumped into his throat. The Red Baron was rapidly bearing down upon young Lt. May. Brown pressed his throttle forward as far as he could and started a climb toward that invisible junction where the world's greatest living ace would bring quick death to the inexperienced boy.

Brown could feel pain gripping his stomach as he urged his ship to greater speed. The baron's plane seemed almost to have dropped from nowhere.

At better than 200 mph the Red Knight of Germany bore down upon the unsuspecting May. A few minutes earlier the baron had been at altitude with his flight commanders, surveying the battle. His job was to get the reconnaissance planes and safeguard the German movements for the "big push," but the temptation of the lone ship had been too great. He could tell from the way that the pilot handled his Camel that inside the cockpit was a green flyer. This would be quick. One pass, a flaming wreck, and then a steep, climbing turn back to altitude to wait and watch for more single wrens.

Brown had reached 2,000 feet and was closing on May and

Richthofen, but he might be too late. Richthofen slid into position behind and slightly above May's Camel. He fired one short burst. The slugs struck May's engine cowling and snapped several wing struts. The surprised May kicked left rudder and side slipped. His startled face looked back, and turned an ashen white as he stared into the cold, steady eyes of the Red Baron of Germany. The "Red Death" seemed almost in the cockpit with him; and it appeared that no human force could turn aside the inevitable doom that awaited him from inside the dark guns. The twin Spandaus spit fire and a short burst of German lead tore into the cockpit. In an instant his right arm was ripped with pain, and blood oozed down his sleeve.

Richthofen slowed his plane to stay on May's tail and to steady his flying platform for a better shot at the doomed aviator.

Brown, his engine straining on its mounts, had reached 5,000 feet, and was now closer to the two airmen. He could see the baron drawing a final bead on the young May. Brown touched his right rudder slightly and added a breath of forward pressure on the stick. Nausea crept over him as the Red Baron slid into his sights. Brown was an experienced aerial gunner and he knew that he was still too far out for accuracy. If he waited just a few seconds more he would close the 1,000 feet that separated him from his enemy, and Germany's most valued flyer would be a certain victim of his guns. But he could not wait. A second's pause and Richthofen would claim his 81st victim. He must swat at the fly to drive him off. He squeezed his trigger. A sharp pain shot through his stomach and he fought off an almost overwhelming dizziness. The tracers struck the tail of the baron's red Fokker. Bullet holes began to march down the fabric. Richthofen jerked his head around in amazement. It all happened in the smallest fraction of a second, but in that time Richthofen had full cognizance of what was taking place. He turned forward to give May one more quick burst before breaking hard over to roll away from the intrusive Capt. Brown. Brown added the faintest pressure to his control stick and the bullets continued in their solemn procession along the baron's fuselage—in a broken, uneven stitch across the cockpit. A bullet struck home and Richthofen slumped forward as Brown's Camel swept past. The bright red Tripe nosed over and dove straight for the ground. The Aussies who had been firing at the Red Baron as he closed on May's Camel, suddenly ceased their fire. All eyes turned toward the earthward-twisting red Tripe. At 50 feet the German ship broke its sharp descent, made a last, futile half sweep, and dropped suddenly to the turf. It hit hard, bounced and stopped.

It was little more than an hour after his takeoff that Capt. Roy Brown was sitting in the briefing shack signing his name to one of the most important combat reports of World War I. Maj. Butler, who had certified Brown's report, picked it up and read it once again:

Date: April 21, 1918
Time: 10:45 A.M.

Place: 62D, 2. (Map designation)
Duty: High Offense Patrols
Altitude: 5,000 feet
Engagement with red triplane
Locality: Vaux sur Somme.
Fokker triplane, pure red wings with black crosses

(1) At 10:35 I observed two Albatroses burst into flames and crash.
(2) Dived on large formation of 15 to 20 Albatros scouts, D-5's and Fokker triplanes, two of which got on my tail, and I came out.
(3) Went back again and dived on pure red triplane which was firing upon Lt. May. I got a long burst into him, and he went down vertically and was observed to crash by Lt. Mellersh and Lt. May. I fired on two more but did not get them.

Signed: A. R. Brown, Capt. Certified: C. H. Butler, Maj. 209th RAF

Back at the scene of the crashed triplane, Lt. Mellersh, who earlier in the battle had been forced down near the very same spot, was on hand to join the Australian gunners as they retrieved the wreck. The occupant was removed from the downed Fokker, and laid out on the ground. A single bullet had entered his right side and had come out the left.

Mellersh opened the dead pilot's tunic and removed his papers and identification cards. Reading them, he turned toward the anxiously waiting Aussies, and nodded his head.

"Blimey," whispered one, " 'E gawt the bloody Baron!"

When the word reached Brown that the death of Baron von Richthofen had been confirmed, he sank into a half stupor as he finally allowed himself to realize the significance of his victory. He gave in a little to the abdominal seizures which he had been fighting off since his landing. The pain seemed to swell up in him, and at last he realized that the job he had really come to do was done. The war was over for him now—he had flown his last combat mission.

The doctors finally insisted that Roy Brown return to his home. Their diagnosis: advanced ulcers. And so the quiet unassuming, unpretentious Canadian, who had stayed in combat long enough to score the most important single victory in the Great War, returned once again to the peace and quiet of the Canadian country that he loved. But as long as he lived, he was always known as the man who downed the Red Knight.

A MOST REMARKABLE ESCAPE

by V. M. Yeates

On the next day, Saturday the sixth of April, rain spread over northern Europe in the early morning, and in places continued all day. In London those with relatives in the R.A.F. hoped that this would be a real day's rest for them, and bore with patience the damping addition to the horrors of week-end shopping; but in Picardy it cleared up in the afternoon and there was plenty of flying, for the enemy was making yet another assault on the defences of Amiens, and there seemed very little reason why they should not carry them, unless it might be their own exhaustion. The British reply to the attack was to bomb from the air more intensely than ever. The clouds lifted to some three thousand feet, so that machines of all descriptions could be used. When C flight arrived at the scene of action soon after three o'clock the air was crowded with machines coming and going, and it was quite difficult to avoid backwash. An instinct made Tom aware that there were Huns about too, waiting to pounce; but none was visible at the moment.

Beal wasted no time, but went right down to a hundred feet. He had thought out a new idea, by which he and Tom would work close together in front, and Miller with the other two would follow a little after, or attack from another angle. He hoped by this to deliver a concentrated attack without their all getting in each others' way. Tom was nearly upset by a shell bursting right underneath his tail, and he lurched as though a giant had given him a push. He hung desperately on to Beal, dropping bombs where he did, not at all sure where. Then he followed him as he went nosing along communication trenches for troops going up. Tom slewed about as much as he could, but Beal seemed entirely unconcerned about bullets; he was after prey. But suddenly Tom saw something that made him go alongside Beal and waggle his wings. There was a bunch of Huns, possibly a dozen, coming down on them. Beal saw them and turned just as they opened fire. He went down in a spin, hit either from the air or from the ground. Tom completed his turn amid an appalling pop-pop-pop-pop-pop-pop of machine guns, and zigzagged westwards. The Huns had dived and pulled out and he was still alive. His Aldis was smashed. He was aware of a group of holes in his left bottom plane. They apparently weren't going to attack again. But there was a crack-crack-crack-crack in a different key. Splinters from a centre-section strut flew in his face. A landing wire broke and the ends rattled about. Something tore a leg of his sidcot. He must be flying straight over a machine-gun nest at about fifty feet. His engine spluttered and his hand switched over to gravity automatically. There was a terrible din going on now his engine wasn't roaring. He was not particularly afraid. His body was functioning as an automaton and his mind was anaesthetized to everything but surprise or curiosity. What was happening, was going to happen? There were bullet holes everywhere. It was preposterous that he wasn't hit. He was going down. He would probably be dead in a second or two. It was impossible to live through this. Then the engine picked up, and he thought he was across the lines, but still a cracking continued. He was certainly across the lines, but the cracking still continued. There could be nothing shooting at him, but the noise went on, and fear returned. What was this unaccountable machine-gun-like row? He couldn't make it out. Was the aeroplane breaking up? Should he land somewhere at once? He throttled down and glided in panic towards the shattered ground. Then he saw a strip of torn canvas that was flapping in the wind on the fuselage just behind him.

He opened out again and climbed away. He was shot to blazes, and it was a miracle that he was alive. There was a smell of petrol. Perhaps it would be better to land as soon as possible. He crept along cautiously on half throttle, and tried to collect his thoughts. What had happened? There had been a dash into Hunland, right on the floor, and here he was, dazed but alive. Beal had gone. They had been shot at from the air and ground at the same time. Beal was dead. What a rattle of guns there had been; that damned staccato chatter. He really didn't remember details.

Someone came alongside him. It was Miller, followed by Smith and Dubois. He waved and joined them, but would not fly faster than eighty miles an hour and they soon left him behind. They came back and had a look at him and amused themselves by fooling about round him. He wouldn't throw a stunt for the world. And there was a damnable smell of petrol. He might burst into flames. Beal, his admirable enemy, had gone and he remained. These twin facts swung round in his head like a planet and moon. Fate manifestly hadn't the interest of the Allies in view. Those Huns had done a good day's work. Where the devil had they appeared from so suddenly? It was weird the way things appeared from and vanished into nowhere upstairs. You had to be as watchful as a goshawk. Then what had happened? The Huns had left him alone and some of their pals on the ground had taken advantage of his preoccupation with them to finish him off; nevertheless their bullets had hit everything but him, and here he was floating insecurely home. He would like to get his bus home. It would break all records. Never had anyone been so shot up and got home. It would be amusing and dramatic if the wing collapsed when he landed, that landing wire being broken. He hoped it would. The rattling and cracking were alarming though they seemed to arise from harmless causes.

He was glad to see home at length; not so profoundly relieved as he expected to be after his unsafe journey; he seemed to have lost some of his capacity for feeling.

His escort let him land first, which he did without losing any time. He made a good landing and watched his damaged wing as he touched earth. It dropped, and scraped its tip along the ground; but this was because the whole aeroplane was tilted, not because it had collapsed. Tom switched off and swung round the pivot of his dropped wing to a standstill.

He climbed out to see what had happened. The tyre of one of the landing wheels was flat, punctured in the air. It struck him as extremely funny to get a puncture in the air. He laughed and laughed and leaned over the bottom plane and laughed till he ached, with his face over a group of six bullet holes that represented a bit of good shooting by one of those Fokkers.

Two mechanics with a spare wheel and tools were the first to arrive. Then Williamson and Hudson. Then Baker and Reeve, very new comers to the squadron, who gazed with reverential horror at the gaping wounds.

"Good God, man," exclaimed Hudson, "what the bloody hell have you been up to? Even your sidcot is shot through. Aren't you hurt?"

"I'm all right. I've only been following Beal. He won't be back."

There was a scorched tear in his right thigh, and a brown mark as though someone had laid a hot poker lightly on his left arm, which meant that a bullet had grazed. A piece was smashed out of a centre-section strut within a few inches of his face; he remembered feeling the splinters blow against him. Several bracing wires were broken, and the petrol tank holed near the top. There were two holes in the floor of the cockpit. The total number of bullet holes was over sixty. It must be one of the most remarkable escapes ever made. He certainly had a reliable guardian angel. For what was the angel working? Wasn't death due till next week? Miller came hurrying up:

"Was Beal shot down?"

"Yes, he went in a spin."

"Didn't he see those Huns d'you think? Holy Jesus, you've caught it!"

It appeared that Miller had seen the Huns in plenty of time and had started climbing, but they had only dived once on Beal and Tom, and cleared off quickly because of the number of British machines in the neighbouring sky. Miller had taken a long range crack at them, but they wouldn't stop to fight. He was sorry about Beal, but he had asked for it, and had nearly done for Tom as well. They'd better go and report.

Tom felt shaky but exhilarated. This was the third Camel of his to be written off by machine-gun fire. After tea, the new wheel being fixed, he taxied the wreck in for dismantling. He cut a bullet out of a spar of the left-hand bottom plane to keep as a souvenir. The whole squadron had been examining the damage and Tom's escape was the evening's wonder. It came on to rain. Beal's decease was not particularly noticed. It was unusual to have a flight commander killed, but Beal had not been with the squadron long and had not secured a big bag of Huns. You got little credit for ground-strafing, although it was the most dangerous, nerve-racking, and perhaps most valuable work that scouts did. Assaults on the trenches were particularly trying, for they were in the most concentrated area of machine guns. It was really safer to go farther back and look for transport and troops on the march; there were machine guns everywhere in Hunland, but not so many a few miles back, and the difference more than compensated for the greater liability to attack from the air; also it was much more fun if you caught anything. Had Beal been able to devote his brief career to aerial combat, no doubt he would have shot down twenty Huns in quick time and his ghost would have been comforted with a posthumous D.S.O.; for he had all the qualifications of a Hun-getter, and his tactics were the essence of that offensive spirit which was sedulously instilled into young pilots by official talkers.

There had been a Captain Trollope, whom Tom knew, killed recently. He had, like Beal, come out to take over a flight in a Camel squadron. During his brief course he shot down six Huns in one day, which earned the M.C.; then he was missing, and men would remember him for a little while as an inspired warrior. But who would know Beal and honour his memory? He had gone out daily to confront incalculable death with risk-oblivious courage, without the stimulus of man-to-man combat; and there was no red triumph of broken or burning enemies reeling down the skies to be entombed in the perky officialese of *Comic Cuts.* He would be forgotten in a week. Bravery was nothing without publicity and popularity. Beal was not unpopular, but he had not been long enough with the squadron to form one of that more stable nucleus of older hands which the imagination envisaged when the tongue said 'the squadron': Mac, Bulmer, Moss, Franklin, Miller, Williamson.

On the fringes of this nuclear group were Tom himself, Hudson, Seddon, Maitland, and Burkett, all of whom seemed in the process of taking root. The rest were here-to-day-and-gone-to-morrow folk whose expectation of life, once they had started jobs, seemed to be about a week then-a-days; perhaps one in ten of them settled down. The more permanent people had their casualties in plenty, but if an expectation of life table for aviators in France had been compiled it would probably have been a sort of inversion of that ordinary one which assures profits to assurance companies. It was difficult to assign reasons for survival. In the first selection youth and immaturity of practical judgment were no doubt adverse factors; and then differences of eyesight and habitual alertness told; and lastly acquired tactical skill and innate cunning. But when all these things were allowed for, it was difficult amid the flying bullets to believe in anything but luck. Everyone got shot up occasionally, and nothing but luck could account for the inches this way or that which made a bullet harmless or fatal; and a succession of lucky chances that resulted in survival lasting over months took on an aspect of destiny. All nonsense, Tom thought. As a condition of war there must be some survivors. But if the survivors liked to think that the piercing eye of destiny had singled each one out as an individual worth keeping alive, why not? They might at some time try to do something to deserve it.

Tom felt more and more worried about Beal as the evening passed, and whisky could not still his conscience. It was impossible not to feel glad that Beal had been killed, and it seemed the most horrible feeling he had ever had. He hadn't realized how much Beal had seized on his imagination as the complete hero, and how much he hated him as a menace to his own life and a reproach to his half-heartedness; or feared. Into what a vile morass of shame he had wandered when his instinctive feeling about the death of one of the bravest men he had ever known was relief! A little comforting maggot of hope wriggled in his brain. It was a vile maggot, and it would not stop wriggling. Those frightful jobs sitting at fifty or a hundred feet over the trenches had probably come to an end.

Miller asked him if he was fit for the early job. They were to go up at six for the usual reconnaissance and morning message to the Huns. Cross would have to be on it.

"I hope he'll be all right," said Tom. "We've had enough casualties lately, and we shan't be much good till some of these new fellows have gained experience."

That was his reply to Beal: casualties. What was the use of destroying the flight? No one had a chance to mature under a flight commander who insisted on too much heroics.

Beal, Beal, Beal: he couldn't get him out of his thoughts. He seemed to hear echoes of his voice flitting about the mess. "Cundall!" Tom jerked round.

"What's the matter?" asked Bulmer.

"My God, you gave me a start. Your voice sounded exactly like Beal's."

"Nerves. Too much ground-strafing. Egg flip's the finest thing for ground-strafing nerves. Hancock, bring four egg flips. What I called you for was a spot of bridge. Here's Franklin and Maitland. What about it?"

"Thanks. Till ten. I'm on the early job."

"You ought to have a rest, but as there's only you and Miller left in your flight I suppose you can't. Probably Mac will be taking you over again to try to rebuild the flight. Cheerio!"

Tom took his egg flip. "Personally I'd be damn glad to have Mac back again, and I know Miller would." He went on playing bridge till eleven as it was raining so steadily and sullenly that the early job seemed impossible. Egg flips were comforting, but Beal haunted him all the time; he was always near; if Tom could have looked round quickly enough, he would have seen him. His voice was entwined in the buzz of conversation.

The batman called him at five o'clock. The morning was fair after a foul night. What a waste of good rain! He fell asleep at once, but after a second the batman was shaking him again. His eyes were glued with sleep, and he ate the hard-boiled dawn egg as if dreaming and went through the running of the engine in indifferent semi-consciousness conditioned by the operations of an automaton. The cold wind of rapid motion revived him as he took off. There was no need to think about taking off; the body attended to that and the dim mental regions of habit; the conscious mind was free to enjoy the solid lift of the plane's bearing on the smooth hard morning air, the wheeling and foreshortening of things terrestrial, the trees that yielded up their splendour and height and diminished into embossed variegations in earth's colour-pattern.

They surveyed the trenches from two thousand feet or so, and everything appeared quiet on their sector. Archie accompanied them assiduously. It was impossible to see far laterally; the red fingers of dawn could not spool the intertangled filaments of mist; but above it was clear, and some black specks appeared in the eastern heights. They dropped their bombs hurriedly and began climbing.

There seemed to be six Huns, quite ten thousand feet above them. They did not want to attack, evidently, but sat up there watching. Then Archie gave them some warning bursts. Dolphins were going over above them, and they made off. Their game was to chivvy solitary Harry Tates or pick off stragglers, not to fight the main intendment of Dolphins or Camels. Miller stayed about a little longer in case they returned, and then, not being on patrol, turned for home.

THEY CALLED HIM THE INDESTRUCTIBLE "BALLOON BUSTER"

by James C. Law

One wheel nearly touched the sandbag of the gun emplacement as the American pilot flew in and flipped the last grenade over the side of the cockpit.

He was heading back for another strafing run when it finally happened. He kicked left rudder and stood the Spad on its wing. There was a rip in the fabric by the cockpit and the force of hot metal tearing through his shoulder twisted him around in his seat. The airplane fell off and headed for the ground. But now the immediate shock of the wound was over, and the pilot eased back on the stick, sweeping over the still-blazing enemy gun emplacements. His own machine guns chattered in return as waves of nausea began to well up in his stomach.

He emptied his guns in this last diving pass and pulled up just high enough to spot the closest clearing. An open field lay dead ahead. The high whistle of the wind abruptly replaced the engine's roar as he cut the throttle and side-slipped down, fighting off the throbbing dizziness.

The little plane bounced off the uneven surface of the field, then settled back, and rolled to a shaky stop.

It was late in the afternoon of September 29, 1918, near the village of Murvaux, France. The American pilot was a twenty-one-year-old second lieutenant from Phoenix, Arizona, whom Eddie Rickenbacker called "the most intrepid air fighter who ever sat in an airplane." His name was Frank Luke, and he had just made aerial history.

Earlier at Austin, Texas, School of Aeronautics he had finished the regular nine weeks' course in seven weeks. At North Island, San Diego, he was first in his class to solo. And he finished final flight training in France at the head of his class in flying, number-two man in gunnery. But the big test was yet to come.

He was assigned to the 27th Aero Squadron, operating near Chateau-Thierry, in early August 1918. During the first week he flew only routine patrols, for new pilots were ushered away from areas where there was likely to be trouble. So Frank Luke learned early that to fight the way he wanted to fight, he would have to go it alone. And at the first opportunity, he headed straight for the enemy lines.

Until this day in mid-August, he had not even seen an enemy plane, so his idea was to head for the one spot where they were sure to be found. He pushed the little biplane to its ceiling and headed for the nearest German airfield.

He throttled back while crossing over the front to avoid detection, but once he was deep into enemy territory, he eased the Spad down, scanning the earth. Finally he saw a cluster of hangars and the dirt runway of the field near the horizon. And ahead of him, at a lower altitude, were six enemy Albatroses. They were flying in formation, heading toward the field from the same direction as Luke.

He pushed the stick forward and dove down to their altitude. Then he opened the throttle and began to close the gap. The German fighters continued serenely on, confident of their safety this far behind their own lines.

Finally Luke was within twenty yards of the closest German ship. He was actually part of their formation and they still had not noticed him! He unloaded a long burst of incendiaries into a startled German's gas tank, then stood the Spad on its nose.

He had drawn his first blood, and yet, because he was so far behind the lines that no other Allied planes or observers could confirm the action, he could not officially claim the kill. There were later occasions, when he fought deep in enemy territory, where there could be no official confirmation of his victories. This was only part of the price he paid for his brand of fighting. But that is the unofficial record. The official record began on September 12, 1918, and it became a fighting record that has never been equalled.

From his first official victory on this date to his last day in action, ending in the field near Murvaux, just seventeen days passed. And yet in this short time, Frank Luke became the leading American ace in the war. In this seventeen day period he had eighteen official victories! Rickenbacker flew at the front for more than eight months and was the leading American ace with twenty-six victories at the end of the war, yet even then, Frank Luke's record in only seventeen days of fighting placed him second.

September 12 marked the opening day of the St.-Mihiel offensive, and Luke's squadron was busy patroling its prescribed sector of the front. The ground troops had begun their advance at dawn but were immediately slowed by accurate German artillery fire.

Frank Luke spotted the observation balloon that was directing the deadly fire. It was strung up about two miles behind the front at the right of the American lines, just outside of his patrol sector. He returned to the airfield to report his find. Here he was told that the balloon had already been seen by the squadron in whose patrol sector it was located. It had, in fact, been under constant attack for most of the day, but without success.

Luke asked permission to enter the neighboring patrol sector and attack the important balloon. A good friend of his, 1st Lt. Joseph Wehner, had just landed to refuel. When he heard about Luke's request, he asked to go along to fly cover for the attack.

Balloon attacks were rarely made on a volunteer basis, simply because there were rarely any volunteers. The observation balloon was the most dangerous target in the air.

It measured about fifty by two hundred feet, a huge, sausage-shaped bag filled with high flammable hydrogen. The observer hung below in a wicker basket. With powerful binoculars and radio communication to the ground, he was an effective observer, usually operating at about 2,000 feet. A lorry on the ground, with a winch on its flatbed, would reel out the balloon at dawn, tow it to wherever it was needed, and pull it back in at sunset.

It was a big, stationary target, to be sure. But few who attacked it survived and of those who did, few repeated the attempt. For on the ground, around the balloon in a huge ring, were batteries of antiaircraft and machine guns. Knowing the exact height of the balloon, they set their shells to explode accordingly. So an attacker had to fly through a wall of exploding shells and machine-gun bullets, pour a long burst of incendiaries into the balloon, since a short burst would seldom ignite the gas, then fly through the fiery wall again on the way out. In addition, enemy fighters were usually hiding in the sun somewhere above, and in any encounter they would have the advantage of altitude on the balloon attacker.

The requests of Luke and Wehner were granted immediately.

When they reached the balloon, Luke peeled off and Wehner began to circle above to cover him from fighter attack. Luke pulled out of his screaming dive beside the balloon and opened fire, but a machine gun had jammed.

He pulled up over the balloon and found himself in the midst of a ring of fire. His plane was jarred by explosions on every side but he whipped around and came back at the balloon, his remaining machine gun chattering. The balloon burst into flames and Frank Luke headed out through the ground fire while his first official victory dropped to earth in flames.

His first success at fighting the *drachen* was a solid confirmation of his fighting skill. Therefore when he volunteered two days later, September 14, for another balloon attack, he was given a flight of planes to fly cover for him. But his job wasn't easier. For there was not one balloon, but a cluster of three!

They were strung up near Boinville and were important to the Germans. They hung at an exceptionally low altitude to discourage attack. In fact, they were so low that the observers in the balloons could not use their parachutes, only recently developed at this time, to save themselves. Because the balloons were so valuable to the Germans it was almost certain that fighters were on guard.

As Luke and his escort approached the target, Luke rocked his wings at the flight leader, pulled away from the formation and nosed his Spad down. He had just begun his dive when a pack of Fokkers dropped through the broken clouds, jumping Luke's squadron mates with blazing guns, trying to break through to stop his one-man attack.

Luke made his run, pouring tracers into the gray bag, but the balloon did not ignite. He came back for a second, then a third pass, and the sky was filled with the smoke of shell bursts. With each dive the ground fire came closer, but he ignored repeated hits and bored through the withering curtain of steel. This was the killing assault and the balloon collapsed into a mass of flaming canvas. Now he turned on his attackers. He defiantly hurled his Spad back into the deadly perimeter and proceeded to strafe the gun positions with his remaining ammunition.

Finally he headed for home, struggling to keep his battered Spad airborne. When he landed, the ground crew shook their heads in amazement. The plane was completely riddled, no longer fit for flying. One slug was found buried in his headrest, not six inches from Luke's head.

A new plane was made ready and the covering flight returned and was re-formed. By late afternoon they were heading back for the two remaining balloons. On this attack, because the first balloon had proved so stubborn, Wehner was to follow Luke down. The quicker you could get in and out of the zone of fire, the better your chances to live and tell about it. And this way, the chances of any dangerous return passes would be lessened.

Again enemy Fokkers engaged their protecting group, and again Luke continued toward one of the balloons, this time closely followed by Wehner.

As they drew nearer the balloons they spied still another enemy formation. The Germans had figured they would break away from the covering planes for the balloon attack. Eight Fokkers were bearing down on them.

Luke and Wehner pushed their throttles wide open and dived, racing the Germans to the balloon. Even before they got within range the balloon's observer jumped, pulling his ripcord in spite of the hopelessly low altitude.

They were beating the Fokkers to the balloon but there was time for only one pass. The ground fire was blistering on all sides of the balloon, but they were diving from almost directly above. Luke had time for only a short burst before he had to pull out, but with the first bullet the great gas bag exploded. They passed through the billowing, expanding smoke, leveled off on the deck and flew for home, leaving the burning balloon and their eight pursuers somewhere behind.

At dawn the next day Luke was in the air again, scouting the Boinville area and planning his attack on the third balloon. While doing so, he spotted a new balloon that the Germans had hurriedly sent up at Bois d'Hingry.

He reported back at the field, told what he had seen, and a new attack was quickly planned. Three five-plane patrols were to rendezvous near the target as he began his first dive. Then, within sixty seconds of his attack, they were to dive after him. So that any victories resulting could be confirmed, our own observation balloons in the area were alerted to watch for the attack. The time was set for 5:05 that afternoon.

As the time drew near, our observers began their watch of the lone remaining Boinville balloon. Suddenly the German antiaircraft gunners jumped into action. Out of the clouds above them came Frank Luke, five Fokkers on his tail. On time to the second, he dived straight at the balloon. According to plan, the three flights of Luke's escorts appeared, diving after him. This placed them on the tails of the German planes, just as they had anticipated.

Meanwhile, Luke had once again successfully penetrated the deadly ground fire and our observers saw the sausage-shaped outline of the Boinville balloon disappear in a ball of fire. But then they saw his plane still heading toward the ground. It vanished below the horizon.

It seemed impossible that he had not crashed. Actually he had pulled out of his dive only a few feet from the ground. Rather than climb up into the still-blazing antiaircraft fire, he immediately landed on the uneven battlefield.

His wheels had hardly stopped rolling when he spied the Bois d'Hingry balloon faintly visible in the distance. He jammed the throttle forward and dodged shell craters and ditches to take off.

He held his Spad a few feet off the ground, flying between splintered trees and over barbed-wire entanglements until he reached the balloon post.

He flashed over the muzzles of the surrounding guns and took them completely by surprise. He pulled back on the stick and climbed upwards toward the balloon, firing as he went. The second balloon to appear in his sights that day, not twenty minutes after the first, fell in flames. Frank Luke headed out through the now angrily awakened antiaircraft fire and started for home.

He landed to find that this plane also had been practically shot out from under him. But a patrol had just returned with news of a new balloon, north of Verdun. There was a little daylight left so Luke headed for Verdun in a new plane. He arrived over the balloon at dusk and for the second time that day surprised the Germans. They were hauling the balloon down for the night when Luke's tracers ripped into it.

Two more balloons had gone up at Reville and Romagne-sous-les-Cottes, the next morning. Luke and Wehner decided to try the twilight attack once more. Between them, they shot down both balloons in just twelve minutes.

There was no flying the next day. The whole front was closed in by bad flying weather, but the day following, September 18, the weather began to break. Luke and Wehner took off together and began scouting the front.

They spotted a group of three balloons just going up. It was unusual for the balloons to be launched this late in the morning. They were normally sent up in the last minutes of protecting darkness before dawn. But there was good reason for the change in procedure. The Germans knew that the balloon killer, who appeared suddenly and was dropping their valuable balloons like over-ripe plums, would not pass such a tempting target.

Luke took the bait, and Wehner headed for his covering position above the first balloon. Luke's Spad got one balloon and headed immediately for the second. Meanwhile Wehner was in a scrambling, falling dogfight. When Luke began his first dive, six Fokkers dropped from their hiding place beneath the clouds and headed after him. Wehner charged in and broke up their dive. Now, as Luke exploded his second balloon, Wehner was slowly losing the one-sided fight he had entered.

As Luke hurried to reach him, Wehner's Spad burst into flame and spun into the ground.

Wehner was dead, and Luke continued his climb towards the other four Germans now diving to meet him. His engine sputtered. His main fuel tank was empty. He switched to his reserve tank—ten minutes of fuel, which had to be hand-pumped to the engine.

Luke held his climb towards the diving Germans. They were all firing at him now. In another second, they would meet head on. Luke didn't budge from his course. The Germans had to break formation and roared on past.

Luke half-rolled his Spad. Pulling the stick back, he split-S'ed after them. As the Fokkers pulled out of their dive, Luke caught the lead ship with a long deflection shot and the pilot slumped forward. Luke's dive had carried him through their formation. Pulling the nose up, Luke tried to line up the second ship in his sights. The Fokker went into a tight turn to the right and Luke turned inside of him, sending a shower of bullets through the Fokker's top wing and into the engine. The plane fell off sluggishly on one wing, then started to spin to the ground. But the two remaining Fokkers were closing in on Luke. He quickly cut his engine, pulled up sharply, and the Germans flashed past and headed for home. Almost as suddenly as it had begun, the battle was over.

On his way back to the field Luke spotted a white cluster of exploding antiaircraft shells. Allied gunners were firing at a German LVG, a two-place reconnaissance plane. Luke headed for the enemy plane, though he expected to run out of gas at any moment.

The German rear gunner opened up but Luke dived below the tail of the LVG and out of the line of fire. He then pulled up and raked the bottom of the ship from nose to tail, killing the German pilot.

The two balloons and three planes brought his total to eleven positive victories. Six days had passed since his first confirmed kill. He had passed Rickenbacker. His buddies began to call him indestructible, and the way he fought, it seemed as though they were right.

As the leading American air ace, Luke had earned a seven-day leave to Paris. He returned to combat on September 26, when the Meuse-Argonne offensive opened, and he added another plane to his score.

Two days later he failed to return to his field. He had shot down a two-place Hanover, then landed at the French airfield at Toul. The French treated "the indestructible" royally that night.

Next morning he walked out into the cold dawn and climbed into his ship. The 220-hp. Hispano-Suiza engine was already warmed up and idling. The French mechanics had refueled the plane and armed the twin Vickers machine guns. They had even left a bag of hand grenades on the floor of the cockpit for him.

Later that day he flew low over an advanced American outpost on the Meuse. He dropped a note telling them to watch three German balloons that were floating a few miles back of the front, near Murvaux.

The observation post watched him nose over for his attack. Suddenly the air was full of Fokkers. There were ten of them. They had been patrolling in relays at 12,000 feet, waiting all day for him. First one, then another of the Fokkers dropped out of the fight in flames. Luke was kicking the little Spad in and out of the swarming Germans like a wild man. For a full five minutes he fought them off. Then his Spad appeared to go out of control and tumble toward the ground.

His plane was falling directly over the three balloons at Murvaux, but Frank Luke wasn't dead. The German gun crews stopped their cheering and watched in stunned silence as he leveled out and opened fire.

The first balloon had already burst into flames before the gun crews recovered. The air around him began to explode as they angrily opened up. Luke hit the second balloon, then the third, and the three thick columns of smoke began to rise. Then the ack-ack caught him.

He knew his war was over as he waited for the German troops in the little field outside of Murvaux. He had emptied his machine guns, and the hand grenades were gone. The pain in his shoulder had eased a bit, but he couldn't fire up the engine by himself. He could only wait.

As German troops spilled into the field Frank Luke pulled himself out of the cockpit. He stood by his Spad waiting for them. They surrounded the ship and the German officer called out to him to surrender. Frank Luke drew his sidearm and emptied the .45 at the enemy.

That was his answer and a signal to the Germans to cut him down with small-arms fire.

He had fought with all he had, and won the Congressional Medal of Honor posthumously for what he did at Murvaux that day. He wasn't quite indestructible, but Frank Luke came as close to it as anyone can get.

World War II
THE REVOLUTIONARY "SPITFIRE"
by Larry Forrester

One day in mid-December, 1938, Bicknell called Tuck into his office and told him to shut the door. Bob knew this wasn't because of the cold —the flight commander's voice had an excited edge to it.

"Listen," Bicknell began the instant the lock had clicked, "you know this squadron's going to be re-equipped with Spitfires?"

"Yes—*one* day," Tuck said cynically, swinging a long leg over a corner of the trestle table. They had been told this months before, but since then there had been only a series of frustrating rumours and he had resigned himself to waiting at least a year. Once or twice he had visited Eastleigh, the Supermarine Company's experimental field in Hampshire, and watched test pilot Jeffrey Quill and his colleagues putting the first production Spits—officially still on the secret list—through their paces. He could hardly believe his eyes—such speed, and such manoeuvrability in a *mono*plane!

Sleek, strong and incredibly high-powered, the Spit represented the fighter of his dreams, and he had fallen in love with her at first sight. Thirty feet of wicked beauty. . . . But it seemed that Air Ministry red tape and shortage of money, which made production painfully slow, would keep them apart for a long time yet.

"It's not going to be as long as you think," Bicknell said. "As a matter of fact I've got a bit of news that ought to make a damned fine Christmas present for you. Pretty soon now, Jeff Quill's going to start checking out a few chaps at Duxford. Each of the future Spit squadrons will send him one pilot to begin with. And you, you lucky bastard—you've been chosen to represent 65."

Tuck just stood gaping at him. Bicknell got up from his chair, grinning broadly, and slapped Bob's shoulder.

"*I* didn't choose you, don't think that. It was the Old Man himself."

"Well I'll be damned!" Tuck breathed, a boyish glee soaking through him—he had been so sure that his commanding officer, Squadron Leader Desmond Cooke, still considered him over-confident and a bit irresponsible. It was, he realized with some confusion and even a little humility, a startling tribute to his flying ability. He felt that he ought to say something rather grave and modest.

"This is wonderful. I really can't see why he should pick me—Lord knows, plenty of the chaps have more experience."

"Too much, in fact—and all on biplanes," Bicknell said, his sagacious, honest face suddenly deadly serious. "This job doesn't need experience so much as flexibility . . . a young quick mind that can accept and absorb new ideas and techniques." His mouth twisted in a tired smile. "Maybe that's just what this whole bloody air force needs—maybe we should apply for nice, new flexible minds to be issued to officers every two or three years." He paused, shrugged, and grew serious again.

"Listen, Tommy—the Spitfire isn't just another new aircraft—a bit faster and more heavily armed, and with a few more clever gadgets. The Spitfire is revolutionary, a new conception in design. At last, it seems we're catching up with progress . . . going into a new age of flying—and that's no bullshine, either!

"Which is just as well, because . . ."—he paused, turned away from Tuck and walked to the window, looking up into the dark grey sky—". . . because the bloody politicians are making a shocking mess of this German problem. Munich was a complete balls-up. My bet is before long we're going to need every Spit and every trained pilot we can find. So for God's sake don't have a prang!"

Jeffrey Quill was a small, lean man, just twenty-five. His puckish face seemed always to have a half-smile, and with his soft casual voice and sporty clothes you might have taken him for an indolent and spoiled youth, until you noticed his eyes—brightly alert, steady and dominating. He had served in the air force from 1931 till '36, then joined Vickers as an assistant test pilot. Now—at the tailend of '38—he had been appointed senior test pilot at the Vickers (Supermarine) Works. Only one man knew more than he about the new Spitfire—its designer, R.J. Mitchell. And Mitchell, his health broken by years of financial worry and overwork, was no longer able to personally supervise the advance test programme or take any part in the training of the first service pilots who were to use his brainchild as the foremost weapon of Fighter Command. Thus to the youthful Quill and his tiny staff fell the huge task, and the frightening responsibility, of getting the R.A.F. swiftly and surely mounted on this new and vastly stronger steed.

They began with half a dozen young pilots, the pick of the squadrons which Air Ministry had earmarked for re-equipment. Quill was glad when Bob Tuck turned up in this group—he instinctively liked this slim, eager young officer who had questioned him so hungrily and intelligently during their previous, brief meetings at Eastleigh. Tuck had shown that he knew by heart the few general performance facts so far released for publication: obviously he was tremendously thrilled by the Spit and, unlike many other pilots, he was not in the least awed by her 'unorthodox' appearance, nor cowed by her high landing speed.

At Duxford, Quill personally took him out to a parked Spitfire which bore the markings K-9796 and began to teach him cockpit drill. For over an hour Tuck sat in the plane while the test pilot, standing on the wing peering in, ordered him to place his hands on various controls. When he had memorized the precise position of each knob, switch, lever and dial—there seemed to be at least three times as many as in the Gladiator—and could flash a hand to it unerringly, Quill made him do it with his eyes tightly closed.

Next, he had to brand into his mind the ritual letters BTFCPUR, which represented the order in which these controls were to be checked and set at the last moment before take-off—brakes, trim, flaps, contacts, petrol, undercarriage and radiator. Other, similar formulae governed the processes of climbing, descending and landing. This took the best part of another hour.

Finally he had to memorize the different speeds, temperatures, pressures, revolutions per minute and other instrument readings necessary for take-off, climbing, straight and level flight, normal cruise, fast cruise, various rates of turn, aerodrome approach and landing. For a while his head was swimming, but they kept at it doggedly and soon he had mastered all this mass of vital operating data: Quill decided they'd had enough theory and it was time for his pupil to put it all into practice.

"Just one more thing," he said, as Tuck fastened his straps. "Be damned careful not to get her nose too far forward on take-off. Once the tail's up you've only a few inches clearance between the prop tips and the deck."

"Right—I'll remember."

"Fine. I'm going to leave you now. Just sit here for a minute or two and go over everything by yourself." He jerked a thumb towards a group of airmen squatting in the grass a few yards away. "When you're all set to go, give the boys a yell." Then, still wearing his lackadaisical half-smile, Quill jumped down and sauntered off.

Left alone, Tuck had momentary qualms. He felt like an impostor, sitting here in this strangely shaped machine . . . looking out through the tiny windscreen at that long, slim, shark's head cowling. . . .

It was so odd not to have the comforting bulk of an upper wing over his head and the familiar latticework of struts and wires on either side. The cockpit was so small his body seemed to fill it, and he had the curious impression that somehow he'd got himself inserted up to the shoulders in a giant bullet. And when he thought of the thousands of horsepower imprisoned in that Rolls Royce Merlin engine just in front of him, waiting to burst into thunderous action at *his* bidding—he realized this Spitfire bore practically no relation to any of the aircraft he'd flown previously. His mouth went dry and his chest was a vast, empty cavern.

There drifted into his momentarily confused brain, like a chill fog, the memory of those terrible first days at Grantham, and he saw Wills' suffering face again and he heard Wills' too-casual voice coming over the gosport, telling him to watch the airspeed, to keep the wings straight, not to be so bloody ham-handed on the stick and not to slam the throttle about like that . . . As always, swallowing the dregs of this old shame again made his spine stiffen in obdurate fury, made him ready to fight with a cold, hard fervour—because fighting like that demanded the concentration of his entire being and so it was the best way, the only way, to exorcise this clammy ghost that was trying to follow him through the years.

Swiftly he tightened his harness, whistling shrilly for the ground crew. They came running to fuss around the aircraft and a few seconds later he pressed the starter button. The single-bladed prop, which looked to him like an enormous plank of wood, turned slowly, hesitantly, then . . .

B-room-bang! The powerful Merlin fired with a deep, crackling roar.

"Chocks away!" Bent figures scurrying through the thin blue exhaust smoke, dragging the heavy blocks from under the wheels . . . A dozen white needles shuddering on the dials before his face, like admonishing fingers waggling at him. . . .

Taking his time, making each movement light yet sure, he eased the throttle forward, opened the radiator wide to prevent overheating, eased off the brakes and taxied carefully to the down-wind side of the field. There he turned her into the wind, stopped and began his cockpit check. As he became absorbed in the mental and physical task all his emotions filtered away into his sub-conscious, and from long habit his muscles relaxed. He could remember every word Quill had said.

He eased the throttle open and she seemed to leap forward. At first he couldn't see ahead because his vision was obscured by that long cowling, so he had to stick his head out and keep her straight by looking along the side of the nose and using a distant tree, on the other side of the field, as a reference point. From the stub exhausts on the side of the cowling, short jets of greenish-blue flame stabbed back towards his face, quivering furiously, roaring like a battery of blowlamps. The thunder of the engine as it surged up to full power seemed to beat on his head like mailed fists.

She gathered speed slowly, as the heavy wooden prop took big, coarse bites at the air, trying to get a firm grip. At just over 60 m.p.h. the tail came up, giving him a clear view ahead, and then she started to accelerate very quickly.

Don't let her nose get too far forward. . . .

Gently he checked the stick, keeping the prop tips clear of the ground. All the time his feet were working nimbly on the rudder, fighting her strong inclination to swing to the right—because at this speed the torque of air spiralling back from the prop struck the tail assembly on the right side with considerable force, trying to veer her round. Then suddenly she was in the air.

When you change hands to retract the undercart, watch your airspeed. . . .

With his left hand he throttled back to climbing revs then tightened the large, milled knob which clamped the lever there. Now, Quill had warned, came a moment of danger; the lever which operated the undercarriage was on the right side of the cockpit, so to retract, it was necessary to change hands on the stick. The retracting lever had to be moved with the right hand to select 'up', and then pumped vigorously for several seconds. It wasn't at all easy to perform large, energetic movements with one hand and at the same time keep the other rock still. At this low altitude, before the new pilot had had a chance to get the 'feel' of the aircraft, a comparatively small, jerky movement on the stick with the left hand could cause either a stall or a dive.

Even the best of beginners, Quill had added indulgently, couldn't be expected to hold her in a steady climb at this point—at least a gentle 'porpoising' movement was inevitable.

He moved his hands unhurriedly. Resisting the temptation to give just one quick glance sideways and downwards towards the undercarriage lever, he kept his eyes on strict vigil, flicking between the airspeed indicator and the distant, hazy line of the horizon. The nose remained precisely in the correct climbing attitude while his right hand sought and found the lever, moved it upwards, pumped it steadily.

The Spitfire's hydraulic muscles flexed, swiftly and smoothly drawing up the undercarriage. *C-loomp c-loomp*—the genteel thuds under his feet as the wheels folded into their belly housings suggested sheer luxury, like the cushioned slammings of giant refrigerator doors. A current of elation sparked through him. He could feel in his hands the touch of sure and responsive mechanism, the delicate poise of this machine, light and quick and graceful as a ballerina. As he slid the hood closed he chuckled aloud. Here in this transparent, streamlined carapace, looking out along the long, tapering nose, he felt drunk with power and speed.

Above the winter clouds, for twenty minutes or so he frolicked joyously—stalling, spinning, looping, rolling. He found himself thinking of this machine as a live creature—gentle and sensitive, with a great heart that throbbed bravely. An understanding and intelligent creature that responded instantly to the most delicate suggestive pressures of its master's hands and feet. He had never dreamed that flying could be like this: he knew that with a little time he could make this 'plane almost a part of him—like an extension of his own body, brain and nervous system.

Descending in a long, gentle dive, he touched 360 m.p.h. Levelling out near the aerodrome, he had to force himself into a more sober frame of mind in order to concentrate on the difficult job of landing a new aircraft for the first time.

He throttled back, opened the radiator wide, slid back his hood and began his approach. At first everything went well. As he turned across wind, he lowered the undercarriage and flaps. Next, turning into wind, he put the prop into fine pitch and eased the stick back: then the long nose reared up and blotted out the ground ahead!

For the barest second he was thrown off balance. And then he remembered. . . .

On the last part of your approach it's a good idea to put her into a gentle side-slip, and then straighten her out just before the wheels touch. . . .

A little rudder and a few degrees of opposite bank, and the nose obligingly swung a little to one side. Now the Spitfire was moving crab-wise through the air, forward and downward in a sort of controlled fall. The wind shrieked in through the open side of the canopy, full in his face, as he looked down at the tilted grassland hurtling to meet him at unnerving speed.

Twenty feet, ten feet, five . . . *now!* He centralized the rudder and took off the bank. Like a soldier coming smartly to attention, the aircraft snapped into the landing attitude.

Stick back, gently but firmly back into the pit of the stomach. A soft jolt, and she was rolling bumpily over the grass. Keep her straight! A touch on one brake, then the other, and she was slowing . . . slowing . . . coming to a standstill in the centre of the field.

How quiet and still was the world! He relaxed for a moment and then, wrapped in a deep, warm gladness, taxied leisurely to dispersal. He knew with a startling certainty that in these last few minutes he'd reached an important milestone in his life.

But he couldn't know *how* important.

He stayed at Duxford for just over a week and returned to Hornchurch on January 9th, 1939, as one of the air force's first qualified Spitfire pilots. The following days were one constant, exhaustive interrogation, but he never wearied of describing to his eager colleagues how wonderful the new fighter was.

Now the Gladiator seemed like an amiable, somewhat rheumaticky old goose, and he seethed with impatience as weeks went by and there was no news about re-equipment. Not until the end of March was he ordered to Eastleigh to collect the first of the new aircraft.

In the mess at Eastleigh he found Jeff Quill and several other pilots he knew. Everyone was in high spirits, and the half-cans of bitter rose and fell merrily. They talked, of course, about the Spitfire, and all the future wonders promised by its success. They talked, too, about another new fighter, the Hawker Hurricane, which somehow had received a great deal more publicity than the Spit, although undoubtedly it was slower, heavier and not nearly so agile.

The Hurricane had smashed a number of records on cross-country flights, and the pilots of 111 Squadron—the only unit so far equipped with this aeroplane—were shooting terrific lines about how much skill and guts it took to handle it. They inferred that it was a kind of monster that had to be tamed and constantly watched—a machine with a sly, malicious intelligence of its own, a killer-plane that only the dashing, devil-may-care elite were permitted to fly.

Undoubtedly 111 had started all this as a huge joke, but the joke was being taken seriously by the public and the press, and the Air Ministry hadn't lifted a finger to dispel the myth. Hence 'Hurricane'—not 'Spitfire'—was the name on every schoolboy's lips and in every newspaper article on Britain's air defences: anyone who flew it was regarded as an 'ace' by the awed, and misinformed, populace.

(This state of affairs must have been galling for the Supermarine Company and for the squadrons taking over the new Spits, but Tuck maintains that it had a more serious repercussion too: for some years most newly trained pilots held the Hurri in almost superstitious dread, and without doubt a number of them crashed while learning to fly it through lack of confidence or sheer nervousness. Their fears were quite groundless, for the Hurricane was in truth an infinitely more sedate and tractable machine than the super-sensitive Spitfire, which reacted full-bloodedly to the slightest movement of the controls—right *or* wrong. Had official steps been taken in 1939 to strangle the legend of the 'killer-plane', after the outbreak of war he believes there would have been fewer serious crashes among trainee pilots of Fighter Command.)

And they talked, that fine day at Eastleigh, about the third of the world's new monoplane fighters, the Messerschmitt 109. But not very much, for none of them knew a great deal about it. All Tuck could say on the subject was that he'd bet his life it had a jolly fine reflector gunsight! Everyone roared with laughter, for they'd all heard the story of Milch and Udet visiting Hornchurch. This led to a variety of other yarns, and their laughter was still ringing in his ears as he left, gay and excited as a bridegroom, to collect his Spit and carry her with his loving hands across the threshold of 65's home.

He started taxi-ing toward the down-wind end of the field so fast that once or twice the tail kicked up and the machine see-sawed clumsily. Then he saw Jeff Quill's car racing across the tarmac to intercept him, and eased up a bit.

Quill was waiting for him at the take-off point, smiling as ever. As the plane rolled to a stop, facing into wind, the test pilot mounted the wing at a single agile spring and said: "Better have a quick little brush-up, eh?"

Tuck had trouble concealing his feverish impatience. He didn't need a refresher—every detail of Spitfire procedure was ready now in the forecourt of his mind, burnished bright by daily polishing—but, after all, it was the best part of three months since he had flown a Spit and he realized that Quill had to be sure. So for the next five minutes he sat there, docilely practising the cockpit drill he could have done in his sleep, moving his hands over levers and switches familiar to him as the pockets and buttons of his uniform.

The Spit was parked only a few feet from the boundary, and the wind of its idling propeller was making a thick hedge sway and flutter. Beyond this hedge lay neat and sombre gardens and a small, very plain brick building—a Crematorium. Neither Tuck nor Quill noticed that, flying stiffly on a short pole close by the hedge there was a plain, red flag.

"Check your magnetos," Quill said at length, getting down from the wing.

Bob locked his brakes, full on, and advanced the throttle. The Merlin's stunning roar seemed to fill the world. The whole aircraft juddered, straining to be off. And behind, the boundary hedge seethed and lashed under the slipstream's torture.

He flicked first one magneto switch, then the other. Carefully he made sure that there was no big drop in the number of revolutions per minute when she was running on only one mag. Finally, he opened up to almost full power, to ensure climbing and take-off revs. Then he throttled back and gave Quill the thumbs-up sign to show him all was well. Quill waved cheerfully, signalling him to take-off. The Merlin's roar rose to a crescendo and in what seemed less than a minute he was streaking up through wispy clouds and Eastleigh was a diminishing patch on the cluttered landscape far below.

High over Hampshire and Essex, riding home in his new Spitfire, he hummed a theme from Mozart, and with the canopy closed the deep drone of the cruising engine seemed to form great chords of harmony. Now and then he plunged into a woof of cloud, pulled up out of it again in a steep climb—playful as a young seal in a summer sea.

He had never been so content. A feeling of inner peace and welling strength filled him, but he entirely failed to recognize the truth: that in some weird way this machine—this marvel in metal which he understood so well, and which seemed to understand him—already was at work altering his character, completing his growing up. He only knew, vaguely, that suddenly he had lost some of the old restlessness, and found an inner balance.

Late that night back at Hornchurch, a 'phone call from Quill at Eastleigh added an odd and embarrassing little postscript to the day.

"There's been one helluva stink down here about your take-off."

"What?"

"Your take-off, chum. The flag was up at the Crematorium—they were burning some poor sod in there just when you revved up."

"My God . . . I forgot all about the flag!"

"It was all such rotten luck, Tommy—couldn't have timed it worse if we'd planned it. Seems the coffin was just starting to sink slowly down into the furnace room—you know the way it's done—when you arrived outside and sat there, just over the hedge, with the engine bumbling and crackling away, and the vibration making the windows rattle and whole place shake. The mourners couldn't hear what the minister was saying, and you know that business about committing the body to the flames or whatever it is—that's the most important part of the whole service. So they had to stop the lift, with the coffin half-way down, and wait for nearly five minutes—while you and I were doing cockpit drill! You can imagine how they felt."

"Yes—terrible! Like I feel now."

"My fault as much as yours—I didn't notice the flag either, and it's my bloody aerodrome. But don't worry, Cocky—my chief's writing an official apology to the vicar and the relatives. It'll probably all blow over."

It must have blown over, for Tuck heard no more. But ever since he has wondered, with undiminishing curiosity, who it was that waited that day, poised midway between this world and dark, obliterating Eternity—waited those few minutes while a young man filled with a frantic yearning made ready and rose into the broad spring sunlight in a new kind of machine that shone like a promise, a machine which so soon was to forge an epic chapter in British history.

Wondered . . . but never dared to find out.

PATROL OVER DUNKIRK

by Paul Brickhill

In darkness he came up out of sleep. A hand was shaking his shoulder and a voice saying: "Wake up, sir. Wake up!" The light clicked on and he blinked and scowled at the batman who stood there.

"Squadron's got to take off for Martlesham at 4 a.m., sir," said the batman. "It's three o'clock now."

"What the hell for?"

"Dunno, sir, but they said it was very urgent."

Still half-asleep and irritable he reached out and strapped on his legs, then thumped the other pilots awake. Mermagen arrived, and said: "I don't know what it's about but we're heading south and not taking any kit. Must be a flap about something."

Dawn glowed in the east as the squadrons shook themselves into formation in the still air, and half an hour later they were landing in sections through feathers of waist-high mist on Martlesham Aerodrome, near Felixstowe, on the East Coast. Another squadron of Spitfires had already arrived, their pilots sipping mugs of tea in a group nearby. Bader strolled over and asked "the form" from a slim, handsome flight lieutenant, elegant in white overalls and with a silver name-bracelet round his wrist.

"Haven't got a clue," said the debonair young man who had aquiline features like a matador, a thin black moustache and a long, exciting scar down the side of his face, the type of young blade, Bader thought, who would make a young girl think of darkened corridors and turning door handles. His name was Bob Tuck.

Mermagen bustled over and said almost casually: "Patrol Dunkirk, chaps, 12,000 feet. Take-off as soon as we're refuelled."

"What the hell!" Bader said. "What's happening over there?"

Mermagen shrugged. "Haven't the slightest idea. Something about evacuating, I think."

One of the pilots said in an injured voice: "I must say it's damned early to go junketing over there. I haven't even seen a paper yet."

It seems odd now that the word Dunkirk did not mean a thing then. The Army had laid a screen of secrecy over the plans for the evacuation and people did not realise that the beaches were filling with exhausted men, least of all the fighter pilots from the north who had not seen the war yet. At least they were going across the water to the edge of France —that was something—but the transition from peace to war is often cushioned and unreal. They did not quite grasp the idea that they might run into German planes over Dunkirk: and, in fact, that day they didn't.

Mermagen led them off in four neat vics of three; they climbed steadily and about 9,000 feet vanished into a layer of fluffy white cloud that stretched beyond the horizon. At 10,000 feet they popped like porpoises out of the cloud and levelled off at 12,000, still in tidy formation . . . unblooded. A Messerschmitt coming up behind could have shot the whole lot down. Far ahead Bader saw a strange black plume floating hugely through the limitless froth they were riding over. Mermagen's voice crackled over the radio: "That looks like it. That smoke. Must be burning oil tanks." For a long time they circled the smoke and ranged over the cloud. Mermagen wanted to dive below the cloud but the controller had said 12,000 feet and such orders (in their inexperience) were orders. They saw nothing else in the sky, and after an hour and a half Mermagen led them away. Under the cloud blood was staining the sand as the Stukas dive-bombed and the Messerschmitt 109's and 110's strafed.

On the way back 222 Squadron was told by radio to land at Manston, and after that were told to fly to Duxford, and at Duxford were ordered off again for Hornchurch, a fighter base just north of the Thames and a dozen miles east of London. "Typical shambles," they grumbled, blasé about the war. At Hornchurch they gazed, startled, and then with mild derision at pilots of other squadrons walking around with pistols tucked in their flying boots and as often as not with beard stubble. The others had been flying over France for several days and were quiet and preoccupied. Still the impact did not strike the 222 pilots, who considered the pistols and beard stubble as "line-shooting."

At 3.30 a.m. Bader was shaken awake again.

"Take-off at 4.30, sir," said the batman.

It was getting beyond a joke.

Unbroken cloud lay over the land at about 4,000 feet, but this day they flew at 3,000. Skirting the North Foreland to pass Dover on the right, he looked down on the grey sea with amazement. Out from the Thames estuary, from Dover and the bays little boats were swarming, slowly converging, heading south-east till they stretched across the sea in a straggling line, trailing feathers of foam, yachts and tugs, launches, ferries, coasters, lifeboats, paddle steamers, here and there a destroyer or a cruiser. It was unbelievable. "God," he thought, "it's like the Great West Road on a Bank Holiday." Far ahead the black smoke rolled thickly up from the edge of Dunkirk, where the oil tanks lay, and all the way in between the swarm of little boats streamed white tails across the water. Hundreds of them.

Mermagen led them across the dirty sand by Gravelines and swung along the beaches towards Dunkirk. At first the men in the distance looked like a wide stain of ants teeming over a flat nest and then, as the planes swept nearer, like flies, thousands and thousands stuck together, packing the sand. No holiday beach was ever like that, but this was no holiday and Bader began to understand that this was war. In the green shallows crawled the vanguard of the little boats, and black lines that were the heads of men threaded the water towards them.

A voice on the R/T said: "Aircraft ahead." Bader saw them in the same moment, about twelve of them, about three miles ahead and a little to the right. He wondered who they were . . . not Spitfires or Hurricanes, and a surprised voice said in his earphones: "Christ, they're 110's!"

A shock sparkled through him. They were coming head-on and in seconds he could see the twin-engines and twin fins. The Messerschmitts veered sharply left, climbing for the cloud . . . must be carrying bombs, avoiding a fight. Mermagen in front pulled up his nose and cartridge cases streamed out of his wings as he fired. But he was a long way out of normal range.

One of the 110's suddenly streamed black smoke, dipped out of the formation and went straight down, flaming. She hit and blew up behind Dunkirk. The other Germans had vanished into the cloud and the sky was clear again. It stayed clear for the rest of the patrol, and when they landed back at Hornchurch everyone clustered round Mermagen excitedly.

"Well I must say," Mermagen said, "I was *most* surprised when that thing fell down."

"By God," said Bader, "so were the rest of us."

But it had been the real thing—if only a taste.

Next morning out of bed at 3.15 again for Dunkirk, and this time not a sign of enemy aircraft, only the ants on the beach and the little boats nosing bravely into the shore. So it was the next day, except that the town was burning and guns flashing round the perimeter. Dunkirk was beginning to mean something. Other squadrons excitedly reported running into packs of Messerschmitts and Stukas, and the bloody fights they had with them. Bader listened intently and with impatience.

Again in the morning up at 3.15, and from the cockpit at 3,000 feet he could no longer see the canals that threaded through the flaming town—smoke brooded heavily and drifted across the stone breakwaters of the harbour. But no German planes. They came and bombed and killed just after the squadron had turned for home. The afternoon was even more frustrating. He led his flight once more over Dunkirk, and after half an hour the engine started misfiring, shaking the plane horribly. For the first time on a battle flight he had to turn back early, and landed in a temper about the war that was raging and always eluded him. A letter awaited, bidding him to answer the charge of speeding at Stevenage. He wrote and asked if they would defer the case for a few days.

In the morning he felt dog-tired when the batman woke him at the same time. Same routine. An odd haze stretched like a ribbon towards London from Dunkirk, and even in the cockpit at 3,000 feet he smelt burning oil and knew what the haze was. Down below the same brave little boats streamed over the water. Dunkirk ahead . . . and over Dunkirk, about three miles away, a gaggle of swift-growing dots. He knew what they were instantly. The 110's wheeled inland without dropping their bombs, but the sky was empty of cloud and the Spitfires leapt after them, blaring on full throttle. No time for thinking, but as he turned his reflector sight on and the gun button to "fire," he knew he was going to shoot. A glance back through the perspex; the straining Spitfires were stringing out in a ragged line and up to the left four grey shapes were diving at them—Messerschmitt 109's, the first he had seen. From the beam they flicked across in front like darting sharks, winking orange flashes in the noses as they fired.

He rammed stick and rudder over and the Spitfire wheeled after them. A 109 shot up in front; his thumb jabbed the firing button and the guns in the wings squirted with a shocking noise. The 109 seemed to be filling his windscreen. A puff of white spurted just behind its cockpit as though someone had used a giant flit-gun. The puff was chopped off . . . for a moment nothing . . . then a spurt of orange flame mushroomed round the cockpit and flared back like a blow-torch. The 109 rolled drunkenly, showing her belly, and in the same moment he saw the black cross on its side. It was true. They did have black crosses. Suddenly it was real and the 109 was falling away and behind, flaming.

Exultation welled sharply up, a fiery thrill running through him as he swung back towards the squadron—but the squadron had gone: not a plane in sight except the plunging torch on the end of the ribbon of black smoke running down the sky behind.

Turning back towards Dunkirk, he did see a plane. From nowhere it seemed a 110 was tumbling down half a mile in front. Incongruously the twin tail was snapped off but still hung to the plane by the control cables, spinning madly like a chimney cowl. Wide-eyed he watched the broken plane erupt into the ground below.

The heady joy of the kill flooded back as he slid out over the water towards England. A glow of fulfilment. Blood runs hotly at the kill when a pilot wins back his life in primitive combat. He had fought a plane and shot at it, impersonally, not seeing the man, and longed to get back and tell everyone, but when he taxied in the joy died. Two of the others were missing.

That afternoon, thirsting for more, he flew back to Dunkirk with the squadron, and on the fringe of the little boats off the breakwater saw a shadow diving on a destroyer. Another shock—black crosses on the wings as a Heinkel 111 swept over the funnels. A white core of water erupted just behind the destroyer and her stern kicked up, the screws foaming out of the water. He was peeling off after the Heinkel, which was swinging back to the coast. Little flashes came from the bomber's glass-house, and Bader pressed his own gun button and the flashes stopped. Good! Killed the gunner! The Heinkel steep-turned sharply inside him. As he pulled up to swing in again two more Spitfires were closing on the bomber, already a mile away. Amazing how fast everything went. No chance of catching them in time. He looked for the rest of the squadron, but they, too, had vanished.

There was the destroyer though, and he banked over to see if they were all right. They seemed to be; they were flashing at him, and then he saw tiny black spots darting past and knew where the flashes came from. A multiple pom-pom. The Navy took no chances in those days. Bader shot away in the other direction. It was, he thought, rather rude of the Navy.

The squadron stayed at Hornchurch. Morning after morning up at 3.15 for the dawn patrol, and other patrols, but always it was the other squadrons that found the enemy, which was infuriating. All Bader saw were the rearguards on the beaches, embattled and dwindling, and it was not pleasant. When not flying the squadron sat all day by their planes, till nearly 11 p.m. when the last light went. Geoffrey Stephenson was missing. They said he had tried a copybook Fighter Command attack No. 2 on a Stuka and the single rear gun had stopped his engine, forcing him down, streaming glycol, in enemy territory.

On 4th June the Prime Minister ordered a last patrol and Bader flew on it. The beach by Dunkirk was empty and the crumbling town lay inert under the smoke. Out of the harbour tacked a single yacht with a little white sail; it must have been the last boat out of Dunkirk and they circled it protectively till low petrol forced them home.

Dunkirk was over and Bader, suddenly exhausted, slept nearly twenty-four hours, waking to find a grim new mood lying over England. You could see what the pilots were thinking by their faces—if it was fighting they wanted they were going to get it. Sobering, but not too daunting. Unreasonably, the country refused to see that it was beaten. Bader went a stage further, refusing to believe that he would, therefore, probably be killed. The possibility, or rather the theory, lay in his mind but he ignored it and like a dried pea it never took root. Having tasted blood, he thought only of flying, fighting and tactics, things he had wanted so long that nothing else mattered, and the thought never obtruded consciously that no one now could think of him with pity or as second to a man who could run. He lived for the coming fight, Britain's, as well as his own.

A letter came from the court in Stevenage saying "Guilty" and fining him £2 10s. Furious, he sent a cheque and a stiff note regretting his inability to attend as he had had to go to Dunkirk.

On a week-end pass he drove down to Thelma, who had gone back to the Pantiles. He had to tell her Geoffrey Stephenson was missing, and after that they did not talk about the war.

The fight seemed a long time coming and the days were unexciting with training—formation, dummy attacks, night flying. The squadron moved north again to Kirton-in-Lindsay and Thelma stayed at the Pantiles. At least for the time being, she thought, nothing was likely to happen to Douglas.

Towards midnight on 13th June Bader was 12,000 feet over the Humber looking for an unidentified aircraft that had been tracked in from Germany. Peering out of the little cockpit he could see nothing but a few pale stars and knew there was little chance of seeing anything else. The Spitfire, with its tiny perspex hood and long nose, was not good for night flying, and seeking a raider in the dark was like being blindfolded and chasing a rabbit in the woods. But then there were no other defences.

"Red One, Red One," the controller's voice said, "weather closing in. Return to base immediately."

He swung steeply down towards the blacked-out land, but the rain cloud moved in faster. On a homing course he was only a few hundred feet up, and right over the airfield before, dimly, he picked up the flarepath suffused through a veil of rain, and swung tightly round it to keep it in sight through the rain-filmed perspex. He floated past the first flare . . . too high. The second flashed behind . . . and then the third before he touched on the downhill runway. The tail was not down and he knew he had misjudged. Stick hard back in his stomach but still the tail stayed up and the flares flashed by. In the same moment he knew he was going to overshoot and that it was too late to open up and take off again; then the tail was down and the brakes were on as hard as he dared.

In front there were no more flares . . . only blackness. An agony of waiting, and then a tearing crash as the plane jolted, slid her belly over the low wall of an aircraft pen, sheering the undercart off, and jarred to a stop. Bricks were suddenly raining down on the metal, and the mind for a moment was a blank. No fear, no shock. He just sat there as he had twice before.

Then he said one short, unprintable word.

A car screeched along the perimeter grass. He took off his helmet and heard the rain pattering on the wings. Tubby Mermagen loomed out of the darkness.

"Douglas," he called anxiously, "are you all right?"

"No," Bader growled. "I'm bloody furious."

"Serves you right," Mermagen said, relieved. "That was a ruddy awful approach."

In the morning Mermagen greeted him with a sly grin and a significant remark: "Well, Douglas, we're losing you."

Bader stared, remembering last night's accident, and thought with a chill of being grounded.

"Where?" he demanded. "I don't want to leave."

"It's all right," Mermagen said soothingly. "You're getting a squadron."

Bader stared again.

"It's not a joke," Mermagen grinned. "Or perhaps it is. Anyway, L.M. wants to see you."

The surge of incredulous joy was cut off a moment later when it occurred to Bader that Leigh-Mallory could not possibly have heard of the latest accident.

He drove to 12 Group Headquarters at Hucknall and stood once more before the A.O.C. Without preamble Leigh-Mallory said: "I've been hearing of your work as a flight commander. I'm giving you a squadron, No. 242."

(Better get it over!)

Bader said: "Yes, sir. . . . Sir, there's one thing I should tell you. . . . I broke a Spitfire last night. Overshot landing."

Leigh-Mallory said mildly: "Well, that happens sometimes, you know."

Wearing his hair shirt to the last, Bader went on: "Sir, the point is that last time you promoted me, to flight commander, I'd also just broken one."

Leigh-Mallory looked grave, then grinned. "Don't worry," he said. "Your new squadron has Hurricanes."

Brisk again, the A.O.C. went on: "242 are a Canadian squadron, the only one in the R.A.F. Nearly all the pilots are Canadians and they're a tough bunch. They're just back from France, where they got pretty badly mauled and lost quite a few aircraft. They were messed around quite a bit; it wasn't their fault and now they're fed up. Frankly morale is low. They need a bit of decent organisation and some firm handling; someone who can talk tough and I think you're the chap to do it. We may need every fighter squadron we've got on the top line soon. The Luftwaffe seems to be gathering across the Channel."

The squadron was at Coltishall, near Norwich, Leigh-Mallory said, and Squadron Leader Bader was to take over as from that moment. He stood up, shook Bader's hand, and said: "Good luck in your first command."

Squadron Leader Bader! Or at least Acting Squadron Leader! How unemotional the interview had been and how deep the content it stirred. Eight weeks ago he had been a flying officer! It hardly even occurred to him that he had caught up with his contemporaries; he was longing to flex his muscles in his first command.

By evening he had driven a hundred miles back to Kirton, packed his kit, telephoned Thelma and was steering the M.G. towards Coltishall.

Almost the first man he saw at breakfast in the morning was Rupert

Leigh. 66 Squadron, apparently, was now also stationed at Coltishall. Shaking his hand on hearing of the promotion, Leigh said: "Now you won't have to call me 'sir' any more. Not that you ever *did,* but it'll be a comfort for you to go on being rude with a clear conscience."

After breakfast the "station master" at Coltishall, the pipe-smoking, phlegmatic Wing Commander Beisiegel, told Bader about his new squadron, and was not comforting. The ground crews were about half English, three or four of the pilots were English and the rest were Canadians. Wild Canadians, the least tractable young officers he had ever seen, and most allergic to commanding officers! God knows what they would think when they heard that the new C.O. had no legs. Already unrest had affected the whole squadron. They needed someone pretty strong and active to discipline them.

It occurred to Bader that he was still wearing only the two rings of the flight lieutenant round his sleeve; he had not yet had time to get the third, thin ring sewn in between, and that would make him look very much a new boy.

"If you don't mind, sir," he said, "I'll drive into Norwich and get the extra braid sewn on before I make my entrance."

He went off in the M.G. and while he was away the news of his arrival reached the squadron. One of the pilots encountered Bernard West, the squadron "plumber" (engineer officer) and said: "Have you seen the new C.O.?"

"No, I haven't." West was greatly interested and a little wary. "What's this one like?"

"Bit unusual," the pilot said cryptically. "I don't suppose we'll be seeing much of him. He's got no legs."

West, a warrant officer of twenty years' service who had seen most things in the Air Force, gaped and groaned.

MIRACLE AT SUNSET

by Ernie Pyle

It was late afternoon at our desert airdrome. The sun was lazy, the air was warm, and a faint haze of propeller dust hung over the field, giving it softness. It was time for the planes to start coming back from their mission, and one by one they did come—big Flying Fortresses and fiery little Lightnings. Nobody paid a great deal of attention, for this returning was a daily routine thing.

Finally they were all in—all, that is, except one. Operations reported a Fortress missing. Returning pilots said it had lagged behind and lost altitude just after leaving the target. The last report said the Fortress couldn't stay in the air more than five minutes. Hours had passed since then. So it was gone.

Ten men were in that plane. The day's accomplishments had been great, but the thought of ten lost friends cast a pall over us. We had already seen death that afternoon. One of the returning Fortresses had released a red flare over the field, and I had stood with others beneath the great plane as they handed its dead pilot, head downward, through the escape hatch onto a stretcher.

The faces of his crew were grave, and nobody talked very loud. One man clutched a leather cap with blood on it. The pilot's hands were very white. Everybody knew the pilot. He was so young, a couple of hours before. The war came inside us then, and we felt it deeply.

After the last report, half a dozen of us went to the high control tower. We went there every evening, for two things—to watch the sunset, and to get word on the progress of the German bombers that frequently came just after dusk to blast our airdrome.

The sunsets in the desert are truly things with souls. The violence of their color is incredible. They splatter the sky and the clouds with a surging beauty. The mountains stand dark against the horizon, and palm trees silhouette themselves dramatically against the fiery west.

As we stood on the tower looking down over this scene, the day began folding itself up. Fighter planes, which had patrolled the field all day, were coming in. All the soldiers in the tent camps had finished supper. That noiseless peace that sometimes comes just before dusk hung over the airdrome. Men talked in low tones about the dead pilot and the lost Fortress. We thought we would wait a few minutes more to see if the Germans were coming over.

And then an electric thing happened. Far off in the dusk a red flare shot into the sky. It made an arc against the dark background of the mountains and fell to the earth. It couldn't be anything else. It had to be. The ten dead men were coming home!

"Where's the flare gun? Gimme a green flare!" yelled an officer.

He ran to the edge of the tower, shouted, "Look out below!" and fired a green rocket into the air. Then we saw the plane—just a tiny black speck. It seemed almost on the ground, it was so low, and in the first glance we could sense that it was barely moving, barely staying in the air. Crippled and alone, two hours behind all the rest, it was dragging itself home.

I was a layman, and no longer of the fraternity that flies, but I could feel. And at that moment I felt something close to human love for that faithful, battered machine, that far dark speck struggling toward us with such pathetic slowness.

All of us stood tense, hardly remembering anyone else was there. With all our nerves we seemed to pull the plane toward us. I suspect a photograph would have shown us all leaning slightly to the left. Not one of us thought the plane would ever make the field, but on it came—so slowly that it was cruel to watch.

It reached the far end of the airdrome, still holding its pathetic little altitude. It skimmed over the tops of parked planes, and kept on, actually reaching out—it seemed to us—for the runway. A few hundred yards more now. Could it? Would it? Was it truly possible?

They cleared the last plane, they were over the runway. They settled slowly. The wheels touched softly. And as the plane rolled on down the runway the thousands of men around that vast field suddenly realized that they were weak and that they could hear their hearts pounding.

The last of the sunset died, and the sky turned into blackness, which would help the Germans if they came on schedule with their bombs. But nobody cared. Our ten dead men were miraculously back from the grave.

And what a story they had to tell! Nothing quite like it had happened before in this war.

The Tripoli airdrome, which was their target, was heavily defended, by both fighter planes and antiaircraft guns. Flying into that hailstorm, as one pilot said, was like a mouse attacking a dozen cats.

The Thunderbird—for that was the name of their Fortress—was first hit just as it dropped its bomb load. One engine went out. Then a few moments later the other engine on the same side went. When both engines went out on the same side it was usually fatal. And therein lay the difference of that feat from other instances of bringing damaged bombers home.

The Thunderbird was forced to drop below the other Fortresses. And the moment a Fortress dropped down or lagged behind, German fighters were on it like vultures. The boys didn't know how many Germans were in the air, but they thought there must have been thirty.

Our Lightning fighters, escorting the Fortresses, stuck by the Thunderbird and fought as long as they could, but finally they had to leave or they wouldn't have had enough fuel to make it home.

The last fighter left the crippled Fortress about forty miles from Tripoli. Fortunately, the swarm of German fighters started home at the same time, for their gas was low too.

The Thunderbird flew on another twenty miles. Then a single German fighter appeared, and dived at them. Its guns did great damage to the already crippled plane, but simply couldn't knock it out of the air.

Finally the fighter ran out of ammunition, and left. Our boys were alone with their grave troubles. Two engines were gone, most of the guns were out of commission, and they were still more than four hundred miles from home. The radio was out. They were losing altitude, five hundred feet a minute—and then they were down to two thousand.

The pilot called up his crew and held a consultation. Did they want to jump? They all said they would ride the plane as long as it was in the air. He decided to keep going.

The ship was completely out of trim, cocked over at a terrible angle. But they gradually got it trimmed so that it stopped losing altitude.

By then they were down to nine hundred feet, and a solid wall of mountains ahead barred the way homeward. They flew along parallel to those mountains for a long time, but they were then miraculously gaining some altitude. Finally they got the thing to fifteen hundred feet.

The lowest pass was sixteen hundred feet, but they came across at fifteen hundred. Explain that if you can! Maybe it was as the pilot said: "We didn't come over the mountains, we came through them."

The copilot said, "I was blowing on the windshield trying to push her along. Once I almost wanted to reach a foot down and sort of walk us along over the pass."

And the navigator said, "If I had been on the wingtip, I could have touched the ground with my hand when we went through the pass."

The air currents were bad. One wing was cocked away down. It was hard to hold. The pilots had a horrible fear that the low wing would drop clear down and they'd roll over and go into a spin. But they didn't.

The navigator came into the cockpit, and he and the pilots navigated the plane home. Never for a second could they feel any real assurance of making it. They were practically rigid, but they talked a blue streak all the time, and cussed—as airmen do.

Everything seemed against them. The gas consumption doubled, squandering their precious supply. To top off their misery, they had a bad headwind. The gas gauge went down and down.

At last the navigator said they were only forty miles from home, but those forty miles passed as though they were driving a horse and buggy. Dusk, coming down on the sandy haze, made the vast flat desert an indefinite thing. One oasis looked exactly like another. But they knew when they were near home. Then they shot their red flare and waited for the green flare from our control tower. A minute later it came—the most beautiful sight that crew had ever seen.

When the plane touched the ground they cut the switches and let it roll. For it had no brakes. At the end of the roll the big Fortress veered off the side of the runway. It climaxed its historic homecoming by spinning madly around five times and then running backwards for fifty yards before it stopped. When they checked the gas gauges, they found one tank dry and the other down to twenty gallons.

Deep dusk enveloped the field. Five more minutes and they never would have found it. The weary, crippled Fortress had flown for the incredible time of four and one-half hours on one pair of motors. Any pilot will tell you it's impossible.

That night, with the pilot and some of the crew, we drank a toast. One visitor raised his glass: "Here's to your safe return."

But the pilot raised his own glass and said instead, "Here's to a God-damned good airplane!"

And the others of the crew raised their glasses and repeated, "Here's to a God-damned good airplane!"

Perhaps the real climax was that during the agonizing homeward crawl that one crippled plane shot down the fantastic total of six German fighters. The score was officially confirmed.

MUSTANGS *VS* MESSERSCHMITTS

by Len Deighton

"Break! Break! Je-susss! Break!"

The up-sun squadron was getting it. Farebrother heard the shouts of joy and terror on the radio, but he was keeping close escort on the bombers. The other squadron was somewhere beyond the cumulus clouds. Nervously he twisted around to scan the sky. His wingman was a nineteen-year-old uncommissioned flight officer who'd just arrived from the replacement depot. It would be rash to depend upon him to spot attackers. He realized how Earl must have felt when first nursing Jamie along.

There were plenty of Germans in the sky, and about five miles away to the south he could see more climbing out of the clouds. He looked below; the Forts were droning steadily on as if they hadn't noticed the impending attack, although he knew that all eyes would be on those swarming midges.

As the Germans came closer he recognized them as Focke-Wulf 190s, "formation destroyers" equipped with a big 21-cm. mortar under each wing to break up the bomber boxes. How long before . . . ? Surely Kevin Phelan had seen them? Ah, here we go. *Phelanski's Irish Rose* was leading the group today, and he began a steep turn that would give them an interception, but not before those long-range mortars had fired at the bomber formation. That's the price paid for the really close escort the bomber crews liked. Now that they were on a collision course, the Focke-Wulfs grew bigger every second. They were in line abreast, and about a thousand yards away, when their wings flickered with flames as the rockets lumbered away.

Big black clouds of smoke appeared amid the bombers as the rocket shells exploded. The Germans were now close enough to rake the bombers with cannon fire. The nearest Fort took hits right from the first. *Scrapbook,* an aged B-17 with weathered green paintwork and a shapely blonde on the nose, reared and bucked. Slices of aluminum flaked off her body, flashed in the dull sunlight, and then folded back into the slipstream like the discarded skin of some great green snake. Only when the stream of cannon shells got to the Plexiglas did the Fort swerve. The top turret's clear glass turned white and shattered. The hammerblows inched along to the cockpit windows and the glassed nose, so that for a moment she disappeared in a snowstorm of broken plastic. Amid the whirling snowflakes, like the tiny Santa Claus in an inverted glass paperweight, men could be glimpsed, arms and legs flailing as they tried to find support in the thin blue sky. The snow flurry melted but the men remained. They twisted and, arms stretched, floated in the Fort's surrounding air before falling away, cartwheeling into the scattered confusion of broken wreckage.

Pilotless, the huge Fort slowly careened and tilted further and further until she rolled right over, breaking in half as her tormentors—the blue-painted Fw 190s—screamed past, twisting through the flying debris.

A Focke-Wulf came through Farebrother's gunsight. He fired and saw strikes near the cockpit, but the German, at full deflection, twisted away and was gone. Another plane charged at him. Instinctively his finger tightened on the trigger, but just in time he recognized the white stars and held his fire. It was huge as it slid toward him. The two planes almost collided, and as the German passed, with only a few feet to spare, *Kibitzer* rocked and wallowed in its turbulent wake.

He turned again to bring another German into view and moved his head to see his wingman, Luke Robinson, still with him. Good boy!

The gunfire was bright in the gray sky. Bang! Bang! His plane shuddered and the stick jerked as bullets plucked the elevator. He dived away. Where was the kid? Yes, he was still following. An explosion to port as a chance shot turned fuel and ammunition into a brilliant orange ball and the subsequent white flash that consumed the aluminum airframe in instantaneous combustion. No shortage of targets; the sky was full of Germans, but as fast as he got one in his sights he'd see the gunfire of another streaking past his wings. Break! He turned away so tightly that he felt the juddering that warns of a high-speed stall; gently does it.

Another German came into his view. Anyone who'd been tempted to believe those intelligence assessments about the Luftwaffe at its last gasp could revise that estimation! The Messerschmitt was still there: a Bf 109G with the big 30-mm. cannon designed to smash up the heavier structures of the bombers. One such shell striking a single-seater is enough to blow it apart. A touch of stick, keep turning. Faster, faster! slowly the Messerschmitt grew in the ring sight. The German turned, and Farebrother eased the stick and held on to him, pressing himself forward against the harness with the insane feeling that he could actually increase his speed by leaning forward. The sun swung gently into his windshield and everything disappeared in the blinding furnace of its light. Eyes closed, keep turning, range and deflection are narrowing. He took a hand off the throttle long enough to unsnap his harness. The risk of smashing his face against the panel was outweighed by the freedom it gave him to look around the sky.

He craned his neck to see around him. He'd done the same thing only half a minute ago, but thirty seconds was time enough for a speck to become an attacker and blow him to blazes. Still the German ahead hadn't seen him. Drop the nose a little to bring the blue aircraft up into the lighted orange circle, a touch of rudder to ease the deflection. The

German was careless, all his attention on his own gunsight. He was stalking; ahead of him, and just below, a crippled B-17 sliding back out of formation, its gunners not at their stations. More rudder. Mustn't make the same mistake—a quick look around for attackers. Good, the wing tips of the Messerschmitt stretched far enough to touch the circle. He squeezed the trigger and felt the kick of the guns. Long smoky trails of gunfire touched the wings and erupted in bright yellow strikes that made the German tip over into a roll and dive, the usual Luftwaffe evasive tactic. Farebrother, ready for it, stuck close on his tail. The Messerschmitt was still in his sights and still taking hits. The prop slowed and stopped. The canopy opened and a black bundle tumbled out, cannoning off the wing and slamming into his own stabilizer before bouncing away spread-eagled. His pale flying coveralls now mottled with red blood, the German pilot sailed past over Farebrother's head.

Farebrother turned his head again to see Luke Robinson. His neck was getting stiff and his back muscles were tired from all this twisting about. If only the kid would stay close enough to be seen in the rearview mirror. Parachutes! There were parachutes—white, American parachutes—above him. Above him! If there were chutes above him, he was below the bombers and that was lower than he wanted to be. Stick back and start climbing; altitude means salvation to a fighter pilot until the last desperate tactic of running for your life at zero feet. Climbing. Luke was still there. Now he saw the bomber boxes sailing through the sky above him. The bombers were trying to tighten formation now that so many had gone down or fallen behind. More parachutes. A Fort trailing smoke, two dropping out of formation, poor bastards. Another explosion seen only out of the corner of his eye, a gigantic flash of yellow light that filled the whole sky. It left no more than a shape of gray smoke, a spider shape, its ever-lengthening gray legs made of smoking debris falling to earth. The unmistakable sight of a fully laden bomber exploding!

"Break! Jamie, break!" MM's voice, where did he come from? Farebrother threw his plane into a violent skid and tumbled inverted into an uncontrolled fall that became a dive as the weight of the Rolls-Royce engine pulled his nose toward the earth. Luke Robinson was still there and the German attacker high and to the left. Good—his shooting is wide! Luke fired a burst but was not positioned for getting hits.

It was dark as they dropped into the billowing cumulus where the world was made of gray jelly and pressed close upon his Plexiglas. Then immediately out of the bottom of the cloud—stratus therefore, not cumulus; even the infallible Farebrother is permitted a mistake now and again. Here under the cloud Germany was sunless, a muted pattern of fields and forest. The only relief from this gray world was the long glittering white wires that came from behind and lit his path. Shit! The Kraut was still on his tail and firing. You bastard! Turn and dive. The bullets are still coming, more throttle. And where the hell was Luke Robinson, what's a wingman for anyway? Farebrother gripped harder on the stick, trying to stop it from vibrating. The wires, curving gently like telegraph lines swaying in the sunlight, came nearer to his port wing. "Break!" Someone's still shouting—Luke or MM. No, it's Rube Wein's voice. So come on over here and heave on the stick and you'll find out!

The throttle was against the fire wall; emergency power. Dive steeper, and steeper still. The white airspeed needle chased around the clock. Faster—350, 400, 450—the white needle caught up with the slower red danger line and Farebrother knew that his airframe was in jeopardy as he used all his strength to pull at the stick. Both hands couldn't hold it still. He braced his feet and pulled so hard that he expected the column to break in his hands. He could feel a dull pain in his belly, his legs were as heavy as lead. There was an insupportable pressure on his head, forcing him down in his seat until he thought his spine would snap. His vision clouded and darkened as the centrifugal effect drained the blood from his brain. He felt the airframe shaking; just a vibration at first and then a pounding, now it was jolting him about in his seat as the wings tried, and failed, to deflect the engine from its chosen trajectory toward the earth. He looked out and saw his wings flapping as if to break off.

No "wires" now, the German was no doubt wrestling with his own controls and waiting for the Mustang's wings to rip off. Farebrother was still trying to pull out of the dive as he lost consciousness.

"Sparkplug Blue Three from Sparkplug Blue Four. I repeat, where are you?" It was the nervous high-pitched voice of Luke Robinson, but eventually his fear overcame the discipline of his radio procedure. "Cap! For Christ's sake. Where the hell are you? It's Luke."

Farebrother was unconscious for only a few seconds, and when the blood pumped back up to his brain and restored his dimmed vision, he saw trees and rooftops flashing past. A small lake, a factory chimney, a farmyard with a dozen people staring up at him. He overtook a train, its smoke trailing across the fields like a long streamer of shiny black silk. He shook his head and only with a tremendous effort of will throttled back and resumed full control of himself and his machine. It seemed so much easier, so much more comfortable, so much more sensible to sit and watch the world rush past. He looked at the instruments and then gently tried the ailerons and rudder.

When he was straight and level, he searched the horizon: not a plane in sight. He checked his wings and looked again to his instruments; all back to normal, but his compass showed him heading east and his fuel was low. By now he must be somewhere near the Polish border. He looked down to find a landmark, but from this height the agricultural land of Silesia seemed flat and featureless. He turned until he was headed northwest, climbed gently up into the overcast, and called up on the radio. Only when he'd tried all the channels did he hear MM's voice, patiently calling him. He answered, "Jamie here, MM. Over."

"Thank Christ. I thought they'd got you, Jamie."

"I blacked out. I think my ears are blocked. I can't hear so well."

"Where the hell are you?"

"Southeast. I'm coming up to find you. Is Luke there?"

"He's here. We're circling till you come. Hurry up, we're all low on gas."

Farebrother broke out through the cloud cover and saw MM, Rube, and Luke Robinson, his wingman, describing lazy circles two or three miles to the west of him. The sunlight was brighter now, the sun was full and frosting the clouds with a blinding white topping. To the north he saw long trailing white threads—the condensation trails of the bombers —the threads bending now as the task force skirted Frankfurt an der Oder. They'd come a long journey to these bleak borderlands of the east, and many of them would never see home again.

Two more single-seaters were skimming the cloud tops by the time *Kibitzer* reached MM and the others. He watched the two strangers suspiciously. Only a week before, a couple of Bf 109s had joined a formation of look-alike Mustangs and clobbered the rear element before getting away scot-free. But these were Jugs, two fat T-bolts who preferred flying home in company. They slid into position behind Luke Robinson, who was flying *Sue-perlative,* one of the newest of the Mustangs; factory-fresh, it was still in natural metal finish. From now on it was to be air force policy to leave aircraft unpainted; it saved a few man-hours in the factory and increased speed. Even old *Kibitzer* had gained ten m.p.h. from her new engine and polished metal finish. For the bombers, locked into their huge formations, the shiny finish seemed a logical modification, but many of the fighter pilots disliked the mirror-flashing attention the new planes got as they turned in the sunlight. Farebrother raised a hand to Luke in salutation. The boy, thankful for a sign that he wasn't going to be blamed for losing Farebrother in the dive, waved back.

After MM set course toward the bombers, one of the Jugs pulled up closer to him, and its pilot ran a finger across his throat to show he was low on fuel. MM made a gesture of acknowledgment and tried again to find a common frequency on the radio, but couldn't reach them. The Jug fell back into battle formation, with about three hundred yards between fighters.

The bombers were stretched out across the river Oder, their target—the sprawling Focke-Wulf plant at Sorau—almost in sight. The air commander, in the lead plane of the task force, had throttled back to accommodate the cripples. Even so, the outermost planes in the formation, which had to keep jockeying the throttles to hold position, had a difficult task. It was little wonder that these outermost planes were subject to so high a proportion of mechanical failures, and little wonder that these were the ones to suffer most from the German fighters. . . .

As the six fighters reached the bomber formation, they could see half a dozen Messerschmitts making concerted attacks on the high squadron of the top box. The fighter pilots could sense the feeling of relief that ran through the minds of the men in this huge task force as they spotted the

American fighters. The formations tightened and there were gunners waving from the open ports of the waist positions.

The Messerschmitt pilots saw the American fighters too, and abandoned the damaged Fortresses, with their windmilling props, idly swinging unmanned guns, their wings and bodies shiny with spilled fuel and leaking hydraulic fluid, their shattered plastic and torn alloy. They abandoned them, but they didn't go far; they circled like sharks some ten miles off to starboard. They didn't seek fighter-to-fighter combat. Their orders were strict: it was the American bombers that had to be destroyed!

MM turned sharply and, to their great credit, the nervous Jug pilots followed him trustingly. Together the mixed formation made for the Messerschmitts, but they didn't go to full throttle, their fuel was too low for that, and far too low for combat. The Messerschmitts climbed away unhurriedly, as if they guessed this was no more than an empty gesture.

Farebrother turned his head to see the bombers plodding on toward their target, searching the horizon for the escorting Fighter Groups which hadn't yet arrived. Who could see the bomber crews without admiring the phlegmatic determination which makes other kinds of courage seem no more than temporary lapses of judgment? They were the real heroes, the ones who came up here day after day as human targets for every weapon an ingenious, dedicated, and tenacious foe could use against them. So in life itself the true measure of courage is to fly on despite the tragedies of accident, sickness, or failure.

"One more time!" It was MM, turning away from the Messerschmitts for one last pass right down the miles of bomber formations. They tucked in tight behind MM, who was now cruising for minimum fuel consumption. Farebrother had his prop at 1,700 revs in fine pitch; now he gave the engine all the manifold pressure he dared. Poor *Kibitzer,* she took it like a lady and didn't complain.

They steered west after leaving the bombers, and no one looked back. Some three thousand feet above them they could see a lone Junkers Ju 88, the "contact holder" following the American bombers and talking all the time to German ground control. Soon the Messerschmitts would go back in to finish their meal.

Below him Farebrother recognized, from the map on his knee, the junction of the river Oder and the Hohenzollern Canal. Not far beyond that were the suburbs of Berlin with all the flak and fighter defenses concentrated around the capital. It was not a healthy place to linger. The bomber force had been routed in from the Baltic, but the six fighters would have to get home by a more direct route if they were to make it across the Channel with props still turning. To the south of Bremen they were met with an untidy cannonade of flak. At first it was eighty-eights well wide of their track, but then came some big 10.5-cm. bursts much nearer. They could hear the radar humming in their earphones, and MM climbed and changed course.

Near Holland's great inland sea, the IJsselmeer, the clouds were less billowing and soon stretched beneath them like flat gray concrete, all the way to where they touched the bottom of the big red disk that was the dying sun. Sandwiched between the strips of pink cirrus overhead and this unending colorless carpet, the six airplanes seemed suspended in space, halted at some great red traffic light hanging in the sky.

"Sparkplug Blue Three from Blue One. You want to take a look at my tail plane? The controls are getting real stiff."

Farebrother narrowed the space between them and went high enough to see properly. "Looks okay to me, MM."

"What do you think, Rube?"

Rube Wein brought *Daniel* in closer, but he too could see nothing wrong with MM's tail. "But you're holed aft of the cockpit, buddy. Could be the control runs or something." Wein's academic prowess was exemplary, but his knowledge of aircraft anatomy was sketchy.

"Are we over the sea, Jamie?" As usual MM had abandoned radio procedure. "Sure I know about the holes, Rube. She's screaming like a banshee—the wind's playing on her like a flute." MM was careful to make his inquiry about the sea sound casual.

Farebrother looked at the map on his knee and then at his clock. "In about four minutes, MM. Over."

"She's giving me real trouble, Jamie. Get up, you bastard . . ." This last remark to his plane, which was becoming more difficult to hold in the turbulent coastal air due to the airflow sucking at the curled edges of the gaping holes. "I'm not bailing out," said MM in response to the silence. "I've got two sure kills on my gun camera and I'm not leaving it."

"For Christ's sake, MM," said Farebrother. Even if it was a joke it didn't amuse him.

All four Mustangs had taken hits; it had been a tough one. And yet there was no pleasure in their victories and their survival. Their last sight of the unprotected bombers was one they couldn't forget, and they felt sullied by their own good fortune. Rube Wein's plane wobbled a little and belched black smoke as the supercharger cut out. He gave it a little throttle to bring him up level with the others.

"You okay, Rube?" said MM. "No glass mountain?"

"I'm okay," said Rube Wein, irritated that MM should reveal and scoff at his reluctantly confessed fears.

"So let's go home," said MM, and all the aircraft pulled in tighter together. The six pilots, alone in their single-seaters, couldn't help each other over the cold dark sea, but some atavistic feeling made them want to fly closer together and MM got comfort from that.

The formation had only just passed over the Dutch coast when Rube Wein came on the radio. "Blue Leader from Blue Two—I can't make it to England." His voice was as calm and matter-of-fact as it always was.

"What in hell do you mean, Rube?" demanded MM indignantly. *He* was the casualty, everyone knew that, so why was Rube trying to steal his thunder?

"I'm out of gas. It's this goddamned blower."

"Shit, Rube, we're practically there now."

"It's no use, MM. I've been nursing her, but the needles are out of sight."

"Have you switched left and right a couple of times?"

"For Christ's sake, MM, I'm not fresh out of Primary Flight Training. It's the blower, like I told you. I'll bail out over Holland. The Resistance guys will maybe smuggle me out or something."

"Now listen, Rube . . ." But MM's advice went unheeded as Rube's wing tip tilted steeply and he began a wing-over that dropped him out of formation belly-up like a dead fish.

Farebrother twisted his head to see how far back Rube would have to fly for a landfall. There were condensation trails high over the coast—German fighters responding to the radar tracks made by the six Americans. As the German planes reached the higher atmosphere, the air condensed to leave a white plume. One after another they became visible against the deepening color of the eastern sky. Rube Wein would be easy meat for them.

"Tell the Colonel I'm sorry." It was Rube Wein's voice again, fainter now and scratchy with static. "I can't swim, see? Explain that, will you, MM?"

"We can't come back, Rube. We're all low on gas."

There was some sort of reply, but it was swallowed up in the rhythms of the German jamming. They listened all the way back over the sea, but they never heard him again.

"Just you and me left now, Jamie," said MM as they crossed the English coast.

"And Luke," said Farebrother hastily. He realized how the new boy must be feeling.

"Oh, sure," said MM. "Sorry, kid. . . . Rube should have hightailed it home long before his gas got so low," said MM, ignoring all radio procedure.

"He'll be okay, Blue Leader," said Farebrother. "I'd say he bailed out long before those fighters got anywhere near him."

There was a double click on the radio as MM jiggled the switch to acknowledge the message. Soon the Thunderbolts waggled wings and dropped out of formation to find their own base.

It was clear at Steeple Thaxted, or relatively so; some puffy stratocumulus, pink-lined to dramatize the lowering sun. The grass was shiny with recent rain, and the reddening sky was reflected on the wet runway. MM took *Mickey Mouse II* into the landing pattern, moving jerkily into finals as he manipulated the stiff controls. He went in a little high, but MM knew the field well enough to effortlessly slip off fifty feet or more so that he was just right as he went over the hedge. Children playing in the paddock near Hobday's Farm stopped their game to watch him, and were surprised at the sudden increase of power that made the engine roar to bursting point, and the little lurch the plane gave as it teetered on the edge of stalling and, wheezing and bawling like an angry old woman, staggered inch by inch back into the air again.

"My gear's jammed," said MM on the radio even before the red flares were fired from the flying control truck. "You guys better go in first. I'll have to belly in, I guess." Retaining control to the end, he added, "Luke first, Jamie next."

Tex Gill jumped up onto *Kibitzer*'s wing as she came to a stop on the hardstand. "We were getting a little worried, sir," he said, looking at his watch and at the bullet holes.

"I got one," said Farebrother. Unlike most other crew chiefs, Tex never asked. "I saw him bail out. But we lost Lieutenant Wein." Farebrother heaved himself out of his seat and stayed there to watch *Mickey Mouse II* come around the circuit. Tex was watching too, but neither of them admitted his concern. "He ran out of gas and turned back to bail out over Holland." Farebrother pulled up the sides of his helmet and prodded a finger in his ears, but he was still a little deafened.

"Everyone liked the Lieutenant," said Tex Gill, still watching MM.

"Ran out of gas," said Farebrother. "His supercharger was on the blink. He came right out over the water before turning back."

Tex Gill looked at his pilot and nodded. Farebrother's face was deeply lined, his eyes bloodshot and darkly underset. Where his oxygen mask had been pressing against his face there were red "scars" curving from nose to jaw. "The stupid bastard should have turned back at the first sign of trouble." To anyone but Tex Gill, Farebrother's voice might have seemed angry, but a pilot had no secrets from his crew chief. He could see in Farebrother's face the desperate bitterness we save for loved ones who die.

"I guess he didn't want to leave Lieutenant Morse without a wingman," said Tex Gill. "Seeing how you had to look after the new young officer." He jumped down from the wing, and Farebrother followed, steadying himself on Gill's shoulder.

"I shot down a Messerschmitt, Tex. The pilot bailed out." Farebrother winced with pain and sat down on the trailing edge of the wing.

"You hurt, Cap?"

"Just cramp." He felt like a fool, but he had to wait until the circulation came back to his leg. "I saw this German pilot, Tex. He sailed past me close enough to touch." Tex Gill said nothing. Farebrother said, "I guess he was dead. He hit his stabilizer, and there was a lot of blood."

"You got some leave coming up, Captain? You sure deserve some."

"A lot of hardware under him. I guess they're tough to handle with cannons and all that junk strapped under the wings."

"There comes Lieutenant Morse," said Gill, easing the parachute harness off Farebrother's shoulder. "He's going to do that real nice, I'd say."

"I can't leave MM now, Tex. And we've got Lieutenant Robinson to think of too."

"You need a rest, Cap," said Tex Gill, deciding there was no point in being too subtle with a man so clearly in a state of shock. "Sometimes . . ." He shifted awkwardly, wondering how to continue. "Sometimes a guy out here on the line sees things the Flight Surgeon misses. You and Lieutenant Morse, you both need a rest."

"You're a good buddy, Tex," said Farebrother, handing him the chute. "And there he goes!"

The main runway was still under repair, so MM had to use the shorter one. He came in wheels up and settled *Mickey Mouse II* gently onto the concrete with plenty of room to spare. He kept its nose up so that the air intake hit first. The plane tilted a bit and made a lot of noise as it slid along, tearing alloy off its underside. Men standing on a nearby revetment saw the Mustang disappear into a cloud of white smoke, but the "smoke" was a spray of rainwater thrown into the air as the plane waltzed down the concrete, and their gasps turned into sighs of relief as the plane came to a standstill and the ambulance and crash wagons went chasing after it.

Farebrother walked to the jeep that was waiting to take them to debriefing. Luke Robinson was already sitting in it. "You want to get in the back seat, Luke?" said Farebrother. The driver looked around but said nothing.

"I'm okay."

"Get in the back seat," said Farebrother, climbing into the back himself and dumping his parachute on the floor.

"I'd rather . . ."

"Get into the back seat, you stupid son of bitch," said Farebrother in a voice that made Robinson shoot out of his seat as if it was red hot.

"Gee, Captain, I'm sorry," he said as he climbed into the back of the jeep.

Farebrother took off his helmet and wiped his face with his hand. To the driver he said, "Drive down the runway and pick up Lieutenant Morse."

"You'd need permission from flying control to drive out there across the airfield. Anyway, this jeep's not marked for it."

"Get going," said Farebrother. His voice was soft but even more intimidating than his previous burst of bad temper. "And that's an order, goddammit. We didn't ride all the way across Europe so you could leave him to walk back from his ship."

The driver turned in his seat to argue, but when he saw Farebrother's face he did exactly as he was told.

I FLEW FOR THE FÜHRER

by Heinz Knöke

28th August, 1944.

The enemy try to cross the Seine on pontoon bridges between Vernon and Mantes. Ceaseless fighter patrols form an umbrella, together with a cordon of concentrated flak to protect the crossing.

During six missions in this sector yesterday the Squadron lost twelve aircraft. We are finished.

This morning the Squadron serviceability report lists only four aircraft as operational. Two others with badly twisted fuselages are capable of non-operational flying only. They are such battered old crates that I am not going to be responsible for sending any of my men into combat in them.

So at 0600 hours there is a telephone call from the Chief Staff Officer at Corps Headquarters. He gives me a furious reprimand.

"This morning you reported only four aircraft available for operations. I have just learned that you can still fly six. Are you crazy? Do you realise the seriousness of the situation? It is nothing but sabotage; and I am not going to tolerate it. Every one of your aircraft is to fly. That is an order!"

He is bellowing like a bull. I have never been reprimanded like this since I finished my basic training as an Air Force recruit. I am so furious that I can hardly control my rage. Why should I have to listen to that arrogant ape? He even has the nerve to accuse *me* of sabotage! Chairborne strategists and heroes of the Staff make me sick. They know nothing of the problems at the Front which we are up against, and they care even less.

I decide to fly one of the worn-out crates myself, and let my wingman, Corporal Döring, take the other. According to the operation orders, we are to take off at 0800 hours and rendezvous with the other Squadrons of the Wing over Soissons. I am then to take over command of the entire fighter formation.

Two minutes before zero hour the engines are started. We roll out from the camouflaged bushes and turn into wind. There is no runway, only a length of soft field. My aircraft lumbers along, gathering flying speed with difficulty, and it is all I can do to coax the old crate into the air in time to clear the trees at the far end of the field.

Döring tries to climb too soon and stalls. His left wing drops and he plunges to crash into the trees. Flames belch forth. Döring is instantly killed—and then we are five.

The order from the Chief Staff Officer at Corps is worse than insanity; it amounts to nothing less than murder!

Base reports by radio to advise me that the other Squadrons are unable to leave the ground, because their fields are being strafed by enemy fighter-bombers.

"Go to sector Siegfried-Gustav."

North of Soissons lies the little town of Tergnier. It is a large railway junction at the point where the Somme Canal meets the River Oise. As a conspicuous landmark it is visible from a great distance. Above it, the Third Squadron of No. 1 Fighter Wing now fights its last air battle against the Americans over French territory.

We encounter more than sixty Thunderbolts and Mustangs in this area. There can be no escape: it is the end. All that remains is for me to give the order to attack. Thus at least a moral victory can still be claimed by my men and myself.

Base still try to give me orders. I turn off the radio; to hell with them now!

My aircraft cannot climb above 10,000 feet. It is very slow and unresponsive. I feel certain that this is its last flight.

The battle does not last for more than a few minutes. Corporal Wagner is the first to be shot down; he does not escape from his flaming aircraft.

Then I see another aircraft on fire, and Flight Sergeant Freigang bales out. His wingman goes down in flames a few moments later.

That leaves only my wingman, Sergeant Ickes, and myself. For us there can be no way out. If this is to be the end, I can only sell my life as dearly as possible. If I ram one of the Yanks I shall be able to take him with me. . . .

Tracers converge on us from all sides. Bullets slam my aircraft like hailstones, and it gradually loses forward speed. Ickes remains close beside me. I keep on circling in as tight a turn as possible. A Mustang gets on to my tail. I am unable to shake it off. My plane is too sluggish, as if it felt too tired to fly any farther. More bullets come slamming into the fuselage behind my head.

With a last burst of power from the engine I pull the aircraft up in a climb, half-roll on to the side, and cut the throttle. The Mustang on my tail has not anticipated this. It shoots past, and now it is in front of me and a little below. I distinctly see the face of the pilot as he turns his head to look for me. Too late, he attempts to escape by diving. I am on him now. I can at least ram him if I cannot shoot him down. I feel icy cold. My only emotion, for the first time in my life, is intense personal hatred of my enemy; my only desire is to destroy him.

The gap closes rapidly: we are only a few feet apart. My salvoes slam into the fuselage: I am aiming for the pilot. His engine bursts into flames. We shall go down together!

There is a violent jolt at the first impact. I see my right wing fold and break away. In a split-second I jettison the canopy and am out of the seat. There is a fierce blast of flame as I am thrown clear, while Messerschmitt and Thunderbolt are fused together in a single ball of fire.

A few moments later my parachute mushrooms overhead. Six to eight hundred feet away and a little higher up there is another open parachute. Ickes.

Overhead and all around us the Americans continue to thunder, circling and milling around like mad. It is a few minutes before it dawns on them that by this time not a single Messerschmitt is left in the sky.

A Thunderbolt comes diving towards me. It opens fire! For age-long seconds my heart stops beating. I throw up my hands and cover my face. . . .

Missed!

Round it comes again, this time firing at Ickes. I can only watch, while the body of my comrade suddenly slumps lifeless. Poor Ickes!

What a foul and dirty way of fighting! War is not the same as a football match; but there is still such a thing as fair play.

I come down to land in a forest clearing. I have no idea whether I am on the German side or behind the enemy lines. Therefore, I start by hiding in the dense undergrowth.

Overhead, the Americans fly away to the west.

It is wonderful to be able to relax. I light a cigarette and lie back on the parachute shrouds, gratefully inhaling the soothing smoke.

As a precautionary measure, I remove the rank-badges from my shoulders and stuff the German Gold Cross into my pocket.

I happen to be wearing an American leather flying-jacket, a dark blue silk sports shirt, rather faded trousers, and black walking-shoes. The whole effect is so un-Prussian that no one will recognise me immediately as a German.

My caution very soon proves justified.

About fifteen minutes after my descent I notice four French civilians at the other end of the clearing. They gesticulate wildly as they talk. With my school French I am able to understand that they must be looking for me. Each one of them wants to search in a different place. I gather that they are under the impression that the parachutist is an American. All four carry arms. Evidently they are underground terrorists of the French Resistance.

I grope for the pistol hidden under my bulky leather jacket.

The four start combing the bushy undergrowth. Discovery is inevitable, sooner or later, so I decide to go out to meet them.

All four look surprised to see me. Four tommy-guns swing round to cover me. Now is the time for me to keep calm and clever. The French have a bitter hatred for us Germans, from the bottom of their temperamental souls. Not that I blame them; no doubt I should feel the same in their place. But if the bastards ever guess that I am German it will mean a bellyful of lead, as sure as God made little apples.

So I walk up coolly, and in the friendliest possible manner greet them in English: "Hello, boys!"

The stern faces of the bandits gradually relax into smiles. They take me for a Yank.

In my best American accent I then proceed to ask them in very broken French to help me find my "comrades":—

"Voulez-vous aider moi trouver mes camerades?"

They immediately explain the position to me. An American armoured unit with Sherman tanks is a little over a mile away. We must be very cautious, however, as the place is still swarming with the lousy Boches. Fighting is going on all round us. In fact I can now hear for the first time the distant gunfire.

The tallest of the Frenchmen—a thoroughly repulsive-looking type—carries a German tommy-gun. I do not like the look of him at all. He remains in the background, suspiciously quiet. Does he doubt that I am what I appear to be?

We make our way through the dense forest until we come to a railway embankment.

There is a sudden chattering from a German machine-gun; it sounds like an M.G. 45, and is quite close. The three Frenchies in front drop flat on their faces. The tall bandit remains standing close to me; evidently he is not going to let me out of his sight. From the other side of the railway comes the grinding clatter of heavy tank engines.

I ask where the line goes.

"Vers Amiens."

Amiens!!? Did I really drift so far west during the dogfight? The city has been in American hands for some time. Blast! I have no desire to spend the rest of the war sitting in a prison camp somewhere in the U.S.A.

The nearest town, I learn, is Nesle. Then the Somme Canal must be somewhere to the north. According to the early morning intelligence reports, it is still being held by our forces. I shall have to head north. But how am I going to get rid of those blasted Frenchies?

More heavy gun-fire is heard. The sound comes from the west. The Frenchmen cautiously cross the tracks and wave to me to follow them. The big fellow stays on my tail with his tommy-gun, otherwise I would be able to bolt back into the forest and then make my way round to the north.

A few hundred yards farther on we come to a highway. It cuts across the landscape, straight as an arrow, and is visible for miles.

The chattering of several machine-guns is again heard off to the left. The first three Frenchmen cautiously cross the road. The big fellow takes two or three paces after them, then turns towards me. Our eyes meet. I can tell that he recognises me. I must be off! There will be no second chance to break away; it must be now or never.

I dash back towards the forest. Then the big fellow is coming after me, before his comrades realise what is happening. He lifts his tommy-gun and starts firing. I drop behind a bank of earth. Bullets thud into the ground all round me.

The bandit empties his clip. He must take his eyes off the target long enough to insert a new one. There is just enough time to draw my pistol and snap up the safety-catch. I leap at the big fellow, who is raising his tommy-gun again, and fire once. It is enough. He goes down with a bullet in the head.

I take his tommy-gun. "Sorry, my friend, but he who hits first lives longest."

Panting, I struggle through the dense undergrowth. Twigs and branches lash at my face. The other three Frenchmen are left behind.

Fifteen minutes later I run into a German patrol. They are soldiers from an armoured unit.

At Chauny the Commanding Officer of a German Air Force unit lets me have his car. It is late at night when I arrive back at my airstrip.

THE BLOND KNIGHT OF GERMANY

by Raymond F. Toliver and Trevor J. Constable

Flying back to his *Gruppe* at Deutsch Brod in Czechoslovakia, Erich found his thoughts turning constantly to the earlier battles with American fighters in Rumania. The P-51 was a fast, maneuverable and rugged bird, as good or better than the Soviet YAK-9. The old model Me-109's used on the Eastern Front, which JG-52 had been forced to send up against the Mustangs in Rumania the previous year, suffered by comparison with the P-51. These older Me-109's, without methanol injection for emergency high-altitude power, or for escape, were at a serious disadvantage in combat with the Mustangs.

Some good men and many aircraft had been lost by JG-52 in the struggle to defend Ploesti and Bucharest. Now that the Americans were ranging into Czechoslovakia with their inexhaustible Mustangs, Erich felt certain he would have to fight them again soon. As he flew closer to the front he reviewed in his mind his first, fierce encounters with USAAF fighters.

Orders leading to the first clash with the Americans came after the disastrous Sevastopol battle and subsequent pell-mell German evacuation of the Crimea. The USAAF chose this time of heavy pressure on the Luftwaffe to begin its attacks on the Ploesti oil fields near Bucharest. Crash orders pulled I/JG-52 out of the Eastern Front battle and assigned the formation to oil-field protection on the Rumanian Front. Erich's squadron was ordered to operate from a grass strip at Zilistea, a few minutes' flying time from Ploesti.

He flew down to Rumania with his squadron, found the Zilistea strip and led his pilots in for a landing. Ground crews sent on ahead to the makeshift base were waiting. Refueling of Erich's squadron had barely finished when the order came to scramble.

He clambered back into his bird and the warm engine caught immediately. Bimmel was missing from the Zilistea advance party, so it was a strange technician who signaled all clear. Erich's *Schwarm* taxied to the end of the strip, Master Sergeant Carl Junger was flying as Erich's wingman, with Lieutenant Puls and Sergeant Wester composing the second *Rotte.* They all took off in good order, closely followed by the second *Schwarm.* The squadron's mission: protect other JG-52 fighters while they tried to get through to the "Fat Dogs"—the bombers.

The Americans had been running their bombing operations over Rumania as if their intention was to make interception of their formations by German fighters as easy as possible. Every day the Americans came over at the same time. Between 1100 and 1300 hours, the USAAF heavies hove into view with the precision of a well-run American railroad. Colonel Dieter Hrabak, JG-52's *Kommodore,* was delighted by the American penchant for accurate timing, even if a little incredulous at first. "We need no standing patrols," he told Erich. "We can bring maximum force to bear on them with minimum effort, and cause them maximum damage, because of the way they plan their operations."

Erich could hear Hrabak's words ringing in his mind as he went racing with his squadron toward Ploesti. The German flak was banging and puffing its black bursts all over the sky. The barrage was massive. Boring through the flak came gaggles of B-17 Fortresses, staggered horizontally and vertically in formations of ten to fifteen ships. Smoke trails reaching earthward showed that the flak had scored a couple of kills. Four miles farther back, droning in on Ploesti from the west, came a second huge gaggle of B-17's.

Erich was on about a level with the Fortresses. He checked his altimeter. Twenty-one thousand feet. No enemy fighter escort was in sight. That meant he would get a shot at the bombers. He drew the stick back and Karaya One went soaring upward, climbing south into the sun in a wide curve. Erich felt the sun was his friend, especially when it was at his back.

The altimeter needle spun up to 25,500 feet as he finished his climbing turn in an ideal position to attack the formation of bombers. A quick glance around him showed him that both his *Schwarms* were intact. He eased the stick forward to dive down on the bombers.

A tight formation of four Mustangs suddenly sliced across his line of vision three thousand feet below, a target too tempting to ignore.

"Attack the fighters," he said into his R/T.

The Me-109's went screaming down on the Mustangs. Erich judged his bounce perfectly, closing in rapidly behind the rear ship in the unsuspecting American formation. The distance between the two fighters shrank rapidly. Three hundred meters . . . 250 meters . . . 200 meters —"closer, Erich"—150 meters . . . 100 meters . . . the white and blue star insignia was close enough to touch. The P-51 filled his windshield. His guns roared for two seconds.

Pieces flew off the American fighter and thundered against Erich's wings. Smoke and fire billowed from the Mustang as Erich pulled left and up, the Messerschmitt easing around to his touch. More debris from the disintegrating Mustang showered against the empennage of Erich's kite. A quick glance back. A big, black and red fireball engulfed what was left of the fighter, while smoking chunks of wing and tail went tumbling earthward.

Erich snapped back to business. "No time to watch fires," he said aloud to himself. The next Mustang was already filling his windshield. Down came the distance again, even more rapidly this time. At 100 meters he pressed his gun buttons. Again he saw a Mustang sag and wobble. No explosion. No matter, Erich. The engine door peeled off the P-51 and inside Erich could see the red glare of an inferno. Emitting a plume of black smoke, the American fighter snap-rolled and fell into an uncontrollable spin. The P-51 was a goner.

Pulling up, Erich watched his second element flame two other Mustangs in quick succession. Looking down he saw the bombers still droning along below them, and nearby but closer, two other P-51's in a turn away from his position. Another perfect bounce beckoned.

"Attack the fighters again," he said on the R/T.

The Blond Knight's *Schwarm* went sweeping after the Mustangs. A perfect attack on the American wingman . . . down came the distance . . . 200 . . . 150 . . . 100 meters. A touch on the gun buttons and half the Mustang's wing sheared off with a bright flash. As the stricken machine went spinning down, Erich could see the pilot clambering out of the cockpit. "Don't watch crashes, Erich. Get the leader."

The American leader had spotted Erich, but it was too late. He pulled his P-51 around to the left in a standard rate turn. Erich thought it was an incredibly clumsy maneuver until he saw that the American pilot still carried his external fuel tanks. Erich pulled Karaya One inside the Mustang's left turn, then pulled his fighter right as hard as he could and clamped down on the triggers. The P-51 rolled over to the other side, as Erich had expected, and flew right into the burst of fire. "Fool!" said Erich aloud. "He should have broken hard left."

Hits sparkled brilliantly on the Mustang's propeller and spangled their way back through the engine compartment and the full length of the fuselage to the tail. A long burst, it finished Erich's ammo, but it looked as though every round found its target. Red and black smoke came billowing from the Mustang, and seconds later a thick, white stream of glycol added contrast to the color pattern.

Diving under his foe and looking up at the riddled P-51, Erich saw a ten-foot tongue of flame licking backward along the empennage. The American pulled up and stalled, then went tumbling earthward. Erich watched the burning wreck for a sign that the pilot might still be alive.

"Jump! Jump! For God's sake, jump!" Erich was calling out as though the American pilot could hear him. The Mustang's canopy flashed clear of the cartwheeling fighter and the pilot struggled clear of his coffin. A sense of relief arose in Erich as the American's chute blossomed.

Erich glanced back and saw wingman Carl Junger was with him watching the crash. There was no point in stooging around here without any ammunition. High contrails were showing. More Mustangs were coming. Time to get out.

"Back to home base at Roman," he said on the R/T.

As they went barreling back in triumph to refuel and rearm, he was quietly talking to himself. "You were lucky today, Erich. Next time, maybe you won't be so lucky." At Roman, Bimmel was waiting to guide him into the parking area after touchdown, all smiles as usual. Switching off, Erich pulled back the canopy and held up four fingers of his left hand for Bimmel to see.

Bimmel beamed as he saw the sign for four victories.

"Mustangs?" Bimmel bellowed the question, knowing Erich would be partially deaf for a few minutes. Erich nodded and Bimmel whistled a little as he set to work once more preparing Karaya One for battle. He filled the ship with fuel, checked the oil, made sure there were full belts for all guns. He wiped the windshield and canopy and made a thorough visual inspection of the fighter.

Three more missions in the next few days were long on fighting but short on success. The Americans came winging in each day on their railroad timetable, so finding the bombers was easy. Attacking the heavies was a rugged task. The beating the Mustangs had taken in the first battle had put the American pilots on their toes. They were sharply alert, aborting Erich's attacks on the bombers. Hard dogfighting and whirlwind battles with the rugged Mustangs produced no results either way. Erich's *Schwarm* had some damaged aircraft, and there were hits on the enemy, but no confirmed kills. The Mustangs were doing a solid job of protecting the bombers, and a single *Schwarm* of Luftwaffe fighters heading for the bomber stream would draw whole squadrons of Mustangs in vigorous defense of the heavies.

Erich's fifth mission against the Americans began like the others, with a good interception at 20,000 feet in clear skies. He held his *Schwarm* at 23,000 feet as top cover for the attacking *Schwarm* assigned to assault the bombers. Watching the four 109's going in to attack, Erich spotted a gaggle of Mustangs plunging down on them from above, probably from 28,000 feet or higher. He hadn't seen the Mustangs, nor had anyone else in his *Schwarm.* They were lucky the American fighters hadn't seen them either, or the German top cover could have been bounced and shot down.

The Mustangs were intent now on bouncing the Me-109's a thousand feet below Erich. Far beneath the bombers, Erich could see two more 109's from another squadron, climbing at full boost and heading for the bombers. Behind this German element were four Mustangs in loose trail, climbing hard and closing fast on the unsuspecting Messerschmitts. Erich snapped on his R/T.

"Look back! Mustangs! Look back! Mustangs!"

The climbing pair of friendly fighters never wavered. They couldn't hear. Damn them. He couldn't do anything more for them now. His job was to protect the other *Schwarm,* with the Mustangs about to attack. Pushing his stick forward, Erich went lancing down after the P-51's, taking them from above and behind.

"Dive down and watch from below," Erich told wingman Junger.

The Mustang leader already had a lone Me-109 bore-sighted and was pouring fire into the German fighter. Three more Mustangs were lined up ready for a firing pass. "Four against one!" Erich saw red. He swept in on the American four from behind at maximum dive speed. Smoke was pouring from the stricken Me-109 as the American leader kept firing. Small pieces of the Messerschmitt were being blasted clear and whipped backward by the slipstream. The American .50-caliber guns were deadly, but not as devastating as the 20-mm cannon on the Me-109.

Four hundred . . . 300 . . . 200 . . . 100 meters . . . the distance came flashing down in split seconds. The Mustang with its checkered tail looked as big as a barn. Erich's windshield was all P-51 as he came rushing in on the rearmost American from below and behind, at a perfect thirty-degree attack angle. He pressed his gun buttons. A blast of fire and an explosion shook Karaya One as the P-51 blew up.

Erich switched instantly to the third Mustang, whose pilot seemed momentarily paralyzed. The Mustang took an all-guns volley of hits from Karaya One and began burning. The American kept flying, and now it was Erich's turn to feel the lash.

"Bubi, Bubi, behind you! Break! Break!" Sergeant Junger's alarm rasped in his headphones.

Erich stroked the stick forward, diving down hard. He felt his eyes bulging in their sockets, and his helmeted head bounced against the canopy as negative G's boosted him hard against his safety belt. In heavy left spirals at full power, the Blond Knight went plummeting down, the Mustangs hot on his tail.

"Back to base on your own. I'll make it alone," he radioed his wingman. That would give Junger a chance. There were too damned many American fighters for him to deal with anyway. The horde of them strung out behind Erich now were determined that this lone Messerschmitt would not escape their vengeance.

Erich looked in his mirror and quickly to each side. Damn! *Eight* of the deadly Mustangs were tearing after him. His negative-G break had momentarily foiled them, and he'd gained some distance as a result, but he was in a tight spot. He began talking aloud to himself, as though acting as his own guardian angel.

"All right Erich, keep your head now, and *fly.* Fly like you never flew before."

The P-51's split into two four-ship elements and sandwiched Erich neatly. They were as fast as he was. That made it rough.

"Hard turns, Erich. Real hard turns, or you'll have bullets in your whiskey stomach."

He reefed Karaya One around hard left and the aerial baseball game began, with the Blond Knight as the ball. Hard right—a blast of gunfire from two of the Mustangs . . . hard left—a storm of tracer from the other side . . . hard right—more gunfire.

"You're lucky, Erich. They're not top shooters. They open fire too soon, too far out. You're lucky again, Erich. If they knew what you know you'd be dead. . . ."

Hard right . . . hard left . . . and in the blood-draining turns where the Mustangs sometimes swung close to him, he fired his own guns.

"You know you won't hit them like that, Erich, but they'll see the tracer. May rattle them a bit. Besides, the sound of your own guns makes you feel better when they've nearly got you."

The eight relentless Americans and the lone German went rat-racing across the Rumanian sky, the roar of the American fifties ringing out at intervals and Erich dodging the tracer. In seconds he could feel the perspiration running down his body under his uniform. His adrenalin-charged body was pouring out sweat. His face was streaming as though he were sitting in a steam bath, and his vest and shirt were saturated. Even his uniform was becoming damp. Hauling the Messerschmitt round in these murderous turns was an ordeal of hard labor.

Amid the periodic hammering of the American guns and the groaning of his overstressed Karaya One, thoughts of the past poured through Erich's head. The sports of his boyhood swam before his mind's eye. "Good thing you liked gymnastics, Erich. Gave you the strength to keep your hide whole. Your coordination is saving you now."

He made another try with his guns when there was a slight chance of hitting a P-51 in one of the tight turns, but this time his guns were dead. All through the numbing turns Erich had kept slowly working his way back toward his base. He was actually gaining slightly on the Mustangs, beating them by a hair in each turn and drawing away a few yards each time.

The Americans might have been losing a few yards, but they were staying glued to the Blond Knight's tail, firing often but wildly. They couldn't quite pull enough lead on their quarry to score a hit, but they were keeping up the pressure. The kill was going to be theirs even if they had to split it eight different ways.

"Keep going, Erich. Keep going. The flak near the base will take these leeches off your tail."

Erich swung into another grinding turn.

"Damn!"

The fuel warning light on the dash glared red. Karaya One was almost out of fuel and he was too far from the base to land the fighter even if he dared.

"Make a fast bailout, Erich. Flip her over on her back, quick but easy."

He released his safety belt. As he came out of the next turn, he tripped the emergency release for the canopy. The plexiglas cover went whipping away in the slipstream and the wind howled and tore around the cockpit. Coming out of the next turn, Erich sucked back on the stick with all his strength, hauling it back into the pit of his belly. As the 109 went soaring upward and over, he released the stick and shot clear of the doomed aircraft.

Sky, earth and trees; wheeling Mustangs and his own booted feet flashed before him in a wild kaleidoscope as he went tumbling earthward. He pulled the D-ring. There was a rustling of silk and cord followed by the plumping sound of the opening umbrella. A bone-bruising jerk shook every joint in his body as he was jarred upright in the parachute harness. He was swinging helpless in his chute surrounded by eight angry Mustangs.

For German fighter pilots it was unthinkable to strafe an enemy pilot hanging in his parachute. They regarded that not as war and fighting between soldiers, but as murder. This chivalrous tradition may have seemed out of place in total war, but the Luftwaffe lived by this code to the end. Swinging under his silk umbrella, the defenseless Blond Knight wondered if his American foes would act the same way. He thought how horrible it would be if they didn't. Was he going to die by mid-air strafing, and fall to earth as a bundle of bloody rags?

A Mustang lined up on him as though for a firing pass. Erich's entrails contracted into a tight ball. For one blinding instant he thought of Usch. Then the American fighter went roaring past a few yards away. An ugly face under a white and yellow helmet glared at Erich through huge goggles that made the pilot look indescribably malevolent. The American's hand went up, there was a manly wave, and the Mustang banked around.*

Erich felt happy to be alive. He felt even happier as the eight Americans formed up on their leader and went streaking off to the north. As he came floating down to the good green earth he told himself again and again, "You are lucky, Erich. You are a lucky boy. By God, you'll have a birthday party tonight."

He came down a little less than four miles from the base, and an army truck took him back to his squadron. The air at HQ was full of bad news. Nearly half the *Gruppe's* aircraft had been shot down. Two pilots were killed and a number of others wounded. Without methanol injection, the old type Me-109 would not cut it against the Mustangs, even with experienced pilots. Higher HQ ordered an immediate halt to fighter attacks on the Americans because of these heavy losses, and the certainty that they would become worse.

Erich Hartmann's *Gruppenkommandeur* during this period was Captain (now Lt. Col.) Willi Batz, a long-time comrade and admirer of the Blond Knight. Batz recalls the struggle to defend Ploesti in these terms:

"In the latter part of May we were forced into combat on two fronts. Fighters were direly needed everywhere, both against the Russians and in the south in Rumania guarding the Ploesti oil fields against American four-engined bombers. I remember well those hard times, because they not only called upon all our resources as fighting pilots, but also placed heavy demands on our ground support forces.

"In defending the Ploesti oil fields, I always made Bubi, at his own

---

* In general, victorious pilots of all nations avoided shooting at parachuting airmen.

request, the head fighter pilot. We always went up together, the whole *Gruppe,* and Bubi would take his squadron and protect the rear against the Mustangs. He accomplished his tasks brilliantly. This type of four-motored aircraft was not familiar to us Eastern Front pilots, but because of Bubi we suffered relatively minor losses. He always managed to protect us, hold the Mustangs in abeyance and keep them off our necks. Only because of Bubi's experience were we able to find success against the bombers. Today [1967] I do not recall how many Bubi shot down in Rumania but I know he was successful against the Mustangs and saved us from greater losses."

Erich reviewed these five battles with the P-51 Mustangs, which had taken place in the spring of 1944, as he droned through his air journey back to Czechoslovakia. Almost a year had passed since he had battled the Americans in Rumania. By now, they would certainly be stronger. When he landed at Deutsch Brod, his comrades in I/JG-52 confirmed his apprehensions. American fighters were penetrating into Czechoslovakian skies regularly. Within a few days, the Blond Knight was again tangling with the Mustangs of the USAAF.

A Russian bombing raid was reported headed for Prague. Erich got the order to scramble. He was to take up a *Schwarm* to intercept the bombers. Bimmel had everything ready and Erich was airborne in minutes, heading for Prague and climbing hard. At 21,000 feet he leveled off and began scanning the skies for the enemy.

The Russian force soon hove into view. Erich counted about thirty bombers, a mixed formation of lend-lease A-20 Douglas Bostons and Russian Pe-2's. Flying top cover was a force of about twenty-five fighters, YAK-11's and P-39 Airacobras. The Red fighters were at about 12,000 feet. Erich switched on his R/T.

"Attack in two elements."

With the sun at his back, Erich was ready to push the stick forward and go diving down on the enemy force. He hesitated. His intuition pricked at him. Then from the corner of his eye he caught sight of a line of contrails, a little higher than his element, descending and closing in from the west. His first thought was that more 109's were coming in to join the attack, but a series of silver flashes from the incoming strangers eliminated them as friends. Polished metal surfaces had long ago been done away with on German fighters. All Luftwaffe ships were painted. They didn't flash in the sun. Polished surfaces usually meant one thing—Americans. Soon the strangers could be recognized. Mustangs!

The silvery craft came in about three thousand feet below Erich and his wingman as they held their altitude. The Mustangs began circling slowly three thousand feet above the Russian top cover. The Americans hadn't seen Erich above them. With the sun behind him and an altitude advantage, he was perfectly set up for a classic bounce. Russians and Americans were now obviously watching each other instead of their tails. The timing was perfect. Erich switched on his R/T.

"We'll make one pass only. Down through the Mustangs, on down through the Russian top cover, and down through the bombers."

At full power the two Me-109's went screaming down on the upper circle of Mustangs. Closing like lightning, Erich's fighter shook briefly with a burst of gunfire and the rearmost Mustang never knew what hit him. The P-51 staggered and went down out of control, tumbling and smoking and dumping debris. In a shallow turn Erich found the next Mustang rushing in to fill his windshield at point-blank range. Erich's burst thundered into the P-51's engine compartment and the American ship nosed up suddenly. With a rolling-out movement, the stricken Mustang went diving down beside Erich, out of control, smoking heavily and shedding chunks of its structure as it rushed to final impact.

Erich's engine was screaming and Karaya One was shuddering as he tore on down at full throttle through the Russian fighter cover. No chance to fire on the fighters. Going too fast. Now the Bostons, rushing up like hell. He squeezed his gun buttons and saw pieces blasted away from one bomber. Hits! Hits! Yes, but nothing mortal. On and down through the bombers and then the brain-glazing pull-out.

The awful suck of gravity on his body drew Erich into a momentary gray-out. He released some of the back pressure on the stick to maintain his vision. As the 109 moaned through its pull-out curve and came up near level with the bombers, Erich checked his tail. His wingman was still with him. What of the second element? He searched the sky.

The second element came slashing down through the Allied formation. Another Mustang came down blazing, but its pilot bailed out and Erich saw the silk billow behind the tumbling flyer. Timing his turn, Erich joined up with the second element as it pulled out, and all four 109's went racing away, their camouflaged aircraft all but indiscernible from above.

Looking back, Erich saw an unexpected and savage consequence of his lightning attack. The Russian YAK's and Airacobras were dogfighting with the Mustangs! The Russians were watching the Americans when Erich drove home his attack. The suspicious Red pilots must have thought the Americans had attacked them. Panic gripped the Russian bomber pilots. They jettisoned their bomb loads, blasting a stretch of empty countryside, then swung around on a reverse course. They were abandoning their mission.

The Russo-American dogfight continued at a furious pace. From the milling droves of planes Erich saw three YAK-11's come flaming down, while a Mustang went limping off to the south belching glycol. Erich shook his head with incredulity. As Allies, the Russians and the Americans seemed to have little trust in each other. Hartmann could not restrain a hearty belly laugh as his Me-109 nosed down and streaked for home.

There would be no more battles between Erich and the Mustangs. The end of the war was imminent. The Americans seemed to know they had won the war, and were confident, numerous and sure of themselves. In big gaggles they felt safe as they ranged over Europe at will, pouncing on every enemy they could find. Sometimes their confidence led to diminished vigilance, as in the battles with Erich Hartmann.

Today Erich writes of vigilance in the air on the basis of his better than eight hundred aerial battles:

"In a kind of auto-suggestion, from my own first crash in training until my last landing on 8 May 1945, I never slept in the air. I always had a bad feeling after take-off, because I never had the idea that I was or could be better than any other pilot in the air at this moment. My stomach felt bad during flight to the instant when I recognized my foes. From that moment, I had the feeling of *absolute superiority.*

"I was afraid in the air of the big unknown factors. Clouds and sun were hate and love in my feeling world. Today I am sure that eighty per cent of my kills never knew I was there before I opened fire. My dogfights were fast and simple on that account. But one factor always worked for me more than any other. I found I could spot enemy planes long before my comrades—sometimes minutes before them. This was not experience or skill, but an advantage with which I was born. My rule for airfighting is this:

"THE PILOT WHO SEES THE OTHER FIRST ALREADY HAS HALF THE VICTORY."

In battling the Americans, Erich Hartmann redressed a technical disadvantage by skill and experience, and downed seven of the formidable Mustangs, whose demise was confirmed. When the odds in combat were eight to one against him and the Mustangs had him cold, he triumphed over their best efforts to outfly him and shoot him down. He lived to tell the tale because his American pursuers had not forgotten their sportsmanship, fought fairly, and did not stoop to murder.

BACK TO BOLOGNA

by Joseph Heller

Captain Piltchard and Captain Wren, the inoffensive joint squadron operations officers, were both mild, soft-spoken men of less than middle height who enjoyed flying combat missions and begged nothing more of life and Colonel Cathcart than the opportunity to continue flying them. They had flown hundreds of combat missions and wanted to fly hundreds more. They assigned themselves to every one. Nothing so wonderful as war had ever happened to them before; and they were afraid it might never happen to them again. They conducted their duties humbly and reticently, with a minimum of fuss, and went to great lengths not to antagonize anyone. They smiled quickly at everyone they passed. When they spoke, they mumbled. They were shifty, cheerful, subservient men who were comfortable only with each other and never met anyone else's eye, not even Yossarian's eye at the open-air meeting they called to reprimand him publicly for making Kid Sampson turn back from the mission to Bologna.

"Fellas," said Captain Piltchard, who had thinning dark hair and smiled awkwardly. "When you turn back from a mission, try to make sure it's for something important, will you? Not for something unimportant . . . like a defective intercom . . . or something like that. Okay? Captain Wren has more he wants to say to you on that subject."

"Captain Piltchard's right, fellas," said Captain Wren. "And that's all I'm going to say to you on that subject. Well, we finally got to Bologna today, and we found out it's a milk run. We were all a little nervous, I guess, and didn't do too much damage. Well, listen to this. Colonel Cathcart got permission for us to go back. And tomorrow we're really going to paste those ammunition dumps. Now, what do you think about that?"

And to prove to Yossarian that they bore him no animosity, they even assigned him to fly lead bombardier with McWatt in the first formation when they went back to Bologna the next day. He came in on the target like a Havermeyer, confidently taking no evasive action at all, and suddenly they were shooting the living shit out of him!

Heavy flak was everywhere! He had been lulled, lured and trapped, and there was nothing he could do but sit there like an idiot and watch the ugly black puffs smashing up to kill him. There was nothing he could do until his bombs dropped but look back into the bombsight, where the fine cross-hairs in the lens were glued magnetically over the target exactly where he had placed them, intersecting perfectly deep inside the yard of his block of camouflaged warehouses before the base of the first building. He was trembling steadily as the plane crept ahead. He could hear the hollow *boom-boom-boom-boom* of the flak pounding all around him in overlapping measures of four, the sharp, piercing *crack!* of a single shell exploding suddenly very close by. His head was busting with a thousand dissonant impulses as he prayed for the bombs to drop. He wanted to sob. The engines droned on monotonously like a fat, lazy fly. At last the indices on the bombsight crossed, tripping away the eight 500-pounders one after the other. The plane lurched upward buoyantly with the lightened load. Yossarian bent away from the bombsight crookedly to watch the indicator on his left. When the pointer touched zero, he closed the bomb bay doors and, over the intercom, at the very top of his voice, shrieked:

"Turn right hard!"

McWatt responded instantly. With a grinding howl of engines, he flipped the plane over on one wing and wrung it around remorselessly in a screaming turn away from the twin spires of flak Yossarian had spied stabbing toward them. Then Yossarian had McWatt climb and keep climbing higher and higher until they tore free finally into a calm, diamond-blue sky that was sunny and pure everywhere and laced in the distance with long white veils of tenuous fluff. The wind strummed soothingly against the cylindrical panes of his windows, and he relaxed exultantly only until they picked up speed again and then turned McWatt left and plunged him right back down, noticing with a transitory spasm of elation the mushrooming clusters of flak leaping open high above him and back over his shoulder to the right, exactly where he could have been if he had not turned left and dived. He leveled McWatt out with another harsh cry and whipped him upward and around again into a ragged blue patch of unpolluted air just as the bombs he had dropped began to strike. The first one fell in the yard, exactly where he had aimed, and then the rest of the bombs from his own plane and from the other planes in his flight burst open on the ground in a charge of rapid orange flashes across the tops of the buildings, which collapsed instantly in a vast, churning wave of pink and gray and coal-black smoke that went rolling out turbulently in all directions and quaked convulsively in its bowels as though from great blasts of red and white and golden sheet lightning.

"Well, will you look at that," Aarfy marveled sonorously right beside Yossarian, his plump, orbicular face sparkling with a look of bright enchantment. "There must have been an ammunition dump down there."

Yossarian had forgotten about Aarfy. "Get out!" he shouted at him. "Get out of the nose!"

Aarfy smiled politely and pointed down toward the target in a generous invitation for Yossarian to look. Yossarian began slapping at him insistently and signaled wildly toward the entrance of the crawlway.

"Get back in the ship!" he cried frantically. "Get back in the ship!"

Aarfy shrugged amiably. "I can't hear you," he explained.

Yossarian seized him by the straps of his parachute harness and pushed him backward toward the crawlway just as the plane was hit with a jarring concussion that rattled his bones and made his heart stop. He knew at once they were all dead.

"Climb!" he screamed into the intercom at McWatt when he saw he was still alive. *"Climb, you bastard! Climb, climb, climb, climb!"*

The plane zoomed upward again in a climb that was swift and straining, until he leveled it out with another harsh shout at McWatt and wrenched it around once more in a roaring, merciless forty-five-degree turn that sucked his insides out in one enervating sniff and left him floating fleshless in mid-air until he leveled McWatt out again just long enough to hurl him back around toward the right and then down into a screeching dive. Through endless blobs of ghostly black smoke he sped, the hanging smut wafting against the smooth plexiglass nose of the ship like an evil, damp, sooty vapor against his cheeks. His heart was hammering again in aching terror as he hurtled upward and downward through the blind gangs of flak charging murderously into the sky at him, then sagging inertly. Sweat gushed from his neck in torrents and poured down over his chest and waist with the feeling of warm slime. He was vaguely aware for an instant that the planes in his formation were no longer there, and then he was aware of only himself. His throat hurt like a raw slash from the strangling intensity with which he shrieked each command to McWatt. The engines rose to a deafening, agonized, ululating bellow each time McWatt changed direction. And far out in front the bursts of flak were still swarming into the sky from new batteries of guns poking around for accurate altitude as they waited sadistically for him to fly into range.

The plane was slammed again suddenly with another loud, jarring explosion that almost rocked it over on its back, and the nose filled immediately with sweet clouds of blue smoke. *Something was on fire!* Yossarian whirled to escape and smacked into Aarfy, who had struck a match and was placidly lighting his pipe. Yossarian gaped at his grinning, moon-faced navigator in utter shock and confusion. It occurred to him that one of them was mad.

"Jesus Christ!" he screamed at Aarfy in tortured amazement. "Get the hell out of the nose! Are you crazy? Get out!"

"What?" said Aarfy.

"Get out!" Yossarian yelled hysterically, and began clubbing Aarfy backhanded with both fists to drive him away. "Get out!"

"I still can't hear you," Aarfy called back innocently with an expression of mild and reproving perplexity. "You'll have to talk a little louder."

"Get out of the nose!" Yossarian shrieked in frustration. "They're trying to kill us! Don't you understand? They're trying to kill us!"

"Which way should I go, goddam it?" McWatt shouted furiously over the intercom in a suffering, high-pitched voice. "Which way should I go?"

"Turn left! *Left,* you goddam dirty son of a bitch! Turn left *hard!"*

Aarfy crept up close behind Yossarian and jabbed him sharply in the ribs with the stem of his pipe. Yossarian flew up toward the ceiling with a whinnying cry, then jumped completely around on his knees, white as a sheet and quivering with rage. Aarfy winked encouragingly and jerked his thumb back toward McWatt with a humorous moue.

"What's eating *him?"* he asked with a laugh.

Yossarian was struck with a weird sense of distortion. "Will you get out of here?" he yelped beseechingly, and shoved Aarfy over with all his strength. "Are you deaf or something? Get back in the plane!" And to McWatt he screamed, "Dive! *Dive!"*

Down they sank once more into the crunching, thudding, voluminous barrage of bursting antiaircraft shells as Aarfy came creeping back behind Yossarian and jabbed him sharply in the ribs again. Yossarian shied upward with another whinnying gasp.

"I still couldn't hear you," Aarfy said.

"I said get *out of here!"* Yossarian shouted, and broke into tears. He began punching Aarfy in the body with both hands as hard as he could. "Get away from me! Get *away!"*

Punching Aarfy was like sinking his fists into a limp sack of inflated rubber. There was no resistance, no response at all from the soft, insensitive mass, and after a while Yossarian's spirit died and his arms dropped helplessly with exhaustion. He was overcome with a humiliating feeling of impotence and was ready to weep in self-pity.

"What did you say?" Aarfy asked.

"Get away from me," Yossarian answered, pleading with him now. "Go back in the plane."

"I still can't hear you."

"Never mind," wailed Yossarian, "never mind. Just leave me alone."

"Never mind what?"

Yossarian began hitting himself in the forehead. He seized Aarfy by the shirt front and, struggling to his feet for traction, dragged him to the rear of the nose compartment and flung him down like a bloated and unwieldy bag in the entrance of the crawlway. A shell banged open with a stupendous clout right beside his ear as he was scrambling back toward the front, and some undestroyed recess of his intelligence wondered that it did not kill them all. They were climbing again. The engines were howling again as though in pain, and the air inside the plane was acrid with the smell of machinery and fetid with the stench of gasoline. The next thing he knew, *it was snowing!*

Thousands of tiny bits of white paper were falling like snowflakes inside the plane, milling around his head so thickly that they clung to his eyelashes when he blinked in astonishment and fluttered against his nostrils and lips each time he inhaled. When he spun around in bewilderment, Aarfy was grinning proudly from ear to ear like something inhuman as he held up a shattered paper map for Yossarian to see. A large chunk of flak had ripped up from the floor through Aarfy's colossal jumble of maps and had ripped out through the ceiling inches away from their heads. Aarfy's joy was sublime.

"Will you look at this?" he murmured, waggling two of his stubby fingers playfully into Yossarian's face through the hole in one of his maps. "Will you look at this?"

Yossarian was dumfounded by his state of rapturous contentment. Aarfy was like an eerie ogre in a dream, incapable of being bruised or evaded, and Yossarian dreaded him for a complex of reasons he was too petrified to untangle. Wind whistling up through the jagged gash in the floor kept the myriad bits of paper circulating like alabaster particles in a paperweight and contributed to a sensation of lacquered, waterlogged unreality. Everything seemed strange, so tawdry and grotesque. His head was throbbing from a shrill clamor that drilled relentlessly into both ears. It was McWatt, begging for directions in an incoherent frenzy. Yossarian continued staring in tormented fascination at Aarfy's spherical countenance beaming at him so serenely and vacantly through the drifting whorls of white paper bits and concluded that he was a raving lunatic just as eight bursts of flak broke open successively at eye level off to the right, then eight more, and then eight more, the last group pulled over toward the left so that they were almost directly in front.

"Turn left hard!" he hollered to McWatt, as Aarfy kept grinning, and McWatt did turn left hard, but the flak turned left hard with them, catching up fast, and Yossarian hollered, "I said *hard, hard, hard, hard, you bastard, hard!*"

And McWatt bent the plane around even harder still, and suddenly, miraculously, they were out of range. The flak ended. The guns stopped booming at them. And they were alive.

Behind him, men were dying. Strung out for miles in a stricken, tortuous, squirming line, the other flights of planes were making the same hazardous journey over the target, threading their swift way through the swollen masses of new and old bursts of flak like rats racing in a pack through their own droppings. One was on fire, and flapped lamely off by itself, billowing gigantically like a monstrous blood-red star. As Yossarian watched, the burning plane floated over on its side and began spiraling down slowly in wide, tremulous, narrowing circles, its huge flaming burden blazing orange and flaring out in back like a long, swirling cape of fire and smoke. There were parachutes, one, two, three . . . four, and then the plane gyrated into a spin and fell the rest of the way to the ground, fluttering insensibly inside its vivid pyre like a shred of colored tissue paper. One whole flight of planes from another squadron had been blasted apart.

Yossarian sighed barrenly, his day's work done. He was listless and sticky. The engines crooned mellifluously as McWatt throttled back to loiter and allow the rest of the planes in his flight to catch up. The abrupt stillness seemed alien and artificial, a little insidious. Yossarian unsnapped his flak suit and took off his helmet. He sighed again, restlessly, and closed his eyes and tried to relax.

"Where's Orr?" someone asked suddenly over his intercom.

Yossarian bounded up with a one-syllable cry that crackled with anxiety and provided the only rational explanation for the whole mysterious phenomenon of the flak at Bologna: *Orr!* He lunged forward over the bombsight to search downward through the plexiglass for some reassuring sign of Orr, who drew flak like a magnet and who had undoubtedly attracted the crack batteries of the whole Hermann Goering Division to Bologna overnight from wherever the hell they had been stationed the day before when Orr was still in Rome. Aarfy launched himself forward an instant later and cracked Yossarian on the bridge of the nose with the sharp rim of his flak helmet. Yossarian cursed him as his eyes flooded with tears.

"There he is," Aarfy orated funereally, pointing down dramatically at a hay wagon and two horses standing before the barn of a gray stone farmhouse. "Smashed to bits. I guess their numbers were all up."

Yossarian swore at Aarfy again and continued searching intently, cold with a compassionate kind of fear now for the little bouncy and bizarre buck-toothed tentmate who had smashed Appleby's forehead open with a ping-pong racket and who was scaring the daylights out of Yossarian once again. At last Yossarian spotted the two-engined, twin-ruddered plane as it flew out of the green background of the forests over a field of yellow farmland. One of the propellers was feathered and perfectly still, but the plane was maintaining altitude and holding a proper course. Yossarian muttered an unconscious prayer of thankfulness and then flared up at Orr savagely in a ranting fusion of resentment and relief.

"That bastard!" he began. "That goddam stunted, red-faced, big-cheeked, curlyheaded, buck-toothed rat bastard son of a bitch!"

"What?"

"That dirty goddam midget-assed, apple-cheeked, goggle-eyed, undersized, buck-toothed, grinning, crazy sonofabitchinbastard!" Yossarian sputtered.

"What?"

"Never mind!"

"I still can't hear you," Aarfy answered.

Yossarian swung himself around methodically to face Aarfy. "You prick," he began.

"Me?"

"You pompous, rotund, neighborly, vacuous, complacent . . ."

Aarfy was unperturbed. Calmly he struck a wooden match and sucked noisily at his pipe with an eloquent air of benign and magnanimous forgiveness. He smiled sociably and opened his mouth to speak. Yossarian put his hand over Aarfy's mouth and pushed him away wearily.

He shut his eyes and pretended to sleep all the way back to the field so that he would not have to listen to Aarfy or see him.

At the briefing room Yossarian made his intelligence report to Captain Black and then waited in muttering suspense with all the others until Orr chugged into sight overhead finally with his one good engine still keeping him aloft gamely. Nobody breathed. Orr's landing gear would not come down. Yossarian hung around only until Orr had crash-landed safely, and then stole the first jeep he could find with a key in the ignition and raced back to his tent to begin packing feverishly for the emergency rest leave he had decided to take in Rome, where he found Luciana and her invisible scar that same night.

ATTACK ON PEARL HARBOR

by Walter Lord

Lieutenant Harauo Takeda, 30-year-old flight officer on the cruiser *Tone,* was a disappointed, worried man as the Japanese striking force hurtled southward, now less than 250 miles from Oahu.

He was disappointed because last-minute orders kept him from piloting the *Tone's* seaplane, which was to take off at 5:30 A.M., joining the *Chikuma's* plane in a final reconnaissance of the U.S. fleet. And he was worried because—as the man in charge of launching these planes—he feared that they would somehow collide while taking off. True, the two ships were some eight miles apart, but it was still pitch black. Besides, when the stakes are so high, a man almost looks for things to worry about.

Nothing went wrong. The planes shot safely from their catapults and winged off into the dark—two small harbingers of the great armada that would follow. Admiral Nagumo planned to hit Pearl Harbor with 353 planes in two mighty waves. The first was to go at 6:00 A.M.— 40 torpedo planes . . . 51 dive bombers . . . 49 horizontal bombers . . . 43 fighters to provide cover. The second at 7:15 A.M.—80 dive bombers . . . 54 high-level bombers . . . 36 more fighters. This would still leave 39 planes to guard the task force in case the Americans struck back.

By now the men on the carriers were making their final preparations. The deck crews—up an hour before the pilots—checked the planes in their hangars, then brought them up to the flight decks. Motors sputtered and roared as the mechanics tuned up the engines. On the *Hiryu,* Commander Amagai carefully removed the pieces of paper he had slipped into each plane's wireless transmitter to keep it from being set off by accident.

Down below, the pilots were pulling on their clean underwear and freshly pressed uniforms. Several wore the traditional *hashamaki* headbands. Little groups gathered around the portable Shinto shrines that were standard equipment on every Japanese warship. There they drank jiggers of *sake* and prayed for their success.

Assembling for breakfast, they found a special treat. Instead of the usual salted pike-mackerel and rice mixed with barley, today they ate *sekihan.* This Japanese dish of rice boiled with tiny red beans was reserved for only the most ceremonial occasions. Next, they picked up some simple rations for the trip—a sort of box lunch that included the usual rice balls and pickled plums, emergency rations of chocolate, hardtack, and special pills to keep them alert.

Now to the flight operations rooms for final briefing. On the *Akagi* Commander Mitsuo Fuchida, leader of the attacking planes, sought out Admiral Nagumo: "I am ready for the mission."

"I have every confidence in you," the admiral answered, grasping Fuchida's hand.

On every carrier the scene was the same: the dimly lit briefing room; the pilots crowding in and spilling out into the corridor; the blackboard revised to show ship positions at Pearl Harbor as of 10:30 A.M., December 6. Time for one last look at the enemy line-up; one last run-down on the charts and maps. Then the latest data on wind direction and velocity, some up-to-the-minute calculations on distance and flying time to Hawaii and back. Next a stern edict: no one except Commander Fuchida was to touch his radio until the attack began. Finally, brief pep talks by the flight officers, the skippers, and, on the *Akagi,* by Admiral Nagumo himself.

A bright dawn swept the sky as the men emerged, some wearing small briefing boards slung around their necks. One by one they climbed to the cockpits, waving good-by—27-year-old Ippei Goto of the *Kaga,* in his brand-new ensign's uniform . . . quiet Fusata Iida of the *Soryu,* who was so crazy about baseball . . . artistic Mimori Suzuki of the *Akagi,* whose Caucasian looks invited rough teasing about his "mixed blood." When it was Lieutenant Haita Matsumura's turn, he suddenly whipped off the gauze mask which had marked him as such a hypochondriac. All along, he had been secretly growing a beautiful mustache.

Commander Fuchida headed for the flight leader's plane, designated by a red and yellow stripe around the tail. As he swung aboard, the crew chief handed him a special *hashamaki* headband: "This is a present from the maintenance crews. May I ask that you take it along to Pearl Harbor?"

In the *Akagi's* engine room, Commander Tanbo got permission and rushed topside for the great moment—the only time he left his post during the entire voyage. Along the flight decks the men gathered, shouting good luck and waving good-by. Lieutenant Ebina, the *Shokaku's* junior surgeon, trembled with excitement as he watched the motors race faster and the blue exhaust smoke pour out.

All eyes turned to the *Akagi,* which would give the signal. She flew a set of flags at half-mast, which meant to get ready. When they were hoisted to the top and swiftly lowered, the planes would go.

Slowly the six carriers swung into the wind. It was from the east, and perfect for take-off. But the southern seas were running high, and the carriers dipped 15 degrees, sending high waves crashing against the bow. Too rough for really safe launching, Admiral Kusaka thought, but there was no other choice now. The Pearl Harbor Striking Force was poised 230 miles north and slightly east of Oahu. The time was 6:00 A.M.

Up fluttered the signal flags, then down again. One by one the fighters roared down the flight decks, drowning the cheers and yells that erupted everywhere. Commander Hoichiro Tsukamoto forgot his worries as navigation officer of the *Shokaku,* decided this was the greatest moment of his life. The ship's doctors, Captain Endo and Lieutenant Ebina, abandoned their professional dignity and wildly waved the fliers on. Engineer Tanbo shouted like a schoolboy, then rushed back to the *Akagi's* engine room to tell everybody else.

Now the torpedo planes and dive bombers thundered off, while the fighters circled above, giving protection. Plane after plane rose, flashing in the early-morning sun that peeked over the horizon. Soon all 183 were in the air, circling and wheeling into formation. Seaman Iki Kuramoti watched, on the verge of tears. Quietly he put his hands together and prayed.

For Admiral Kusaka it had been a terrible strain, getting the planes off in these high seas. Now they were on their way, and the sudden relief was simply too much. He trembled like a leaf—just couldn't control himself. And he was embarrassed, too, because he prided himself on his grasp of Buddhism, *bushido,* and *kendo* (a form of Japanese fencing)—all of which were meant to fortify a man against exactly this sort of thing. Finally he sat on the deck—or he thinks possibly in a chair—and meditated Buddha-fashion. Slowly he pulled himself together again as the planes winged off to the south.

Commander Mitsuo Fuchida knew they must be nearly there—they had been in the air now almost an hour and a half. But a carpet of thick white clouds stretched endlessly below, and he couldn't even see the ocean to check the wind drift. He flicked on the radio direction finder and picked up an early-morning program from Honolulu. By twisting his antenna he got a good bearing on the station and discovered he was five degrees off course. He made the correction, and the other planes followed suit.

They were all around him. Behind were the other 48 horizontal bombers. To the left and slightly above were Lieutenant Commander Kakwichi Takahashi's 51 dive bombers. To the right and a little below were Lieutenant Commander Shigeharu Murata's 40 torpedo planes. Far above, Lieutenant Commander Shigeru Itaya's 43 fighters provided cover. The bombers flew at 9000 feet, the fighters as high as 15,000. All of them basked in the bright morning sun that now blazed off to the left.

But below, the clouds were still everywhere. Fuchida began to worry—would it be as bad over Pearl Harbor? If so, what would that do to the bombing? He wished the reconnaissance planes would report—they should be there by now. And then through the radio music he suddenly heard a weather broadcast. He tuned closer and caught it clearly:

". . . partly cloudly . . . mostly over the mountains . . . ceiling 3500 feet . . . visibility good."

Now he knew he could count on the clouds to break once he reached Oahu. Also that it would be better to come in from the west and southwest—those clouds over the mountains made an eastern approach too dangerous. Then, as if to cap this run of good luck, the clouds below him parted, and almost directly ahead he saw a white line of surf breaking against a rugged green shore. It was Kahuku Point, Oahu.

Lieutenant Toshio Hashimoto, piloting one of Fuchida's bombers, was simply charmed. The lush green island, the clear blue water, the colored roofs of the little houses seemed in another world. It was the kind of scene one likes to preserve. He pulled out his camera and snapped some pictures.

For fighter pilot Yoshio Shiga, this warm, sunlit land had a deeper meaning. Back in 1934 he had been to Honolulu on a naval training cruise . . . a visit full of good times and pleasant memories. To see Oahu again, still so green and lovely, gave him a strange, nostalgic feeling. He thought about it for a moment, then turned to the business at hand.

The time had come to deploy for the attack, and Commander Fuchida had a difficult decision to make. The plan provided for either "Surprise" or "Surprise Lost" conditions. If "Surprise," the torpedo planes were to go in first, then the horizontal bombers, finally the dive bombers, while the fighters remained above for protection. (The idea was to drop as many torpedoes as possible before the smoke from the dive bombing ruined the targets.) On the other hand, if the raiders had been detected and it was "Surprise Lost," the dive bombers and fighters would hit the airfields and antiaircraft defenses first; then the torpedo planes would come in when resistance was crushed. To tell the planes which deployment to take, Commander Fuchida was to fire his signal gun once for "Surprise," twice for "Surprise Lost."

Trouble was, Commander Fuchida didn't know whether the Americans had caught on or not. The reconnaissance planes were meant to tell him, but they hadn't reported yet. It was now 7:40 A.M., and he couldn't wait any longer. They were already well down the west coast and about opposite Haleiwa. Playing a hunch, he decided he could carry off the surprise.

He held out his signal pistol and fired one "black dragon." The dive bombers began circling upward to 12,000 feet; the horizontal bombers spiraled down to 3500; the torpedo planes dropped until they barely skimmed the sea, ready for the honor of leading the assault.

As the planes orbited into position, Fuchida noticed that the fighters weren't responding at all. He decided that they must have missed his signal, so he reached out and fired another "black dragon." The fighters saw it this time, but so did the dive bombers. They decided it was the second "black dragon" of the "Surprise Lost" signal. Hence, they would be the ones to go in first. In a welter of confusion, the High Command's plan for carefully integrated phases vanished; dive bombers and torpedo planes eagerly prepared to slam into Pearl Harbor at the same time.

They could already see it on their left. Lieutenant Shiga was attracted by the unusual color gray of the warships. Commander Itaya was struck by the way the battleships were "strung out and anchored two ships side by side in an orderly manner." Commander Fuchida was more interested in counting them—two, four, eight. No doubt about it, they were all there.

Planes were approaching, and from more than one direction. Ensign Donald L. Korn, officer of the deck on the *Raleigh,* noticed a thin line winging in from the northwest. Seaman "Red" Pressler of the *Arizona* saw a string approaching from the mountains to the east. On the destroyer *Helm,* Quartermaster Frank Handler noticed another group coming in low from the south. The *Helm*—the only ship under way in all of Pearl Harbor—was in the main channel, about to turn up West Loch. The planes passed only 100 yards away, flying directly up the channel from the harbor entrance. One of the pilots gave a casual wave, and Quartermaster Handler cheerfully waved back. He noticed that, unlike most American planes, these had fixed landing gear.

As the planes roared nearer, Pharmacist's Mate William Lynch heard a *California* shipmate call out, "The Russians must have a carrier visiting us. Here come some planes with the red ball showing clearly."

Signalman Charles Flood on the *Helena* picked up a pair of binoculars and gave the planes a hard look. They were approaching in a highly unusual manner, but all the same there was something familiar about them. Then he recalled the time he was in Shanghai in 1932, when the Japanese Army and Navy invaded the city. He remembered their bombing technique—a form of glide bombing. The planes over Ford Island were diving in the same way.

In they hurtled—Lieutenant Commander Takahashi's 27 dive bombers plunging toward Ford Island and Hickam . . . Lieutenant Commander Murata's 40 torpedo planes swinging into position for their run at the big ships. Commander Fuchida marked time off Barbers Point with the horizontal bombers, watching his men go in. They were all attacking together instead of in stages as originally planned, but it would apparently make no difference—the ships were sitting ducks.

A few minutes earlier, at 7:49 A.M., Fuchida had radioed the signal to attack: "To . . . to . . . to . . . to . . ." Now he was so sure of victory that at 7:53—even before the first bomb fell—he signaled the carriers that the surprise attack was successful: "Tora . . . tora . . . tora . . ."

Back on the *Akagi,* Admiral Kusaka turned to Admiral Nagumo. Not a word passed between them. Just a long, firm handshake.

Commander Fuchida, the Japanese leader, didn't even try to cover his tracks on the flight back to the carriers. There just wasn't enough gas for deception. As fast as the bombers finished their work, they rendezvoused with the fighters 20 miles northwest of Kaena Point, then flew back in groups. The fighters had no homing device and depended on the larger planes to guide them to the carriers.

Fuchida himself hung around a little while. He wanted to snap a few pictures, drop by all the bases, and get some idea of what was accomplished. The smoke interfered a good deal, but he felt sure four battleships were sunk and three others badly damaged. It was harder to tell about the airfields, but there were no planes up, so perhaps that was his answer.

As he headed back alone around eleven o'clock, a fighter streaked toward him, banking from side to side. A moment of tension—then he saw the rising sun emblem. One of the *Zuikaku*'s fighters had been left behind. It occurred to Fuchida that there might be others too, so he went back to the rendezvous point for one last check. There he found a second fighter aimlessly circling about; it fell in behind, and the three planes wheeled off together toward the northwest—last of the visitors to depart.

At his end, Admiral Kusaka did his best to help. He moved the carriers to within 190 miles of Pearl Harbor. He wasn't meant to go closer than 200 miles, but he knew that even an extra five or ten miles might make a big difference to a plane short of gas or crippled by enemy gunfire. He wanted to give the fliers every possible break.

Now everything had been done, and Admiral Kusaka stood on the bridge of the *Akagi* anxiously scanning the southern horizon. It was just after 10:00 A.M. when he saw the first faint black dots—some flying in groups, some in pairs, some alone. On the *Shokaku,* the first plane Lieutenant Ebina saw was a single fighter skimming the sea like a swallow, as it headed for the carrier. It barely made the ship.

Gas was low . . . nerves were frayed . . . time was short. In the rush, normal landing procedures were scrapped. As fast as the planes came in, they were simply dragged aside to allow enough room for another to land. Yet there were few serious mishaps. As one fighter landed on the *Shokaku,* the carrier took a sudden dip and the plane toppled over. The pilot crawled out without a scratch. Lieutenant Yano ran out of gas and had to ditch beside the carrier—he and his crew were hauled aboard, none the worse for their swim.

Some familiar faces were missing. Twenty-seven-year-old Ippei Goto, who this morning had donned his ensign's uniform for the first time, failed to get back to the *Kaga.* Baseball-loving Lieutenant Fusata Iida didn't reach the *Soryu.* Artistic Lieutenant Mimori Suzuki never made the *Akagi*—he was the pilot who crashed into the *Curtiss.* In all, 29 planes with 55 men were lost.

But 324 planes came safely home, while the deck crews waved their forage caps. The men swarmed around the pilots as they climbed from their cockpits. Congratulations poured in from all sides. As Lieutenant Hashimoto wearily made his way to his quarters on the *Hiryu,* everyone seemed to be asking what was it like . . . what did he do . . . what did he see.

Now that it was all over, many of the pilots felt a curious letdown. Some begged for another chance because they missed their assigned targets. Others said they were dissatisfied because they had only "near-misses." Commander Amagai, flight deck officer of the *Hiryu,* tried to cheer them up. He assured them that a near-miss was often an effective blow. Then he had an even brighter idea for lifting their spirits: "We're not returning to Tokyo; now we're going to head for San Francisco."

At the very least, they expected another crack at Oahu. Even while Commander Amagai was cheering up the pilots, he was rearming and refueling the planes for a new attack. When Lieutenant Hashimoto told his men they would probably be going back, he thought he detected a few pale faces; but, on the whole, everyone was enthusiastic. On the *Akagi,* the planes were being lined up for another take-off as Commander Fuchida landed at 1:00 P.M.—the last plane in.

When Fuchida reported to the bridge, a heated discussion was going on. It turned out another attack wasn't so certain after all. For a moment they postponed any decision, to hear Fuchida's account. After he finished, Admiral Nagumo announced somewhat ponderously, "We may then conclude that anticipated results have been achieved."

The statement had a touch of finality that showed the way the admiral's mind was working. He had always been against the operation, but had been overruled. So he had given it his very best and accomplished everything they asked of him. He had gotten away with it, but he certainly wasn't going to stretch his luck.

Commander Fuchida argued hard: there were still many attractive targets; there was virtually no defense left. Best of all, another raid might draw the carriers in. Then, if the Japanese returned by way of the Marshalls instead of going north, they might catch the carriers from behind. Somebody pointed out that this was impossible—the tankers had been sent north to meet the fleet and couldn't be redirected south in time. Fuchida wasn't at all deterred; well, they ought to attack Oahu again anyhow.

It was Admiral Kusaka who ended the discussion. Just before 1:30 P.M. the chief of staff turned to Nagumo and announced what he planned to do, subject to the commander's approval: "The attack is terminated. We are withdrawing."

"Please do," Nagumo replied.

In the home port at Kure, Admiral Yamamoto sensed it would happen. He sat impassively in the *Nagato*'s operations room while the staff buzzed with anticipation. The first attack was such a success everyone agreed there should be a second. Only the admiral remained noncommittal. He knew all too well the man in charge. Suddenly he muttered in almost a whisper: "Admiral Nagumo is going to withdraw."

Minutes later the news came through just as Yamamoto predicted. Far out in the Pacific the signal flags ran up on the *Akagi*'s yardarm, ordering a change in course. At 1:30 P.M. the great fleet swung about and headed back home across the northern Pacific.

THE MILK RUN

by James A. Michener

It must make somebody feel good. I guess that's why they do it. —The speaker was Lieut. Bus Adams, SBD pilot. He was nursing a bottle of whiskey in the Hotel De Gink on Guadal. He was sitting on an improvised chair and had his feet cocked up on a coconut stump the pilots used for a foot rest. He was handsome, blond, cocky. He came from nowhere in particular and wasn't sure where he would settle when the war was over. He was just another hot pilot shooting off between missions.

But why they do it—Bus went on—I don't rightfully know. I once figured it out this way: Say tomorrow we start to work over a new island, well, like Kuralei. Some day we will. On the first mission long-range bombers go over. Sixty-seven Japs come up to meet you. You lose four, maybe five bombers. Everybody is damn gloomy, I can tell you. But you also knock down some Nips.

Four days later you send over your next bombers. Again you take a pasting. "The suicide run!" the pilots call it. It's sure death! But you keep on knocking down Nips. Down they go, burning like the Fourth of July. And all this time you're pocking up their strips, plenty.

Finally the day comes when you send over twenty-seven bombers and they all come back. Four Zekes rise to get at you, but they are shot to hell. You bomb the strip and the installations until you are dizzy from flying in circles over the place. The next eight missions are without incident. You just plow in, drop your stuff, and sail on home.

Right then somebody names that mission, "The Milk Run!" And everybody feels pretty good about it. They even tell you about your assignments in an offhand manner: "Eighteen or twenty of you go over tomorrow and pepper Kuralei." They don't even brief you on it, and before long there's a gang around take-off time wanting to know if they can sort of hitch-hike a ride. They'd like to see Kuralei get it. So first thing you know, it's a real milk run, and you're in the tourist business!

Of course, I don't know who ever thought up that name for such missions. The Milk Run? Well, maybe it is like a milk run. For example, you fill up a milk truck with TNT and some special detonating caps that go off if anybody sneezes real loud. You tank up the truck with 120 octane gasoline that burns Pouf! Then instead of a steering wheel, you have three wheels, one for going sideways and one for up and down. You carry eight tons of your special milk when you know you should carry only five. At intersections other milk trucks like yours barge out at you, and you've got to watch them every minute. When you try to deliver this precious milk, little kids are all around you with .22's, popping at you. If one of the slugs gets you, bang! There you go, milk and all! And if you add to that the fact that you aren't really driving over land at all, but over the ocean, where if the slightest thing goes wrong, you take a drink . . . Well, maybe that's a milk run, but if it is, cows are sure raising hell these days!

Now get this right, I'm not bitching. Not at all. I'm damned glad to be the guy that draws the milk runs. Because in comparison with a real mission, jaunts like that really *are* milk runs. But if you get bumped off on one of them, why you're just as dead as if you were over Tokyo in a kite. It wasn't no milk run for you. Not that day.

You take my trip up to Munda two days ago. Now there was a real milk run. Our boys had worked that strip over until it looked like a guy with chicken pox, beriberi and the galloping jumps. Sixteen SBD's went up to hammer it again. Guess we must be about to land somewhere near there. Four of us stopped off to work over the Jap guns at Segi Point. We strafed them plenty. Then we went on to Munda.

Brother, it was a far cry from the old days. This wasn't The Slot any more. Remember when you used to bomb Kieta or Kahili or Vella or Munda? Opposition all the way. Japs coming at you from every angle. Three hundred miles of hell, with ugly islands on every side and Japs on every island. When I first went up there it was the toughest water fighting in the world, bar none. You were lucky to limp home.

Two days ago it was like a pleasure trip. I never saw the water so beautiful. Santa Ysabel looked like a summer resort somewhere off Maine. In the distance you could see Choiseul and right ahead was New Georgia. Everything was blue and green, and there weren't too many white ack-ack puffs. I tell you, I could make that trip every day with pleasure.

Segi Point was something to see. The Nips had a few antiaircraft there, but we came in low, zoomed up over the hills, peppered the devil out of them. Do you know Segi Passage? It's something to remember. A narrow passage with maybe four hundred small pinpoint islands in it. It's the only place out here I know that looks like the South Pacific. Watch! When we take Segi, I'm putting in for duty there. It's going to be cool there, and it looks like they got fruit around, too.

Well, after we dusted Segi off we flew low across New Georgia. Natives, and I guess some Jap spotters, watched us roar by. We were about fifty feet off the trees, and we rose and fell with the contours of the land. We broke radio silence, because the Japs knew we were coming. The other twelve were already over target. One buddy called out to me and showed me the waterfall on the north side of the island. It looked cool in the early morning sunlight. Soon we were over Munda. The milk run was half over.

I guess you heard what happened next. I was the unlucky guy. One lousy Jap hit all day, on that whole strike, and it had to be me that got it. It ripped through the rear gunner's seat and killed Louie on the spot. Never knew what hit him. I had only eighty feet elevation at the time, but kept her nose straight on. Glided into the water between Wanawana and Munda. The plane sank, of course, in about fifteen seconds. All shot to hell. Never even got a life raft out.

So there I was, at seven-thirty in the morning, with no raft, no nothing but a life belt, down in the middle of a Japanese channel with shore installations all around me. A couple of guys later on figured that eight thousand Japs must have been within ten miles of me, and I guess that not less than three thousand of them could see me. I was sure a dead duck.

My buddies saw me go in, and they set up a traffic circle around me. One Jap barge tried to come out for me, but you know Eddie Callstrom? My God! He shot that barge up until it splintered so high that even I could see it bust into pieces. My gang was over me for an hour and a half. By this time a radio message had gone back and about twenty New Zealanders in P-40's took over. I could see them coming a long way off. At first I thought they might be Jap planes. I never was too good at recognition.

Well, these New Zealanders are wild men. Holy hell! What they did! They would weave back and forth over me for a little while, then somebody would see something on Rendova or Kolombangara. Zoom! Off he would go like a madman, and pretty soon you'd see smoke going up. And if they didn't see anything that looked like a good target, they would leave the circle every few minutes anyway and raise hell among the coconut trees near Munda, just on chance there might be some Japs there. One group of Japs managed to swing a shore battery around to where they could pepper me. They sent out about seven fragmentation shells, and scared me half to death. I had to stay there in the water and take it.

That was the Japs' mistake. They undoubtedly planned to get my range and put me down, but on the first shot the New Zealanders went crazy. You would have thought I was a ninety million dollar battleship they were out to protect. They peeled off and dove that installation until even the trees around it fell down. They must have made the coral hot. Salt water had almost blinded me, but I saw one P-40 burst into flame and plunge deeply into the water off Rendova. No more Jap shore batteries opened up on me that morning.

Even so, I was having a pretty tough time. Currents kept shoving me on toward Munda. Japs were hidden there with rifles, and kept popping at me. I did my damnedest, but slowly I kept getting closer. I don't know, but I guess I swam twenty miles that day, all in the same place. Sometimes I would be so tired I'd just have to stop, but whenever I did, bingo! There I was, heading for the shore and the Japs. I must say, though, that Jap rifles are a damned fine spur to a man's ambitions.

When the New Zealanders saw my plight, they dove for that shore line like the hounds of hell. They chopped it up plenty. Jap shots kept coming after they left, but lots fewer than before.

I understand that it was about this time that the New Zealanders' radio message reached Admiral Kester. He is supposed to have studied the map a minute and then said, "Get that pilot out there. Use anything you need. We'll send a destroyer in, if necessary. But get him out. Our pilots are not expendable."

Of course, I didn't know about it then, but that was mighty fine doctrine. So far as I was concerned. And you know? When I watched those Marine F4U's coming in to take over the circle, I kind of thought maybe something like that was in the wind at headquarters. The New Zealanders pulled out. Before they went, each one in turn buzzed me. Scared me half to death! Then they zoomed Munda once more, shot it up some, and shoved off home.

The first thing the F4U's did was drop me a life raft. The first attempt was too far to leeward, and it drifted toward the shore. An energetic Jap tried to retrieve it, but one of our planes cut him to pieces. The next raft landed above me, and drifted toward me. Gosh, they're remarkable things. I pulled it out of the bag, pumped the handle of the CO_2 container, and the lovely yellow devil puffed right out.

But my troubles were only starting. The wind and currents shoved that raft toward the shore, but fast. I did everything I could to hold it back, and paddled until I could hardly raise my right arm. Then some F4U pilot with an IQ of about 420—boy, how I would like to meet that guy—dropped me his parachute. It was his only parachute and from then on he was upstairs on his own. But it made me a swell sea anchor. Drifting far behind in the water, it slowed me down. That Marine was a plenty smart cookie.

It was now about noon, and even though I was plenty scared, I was hungry. I broke out some emergency rations from the raft and had a pretty fine meal. The Jap snipers were falling short, but a long-range mortar started to get close. It fired about twenty shots. I didn't care. I had a full belly and a bunch of F4U's upstairs. Oh, those lovely planes! They went after that mortar like a bunch of bumblebees after a tramp. There was a couple of loud garummmphs, and we had no more trouble with that mortar. It must have been infuriating to the Japs to see me out there.

I judge it was about 1400 when thirty new F4U's took over. I wondered why they sent so many. This gang made even the New Zealanders look cautious. They just shot up everything that moved or looked as if it might once have wanted to move. Then I saw why.

A huge PBY, painted black, came gracefully up The Slot. I learned later that it was Squadron Leader Grant of the RNZAF detachment at Halavo. He had told headquarters that he'd land the Cat anywhere there was water. By damn, he did, too. He reconnoitered the bay twice, saw he would have to make his run right over Munda airfield, relayed that information to the F4U's and started down. His course took him over the heart of the Jap installations. He was low and big and a sure target. But he kept coming in. Before him, above him, and behind him a merciless swarm of thirty F4U's blazed away. Like tiny, cruel insects protecting a lumbering butterfly, the F4U's scoured the earth.

Beautifully the PBY landed. The F4U's probed the shoreline. Grant taxied his huge plane toward my small raft. The F4U's zoomed overhead at impossibly low altitudes. The PBY came alongside. The F4U's protected us. I climbed aboard and set the raft loose. Quickly the turret top was closed. The New Zealand gunner swung his agile gun about. There were quiet congratulations.

The next moment hell broke loose! From the shore one canny Jap let go with the gun he had been saving all day for such a moment. There was a ripping sound, and the port wing of the PBY was gone! The Jap had time to fire three more shells before the F4U's reduced him and his gun to rubble. The first two Jap shells missed, but the last one blew off the tail assembly. We were sinking.

Rapidly we threw out the rafts and as much gear as we could. I thought to save six parachutes, and soon nine of us were in Munda harbor, setting our sea anchors and looking mighty damned glum. Squadron leader Grant was particularly doused by the affair. "Second PBY I've lost since I've been out here," he said mournfully.

Now a circle of Navy F6F's took over. I thought they were more conservative than the New Zealanders and the last Marine gang. That was until a Jap battery threw a couple of close ones. I had never seen an F6F in action before. Five of them hit that battery like Jack Dempsey hitting Willard. The New Zealanders, who had not seen the F6F's either, were amazed. It looked more like a medium bomber than a fighter. Extreme though our predicament was, I remember that we carefully appraised the new F6F.

"The Japs won't be able to stop that one!" an officer said. "It's got too much."

"You mean they can fly that big fighter off a ship?" another inquired.

"They sure don't let the yellow barstards get many shots in, do they?"

We were glad of that. Unless the Jap hit us on first shot, he was done. He didn't get a second chance. We were therefore dismayed when half of the F6F's pulled away toward Rendova. We didn't see them any more. An hour later, however, we saw thirty new F4U's lollygagging through the sky Rendova way. Four sped on ahead to relieve the fine, battle-proven F6F's who headed down The Slot. We wondered what was up.

And then we saw! From some secret nest in Rendova, the F4U's were bringing out two PT Boats! They were going to come right into Munda harbor, and to hell with the Japs! Above them the lazy Marines darted and bobbed, like dolphins in an aerial ocean.

You know the rest. It was Lt. Comdr. Charlesworth and his PT's.

Used to be on Tulagi. They hang out somewhere in the Russells now. Something big was on, and they had sneaked up to Rendova, specially for an attack somewheres. But Kester shouted, "To hell with the attack. We've gone this far. Get that pilot out of there." He said they'd have to figure out some other move for the big attack they had cooking. Maybe use destroyers instead of PT's.

I can't tell you much more. A couple of savvy Japs were waiting with field pieces, just like the earlier one. But they didn't get hits. My God, did the Marines in their F4U's crucify those Japs? That was the last thing I saw before the PT's pulled me aboard. Twelve F4U's diving at one hillside.

Pass me that bottle, Tony. Well, as you know, we figured it all out last night. We lost a P-40 and a PBY. We broke up Admiral Kester's plan for the PT Boats. We wasted the flying time of P-40's, F4U's, and F6F's like it was dirt. We figured the entire mission cost not less than $600,000. Just to save one guy in the water off Munda. I wonder what the Japs left to rot on Munda thought of that? $600,000 for one pilot. —Bus Adams took a healthy swig of whiskey. He lolled back in the tail-killing chair of the Hotel De Gink.—But it's sure worth every cent of the money. If you happen to be that pilot.

DROPPING THE BOMB OVER HIROSHIMA

by Joseph L. Marx

34°17′N, 132°22′E	Time: 09:15	Head: 265
Airspeed: 200	Temp: −22°C	Alt: 31,600

The *Enola Gay* was so close to schedule it was almost uncanny. Colonel Tibbets, the perfectionist, had trained himself and the rest of the outfit so thoroughly that they were not surprised when they realized that everything had been executed precisely according to plan. They had come to expect it. At 08:50, when they passed over the tip of Shikoku Island, *The Great Artiste* dropped back about 1,000 yards, and Captain Marquardt's #91, which had already fallen a little behind, made a full 360 degree turn to let the other two pull farther ahead.

Tibbets and Lewis took over from the automatic pilot, and the crew members, with the exception of Jake Beser, all pulled on their cumbersome flak suits. Jake had made his last check of the Japanese radar and radio wavelengths and he had gone forward to tell Jeppson, Parsons and Tibbets that there would be no interference. He didn't get into his flak suit but he did drape it around himself. "I never could wear the thing; it was too heavy to move around in," he says.

Ted Van Kirk made a final check with Stiborik's radar (the two calculations agreed) for wind speed and direction, and the plane's airspeed and ground speed, which he fed to Tibbets and Lewis and Ferebee. Van Kirk carefully noted in his log that there were eight large ships in view in the harbor at Hiroshima.

Colonel Tibbets' voice came over the intercom: "We are about to start the bomb run. Put on your goggles and place them on your forehead. When you hear the tone signal, pull them down over your eyes and leave them there until after the flash."

The men on the three planes had been warned many times not to look at the detonation without their goggles. They were special Polaroid glasses, shaped like welder's goggles to prevent the light from entering from above, below, or the sides. Light could reach the eye only through the lens, and the lens had quinine crystals to keep out all but purple light. The men put on their goggles, but Major Ferebee, the bombardier, had to keep his off.

This was Tom Ferebee's moment. Except for a few moments during the bomb run, he had been taken "along for the ride." Ferebee was a big, good-looking, dark haired man of twenty-six who sported a bristling black "overseas moustache." He was born and raised in Mocksville, a small town in North Carolina's central hills, about thirty miles southwest of Winston-Salem.

Tom Ferebee's ambition had been to be a baseball player. He was a pretty good shortstop and had had a spring tryout with a major-league team. Branch Rickey had been interested in him and had advised him to finish his education. Ferebee never did get back to professional baseball and has always wondered whether he would have made the grade. The war came along and he joined the Air Force, and after completing his training, he found himself flying as a B-17 bombardier with Tibbets and Van Kirk over Europe and North Africa.

After sixty-three combat missions, he returned with them to the States to be an instructor. Ferebee was tapped by Colonel Tibbets to come to Wendover as group bombardier for the 509th. He was one of the men who had to know something about the weapon. He had to know why it was expected to be dropped visually from 30,000 feet or better. Normal bombardiers' training was considered complete after twenty-five drops, twenty visual and five by radar. The bombardiers of the 509th Composite Group had a different instruction schedule. They were already trained in the craft when they started and they made as many as thirty visual drops a week.

The bombing on the 509th's Special Bombing Mission #13 was routine. Ferebee was considered a crack bombardier, nerveless and impossible to rattle. He claims that there were others equally qualified who would have done the job just as well. Nevertheless, he had been chosen for the job and he did it perfectly. He makes it sound simple:

"Since I knew what we were actually carrying and what the effects could be, naturally I was concerned that we deliver it in the proper place. Fortunately, we had a very good flight to the target area. And the rest of the crew that were concerned with the bomb lined me up. My part of the mission was easy and I was able to see the target area some distance out. I was briefed that I had to bomb visually, that I couldn't bomb any other way."

The weather report had indicated that they would be able to bomb visually, and approaching the city they saw the same hole in the cloud cover that Major Eatherly had noted. Each member of the crew performed a previously assigned task. Bob Caron is not certain, but he thinks he remembers saying a prayer. Tibbets and Lewis flew the plane. Duzenbury checked the engines and gear to make sure that nothing would prevent the craft from becoming a smooth, level, even-flying platform for bombing. The *Enola Gay* had to meet all these requirements because it was being used to aim a five-ton projectile at a speed of four and a half miles a minute from a height of five miles, in order that the bomb would detonate less than 2,000 feet above a specific target with an error of less than 250 yards.

Stiborik watched his radar screen. Caron and Shumard watched for possible enemy interceptors. Van Kirk checked his navigation again, but there was no need to; the destination was visual now. Dick Nelson wondered what kind of a message he would soon be sending back.

Morris Jeppson checked his console for the last time and signaled to Captain Parsons that everything inside the bomb was functioning as it should. And then Lieutenant Jeppson did something that might have alarmed the rest of the crew if they had been paying close attention to him. After buckling his parachute on his harness, as the others did, he got his oxygen mask ready and attached it to the emergency oxygen bottle. "It suddenly occurred to me that the blast from this bomb might blow out the windows of the pressurized cabin. If that happened, I didn't want to be caught without oxygen."

Captain Parsons went forward to tell Tibbets that the bomb was in order, and he stood behind the colonel in the cockpit. Soon, through the huge hole in the clouds, they saw the outline of a city that was familiar to them from many aerial photos and charts. Tibbets asked Parsons whether he agreed that they were over the target, and Captain Parsons said that he did.

At 09:12 they came to the I.P. (Initial Point, for starting a bomb run) exactly on schedule. The aiming point on the ground was fifteen and one-half miles ahead. Major Ferebee put his left eye to the Norden bomb sight.

In a bomber, once the I.P. has been reached, the bombardier usually takes over the plane. But Ferebee and Tibbets had been working together for a long time and had developed their own system. When they operated together, the bombardier did not take over the craft until the last ninety seconds.

Ferebee called a minute adjustment to Tibbets, who answered with the customary "Roger."

At 09:13:30, Tibbets called out to Ferebee, "It's all yours."

Everyone waited and looked. This was the climax of months of training, and what should have been dramatic seemed strangely quiet and anticlimactic. They felt almost as though they were watching something outside themselves that had been preordained. There was a feeling of unreality in this smooth, on-schedule flight and in the peaceful-looking city basking in the sun below. Only a few wispy clouds interfered with their view.

The *Enola Gay*'s course was 265 degrees, only 5 degrees south of due west. They were almost six miles above sea level and approaching their target at a ground speed of 285 miles per hour. The scene below had been studied so intensively that it was as familiar to the men as their places on the plane. And to Tom Ferebee, his face fastened to the eyepiece of his bomb sight, it was particularly familiar.

The city unrolled under his scanning eye just exactly as it was expected to. At 09:14:17, the aiming point (the center of a bridge) appeared on the crosshairs of his sight. He yelled out that he had it, and he started the automatic process that would release the bomb in sixty seconds.

Forty-five seconds later, the radio tone began, signifying that the bomb would drop in exactly fifteen seconds. The men on the *Enola Gay, The Great Artiste,* and #91 heard the continuous radio tone and pulled down their goggles. Hundreds of miles away, *Jabbit III, Straight Flush,* and *Full House,* flying home to Tinian, picked up the tone on their radios and knew what it meant. Even farther away, on Iwo Jima, Captain McKnight, sitting in the cockpit of *Top Secret,* heard it on his radio and called out the news to the members of his crew standing around the reserve plane.

At 09:15:17, responding to the programmed command set in motion a minute earlier by Ferebee, the *Enola Gay*'s pneumatically operated bomb-bay doors sprang open and Little Boy #1 tumbled out. Ferebee cried out that it was clear and Ted Van Kirk observed in his log: "Bomb away."

The instant the bomb left the bay it broke an electrical contact and the radio tone stopped. At the same moment the plane jumped up, suddenly five tons lighter.

Ferebee watched the bomb. It fell broadside at first and then, as the carefully engineered tail fins caught the rarefied air, it straightened out for a nose-first dive.

When the radio tone stopped, *The Great Artiste*'s bombardier, Tex Beahan, hit the switch that opened the bomb-bay doors in his plane, releasing three instrument packages which were soon swinging on their individual parachutes as they floated earthward.

As soon as the drop began, the two planes went into their appointed maneuvers. The *Enola Gay* made a sharp diving turn to the right, *The Great Artiste* a matching turn to the left. As his plane turned in the thoroughly rehearsed maneuver, Bob Lewis scanned the panel before him and realized that he couldn't see the instruments at all. He snapped up his Polaroid glasses. He knew that he was supposed to have a grace period of forty-three seconds before the flash.

The plane made a turn of 155 degrees and dropped at least 1,000 feet, picking up speed and giving "tail-end Charlie" Bob Caron a roller-coaster ride. Many of the men counted to themselves as the plane sped away, trying to get out of the danger zone before the blast. The scientists had predicted that the plane would not be in danger as long as it got far enough away. But only one atomic bomb had ever been detonated before this one, and none had ever been dropped from a plane. The scientists could not be certain.

In their nervousness or hurry, the men counted quickly.

Jeppson remembers that when his own personal countdown reached forty-three, all he could think was, It's a dud.

Bob Caron, the official observer, had the best view. As tail gunner, he was facing back toward where they had just been. Bob has said that although he had nothing to do with the bomb, he tensed as the others did when the craft went into the bomb run. Bob could hear the fifteen-second warning signal before the bomb was dropped, and the startling silence as the release of the bomb broke the electrical contact.

The plane went into its predetermined escape maneuver, which Bob Caron described as "a right-hand diving turn at the limit of the plane's capabilities or even possibly exceeding its limits, its red-line limits. The turn really threw the tail around and you got a lot of side Gs, vertical Gs, and just plain Gs being thrown at you from every direction." It was as though the big plane were playing snap-the-whip with him at the tip.

As soon as they settled into their new northeasterly course, Colonel Tibbets asked him on the intercom whether he had seen anything yet. Bob had to answer in the negative. When he looked back and a little to the right, he could not see the falling bomb. In fact, wearing his special goggles, he couldn't really see anything at all.

Then suddenly the world dissolved in a bright purple flame.

Bob's eyes closed instinctively with the flash. I must be blinded, he thought, and remembered that when he had looked through the glasses at the sun a second before he had seen only a faint light. "It was too much for me. I forgot to report it on the intercom. Besides, it wasn't necessary, no one could have missed that, whether or not he was looking."

Bob Caron had every right to say that. He had looked directly into the center of an atomic detonation. In a space of time so small it could only be reckoned in milliseconds and measured electronically, he had seen the release of a power that generated, literally instantaneously, a temperature of one hundred million degrees.

Tom Ferebee, who had had to remove his goggles for his bomb sight, forgot to put them back on. To him, the flash was "like an enormous flashbulb going off in my face."

The mushroom cloud began to form almost at once. But first came the shock wave. Bob Caron was the first person to see and try to describe this phenomenon coming toward him in a plane. It looked like a shimmering heat wave, a visible reaction to the tremendous concussion. He could see the wave because the detonation forced the atmosphere violently away from it, outward in an expanding circle like the ripples caused by a stone dropped into a still pond. Behind the air compressed by the blast was a vacuum which condensed the moisture in the air and made it visible.

The scientists had estimated that the shock wave would reach the plane about a minute after the bomb was dropped. Before the minute elapsed, however, the nose of the *Enola Gay* was pulled up and the plane was traveling considerably slower. There would be less strain on the craft's frame at a slower speed, and the shock wave, traveling at about twelve miles a minute, would go past the plane faster.

When the wave hit the plane, Captain Parsons called out that it was flak. But then he realized what it was and said that it wasn't flak at all but the shock wave.

The force of the shock wave was like a burst of flak just beneath the plane. No matter where he was stationed on the plane, each man felt as though the antiaircraft burst had exploded just below or next to his place. Bob Lewis said it felt as though some giant were hitting the plane with a telegraph pole, and later Capt. George Marquardt said he had the feeling that a huge hand had struck the plane right next to him.

Before they could settle down, Caron called out on the intercom that another one was coming. This was the "echo wave" predicted by the scientists. It was caused by the reflection from the earth's surface of the first shock wave. It was a much milder disturbance.

Eleven men in the plane felt the shock wave with surprise, even though the scientists had warned them of it. Bob Caron, in the tail, wasn't surprised. Perhaps this was because he could see it coming. "Back in the tail where I sat," he said, "it felt like the usual lumps you get when you're shaken around."

Again Colonel Tibbets called back to ask if he could see anything yet, and again Caron had to say no. Then he saw the mushroom cloud and called out that it was coming.

"It seemed to be coming at us, but of course it was a good distance away," Caron said. "I don't think I was afraid. It was interesting and awesome but more of a spectacle than something directly frightening to me. I had this little hand camera, a K-20 with a pistol grip, and I was trying to get pictures with it. My view was partially blocked by the turret, so I asked the colonel to turn a couple of degrees to the right. He did and I started shooting pictures, shooting 'em like mad, out of the side turret window. I found out later that most of my pictures were of the framework of the turret, but they did get some, seven I think, that were satisfactory.

"I kept shooting pictures and trying to get the mess down over the city. All the while I was describing this on the intercom, doing the narration and description so that those who didn't have as good a view as I did could get the picture. The mushroom itself was a spectacular sight, a bubbling mass of purple-gray smoke and you could see it had a red core to it and everything was burning inside. As we got farther away, we could see the base of the mushroom and below we could see what looked like a few-hundred-foot layer of debris and smoke and what have you.

"I was trying to describe the mushroom, this turbulent mass. I saw fires springing up in different places, like flames shooting up on a bed of coals. I was asked to count them. I said, 'Count them?' Hell, I gave up when there were about fifteen, they were coming too fast to count. I can still see it—that mushroom and that turbulent mass—it looked like lava or molasses covering the whole city, and it seemed to flow outward up into the foothills where the little valleys would come into the plain, with fires starting up all over, so pretty soon it was hard to see anything because of the smoke."

The reaction of the men to the scene was characteristic in some instances. In others it was unexpected. Bob Lewis is reported to have said two things and he isn't sure that he said either. According to some he said, "My God, look at that sonofabitch go." Others report that he said, "My God. What have we done?" That, at least, is written in the log he was keeping for Bill Laurence.

This, he says, wasn't a statement but a question. It wasn't meant to ask what have we on the *Enola Gay* done, but what have we, mankind, made that can produce such utter devastation? "The effect was so spectacular it was impossible not to be stunned," he said. "And what shook me up as much as anything was that Captain Parsons, calm, quiet, and knowing more about the bomb than any of us, seemed to be as amazed as we were."

Captain Parsons' assistant, Lieutenant Jeppson, kept his eyes on the console for a time, even though the intricate wiring system was no longer connected to anything and the rows of lights were now blank. The service magazine *Yank* reported that he said, "Jesus Christ, if people knew what we were doing, we could have sold tickets for $100,000!"

Colonel Tibbets' reaction was primarily of relief. "We felt the blast about a minute after it occurred. We had gone into the planned 155-degree turn, and we continued right on around after the shock wave hit us and made a 180-degree turn so we'd come right back, headed at the target again to take a look at it. We wanted to see it from two points of view. One, to see what happened from an atomic explosion; also, we had cameras and photographic equipment to take pictures that could be returned to the Intelligence people for their analysis.

"I had been expecting the shock wave, having been told by the scientists it would be coming. It's much like sitting or standing and waiting, knowing somebody's going to slip up behind you and hit you on the back. There was a definite feeling of relief after we dropped the bomb. Here was the successful climax to about eleven months of awfully hard and demanding work."

Jake Beser had a similar feeling. "In a way, it was a big relief. There had been a lot of tension in the buildup of this thing. You must remember we didn't know until just a few days before the mission that the weapon had been successfully tested in the States. When the shock wave came up to our level it rattled the skin of the airplane like flak, and there was all kinds of excitement, talking back and forth. Paul announced on the intercom, 'Fellows, you have just dropped the first atomic bomb in history.' There were so many things happening and guys were running around to the windows.

"When the colonel put the plane into the planned maneuver it was a pretty tight turn and the centrifugal force had me pretty well pinned down to the seat until we broke out of it. Then when I got to the window all I could see was the fire and corruption down below; I couldn't see much of Hiroshima. The cloud was already up by the time I got to where I could see. That city was burning for all she was worth. It looked like . . . well, did you ever go to the beach and stir up the sand in shallow water and see it all billow up? That's what it looked like to me."

Bob Shumard, also in the rear compartment, remembers the brightness of the flash. "These special Polaroid goggles we had, they seemed to black out everything so you couldn't see anything at all. But the light was so intense when that bomb was detonated that it even pierced those glasses. I turned toward the detonation and it seemed that everything was coming right back up to us. Of course, we were very high but it seemed like everything was erupting right back at us. I was scared. It's just like a real close flak burst, it scares you, you know. It was a boiling action and full of all kinds of colors, but you could tell there was nothing but death in that cloud."

The other man in the rear compartment, Joe Stiborik, had not been looking for the flash. "I'd been instructed to watch my radarscope and see if there was any reaction on the scope. But in the turn, the radar set went out. There was no reaction on the scope at all, it went blank. Later, when I was certain nothing would appear on the scope, I was able to look out at the city but all I could see was fire and smoke, mostly smoke."

Ted Van Kirk's first reaction was rather like Tibbets': "What a relief. We'd gotten the thing there and we'd done the mission we started out to do. The task we'd been assigned had been completed successfully. This was very important.

"Thirty seconds or so after the explosion, we turned the plane so we could take a look and see what happened. I think the thing that amazed us most was the cloud that formed and was well above our altitude, over 30,000 feet. The entire city of Hiroshima was more or less covered with black smoke. I thought it resembled a cauldron of boiling black oil. It blotted out any detailed observation of the damage to the city."

M/Sgt. Wyatt Duzenbury, the flight engineer, was concerned with the performance of his craft and its safe return. Sergeant Duzenbury was born in Lansing, Michigan, April 6, 1913. He was thirty-two and the oldest Air Force man on the plane. He had joined the Air Force in 1942, and after the usual basic training and sorting-out period had been designated as a flight-engineer trainee. He checked out as one in 1942 and had been one ever since.

Sergeant Duzenbury had done test work on the B-29 with Colonel Tibbets and Captain Lewis when it was still in its experimental classification. He probably knew the inner workings of the craft as well as any flight engineer in the service, and he was one of the original men selected by Colonel Tibbets when the 509th was organized. In addition to his knowledge of the plane, Duzenbury's calmness under pressure was undoubtedly a factor in his selection.

The flight engineer on a plane is rather like the chief engineer on a ship. The pilot and copilot give the orders, set the speed, rate of climb, etc., and with material furnished by the navigator they select the course. The flight engineer sees that the engines are running properly—not using too much fuel, not overheating, each delivering the proper power—and that all the allied systems in the plane are functioning as they should.

Of his own experience on the flight Duzenbury said: "We had been in training for a number of months. We had something unusual, and we didn't know what it was. It was different from the normal units, 500 and 1,000 pounders. We knew we were being groomed for something special. It was a big project and the amount of security was extreme. I had no idea that I was going to be on the drop until we were briefed for the mission. The briefing didn't tell us what it was. We saw the picture of the bomb that exploded at Alamogordo, so we knew what we could expect. The briefing told us how to act at the time of the explosion.

"We were told about the light. They issued us the special kinds of goggles, blackout goggles to protect our eyes from the tremendous amount of light. When the drop was made, you first felt the release of the weight. My personal feelings at the time were how this would affect the operation of the aircraft. That was my primary purpose, to follow my instruments, and my engines, and to see how the blast might affect them. I had no idea what would happen.

"I was at the flight engineer's panel, and in the B-29 we rode backward. I saw that initial flash of light. I had the goggles on, and was constantly opening and closing them, so I could keep track of the instruments. When you engineer an airplane, you can't completely ignore the instrument panel, you keep checking it. I would flash the goggles open long enough to take a look at the instrument panel and then close them again. After the initial flash, I took them off.

"We felt a couple of distinct shock waves. I had a hatch by the right side of the airplane but my position overlooked the right wing. The only thing that I observed was that when we turned, I saw the mushroom cloud which was up to our altitude shortly after the bomb was detonated. That's the only thing I observed, not the actual detonation of the bomb."

Dick Nelson, the radio operator, said: "I didn't have a window, but there were enough openings in the aircraft to see the flash. By the time I got to a window, there wasn't much to see below. The whole town was a mass of dust and flames and smoke. The most vivid thing, the most awesome, was the tremendous cloud rising from it. When you realize that when an ordinary explosive is dropped from that altitude, you see hardly any smoke—but there was a cloud so large and so high it was almost up to us."

While they were still cruising along, broadside to the city, Dick Nelson had some work to do. First, he had to send back the usual strike report prepared by Tibbets and Ferebee.

It was a perfectly normal, brief strike report, and it said that their primary target had been bombed visually with good results, one-tenth cloud cover, no fighter opposition, no flak.

While Nelson was sending this message, Captain Parsons was working on his own report. He tried to estimate the effect of the detonation and to compare it with the test at Alamogordo. The standard strike report did not provide the detailed information that informed military men, scientists and statesmen on Tinian, General Groves and his staff at the Pentagon, and Secretary Stimson and President Truman were awaiting.

Parsons wrote out his message to General Farrell in the agreed-upon code and gave it to Nelson to transmit: "82 V 670. Able, Line 1, Line 2, Line 6, Line 9."

On Tinian General Farrell and the men waiting with him received the strike report and learned that the bomb had been dropped. Then Captain Parsons' message came in and Farrell translated it quickly for the others: "Clear cut, successful in all respects. Visual effects greater than Trinity. Hiroshima. Conditions normal in airplane following delivery, proceeding to regular base."

Vietnam
THE RESCUE
by Walter J. Boyne and Steven L. Thompson

November 1971
Bien Hoa AB
Vietnam

He enjoyed running his fingers over the crudely carved wooden sign on his desk. Against a background of command-pilot wings complete with star and wreath, the first line read: MAJOR LAWRENCE A. WHITE, USAF; the second, OPERATIONS OFFICER; the third, 32 AIR TRANSPORT SQUADRON; the fourth, VNAF.

It was damn near a command. He'd never been so happy, reliving the role he had played the first time he'd come to Vietnam. They had been sent over to supplement the Vietnamese efforts to defend themselves, to train them. By 1965 the Americans had taken over, reduced the Vietnamese to a subordinate role. Now "Vietnamization" was in full swing, and Larry was back training Vietnamese. This time, though, he was a wheel, with an office.

The Vietnamese had almost reversed their roles. Then they'd been young, terribly eager but relatively untrained. Now they were older, no longer eager, but excellent pilots. He flew as many missions as he could, sometimes as instructor pilot, sometimes just along for the ride.

The airplane was better too; he'd loved the old C-47, but now they had Fairchild C-123s, twin piston-engine high-wing transports fitted with a J47 jet engine under each wing. The jets gave plenty of power to get in and get out, and the way the flak was building up in the South, you had to have speed to survive.

He wondered how many wood, screen, and corrugated tin shacks exactly like his own dotted Vietnam. It didn't matter, here he was king, this was his castle. In the corner were two more ceramic Vietnamese elephants to mail back to Micky; she had plenty, he knew, but they were great gifts, and she always loved anything he sent. Nowadays the system was so pat he just put an address on them, didn't even wrap them, and they'd get through, unharmed.

The mission today would be like the missions yesterday, the missions for the past week. The North Vietnamese had a garrison surrounded at Kham Loc. The only supplies the garrison could get were parachuted in from the C-123s and C-130s. The planes couldn't land anymore; the fire was too hot. A mixed Vietnamese and USAF ground control team had been calling in the support fire from the F-4s, A-1s, and B-52s. They were supposed to have been evacuated last night. Hulks of burned-out transports lined the wretched pierced-steel plank runway, too damaged even to merit mortar fire from the enemy. When they air dropped supplies at least half landed in enemy hands, but it didn't matter. Time was running out; it was Stalingrad, Dien Bien Phu again, on a smaller scale.

He met the mission commander and his copilot at the airplane; he glanced at their mission folder. Their call sign was "Victor One," another of the war's little ironies. The two pilots said they had preflighted, but White walked around it just the same, just checking. He'd stayed alive a long time, just checking. He spent some time in the cavernous fuselage, making sure everything was rigged right for a quick release. The Vietnamese airmen were quiet, surly; they resented his looking.

The two Vietnamese pilots were in their seats, starting engines, when he crawled aboard. Their methods were strangely similar, strangely different from the U.S. types, who were less precise, more relaxed, but exacting. The Vietnamese formally parroted the checklist and response, but seemed indifferent, aloof, apt to overlook something in their coldness. He watched them, sometimes reaching surreptitiously down to place a switch in the right position after it had been called and responded to, ignored. He had to do it covertly; to call it out would cause a loss of face.

The flight to Kham Loc was easy except for the radio. The VC were making a final attack, and the air was filled with cries for support from fighter bombers and B-52s. The Vietnamese pilots looked worried; the flak was reported to be heavy.

There was a circus of aircraft on station. Some had already dropped; he saw a C-130 trailing off in the distance, two engines out on one side, streaming smoke. Black smoke boiling off the end of the runway showed where something had gone in; it was JP-4-type smoke, so it was either a fighter or a C-130.

The radio chatter was intense; suddenly a voice familiar from their past few days' missions came on. "Hey, anybody, this is Golfball, we're still here, over."

"Roger, Golfball, this is Hector Two. Where are you?"

"We're holed up here down by the second C-130, the one with the fuselage burned out, about fifteen hundred feet from the south end of the runway."

"Roger, stand by."

"Victor One, go to Echo channel."

Larry watched as the pilot switched over. He tapped him on the shoulder, waved his mike; this was no time for a language barrier.

"Roger, Hector, Victor One."

"Did you hear Golfball?"

"Roger."

"Look, I'm too heavy to make a stop and go there, the strip's too short. By the time I taxied back and turned around, they would have nailed me with mortars. Do you think you can do a short field landing, take Golf on, and get out?"

"Let me look."

There was about four thousand feet of runway, according to the chart, but it was pockmarked with shell holes. Still, if he offloaded the cargo, flew right at the stall, and used full reverse just before he hit, it might be possible. Provided they didn't shoot him out of the air.

"Hector, Victor One. I'm just going to jettison this stuff at altitude; if I make a low pass and they hit me, I couldn't make a try at it. Then I'll try. You transmit to Golf to watch and run to get in about a hundred yards from where they are now; I won't be able to stop any slower than that. Tell them it's a one-time deal; if they don't make it I wouldn't be able to try again, because they'll be alert. First time we might surprise them, over."

"Roger, Victor, good show. We'll watch what you are doing and try to divert some more fighter bombers in to suppress the flak."

Larry had been watching the VNAF pilots; they understood what he had said, and didn't like it. They argued about jettisoning the supplies at altitude, saying the troops needed them. Finally they gave in, flew a pattern at eleven thousand feet, dropped the cargo. It spread out over the jungle; probably 10 percent or less landed in the drop zone.

Larry said, "Let me in the left seat."

The VNAF pilot shook his head, reefed the control around to leave.

White pulled his .38 pistol out of his pocket, jammed it against the aircraft commander's head. "Get your ass out of that seat or I'll blow your fucking brains out."

The copilot moved as if to intervene and Larry cocked the pistol. "Move you bastard, I don't have time to fuck with you."

The man slipped out of his straps, and went to the back of the cockpit.

"Hector, Victor One."

"Ah roger, Victor, go."

"Hector, I'm going to put this mother in the stall mode and drop straight down off the end of the runway, as straight and as slow as I can. When I get low I'll pop the gear and try to stick it on the end of the runway. Is Golfball ready?"

"Roger, they're ready; Charlie's been probing for them with mortars."

White went through the drill of lighting up the J47 jet engines; he slowed the C-123 down, bled the airspeed off, dropped full flaps. Unused to the treatment, the airplane groaned, and all the sounds of air whistling changed; it felt different in White's hands, flying only reluctantly, ready to fall.

The Vietnamese aircraft commander had disappeared, back into the hold; he was probably lying down next to the landing gear area, looking for protection from the spray of flak he knew was coming. The copilot looked more angry than scared.

White pulled the throttles to idle; as the nose dropped, he kept trimming back to keep the nose from pitching forward. The C-123 began to fall like an elevator, and now the flak picked up and began hammering it. He could hear the hits, but all the gauges looked good.

The jungle came up like the bottom of a roller-coaster track; he thought he was too low, added power, fought the trim that bucked the nose upward, realized he was too high, jerked the throttles back. The copilot had turned his head away. A hailstorm of small-arms fire rose up; it was like flying into a shooting gallery.

At the tree line he poured on power, dragged it over, chopped the throttles, and hit the runway hard; he threw the engines into reverse, blowing up a cloud of dust and smoke. Ahead, mortar rounds came toward him. He heard the back door open; the aircraft commander ran forward, called, "All aboard, we go!"

The engines, shuddering from the hard reversal, worked back into full thrust. He saw a line of mortar shells walking down the side of the runway, straight toward him. The C-123 broke ground between impacts, the mortar bursts bracketing it nose and tail.

"Good show, Victor, that's a fucking Medal of Honor if I ever saw one!"

The trembling set in on the way back. The crew from Golfball, two USAF officers and an enlisted man, along with two Vietnamese, came forward. The Golfball C.O. slapped him on the back.

"Goddamn it Major, you saved our ass! They aren't going to be able to hold for the rest of the day. We'd have been on the way to the Hanoi Hilton tonight." Even the Vietnamese crew was jubilant.

When they landed, White walked around the 123. It was ripped with shrapnel; the fuselage was punctured with two rows of holes that must have been 20 mm, but hadn't exploded on contact, entering high on the right and leaving through the roof. There were small-arms hits everywhere, and some skin torn loose by shrapnel of some sort, probably from a mortar round. But there wasn't a hole in anything vital; the plane could be fixed with sheet metal and rivets. It was a tank.

He spent the afternoon getting congratulatory calls and telegrams. He got a personal call from General Martell, the Seventh Air Force commander, telling him he was being put in for the Medal of Honor.

Next morning some different calls came in.

"Major White? This is Colonel Hansen at Seventh. Let me congratulate you on your rescue yesterday; it was brilliant."

"Thank you, sir."

"But I've got a problem; I've got a complaint from the commander of the VNAF that you pulled a gun on Major Ky, said you'd blow his brains out."

White gulped. "Yes sir, I believe I specified his 'fucking brains.' "

"Don't screw around, White, this is serious. They want you court-martialed; word around here is that Ky claims to be some kind of distant relative of Nguyen Cao Ky. I don't know what we can do to stop it."

White was furious. "The man should have been shot; he was preparing to fly away, desert the scene of combat."

"You have any witnesses?"

White blanched; he had been the only American on board when it happened. He hadn't even told the Golfball team about it; he didn't want to blow his own horn.

"No, sir, but that's what happened. Why else would I have to use a gun?"

"You sit tight, son; I'm putting you under house arrest right now. There'll be a team in a chopper in about forty minutes. You pack your gear."

White slammed the phone across the room. He didn't even know who would do the court-martialing, the USAF or the Vietnamese. He could win the USAF fight, but if they let the Vietnamese do it, he'd be in a tiger cage on some godforsaken island prison.

The chopper came in, complete with two security policemen in chrome helmets. Hansen was with them, wearing a sidearm, waving a warrant.

They threw White's bags on and scrambled away in less than ten minutes. Hansen reached in his pocket and pulled out a pint bottle of Jack Daniel's. "Take a pull on this, Major, you've been through hell in the last twenty-four hours."

"What's going to happen to me, Colonel?"

"Well, we're going to land at Ton Son Nuit right next to a Navy P-3. You are going straight to Clark Field, and then you are going home. Fuck those guys and their court martial. You are a goddamn hero, and if we can't get you a Medal of Honor, General Martell says he'll personally get you an Air Force Cross."

Relief swept across White; the only thing he regretted was losing the nearest thing to a command he ever had. Well, he had his wooden nameplate tucked into the B-4 bags; the ceramic elephants were lost, but he knew Micky would understand.

FIFTEEN SAMS FOR GEENO

by Jack Broughton

As we took the belated and hesitant step of pressing the attack against North Vietnam's symbolic experiment in industrialization, the Thai Nguyen steel complex, my buddy Geeno was notified that his next assignment in the States would take him back into research, back to the big puzzle palace. Although Geeno was one of our more aggressive leaders and gave it all he had every time, he had already gone the advanced education route to the big degree that led him to a strictly support position. Only the real-life facts of the Vietnamese operation—the Defense Department does not like to call it a pilot shortage in so many words—had allowed him to escape to the fighter pilot's primary job of driving a machine in combat. Now, as the war heated up, he was not too pleased with the prospect of heading back into the administrative jungle. How much that thought pressed him to overextend himself while he had the chance I shall never know, but he sure pulled it all out.

The personnel mill seemed to be constantly out of rig, not sending enough qualified pilots down the pipeline, or once in a great while sending too many; and there is a never-ending flow of people like Geeno who are unhappy with the friendly personnel officer and their new assignments. Some of the reasons why it works like this make sense of a sort. Others don't.

You can't have the same younger people fighting the battle interminably or they run out of longevity. Even if they don't, you can only put a guy in the way of getting killed so many times before he loses his enthusiasm for the role. And besides, you get just plain tired. So you replace them with older men pulled in from some remote installation who once flew fighters or maybe never did but wear the set of feathers on the chest anyway. Now, even the most single-minded fighter pilot will admit that someone has to fill these vacated spots, but that is a lot less easy to accept when it applies to you as an individual. The real catch, however, is that it takes a different breed of cat to drive a fighter properly. For years we have shuffled our pilots into jobs that have little or nothing to do with combat, but they aren't standardized components and they don't convert back from a desk or a transport simply because a computer spits out a set of orders. Conversion or retraining takes time; often, it doesn't work. Aging, too, is a factor that should not be ignored where it means that the pilot has been forced to lose the razor-edge of frequent and demanding single-seat flight. If some of our best people are lots older than they were back in Korea and still going strong, it's usually because they have been close enough to the machines to keep their hand in, growing and aging with the machinery, learning to use to perfection every assist the system affords.

All of this is by way of trying to give you some idea of how Geeno, and too many others like him, felt as he neared the end of his tour. When I got to the base, he was the operations officer of one of the squadrons and, in conjunction with his strong and feisty squadron commander, ran about as tight a ship as can be run. Trying to get that pair to bend gracefully to a decision that offered assistance to anyone other than themselves was like ramming your head into the wall. To say they were strong-willed would be to water down the facts. They were just plain stubborn, but fortunately, they were quite often correct. One of the challenges that a combat commander faces is that of recognizing strong people and blending their smarts and their drive into a successful operation. I was able to do this in the case of Geeno and his boss quite easily, perhaps because I too have been accused by some of the learned ones of being of a somewhat hardheaded nature. Naturally I deny this, you know; we all know someone who is this way but naturally it is not us. Besides that, I made out their efficiency reports.

It is a big kick to me to see how people evaluate others on the efficiency report (ER) system that we use as a report card on our folks. If you read between the lines you can often get a fair overview of the person. If you read only the written words, you are bound to get a phony picture as the ER has become the most abused weapon in the history of military warfare. It is the manna of the promotion system, and bastardized descriptions of the performance of officers, as the promotion pendulum swings from extreme to extreme, are something to behold. If we had people who were as good and as bad as they are described in the hallowed ER files of the Pentagon, we would have no trouble winning the war with Ho Chi Minh. We could well afford to take all those who show up so badly and arm them with sticks to become a sacrifice force to walk through Laos to the North Vietnamese border. While these worthless souls paid the supreme price for failure to please their rater with their social grace, or their overdedication to some facet of their mission, the other group could walk up the waters of the Gulf of Tonkin and sway the land of Ho and perhaps that of Mao with their documented abilities to "get along well with peer, subordinate and supervisor alike under even the most demanding situations" or their "clearly superior ability to see the big picture that allows him without fail to solve any problem in the most cost effective and timely manner." If you think that I consider this system to be a farce you are correct. The only nice thing I can say about it is that I do not have a better system up my sleeve. The problems associated with ranking such a huge group as the Air Force into a neatly cataloged mass of tickey-tackey defies true solution. The ability to hire, fire, pay, train and reward those who work directly for any given supervisor has been so completely withdrawn into the bowels of the system that if you accept the career you must accept the rating system. You don't have to like it but you must accept it—it is all-powerful, something like James Michener's Oro, the red god of Bora Bora.

The ER is good for a laugh once in a while. Since your fate in this business hangs on it, there can be considerable consternation if you have one coming up and you know deep down inside that you have riled the powers that be. Geeno's boss had no problems with me, but there were those in our channels who looked upon his determination with less enthusiasm than I did. By the same token, he knew that I was the drone who prepared the actual papers that were later emblazoned with the big signature, and he knew that I would somehow or other manage to allow a peek at the finished product. Another facet of this monster that I confess I do not understand is the current vogue for not showing the report card to the man being rated. We used to, and I personally thought this gave people a fair understanding of how they stood with the guy they worked for. I hate leaving work at the end of the day with that gnawing in your stomach that indicates you don't know how well you are pleasing the one who has so much go or no-go power over your future in the Air Force. Perhaps it is difficult for some to talk frankly with those who toil for them, and to be constructive in their criticism. In that I do not personally have this problem, I am intolerant of those who do, and I would suggest another block on the form to be filled in by those with such a problem. It could just say, "I am too chicken to discuss this man's performance to his face, yes or no." In fact, the man being rated is not precluded from seeing the report: he can do so simply by traveling a few thousand miles to the major air command headquarters and making an appointment to review his records file. Now I ask you, is this cost effective?

When it came time to prepare the ER on Geeno's boss, I decided it was time to have a bit of fun out of the grim business that took all of our conscious and many of our less than conscious moments. I sat down at the typewriter on a Sunday afternoon when I was not flying and dashed off the report that follows. I then went up to my trailer and called him on the phone saying I had something I wanted to discuss in private. He responded, and when he entered the trailer I managed to have the report on my desk, not quite concealed, where he was bound to see it. The curiosity factor was tremendous and he about flipped trying not to look at this all-powerful piece of paper that had his name and some wildly out-of-place markings on it. After a few minutes of idle chatter, I broke down and showed him the farce with a straight face. Concern changed to disbelief and then to laughter as he read through the paper. It went like this:

This Lieutenant Colonel is a most impressive officer with an intense interest in flying. *Fly, fly, fly, that's all the son of a bitch does. Every time you need him to get something done he's airborne. Try and pin him down for a decision—"the Colonel is flying."* During this reporting period his squadron has set several records for combat flying time and for the biggest number of fighter combat sorties from a single squadron. *Sure—what's so tough about that? He's got those poor pilots so scared of coming in second in anything that they pad more time than they fly. Who ever heard of a seven-hour mission to the bottom of route pack one? And those bandits in his maintenance section—those bastards would steal a rose off their grandmother's grave. The rest of the poor slobs on the flight line work their tails off and his guys run around all night stealing parts and switching aft sections.* He has welded his entire squadron into a tightly knit and cohesive unit. *You bet your ass he has —they all lie and cover up for each other like a bunch of cell mates. Call him on the phone and what do the airmen say? "Sorry sir, he's in an important conference and asked not to be disturbed." He's in the sack and they know it.* His dynamic personality has made a lasting impression on the local nationals and brought about a new era in Thai-US relations. *Who'll ever forget the night the Thai commander had us over to his place? He even ran out of Thai whiskey—and that funny little dance he did in his bare feet between the broken bottles.* He has been decorated, and decorated, and decorated. *That's all those poor Lieutenants and Sergeants do down there is make up decorations for him. They even tried to get him another Silver Star for making last week's staff meeting on time—for once.* I recommend that he be assigned at the highest possible staff level, preferably to the Pentagon. *That place is so jumbled up and big, that with his ability to get lost in the shuffle it is hard to see how he can do any harm up there.*

As we progressed through the lines, we decided the levity was too good to hold to ourselves so I called the other two squadron commanders over and we all had a big guffaw. One of the other squadron commanders was now Geeno. When we had lost Don, we wanted to replace him immediately with a strong commander from within our own resources. Geeno was the logical choice, and though he took Don's job with the heavy heart that we all shared, he waded right into the problems he faced, and within a few days you would have thought that he had been a combat squadron commander for years. Unfortunately, we were not to have the benefit of Geeno's tough but gentle personality for very long. He believed in his mission too much, and he immersed himself so far in the details of his charges that a few weeks later we lost him.

It was a Saturday morning and Geeno had drawn the early briefing and takeoff as the mission commander for both the Korat wing and ourselves against that lousy Thai Nguyen railroad yard, which served the steel mill (at that time we had not yet been turned loose on the mill itself). This was one of the many wild setups over there and the North Vietnamese naturally wanted to extract the maximum price for letting us clobber that complex. They had enough stuff in there to protect both the rail yards and the steel plant, but as they were always pretty sure of our restrictions and what we could and could not hit, they could quite well afford to orient all their guns toward the protection of the rail yards and trust to luck and intelligence for the protection of the steel plant. We made their tasks lots easier in many respects.

Their Sam and Mig defenses were not hampered by being divided between the two targets lying one on top of the other, and they had excellent area defense. They had positioned their Sams in such a manner that they could cover our ingress to the target area of Thai Nguyen from any angle and protect both the yards and the mill. They had the benefit of lots of practice in tracking us as we came down Thud Ridge; and because they knew we would avoid both the Mig sanctuaries at Phuc Yen and Kep and the magic inner circles at Hanoi and Haiphong, they were able to look at us all the way in and have a fair shot whenever the missile gear indicated conditions to be favorable.

The Migs were also in a favorable posture since they were based on both sides of the Ridge—at Phuc Yen to the west and Kep to the east. I have often marveled at the Migs' amazing lack of success. I know airplanes very well and my three years of leading the USAF demonstration team, The Thunderbirds, did nothing to dim my perception of relative maximum performance capability among different aircraft. I have fought with the Migs in two wars now—be they declared, recognized, popular or not—and I have yet to see any general indication that the Mig drivers we have faced thus far are using the maximum skill or technical capability available to them. I don't think you will find a truly professional fighter pilot who would not sell his front seat in hell to be a Mig squadron commander in the face of an American fighter-bomber attack, should such a transformation be possible in our world of reality. Please remember I am only speaking professionally and am not expressing any desire to go the rice and fish route. I am simply saying that they could murder us if they did the job properly.

They don't go first class and our guys are both good and dedicated. I guess that is the difference. I have had a batch of them on my tail when they have had a better aircraft that could go faster, turn better, and outaccelerate me. I have been on the low end of odds as high as 16 to 2—and that's pretty lousy. (In this particular case of the poor odds, they hung me up for twenty-three minutes, an almost unheard-of time period for aerial combat even in the early Korea days when this occurred. They didn't scratch me, only because their cannon couldn't hit the round side of a broad.) I have had them come up from under my tail spewing red tracers that looked like a runaway Roman candle burst at the seams. Had those guns been properly harmonized, they would have nailed me without a doubt.

They have still not learned their lessons well and I suspect they do not do their homework properly. With the advantages they have going for them, I am sure glad that the majority of those we have tangled with to date are not as clever in this game as our guys are. Anyone who reads the air-to-air results and feels that American technology has scored another victory over the competition of the world is sadly misled. We have been able to take advantage of their mistakes and they have not seen, or have ignored, or have been inept enough not to take advantage of, our mistakes. I scream caution at the top of my lungs that we have not yet met the first team of Mig drivers but I have failed to observe a flow of listeners to my door. As a matter of fact, it becomes less popular and less rewarding each day to scream about basic convictions in the conduct of any struggle between men and machines. I feel very strongly that our inability to talk of practicality or to accept the word of those who physically do the job is hurting us all the way from the drawing board to the battlefield. Is our level of incompetence so high that the doer can never be heard? Is it inconceivable that a captain could know something from practical experience that a general doesn't know? I often wonder if Hannibal had any elephant drivers who tried to get the big message to him at the base of the Alps, but were swallowed up in a system that wanted to hear only good about itself.

But Geeno's problems were faster moving than Hannibal's and the Sams, the Migs and the flak were all zeroed in and waiting for him that bleak morning when he headed north for the last time—and he knew they were waiting. Like the rest of the Thud drivers, he never lacked a knowledge or appreciation of the forces aligned against him, but only a few flinched from the blanket of steel that waited, always active, always eager, never compromising. We had only four who couldn't hack it, four only whose fear overcame them and dealt them the gravest defeat man can suffer—to surrender to the cowardice that made them quit in the face of the enemy while those they had lived with went forth to take their chances on dying or rotting away in prison in order to defend their supposed right to default on their brothers-in-arms and still go forth unblemished. This is wrong and our system is wrong to tolerate it. You try and change it if you will. I have already tried and been rebuffed. No matter what demands the leadership imposes, the combat soldier who falters and fails in the face of the enemy's fire is an unspeakable wretch whose own insides must someday devour him.

There is no telling what type may display the unpardonable sin of reneging under fire. Our four covered the spectrum. We had one who had been a professional fighter pilot for about ten years. He loved the travel, adventure and challenge of the peacetime forces. He liked his aircraft and thought well of her demonstrated prowess on the gunnery range with the practice bombs and shells. When the press of events called him to the day when the gunnery range fired back and airplanes exploded and people died, he crawled on his belly and surrendered his image of a man because he was afraid. Another was a bomber guy who got caught up in the personnel conversion to this different machine. He was out of his element, almost as far out of his element as those poor slobs who have been rotting in Hanoi for over two years, so he fell on his face and cried, "I can't take it." He had been professionally raised under a banner that unfortunately says "Peace Is Our Profession" and he wasn't capable of transforming himself to the knowledge that war is our profession, as most of the rest of the bomber guys did. Our third failure was a lieutenant who almost cracked up earlier while pulling alert pad duty with nobody even shooting at him. Perhaps I should have spotted him then, but it took only a few lousy 37-millimeter shells, bursting woefully out of range, to surface this clever dodger in uniform. He decided that he would like to be a ground officer during the period of hostilities, and the last I heard he was getting away with it.

Our fourth was our worst. He wears the U. S. Navy ring of an Annapolis graduate. I always knew the Navy was smart, but how they figured this clown out ten years ago and got him transferred to the Air Force is beyond me. He was the worst in that he knew better and had demonstrated the capability, under fire, to do the job. He quit around the halfway mark when he was approaching the stage where he would have been of real value to us. Among other things, he developed a fear of heights after ten years as a jet pilot. He learned all the rules and all the angles and he played them to the hilt. When all else failed him, he managed a hardship discharge. Hardship indeed, that this leech defaced the profession as long as he did.

So do you suppose that Geeno was scared as he blasted off in the murk of a predawn departure from our own private piece of jungle? I suppose he was. Anyone who isn't scared is an idiot. It is completely plausible and quite a scintillating experience to be able to translate this being scared into the most dynamic courage and a determination to get the job done properly. Geeno knew what his job was. He had to lead two wings of F-105's to one of the nastiest targets in the North, and he and his three flight companions were to still the flak so the first wave of strike aircraft could penetrate and get the job done.

When you are in the spot of leading both wings and are also the flak suppression flight for your own wing, the first one in on the target, you can't help feeling a tremendous sense of responsibility. In this situation, more than any other, you know that the responsibility for the whole tribe is in your lap. More than that, you know that the success or failure of the strike itself is your baby doll. No matter how well it is planned and no matter how many instant experts are sitting on the ground ready to advise on something they have never done, you have the ball. Your word is sought after in the confusion of the departure. You call the shots as men and machines struggle to the end of the runway and fight to leave the arming area in proper order. Your burner light is the infallible signal to all concerned, "Yes, this is it, we're really going," and the degree of confidence, calm and expertise that you exude does more than you know to determine the results, and even the survival of your troops.

This was brought home to me most clearly during a discussion with one of the docs who was working on a potential fear-of-flying case. Actually the guy had the fear, and it seemed like every time he moved he got exposed to something else to increase his fear, but he was a good man and he utilized every bit of smart and stamina he had, and while I am sure that he never beat the fear, he controlled it and stuck with the task. While trying to help this pilot, the doc was discussing the emotions of people faced daily with the violent loss of those they sweat next to and he said something to the effect that all rational men had a sense of fear. He said, "Don't you think the colonels who lead you in this wing feel fear?"

The pilot responded in amazement, "You mean they actually get scared too?" It's what you do with the emotion that counts.

Geeno picked up his specific responsibility for this Saturday morning mission the evening before. When the frag arrived there was always much interest in what we were doing the next day and a shuffle to see who would fill which spot. In a wing like ours where the leaders led, you always had to give the boss first crack at the next day's work. Depending on who had to meet the visitors the next day—and there were almost always visitors—who had what meeting or what additional duty plans, the boss would decide on his availability and choice of mission time. Other things being equal, that 0200 wakeup was not too popular with those of us in the command bracket. It is great to be skimming along when the sun comes up, and you get the feeling that you are in the saddle on this new day and that you are running things and all will be good. You also get a feeling of accomplishment when you land early and know that before most people have stirred you have done a good job. And you get so tired you hurt. The primary duty jocks who have been flight planning most of the night could sneak away to the sack for a few hours, but the leaders always had something to make that move inappropriate, and the next thing you knew you had worked yourself out of daylight and into night. We all gave the continuing early schedule a try at one time or another, and we all managed to get falling-down sick doing it. So on this particular Friday afternoon, both the boss and I declined and the early one rotated to Geeno, the next squadron commander in line.

Immediately after the stand-up briefing he gathered his flight leaders and his planners in the big briefing room and they started through the mass of detail necessary to select and chart the route for the next morning. Every detail of ingress and egress was probed and once the mission commander was satisfied with his plan of action, the selected individuals from each participating flight set to work to prepare the maps, charts and cruise data for their flight members. This particular planning session did not have to get too involved as most everyone knew the area and the target quite well. There was not too much freedom of choice on routes, and there was nothing new to say on defenses in that area. They were all still there and everyone would get to see all of them in the morning. Having put his charges to work there was little else for him to do other than to make sure he knew each and every particular of the route he had selected as well as the details of the drill he would employ in marshaling and leading the next day.

Very little went right in the morning. The first problem was getting enough aircraft in commission. After much hassling and reconfiguration the last-minute efforts of the flight line people and the harried schedulers paid off and aircraft numbers, pilots, flight call signs and bombloads started to fall into place. It is most important that all the scheduled blocks be filled and that each flight performs as a flight of four. The maintenance troops are always hard pressed to get enough of the occasionally recalcitrant monsters all the way in commission, with all systems working. Should they fail to do so, which they seldom do even under the worst of time compressions, it results in more than a departure short one or two aircraft, worse than an effort launched with less than planned bomb coverage on target. It becomes an effort wherein one or more flights are no longer self-sustaining portions of the strike, since they cannot render mutual support between the elements of two. The offensive as well as the defensive plan is short one pair of eyes and one man and machine combination that fits perfectly into the jigsaw of mutual support. The flight short one man automatically becomes a pair plus a straggler, and Thai Nguyen was no place for stragglers.

This particular predawn scramble paid off and the full force was launched as planned. Geeno ran into weather on his refueling effort but managed to get the job done in style, and all his charges dropped off the tanker, and headed for Thud Ridge. As they approached the target area the weather they had experienced during refueling was still with them and by now had become a threat to the success of the mission. From the river on in, the area was covered with a middle layer of broken to overcast clouds. While a cloud layer of this kind is not in itself too difficult to penetrate, it makes a great difference in your tactics against the defenses and your actual run on the target. Whether you stayed above the clouds, went below them, or tried to hide inside them, you were in for trouble.

If you stay on top on the way to the target you can look for Migs, but you cannot see the ground for that extra double check on your approach, nor can you see the Sams as they kick up a boiling caldron of dust when they leap from their launch sites. If you can't see them on the way up when they are relatively slow and struggling both to accelerate and to guide, you are in trouble, for by the time they come bursting up through the undercast, accelerate and guiding on course for you, your chances of evading them are slim. If you duck just under the clouds you have a better visual shot at the Sams and better visual navigation, but you give both the Sam people and the ground gunners a perfect silhouette of your force against the cloud backdrop, at the same time telegraphing your exact altitude for both sighting and fuzing purposes. If you go far below the clouds, up goes the fuel consumption and up goes the exposure to smaller guns on the ground. About the only other piece of airspace available is inside the clouds themselves, and herding a large formation of heavily loaded machines through uncontrolled airspace that is full of turbulence and rocks, thundering blindly into and over an area where the defenders have no qualms about firing guns or Sams into the clouds if they or their radar even think you are there, is not a generally approved tactic. Those who have inadvertently found themselves in this thrilling situation usually do their utmost to avoid a repeat.

Geeno was in the process of initiating a gradual descent to a position under the clouds that appeared to be the best compromise available under the conditions when Sam helped him to expedite both his decision and his descent. Three Sams launched and headed directly for the lead flight like lumbering white telephone poles. It quite obviously does not take them too long to get out of that lumbering stage and the closer they get and the faster they go the more rapidly you must react. Geeno still had visual contact with the ground and was able to spot this flight of three en route toward his charges. He bellowed out the warning on the radio and took his flight down to the deck, under the approaching missiles. You can practice all you want and brief all you want, but when those things are pointed your way, the old adrenaline flows, the palms get sweaty and the voice gets squeaky. If you are worried about your circulation, a few rides in that area will convince you that the old pump is really putting out.

The rest of the force had been well alerted by Geeno's call and were able to watch the air show as he and his flight parried the Sams and continued on toward the target. There was little doubt that the defenses were ready that morning and when you started getting tapped that far out you could bet the rest of the ride would be wild. In one way it sort of helps to have some successful action of that kind before you get right on the target, as it seems to act almost like a warm-up session before a deadly ball game. As long as you win that first one you have some feeling of accomplishment along with the definite knowledge that the ball game is on. It does not do a thing for the radio chatter, however, and a lot of people immediately have a great number of important things that they just have to say right now. This was the worst possible time for a garbaged-up radio channel. You want the air clear for calls alerting the rest of the flights to the posture and actions of the defenses. There is no telling how many people and aircraft we have lost simply because some blabbermouth was making a worthless transmission that blocked out a warning call. It was a problem requiring constant attention and it was not uncommon to have to chew some guy out on the radio and tell him to shut up.

Fortunately, the chatter died rapidly or Geeno would probably never have made it to the target. He was now definitely committed to an approach under the clouds and the countdown proceeded as the tick marks fell behind on the run-in line on his map and the exaggerated pencil mark alongside his course line said silently that two minutes from now all hell would break loose above the rail yards. This was where you liked everything smooth, so you could navigate perfectly and get the approach and roll-in that you wanted without slinging some poor wingman off by himself as the speed built toward maximum. But there were no smooth skies available at the two-minute marker that day. A second volley of three Sams hurled clouds of dust and dirt on their masters and leaped eagerly toward the lead flight. Navigation be damned, you had to beat those Sams or the navigation would be of no value, so Geeno sounded the alarm again and hauled all of his flights down to the treetops at breakneck speed. The maneuver was too much for the Sams' stubby little wings trying to accept their radar's guidance, and two of them stumbled hopelessly, only to stall themselves out and tumble earthward, while their lone companion screeched ballistically skyward, ever accelerating, to explode in isolation at the end of its snow-white contrail. But the Sams had accomplished one thing: they forced Geeno into a major decision at a time when he would just as soon have had nothing to think about but the mechanics of the attack. He had to decide whether he would blast that Sam site or continue as planned.

By this time in our war, a Sam site that revealed itself was fair game, one of the targets we liked to destroy. This guy was wide open and had showed his colors to an entire strike force loaded for bear. The three dust pillars from the launch pad stretched upward like three large surveyor's poles saying, here, right in the middle of these three, here is Sam, and nothing Sam's masters could do would make those indicators disappear for several minutes. It was a great target, the kind a fighter pilot loves. There would be guns protecting the site, more missiles on the launch rails and maybe more in concealed storage, and that silly little control van in the very center. A few loads of bombs could do a lot of good in the middle of that site. It would have been a legal decision nobody could criticize, but the thought wouldn't go away that he was the leader, the guy who had to get this wing and another wing in and out of that gruesome rail yard. He was also the guy they were depending on to draw that flak at the yards and then paste it good so that all following could have a better chance of completing their runs. He knew it was going to be hard as hell to straighten this gaggle out after the Sam-evading maneuvers and get a decent run at the target, but the yards were the target, the one they had briefed on for so long, the one they wanted to knock out so badly so they wouldn't have to come back here for it again. The decision was instantaneous and automatic and Geeno squared his forces away and pushed for the yards already coming into view at 600 per.

(I faced a similar one about that time when I was suppressing the flak around a cozy little spot closer to town. The flak was fierce and my course took me right over the hallowed sanctuary of Phuc Yen airfield, which was still off limits. As I pulled up there were four Mig-21's in run-up position on the end of the runway, getting ready to take off and jump the guys behind me in the force. They, of course, were taboo as their wheels had not yet bounced off the concrete, but I had weapons on board that would leave no big postholes for identification and it would sure be great to knock those four out all at once. But the guys behind me could probably outdo the Migs, one way or the other, and I knew that the flak in front of me would get nothing but more accurate unless I hammered it for the guys behind me. I pressed on to suppress the flak. As advertised, they rolled down the runway, sucked up their gear, made a 180-degree turn, and were all over the second flight behind me. It's probably a good thing that I didn't cream those four Mig-21's as somebody would have squawked about it, and with my luck they would have court-martialed me. I'm so dumb about things like that, I probably would have told the truth anyway. Hindsight is wonderful.)

Geeno's problems were compounding rapidly and as he reached up for bombing altitude he found the cloud deck lowering right over the target and another decision was upon him. The weather wasn't as good as it had looked and the flights were coming up from behind like six hundred. Was it good enough? Could these pros get in under here, knock the target out and get back out with their skins? The micro-second evaluation by the trained eye said yes—yes they could change the mechanics of their prebriefed attack, they could convert dive angles and airspeeds and sight pictures to change the amount of lead angle required to get the bombs in there. They could get whatever altitude the clouds and the gunners would give them and as they rolled in, they could tell how high they were and what the angle was to the desired impact point and they could tell when it looked just right and bomb and get the hell out of there. Yes, it was a go, and Geeno so announced on the radio.

The dizzy guns didn't light up the way they should have. The fire was only light and yet he knew that a goodly portion of the defenses in the North were concentrated down there. To bomb on the minuscule elements that revealed themselves would have helped, but only a little. What was the matter with those clods, were they asleep? Surely he hadn't surprised them, not after they had been hosing Sams at him for five minutes. He went as high as the clouds would allow and he had to make a move right away. This was Geeno's big decision, the instantaneous awful decision of a lifetime and he did the unheard of. He stayed up on top, and he calmly circled over the wildest array of weapons ever assembled in the history of ground-to-air warfare. He circled because they would not fire at him and if they did not show themselves he could not blast a channel for his strike aircraft and some of his boys would get hurt.

As he swung past the end of the yards, Sam broke the relative lull and the seventh, eighth and ninth launches of the day reached for him. As he swung violently out of their guidance capability he tried to set his lead element up to bomb the newly revealed and threatening site, but his evasive gyration had not only thrown the Sams off, it had swung him out of position to strike the site as its defending guns let fly all the lead they owned, since their charges had revealed their position during launch. His third and fourth aircraft, in the second element, were in good position, and satisfied that they could knock out this threat, he directed them to hit the site, calmly turned his back on them and proceeded to weave his way between the clouds and the rising crescendo of heavy gunfire that now committed itself fully from the other end of the yards. Those were the ones he wanted, the big ones that had remained hidden and were now making up for lost time.

He somehow made it back toward them and knew he had found the target he wanted. Two bombloads were on the Sam site and he still had his own and his wingman's bombs for these guns. Up and over he went for his bomb run and the timing was great as the first strike flight was approaching their own roll-in. He had to hurry—but not too fast. Sam had other ideas and, in the day's duel between Geeno and Sam, Sam was not to be denied. A site commander who had remained concealed must have realized the gravity of the threat with the suppressors on the run and the strike birds right on their tail, and he salvoed all six of his Sams directly at Geeno in a desperate attempt to get this wild one who had flaunted the strongest of defenses by loitering above them. There was no warning and there was no evasive action. All six Sams guided perfectly, all six proximity fuzes functioned, and Geeno was obscured in a six-sided puff ball of ugly red, brown and gray.

His Thud flew out the other side of the blossoming cloud, faltered for a moment, then rolled over for its final dive. His wingman had been wide of the burst and his bombs did the job. I hope Geeno knew.

Things were still moving at breakneck speed and the strike force was at work. There was no faltering, no hesitation, just deadly split-second precision work. You don't look for anybody else and you don't think about anybody else during these seconds when your ass belongs to Uncle Sam. Most of the time you can't assimilate anything else, and you definitely can't analyze it until later anyway; nor, even if you could, could you do anything about it. Each one of us understands that, but we don't particularly care to dwell on it. The strike was a beauty and everyone put them right in there and everyone got out. Everyone, that is, except Geeno—the fighter pilot commander who bet his life that he could knock out the toughest guns in the world and save his buddies.

FORCED TO EJECT OVER HANOI

by Stephen Coonts

On December 28, 1972, Jake and Tiger learned they were scheduled for their fifth SAM-suppression mission; this time the target was on the northern edge of Hanoi.

"Maybe our best route is to go all the way around the city," Tiger suggested.

Jake examined the wall chart. Concentrations of flak and SAMs were shown by color-coded pinheads. Hanoi was a pin cushion. Well, he and Cole had been there before. He came back to the table where Tiger had laid out his charts. "Uh-huh," he said. Then he asked, "When will the big mothers be along?"

"The B-52s roll in about ten minutes after our drop time of 1933."

Jake inspected the aerial photos of the SAM site, which Steiger had collected. They revealed the classic tactical deployment of the SA-2 surface-to-air missile system: six missiles on their trailer launchers were arranged in a circle around a semitrailer with a radar antenna. The launchers sat in indentations gouged in the earth, so that if a missile was destroyed or blew up on the launcher, the blast would be deflected away from the other missiles and the semitrailer with the electronic control equipment. Off to one side Jake could make out two parked tractors. He had seen photos of hundreds of sites that looked just like this. He checked the date; the photos were more than eighteen months old.

There was a blur in the upper-right corner. He knew it was a gun shooting at the Vigilante that had taken the picture.

He tossed the photos back on the table and examined the route Tiger had marked out. The bombardier planned to coast-in just south of the lighthouse at the entrance of Haiphong harbor, proceed straight to an island in the river on the northern edge of Hanoi, and turn to the attack heading. After bombing, they would move left in a sweeping turn that would let them circumnavigate the city and would spit them out on the southeast side, headed for the ocean and safety. The pilot studied a sectional chart that showed in detail the terrain around the island, tonight's Initial Point, and around the target. Maybe there would be enough light to see the rivers. Like hell!

"Another good navy deal," he said and patted his bombardier on the shoulder. He paused again at the flak chart, then went off to the wardroom for a cup of coffee before the brief.

The Augies had a tanker hop and were in the locker room when Jake and Tiger entered. Little Augie had not exchanged a word with Jake since he had returned from Cubi. Now he spoke. "Where're you headed tonight?"

Grafton told him but didn't bother to look at the diminutive pilot. Little Augie lingered, watching Jake inspect the cartridges for his .357 Magnum and then carefully load it. Jake had returned his issue .38 to supply long ago so he could carry this more powerful weapon.

"If you get bagged tonight, can I have your stereo?"

Jake grinned. Apparently whatever sins Little Augie thought him guilty of were forgiven. "If you can find it," Jake told him. Unlike almost everyone else, he had not bought an expensive Japanese sound system at the Cubi Point Exchange. Little punched him on the shoulder and walked out of the locker room.

Jake put the contents of his pockets, including his wallet, onto the top shelf of the locker. He placed a folded cardcase, which contained a green navy ID card, a Geneva convention card, and a twenty-dollar bill, in one of the big chest pockets of his flight suit. Like most airmen, he carried several thousand dollars worth of small, navy-issue gold wafers in his survival vest in case he had to barter with or bribe local people, but he brought nothing else of monetary or personal value. Except the ring. This he had in the left sleeve pocket of the flight suit where he had kept the sand dollar.

Dressed, with helmet bag in hand, he paused before closing his locker. He examined its contents, as he had done on every mission before. Morbidly, he knew that if he were shot down or killed, Sammy Lundeen would have the job of clearing out these little pieces of his life. Well, he had logged the same number of landings as takeoffs, so far. He felt for the ring, assured himself the pocket was completely zipped, then slammed the locker door and spun the combination lock.

They launched at twilight. Jake took the *Intruder* to 20,000 feet and cruised leisurely up the Gulf. Spectacular reds and oranges and yellows, afterglow of the setting sun, filtered through the clouds that lay over the mountains in Laos. Deep blues and purples began to vanquish the lingering gold. He had witnessed many sunsets and sunrises from the sky, but the pageant never failed to move him. Someday he would share a sunset aloft with Callie.

"The system looks real good," Tiger announced. Jake engaged the autopilot. The steady beep of a search radar was clearly audible now. "Commie sonsuvbitches have found us," Tiger muttered.

A falling star caught Jake's eye. What could he wish for? To survive? To get back to Callie safely? He also wished for more stars, and as the minutes passed his wish was granted.

"I've got an update on the lighthouse." The lighthouse on the Do Son peninsula, which jutted out into the mouth of Haiphong harbor, had not been illuminated for years. "We have six minutes to kill. How about a six-minute turn to the right?"

Jake nudged the stick over, then released it. The autopilot held the warplane at the selected angle-of-bank. "You're pretty talkative tonight," he told the bombardier.

"Checklist," Tiger prompted. Together they set the switches on the armament panel, double-checked the ECM panels, and watched the compass and clock hands rotate. As they completed their turn, Tiger checked their position again. The steering on the VDI in front of the pilot swung to the coast-in point. Jake caught Tiger's eye for a second, then turned the autopilot off. When they had descended a thousand feet, Jake turned off the exterior lights, IFF, and TACAN. "Devil Five Oh Oh, strangling parrot."

"Black Eagle copies, Five Double-nuts."

The plane descended toward the sea. The beeps of the enemy radar sounded closer together now. The operator was in a sector search, painting them repeatedly, measuring their course and speed. Jake leveled off at 500 feet and allowed the speed to bleed off to 420 knots. "Three miles to coast-in," Tiger informed him. The enemy radar was back on area sweep. Perhaps their plane had faded in radar return from the sea.

Jake blinked the perspiration from his eyes and looked ahead for the silver ribbon of sand that divided the land and sea. A mile out, he saw it and the thin, wavering lines of breakers washing ashore. He thought of Callie on the beach.

"Black Eagle, Devil Five Oh Oh is feet dry."

"Roger Five Oh Oh. Feet dry at 1919." Fourteen minutes to the target.

The starlight reflected off the paddies and wide creeks flowing to meet the sea. No flak came up at them yet. The search radar still beeped, about once every twelve seconds, but at 400 feet over the table-flat delta they were invisible in ground return.

From the left the first flak of the night shot out in their direction. Jake concentrated on maintaining altitude and heading.

Tiger called the IP; Jake flipped on the master arm switch and advanced the throttles to the stops as he laid the plane into the turn. Halfway through the heading change a row of guns erupted ahead. The pilot saw the streams of tracer rise and reacted instinctively, rolling the plane almost ninety degrees to squeeze it through an empty space between the tracers. They were almost on the outskirts of Hanoi.

As he entered the gap another gun opened up.

Horrified, Jake momentarily froze as the molten finger of death reached for him. The *Intruder* shuddered from the blows; then, suddenly, it was through the flak into the dark void beyond. It was all over in less than a heartbeat.

As Jake rolled the wings level, the brilliant red of the left engine fire-warning light filled the cockpit. A look in the rear-view mirror showed no visible fire yet. But the exhaust gas temperature on the sick engine had risen to more than 700 degrees centigrade, and the RPM had dropped by more than ten percent. Jake felt the warplane shimmy through his seat, the floor, the throttles, and the stick. The bird was badly hurt. Quickly he shut off the flow of fuel to the left engine.

The bombardier leaned away from the scope hood and peered at the engine instruments in front of Jake's left knee. "How bad is it?" The fire-warning light reflected off his helmet visor.

"Left engine's gone. Do you have the target?"

Tiger put his face back to the scope hood. "Come left ten degrees."

Jake centered the steering. He glanced at the mileage readout between his knees. Eight more miles to go. The attack light lit up on the VDI, and Jake squeezed the commit trigger. As the plane slowed to only 350 knots the left generator dropped off the line. With only one generator they would have the radar and computer but not the ECM. Jake's earphones were silent, and it wasn't because the gomers had shut down for the night. All the console lights on the bombardier's panels were now dark.

Those lucky fuckers! Smacked us with a cheap shot!

The hydraulic gauges captured Jake's eyes. One of the two hydraulic systems showed zero pressure. And only one of the pumps in the other system was still working. Damn. From four pumps to one, just like that.

He looked at the computer steering symbol. Almost centered. The fire-warning light was so brilliant that he reached to cover it with his hand, but then it went out. The cockpit was dark again.

"Three more miles," Tiger called.

More flak ripped the night. Jake tried to ignore it, to concentrate on flying a perfect run. Something ahead caught his eye.

A blazing streak of pure white fire hurtled toward them. Quicker than thought Jake pulled back the stick, and the enemy missile tore by. God, too close! Jake tweaked the nose of the Intruder, pointing it straight at the offending missile launcher.

"I've got the radar van," Cole advised.

Jake watched the release marker descend the VDI. He savagely mashed the pickle to back up the computer-derived release signal.

The bombs did not release.

Jake pressed the pickle button again and again. No release.

He cycled the master armament switch, selected a manual release, and punched the pickle button. Nothing.

Heavy flak ahead. "Can you find it again?" he demanded of Cole.

"Yeah."

Jake lowered the left wing and turned south. This time he planned on jettisoning the bomb racks with the emergency release. The Rockeyes would not spread out but would remain in their cases, attached to the racks. There'd be hell to pay when they exploded all together. "We're not whipped yet," he said to Cole. "Better tell 'em we're in trouble."

The bombardier got on the radio as they turned.

More fire from heavy weapons rippled through the air, but not too close. Jake nursed the plane through the turn, frequently checking the pressure gauge for the lone hydraulic pump. Because the plane's controls were actuated by hydraulic pressure, a violent jerk on the stick could overload the pump and leave the pilot dependent on the electrically driven backup pump, which had a very limited output. The backup pump was working—the BACKUP HYD light was lit on the annunciator panel—but it would only give him enough pressure to operate the stabilator and rudder at reduced effectiveness. The tightrope was fraying.

"What type weapon do you want selected?" Dropping the racks was Jake's only choice. Of the more than fifty preprogrammed options available to tell the computer about the ballistic trajectory of the weapons, none of the options fit the dropping of the entire bomb rack. So Cole had asked the crucial question.

"What do you think?" asked Jake.

"The racks will go down about like a retarded Snake, maybe a little flatter," said Cole. "We'll use that, and I'll type in a correction."

The pilot checked the airspeed indicator. Steady at 325 knots. Very slow, but they would pick up thirty knots or so when they dropped the weapons.

Fireballs tore around them. Something smashed into a wing and the stick wiggled hard in Jake's fist. He shot a glance at the left wing. All okay. But on the right wing fuel was erupting through two holes and being blasted back into the slipstream.

Oh, Jesus! Sweet Jesus, help us get out of this alive.

"I've got the target and we're in attack," Tiger said. The last spurts of the right-wing fuel siphoned away. There was still a ton in the left wing but both wings drained through a common pump, which needed fuel from both wings to be effective. Jake had no choice. He opened the wing dumps and let the unusable fuel pour into the slipstream. They still had nine thousand pounds internal, and if they could make it to the tanker in the Gulf they'd have a chance.

"Two miles." The pilot readied his finger over the emergency jettison button. The release marker was marching down.

"Gimme one second's warning," he reminded Tiger. The circuit had a safety feature that required the button be held at least a second to prevent inadvertent jettisoning.

"Now!"

Jake depressed the button and held it. Whump! He slammed the stick over and turned left hard. The hydraulic pressure and the airspeed sagged, but he had to escape the impact area or they would be caught in the blast. The bombs exploded. A blinding light flashed in the mirrors, and the concussion buffeted, but did not harm, the plane. The *Intruder* was headed south over the city.

Tiger keyed his radio mike and spoke to the Black Eagle controller, safe and snug in his E-2 over the Gulf. "Five Double-nuts is off target and coming out."

"Roger that. Are you declaring an emergency?"

"Affirmative. We're going to need a tanker as soon as we're feet wet."

Jake selected the main internal tank on the fuel gauge and dodged flak while he waited for the needle to register the correct amount.

My God! Only five thousand pounds left. The tank must be spewing the stuff out. There won't be enough fuel to make it even to the tanker. We're going to have to eject! But where? Just to make it out of North Vietnam would be tricky.

Tracers rose ahead in shimmering curtains of fire. Now they were over Hanoi, and the flak was in front and on all sides. The black shapes of rooftops and trees stood out clearly in the starlight and the eerie glow of the tracers. Jake descended until he was skimming the rooftops. Hell, just to make it out of Hanoi would be a trick and a half.

At this height, in this light, they were visible to every man, woman, and child with a weapon. He felt the thumps of small-arms bullets penetrating the side of the aircraft. The hounds had the fox nearly at bay.

As he pointed out the fuel indicator to Cole a stream of fire came from the right and headed straight for the windshield. Jake porpoised up and over the stream and both men flinched, a useless reflex. They were lucky. Thumps in the tail only.

"What's your position?" someone asked on the radio.

"Right over Hanoi," Grafton shouted. Illuminated by tracers, the city looked like an open door into hell. Every building seemed to have a coven of antiaircraft guns mounted on it.

"The radio is dead," Tiger said.

More thumps from something hitting the plane. The annunciator panel, normally dark, glowed with yellow lights. Left generator gone, left speed drive out, hydraulic pumps, fuel filter. . . . Why the fuel filter? Jake didn't have time to think about it. Yellow fireballs wound out at them and something smashed against the wings.

The bird was dying. Jake glanced at Tiger. "You can jump ship now if you want—"

"Keep rolling the dice," Tiger said.

Jake swung into a hard right turn and spoke into the dead radio. "Devil Five Oh Oh's turning west. We're going to Laos."

He concentrated on keeping the nose up and flying just above the buildings. The gunners could see the plane in this light, so he needed to be as low as possible to make their aiming more difficult. On the chance that the transmissions might be heard, the bombardier continued to report their intentions over the radio.

Ahead, to the left, a gunner opened up with a long continuous burst. The tracers came in a flat arc. Jake pulled up slightly and the shells streaked underneath. But the gunner corrected. The pilot retarded the single throttle momentarily and the plane decelerated, causing the stream of tracers to pass ahead of them. Jake shoved the throttle back to the stops and dived as low as he dared. The tracers seemed to correct in slow motion. "You'll burn the fucking barrel up," he screamed at the enemy gunner. Ahead loomed a building taller than its neighbors. The plane banked around the right side and the shells slammed into the building.

Flashes. White flashes off to the right. Jake narrowed his eyes in that direction. Trip-hammer flashes, a dozen a second, marched across the city.

"B-52 raid," Tiger whispered in awe.

The city lay naked in the pulsating light of the bombs. The *Intruder,* rocked by concussion waves, hung suspended in the popping-light universe of flashing bombs and white-hot fireballs. For almost a minute the unseen B-52s scourged the city. The A-6 shot into the darkness over the rice paddies. In the rear-view mirror, Jake saw fires burning and the streaks of flak still rising.

"Sweet Jesus," Tiger Cole said.

"We're gonna make it, man," Jake said, his voice cracking.

The fuel gauge showed four thousand pounds. Occasional flashes of burp guns lit the night—pinpricks after what they'd been through. Grafton floated the plane up to almost 500 feet on the radar altimeter. The barometric altimeter was frozen.

"Come right five degrees," Tiger said. "The computer quit a while back but the radar still works. We're coming into the mouth of a valley, and I'll steer us up it."

The land was rising. Jake nudged the plane up to hold at 500 feet above the ground. The darkness outside the plane was complete. They flew on, Tiger ordering minor heading changes.

The left fire-warning light came on again. It was distractingly bright, so Jake smashed it with his flashlight. He watched the fuel indicator. Thirty-two hundred pounds. They topped the crest of the valley and continued to climb. In a moment they went beyond the maximum altitude of the radar altimeter, and it stopped working, as it was designed to do.

"Swing left ten and hold that course."

Tiger turned the radio transmitter to Guard, an emergency frequency that was always monitored. These calls went out over a separate transmitter, so maybe they were being heard by someone even though the crew's earphones remained silent. Jake's eyes were itching. He loosened his oxygen mask and sniffed the cockpit air. Something burning. He turned off the air-conditioning switch. The smell hung in the cockpit. He replaced his mask and cinched it tight.

Jake could actually see the needle on the fuel indicator dropping. Where was that fuel going? It had to be spraying into the left engine bay through the holes smashed by the flak shells. If it ignites, we'll be strumming harps with Corey Ford and the Boxman. Those engine burner cans and the tailpipe have to be still hot enough to ignite that fuel. He rechecked the engine/fuel master switch to ensure that no electrical power was reaching the burner-can igniters. The switch was off, but he didn't remember toggling it, although if he hadn't they probably would be dead by now.

Twenty-three hundred pounds on the dial. Almost three hundred pounds a minute was disappearing, partly into the right engine and partly into the air. Jake calculated that was eighteen thousand pounds an hour. They had eight more minutes, maybe another fifty miles.

Every mile they traveled increased their chances of being rescued instead of captured. The Air Force SAR teams could pick them up in Laos, but North Vietnam was too heavily defended for a helicopter to survive.

Come on, baby! Don't fail us now.

Eighteen hundred pounds left. His gut was tied in a knot and he had trouble thinking about their dilemma. "Have you ever jumped before?" he asked Tiger Cole.

"Yep, and I broke my leg."

The terror of every combat pilot had finally become real for them. They would have to eject into enemy territory and survive on their wits and what little equipment they carried in their survival vests. Failure to be rescued meant death or imprisonment in a tiny cell. Capture itself was a living death.

Twelve hundred pounds. The low-fuel warning light was lit.

A faint glow in the clouds caught his attention. He adjusted the mirror. A yellow tongue of flame flickered under the left wing.

"We're on fire," he shouted. They would have to eject *now.*

"Not yet," Cole said and put his left arm across the pilot's chest. "Maybe a few more miles."

"Burning jets have a nasty habit of exploding, you know," said Jake. In his mind he could see the line in the operating manual for the A-6 Intruder: "At the first sign of visible fire, eject."

The nose of the airplane dipped. He tugged the stick aft, but the nose continued down. There was no pressure at all on the hydraulic gauges. The fire had melted the hydraulic lines.

Tiger stopped talking on the radio and looked at Jake.

Slowly, slowly, the nose started back up, but the plane rolled left. Jake waggled the stick and rudder. No response. Devil 500 was finished.

The two men looked into each other's eyes.

Tiger Cole reached up with both hands, grasped the primary ejection handle, and pulled it down over his head in a swift, clean motion. Instantly he was gone in a thunderclap of noise, wind, and plexiglas.

One last time, out of habit, Jake's eyes swept the instrument panel, then he pulled the alternate firing handle between his legs. In the fraction of a second before the ejection seat smashed its way upward through the plexiglas, the image of the panel and the yellow fire reflected in the mirror indelibly seared his memory.

Something was hammering at his body, pounding every inch of his chest, arms, legs, and neck. Even as he realized it had to be drops of rain, a tremendous jolt tore at his crotch as his parachute opened.

After the deafening rush of wind on ejection there was silence. He could not see a thing. In a near panic, he groped above him for the parachute risers. The straps rising from his shoulders were firm as steel cables. Reassured, he tried to think.

Why was he blind? He wasn't; there simply wasn't enough light to see by. Firmly grasping the nylon straps on each side of his neck, he let the seconds tick by. His ears momentarily picked up the faint whine of a jet engine.

The oxygen mask! If he were knocked out on landing and still had it on, he would suffocate when the oxygen in the seat pan ran out. He had to get rid of it. With his right hand he fumbled for the catches that held the mask to his helmet. He had no dexterity, and terror threatened to overwhelm him. He fought down the killing panic and fingered the place where the catches had to be. He found them and disconnected the mask and threw it out into the darkness. Through it all, he kept a death grip on the left riser.

Again using his right hand, he felt for the quick-release fittings on the lap belt. He would have no need for the seat pan, which was for landing in water. He unlatched the right-hand fitting and was aware of the weight shifting on the back of his thighs. Carefully changing hands on the risers, he struggled with the left fitting. Finally the weight on his legs vanished as the seat pan fell away. His right hand automatically seized the right riser again.

He heard the dull boom of a distant explosion. His airplane, probably. The end of Devil 500.

A faint breeze fanned his face. Somewhere below, the jungle waited. When will it come up? The darkness was total. He thought of his flashlight in the survival vest, but he didn't want to risk losing it on landing.

The pounding of his heart and the gentle kiss of the wind and rain and the reassuring tautness of the riser straps were the only sensory stimuli in the dark silence.

He begin to think. Would he land in trees or a paddy or a rock-strewn creek? Would he be dashed against a cliff? He hooked his legs together to protect his crotch and placed his left hand on his right shoulder and his right hand on his left, then lowered his face into the crook of his elbows. Now to wait.

His body was tense, awaiting the impact. Relax, he told himself. No, stay tense. Keep those legs together and protect the family jewels.

Something tore at his legs, then smashed into his body. He was pummeled by a series of rapid, rock-hard blows, and he felt his legs become separated and a fire of agony ripped up his left side. He was tumbling and his arms were flailing, searching for the risers that were no longer there. He took bullwhip lashes across the lower part of his face. Then he lost consciousness.

THE ELEMENTS

by Antoine de Saint-Exupéry

When Joseph Conrad described a typhoon he said very little about towering waves, or darkness, or the whistling of the wind in the shrouds. He knew better. Instead, he took his reader down into the hold of the vessel, packed with emigrant coolies, where the rolling and the pitching of the ship had ripped up and scattered their bags and bundles, burst open their boxes, and flung their humble belongings into a crazy heap. Family treasures painfully collected in a lifetime of poverty, pitiful mementoes so alike that nobody but their owners could have told them apart, had lost their identity and lapsed into chaos, into anonymity, into an amorphous magma. It was this human drama that Conrad described when he painted a typhoon.

Every airline pilot has flown through tornadoes, has returned out of them to the fold—to the little restaurant in Toulouse where we sat in peace under the watchful eye of the waitress—and there, recognizing his powerlessness to convey what he has been through, has given up the idea of describing hell. His descriptions, his gestures, his big words would have made the rest of us smile as if we were listening to a little boy bragging. And necessarily so. The cyclone of which I am about to speak was, physically, much the most brutal and overwhelming experience I ever underwent; and yet beyond a certain point I do not know how to convey its violence except by piling one adjective on another, so that in the end I should convey no impression at all—unless perhaps that of an embarrassing taste for exaggeration.

It took me some time to grasp the fundamental reason for this powerlessness, which is simply that I should be trying to describe a catastrophe that never took place. The reason why writers fail when they attempt to evoke horror is that horror is something invented after the fact, when one is re-creating the experience over again in the memory. Horror does not manifest itself in the world of reality. And so, in beginning my story of a revolt of the elements which I myself lived through I have no feeling that I shall write something which you will find dramatic.

I had taken off from the field at Trelew and was flying down to Comodoro-Rivadavia, in the Patagonian Argentine. Here the crust of the earth is as dented as an old boiler. The high-pressure regions over the Pacific send the winds past a gap in the Andes into a corridor fifty miles wide through which they rush to the Atlantic in a strangled and accelerated buffeting that scrapes the surface of everything in their path. The sole vegetation visible in this barren landscape is a plantation of oil derricks looking like the after-effects of a forest fire. Towering over the round hills on which the winds have left a residue of stony gravel, there rises a chain of prow-shaped, saw-toothed, razor-edged mountains stripped by the elements down to the bare rock.

For three months of the year the speed of these winds at ground level is up to a hundred miles an hour. We who flew the route knew that once we had crossed the marshes of Trelew and had reached the threshold of the zone they swept, we should recognize the winds from afar by a grey-blue tint in the atmosphere at the sight of which we would tighten our belts and shoulder-straps in preparation for what was coming. From then on we had an hour of stiff fighting and of stumbling again and again into invisible ditches of air. This was manual labor, and our muscles felt it pretty much as if we had been carrying a longshoreman's load. But it lasted only an hour. Our machines stood up under it. We had no fear of wings suddenly dropping off. Visibility was generally good, and not a problem. This section of the line was a stint, yes; it was certainly not a drama.

But on this particular day I did not like the color of the sky.

The sky was blue. Pure blue. Too pure. A hard blue sky that shone over the scraped and barren world while the fleshless vertebrae of the mountain chain flashed in the sunlight. Not a cloud. The blue sky glittered like a new-honed knife. I felt in advance the vague distaste that accompanies the prospect of physical exertion. The purity of the sky upset me. Give me a good black storm in which the enemy is plainly visible. I can measure its extent and prepare myself for its attack. I can get my hands on my adversary. But when you are flying very high in clear weather the shock of a blue storm is as disturbing as if something collapsed that had been holding up your ship in the air. It is the only time when a pilot feels that there is a gulf beneath his ship.

Another thing bothered me. I could see on a level with the mountain peaks not a haze, not a mist, not a sandy fog, but a sort of ash-colored streamer in the sky. I did not like the look of that scarf of filings scraped off the surface of the earth and borne out to sea by the wind. I tightened my leather harness as far as it would go and I steered the ship with one hand while with the other I hung on to the longeron that ran alongside my seat. I was still flying in remarkably calm air.

Very soon came a slight tremor. As every pilot knows, there are secret little quiverings that foretell your real storm. No rolling, no pitching. No swing to speak of. The flight continues horizontal and rectilinear. But you have felt a warning drum on the wings of your plane, little intermittent rappings scarcely audible and infinitely brief, little cracklings from time to time as if there were traces of gunpowder in the air.

And then everything round me blew up.

Concerning the next couple of minutes I have nothing to say. All that I can find in my memory is a few rudimentary notions, fragments of thoughts, direct observations. I cannot compose them into a dramatic recital because there was no drama. The best I can do is to line them up in a kind of chronological order.

In the first place, I was standing still. Having banked right in order to correct a sudden drift, I saw the landscape freeze abruptly where it was and remain jiggling on the same spot. I was making no headway. My wings had ceased to nibble into the outline of the earth. I could see the earth buckle, pivot—but it stayed put. The plane was skidding as if on a toothless cogwheel.

Meanwhile I had the absurd feeling that I had exposed myself completely to the enemy. All those peaks, those crests, those teeth that were cutting into the wind and unleashing its gusts in my direction, seemed to me so many guns pointed straight at my defenseless person. I was slow to think, but the thought did come to me that I ought to give up altitude and make for one of the neighboring valleys where I might take shelter against a mountainside. As a matter of fact, whether I liked it or not I was being helplessly sucked down towards the earth.

Trapped this way in the first breaking waves of a cyclone about which I learned, twenty minutes later, that at sea level it was blowing at the fantastic rate of one hundred and fifty miles an hour, I certainly had no impression of tragedy. Now, as I write, if I shut my eyes, if I forget the plane and the flight and try to express the plain truth about what was happening to me, I find that I felt weighed down, I felt like a porter carrying a slippery load, grabbing one object in a jerky movement that sent another slithering down, so that, overcome by exasperation, the porter is tempted to let the whole load drop. There is a kind of law of the shortest distance to the image, a psychological law by which the event to which one is subjected is visualized in a symbol that represents its swiftest summing up: I was a man who, carrying a pile of plates, had slipped on a waxed floor and let his scaffolding of porcelain crash.

I found myself imprisoned in a valley. My discomfort was not less, it was greater. I grant you that a down current has never killed anybody, that the expression "flattened out by a down current" belongs to journalism and not to the language of flyers. How could air possibly pierce the ground? But here I was in a valley at the wheel of a ship that was three-quarters out of my control. Ahead of me a rocky prow swung to left and right, rose suddenly high in the air for a second like a wave over my head, and then plunged down below my horizon.

Horizon? There was no longer a horizon. I was in the wings of a theatre cluttered up with bits of scenery. Vertical, oblique, horizontal, all of plane geometry was awhirl. A hundred transversal valleys were muddled in a jumble of perspectives. Whenever I seemed about to take my bearings a new eruption would swing me round in a circle or send me tumbling wing over wing and I would have to try all over again to get clear of all this rubbish. Two ideas came into my mind. One was a discovery: for the first time I understood the cause of certain accidents in the mountains when no fog was present to explain them. For a single second, in a waltzing landscape like this, the flyer had been unable to distinguish between vertical mountainsides and horizontal planes. The other idea was a fixation: The sea is flat: I shall not hook anything out at sea.

I banked—or should I use that word to indicate a vague and stubborn jockeying through the east-west valleys? Still nothing pathetic to report. I was wrestling with chaos, was wearing myself out in a battle with chaos, struggling to keep in the air a gigantic house of cards that kept collapsing despite all I could do. Scarcely the faintest twinge of fear went through me when one of the walls of my prison rose suddenly like a tidal wave over my head. My heart hardly skipped a beat when I was tripped up by one of the whirling eddies of air that the sharp ridge darted into my ship. If I felt anything unmistakably in the haze of confused feelings and notions that came over me each time one of these powder magazines blew up, it was a feeling of respect. I respected that sharp-toothed ridge. I respected that peak. I respected that dome. I respected that transversal valley opening out into my valley and about to toss me God knew how violently as soon as its torrent of wind flowed into the one on which I was being borne along.

What I was struggling against, I discovered, was not the wind but the ridge itself, the crest, the rocky peak. Despite my distance from it, it was the wall of rock I was fighting with. By some trick of invisible prolongation, by the play of a secret set of muscles, this was what was pummeling me. It was against this that I was butting my head. Before me on the right I recognized the peak of Salamanca, a perfect cone which, I knew, dominated the sea. It cheered me to think I was about to escape out to sea. But first I should have to wrestle with the gale off that peak, try to avoid its down-crushing blow. The peak of Salamanca was a giant. I was filled with respect for the peak of Salamanca.

There had been granted me one second of respite. Two seconds. Something was collecting itself into a knot, coiling itself up, growing taut. I sat amazed. I opened astonished eyes. My whole plane seemed to be shivering, spreading outward, swelling up. Horizontal and stationary it was, yet lifted before I knew it fifteen hundred feet straight into the air in a kind of apotheosis. I who for forty minutes had not been able to climb higher than two hundred feet off the ground was suddenly able to look down on the enemy. The plane quivered as if in boiling water. I could see the wide waters of the ocean. The valley opened out into this ocean, this salvation. —And at that very moment, without any warning whatever, half a mile from Salamanca, I was suddenly struck straight in the midriff by the gale off that peak and sent hurtling out to sea.

There I was, throttle wide open, facing the coast. At right angles to the coast and facing it. A lot had happened in a single minute. In the first place, I had not flown out to sea. I had been spat out to sea by a monstrous cough, vomited out of my valley as from the mouth of a howitzer. When, what seemed to me instantly, I banked in order to put myself where I wanted to be in respect of the coast-line, I saw that the coast-line was a mere blur, a characterless strip of blue; and I was five miles out to sea. The mountain range stood up like a crenelated fortress against the pure sky while the cyclone crushed me down to the surface of the waters. How hard that wind was blowing I found out as soon as I tried to climb, as soon as I became conscious of my disastrous mistake: throttle wide open, engines running at my maximum, which was one hundred and fifty miles an hour, my plane hanging sixty feet over the water, I was unable to budge. When a wind like this one attacks a tropical forest it swirls through the branches like a flame, twists them into corkscrews, and uproots giant trees as if they were radishes. Here, bounding off the mountain range, it was leveling out the sea.

Hanging on with all the power in my engines, face to the coast, face to that wind where each gap in the teeth of the range sent forth a stream of air like a long reptile, I felt as if I were clinging to the tip of a monstrous whip that was cracking over the sea.

In this latitude the South American continent is narrow and the Andes are not far from the Atlantic. I was struggling not merely against the whirling winds that blew off the east-coast range, but more likely also against a whole sky blown down upon me off the peaks of the Andean chain. For the first time in four years of airline flying I began to worry about the strength of my wings. Also, I was fearful of bumping the sea—not because of the down currents which, at sea level, would necessarily provide me with a horizontal air mattress, but because of the helplessly acrobatic positions in which this wind was buffeting me. Each time that I was tossed I became afraid that I might be unable to straighten out. Besides, there was a chance that I should find myself out of fuel and simply drown. I kept expecting the gasoline pumps to stop priming, and indeed the plane was so violently shaken up that in the half-filled tanks as well as in the gas lines the gasoline was sloshing round, not coming through, and the engines, instead of their steady roar, were sputtering in a sort of dot-and-dash series of uncertain growls.

I hung on, meanwhile, to the controls of my heavy transport plane, my attention monopolized by the physical struggle and my mind occupied by the very simplest thoughts. I was feeling practically nothing as I stared down at the imprint made by the wind on the sea. I saw a series of great white puddles, each perhaps eight hundred yards in extent. They were running towards me at a speed of one hundred and fifty miles an hour where the down-surging windspouts broke against the surface of the sea in a succession of horizontal explosions. The sea was white and it was green—white with the whiteness of crushed sugar and green in puddles the color of emeralds. In this tumult one wave was indistinguishable from another. Torrents of air were pouring down upon the sea. The winds were sweeping past in giant gusts as when, before the autumn harvests, they blow a great flowing change of color over a wheatfield. Now and again the water went incongruously transparent between the white pools, and I could see a green and black sea-bottom. And then the great glass of the sea would be shattered anew into a thousand glittering fragments.

It seemed hopeless. In twenty minutes of struggle I had not moved forward a hundred yards. What was more, with flying as hard as it was out here five miles from the coast, I wondered how I could possibly buck the winds along the shore, assuming I was able to fight my way in. I was a perfect target for the enemy there on shore. Fear, however, was out of the question. I was incapable of thinking. I was emptied of everything except the vision of a very simple act. I must straighten out. Straighten out. Straighten out.

There were moments of respite, nevertheless. I dare say those moments themselves were equal to the worst storms I had hitherto met, but by comparison with the cyclone they were moments of relaxation. The urgency of fighting off the wind was not quite so great. And I could tell when these intervals were coming. It was not I who moved towards those zones of relative calm, those almost green oases clearly painted on the sea, but they that flowed towards me. I could read clearly in the waters the advertisement of a habitable province. And with each interval of repose the power to feel and to think was restored to me. Then, in those moments, I began to feel I was doomed. Then was the time that little by little I began to tremble for myself. So much so that each time I saw the unfurling of a new wave of the white offensive I was seized by a brief spasm of panic which lasted until the exact instant when, on the edge of that bubbling cauldron, I bumped into the invisible wall of wind. That restored me to numbness again.

Up! I wanted to be higher up. The next time I saw one of those green zones of calm it seemed to me deeper than before and I began to be hopeful of getting out. If I could climb high enough, I thought, I would find other currents in which I could make some headway. I took advantage of the truce to essay a swift climb. It was hard. The enemy had not weakened. Three hundred feet. Six hundred feet. If I could get up to three thousand feet I was safe, I said to myself. But there on the horizon I saw again that white pack unleashed in my direction. I gave it up. I did not want them at my throat again; I did not want to be caught off balance. But it was too late. The first blow sent me rolling over and over and the sky became a slippery dome on which I could not find a footing.

One has a pair of hands and they obey. How are one's orders transmitted to one's hands?

I had made a discovery that horrified me: my hands were numb. My hands were dead. They sent me no message. Probably they had been numb a long time and I had not noticed it. The pity was that I had noticed it, had raised the question. That was serious.

Lashed by the wind, the wings of the plane had been dragging and jerking at the cables by which they were controlled from the wheel, and the wheel in my hands had not ceased jerking a single second. I had been gripping the wheel with all my might for forty minutes, fearful lest the strain snap the cables. So desperate had been my grip that now I could not feel my hands.

What a discovery! My hands were not my own. I looked at them and decided to lift a finger: it obeyed me. I looked away and issued the same order: now I could not feel whether the finger had obeyed or not. No message had reached me. I thought: "Suppose my hands were to open: how would I know it?" I swung my head round and looked again: my hands were still locked round the wheel. Nevertheless, I was afraid. How can a man tell the difference between the sight of a hand opening and the decision to open that hand, when there is no longer an exchange of sensations between the hand and the brain? How can one tell the difference between an image and an act of the will? Better stop thinking of the picture of open hands. Hands live a life of their own. Better not offer them this monstrous temptation. And I began to chant a silly litany which went on uninterruptedly until this flight was over. A single thought. A single image. A single phrase tirelessly chanted over and over again: "I shut my hands. I shut my hands. I shut my hands." All of me was condensed into that phrase and for me the white sea, the whirling eddies, the saw-toothed range ceased to exist. There was only "I shut my hands." There was no danger, no cyclone, no land unattained. Somewhere there was a pair of rubber hands which, once they let go the wheel, could not possibly come alive in time to recover from the tumbling drop into the sea.

I had no thoughts. I had no feelings except the feeling of being emptied out. My strength was draining out of me and so was my impulse to go on fighting. The engines continued their dot-and-dash sputterings, their little crashing noises that were like the intermittent cracklings of a ripping canvas. Whenever they were silent longer than a second I felt as if a heart had stopped beating. There! that's the end. No, they've started up again.

The thermometer on the wing, I happened to see, stood at twenty below zero, but I was bathed in sweat from head to foot. My face was running with perspiration. What a dance! Later I was to discover that my storage batteries had been jerked out of their steel flanges and hurtled up through the roof of the plane. I did not know then, either, that the ribs on my wings had come unglued and that certain of my steel cables had been sawed down to the last thread. And I continued to feel strength and will oozing out of me. Any minute now I should be overcome by the indifference born of utter weariness and by the mortal yearning to take my rest.

What can I say about this? Nothing. My shoulders ached. Very painfully. As if I had been carrying too many sacks too heavy for me. I leaned forward. Through a green transparency I saw sea-bottom so close that I could make out all the details. Then the wind's hand brushed the picture away.

In an hour and twenty minutes I had succeeded in climbing to nine hundred feet. A little to the south—that is, on my left—I could see a long trail on the surface of the sea, a sort of blue stream. I decided to let myself drift as far down as that stream. Here where I was, facing west, I was as good as motionless, unable either to advance or retreat. If I could reach that blue pathway, which must be lying in the shelter of something not the cyclone, I might be able to move in slowly to the coast. So I let myself drift to the left. I had the feeling, meanwhile, that the wind's violence had perhaps slackened.

It took me an hour to cover the five miles to shore. There in the shelter of a long cliff I was able to finish my journey south. Thereafter I succeeded in keeping enough altitude to fly inland to the field that was my destination. I was able to stay up at nine hundred feet. It was very stormy, but nothing like the cyclone I had come out of. That was over.

On the ground I saw a platoon of soldiers. They had been sent down to watch for me. I landed near by and we were a whole hour getting the plane into the hangar. I climbed out of the cockpit and walked off. There was nothing to say. I was very sleepy. I kept moving my fingers, but they stayed numb. I could not collect my thoughts enough to decide whether or not I had been afraid. Had I been afraid? I couldn't say. I had witnessed a strange sight. What strange sight? I couldn't say. The sky was blue and the sea was white. I felt I ought to tell someone about it since I was back from so far away! But I had no grip on what I had been through. "Imagine a white sea . . . very white . . . whiter still." You cannot convey things to people by piling up adjectives, by stammering.

You cannot convey anything because there is nothing to convey. My shoulders were aching. My insides felt as if they had been crushed in by a terrible weight. You cannot make drama out of that, or out of the cone-shaped peak of Salamanca. That peak was charged like a powder magazine; but if I said so people would laugh. I would myself. I respected the peak of Salamanca. That is my story. And it is not a story.

There is nothing dramatic in the world, nothing pathetic, except in human relations. The day after I landed I might get emotional, might dress up my adventure by imagining that I who was alive and walking on earth was living through the hell of a cyclone. But that would be cheating, for the man who fought tooth and nail against that cyclone had nothing in common with the fortunate man alive the next day. He was far too busy.

I came away with very little booty indeed, with no more than this meagre discovery, this contribution: How can one tell an act of the will from a simple image when there is no transmission of sensation?

FIRST ACROSS THE TASMAN SEA—ALONE

by Francis Chichester

It was 9.30 a.m. local time. I could not get back to salute the people on the jetty—I just felt burnt out. A stiff breeze chased the seaplane along, and the sea glittered in the sunlight coming from behind my right shoulder. The sun seemed too far north for so early in the day: was my compass wrong? I uncased the slide rule, and computed the sun's true bearing. Of course, I had forgotten that it was nearly mid-winter, and the sun at its farthest north; the compass was all right. As the tailwind was drifting the seaplane slightly off course to the north, I changed direction ten degrees to the south. Observing for drift was an irksome fatigue; I wanted only to sit and muse. It seemed to me that with Australia presenting a face nearly 2,000 miles long it did not much matter whether I made a bull's-eye of Sydney or not. My wits were certainly bemused, otherwise I would have realized that this Australian coastline had a receding chin, and that every degree I flew south of the course rapidly increased the distance to land which might soon become greater than my range, whereas every degree north of the course would have shortened the flight over the sea.

Fifty-five minutes out, the mountains were still visible 100 miles astern, like two tiny warts on the face of the ocean. It seemed perfect weather, with a tailwind of forty m.p.h. I was nearly a quarter of the way across in one hour. But the wind had backed, and I was ten miles off course to the south as a result. At 160 miles out I had a shock: the engine backfired with a report loud above the roar—a thing it had never done before in full flight. Was there another piece of skin in the carburetor? I sat utterly still, waiting for the final splutter and choke. The engine continued firing. I reached up and tried the starboard magneto; it was all right. I tried the port, and the engine dropped fifty revs, firing roughly and harshly. A defective magneto—the only parts I had not repaired myself! The engine ran harshly for two minutes while I listened intently, then suddenly it broke into an even smooth roar again. Thank God it was not the carburetor! And I did have two magnetos.

By the end of the second hour the wind had backed still more to the north, but still was driving the plane onwards. I had covered 217 miles, nearly half-way, in two hours. Again through the change of wind I had not corrected enough for drift, and was now twenty-five miles off course to the south. Every mile to the south added length to the flight, but it did not seem to make much odds in such perfect conditions. I changed course another ten degrees to northward.

Then came clouds, and I could see that I might be unable to get a sextant shot. I did not worry much at first—there did not seem much to worry about with a target 2,000 miles wide ahead. But the wind was increasing, and backing persistently. At 250 miles out the sky was completely shut off by dull grey, threatening cloud. I spurred myself to make some hurried drift observations; the wind had increased to fifty m.p.h. from the north-east, and the seaplane was forty-three miles off course to the south. With the drift, we were heading obliquely for the receding part of Australia. Forty-three miles off course seemed a lot, and I wished that I had not allowed it to build up so much. I changed course another ten degrees northwards.

At three hours out heavy rain stung my face. The drift to the south was becoming alarming; the wind had backed till it was now right in the north. I changed course another ten degrees to the north, which put the wind dead abeam. I dared not correct the drift more than that, or I should have made a head wind of the gale, which I sensed would destroy my chance of reaching the mainland. The seaplane was drifting forty degrees to the south, and moving half sideways over the water, like a crab. The rain became a downpour—I had forgotten that it could rain so heavily. I kept my head down as much as possible, but the water caught the top of my helmet, streamed down my face and poured down my neck. We seemed to strike a solid wall of water with a crash. I ducked my head, and from the corner of my eye I could see water leaving the trailing edge of the wings in a sheet, to be shattered instantly by the air blast. On either side of my head the water poured into the cockpit in two streams, which were scattered like windblown waterfalls and blew into my face. I was flying blind, as if in a dense cloud of smoke. I throttled back, and began a slanting dive for the water. Panic clutched me: if I got out of control, I would be too low to recover. But panic meant dying like a paralysed rabbit. I remember saying out loud, "Keep cool! Keep cool! K-e-e-p c-o-o-l!" The seaplane passed through small sudden bumps, which shook it violently. I looked over at the air speed indicator on the strut, but I could not see either the pointer or the figures in the smother of water. I had to make do with the rev indicator; if the revs increased, the dive was steepening. I felt that I had to find the surface of the sea, for I dared not try to climb blind. If I lost control and tried to spin out, the sea would not show up quickly enough to level off. I sat dead still, moving only my eyes from compass to rev indicator to vertically downwards over the cockpit edge. When the engine speed increased, I used the control-stick lightly with finger and thumb to ease up the plane's nose. There was more chance of the seaplane's flying itself level than of my keeping it level, flying blind. Thank God it was rigged true.

At last I saw a dull patch of water below the lower wing rushing up at me. I pushed the throttle, the engine misfired, and failed to pick up. I thrust the lever wide open as I flattened the seaplane out above the water; the engine spluttered, broke into an uneven rattle and backfired intermittently; its roughness shaking the whole plane. But the plane kept up, and lumbered on. I concentrated on flying. The engine continued with an uneven tearing noise. The sea was only visible a plane's length ahead, where it merged in the grey wall of rainwater. I was flying in the centre of a hollow grey globe, with nothing to help me to keep level except the small patch where the globe rested on the sea. I hugged every wave, rising or falling with it, and the seaplane jerked its way along. The water poured over my goggles, distorting my sight; it ran down my face and neck, and streams of it trickled down my chest, stomach and back. I dared not take my eyes off the water to look at the compass or the rev indicator. One thing helped me—the violence of the gale itself. Although the seaplane headed in one direction, it was being blown sideways, so that it crabbed along half left, and I could see the next wave between the wings instead of its being hidden by the fuselage. I steered by the drift, keeping the angle of it constant. Otherwise I should have wandered aimlessly about the sea. There was a furious cross sea. Waves shot upward, to lick at the machine, but were slashed away bodily southwards by the wind. The tails of spume streaking south across the wave troughs enabled me to steer a straight course. I knew that I was flying as I had never flown before, but I also knew that I could not last long at that pace. At any moment I expected a muscle to lag, and the seaplane to strike a wavecrest. Suddenly I found myself flying straight into the water, and snatched back the stick to jump the seaplane's nose up, thinking my eye and hand had at last failed me. Then I realized that the rainfall had eased while I was in the trough between two rollers, and that the crest of the swell ahead had unshrouded above me. Next instant the seaplane shot into the open air. I rose 30 feet, and snatched the goggles up to my forehead. It seemed like 3,000 feet.

The compass showed that I was fifty-five degrees off course, headed to miss even Tasmania. That seemed strange, for I thought that I could fly accurately by the drift. I soon saw what had happened—the wind had backed another forty-five degrees, and was now north-west. I had to think hard. I picked up the chart case on which my chart was rolled, but the soaked chart was useless. Before the storm I had been drifted so far south that I was right on the edge of the chart; during the storm I was blown farther south at the rate of a mile a minute, and was now far off it. I had a small map of Australia torn from a school atlas on the island. There was not enough sea area on it to show Lord Howe Island's position, but it was the only thing to use. Where was I before the storm? The position on the school map came right in the middle of a city plan of Sydney in the corner.

I flew up to another line squall ahead, parallel to the previous storm, and stretching from horizon to horizon, but I could see the water on the other side, as through a gauzy curtain. The rain was heavy, but the engine still carried on. We flew through the curtain of rain into an immense cavern of space between the illimitable vault of dull sky above, and the immeasurable floor of dull water below. It was solitary in that great space. Some slanting pillars of rain leaned against the wind, trailing across the dull floor of water like spirits of the dead drifting from the infernal regions. The vastness lent it all a nightmare air. In one place the vaulted ceiling bulged downwards with two black-cored squall clouds, each linked to the sea by a column of waterspout. Between the two columns another waterspout, a slender grey-white pillar was rising from the sea's surface. At a good height it burst at the top, like smoke expanding after an explosion. I flew straight towards it, fascinated. Suddenly the engine burst into a rough clatter again, and I realized that I must not fly near that thing; the disturbance capable of twisting it from the sea must be terrific.

I thought I saw land away to the north-west, purple foothills with a mountain range behind, but when I looked for it again later it had disappeared; land was still 160 miles away. At the foot of a great storm-cloud I saw smoke—a ship. It offered me a new lease of life, and I immediately turned towards it. It lay at the edge of the storm like a duck at the foot of a black cliff. I swooped down and read the name *Kurow* on the stern. It was an awesome sight. The bows slid out of one comber, and crashed into the next, to churn up a huge patch of seething water. When a cross swell struck her, she lurched heavily, slid into a trough and sank, decks awash, as if waterlogged; but wallowed out, rolling first on one beam and then the other, discharging water from her decks as though over a weir. There was no sign of life on board, and I could not imagine anything less capable of helping me. I felt as if a door had been slammed in my face, turned and made off north-west to round the storm. I felt that I would rather go fifty miles out of my way than face another storm. I had been only four hours thirty-five minutes in the air: it seemed a lifetime.

Round the storm we flew into calm air under a weak hazy sun. I took out the sextant and got two shots. It took me thirty minutes to work them out, for the engine kept backfiring, and my attention wandered every time it did so. The sight in the end was not much use; the sun was too far west, but I got some self-respect from doing the job.

Suddenly, ahead and thirty degrees to the left, there were bright flashes in several places, like the dazzle of a heliograph. I saw a dull grey-white airship coming towards me. It seemed impossible, but I could have sworn that it *was* an airship, nosing towards me like an oblong pearl. Except for a cloud or two, there was nothing else in the sky. I looked around, sometimes catching a flash or a glint, and turning again to look at the airship I found that it had disappeared. I screwed up my eyes, unable to believe them, and twisted the seaplane this way and that, thinking that the airship must be hidden by a blind spot. Dazzling flashes continued in four or five different places, but I still could not pick out any planes. Then, out of some clouds to my right front, I saw another, or the same, airship advancing. I watched it intently, determined not to look away for a fraction of a second: I'd see what happened to this one, if I had to chase it. It drew steadily closer, until perhaps a mile away, when suddenly it vanished. Then it reappeared, close to where it had vanished: I watched with angry intentness. It drew closer, and I could see the dull gleam of light on its nose and back. It came on, but instead of increasing in size, it diminished as it approached. When quite near, it suddenly became its own ghost—one second I could see through it, and the next it had vanished. I decided that it could only be a diminutive cloud, perfectly shaped like an airship and then dissolving, but it was uncanny that it should exactly resume the same shape after it had once vanished. I turned towards the flashes, but those too, had vanished. All this was many years before anyone spoke of flying saucers. Whatever it was I saw, it seems to have been very much like what people have since claimed to be flying saucers.

I felt intensely lonely, and the feeling of solitude intensified at every fresh sight of "land", which turned out to be yet one more illusion or delusion by cloud. After six hours and five minutes in the air I saw land again, and it was still there ten minutes later. I still did not quite believe it, but three minutes later I was almost on top of a river winding towards me through dark country. A single hill rose from low land ahead, and a high, black, unfriendly-looking mountain range formed the background. A heavy bank of clouds on top hid the sun, which was about to set.

Well, this was Australia. Away to the south lay a great bay, and at the far side I spotted five ships anchored. They were warships. I flew south, and crossed the bay. Flying low between the two lines of ships I read HMAS *Australia,* HMAS *Canberra.* On the other side there appeared to be an aircraft-carrier. My heart warmed at the thought of getting sanctuary there, but all the ships had a cold, lifeless air about them. I supposed that I must fly on to Sydney. I flew over an artificial breakwater near a suburb of red-bricked, red-tiled, bungalows and houses like a small suburb in a dull-brown desert, with only a few sparse trees of drab green. There was not a sign of life, and not a wisp of smoke from the chimneys. Had the world died in my absence? If there was anyone left alive, there would surely be a watchman on one of the warships. I turned and alighted beside the *Australia,* its huge bulk towering above me. The seaplane drifted past and away from it, bobbing about on the cockling water. There was dead silence except for the soft *chop chop chop* against the float. I felt a fool to drop into this nest of disdainful battleships. I stood on the cockpit edge, and began morsing to the *Canberra* with my handkerchief. An Aldis lamp at once flashed back at me from the interior of the bridge. A motor-launch shot round the bows of the warship. I cancelled my signal, and stood waiting.

"How far is Sydney?"

"Eighty miles."

I dreaded the thought of Sydney, and its crowds, but my job was to reach it. The launch was crowded with sailors, and at 20 yards their robust personalities gave me a feeling of inferiority. I felt that I had to get away quickly. I asked the launch to tow me to the shelter of the breakwater, and a sailor slipped me a tow rope efficiently. I climbed out on to the float to swing the propeller, and as I swung it I noticed mares' tails of sticky black soot on the cowling, due to the backfires. I wondered if the engine still had enough kick to get me away, but as soon as the seaplane started moving forward and pounding the swells, the futility of trying to take off was obvious. That settled it; I had to ask for help. The launch approached again. "We'll tow you to *Albatross,*" an officer said. I made fast the tow line and I was towed up to the aircraft carrier, where I made fast to a rope dangling from the end of a long boom. I released the pigeons, feeling sorry for them, and they took off flapping and fluttering, presumably for their home loft near Sydney. A sailor let down a rope ladder from the boom, and I grappled clumsily up it, my feet often swinging out higher than my head. I made my way along the boom to the deck where a commanding figure, with much gold braid, was waiting for me. "Doctor Livingstone, I assume," he said, looking hard at me. "At any rate, you have managed to discover the only aircraft carrier in the Southern Hemisphere. Come along to my cabin."

I felt like a new boy in front of the headmaster. "Did I say, when you came aboard, 'Doctor Livingstone, I *as*sume?' Of course, I meant, 'Doctor Livingstone, I *pre*sume?'." But Captain Feakes of the Royal Australian Navy was a great host. He gave me whisky and soda and made me feel like a long-expected, favourite guest. Yet I felt isolated, and drained of personality, horribly cut off from other people by some queer gulf of loneliness. I had achieved my great ambition, to fly across the Tasman Sea alone, I had found the islands by my own system of navigation which depended on accurate sun-sights worked out while flying alone, something which no one had ever done before and perhaps no one ever would do in similar circumstances. I had not then learned that I would feel an intense depression every time I achieved a great ambition; I had not then discovered that the joy of living comes from action, from making the attempt, from the effort, not from success.

Squadron-Leader Hewitt of the Australian Air Force arrived and offered to lift the seaplane on board *Albatross.* I asked him to let me do the job of hooking on. It was dark when I went on deck. An arc-lamp shed a brilliance high up but only a dim light reached the seaplane as she was towed slowly under the lowered crane-hook. Standing on the top of the engine of the bobbing seaplane I tried to catch the ponderous hook; it was a giant compared with the one at Norfolk Island, with a great iron hoop round it, probably a help in hooking on big flying-boats, but only adding to my difficulties. I had to duck the hoop to catch the hook with one hand, and reach under it with the other to keep the two sling wires taut with the spreaders in place and the middle points of the wires ready for the hook. The hook itself was so heavy that I could not lift it with my arm outstretched. The seaplane was rolling, and also there was a slight movement of the aircraft carrier, sufficient to tear the hook from my grasp, however tightly I clung with my knees jockeywise to the engine cowling. At last I had the wires taut and the hook in place under them, when either the seaplane dropped or the aircraft carrier rolled unexpectedly. The hook snatched and lifted the seaplane with my fingers between the hook and the wires. The pain was excruciating, as the wires bit through my fingers. I shrieked. I felt ashamed; but I knew that my cry was the quickest signal I could give the winchman. The hook lowered, and I sat on the engine top, knees doubled up, leaning against the petrol tank. I could not bear to look at my hand. The hook swung like a huge pendulum above me. I felt, well, I had bragged of my skill at this job; I should just have to get on with it. I cuddled the round of the iron hook in the palm of my right hand, and rested the wires in the crook of my thumb of the other hand. Everything went easily. "Lift!" I said. The water fell away, and at last the seaplane swung inboard, stopped swinging, and dropped softly on to padded mats. I said to a man standing by, "Help me down, will you? I am going to faint."

When I came to I was in the ship's hospital. My right hand was crushed, but I lost only the top of one finger. The surgeon cut off the crushed bone and sewed up the flesh. I then became the guest of the wardroom officers as well as of Captain Feakes, and it is hard to recount such marvellous hospitality. It was like staying in the best club with the mysterious fascination of naval life added.

IN A TYPHOON'S EYE

by Royal Leonard

The last day of June 1941 dawned hot and muggy on the ground, but it was cool and crisp at twelve thousand feet in the air. I was on my unsuspecting way to keep a date with a typhoon.

The evening of the twenty-ninth I had laid over at the bomb-shattered field of Kweilin, four hundred miles from Hong Kong. Radio advices from the British Crown colony, which was to become an Imperial Japanese colony six months later, told of a typhoon stalking outside the great harbor.

The Chinese know the typhoon as *tai fung.* Its name is composed of two Cantonese syllables which mean "big wind." The English name is a corruption of this description. Actually the typhoon is a whirlpool of air built up by atmospheric masses of unequal pressure. It might be called an invisible doughnut of weather, a platter of wind and rain with a hole in the center called the "eye." Meteorological instruments have recorded that the middle is calm, the "big wind" rotating about it at a rate sometimes reaching over one hundred miles an hour. The typhoon itself moves comparatively slowly, at a rate of about twenty miles an hour. The course of a typhoon, like that of cyclones and whirlwinds, is unpredictable. Sometimes it will veer like a drunken man; sometimes it will halt completely; sometimes it will maintain an equable, predictable course. The diameter of the windless center of the typhoon is also a puzzle, since the thickness of the wind doughnut is nearly unknown. This cannot be determined until after the holocaust of wind is past, and then only by rough guesswork. But on Thirty-and-Six, as the Chinese call the last day of June, I found out.

Unwittingly and unwillingly, I kept my date to fly through the eye of a typhoon. I not only flew through the eye, but I flew down the center, out via one diameter, up through the other diameter, and over the top. In the words of an amazed British air official, I was the "only fool in existence who had luck enough to fly through and come out in one piece."

Man-made dangers would have made the flight ticklish enough. Japanese troops held Canton, and their air patrols were constantly in the sky. They had already evinced their willingness to shoot down commercial airliners of any nation, both from the ground and in the air. Their particular prey was still the C.N.A.C. line. Moreover, I was the special target of their active dislike. Not only was I flying for an airline in which the United States had a large vested interest together with the Nationalist government, but I had also been the personal pilot of Generalissimo Chiang Kai-shek for the past three years. Before that I had flown for the Young Marshal, Chang Hsueh-Liang, a deadly enemy of Japan, who had proffered the anti-Japanese policy to the Generalissimo. And I was still on call as pilot for the man who had been thwarting Japan's Chinese designs for four years. Nevertheless, it was my job to cross the Japanese lines and put down in Hong Kong. The Japanese knew that several of us were sneaking loads across their lines, and they were especially vigilant. Planes were even then being moved up for the push on Hong Kong.

We flew only at night or in bad weather. From Kweilin the usual method was to follow a secret route approximately south-southeast to a point seventy or eighty miles above Hong Kong, then put on full speed and zigzag across the Japanese air patrols out of Canton. The passengers and freight who went with me took their chances—but there was never a letup in the reservations of freight room—it was signed for weeks beforehand.

I was flying a C.N.A.C. Douglas DC-2. It was seven years old, the oldest ship in the whole C.N.A.C. fleet. A wing had been crumpled in an earlier landing, and the whole portside had been rebuilt by native personnel in China. My flight had to be timed almost to the minute, and I had to cross the Japanese lines under cover of darkness if the weather was good. The landing at Hong Kong I wanted to be made precisely at daybreak, since I was heading into unknown weather. If the typhoon was raging, I would need the dawn light for landing. The British Kowloon airport was fronted on the sea and backed by 3000-foot mountains. Light was imperative for a good landing, as it was difficult enough to put down there under the most favorable circumstances. We could not expect help if we met disaster en route, as we were really blockade runners of the air, flying over Japanese territory without official authorization or cognizance.

I had a full load of twelve passengers—two of them American missionaries. There were 525 gallons of gas in my tanks, enough for six hours (the flight would normally take about two hours with luck and the usual tail wind). The 10-ton ship had a baggage load of about six hundred pounds, which put the total about three hundred pounds above the prescribed weight load. This, however, was nothing unusual. There were so many people and so much freight to be moved in China that could not be sent any other way than by plane that we often flew with seven hundred pounds of overload.

There were no weather reports from Hong Kong. They had long since ceased giving them, as they aided the Japanese. The news of the typhoon was broadcast as in an emergency category rather than as a weather bulletin. The British meteorologists calculated that it would strike about 6 P.M. at Hong Kong and pass north and west during the night. On the basis of that report I put down in the mud puddle of a field at Kweilin to wait until the typhoon passed over my destination. Two other pilots were waiting there too. One was Woody; the other was Frank Higgs, famous because of his one continuous thick black eyebrow right above his eyes and because he was caricatured in Terry and the Pirates as "Dude Hennick." They both agreed that I should take off first. I wanted them to fly first into the unknown weather, but I finally became tired of the Alphonse-and-Gaston technique. Besides, I was sure that the typhoon was past. The only thing I was worried about was that I thought I was getting off too late.

We took off without trouble, heading southeast. In the darkness I could see little shreds of clouds in the sky. The sunset had been, I recalled, a bright yellowish red. There had been flashes of lightning on the southern horizon, and they still continued. The air was unusually still, so still that I had slept under a lighted punk stick at Kweilin to keep the mosquitoes away. It was three in the morning, 19.07 Greenwich Meridian Time, when I took off. The radio at Hong Kong was shut off because of lack of personnel. My co-pilot Yue, who had learned flying in the Cantonese air force, could keep the Douglas level, but flying a compass course was beyond him. He had the reputation of being able to lose himself at least twice a month. The country below us was amazingly rugged and mountainous. Flying at twelve thousand feet, it looked as though millions of ice-cream cones, upside down, were jammed together all over the landscape, cones over one thousand feet high.

The faint light of early dawn was livid green. The wind suddenly picked up. It scattered the clouds and, since we were driving straight into it, held us back considerably. At three-thirty the Hong Kong radio station came on the air to give us a bearing. We were three hundred miles from the British Crown colony, speed one hundred and sixty miles an hour. The wind increased, and I noticed a strong drift. I had allowed for ten degrees, which indicates a fairly strong wind, but I was forced to allow for twenty degrees, then thirty. My bearings on Hong Kong were changing rapidly. I had descended to ten thousand feet, going through a thin stratus at eleven thousand feet. The wind was picking up tremendous force. Suddenly we discovered that we were due west of Hong Kong, and I put the throttles all the way forward. Bobbing up and down like a cork in the rapids, we flew and flew. I calculated that I must be near the harbor.

Suddenly, below me, I saw a hole in the stratus clouds. It was approximately a mile across and looked as though it had been bored through the atmosphere with a Celestial brace and bit. At the bottom I could see water, furious waves smashing against rugged, rocky-shored islands. The whole view was as sharply defined as a scene in the movies.

"God must have cut this out with a biscuit cutter," I muttered. I started to spiral down to get below the clouds. In this hole, which I later discovered was the eye of the typhoon, the atmosphere was smooth as silk, but the clouds were thick about it. I went down to fifteen hundred feet before I could get under the ceiling and noticed that the air was filled with heavy rain squalls, driving every which way with the force of a fire hose. It was now sunup, five o'clock in the morning. I headed out of the typhoon's eye toward Hong Kong.

I had flown perhaps a mile, when suddenly the DC-2 leaped like a bucking bronco three hundred feet straight up. During the next fifteen minutes, with my air speed still at one hundred and sixty miles an hour, I went ten miles. The air was so rough that I was forced to throttle down. The churning currents of air smashed the plane about unmercifully.

Hong Kong was in sight. In the harbor I could see British warships at anchor. They were being overwhelmed with huge waves that rolled their masts in arcs of nearly one hundred degrees. The water had backed up so high that it was breaking over the great Kowloon-Hong Kong sea wall. I was afraid that the landing field, which faces directly on the harbor, would be washed away. I was coming in under full power at five hundred feet. The rain was drowning the cockpit in a Niagara of water, in such solid sheets that I could only get an occasional glimpse of where I was going.

Loh, my radio operator, shouted in my ear: "Hong Kong wind thirty-five miles an hour." I could not believe it. Loh checked back and insisted that he was right. Later I discovered that he meant *one hundred and thirty-five* miles an hour. I started to go in, with my landing flaps up. There was a lull in the roughness as I approached the field. Suddenly the air turned into a maelstrom. Terrific gusts struck from all directions. Within a second we were smacked sideways, forward, backward, up and down. The high mountains that form a ring directly behind the Hong Kong landing field cause the wind to boil down their sides in unpredictable waves. One second my landing wheels were barely missing the ground. The next they dangled hundreds of feet in the air. I shouted to Yue to raise the landing gear that I had lowered—it made a drag on the plane which I wanted removed—but he was too terrified with fear.

Loh shouted to me again.

"British weatherman say typhoon still here! Blowing 113 miles an hour!"

This was no place for me or my passengers. I went to the widest part of the bay, then headed into the wind for my climb back through the typhoon.

From two thousand to five thousand feet the rain was more intense than ever. We endured the most terrific bumps we had yet encountered. It felt as I imagine one must feel riding in a speedboat, going at one hundred miles an hour through 30-foot waves—sideways, up and down, corkscrewing all over the sky. At six thousand feet the air was still rough and the water was pouring down the windshield in a continuous stream, but I had control at the throttled-down speed of one hundred and twenty miles an hour. Ten thousand feet was smooth by contrast. At twelve thousand feet I was on top of all the clouds and the air was smooth. I was surprised at the clear weather and the absence of a static condition.

Often, in storms, blue St. Elmo's fire crackles all over the metal skin of the Douglas, until it looks like a flying Christmas tree. The only electrical display of the typhoon consisted of a few flashes of lightning off the center to the west. We finally headed north to Namyung, two hundred miles away from Hong Kong. The wind was still ninety miles an hour at that point, but I managed to put the ship down safely.

That was the end of my experience with the typhoon. I felt as a tenderfoot might after just getting off the wildest of bucking broncos. My knees buckled under me as I walked across the rain-swept Namyung field.

The plane, as verified by mechanics afterward, was in perfect condition. Not a rivet was strained, and inside the cabin only one seat had been broken. One of the passengers, an American businessman, had not strapped himself in. He thought only sissies did that. As a result, his frantic grip had ripped his tubular chair from the floor of the cabin. Later I discovered that the area of the typhoon was about five hundred miles in diameter. The readings of my instrument board during the height of the shaking-up are still a mystery to me. When I looked at them it was like trying to read a newspaper in a vibrating reducing machine.

Higgs and Woods were waiting for me at the Namyung field with grins plastered over their faces. They had played it safe and landed there without attempting Hong Kong.

"Hey, boy!" they hailed me. "What goes? You look all in. Been working hard?"

"Sure have," I told them. "Just licked a typhoon."

SUCKED UP IN A THUNDERCLOUD

by David Lampe, Jr.

Too warm for a flying suit. In slacks and shirt, Derek Piggott squinted skyward. On the point of spilling, cumulus clouds had been piling ominously since morning. Warm and muggy, southern England was perfect for gliding on July 15, 1955—perfect till spikes of lightning began raking cloudbanks a mile from Lasham Airfield.

No use stringing wires up into an electrical storm. Small, loose-jointed, 34-year-old Derek Piggott, Lasham's chief glider instructor, ordered winches and tow cars off the runway. Only the *Tiger Moth* biplane continued kiting the sailplanes aloft.

Imperial College Gliding Club's new *Skylark* sat idly. Piggott got the orange glider onto the grassy runway, and climbed into the pod-like cockpit. He planned to try for a 3,000 meter height gain for his Gold-C, an international gliding achievement badge. And if the weather held, he might reach Diamond-C altitude—a 5,000 meter free climb. Only about five days a year are good for such flying in England; this seemed such a day. Earlier, a jet pilot told Lasham the top of the cumulus reached 30,000 feet. Soggy clouds suck gliders swiftly upward.

Shuddering as the *Tiger Moth* towed it aloft, the *Skylark* felt like an airborne eggshell—a feel Piggott liked. Slouching in his seat he sighted along the tow rope, left hand loose on the control column, body sensitive to the glider's movement. Air tows always recalled combat formation flying. The *Moth* sheered southward from the storm clouds heaped over Lasham's dispersal area. Lightning still snicked nearby as Piggott lifted 1,800 feet into the clear air. To notch the barograph flight-recorder in the cockpit, he pushed the control column hard forward and the *Skylark* dove 100 feet. Piggott pulled the tow-line releasing cable and heeled the *Skylark* on its left wing to show the *Moth* he'd cut free. As his airspeed lowered, the vibration faded and the slipstream's whistle softened to a hiss. He hovered, feeling gently for a thermal updraft.

On the edge of the storm he found it. Tilting the stick, he began an upward spiral. At 3,500 feet, white murk wrapped his glider. He was in a gentle 30-degree rise—a spiral ramp inside an invisible, vertical tunnel. Only the soft slipstream whistle and his own sensitivity told him he was moving—soaring on instruments as he was blown upward on the rim of the storm. Derek planned to cruise northeast through the clouds to compensate for drift. On the instrument panel the glider's variometer had a pair of plastic columns, one marked "up," the other "down," a sensitive little ball afloat in each. The scale between them indicated climb or descent rate in feet-per-second. Sensibly, Piggott wouldn't rely on the variometer in the clouds. Instead he'd check his wristwatch against the altimeter. At 4,000 he did this and pencilled a notation. In five minutes he checked his watch again. The ship was climbing at 14 feet per second —fast but not dangerous.

Ten after four—11,000 feet—air still warm in the snug cockpit. At 12,000, nearing icing level, everything was normal. At 13,000—still going up. At 14,000—trouble! Piggott's body jolted forward. The glider fell and bounced high on an updraft; then slammed downward, then upward again! Piggott steadied the stick lightly, remembering he musn't overcontrol. A sudden ominous noise, a squeaking twisting howl, came from above his head where a pair of clamps held the wing in place. The glider sounded ready to rip apart. To keep from banging his head, Piggott braced hard back in his seat and checked his safety belts with his free hand. The beads in the variometer kept a zany up-down dance as the glider pitched in the turbulent air. The altimeter needle swung back and forth. Derek imagined a bail-out from 14,000 in shirtsleeves and slacks! The cockpit was warm; outside he'd freeze.

More noises! Loud splatting on the wing and tail surfaces—hailstones pelting the glider, crescendoed into sound reminiscent of ack-ack barrage. The storm kept lifting the plane and slamming it forward. The pilot had done plenty of storm and instrument flying in gliders, but never like this. Airspeed wavered between 40 and 50 knots, so Piggott put on the air brakes and the bucking slowed. For a moment he was gliding again, hissing upward through the lashing hail, still all in one piece. He retracted the brakes and slid open the small clear-vision panel on the side of the plexiglass canopy. A burst of pea-size hailstones sprayed his lap.

The hail thinned and the *Skylark* soared peacefully again, but not for long. Like flash bulbs set off behind him, lightning played in the white clouds. No thunder roared, and the white lights weren't strong enough to blind, yet Derek began to feel an occasional tingle from the control column and rudder pedals—static electricity, common in gliders, especially during take-offs.

Still no thunder. Then giant shreds of lightning suddenly began flailing the *Skylark's* fuselage! He gauged the jagged bright stalks at maybe half an inch thick, until lashing toward him, Derek saw a blinding bolt like an oversized spark from an atom smasher. It hit the *Skylark's* nose with a pistol noise, entered the cockpit and jumped from Piggott's right to his left rudder pedal! He felt the current run through the soles of his shoes, and guessed they must be damp. A pungent ozone smell filled the cockpit as the lightning continued to thrash soundlessly near the glider. The loudest noise was still the slipstream whistle, interrupted only occasionally by a distant thunder boom. Was being in the storm's core keeping him from hearing it? Sparks kept bouncing off the glider's fiberglass nose and snicking past at what seemed incredibly slow speeds. Flashes now came every few seconds and the control column grip began to feel as if it had been plugged into a live light socket—and English house current is 220 volts! Piggott's arm stiffened and his eyes ached as the current bucked through him.

It happened again and again! The worst electric shocks he'd ever felt in his life, and he could do nothing to avoid them. He must keep his sweaty hand on the control column. No use kidding himself. He was scared, good and scared. The last bolt of lightning hit so hard that he yelped, *"Yow!"*

The *Skylark* spiraled higher and the lightning died but Piggott began a new line of worry—anoxia—the sickness caused by lack of oxygen. A pilot can't tell when he's becoming anoxic, isn't sure when he's tight in its grip. Anoxia feels like a weird binge, but it can kill. First its victim gets light-headed, over-confident, uncertain of his reactions and his plane's response. He does odd, unaccountable things, takes risks he'd never take if he were breathing enough oxygen. Typically Piggott stopped worrying about anoxia. The *Skylark* carried no oxygen gear, anyway.

He wanted to unkink his course, to come out of the spiral, so he shoved over the stick. The glider should have felt to him as if it were actually curving in the opposite direction. But when the compass showed he was flying straight, he *felt* he was flying straight. He shook his head in disbelief and mumbled to himself that this doesn't look right. The compass hadn't been jumpy, even in the worst of the electric storm, and now it kept a steady heading. Soon he was out of the shock area, and headed into new trouble. The control column was stiffening, not yielding when he eased it from side to side, to and fro.

Ice! He could feel the controls champ against the accumulating frost. As he soared higher the controls became more rigid. Soon he needed both hands to shift the column. Finally he took the chance, jolted the controls and the glider leaped as the ice fell away and the column worked again. But at 15,000 feet ice heavily sheathed the *Skylark's* nose and was building up on the leading edges. The trim tab was as far down as it would go, but the glider was nose heavy. Ice wasn't yet blocking the instruments. Or was it? He shook his head hard and squinted at the dials on the panel. Could they all be wrong? He wasn't certain. He was gasping, had been gasping ever since the first lightning struck him. Must have breathed up all the fresh air in the cockpit. Must watch out for anoxia! Poking his right hand through the small clearvision slot he deflected fresh, cold air into the cockpit.

The altimeter said 16,000 feet. Or did it say 6,000? Sixteen or six? In a glider the needle that reads feet in tens of thousands isn't often used. Derek swayed his body, dipped his head forward and threw it back, giggled like a child and squinted at the instruments. He was at 17,000—18,000—still going up. He should have turned and dipped down out of the rising damp, but all he could remember was his first flight plan.

Occasional hail flurries pelted the *Skylark* but he didn't hear them. He was too intent on the instruments swimming in front of him. "Anoxia," he mumbled aloud. "Mus'n't get anoxic." His eyelids felt sandbagged and his head weighed a ton. He remembered that one of his friends had gone to 17,000 feet to get a Diamond-C. Just to be sure of his Diamond-C, Derek decided, he'd soar to 19,000.

The thermal thrust the glider upward swiftly. He circled into a stronger thermal patch, squinted at the altimeter. The dial read 20,000 feet. Piggott's body became limp, then stiffened in the safety harness. He nearly fainted but shook his head, poked his right hand through the clear-vision slot and deflected in new air. On the ground he'd never dream of climbing so high without oxygen. Derek didn't know that the altimeter wasn't accurate, that its faulty dial showed him to be several thousand feet lower than he actually was! Reaching over, he worked the air brake control lever. The hissing slipstream quieted as his pace checked. Slowly he began to descend. Another lifting eddy caught him. He peered at the instruments, scrutinized them carefully. Might as well go back upstairs. Jus' to make sure. Pulling in the air brakes, he shot skyward. The glider stayed on its even spiral, lifting easily, climbing within the solid white cloud. Piggott's body sank limply back in the seat.

Later he didn't remember having passed out. Only the barograph recorded the story. He had risen so swiftly that the barograph's needle had to lean over backward to record on the revolving cylinder. A six kilometer instrument, the barograph recorded only to 23,200 feet. Piggott's climb carried him upward right off the top of the smoked paper!

How he flew the plane without being conscious, he'd never know. But if the barograph could be trusted—and it was checked and double-checked—he had shot above 25,000 feet, dove at several thousand feet a minute, again tracing a backward curving line on the smoked paper. Consciousness crept back into Derek's mind. He didn't feel himself regaining it because he'd never felt himself passing out. Only the barograph could relate the story.

Finally able to look around, to inventory his position, to squint at the altimeter, he saw he was down to 16,000 feet. The variometer's right-hand bead danced. He was descending. Almost wantonly he slammed open the air brakes and felt himself heel harder downward through the mist. The *Skylark* corkscrewed to 10,000 feet easily, emerged beneath the overcast and slashed through a mixture of rain and hail. Derek breathed deeply, sucking the thickening air into his lungs. His head felt light, giddy, awful.

Alton, the town nearest Lasham Airfield, should be below him. He lived in Alton. The town he saw didn't look familiar. Ah! there was the hospital! Alton! Home! Faraway he saw Friendship Pond. But anoxic, he had to circle round and round Alton before he could remember the way back to Lasham. Several times he tried to veer west toward the field, but each time he had to hover back over the hospital because he felt lost. The rain was slowing as he finally circled at 6,000 feet over Lasham's parked gliders. It was 5:45. He'd flown an hour and a quarter.

If he hadn't been deep in anoxia and shock, he'd never have chanced the victory loops he did before landing. Shaking all over when he skidded the *Skylark* to a stop, he could barely climb from the cockpit. Lightning had pinholed the glider's fiberglass nose and splayed the fabric covering. Slits slashed all over the elevator—hailstones or loosened ice. One side of the rudder was perforated badly. The leading edges of the wings were full of dents.

Lightning burns scarred the fuselage. Where lightning had struck the rudder, it ripped away a large splint and left an ugly burn.

Piggott took two days to recover from anoxia. He got his Diamond-C and set a British glider climb record. And possibly he holds a world record for surviving anoxia.

HUMILITY LEARNED

by Ernest K. Gann

AM-21 is a puny and miserable couplet for the expanse of America it is supposed to designate. It fails utterly to suggest the easygoing beauty of the route in all seasons, its pleasures or its discomforts. Nor can such an insipid formula embrace the remarkable variety of the route, which is enough, without the need of spectacle.

The eastern terminus of the route is now Newark, an unsightly beginning to such a mixture of tranquillity and beauty. Just west of Newark, even before the climb to cruising altitude is completed, the threshold of the Alleghenies rises gently against the horizon.

The first specified landing for any flight embarking on the route is Wilkes-Barre. The airport is laid out upon a flat which stretches between two steep ridges. As a result, the location becomes a drafty tunnel where even a mild wind multiplies upon itself and, contrary to all the laws of nature, moves unpredictably back and forth across the draw rather than flowing with its contour. The strength of any wind is as fickle as its direction, and in the near vicinity of the field itself the downdrafts are notoriously treacherous. Hence the landing at Wilkes-Barre is often passed over by the more conservative pilots. Ross, however, rarely refuses the challenge, though the wind may blow thirty miles an hour directly across the single runway. On this first landing I am too preoccupied with my own simple duties to appreciate his skill and supreme self-confidence.

Once away from Wilkes-Barre, the route, which is actually an ever-changing combination of air space and terrain, veers northward toward upper New York State and Syracuse, the next point of landing. As the Alleghenies drop into minor ridges of the earth and the scars of mining along the hill flanks become obscure, all the land below begins to roll like a gentle sea. The ruggedness vanishes as quickly as it commenced in the east. In the vicinity of Binghamton the strange enchantment and quietly lush beauty of AM-21 begin.

In spring the land below is charged with life. The fields are a soothing green to match the easy configuration of the valleys, and the hillsides are speckled with fat brown cattle. The newly tilled soil in the flats and minor depressions along streams is a rich, warm umber. It blends delicately with the near black-green outlining the shaded roads, which are so pleasantly few and almost deserted.

The light at noon, which is customarily the time of flight transit over this region, is always of a peculiarly mellow quality, as soft and agreeable as the land below. In spring the air is tranquil. The heat of the earth is not yet sufficiently retained, so that as day progresses it will rise from the brown and sink into the green, thus transforming the lower air mass into a rocking ocean of discomfort.

Now, in spring, everything below is sharply etched, and from six thousand feet a farmer sitting on his tractor is as clear-cut as the furrows dribbling out behind him.

The stewardess brings two box lunches to the cockpit. She opens one for Ross and sets it upon his lap. With the same solicitude she might show a wayward dog, she places the other box on the floor for me.

There is no automatic pilot on a DC-2 so I am obliged to fly the ship until Ross has eaten. This is a task I am more than willing to perform since, by maintaining near perfect course and altitude, I may possibly redeem faults which have already created a certain coolness between us. First of all, my arithmetic talent became dulled with excitement, and I made an eleven-minute error in recording our flight time between Newark and Wilkes-Barre. Such an error could represent only stupidity or unforgivable carelessness. Ross's strong sense of exactitude was so insulted that he chose to erase and make the correction himself while I labored to overcome a second mistake.

On arrival in Wilkes-Barre I could not find either the mail or baggage destined for that city. Somehow I became convinced it was stowed near the bottom of the bin instead of on top, where it should have been. There followed an embarrassing delay while I heaved bags and suitcases about the passageway and, sprawling across them, sought in the ill-lighted bin for what should have been so handy. The items were eventually discovered by the ground agent, who had the imagination to look in the tail compartment. Neither he nor Ross took this casually, since the ensuing delay of eight minutes would require them to write explanatory letters to the company.

I did not witness our take-off from Wilkes-Barre in its entirety. Ross, as if bound to demonstrate my true usefulness aboard, nicely managed without my assistance. I was still reloading the baggage bin as we left the ground.

I had just resumed my seat when further trouble occurred. Ross shivered and said he was cold. The drop in temperature was confirmed almost immediately by the stewardess, who came forward long enough to complain of a chill in the cabin. I knew at once that my trials were just beginning, for co-pilots are the janitors of the sky, and it would now become my duty to nurse the heater of a DC-2 back to life.

This contraption is located in the passageway between the cockpit and the cabin. It has brought many co-pilots almost to tears. Others, more combative, have been forcibly restrained from smashing it to bits with the crash ax. The heater consists of a cylindrical-shaped boiler which is somewhat larger than a football. It obtains its heat from the exhaust of the right engine and is festooned with valves, the majority of which are usually stuck fast. The entire assembly has a certain human quality—recalcitrant, self-indulgent, and capricious. Everyone is agreed that it was designed by a maniac barely thwarted in his attempt to create an infernal machine. Captains have been known to cherish co-pilots who can keep a DC-2 heater operating, and others have made life aloft very unhappy for those who cannot.

The diagrams drawn in Lester's school could never illustrate the fiendish personality now knocking and sputtering complaints loud enough to be heard above the sound of the engines. I gingerly turn one of the valves, which, according to my memory, is supposed to lock off the system and permit the addition of water. I wait a moment, dubious, and quite resigned to the possibility of an explosion. The boiler becomes ominously silent. Ross calls from the cockpit, urging me to hurry. He claims he is freezing.

In desperation I bend down until it is possible to examine the glass sight gauge on the boiler. There seems to be an adequate supply of water. Perhaps there is too much? I smack the boiler with my fist; then, after a brief struggle, I resolutely turn a valve near the top of the boiler. The results are instantaneous and spectacular. A jet of steam hisses from some unseen outlet and at once obscures everything within the passageway. Now, thoroughly alarmed, I reach frantically into the seething cloud of vapor and manage to close the valve. Nothing has worked according to the book.

Ross calls me back to the cockpit in a voice vibrant with authority. He waves his hand as a sign for me to sit down and take over the controls. Then, with a great and all-enduring sigh, he strides back to the heater. He is gone only a few minutes before I feel a telltale draft of heat across my ankles.

Ross returns to eat his lunch in silence, although as he munches on his sandwiches I am well aware that he is examining me without enthusiasm. I am therefore astonished when he fails to take over the flying as we approach Syracuse airport. Certainly I must have misunderstood his casual hand wave. It would normally indicate the landing would be mine.

My eyes question, yet he nods his head affirmatively. This, then, will certainly be the end. My past performance with a DC-2 was anything but heartening, and I have never seen Syracuse airport in my life. Ross is either joking or has mistaken me for a more experienced man, which, in view of the morning thus far, is unlikely.

There is no rule or custom to dictate a captain's generosity. He may, if he pleases, never give away a landing or a take-off, both of which are as sweetmeats to any co-pilot. Many co-pilots go for months without touching the controls except when safely at cruising altitude. To refuse Ross's offer now would be unthinkable.

Trying not to dwell upon my adventure with McCabe, I ease the ship down through a thin deck of broken clouds. Ross has apparently lost all interest in our progress. He is thoughtfully chewing on a cooky, cupping his hand beneath it to prevent any possibility of a crumb falling on his trousers.

As we break out beneath the clouds, the airport is just over the nose. My former flying sense returns and I am alert to a multitude of signs and revelations, each important to a good approach and proper landing. An experienced barnstormer desiring to remain whole and also solvent must discipline himself to observe and evaluate considerable information before he attempts a landing on any strange field. He must do this without help from the ground, depending entirely on the lore accumulated by the very early birds. Handed down from veteran to neophyte, it becomes an integral part of his professional stock.

Though we are still three miles away, I instinctively compare the cloud shadows moving across the field with the wind sock on top of the hangar and find that the wind aloft is different from that on the ground. I must allow and compensate for this difference, executing the final turn somewhat sooner and thus permitting the plane to be carried on the invisible wind until it is aligned with the western runway.

The wind is gusting, according to the sock. By the manner in which the tree leaves are whipped and laid back until they glitter in the sunlight, I judge that its force is now close to thirty miles an hour. I must concern myself with those trees. They border the end of the runway, and their cool shade is certain to create vertically descending air, a downdraft not necessarily dangerous if the trees are given sufficient clearance, but a smooth and regular approach is the prelude to a good landing. A good pilot thinks far ahead of his airplane, knowing that his mind may become instantly and terribly crowded if things go wrong.

We descend. A glance at Ross finds him at ease, although I know that he has seen all that I have seen and added to it his familiarity with the field itself.

We pass over the trees at exactly ninety miles an hour. I chop off the power to the engines. The approach has been so proper and satisfying that Ross cannot fail to appreciate my careful planning. And now the final glide is right, a good angle, neither too fast nor too slow, just enough reserve of speed to handle the gusts.

We swoop over the edge of the field and sink gracefully to the runway. I spin the stabilizer crank and ease back on the control yoke. It must be a perfect landing.

My self-satisfaction dies before it is truly born. For once again I have literally flown this airplane straight into the ground. Its resentment is immediate and dramatic. The stiff-legged brute leaps crazily back into its element and proceeds down the runway in a series of ludicrous vaultings.

Ross is quick and his hands powerful. He tames the ship in an instant. We roll on smoothly and I wallow in vileness, waiting for Ross to heap ashes on my head.

I am almost disappointed to discover him smiling. And his measured comment only increases my despondency.

"There are two kinds of airplanes—those you fly and those that fly you. With a DC-2 you must have a distinct understanding at the very start as to who is the boss."

My spirit revives slightly during the fifteen minutes required for refueling, unloading, and loading. We again prepare for take-off. The next landing will be Rochester, a mere ninety miles. Reviewing the events of the morning and hopefully applying the law of averages, I cannot imagine how I can commit any more misdemeanors this day.

Ross taxis to the end of the runway, handling the DC-2 as if it were an obedient quarterhorse, despite the increasingly gusting wind.

The landing gear of a DC-2 is retracted and lowered by hydraulic power. Once the landing gear is down a steel pin is inserted just above the retraction lever so that it cannot be moved inadvertently once the ship rests on its wheels. This pin is normally removed just before actual take-off unless both pilots forget about it, in which event there is an embarrassing delay in raising the landing gear. And though the pause may be only a few seconds it can be a very important interval because take-off is a critical time for a DC-2. If one engine should fail just after breaking from the ground, a twin-engined airplane can proceed with relative safety provided it is free of landing-gear drag. If not, there is trouble—very sudden and very serious.

For this reason the landing gear is always retracted soon after safe flying speed is attained. On no account must this moment be anticipated lest, faltering in a semi-stall, the ship sink back to earth. Then, at the very least, the whirling propeller tips will be smashed, which, in turn, must almost certainly result in a crash belly landing, with an excellent possibility of fire.

The signal for pulling the lever and so raising the landing gear is made by the captain, who will smartly raise his hand, palm upward. At the same time he is supposed to command "Gear Up!" in a voice clearly audible above the engines.

Now, as Ross runs up the engines, I remove the safety pin from the gear lever. I watch Ross anxiously. I am pathetically eager to perform my co-pilot's duties quickly and efficiently. As he shoves the throttles forward and we start down the runway, I place my hand ready on the gear lever. I feel the tail lift. I bend down and slightly forward, my eyes fixed on Ross's hand, waiting for the signal. I believe that we already have good speed, but I am watching his hand, not the indicator. His hand moves as if to leave the throttles. Take-off noise level in a DC-2 cockpit is terrific. I am certain Ross has called "Gear Up!" I yank up the gear lever.

"Jesus! Man!"

Ross fights the control wheel, jockeying it desperately.

I glance at the air speed, then out the window. We are hanging in the air, sinking, then hanging again. Ross did *not* give a signal. Anxiety has duped me. I have deliberately pulled the gear out from under him!

The entire ship shudders in agony, a sensation which is transmitted directly to my bowels.

Then, just as suddenly, we are in smooth flight, and the ground falls away. In a magnificent display of flying skill, Ross has safely completed an abortive take-off.

I cannot look at him—yet I must. This has been no minor error which can be erased with the end of a pencil. I have, with my foolish hand, endangered the lives of every soul on this airplane. No matter how innocent in intent, the deed is unforgivable. Sick to the depths of my being, utterly demoralized, I cannot find the simplest words of apology. I would not be displeased if Ross pulled out his mail gun and put a bullet through my offending hand. He would be more than justified. His pride is never to put a scratch on an airplane and I, in one accursed moment, have brought him perilously close to ruin.

As we climb safely over the western hill the tautness leaves Ross's body. He raises a finger to his brow and flicks away invisible sweat. Then he meets my eyes, and the hard muscles about his jaw relax. I can see no anger in his face, not even accusation. Only his breathing, which is still quick, betrays the passing of a crisis. Fear is no stranger to him, and through much involuntary practice he has learned to extinguish it quickly once the torch is removed. He speaks slowly, enunciating each word with such care that the effect is comical, as he intends.

"If you ever do that again, I'll cut you out of my will."

No abuse. No recounting of my crime or its so obvious potentialities. Not the slightest show of resentment. My near despair, brought on by the series of blameworthy incidents ever since I entered Lester's school, somehow melts away. I keep my silence, thinking only that Ross is one of the great persons of the air.

In a moment he waves for me to take over the controls. Then he snatches up the logbook and methodically writes down our time of take-off as if nothing unusual had occurred. I envy the steadiness of his hand and am vastly grateful for his sensitivity. Surely he knows that my only self-redemption is in actually flying.

I have yet so very much to learn.

Ross is but one of the captains holding a bid on AM-21. The others thus engaged are Dunn, who can barely squeeze his enormous bulk into a cockpit; Hunt, who is equally big although not so ponderous; Shoff, slight and already somewhat wrinkled in the face despite his youth; and Lewis, habitually stooped and somehow always a trifle forlorn. There is Konz, who was once an oboe player in the Rochester Symphony. There is also Brooks, who is handsomely gray and ever loquacious; Mitchell, paper-thin and as alert as a sandpiper; and Keim, the growling maverick of the lot. All of these men are forthright individuals of much flying experience, and they are thoroughly versed in the special features of the route as well as the idiosyncrasies of the DC-2.

Beyond Syracuse, AM-21 proceeds almost directly west, leaving the lovely Finger Lakes and their higher encompassing hills several miles to the south. The route parallels the Erie Canal as far as Rochester. Here the terrain becomes flatter, permitting flight all the way to Buffalo as low as two thousand feet. The land between Syracuse and Buffalo is like a gay and harmoniously colored mosaic, and the villages, long ago established to receive the bounty of the canal, are settled in sophisticated peace.

In summer the prevailing westerly winds brush across the yellow grain in the fields, the hedgerows, and the tops of the trees in such a playful manner that the whole region appears to be alive and in rippling motion. In autumn, when the colors turn and become even more jolly, the welcome of the land is almost audible.

West of Buffalo the route follows the gently swerving south shore of Lake Erie. Here too the terrain is remarkably flat, although the oriental splendor of colors is replaced by a nearly solid green. The lake, so like a sea, stretches to the horizon from any altitude less than fifteen thousand feet, and only on the clearest days may the shore of Canada be seen.

AM-21 calls for a landing at Erie, which stands upon the lake shore and which is such a peculiarly uninspiring city from the air that few pilots pay it even the compliment of a downward glance. The route then continues west along the lake shore to Cleveland.

The captains flying AM-21 know much more of the route than its geographical pleasantries. And they are concerned with the sky as well as the land. They know that an east wind flowing across Syracuse in summertime is likely to carry fog along with it and may quickly seal off the airport. They know a way to approach Syracuse from the west without using the radio range leg. In haze or heavy summer rain, they know that in spite of poor visibility it is quite safe to drop down as low as seven hundred feet and follow the eastbound railway tracks until they make a junction with a certain sharp twist in the canal. Then, banking away to the southwest as the hill of Syracuse looms darkly upon their left wing, they follow this mass until it melts away. Now they execute a one-minute left turn, reversing their course to the northwest. Continuing, they descend cautiously until the hill reappears once more on their left. They are now in a flat and narrow valley which leads directly to the end of the northeast runway.

These men know that, in wintertime, icing of consequence is rare along AM-21, and that if it should come they may safely descend to a low cruising altitude and so carry the burden in better style. They know too that radio reception is freakish in all seasons and the eastern leg of the Rochester range should always be regarded with suspicion.

At Rochester they are mindful of ground fog, which is prone to collect very quickly on still summer nights and quite surprise the unwary.

Though only a few feet thick and nearly invisible from aloft, it hangs just above the surface and can completely blind a pilot during the last and most important moment of flare-out for landing. And, like Syracuse, Rochester has a special approach most useful in poor visibility when the landing must be accomplished to the north. Then the railroad track is picked up just west of the field and held until a certain marshaling yard is intersected by a parade of high-tension towers. With this combination below, easily visible in snow or rain, the key is in the lock. A turn is made to the north, and the descent begins. By the time the landing gear is put down and final approach speed attained, the end of the desired north runway will appear just over the nose.

Even on fine days Rochester demands alertness because clear weather brings out the small training planes of which Rochester has an uncommon share. They must be watched with the greatest solicitude, for if there is one solid, deep-rooted, ever-present fear known to all airline pilots, it is the hanging sword of midair collision. No other prospect except structural failure, which is so rare as to be virtually ignored, can render a pilot so entirely helpless.

A true route pilot is no more to be surprised by the geographical eccentricities found in his daily work than a mailman plodding his customary rounds. The AM-21 captains know that in wintertime Buffalo can become one of the coldest airports in the world and that reports of blowing snow, which can instantly hide or as suddenly reveal a runway, are almost standard for the season. If radio reception is poor, as it so often is in snow, even the best route captains will sometimes miss lining up with the proper runway and must at the last moment up-gear, shy away, and circle for another try.

AM-21 captains know that farther west Erie can be easily found in the worst visibility and radio conditions, simply by following the lake shore. And they may fly as low as their individual natures permit the disregard of regulations, without fear of hitting anything. AM-21 is not for the automation pilot whose route manual is an ironbound scripture from which even the slightest deviation is sinful. Such pilots do not like the route and its frequent demands for resourceful improvisation; nor does it seem that the route likes them, if the performance record of such occasional experiments is honestly evaluated. The rule sticklers pass over too many fields on AM-21. They cancel too frequently when a safe landing could be made.

Due in part to its special terrain and freakish weather, a certain maxim of flying becomes more apparent on AM-21 than on most other routes. The timid, super-cautious pilot is not necessarily the safest. Coupled with knowledge, a touch of boldness is required, and thus it is that captains on AM-21 have long established both a special pride and a tradition. No one envies their environment and the attendant extremes of heat and cold. The frequent landings and comparatively little night flying mean lower pay and much more work to achieve the same number of hours by the end of the month. Yet, as perverse and contrary as the route itself, the pilots of AM-21 are not easily persuaded to fly any other.

When Gay, Carter, Mood, and the others learn of my assignment, they express pity in various degrees. To them, flying fast and high on longer routes between greater cities, I have been sent into exile. I am a mere grasshopper. The planes are antiques, soon to be retired, the captains notorious taskmasters, and the weather always distressing. They do concede the route offers superb training.

OVER THE MATTERHORN—?

by Richard Halliburton

Back in Paris, after a leisurely flight from Fez through Seville, Lisbon and Madrid, Moye and I found ourselves no less eager to continue our exploration of the world by air. The Flying Carpet, now thoroughly overhauled, was ready to take us anywhere we wished to go.

We spread the map of Europe before us. Moscow beckoned, Norway beckoned, Sicily beckoned. We chose the Alps.

Some years before I'd spent a month wandering among those ice-clad peaks. I'd gone up the valley of the Visp to Zermatt, and from there, with one of my schoolmates, climbed the bloodthirsty Matterhorn. It had been one of the great moments of my youth—that savage battle with the snow and the wind, the heights and the chasms. For experienced Alpinists the conquest of the Matterhorn is no longer considered a great climbing feat. It is by no means the highest of the Alps—there are five peaks higher, four of which literally look down upon the Matterhorn. But for me, who at that time had done no climbing at all, this first battle with a mountain in the clouds was a terrific struggle. I was violently seized with mountain nausea; my head almost burst from the rare atmosphere; my heart stopped beating from sheer fright when I lost my grip on the suspended chains and slithered down a five-thousand-foot precipice toward Switzerland—as far as the climbing-rope fastened to my waist allowed.

Even so, I had crawled on, and the summit was attained, and the world far below rolled away in homage from the foot of this iceberg throne.

But it had been a costly victory. My face was frostbitten, my ankle was wrenched, and the seat of my pants was worn through.

Now for my revenge!

From the moment we turned south again from Paris I began to plot against the Matterhorn. Three miles high, was it? My Flying Carpet could climb higher. Wreathed in a barrage of mist and clouds? We could swoop over them and around them at will. The time before I had only unaccustomed legs and sea-level lungs to fight with. Now I had two hundred and twenty-five winged horses to draw my scarlet Carpet through the Alpine thunder, and Moye's relentless grip to hold the reins.

At Geneva we girded ourselves for the battle. Then up the lake we advanced—over Lausanne—over Montreux—over the Castle of Chillon—into the teeth of the sky-scraping barriers. The Rhone Valley closed in two miles below; the river trickled down, walled by the gleaming titans of the Alps. Vast flocks of clouds roamed beneath. Mont Blanc, thirty miles away, blocked out the sky with its white magnificence.

How unfamiliar, from the air, these mountains seemed! On the previous visit, one vista at a time had been revealed, beautiful but fixed. Now all Switzerland rolled by below, changing, towering, hiding, falling. The miracle of flying, long since a commonplace, gripped me anew. Flight! It *was* a miracle. One moment our Carpet almost touched a glittering mountaintop. The next, the whole world fell away, and only space, bottomless, infinite space, gaped hungrily beneath. Now the clouds blanketed our view; now the sun burst through against the glaciers and half-blinded with a dazzling light.

What was this apparition there below me? Surely not the earth on which I lived, but rather some strange, nameless, frozen star. I did not belong to it; I never saw it before. Tiny clusters of tiny houses inhabited by tiny specks could be seen in the valleys far beneath. But they were merely colonies of specks. Their existence was of no importance. Their life, their death, their happiness and wretchedness, their works and wars, were all reduced to complete insignificance beside these terrible peaks of ice. At moments during this journey above the summit of a continent, I felt as detached from the earth as from the moon. They seemed equally remote.

Captain Stephens suddenly gave our Flying Carpet a sharp right-angle turn. We had reached the tributary valley of the Visp. Here the mist came down like an angry ocean and half-filled our canyon corridor, but the towering giants all about us still marked the way.

Closer and closer pressed the spires, white as the mountains at the poles. Above them the sky had turned to a blue so deep that it was almost black. Under this indigo dome, across the jagged iceberg sea, the Flying Carpet, scarlet-bodied, black-cowled, wings and tail of polished gold, flashed and sparkled through the flood of sun.

The jaws of the canyon, at its narrowest point, now waited just ahead, the right flank guarded by the incomparable Weisshorn, the left flank by the pinnacle of the Dom. We rushed between them at full speed, fearful that these Alpine Symplegades would clash together across the chasm and destroy our Fire Bird before we could sail through.

We escaped, but the mountains marshaled themselves anew. The Dent Blanche, as if in league with the foe, loomed out of the clouds to hold the west; in the east, Monte Rosa, next to Mont Blanc the highest of them all, blocked the way into Italy. Eight thousand feet below us, through a rift in the barrage of fog, we caught a glimpse of the village of Zermatt, shrinking deep into the valley as if in mortal dread of the terrible frozen monsters hanging over it.

And straight before us, with its head lifted in mighty isolation, the Matterhorn, the tiger of the Alps, awaited the onslaught of the Flying Carpet and its crew.

At a hundred miles an hour we rushed toward its soaring northern precipice. How appallingly sheer it looked! How did climbers ever scale it? How did God ever build it? But this was no time to soliloquize—for while we were still half a mile away, a great bank of clouds condensed right in front of us, and completely blocked our vision. Moye did a sudden wing-over, and we turned on our tracks. But the blinding fog was now behind us as well, and all about us. We must get out at once. This shifting mist might at any moment reveal—too late!—another fang of ice lifted in our path. Moye, noting through the rifts clear skies above, pulled us upward in a spiral, at the sharpest angle such thin air permitted. But we had to climb a thousand feet before we emerged completely from the clouds, which now rolled in vast waves below us.

The altimeter registered fourteen thousand feet—eight hundred feet more, and we could clear the Matterhorn.

But which one *was* the Matterhorn? All the mountaintops, so easily identified from below in the valley, seemed to have shifted, and changed their appearance. An entire archipelago of islands swam below us in the white and tossing sea, all looking more or less alike. Their familiar aspects were so distorted from this height that we could no longer identify my old enemy among a dozen others.

It seemed impossible to believe. A moment before, the great peak had soared before us, distinct and challenging—and now we couldn't even find it!

We resorted to our maps.

"It should be that one," Moye indicated, pointing over the side.

Ridiculous!—that strange peak couldn't be it! As though I wouldn't recognize my mountain. Hadn't I sat on top of it long enough!

"It's *this* one," I insisted, none too sure myself, directing Moye to a peak whose sheer and savage bulk looked familiar.

Its summit still rose well above us. We climbed to fifteen thousand feet. This, I knew, was somewhat above the level of the Matterhorn's utmost point. But it was not high enough, for the winds were blowing a violent blast that warned us to go higher and farther out of reach of the treacherous spire.

Oh, those winds! The peak was now up in arms. What devilish contraption was this that came roaring defiantly over its head, bearing two men from earth? Winds! Assault them! Break them and destroy them, winds! And the winds rushed at us with a breath that froze and a fury that almost hurled us from our seats.

But Moye, at the helm, was undismayed. Into the very thick of the battle, we climbed yet another thousand feet—sixteen thousand now—got a running start, nosed downward and swooped exultantly right over the top of the outraged mountain.

I looked overboard, straining my eyes to recognize some distinguishing feature of the summit.

I recognized nothing. Perhaps this wasn't the Matterhorn at all. It was probably some other confounded peak.

I glanced back at Moye and shook my head, and cursed all the mountains in Switzerland.

We were now hopelessly confused. I knew that the Matterhorn had two vast precipices sliced from its northern and eastern slopes—but all the other mountains seemed just as precipitous. The Gorner Glacier would get us straightened out—but it was completely lost beneath the sea of clouds.

Fortunately, the clouds were not stationary. They shifted and rose and fell, hiding peaks here, disclosing others there, though the valleys remained always submerged. And every time a new pinnacle appeared, the Flying Carpet, colder and colder, and angrier and angrier, went charging after it. In this grim game of hide-and-seek, we probably flew over some of the mountains twice.

At the summit of one pinnacle, resting on the topmost rock, we noticed two figures of climbers . . . black dots against the snow. With what excitement they waved at us, and we back at them! How astonished they must have been, after spending perhaps a day and a night toiling upward to this needle's point, to behold our gold and scarlet Carpet appearing out of the cold thin void and diving *down* to have a look at them. But whether their mountain was the Matterhorn or Pike's Peak, we hadn't the slightest idea. We circled five hundred feet above them, and dropped a note, tied to a monkey-wrench: *"Where* is the Matterhorn?" But our aim was poor; the note missed the rock by a hundred feet and went bounding down into the abyss.

We took a photograph of this peak, as we had of a dozen others, and fled. We must get out of these increasingly ominous clouds. We were being forced higher and higher as the mist, vapor climbed after us. All Switzerland was about to be submerged. But for one glorious moment, the tips of just the six highest of the Alps, armored in plates of gleaming ice and drenched in sunshine, rose higher than the fog. Mont Blanc, the loftiest island, far in the west, was unmistakable. On billows of fleece floated the summit snows of the cluster below us, a cluster containing Monte Rosa and Lyskamm and the Weisshorn and the Dom—*and* the Matterhorn; but we still didn't know which was which—and by now we didn't give a damn.

Then as we looked, there came a great surge in the cold and rolling ocean. All five of the peaks sank beneath the veil, and only Mont Blanc beckoned across this boundless sea.

Three miles high, we fled over the clouds toward the one remaining beacon, en route to Geneva. What canyons, what glaciers, what crags and depths, were hidden below, we could not tell. Mont Blanc alone joined us to the earth.

Europe's highest mountain was now only a mile away. We shot forward through the freezing sky at our utmost speed. Fly, old Carpet, fly! There was not going to be any argument about this mountain! Half a mile remained—two hundred yards. Hep! Over we went!—found a hole in the fog above Lac Leman, and tumbled home.

Next day the manager of the Geneva airport came to see us.

"We've just had a phone call from Zermatt," he said. "Two German climbers were on top the Matterhorn yesterday and saw a red-and-gold airplane fly right over their heads and try to drop a note. They wanted to report it, and to find where the plane came from. I told them you flew that way yesterday, and were undoubtedly over the Matterhorn—"

"Undoubtedly!" Moye and I exclaimed in unison.

CLEAR ICE! THE EMPEROR'S ACTING UP!

by David Beaty

Cavendish had seen the cloud from the rest compartment, where he had been eating a solitary dinner. He walked up to the front and stood between the two pilots. "There seems more in that weak front than they forecast, Captain Bellamy."

"Yes. I've been watching the temperature going up over the last hour." He pointed it out. Only −7°. "Might have to climb . . . if we get any ice."

"One thing," Cavendish said in a reassuring tone, "if we *do* have to go up, in this warm air, we won't get anywhere near −40."

"I'd have gone up anyway. Except there's that cold air on the other side of the front." Bellamy turned to Seawood. "You go back and have dinner now."

The First Officer carefully got out of the right-hand seat. Just as carefully, Cavendish settled his huge bulk down on the cushion, as soon as it was vacant. Bellamy was looking up through the panel, hoping to see a star or two to prove this sudden darkness was just ragged, unimportant layer cloud. But there was nothing. Only solid blackness, and the tiny reflection of the green instrument lighting on the glass. He took a handkerchief from his pocket and wiped the sweat off his hands. The Emperor had started to rock very slightly from side to side. As a precaution against sudden turbulence he had disengaged the automatic pilot.

Cavendish peered out into the night. "This haze makes things difficult."

"Yes."

"We're not in cloud."

"Not *yet.*"

The temperature gauge had gone up another degree. They sat together in silence; Cavendish watching out for the slightest sign of heavy cumulus that might mean ice, Bellamy's eyes alternating between the blind flying instruments and the temperature.

Cavendish said, "Mind if we have all the lights out?"

"Go ahead."

Cavendish pulled the curtain behind the pilots tight shut. Then he turned out the tiny glow over the instruments. Only the phosphorescent numbers and needles stood out now.

Cavendish still kept staring ahead. He said suddenly, "Isn't that a cumulus head?"

Bellamy looked up. "Where?"

"Over to starboard."

Bellamy turned his head. "Can't see anything."

"No." Cavendish relaxed a little. "Impossible to tell, really. Pitch black outside. Just thought I caught a shadow that was blacker than the rest."

"All the same," Bellamy said. "I don't like it. I think we'll climb."

"Temperature still going up?"

Bellamy was just about to answer, when a sudden overwhelming clatter of ice and rain broke in a great splintering mass over the nose. In two seconds, the windscreens changed from black to white.

Cavendish shouted, "Clear ice!"

It was as though an iceberg had disintegrated on top of them. Though the pilots had immediately switched on all the alcohol anticers, all the windows were tightly bandaged up. Nothing could be seen but wet shining whiteness.

Bellamy knew he had to act quickly, before the whole aircraft was suffocated. This was the most dangerous form of ice—almost perfectly clear, heavy and quick-forming. He said to Cavendish as he pulled back on the stick, "Let's get out of here!"

"Want me to take her up?"

"Please."

Cavendish put his hands on the control column and moved it even further towards him. The rate of climb shot up. Bellamy went back to tell Hooper to get a clearance to 25,000. This was very definitely a time when immediate action, permission or not, was essential. There were few aircraft on this route, anyway; but all the same, he would feel happier when Control had cleared them. Rawlings had already put on the fractional increase that separated cruise and climb power on Cruttwell's jet engines.

Unseeing, blinded by ice, Able Dog's nose rose up steeply as she started a powerful leap upwards through the freezing air. As Bellamy stood impatiently beside the Radio Officer, still keeping an eye on the temperature gauge, Cavendish edged the control column further back, anxious to shake off the icy clinging fingers of the cloud: up into the colder, drier air where the ice would lessen.

The Emperor responded magnificently. Her propellors slashed through the stuff, sending it clanging in great chunks against her metal sides. The altimeter needle never wavered as it clocked in each thousand feet of height gained. The vibration inside the aircraft increased. She shuddered a little. That was all. And the temperature gauge, very reluctantly at first, started to go down as the altimeter went up: −11, −12, −13. Every degree meant less of this throttling wet ice.

Bellamy came back to the front for a moment. "All right?" he asked Cavendish.

The older pilot pointed to the altimeter, already at 22,000 feet. "Climbing well."

Then Hooper called out, "Got clearance, sir"; and Bellamy felt that the sudden crisis was over. They would probably be clear of cloud now, if they could see out. The tension on the flight deck relaxed as he went aft to the navigation compartment. Leaning on the table, with his chin cupped in his hand, he discussed with Douthwaite the flight plan at the new altitude. The temperature was still only −20°, well below the suspected danger point for the boosters.

Bellamy said, "Of course, the temperature'll go down sharply past this front. May have to go down. But I'll keep my eye on it."

Alone in the curtained-off tip of the nose, Cavendish relaxed his tight grip of the stick. The needle on the altimeter was still gaily turning. They were past 24,000 now. Only another thousand feet to go—they'd done it easily.

He watched the pointer pass the new altitude. Then he eased gently forward on the control column.

Nothing happened. Only the altimeter moved—up and up, past 26,000, pressing on tirelessly to 27,000.

He called, "Cruise Power." Not that the small decrease would make much difference, but with everything set up, he could devote all his attention to the problem on hand. Very slightly harder, he pushed forward on the control column.

It still didn't move.

Incredulously, he looked to see if the automatic pilot was engaged. But all the levers were back. Out.

He pushed forward again much harder. The metal stick quivered a little under the pressure. But it stayed where it was.

Then his eye caught the altimeter reading. With the present high angle of the wings' attack, they were still shooting upwards, just passing 28,000.

Settling himself lower in the seat, with all his might, he strained against the control column. But he could not shift it. He tried the ailerons. Then, more gingerly, the rudders. Both were working perfectly normally.

Sweat began to pour down his face. He leant his whole big body against the damned thing. Still nothing gave.

He turned his head and called, "Captain Bellamy!"

Bellamy came up to the front immediately and leapt into the left-hand seat. "What's the trouble?"

"These damned elevators!"

Bellamy tried them. Both pilots pushed together. "Stuck solid!" Then he saw the reading on the altimeter: 31,000 feet and still going up. "Christ!"

Cavendish said, "I think it's ice over the hinges of the elevators. Jammed them solid in the up position."

"Hope to God it's not the boosters." He tried the emergency position; but there was no change. Only the windscreens were altering: the alcohol had eaten away at the ice, clearing a hole in the centre through which the stars shone, bright and alive around them. But they could also see the lumps of jagged ice, inches thick on the wings.

"I think you're right," Bellamy said.

He put the de-icer boots on, to get the ice at least off the wings and tailplane. Then he saw the temperature gauge: −32° Centigrade, and still going down. "Mightn't be the boosters now," he said grimly. "But if we don't watch out . . . it damn soon will be!"

He put his hands on the throttles. Very cautiously, he was bringing them back. Cavendish said, "For God's sake, don't stall her!"

"We've *got* to stop her climbing."

At the best of times, the Emperor's stall was vicious and sudden. In this nose-up attitude, with the elevators locked, what would happen was best not thought about. To make matters worse, with the ice they still carried, the stalling speed would be anybody's guess.

They had passed 34,000 feet now, but as the power from the engines was reduced, they were slowing up. But at the back of Bellamy's mind was the certainty that now they were passing the front, the temperature up here would take an alarming drop, way past −40°. He watched it going back on the dial, as he reduced power on the engines.

The climb had slowed up to a lazy progression upwards. He eased back the four levers just a fraction further.

And then, suddenly, with no warning at all, a great shudder ran through the whole aircraft. She quivered and wobbled like a giant jelly. Bellamy slammed all the throttles into the take-off position.

He yelled to the crew, "Strap yourselves in!", and switched on the passenger seat belt sign.

The trembling continued. Without the use of the elevators, there was a lag on the speed building up. The Emperor tottered at the top of the sky, trying to make up her mind what to do. Her metal plates seemed to go mad and melt into a shivering, clanging mass of metal.

And then, only seconds after the first tremors but like years to Bellamy, she gave up the ghost. The juddering ceased abruptly. With a whimper, the huge nose dropped. The navigator's pencils bounced off the table. As though suddenly deprived of all air to fly in, Emperor Able Dog plunged like a stone down towards the sea.

Payton was the only one in the passenger cabin to notice the seat belt sign come on. Feeling the juddering, his mind harked back to Labrador. Immediately, he felt for the webbing straps.

But it was too late. Before he could fasten them, the aircraft had lurched forward at an alarming angle. He was hurled against the seat in front. Tightly, he clung to the strawberry-pink upholstery; while the others, caught more unawares, were spilled like dice on the floor in all sorts of attitudes.

Eastlake had crashed over two seats, and was upside-down with his legs in the air. The Chairman hung grimly on to the arm of the vacant chair across the aisle. Brocklehurst had smashed his face hard against the porthole. Hamilton, who was standing up at the time, was knocked nearly unconscious against the rear bulkhead.

After the first cries of surprise, nobody said anything. Unsure whether they were upside-down or sideways, they lay where they had been thrown. Riley gave a groan, but it was the bump on his head that he was groaning about. Cruttwell had a gash right down his cheek that was now red and bleeding. The two girls, flattened on the galley floor, had their eyes tight closed.

They were all in such unlikely attitudes, that there could now be no remedy. They knew they were going downwards. The engines were curiously soft; but a gale seemed to whine and howl against the outside of the fuselage.

Sir James tried to get straight, but he fell back. Only Enderby-Browne was still upright, his legs propped hard against the seat in front of him.

But this descending motion was not an unpleasant sensation. As the seconds went by, they became, one by one, past being afraid. An inability to do anything anyway made them lie there passive, warm, comfortable even in the mêlée of bodies around them, waiting for whatever power there was that controlled these things to do what he wished with them.

The seconds stretched into minutes. They were still going down. And now they were turning. Right at the back, Lalette and Angela began to feel giddy and sick. Their eyes watered. Their heads went round and round. Everyone was conscious that somewhere, at some time soon, the air must end with the hard surface of the sea.

But the minutes passed, and nothing happened. Hearteningly, the engines started to roar up; yet the twisting and turning still went on; they were all pinned where they were by the invisible rotating strength of centrifugal force.

Up at the front, strapped in their seats, both pilots fought to make the Emperor recover. Bellamy yelled, "Is she spinning?"

The turn indicator was rate four to the left.

Cavendish shouted back, "God knows!" The turn indicator had swung central again.

"Can't feel anything in the rudders."

"Nothing in the ailerons, either."

Bellamy flung himself against the control column with all his might. "These damned elevators! Won't shift an inch!"

He had tried full travel on the trimmers. Nothing seemed to make any difference. The Emperor, descending now past 11,000 feet, had lost over three miles in height. She seemed to have forgotten all sense of behaving like an aeroplane. More like a huge hunk of metal, irregularly shaped, that twisted and turned, slowed up and spurted down: up on the port wing one minute, starboard the next: skidding and slipping in the darkness, the airspeed fluctuating wildly: now seemingly on the point of recovering, flat and much more steady, until once more the nose dropped violently, the shuddering started up, and she heeled over again, hard on her side.

Bellamy called out, "She's turning to the left again! I'm trying power on the port engines. Throttle back the starboards!"

He was trying to stop the spinning motion by counteracting it with asymmetrical engine power, now the rudders and ailerons were flabby and unresponsive and the elevators solid in the up position.

The nose steadied a little. The speed built up. Then up on her right wing she went. The altimeter needle unwound past 9,000 feet. There was a mile and a half of air left before the cold waters of the Atlantic began.

Bellamy still attempted to help her out of her paroxysms with the motors. Sometimes, there was more feel in the rudders: once, just on 5,000 feet, well below the freezing level now, they seemed to respond normally. But it was only for a moment, before the giddy shimmying rotation continued.

Cavendish said quietly, "Three thousand feet. Turning to starboard now!"

In a last desperate effort to right her, Bellamy tried take-off power on the starboard side, none on the port. Full rudder was already rammed hard on.

The aircraft went down another thousand feet. But she was descending slower. Bellamy saw the speed build up. Abruptly, the turning ceased. All juddering stopped. He banged the four throttle levers wide-open; and at last he felt life flowing back into the rudders and ailerons. The Emperor seemed to stop quite still for a moment. A calm descended over the whole of her fuselage. And then, quite undisturbed, she roared majestically up into the night, while the hard-working hand of the altimeter began rapid amends for butter-fingering five miles' worth of thin air.

The Emperor had reached 6,000 feet before either of the pilots spoke. Then Cavendish observed drily, "This aircraft continues to astonish me, Captain Bellamy."

Bellamy could still feel the emptiness inside him; the hard hammering of his heart. He turned his sweat-soaked face towards the older pilot. "She has her moments."

He saw Cavendish was smiling: the unperturbed, patient smile of long experience with fractious aeroplanes. "On top of her other virtues . . . what do we find but a remarkable gift for aerobatics!"

In spite of himself, Bellamy smiled back. His mind had been a blank over what he was going to do, still stunned by that terrifying spiral through the sky. Cavendish looked completely calm, as though he had been immunised against any feelings of near-disaster. His indomitable attitude, as he sat in the right-hand seat unmoved and unshaken, was in itself an immense encouraging comfort.

Bellamy said, "She'll be wanting to do an encore . . . if we don't watch out."

"I'd been thinking about that."

"It can't be ice now." Bellamy banged at the elevator control column, still stuck fast. "We got way below the freezing level." He took out his torch and shone it on the wing. "Not a sign of the stuff out there now."

"It was ice to begin with. Then I fancy when we got beyond 33,000 feet the elevator booster cylinders contracted in the cold temperatures. And jammed the pistons."

"Thank God the rudders didn't join them!" Bellamy bent over the throttle levers, bringing back the power on the engines. There was a greater feeling of security, now they had some height beneath them. But the angle of attack of the wings was very steep, causing an immense drag as the pilot tried to make the aircraft mush. "We've got to get the nose down somehow!"

They talked it over while the aircraft climbed, slowly and steadily up into the clear sky. The front was behind them now, and they were flying in a cold airstream from the north. When they had agreed on a course of action, Bellamy climbed out of his seat and went aft. He had a word with Douthwaite, Hooper and Seawood; the First Officer opened up a hatch in the floor for them, and all three disappeared into the baggage compartment.

In the passenger cabin, everyone had picked themselves up, and in a dazed silence had obeyed the sign to strap themselves in. Enderby-Browne had taken out the first-aid kit, and now Cruttwell's cheek had been dressed, sat with it on his lap, waiting like everyone else for the next plunge downwards to the sea.

Immediately Bellamy came into the compartment, the Chairman called out, "What's happened, Bellamy? What's wrong?"

The pilot told them all as briefly as possible. Then he explained what they intended to do. "As you can guess, the important thing is to *stop climbing.* All the same, we're going up to 19,000 feet, where we'll get a reasonable speed and where the upward effect of the elevators won't be so great. We can't go higher, in case of colder temperatures."

He paused, looking at the anxious faces around him. "But fortunately, the Emperor is very sensitive on fore and aft trim. All the cargo in the holds is now being moved forward. I want you to bring everything movable in the cabin and the galley up front. And then come up yourselves too. We want every available pound we can get crammed into the nose. That way, we may be able to balance out the up effect of the elevators."

"Like a pair of scales, Captain," Riley suggested.

Bellamy nodded. "Something like that."

Everyone in the cabin set to with a will, glad at last to be able to do something to help themselves, pushing and pulling everything that would move as far forward as they could. In a forlorn hope, Bellamy sent Rawlings and Eastlake back into the tail cone, to see if they could do anything about the jammed booster cylinders.

They were down there fifteen minutes. By the time they returned, dirty and dusty, all the other inhabitants of the Emperor were squeezed tightly together on the flight deck.

"Manage to do anything?" Bellamy asked them from the left-hand seat.

Eastlake shook his head. "Nothing."

But there he was wrong. By moving their combined weights of 331 pounds from the tip of the tail to the front of the nose, they achieved at last in the Emperor that balance that had been wanting. The altimeter stopped turning. Throttled back a little certainly, and in rather a begging attitude, Able Dog was nevertheless staying perfectly level around 19,000 feet, and yet still maintaining a reasonably good airspeed.

"Nice to be able to work," Douthwaite observed, as he sent up through the throng a new course of 072°, "without going round in circles!"

He saw Lalette, squashed against Cruttwell, and grinned at her. She tried to grin back.

But now that the emergency was apparently over, and there was nothing else to do but stand waiting in this crush, she felt her body take the delayed shocks of the past half-hour. She was suddenly cold. She hunched herself over her folded arms, as though to conserve the dwindling heat of her body, pressing her legs against the metal sides of the cockpit to stop their shuddering.

Instinctively, she pressed herself as far as possible into the dimly-lit, frighteningly crowded flight deck until she stood close behind Bellamy's seat. His nearness gradually comforted her. If she put out a hand, she could touch him. But because she knew she could, she no longer needed to. Instead, she looked along the shadow of the port wing, watching the red navigation light on its tip join the pattern of the stars.

She shifted her half-numbed foot. Around her, heads were bent, eyes peered only half-seeing at the endless black future that stretched in front of them. In the pale green glimmer from the instruments, the faces and hands of the pilots shone as though carved of undersea rock.

Lalette said to Bellamy, "Would it make a lot of difference if I went to the galley for coffee?"

"It would make some." He turned and smiled at her. "But I think it's worth it. So long as you're quick."

She was back soon, with the first tray. She reached her hand out for a cup for Sir James. "Two lumps for you, isn't it, sir?"

But he waved the cup away. "Workers first!" He nodded at the pilots. Lalette put in one lump of sugar and passed it to Bellamy. "Your coffee, sir."

As he took it, for a moment his fingers pressed over hers. "Thanks," he said. "Just what we all needed."

The cockpit began to be filled with conscientious human jollity, as Lalette went aft for the second tray of cups.

But after the coffee had gone, silence descended once more. There was an almost itching discomfort in so many people jam-packed together.

Bellamy rubbed the side of his head and the back of his neck. Then he straightened his shoulders as though throwing off the weight of the anxious souls behind him. For a second, he spared a thought for the girls, hoping that neither of them would feel this suffocating claustrophobia and become hysterical. When Lalette began to speak again, he listened with an ear trained to the nuances of dangerous vibrations, searching in the even tenor of her voice for the too high pitch, the confused hesitations, the beginning of the breaking point into tears.

But there was nothing. She was asking Captain Payton about the stars. Her voice was quiet, polite, interested. He could feel her lean forward a little. He could imagine her hand moving lightly, pointing across millions of miles of darkness to the ordered pattern of the now clear sky.

"Altair," said Payton. "Now look up! No, a bit to your right."

"That bright one? Beyond the Little Bear? Yes? What's that?"

"Deneb."

They were all looking out now. As if the whole sky were open to them, as if the cabin had been flung wide open, the heavy silence broke, the tenseness eased and flowed away.

Bellamy bent forward and looked at the instruments. Sir James leaned across to him and asked, "Did we send an emergency signal, Captain?"

Bellamy shrugged his shoulders. "No point. State we were in, nobody could have helped us. And now"—he looked out at the steady wings stretched out under the orderly sky—"there's no need."

"How are we doing?"

"Not bad, sir. Considering everything . . . she's going very well." He put out his hand for a piece of paper on which Douthwaite had written: *25 West.* Course *078° to 20 West. Estimate 06.10.*

Bellamy pursed his lips as he read it. They were going slower than he'd hoped. There was still another eight hundred miles of sea to go.

It was like that, all bunched in the nose of the Emperor, that dawn discovered them two hours later. The door to the passenger cabin swung to and fro, disclosing the empty cabin beyond them. Finding that the Emperor stayed where she was without her yen to climb, they found also that the close proximity was even comfortable. Riley made some crack about coming home with the milk. Eastlake (whose shiny hair was ruffled, his immaculate appearance spoiled) pressed close to Sir James, and said wryly, "It's my boosters again. Jammed pistons. On the elevators. And this time, they haven't come unstuck."

But it was no time for recrimination, for allotting the blame. Sir James recalled the whole question of the Mark II booster cylinders—from London through New York to Bermuda—very vividly in his own mind. Thoughtfully, he looked out of the port windscreen, and watched the red line on the eastern horizon gradually disappear, and a pearly grey explosion of light take its place. The cabin, before a small black hole with the flickering dials of the instruments as the only illumination, became a strip of metal with too many people standing on it. Beards began to show; the deep lines of fatigue cut into the faces of all those around him.

Looking at them, he was touched by the rather ragged scene before his eyes, all bunched together behind the pilots, everyone contributing their assorted weights to the eventual home-coming, while above them, glittering in the colours of a new day, the immense universe lay unbroken for millions of miles above their heads and below them washed the waves of the oldest ocean in the world—as though they were poised on a scale between the disaster of going too high, and the disaster of going too low, by the odd counterbalance of the tight-packed weight of humanity on the flight deck.

There was still cheerfulness. The aircraft seemed quite content to go on flying like this, without giving further trouble. Her ground speed, reduced by her begging attitude and the slight hindrance of a beam wind, was over 200 knots. Two hours from the estimated time of arrival over London, Bellamy obtained descent clearance, and by throttling back the engines still further, managed to begin a very slow descent.

The sky had lightened. Down below them now, they could see the slightly ruffled surface of the sea. Everyone immediately started to look at their watches, waiting for the moment when the coast of England would come out of the morning mist to greet them.

The time passed more slowly, now they were counting the minutes. Once or twice, small chunky clouds, low down, seemed to look like hills. And then suddenly, Seawood, squeezed behind the right hand seat, stretched out his hand and pointed out to starboard. "Land!"

A craggy piece of rock came jutting out of the horizon. It grew larger and longer—a cliff edged with green, with a beach in front of it and a chequer-board of fields and hills beyond. As they flew over the yellow stretch of sand that stretched like a winner's tape below them, everyone's spirit soared. The Emperor had at last come home.

And then, invisibly as a germ, a thought crossed their minds. Though the present danger had been overcome, and everyone was safe and comparatively comfortable, ahead lay the best-not-thought-about hazard of coming in for a landing at London.

THE CRASH

by Piers Paul Read

The copilot, Lagurara, was again at the controls of the Fairchild as it took off from Mendoza airport at eighteen minutes past two, local time. He set his course for Chilecito and then Malargüe, a small town on the Argentine side of the Planchon Pass. The plane climbed to 18,000 feet and flew with a tail wind of between 20 and 60 knots.

The land beneath them was sparse and arid, marked by river beds and salt lakes which bore the tracery of bulldozers. To the right rose the cordillera, a curtain of barren rock reaching toward the sky. If the plain below was mostly infertile, these mountains were a desert. The brown, gray, and yellow rock was untouched by even the smallest trace of vegetation, for their height sheltered the mountains on this side from the rain which was blown in from the Pacific on the western side of the range. Here, on the Argentinian side, the soil which lay between the folds and cracks of the mountains was no more than volcanic dust. There were no trees, no scrub, no grass. Nothing broke the monotonous ascent of these brittle mountains except the snow. Above 13,000 feet it was perpetual, but at this time of year it lay at much lower altitudes, softening the lines of the mountains and piling up in the valleys to a depth of more than a hundred feet.

The Fairchild was equipped not only with an ADF (Automatic Direction Finder) radio compass but also with the more modern VOR (VHF Omnidirectional Range). It was therefore a matter of routine to tune to the radio beacon at Malargüe, which was blocked at 15:08 hours. Still flying at 18,000 feet, the plane now turned to fly over the cordillera along air lane G 17. Lagurara estimated Planchon—the point in the middle of the mountains where he passed from Air Traffic Control in Mendoza to that in Santiago—at 15:21 hours. As he flew into the mountains, however, a blanket of cloud obscured his vision of the ground beneath. This was no cause for concern. Visibility above the clouds was good, and with the ground of the high cordillera covered with snow, there would, in any case, have been nothing by which they could have identified Planchon. Only one significant change had taken place: the moderate tail wind had now changed to a strong head wind. The ground speed of the plane had therefore been reduced from 210 to 180 knots.

At 15:21 Lagurara radioed Air Traffic Control in Santiago to say that he was over the Pass of Planchon and estimated to reach Curicó—a small town in Chile on the western side of the Andes—at 15:32. Then, only three minutes later, the Fairchild once again made contact with Santiago and reported "checking Curicó and heading toward Maipú." The plane turned at right angles to its previous course and headed north. The control tower in Santiago, accepting Lagurara at his word, authorized him to bring the plane down to 10,000 feet as he came toward the airport of Pudahuel. At 15:30 Santiago checked the level of the Fairchild. It reported "level 150," which meant that Lagurara had already brought the plane down 3,000 feet. At this altitude it entered a cloud and began to jump and shake in the different currents of air. Lagurara switched on the sign in the passenger cabin which ordered passengers to fasten their safety belts and to stop smoking. He then turned to the steward, Ramírez, who had brought Ferradas a gourd filled with maté, the bitter tea of South America, to return to the galley and make sure that the unruly passengers did as they were told.

Inside the passenger compartment there was a holiday atmosphere. Several of the boys were walking up and down the aisle, peering out of the small windows to try and catch a glimpse of the mountains through a gap in the clouds. They were all in high spirits; they had their rugby ball with them, and some were throwing it up and down the passenger cabin over their heads. At the back of the plane a group was playing cards, and farther back still, by the galley, the steward and the navigator, Martínez, had been playing a game of *truco,* a kind of whist. As the steward made his way back from the cockpit to resume the game, he told the boys still standing in the aisle to sit down.

"There's bad weather ahead," he said. "The plane's going to dance a little, but don't worry. We're in touch with Santiago. We'll be landing soon."

As he approached the galley he told four of the boys at the back to move forward. Then he sat down with the navigator and took up his hand.

As the plane entered another cloud bank it began to shake and lurch in a manner which alarmed many of the passengers. There were one or two practical jokes to hide this nervousness. One of the boys took hold of the microphone at the back of the plane and said, "Ladies and gentlemen, please put on your parachutes. We are about to land in the cordillera."

His audience was not amused, because just at that moment the plane hit an air pocket and plummeted several hundred feet. Roberto Canessa, for example, feeling alarmed, turned to Señora Nicola, who sat with her husband across the aisle, and asked her if she was afraid.

"Yes," she said. "Yes, I am."

Behind them a group of boys started to chant "Conga, conga, conga," and Canessa, with a show of courage, took a rugby ball which he had in his hands and threw it to Dr. Nicola, who in his turn threw it back down the cabin.

Eugenia Parrado looked up from her book. There was nothing to be seen from the window but the white mist of cloud. She turned the other way and looked at Susana's face and took hold of her hand. Behind them Nando Parrado and Panchito Abal were engrossed in conversation. Parrado had not even fastened his seat belt, nor did he do so when the plane hit a second air pocket and sank like a stone for a further few hundred feet. A cry of *"¡Ole, ole, ole!"* went up from the boys in the cabin—those, that is, who could not see out of a window—for the second fall had brought the plane out of the clouds, and the view which opened up beneath them was not of the fertile central valley of Chile many thousands of feet below but of the rocky edge of a snow-covered mountain no more than ten feet from the tip of the wing.

"Is it normal to fly so close?" one boy asked another.

"I don't think so," his companion replied.

Several passengers started to pray. Others braced themselves against the seats in front of them, waiting for the impact of the crash. There was a roar of the engines and the plane vibrated as the Fairchild tried to climb again; it rose a little but then there came a deafening crash as the right wing hit the side of the mountain. Immediately it broke off, somersaulted over the fuselage, and cut off the tail. Out into the icy air fell the steward, the navigator, and their pack of cards, followed by three of the boys still strapped to their seats. A moment later the left wing broke away and a blade of the propeller ripped into the fuselage before falling to the ground.

Inside what remained of the fuselage there were screams of terror and cries for help. Without either wings or tail, the plane hurtled toward the jagged mountain, but instead of being smashed to pieces against a wall of rock it landed on its belly in a steep valley and slid like a toboggan on the sloping surface of deep snow.

The speed at which it hit the ground was around 200 knots, yet it did not disintegrate. Two more boys were sucked out the back of the plane; the rest remained in the fuselage as it careered down the mountain, but the force of deceleration caused the seats to break loose from their mountings and move forward, crushing the bodies of those caught between them and smashing the partition which separated the passenger cabin from the forward luggage area. While the freezing air of the Andes rushed into the decompressed cabin and those passengers who still had their wits about them waited for the impact of the fuselage against the rock, it was the metal and plastic of the seats which injured them. Realizing this, some of the boys tried to undo their safety belts and stand up in the aisle, but only Gustavo Zerbino succeeded. He stood with his feet planted firmly on the floor and his hands pressed against the ceiling, shouting, "Jesus, Jesus, little Jesus, help us, help us!"

Another of the boys, Carlitos Páez, was saying a Hail Mary, begun when the wing of the plane had first touched the mountain. As he mouthed the last words of this prayer, the plane came to a stop. There was a moment of stillness and silence. Then, slowly, from all over the tangled mess within the passenger cabin came the sounds of life—groans and prayers and cries for help.

THE FLIGHT TO EAST HAMPTON

by Jim Shepard

His idea had been buttressed month after month with information from *The Lore of Flight,* the Cessna manual, from the public library, from conversations with Carver, from hours spent hanging around the airport, and from the Rand McNally road map of Long Island. The working out of its details and problems had completely taken the place and function of dice baseball, growing in intensity as it became less and less of a game, as his other alternatives fell away and lost their power or potential. Whether it was cause or effect of the death of his Oriole and Viking visions, he didn't know. He had watched Mr. Carver take off. He had discussed the process with him. He had absorbed the manual. He had never successfully driven a car before, but was convinced he could fly the plane. He could take off, he could maintain level flight, and he was willing to bet—although it was the chanciest part by far—that he could land as well. The Cessna 152 was, as both *The Lore of Flight* and the Cessna manual had assured him, an exceedingly simple aircraft, a trainer of sorts, a beginner's machine. He'd gone over and over the procedures in his head night after night, imagining and remembering the plane's responses, the pictures in his head allowing flights from his desk chair. He'd taken all questions to Mr. Carver or the library and had been satisfied with the answers.

The weather was ideal and he'd be flying VFR, navigating visually, so his radio contact with the tower would be minimal and voice identification impossible. He could bluff his way onto the runway with only the few phrases Carver had used. His bike with the front wheel turned around would fit in the front passenger's seat. According to the specifications in the Cessna manual, there was room. He'd checked his bike with a tape measure.

He was already on Ferry Boulevard, sweeping from shadow to sun to shadow as he flew past the widely spaced trees. He wasn't sure how much time he had or when the alarm would be sounded. And he wasn't sure—he forced the thought from his mind as he pedaled, ducking and leaning forward and pumping furiously—if he could even go through with it, sitting in the cockpit with the engine roaring and the runway stretching flat and terrifying before him.

He would fly to East Hampton. If all went as expected, there would be no notice taken of his flight until too late, nothing considered unusual.

Once in the air he would simply cross the Sound and Long Island and bear east along its southern coast. If he appeared from the south, with the wind the usual prevailing westerly, they would tell him to land on runway 28, at the end of which was the dirt path to the road he had glimpsed on his earlier trip. Rand McNally had identified it as Wainscott Road, which after 1.3 miles turned into the East Hampton Turnpike, which passed through Sag Harbor going north 3.3 miles later. He would set the plane down, run the entire length of tarmac to the tree line, engage the parking brake, leave the engine running, and disembark with his bike on the side away from the Hamptons' service building. There was no tower there and he would not be visible behind the fuselage. He'd take the bike and bag and leave the plane where it was, unharmed, a decoy, a ghost ship. He'd ride to Sag Harbor and then North Haven, take the ferry to Shelter Island, ride to the docks along Ram Island Drive, wait until dark, and take one of the rowboats he had seen so casually tethered to Long Beach Point across less than a mile of bay. At night it would be north-northwest on the compass. It was over a mile long and would be hard to miss. He'd never rowed a boat before for any distance; but, then, he'd never flown a plane before, either, he'd reasoned when that part of the plan had been taking shape. From there he'd go to Plum Island, northeast, and from there if possible due east across another mile or so of Sound—lonely, wild water—to Great Gull Island, devoid of any civilizing symbols and marks on the Rand McNally map and distant and alone out beyond the jaws of eastern Long Island's north and south peninsulas.

Avco slipped by hardly noticed, as did the airport fence, sunlight beading along its links in rapid succession, and just past stacks of steel drums and an Army trainer he turned onto the access road, bumping over the patched and broken concrete. The small brick Bridgeport Flight Service sat at the terminus of the dead end, and halfway down was the melancholy Windsock Restaurant, its windows broken, seemingly abandoned. He swung a sharp right opposite it through the opening in the interior fence to the hangar area. He slowed as the space opened in front of him.

Planes of all shapes and colors stood tethered and silent before him, set at random angles in a wide arc. From their wing struts and tails, ropes stretched to metal bars sunk in concrete. He eased to a halt straddling the bike, sweat running into the corners of his eyes. There was no sound, no movement. At this time of day he knew there might be only two or three men in the area, and they would almost certainly be seeking refuge in the manager's air-conditioned office. He slipped the key ring from his pocket and located the Cessna keys, the firm's name embossed in raised letters on the bow of the key. Then he untied the bag and pulled out the manual and checklist, no bigger together than the monthly missalette at church, retied the bag, and pedaled silently through the grove of struts and wings, quickly weaving his way to the blue-and-white Cessna parked with its tail to him and its nose to the runway. He glided up to its fuselage as if on rails, and was off the bike and fitting the key to the passenger door in seconds.

The handlebars caught and grabbed on the metal skin of the fuselage, balking at the smallish cavity of the door, but he angled them around, hefting the bicycle frame waist-high. The delay was agonizing. Finally it slid in and lay reasonably stable, and he shut the door and moved quickly to the tail. He had the preflight checklist memorized so completely he could visualize the pages in his head. He had them visualized so well—he knew them so well—that he could take shortcuts, save time. He unhooked the rudder gust lock, a metal band around the tail resembling a giant bobby pin, by impatiently spinning the wing nut off that held it together, and set it on the pavement behind him. He disconnected the tail tie-down, unlooping the knots, his fingers fumbling next to the smooth aluminum underside of the tail. He checked the control surfaces for freedom of movement and disconnected the wing tie-downs, flipping the freed ropes from the struts. He gave the tires a shove and hurriedly rolled a nearby stepladder up to the wings to check the fuel quantity visually, then rolled it away. He pulled the canvas cover from the Pitot tube: with the cover on, there would be no ram air input, and with no ram air input, his airspeed indicator and altimeter would not function. The cover still in his hand, he unlocked the other door and clambered aboard, flooded with relief to be finally off the tarmac, but still moving quickly, his hands shaking, pulling out the manual and double-checking the exterior checklist. He'd skipped some checks—oil, landing lights, air filter—gambling somewhat but feeling as though he were pressing his luck to the limit with every moment he stayed outside the plane. From his seat the instrument panel spread before him precisely as expected, the flight controls stabbing upward in a pair of elegant bull's horns. It was a three-dimensional model of the manual's full-page black-and-white photograph. That's all, he told himself. Yet he still shook, and his hand jittered across the plastic surface of the flight control when he reached out to touch it, his sweat leaving a momentary mist of a trail.

Keep moving, he thought. Keep moving, keep moving, keep moving, or you'll never do it. His hands flew.

1. A. *Remove control wheel lock.*
   B. *Check ignition switch* OFF.
   C. *Turn on master switch and check fuel quantity indicator; turn master off.*
   D. *Fuel selector valve on* BOTH.
   E. *Check door security; lock with key if children are to occupy any seats.*

He gazed through the windshield, the sun glaring it in streaks. It all seemed too easy. He fought the terrifying feeling that he had forgotten or bungled a single fatal detail. He folded the manual open to page 1–4 and propped it up on the seat beside him.

STARTING THE ENGINE

1. *Mixture—rich.*
2. *Carburetor heat—cold.*
3. *Primer—two to six strokes as required.*

The mixture knob was at the right center of the console, a white plastic knob a bit bigger than a thimble. He turned the indicator to "Rich." The carburetor heat control was its symmetric twin. The primer was on the lower left of the panel just above his left knee. He slipped two fingers behind it and pulled, half expecting it not to give. It did. He pumped it in and out twice more, priming the engine with fuel.

4. *Throttle—Open 1/8".*

It was right where his diagram had placed it. He crept it out an eighth of an inch.

5. *Master switch* ON.
6. *Propeller area—Clear.*

It had better be, he thought, not even looking up.

He swallowed. Outside the windshield the runway stretched silent under the sun, oblivious. He felt cold. He threaded the brother of the door key into the ignition—number 7 on the checklist—and turned it firmly, and the engine caught, coughing, terrifying him, the noise an explosion in a church, and gained power and volume with a steady surge. Events seemed to accelerate and he wanted to get off the runway and into the air as soon as possible, fearing last-minute police cars or security guards, remembering his sail collapsing in the storm so many months ago, unable completely to believe that he wasn't overlooking something, some fundamental, foolish detail. Stay with the checklist, he told himself. Move fast. Don't fool around. Shit or get off the pot.

TAXIING

When taxiing, it is important that speed and use of brakes be held to a minimum and that all controls be utilized (see Taxiing diagram, figure 2–4) to maintain directional control and balance.

The wind sock fluttered orange and fragile in the distance, indicating the wind direction and his next move, as outlined by figure 2–4: right-wing aileron slightly up, elevator neutral. He eased his toe off the brake, the arches of his feet still firm in the rudder stirrups, and opened the throttle. The plane began to roll.

He experienced at first that moment of sheer terror when he felt completely inadequate to the task of controlling the vibrating, deafening machine he was setting into motion, but it responded, he began to see, to the gentlest deflections of the flight controls. He wobbled steadily forward, jerking a bit from too much brake, learning by trial and error as he rumbled along how to guide the twelve-hundred-pound plane smoothly. He braked at the turn onto the access road that fed the runway.

The tower stood squat and imperturbable in the distance, an occasional bird crossing behind it. He switched on the receiver, lifted the microphone from its hook, closed his eyes, and pressed the button. He'd already be on the tower frequency.

"Tower, this is 9–0 Zulu," he said. "Request clearance for taxi."

He released the button and the cockpit filled with static. He waited and there was no answer. His ears were hot and his fingers slippery on the black plastic.

"Roger, Zulu," crackled a voice. "Take off runway 24."

He rehung the microphone and wiped his forehead. There was no alarm, no sudden activity, no yellow jeep. The sun beat down on the pavement. A Funny Bones wrapper, identifiable at forty feet, blew across the tarmac.

He turned left, following the painted yellow lines; the sun slipped behind him, and the shadows of his wings crossed the pavement before the plane like cool ripples. Runway 24 was the closest to him, the longest, and stretched to the south, which meant he'd take off over the marshes and Burma Road and be above the Sound in seconds. He rolled cautiously to the very end of the runway, the white "2" and "4" sweeping away from him majestically, and set the parking brake. His finger skimmed the checklist columns of the manual. He checked the flight controls, the fuel-selector valve, elevator trim, suction gauge, magnetos, and carburetor heat. He ran the engine up to 1700 rpm and past it, up to full throttle, or as near as he dared go—2100 rpm—and back down. He rechecked the locks on the doors. He buckled his seat belt. He was ready to go.

"Tower, this is 9–0 Zulu asking takeoff clearance," he said, the microphone brushing his lips. His gums felt dry.

"Roger Zulu, 24 cleared for takeoff." The answer was prompt, listless: just another day at the airport.

He released the parking brake and edged onto the runway, pivoting to his right before braking to a halt with the tarmac vast and endless before him, rushing straight-edged off to a single point over his cowling. He nudged the wing-flap switch until the indicator read 10 degrees up. His feet firm on the brakes, he opened the throttle fully.

> The takeoff is a simple procedure: lining the aircraft into the wind, the pilot gives full throttle and releases the wheel brakes. As the aircraft accelerates, airflow over the wings begins to generate lift. When the lift nearly equals the weight, the pilot eases back the control column.

With his toe off the brake, yet hovering near, he felt the surge and rush of the Cessna down the tarmac even as the flat repetition of images in his peripheral vision seemed to indicate little or no movement, and he remembered to keep the nose of the plane on the horizon as it bumped and shook over the cowling, and he stayed straight on, keeping the centerline centered in front of him, the pavement blurring by, and he felt the wings trying to leave the ground and he was up, prematurely, having waited too long on the control column, and he bounced, hard, frightening himself, but continued to sweep forward and this time pulled the control surface back smoothly and firmly, having the impression from the corner of his eye of the tower and parking lot to his right as colored streaks, and the plane swept off the ground, the left wing dipping a bit with runway to spare, the marshes appearing below, when he dared to look to his left, as yellow and soft as a wheat field with the black shadow of the plane speeding across them. He whooped and cheered, pounding the dashboard, his laughter mixing with the noise of the engine.

He flashed low across the wetlands, the clouds above and land below recalling to him a fleeting memory of the thermocline corridor at the beach, and he continued to climb as he passed over the strip of sand and road that was Long Beach, noting a running child, the dot of a beach ball, a cyclist at rest with one foot on the ground. Then the beach was behind him and the Sound ahead, blue and choppy. The triangular rainbow of a catamaran sail slipped by. And ever more to his left, away from him, was Port Jefferson, his first navigational objective.

> In flight the pilot will also want to turn. This is not accomplished by merely turning the rudder as is the case with a ship, but by a combination of aileron, rudder, and elevator movement and an adjustment of engine power.

Trying to remember everything at once and apprehensive, he turned the flight controls, pulling them back slightly as he did and easing out the throttle. The horizon reeled slowly in front of him, the twin stacks of the heavy industry in Port Jefferson harbor centering themselves over his cowling, and he applied opposite rudder and leveled out, elated. He was flying, two thousand feet off the ground without the benefit of a lesson.

Small boats appeared and disappeared below, flecked across the dark water. He allowed himself only the briefest glimpses, concentrating on the altimeter. In minutes he seemed to be coming up on the harbor at Port Jefferson, a small spit of land rising from his left to a steep bluff. Hundreds of boats were sheltered in its lee like orderly flotsam. There was a long knife edge of breakwater and then the darker blue of the channel and a freighter of some sort, maroon and black with its rust visible even from his height. He passed over the town as it climbed the hills from the harbor as if in an attempt to meet him, and he began to have the vague impression of trees and roads below, his eyes fixed on the compass and altimeter. The engine roared reassuringly and he made constant minute adjustments, concentrating. The cockpit hung pendulum-like beneath the great wings and the sun swept in the canopy and glittered on the fuselage. Ahead of him, rising like a sheer wall to an awesome height, was a snow-white anvil-shaped cloud filling his field of vision as he hurtled into it, having kept his eyes too long on the instruments. The sun disappeared and he was in a world of gray, all sensation of movement gone and the engine racketing abstractly in the half gloom. He fought panic and kept his eyes on the altimeter as it dipped and rose, thinking, Maybe it will stop, it's got to stop somewhere, and as it continued his fear mounted and he was no longer sure of his compass headings. He had to try something else and he had to trust his memory and ability.

EMERGENCY PROCEDURES: Disorientation in Clouds.
Executing a 180° turn in clouds.
Upon entering the clouds an immediate plan should be made to turn back as follows:

He located the clock and put his finger physically on the glass over the minute hand, trying to calm himself. When the sweep second hand indicated the nearest half minute, he banked to the left, holding the turn coordinator—a small white symbolic airplane wing on a black field—opposite the lower left index mark, waiting, waiting, for the second hand to complete its revolution. When it did, he leveled off, checking the compass heading to insure it was the opposite of the previous one and climbing to restore altitude. He could hear himself breathing, panting like a dog. Outside the cockpit everything was still softly opaque. He fought the urge to dive or climb. The gray remained, fog or wool, and his fear grew and he was ready to call on God when the gray swept away and sunlight flooded him, glancing blindingly off the cowling. He whooped even as he blinked and averted his eyes.

After a few moments he swung the plane around to the left again, returning to the cloud but letting the altimeter slip until it read 2000 and he was passing underneath the flat white ceiling, the light losing some of its warmth, bumps and irregularities appearing on the underside and rushing past. He passed a highway, ribboned with moving cars. A shopping center like an arrangement of low boxes. Clusters of towns. More highways. He found himself out from under the cloud, in the sun again, with the shore and the Atlantic uneven strips on the horizon. Towns, trees, roads, fields. Farmland. Low fences with animals (cows?) spotting the land. A bridge across a narrow bay. Marshes and beach houses. The white lines of sand and breakers and he was back over ocean again, banking up and around with blue sky and white clouds spinning across the windshield. When he leveled out, the compass on the dash was reading E-NE and he was following the long thin strip of land to his left between a large bay and the Atlantic, the land a joyous tan in the sun and a directional indicator to East Hampton Airport.

He seemed to be safely south of the clouds and flew level, free and happy. He laughed aloud again in delight, bobbing his wings a bit to echo his feelings.

The radio crackled, harsh and startling. "Aircraft 9-0 Zulu, are you on frequency?"

He stared silently out the window, everything falling apart in front of him.

"Aircraft 9-0 Zulu repeat are you on frequency?"

The tone recalled Sister Theresa seeing him on the roof, his father hearing of the detention. Broken windows, ruined dress pants, late arrivals, and poor report cards. They knew the plane was missing, they knew he had it and they knew it was still in the air.

He sat immobilized by the shock of his failure. It had been crucial that he land undetected, to allow for his unnoticed disappearance on the bicycle, but he couldn't land undetected anywhere now with the designation he was sporting on the side of his fuselage. His plan had been destroyed, that quickly, that easily. He wiped his eyes furiously. He had to think. It couldn't be all over after everything he'd been through. Below him breakers ran a jagged white track along the shore, curving and growing in distant foamy lines. He was passing a very large airport to his left, and the land below opened into a great irregular bay closed to the sea by a long spit crested with dunes. If it was Shinnecock Bay, as he guessed it was from the map, Southampton was directly east, and he would be approaching East Hampton Airport in minutes.

He couldn't land there, he thought. He couldn't just quit. But where else could he go? What other airport could he find from the air without navigational aids? Montauk had an airport, he knew, but that was as good as giving up: they'd be waiting there as well, and it was exposed and isolated, with nowhere to go once he landed.

"Biddy. Biddy, this is your father. What the good Christ do you think you're doing?"

He stared at the radio, stunned. The engine's roar changed in pitch to signal he'd let the nose drop, and he corrected it.

"Biddy, tell us where you are." His father sounded as though the lifeboats were sinking or he was hanging from a cliff. On the radar screen his blip would be indistinguishable from any others. "Biddy, you got up all right but how are you going to get down? Biddy! Let them talk you down!" His father's last cry shook him, and he reached for the microphone. The crackling continued.

"Aircraft 9-0 Zulu, are you on frequency? Aircraft 9-0 Zulu, are you on frequency? Acknowledge."

The coast was flowing steadily under the cowling as the Cessna's nose ate up space and distance. There was literally nowhere to go. He began to cry, from frustration and tension. I could go right to Great Gull Island, he thought. I could go right to it and land in the water.

But he recognized the absurdity of the idea: he'd destroy the plane, kill himself. Or hurt himself and drown. And how could that possibly go undetected?

The voice on the radio asked again if he was on frequency. His father's voice broke in. "Biddy," he said. "Please."

The blue sky hung unbroken before him. The extent to which he'd hurt people had been reflected in his father's final cry, and it had been much more than he had guessed. Every action he was taking was connected to others and hurting in ever-widening circles and ways and there was no longer any hope of preserving the illusion of his actions enjoying a total independence in the world, of his escape taking place in a vacuum. Was any of this going to make him, or anyone else, or anything about his life, any better?

East Hampton Airport rolled into sight over the drum of the horizon. He lifted the microphone and pushed the "Send" button. "I'm all right," he said. "I'll be right down." He lowered it to his lap at the answering gabble of voices and shut off the receiver. He turned the frequency to 132.25 for East Hampton. He glanced into the distance in the northeast, trying for a glimpse, at least a glimpse, after having come this far, of the north fork and Plum or Great Gull Island in the haze. But it all remained indistinct and imprecise, however beautiful. He switched the receiver back on and raised the microphone.

"East Hampton, this is 9-0 Zulu," he said. His back hurt and his head ached. "What's your active runway?"

"Ah, Roger, Zulu, we have traffic taking off and coming in on 28." There was a pause. "Ah, 9-0 Zulu, do you want to be talked down? Acknowledge."

He pressed to answer, the radio silence hissing expectantly. "No," he said. "No, thank you." He switched off the receiver.

He was approaching from the southeast. There were no clouds over the airport, and no traffic he could make out. A far-off V of birds stroked across the sky toward the land.

Below him houses and gray roads rolled by, breaking the irregular green of the trees: he was away from the coast. The airport grew larger, the three runways a gray triangle pointed at him, the service area as vivid against the dark green pines as he remembered. Far below he could make out tiny multicolored ovals drifting up toward him—balloons, he realized with a start, their threadlike strings undulating behind. The sun caught on a random car windshield, sparkling like a diamond.

He pushed left rudder hard and went into a bank, thrusting the control column forward and the nose down as he did. The sky went over the top of the canopy and the ground centered itself on the windshield and began to climb slowly to meet him. The altimeter was dropping, the needle retreating from 3 past four calibrated notches to 2 and still descending when he checked the airspeed indicator, just leaving the green arc of normal operating range at 130 mph and making its way through the yellow, labeled CAUTION. He eased back on the throttle, keeping the indicator away from the red line, and the triangle of runway shook gently and grew in size in his windshield, tilting from the level as his wings did, and when he felt he couldn't go any lower he began to pull up, the ground rushing along under him like a film out of control, vague shapes and colors streaking by, blurring and disappearing in an instant. Tree after tree swept past and roads and a hill and the airport suddenly loomed in front of him from out of the trees like someone rising from tall grass, the central buildings rushing at him, and he was too low too low the wheels his belly would hit surely and he was over, skimming the billowing carpet of treetops again, the altimeter creeping higher as he pulled up and around.

Climbing, he turned on the receiver. There was a loud burst of static. "Uh, 9-0 Zulu, have you lost your mind? Acknowledge."

His climb and bank were carrying his nose around to the sun, which flooded white and blinding across the canopy. He leveled out east of the airport, the plane sideslipping a bit as he did, and came around again, on line with the runway. He eased the nose up and the throttle forward and his airspeed began to drop.

He lifted the microphone from his lap. "This is 9-0 Zulu. Can I have landing clearance?" he said.

A voice crackled back. "Jesus Christ, by all means, Zulu."

He was already on his approach. He extended his flaps. A utility right-of-way flashed by beneath him, the power lines and treetops closer than he expected.

"Watch your airspeed, Zulu," the radio said. Things seemed to slow. Trees drifted by. The curve of a road. A field with a white dog outlined against tall weeds.

"Keep your nose up, Zulu. Keep it on the horizon. Stay level. Watch your airspeed." He did. It read 90. Everything was spinning by him. He was so low he saw only trees and then they stopped and it was flat and wide before him, gray streaked with black, and the white number 28 glided up to meet him and he could hear the radio as if it were in someone else's cockpit—"Ease back! Ease back!"—and, keeping the top of his cowling in line with the horizon, easing the nose still farther back, cutting the power still more, he caught one last glimpse of the airspeed indicator, vaguely remembering it as too high, before he hit.

He bounced, jerking forward and upward in the seat as if catapulted, his shoulder harness straining against him, the wings outside the cockpit swaying against the level ground flashing past. And he lifted the nose still more and cut the throttle almost to nothing, and the plane seemed to hesitate in the air before dropping again, like a sofa, to the runway, the concussion nearly shaking his hands from the wheel but leaving him on the tarmac, rolling instead of flying, with quite a distance of safety margin still to go. He rolled and rolled and began to slow and his toes found the brakes again, a little too soon, but again, learning quickly, and he taxied to the very edge of the runway and bumped off onto the access area, turning until trees and trunks filled his vision and the plane rolled to a stop. He reached forward to switch the engine off and the propellers began to materialize, blurs cutting a half circle in front of him before hacking and chopping to a halt, gleaming and smooth. He wasn't used to the silence, and small noises seemed out of proportion, welcome.

Across the long bisection of runways to his right he could make out a lone police car, a bar of red-and-blue lights on its roof, approaching on the access road from the parking area, its tires audible on the gravel. There had been no foam on the runway, no battery of rescue vehicles, no SWAT team. And no crash. There was just a lone police car, in no discernible hurry. As it grew closer, he unbuckled his harness, anxious to get the bike and the bag out of the cargo area himself. He wanted no help at this point. He'd come this far, he had a way to go, and he wanted to be ready by the time they arrived.

HELL AT 40,000 FEET

by Martin Caidin

It is 1943. At 40,000 feet it is bitterly cold. A screaming wind bursts upward through the open bomb-bay doors of the B-17 *Fortress,* tears with ice-needle fingers at the clothes of the man standing at the edge of the bay looking down into the abyss.

Seventy degrees below zero, cold impossible to comprehend but terribly real and dangerous, severe enough to freeze a man's hand rock-hard within seconds.

There is another enemy: the cruel, thin air of this height. On the face of the man staring down at the featureless surface of the earth is an oxygen mask, its rubberized bladders alternately sucking empty and then puffing into a bloated bag, like lungs exposed nakedly to the air. Only that mask and its bladders lie between life and unconsciousness within ten to fifteen seconds should the mask fail, clog, freeze, or suffer even a minor leak.

The man is Lieutenant Colonel W. R. Lovelace of the Army Air Forces, and he is preparing to step out into the emptiness of the gaping bomb bays and attempt an unprecedented parachute descent to the earth far, far below. The oxygen equipment worn by the colonel? Untried, untested, unproven at this height, under the extreme conditions of terrible cold and rarefied air.

Colonel Lovelace is completely out of his element. He has no business here. He has never made a parachute jump. He is a surgeon with skilled hands who belongs in an operating room, saving the lives of men in need of probing and cutting and healing. And yet, here he is at 40,000 feet, prepared to make a jump that has every chance of wresting his life from him.

Only one other man in the entire world has ever stepped into the awesome emptiness of this height for a parachute jump. But the Russian major who dropped away from his airplane departed the stratosphere as quickly as his falling body would drag him down to denser, safer, warmer air; inside of a minute and a half, the Soviet officer dropped free of the perils of altitude, to be embraced by the thick ocean of air closer to the earth.

Colonel Lovelace is going to attempt something that no man has ever done. Most doctors are certain he will be dead long before his feet ever touch the ground. Lovelace is going to open his parachute immediately upon leaving the great bomber!

It will take him twelve minutes to reach a level where he can breathe without his vital oxygen bottle. There is the danger that the opening shock of the parachute may hammer him senseless; the equipment may snap free; the hose-line may fail—perhaps it will freeze. In 1943 engineers know precious little about the effects of such severe cold and wind.

As far as Lovelace is concerned, it is imperative that he make this jump. Pilots and their crews already are fighting in mortal combat at this height. Can they survive a jump if they are forced to bail out at this altitude? Will their equipment keep them alive? The colonel believes that Air Force doctors should hardly send men into combat, with aviation-medicine equipment, without knowing if that equipment will give the men a chance to survive. There is only one way to find out. All it takes is a single step.

Colonel Lovelace takes a deep breath; he is ready for that step.

"Forty thousand feet seems much farther, looking straight down," he explained later, "than it does when you look out the side of a ship. It looks like a hell of a long ways. As we approached the altitude at which I wanted to leave the ship, things had been happening pretty fast and I was busy getting my equipment ready. You can't avoid a certain feeling of apprehension just before you jump, but the most careful preparations had been made and I didn't worry at all.

"I turned on my oxygen supply in the bottle zippered in my flying suit. Then I disconnected from the ship's supply and went on the bottle. I saw the oxygen pressure needle on my emergency equipment beginning to come around, and I knew I was all set.

"I stood there maybe forty-five seconds—that was the longest part of the jump! Then I went out feet first."

Lovelace falls through the bomb-bay opening. He goes out with the terrific roar of the wind and the engines pounding in his ears. There is a blur of metal and a flash of sky as his head passes the belly of the *Fortress,* then his body clears the bomber. The force of the airstream slaps him around, and he hurtles backward in mid-air. He sees the B-17 as he begins his fall, hears the now faint sound of its engines.

It takes only a second or so for his body to reach the limit of the static line. The line pulls taut, yanks the pilot chute from its folds. In an instant the full parachute comes out and snaps open.

The terrible jolt—a sudden, violent wrenching of every muscle, of every bone—jars him. He experiences immediate deceleration. In a fraction of a second he is brought from his high speed to a virtual halt. The force of the deceleration is the same as if he were hurled face first into a brick wall in the sky.

In that terrible moment before unconsciousness snatches him from pain, all the air is pounded from his lungs. There is a timeless moment in which he sees the leather glove and the silk glove beneath it fly away from his left hand. He sees it almost as if he were in a dream. Even as he is blacking out, his brain seeming to register things in slow motion, he realizes that he has suffered a blow of at least six times the force of gravity, perhaps even more. With all his equipment, the colonel in an instant has been exploded all the way to a weight of more than 1500 pounds! And that is all he knows as blackness envelops him.

His limbs sag. The next moment he hangs limp in the parachute harness, his left hand exposed to the brutal cold of eight-mile height. He falls, seemingly lifeless.

In the B-17, Dick Williams, the pilot, has racked the heavy bomber around as steeply as the thin air will permit. He comes around in a diving turn so the crewmen can spot the parachute and see how Colonel Lovelace is faring.

Someone shouts—but the sighting of the parachute is followed with a cry of dismay. "I think he killed himself!" one man calls.

It does look as if the colonel is dead, as he swings inertly in his harness. The parachute drops him toward the earth at the rate of forty feet per second. As he falls, his body swings limply from side to side, but in a wild and swooping arc of at least 45 degrees. It is a frightening sight for the men in the B-17, for at the end of each swing, the far side of the parachute canopy "laps in."

This is a partial collapse of the chute. The wild oscillations threaten to collapse the canopy at any instant and streamer the chute, and this is a sure warrant of death. Somehow, the chute holds each time.

Acutely aware that, even if he has survived the terrible shock of the parachute opening and is still alive, Colonel Lovelace may be doomed to death at any moment, the B-17 crewmen follow him down, searching anxiously for any sign of life.

"Maybe he hit the plane as he went out," someone offers in the way of explanation, "or maybe the static line clipped him." Maybe. Maybe. They talk without any real knowledge, and they know this, even as they conjecture that the opening jerk of the parachute might have caused him to be struck about the head with some of his equipment, or even his own fist. Perhaps the oxygen line snapped, and he blacked out from lack of oxygen. Even, as they watch, he may be strangling to death.

Nine agonizing minutes pass. In this eternity of waiting, Lovelace drifts down from 40,200 feet to 22,000 feet, still more than four miles above the earth. At this height the earphones of the B-17 pilot crackle. Lovelace has been spotted by Boeing test pilots Bob Lamson and Cliff Dorman, who are circling at a lower altitude in an AT-6 trainer. The initial excitement of the sighting vanishes, for Lamson reports that there is still no sign of life. The colonel's body dangles helplessly in the oscillating parachute.

Somewhere during this part of the descent, Lovelace stirs to consciousness. He is still very far up. How high, he cannot tell. He looks "down a great distance" and then blackness once more engulfs him.

He drifts toward a layer of broken clouds, the AT-6 buzzing helplessly around his inert figure, Lamson and Dorman trying desperately in some way to help their friend. But they are only observers.

At 8000 feet Lovelace drops through a large hole in the clouds, and

Lamson fairly screams into his mike. "He's *alive!* He's alive! I can see him moving!"

Lovelace is fighting his way back to consciousness. The sound of the AT-6 engine helps bring him to, and he raises his right hand in a feeble gesture of recognition.

The colonel is in bad shape, and he suffers a deep, burning pain. He is in shock, his body fighting the effects of hypoxia—oxygen starvation. He suffers from severe nausea, and his left hand is frozen almost solid.

Lamson notes with gratitude that just before Lovelace is about to hit the ground he slowly moves his legs. But the colonel's effort to prepare himself for the impact is futile. The earth rushes up at him, and he strikes the ground stiffly. Fortunately, he has fallen onto the flat expanse of a wheat field.

He topples helplessly to the ground, and the chute billows out. For several seconds it drags him along the ground. Luck stays with him, however, and the billowing silk collapses.

Right overhead is the AT-6, Lamson clawing around in a tight turn as he swings into the wind to land. Lovelace feebly waves a hand, and Lamson loses no time in following procedure. He radios the B-17 that Lovelace is alive, specifies his position, and asks for help. Then the AT-6 swings around sharply and slides to the ground.

Lamson leaps from the cockpit and runs to the colonel. Lovelace stirs feebly and cries, "God! I'm glad to see you!"

His face is the color of chalk. He can barely move his limbs. His left hand is a sickly, frozen white. The effects of his descent—nausea, shock, frozen hand, hypoxia—have taken a visible toll.

But all he says to Lamson is, "I'm all right. My hand hurts, and I feel just a little sick."

Lamson uses a portable oxygen bottle to feed pure oxygen to the colonel, who is trying to keep his frozen hand in the direct rays of the sun. He needs the oxygen badly. The rescue team arrives, and the doctor who checks over Lovelace orders him into the hospital immediately. There he is placed under oxygen. That evening the doctors permit him to drink some tea, but that is all.

By morning, however, Lovelace is on the upgrade. Later he recalls, "I didn't feel much like talking after I hit the ground. I noticed that I could form sentences all right, but some of the words—an average of one word per sentence—seemed to me to come out badly. I would attribute all that to lack of oxygen.

"They used to tell the men who might be in a spot where they had to make a high-altitude parachute jump to take a deep breath and hold it. But when you are bailing out there are a million things to think of, and I don't believe a jumper would ever be able to hold his breath. Even if he could, the deceleration would knock it out of his lungs."

Colonel Lovelace accomplished his perilous mission in one of the most amazing first jumps any man has ever made. Twenty years later, a parachute opening at 40,000 feet is still considered one of the most dangerous experiences any man can face, even with modern equipment and space-age medical research. From the lessons of Lovelace's jump, the Army Air Force was able to tell its fliers that, with emergency equipment, they could get out at high altitude and survive. But the Army recommended that the men ride their disabled planes down as far as they could do so in safety and, if they must get out, free fall as long as possible.

They're still telling them the same thing today.

YEAGER BREAKS THE SOUND BARRIER

by Tom Wolfe

At the end of the war the Army had discovered that the Germans not only had the world's first jet fighter but also a rocket plane that had gone 596 miles an hour in tests. Just after the war a British jet, the Gloster Meteor, jumped the official world speed record from 469 to 606 in a single day. The next great plateau would be Mach 1, the speed of sound, and the Army Air Force considered it crucial to achieve it first.

The speed of sound, Mach 1, was known (thanks to the work of the physicist Ernst Mach) to vary at different altitudes, temperatures, and wind speeds. On a calm 60-degree day at sea level it was about 760 miles an hour, while at 40,000 feet, where the temperature would be at least sixty below, it was about 660 miles an hour. Evil and baffling things happened in the transonic zone, which began at about .7 Mach. Wind tunnels choked out at such velocities. Pilots who approached the speed of sound in dives reported that the controls would lock or "freeze" or even alter their normal functions. Pilots had crashed and died because they couldn't budge the stick. Just last year Geoffrey de Havilland, son of the famous British aircraft designer and builder, had tried to take one of his father's DH 108s to Mach 1. The ship started buffeting and then disintegrated, and he was killed. This led engineers to speculate that the shock waves became so severe and unpredictable at Mach 1, no aircraft could survive them. They started talking about "the sonic wall" and "the sound barrier."

So this was the task that a handful of pilots, engineers, and mechanics had at Muroc. The place was utterly primitive, nothing but bare bones, bleached tarpaulins, and corrugated tin rippling in the heat with caloric waves; and for an ambitious young pilot it was perfect. Muroc seemed like an outpost on the dome of the world, open only to a righteous few, closed off to the rest of humanity, including even the Army Air Force brass of command control, which was at Wright Field. The commanding officer at Muroc was only a colonel, and his superiors at Wright did not relish junkets to the Muroc rat shacks in the first place. But to pilots this prehistoric throwback of an airfield became . . . shrimp heaven! the rat-shack plains of Olympus!

Low Rent Septic Tank Perfection . . . yes; and not excluding those traditional essentials for the blissful hot young pilot: Flying & Drinking and Drinking & Driving.

Just beyond the base, to the southwest, there was a rickety wind-blown 1930's-style establishment called Pancho's Fly Inn, owned, run, and bartended by a woman named Pancho Barnes. Pancho Barnes wore tight white sweaters and tight pants, after the mode of Barbara Stanwyck in *Double Indemnity.* She was only forty-one when Yeager arrived at Muroc, but her face was so weatherbeaten, had so many hard miles on it, that she looked older, especially to the young pilots at the base. She also shocked the pants off them with her vulcanized tongue. Everybody she didn't like was an old bastard or a sonofabitch. People she liked were old bastards and sonsabitches, too. "I tol' 'at ol' bastard to get 'is ass on over here and I'd g'im a drink." But Pancho Barnes was anything but Low Rent. She was the granddaughter of the man who designed the old Mount Lowe cable-car system, Thaddeus S. C. Lowe. Her maiden name was Florence Leontine Lowe. She was brought up in San Marino, which adjoined Pasadena and was one of Los Angeles' wealthiest suburbs, and her first husband—she was married four times—was the pastor of the Pasadena Episcopal Church, the Rev. C. Rankin Barnes. Mrs. Barnes seemed to have few of the conventional community interests of a Pasadena matron. In the late 1920's, by boat and plane, she ran guns for Mexican revolutionaries and picked up the nickname Pancho. In 1930 she broke Amelia Earhart's air-speed record for women. Then she barnstormed around the country as the featured performer of "Pancho Barnes's Mystery Circus of the Air." She always greeted her public in jodhpurs and riding boots, a flight jacket, a white scarf, and a white sweater that showed off her terrific Barbara Stanwyck chest. Pancho's desert Fly Inn had an airstrip, a swimming pool, a dude ranch corral, plenty of acreage for horseback riding, a big old guest house for the lodgers, and a connecting building that was the bar and restaurant. In the barroom the floors, the tables, the chairs, the walls, the beams, the bar were of the sort known as extremely weatherbeaten, and the screen doors kept banging. Nobody putting together such a place for a movie about flying in the old days would ever dare make it as dilapidated and generally go-to-hell as it actually was. Behind the bar were many pictures of airplanes and pilots, lavishly autographed and inscribed, badly framed and crookedly hung. There was an old piano that had been dried out and cracked to the point of hopeless desiccation. On a good night a huddle of drunken aviators could be heard trying to bang, slosh, and navigate their way through old Cole Porter tunes. On average nights the tunes were not that good to start with. When the screen door banged and a man walked through the door into the saloon, every eye in the place checked him out.

If he wasn't known as somebody who had something to do with flying at Muroc, he would be eyed like some lame goddamned mouseshit sheepherder from *Shane.*

The plane the Air Force wanted to break the sound barrier with was called the X-I at the outset and later on simply the X-I. The Bell Aircraft Corporation had built it under an Army contract. The core of the ship was a rocket of the type first developed by a young Navy inventor, Robert Truax, during the war. The fuselage was shaped like a 50-caliber bullet—an object that was known to go supersonic smoothly. Military pilots seldom drew major test assignments; they went to highly paid civilians working for the aircraft corporations. The prime pilot for the X-I was a man whom Bell regarded as the best of the breed. This man looked like a movie star. He looked like a pilot from out of *Hell's Angels.* And on top of everything else there was his name: Slick Goodlin.

The idea in testing the X-I was to nurse it carefully into the transonic zone, up to seven-tenths, eight-tenths, nine-tenths the speed of sound (.7 Mach, .8 Mach, .9 Mach) before attempting the speed of sound itself, Mach 1, even though Bell and the Army already knew the X-I had the rocket power to go to Mach 1 and beyond, if there *was* any *beyond.* The consensus of aviators and engineers, after Geoffrey de Havilland's death, was that the speed of sound was an absolute, like the firmness of the earth. The sound barrier was a farm you could buy in the sky. So Slick Goodlin began to probe the transonic zone in the X-I, going up to .8 Mach. Every time he came down he'd have a riveting tale to tell. The buffeting, it was so fierce—and the listeners, their imaginations aflame, could practically see poor Geoffrey de Havilland disintegrating in midair. And the goddamned aerodynamics—and the listeners got a picture of a man in ballroom pumps skidding across a sheet of ice, pursued by bears. A controversy arose over just how much bonus Slick Goodlin should receive for assaulting the dread Mach 1 itself. Bonuses for contract test pilots were not unusual; but the figure of $150,000 was now bruited about. The Army balked, and Yeager got the job. He took it for $283 a month, or $3,396 a year; which is to say, his regular Army captain's pay.

The only trouble they had with Yeager was in holding him back. On his first powered flight in the X-I he immediately executed an unauthorized zero-g roll with a full load of rocket fuel, then stood the ship on its tail and went up to .85 Mach in a vertical climb, also unauthorized. On subsequent flights, at speeds between .85 Mach and .9 Mach, Yeager ran into most known airfoil problems—loss of elevator, aileron, and rudder control, heavy trim pressures, Dutch rolls, pitching and buffeting, the lot —yet was convinced, after edging over .9 Mach, that this would all get better, not worse, as you reached Mach 1. The attempt to push beyond Mach 1—"breaking the sound barrier"—was set for October 14, 1947. Not being an engineer, Yeager didn't believe the "barrier" existed.

October 14 was a Tuesday. On Sunday evening, October 12, Chuck Yeager dropped in at Pancho's, along with his wife. She was a brunette named Glennis, whom he had met in California while he was in training, and she was such a number, so striking, he had the inscription "Glamorous Glennis" written on the nose of his P-51 in Europe and, just a few weeks back, on the X-I itself. Yeager didn't go to Pancho's and knock back a few because two days later the big test was coming up. Nor did he knock back a few because it was the weekend. No, he knocked back a few because night had come and he was a pilot at Muroc. In keeping with the military tradition of Flying & Drinking, that was what you did, for no other reason than that the sun had gone down. You went to Pancho's and knocked back a few and listened to the screen doors banging and to other aviators torturing the piano and the nation's repertoire of Familiar Favorites and to lonesome mouse-turd strangers wandering in through the banging doors and to Pancho classifying the whole bunch of them as old bastards and miserable peckerwoods. That was what you did if you were a pilot at Muroc and the sun went down.

So about eleven Yeager got the idea that it would be a hell of a kick if he and Glennis saddled up a couple of Pancho's dude-ranch horses and went for a romp, a little rat race, in the moonlight. This was in keeping with the military tradition of Flying & Drinking and Drinking & Driving, except that this was prehistoric Muroc and you rode horses. So Yeager and his wife set off on a little proficiency run at full gallop through the desert in the moonlight amid the arthritic silhouettes of the Joshua trees. Then they start racing back to the corral, with Yeager in the lead and heading for the gateway. Given the prevailing conditions, it being nighttime, at Pancho's, and his head being filled with a black sandstorm of many badly bawled songs and vulcanized oaths, he sees too late that the gate has been closed. Like many a hard-driving midnight pilot before him, he does not realize that he is not equally gifted in the control of all forms of locomotion. He and the horse hit the gate, and he goes flying off and lands on his right side. His side hurts like hell.

The next day, Monday, his side still hurts like hell. It hurts every time he moves. It hurts every time he breathes deep. It hurts every time he moves his right arm. He knows that if he goes to a doctor at Muroc or says anything to anybody even remotely connected with his superiors, he will be scrubbed from the flight on Tuesday. They might even go so far as to put some other miserable peckerwood in his place. So he gets on his motorcycle, an old junker that Pancho had given him, and rides over to see a doctor in the town of Rosamond, near where he lives. Every time the goddamned motorcycle hits a pebble in the road, his side hurts like a sonofabitch. The doctor in Rosamond informs him he has two broken ribs and he tapes them up and tells him that if he'll just keep his right arm immobilized for a couple of weeks and avoid any physical exertion or sudden movements, he should be all right.

Yeager gets up before daybreak on Tuesday morning—which is supposed to be the day he tries to break the sound barrier—and his ribs still hurt like a sonofabitch. He gets his wife to drive him over to the field, and he has to keep his right arm pinned down to his side to keep his ribs from hurting so much. At dawn, on the day of a flight, you could hear the X-I screaming long before you got there. The fuel for the X-I was alcohol and liquid oxygen, oxygen converted from a gas to a liquid by lowering its temperature to 297 degrees below zero. And when the lox, as it was called, rolled out of the hoses and into the belly of the X-I, it started boiling off and the X-I started steaming and screaming like a teakettle. There's quite a crowd on hand, by Muroc standards . . . perhaps nine or ten souls. They're still fueling the X-I with the lox, and the beast is wailing.

The X-I looked like a fat orange swallow with white markings. But it was really just a length of pipe with four rocket chambers in it. It had a tiny cockpit and a needle nose, two little straight blades (only three and a half inches thick at the thickest part) for wings, and a tail assembly set up high to avoid the "sonic wash" from the wings. Even though his side was throbbing and his right arm felt practically useless, Yeager figured he could grit his teeth and get through the flight—except for one specific move he had to make. In the rocket launches, the X-I, which held only two and a half minutes' worth of fuel, was carried up to twenty-six thousand feet underneath a B-29. At seven thousand feet, Yeager was to climb down a ladder from the bomb bay of the B-29 to the open doorway of the X-I, hook up to the oxygen system and the radio microphone and earphones, and put his crash helmet on and prepare for the launch, which would come at twenty-five thousand feet. This helmet was a homemade number. There had never been any such thing as a crash helmet before, except in stunt flying. Throughout the war pilots had used the old skin-tight leather helmet-and-goggles. But the X-I had a way of throwing the pilot around so violently that there was danger of getting knocked out against the walls of the cockpit. So Yeager had bought a big leather football helmet—there were no plastic ones at the time—and he butchered it with a hunting knife until he carved the right kind of holes in it, so that it would fit down over his regular flying helmet and the earphones and the oxygen rig. Anyway, then his flight engineer, Jack Ridley, would climb down the ladder, out in the breeze, and shove into place the cockpit door, which had to be lowered out of the belly of the B-29 on a chain. Then Yeager had to push a handle to lock the door airtight. Since the X-I's cockpit was minute, you had to push the handle with your right hand. It took quite a shove. There was no way you could move into position to get enough leverage with your left hand.

Out in the hangar Yeager makes a few test shoves on the sly, and the pain is so incredible he realizes that there is no way a man with two broken ribs is going to get the door closed. It is time to confide in somebody, and the logical man is Jack Ridley. Ridley is not only the flight engineer but a pilot himself and a good old boy from Oklahoma to boot. He will understand about Flying & Drinking and Drinking & Driving through the goddamned Joshua trees. So Yeager takes Ridley off to the side in the tin hangar and says: Jack, I got me a little ol' problem here. Over at Pancho's the other night I sorta . . . dinged my goddamned ribs. Ridley says, Whattya mean . . . *dinged?* Yeager says, Well, I guess you might say I damned near like to . . . *broke* a coupla the sonsabitches. Whereupon Yeager sketches out the problem he foresees.

Not for nothing is Ridley the engineer on this project. He has an inspiration. He tells a janitor named Sam to cut him about nine inches off a broom handle. When nobody's looking, he slips the broomstick into the cockpit of the X-I and gives Yeager a little advice and counsel.

So with that added bit of supersonic flight gear Yeager went aloft.

At seven thousand feet he climbed down the ladder into the X-I's cockpit, clipped on his hoses and lines, and managed to pull the pumpkin football helmet over his head. Then Ridley came down the ladder and lowered the door into place. As Ridley had instructed, Yeager now took the nine inches of broomstick and slipped it between the handle and the door. This gave him just enough mechanical advantage to reach over with his left hand and whang the thing shut. So he whanged the door shut with Ridley's broomstick and was ready to fly.

At 26,000 feet the B-29 went into a shallow dive, then pulled up and released Yeager and the X-I as if it were a bomb. Like a bomb it dropped and shot forward (at the speed of the mother ship) at the same time. Yeager had been launched straight into the sun. It seemed to be no more than six feet in front of him, filling up the sky and blinding him. But he managed to get his bearings and set off the four rocket chambers one after the other. He then experienced something that became known as the ultimate sensation in flying: "booming and zooming." The surge of the rockets was so tremendous, forced him back into his seat so violently, he could hardly move his hands forward the few inches necessary to reach the controls. The X-I seemed to shoot straight up in an absolutely perpendicular trajectory, as if determined to snap the hold of gravity via the most direct route possible. In fact, he was only climbing at the 45-degree angle called for in the flight plan. At about .87 Mach the buffeting started.

On the ground the engineers could no longer see Yeager. They could only hear . . . that poker-hollow West Virginia drawl.

"Had a mild buffet there . . . jes the usual instability . . ."

Jes the usual instability?

Then the X-I reached the speed of .96 Mach, and that incredible caint-hardlyin' aw-shuckin' drawl said:

"Say, Ridley . . . make a note here, will ya?" *(if you ain't got nothin' better to do)* ". . . elevator effectiveness *re*-gained."

Just as Yeager had predicted, as the X-I approached Mach 1, the stability improved. Yeager had his eyes pinned on the machometer. The needle reached .96, fluctuated, and went off the scale.

And on the ground they heard . . . that voice:

"Say, Ridley . . . make another note, will ya?" *(if you ain't too bored yet)* ". . . there's somethin' wrong with this ol' machometer . . ." (faint chuckle) ". . . it's gone kinda screwy on me . . ."

And in that moment, on the ground, they heard a boom rock over the desert floor—just as the physicist Theodore von Kármán had predicted many years before.

Then they heard Ridley back in the B-29: "If it is, Chuck, we'll fix it. Personally I think you're seeing things."

Then they heard Yeager's poker-hollow drawl again:

"Well, I guess I am, Jack . . . And I'm still goin' upstairs like a bat."

The X-I had gone through "the sonic wall" without so much as a bump. As the speed topped out at Mach 1.05, Yeager had the sensation of shooting straight through the top of the sky. The sky turned a deep purple and all at once the stars and the moon came out—and the sun shone at the same time. He had reached a layer of the upper atmosphere where the air was too thin to contain reflecting dust particles. He was simply looking out into space. As the X-I nosed over at the top of the climb, Yeager now had seven minutes of . . . Pilot Heaven . . . ahead of him. He was going faster than any man in history, and it was almost silent up here, since he had exhausted his rocket fuel, and he was so high in such a vast space that there was no sensation of motion. He was master of the sky. His was a king's solitude, unique and inviolate, above the dome of the world. It would take him seven minutes to glide back down and land at Muroc. He spent the time doing victory rolls and wing-over-wing aerobatics while Rogers Lake and the High Sierras spun around below.

On the ground they had understood the code as soon as they heard Yeager's little exchange with Ridley. The project was secret, but the radio exchanges could be picked up by anyone within range. The business of the "screwy machometer" was Yeager's deadpan way of announcing that the X-I's instruments indicated Mach 1. As soon as he landed, they checked out the X-I's automatic recording instruments. Without any doubt the ship had gone supersonic. They immediately called the brass at Wright Field to break the tremendous news. Within two hours Wright Field called back and gave some firm orders. A top security lid was being put on the morning's events.

APPROACH TO CHAUMONT

by Richard Bach

The wide needle of the TACAN wobbles, the distance-measuring drum turns through 006, and it is time to put my set of plans into action.

I begin the left turn into the holding pattern, and my right glove half-turns the cockpit light rheostats, soaking itself in soft red. The IFF dial goes to Mode Three, Code 70. I should now be an identified and expected dot on the radar screen of Chaumont Radar. Thumb down very hard on microphone button, throttle back, speed breaks out and the rumble of shattering air as they extend from the side of the plane. "Chaumont Approach Control, Jet Four Zero Five, high station on the TACAN, requesting latest Chaumont weather." There is a sidetone. A good sign. But there is no reply.

Fly along the pattern, recheck defrosters and pitot heat *on,* a quick review of the penetration: heading 047 degrees outbound from the holding pattern, left descending turn to heading 197 degrees, level at 3,500 feet and in to the 12-mile gate.

I level now at 20,000 feet, power at 85 percent rpm and ready in my mind for the letdown.

". . . measured nine hundred feet overcast, visibility five miles in light rain, altimeter two niner eight five."

I have never had a more capricious radio. Hard down on the plastic button. "Chaumont Approach, Zero Five leaving flight level Two Zero Zero present time, requesting GCA frequency." Stick forward, nose down, and I am through 19,000 feet, through 18,000 feet, through 17,000 feet, with airspeed smooth at 350 knots.

". . . ive, your radar frequency will be three four four point six, local channel one five."

"Roj, Approach, leaving your frequency." In the left bank of the turn, I click the channel selector to one five. And back to the instruments. Look out for vertigo. "He went into the weather in a bank, and he came out of it upside down." But not me and not tonight; I have come through worse than vertigo, and I have been warned. "Chaumont Radar, Jet Four Zero Five, how do you read on three four four point six." A pause, and time to doubt the errant radio.

"Read you five square, Zero Five, how do you read Radar?" So the radio becomes better as I descend. Interesting.

"Five by."

"Roger, Zero Five, we have you in positive radar contact one eight miles north of Chaumont. Continue your left turn to heading one three five degrees, level at two thousand five hundred feet. This will be a precision approach to runway one niner; length eight thousand fifty feet, width one hundred fifty feet, touchdown elevation one thousand seventy five feet. If you lose communication with Radar for any one minute in the pattern or any thirty seconds on final approach . . ."

I am gratefully absorbed in familiar detail. Continue the turn, let the nose down a little more to speed the descent, recheck engine screens retracted and pneumatic compressor *off* and oxygen 100 percent and engine instruments in the green and hook again the lanyard to the D-ring of the parachute ripcord. My little world rushes obediently down as I direct it. Concentrating on my instruments, I do not notice when I again enter the cloud.

The voice continues, directing me through the black with the assurance of a voice that has done this many times. The man behind the voice is an enlisted man, to whom I speak only on official business. But now I give myself and my airplane wholly to his voice and rank is a pompous thing. Microphone button down.

"Zero Five is level . . ." No sidetone. I am not transmitting. Microphone button down hard and rocking in its little mount under the left thumb. "Zero Five is level, two thousand five hundred feet, steady one three five degrees." Flaps down. Airspeed slows through 220 knots. Left glove on the clear plastic wheel-shaped handle of the landing gear lever. A mechanical movement: pull the handle out a quarter-inch and push it down six inches. At the instant that the lever slams down into its slot, the tall hard wheels of my airplane break from their hidden wells and press down, shuddering, into the rush of cloud. Three bright green lights flare at the left of the instrument panel. Speed brake switch forward.

"Zero Five has three green, pressure and brakes." Tap the brakes.

"Roger, Zero Five, you are now one zero miles from touchdown, recheck your gear, the tower has cleared you for a full-stop landing. Turn heading one seven five, stand by this frequency for final controller." Inside the rain-spattered red-checkered Ground Control Approach van at the side of Chaumont's only runway, the search controller looks across to his companion, framed dimly in the green light of his own radar screen. "He's all yours, Tommy." Tommy nods.

"Jet Zero Five, this is your final controller, how do you read?" He already knows that I can hear him very well. The procedure is part of a time-honored ritual.

"Zero Five reads you five by." And I say with him to myself his next words, the lines assigned to him in the script for his role as GCA Final Approach Controller.

"Roger, Zero Five," we say. "You need not acknowledge any further transmissions, however there will be periodic transmission breaks on final approach which will be identified." Fuel aboard shows just under 2,000 pounds on the big tank gage. At my airplane's present weight, I should fly down final approach at 165 knots. "Repeat the tower has cleared you for a full-stop . . ."

When I am under the direction of a good GCA operator, I might just as well be on the ramp and shutting down my engine, for my landing is absolutely certain.

". . . you are thirty seconds from the glide path, correcting left to right on the centerline. Turn heading one eight zero. One eight zero. Transmission break." He lifts his foot from the microphone pedal on the floor under his screen, giving me a few seconds to speak. I have nothing to say to fill his silence, and his foot comes down again. "One eight zero is bringing you out on centerline, drifting slightly from left to right. Ten seconds to glide path. Turn one seven niner. One seven niner . . ." That is a little compliment for me. One-degree corrections are very small, very precise, and require smooth aircraft control from the pilot. I hear one-degree corrections only in still air, only when I am flying well. A smile under the oxygen mask. He should have seen me thirty minutes ago.

"On glide path, begin descent. Suggest an initial rate of descent of seven hundred fifty feet per minute for your aircraft . . ." What could be simpler than flying a GCA through the weather to the runway? There are the cross-barred pointers of the Instrument Landing System to accomplish the same job, but the ILS is not human. Technically, an ILS approach is more consistently accurate than a GCA, but I would much rather work with a good man behind a good radar, in any weather. Speed brakes out with left thumb aft on sawtooth switch. I lower the nose, visualizing as I do the long slide of the invisible glide slope in front of me. The rate of climb needle points on the *down* side of its scale to 1,000 feet per minute, then moves back to 800 feet per minute.

"Rolled out nicely on glide path . . . on centerline . . . drifting now slightly left of centerline, turn heading one eight three degrees, one eight three. On glide path . . ." Airspeed is 170 knots, back on the throttle for a second, then up again. Airspeed 168. Back again and up again. 165.

"Going five feet low on glide path, adjust your rate of descent slightly . . . on centerline . . . transmission break." I think the stick back a little, think it very slightly forward again.

"Up and on glide path, resume normal rate of descent. On centerline . . . on glide path . . . on centerline . . . an excellent rate of descent . . ." Sometimes, I would bet, a GCA operator runs out of things to say. But he is required to give continuous direction to aircraft on final approach. What a boring life he must lead. But bored or not, I am very glad to hear him.

"On glide path . . . doing a nice job of it, lieutenant . . . on centerline . . . tower reports breaking action good . . ." How does he know that I am a lieutenant? I could be a major or a colonel out in the night weather to check on the standardization of GCA operators. But I am not, I am just a man happy to be through a storm and grateful to hear again a voice on my long-silent radio.

". . . you are two miles from touchdown, on glide path, going ten feet left of centerline, turn right heading one eight four degrees . . . one eight four. On glide path correcting back to centerline . . . one eight four . . . a mile and a half from touchdown . . ."

I look up, and realize suddenly that I have been out of the cloud for seconds. The red and green and twin white rows of runway lights stretch directly ahead. Back a fraction on the throttle, slowing down.

". . . one mile from touchdown, going ten feet low on the glide path . . ." Here it comes. I know it, the final controller knows it. I drop below the glide path when I have the runway in sight. If I were to stay completely under his direction, I would touch down some 600 feet down the runway, and that is 600 feet I can well use. It takes normal landing distance and 2,000 feet more to stop my airplane if the drag chute fails on a wet runway. And regardless of drag chute, regardless of airplane, I learned as a cadet to recite the three most useless things to a pilot: Runway behind you, altitude above you, and a tenth of a second ago.

Though I listen offhandedly to the GCA operator's voice, I fly now by only one instrument: the runway. Landing lights on. Left glove reaches ahead and touches a switch down to make two powerful columns of white light pivot from beneath my wings, turning forward to make a bright path in the droplets of rain.

". . . one quarter mile from touchdown, you are going thirty feet below the glide path, bring your aircraft up . . ." I wish that he would be quiet now. I need his voice in the weather, but I do not need him to tell me how to land my airplane when I can see the runway. The columns of light are speeding over white concrete now, redlights, greenlights flash below.

". . . thirty-five feet below glide path, you are too low for a safe approach, bring your aircraft up . . ."

Quiet, GCA. You should have more sense than to go to pieces when I begin the flareout. Either I am happy with a touchdown on the first few hundred feet of runway or you are happy with my airplane landing 600 feet along a wet runway. Stick back, throttle to *idle,* stick back, a bit of left aileron . . . I feel for the runway with my sensitive wheels. Down another foot, another few inches. Come on, runway.

Hard rubber on hard concrete. Not as smooth a touchdown as I wanted but not bad, stick forward let the nosewheel down, squeak of 14-inch wheel taking its share of 19,000 pounds of airplane, right glove on yellow drag chute handle and a quick short pull. Glove waits on handle ready to jettison the chute if it weathervanes and pulls me suddenly toward the edge of the runway. I am thrown gently forward in my shoulder harness by the silent pouf of a 16-foot ring-slot parachute billowing from the tail. Speed brakes in, flaps up, boots carefully off the brakes. The drag chute will stop me almost before I am ready to stop. I must turn off the runway before I may jettison the chute; if I stop too soon and have to taxi to the turnoff with this great blossom of nylon behind me, I would need almost full power to move at more than two miles per hour. It is an effective drag chute.

We roll smoothly to the end of the runway, and even without braking I must add a burst of throttle to turn off at the end. Boot on left pedal and we turn. Drag chute handle twisted and pulled again, as I look back over my shoulder. The white blossom is suddenly gone and my airplane rolls more easily along the taxiway.

Left glove pulls the canopy lock handle aft, right glove grips the frame and swings the roof of my little world up and out of the way, overhead. Rain pelts lightly on my face above the green rubber mask. It is cool rain, and familiar, and I am glad to feel it. Landing lights *off and retracted* taxi light *on,* ejection seat safety pin from the G-suit pocket and into its hold in the armrest, UHF radio to tower frequency.

"Chaumont Tower, Jet Four Zero Five is clear the active runway, taxi to the squadron hangar."

"Cleared taxi via the parallel taxiway, Zero Five. We had no late estimate on your time of arrival at Chaumont. Did you have difficulties enroute?"

Tower feels chatty this evening. "A little radio trouble, tower."

"Read you five square now, Zero Five."

"Roj."

Right glove presses the shiny fastener at the side of my mask as I glide between the rows of blue taxiway lights, pushed by the soft sigh of engine at 50 percent rpm. Cool rain on my face. We trundle together in a right turn, my airplane and I, up a gentle hill, and follow after the green letters of a Follow Me truck that appears suddenly out of the darkness.

Above this dark rain and above the clouds of its birth is a world that belongs only to pilots. Tonight it belonged, for a moment, only to me and to my airplane, and across the breadth of it to the east, to another pilot and another airplane. We shared the sky tonight, and perhaps even now he is tasting the cool raindrops as he taxies by a runway that is as much a target in my intelligence folders as Chaumont Air Base is a target in his.

And I understand, in the rain, that although tonight there has been only he and I in our airplanes, tomorrow it will be some other one of Us and some other one of Them. When my little scene is played and I am once again back in the United States and a pilot of the New Jersey Air National Guard, there will still be someone flying the European night in a white-starred airplane and one in a red-starred one. Only the faces in the cockpits change.

Share work, share dedication, share danger, share triumph, share fear, share joy, share love, and you forge a bond that is not subject to change. I'll leave Europe for America, he'll leave Europe for Russia. The faces change, the bond is always there.

Hard on the right brake, swing around into the concrete pad of a parking revetment, nose pointing out toward the taxiway and the runway beyond. Taxi light *off,* check that the ground crew from the Follow Me truck slide the chocks in front of the tall wheels.

May you have the sense and the guidance to stay out of thunderstorms, distant friend.

Throttle back swiftly to *off.* The faithful spinning buffoon in steel dies with a long fading airy sigh, pressing the last of its heat, a shimmering black wave, into the night. Sleep well.

A slap on the side of the fuselage. "Run-down!" the crew chief calls, and I check my watch. It took 61 seconds for the turbine and the compressor to stop their sigh. Important information, for a maintenance man, and I enter the time in the Form One.

Inverter *off,* fuel *off,* UHF radio *off,* and at last, battery *off.* There is one last heavy click in the night as the battery switch goes to *off* under my glove, and my airplane is utterly and completely still.

In the beam of my issue flashlight, I write in the form that the UHF radio transmitter and receiver operate erratically above 20,000 feet. There is no space in which to enter the fact that the Air Force is lucky to have this airplane back at all. I log 45 minutes of night weather, one hour of night, one TACAN penetration, one GCA, one drag chute landing. I sign the form, unsnap the safety belt and shoulder harness and survival kit and G-suit and oxygen hose and microphone cable and soft chinstrap.

A blue Air Force station wagon arrives, splashing light on my nosewheel, and the sack from above the guns is handed down.

I lay my white helmet on the canopy bow in front of me and climb stiffly down the yellow ladder from the lonely little world that I love. I sign a paper, the station wagon leaves me in the dark. Helmet in hand, scarf pressed again by the wind, I am back on the ground of my air base in France, with a thousand other civilians in uniform, and with 31 . . . no, with 30 . . . other pilots.

My airplane is quiet, and for a moment still an alien, still a stranger to the ground, I am home.

THE EXPERIMENTAL FLIGHT OF THE US-XP

by Jon Cleary

They passed 10,000 feet and Duke plugged his mask into the bomber's oxygen supply. Another half an hour, another 25,000 feet, before it would be time for him to get off. He sat back on the uncomfortable bench seat, stretching his legs, looking disinterestedly at the sergeant and the corporal, his two line tenders, sitting opposite him. This was the sixth drop he had made in the US-XP and each time Grabowski and Fuller had come up with him. They knew their job and he could depend on them. This was his last flight and he wondered if they were as bored with the test flights as he had now become.

Midge Filene, the bomber pilot, looked back over his shoulder. His voice, flat and croaky as a Jewish mynah bird's, came over the intercom. "You got a good day for it, Colonel. Looks like the cover will be less than predicted. About two-tenths, I'd guess."

Filene, a bald wiry little man who looked like a plucked eagle, had been twelve years in the Air Force and was a major. He called both Duke and Matt by their first names down on the base, but here in the air they were always "Colonel" to him; he was proud of his own rank and he respected other men's, especially that of those above him. He expected some day to be called "Colonel" himself.

Duke had been pleased when his and Matt's promotions had come through on the same day five months ago. He knew that the silver maple leaf of a lieutenant colonel meant more to him than it did to Matt; but he would have been genuinely upset had he been promoted ahead of Matt. The latter was not unambitious, but he looked upon promotion primarily as a source of more money; he had not become mercenary, but he and Jane were now putting money away for the children's later education. Duke himself, while not careless of the extra pay, was ambitious, as he had always been. It was not improbable that he would make brigadier general within the next ten years, before he was forty-five. He might some day even make general, although he had missed his chance of being one at eighteen.

"Twenty thousand," Midge Filene said over the intercom. "Just crossed the Utah state line."

"How do you know, skipper?" said Begley, the co-pilot.

"It's that dotted line running down the desert there, see?" said Filene.

Grabowski and Fuller grinned politely at Duke, showing they appreciated the humor of their superior officers. Filene was loaded with corny old jokes: Duke sometimes wondered if he had studied Joe Miller's Joke Book instead of the Officer's Manual. Every time Duke went out of Filene's bomber in a drop, he was presented with a corsage of corn; he was pretty sure that Filene stayed up half the night looking up suitable jokes. Duke grinned back at the two men opposite him, wondering what they really thought of him, Filene and the other officers on board. As a test pilot he had little to do with the enlisted men. Each time he went up they presented him with a plane; when he came back he returned it to them. The rest of the time they were strangers.

He and Matt had now been four years at Edwards Air Force Base at Muroc Dry Lake in California. Their tours of duty had been extended twice, but they knew now they were in their last inning. Next week they were both going to the National Aeronautics and Space Administration's Laboratory at Langley Air Force Base in Virginia for two months to assist in experiments on space-flight simulators. After that it looked like desk duty in Washington for an indefinite period.

It had taken Duke less time to settle down out here in California than it had Matt; the latter had been worried for months about Jane's attitude toward the job. Both men had had their escapes during the test flights; it would have been remarkable had they not over four years of such flying. But Jane had never asked questions of Duke as to what went on, and he and Matt had an implicit agreement that the day's work would never be discussed in front of her. They had adopted the façade that every day was routine flying; and to all outward appearances Jane was now reconciled to the job. She and Matt had taken a house in Lancaster, where the children could go to school, and Matt drove out every morning; one or two week ends a month, if Matt wasn't needed for duty, they drove up to Lake Mead in Nevada, where Matt kept a power boat. Duke guessed that it was a drab life for Jane, but she did not appear to complain. She, Matt and the children seemed to have a happy and contented life, and he was glad for them.

He had tried to tell himself that he was happy and contented with his own life, but there were times when doubts pricked at him like exposed nerve ends. Never when actually flying: *then* he was happy and content, sometimes excited to the point of ecstasy. He had become bored with test piloting because of the isolation here at Edwards; as a virtually bachelor officer he lived on the base. The desert was fine for flying, but it offered no social life nor diversion: not unless you were an amateur naturalist, which he was not. He was sick of the sight of bare mountains, Joshua trees and the cactus trees that dotted the desert like the phallic remains of a million horny Indians, as Matt had described them. Washington, even at a desk, would be welcome. At least for a while.

The doubts had begun some months ago. He could not be sure when he had first felt the irritation of them: on the long drive back from Malibu, after a week end with Debbie Fairfax, or coming back from the three or four visits a year he made East to Cleo and Caroline. There would be no emptiness of feeling, but more a feeling of non-fulfillment; it was as if he had climbed a mountain to find there was no view. He would have enjoyed his time with Debbie, and even more so with Cleo and Caroline; but the taste of enjoyment would be gone before he was halfway home. He remembered Cleo, in one of her surprising moments, telling him that suffering was a part of happiness, and he had begun to wonder if that was his trouble: had he lost the capacity to suffer? He was not convinced that Cleo's philosophy was correct, but he had no counterargument. He had no *desire* for suffering: that way led only to self-pity. But over the past year experience had begun to repeat itself. Boredom had turned into a slide at the bottom of which was melancholia. He was not pessimist enough to accept the inevitability of such an end, but he had begun to recognize the danger of it. Once he got away from the dead atmosphere of the desert, the vast lifelessness of it that month after month filtered like sand into your soul, he would be all right again. Soon the rut of the last four years would come to an end.

Part of the rut (he grinned at the pun: it was corny enough to exchange for one of Midge's jokes) was Debbie Fairfax. He had met her at a party in Brentwood, where he had gone with one of the other officers from the base. She was a film editor, working for one of the better independent producers, a dark-haired, plumply good-looking girl who had come out from Pennsylvania to be a film star and had never made it past the extra ranks. She was a sensible girl who had some creative ability, and after two years of being no more than a passing flash on the screens of the world she had looked around for another job. She had slept with an aging film editor, whose fading virility had not allowed him to make love all the time; on his tired days he had taught her to cut film, had explained to her other rhythms than the ones they had practiced in bed. She had then met the independent producer, who had fortuitously had a vacancy in his bed and on his staff. She had proved her worth in both places, and though the producer had stopped sleeping with her after three months, when he had gone back to his wife, he had kept her on as an assistant editor. Now she was his senior editor and his wife's best friend.

"Thirty thousand, Colonel. We're over Wendover. Time you got ready. Mind the step as you go out."

Filene must be getting bored, too: that was one of his earliest jokes and one of his worst. Duke stood up and Grabowski and Fuller rose from their bench, looking men glad at last to be getting to work. They took hold of the long oxygen line and followed him to the bomb bay. Fuller bent down and pulled back the door of the bay. The wind blasted in at them, cold and sharp as a huge blade of ice. Below the opening, like a white needle-nosed shark that had been caught in the ocean of the sky, hung the US-XP. The wind shrieked past it, making it sound almost as if it were alive. In another twenty minutes it *would* be alive and far more dangerous than any shark.

The US-XP was not the latest of the experimental aircraft being tested for the Air Force. There were five or six later prototypes, all of which had been flown; but the US-XP had not been junked as being superseded. Soon it would be obsolete, but as of now it still had something to teach the designers. Duke had an affection for it because it was still a *plane:* some of the later prototypes did not deserve the title of airplane and offered very little that resembled real flying. In the US-XP the pilot still had a sense of being in full control of his aircraft, even if the margins for error were razor-thin.

Duke slid down through the opening into the cockpit below, feeling the wind tearing at him, trying to blow him out into the open sky. The oxygen line whipped against his helmet; instinctively he turned away so that the line would not hit his face plate. Then he was in the cockpit, out of the worst of the wind. He nodded up at Grabowski, and behind the pig-snout of his mask the sergeant winked encouragingly. Duke took a deep breath, then quickly disconnected the oxygen line from the bomber's supply and plugged it into that of the US-XP. Fuller and Grabowski pulled the hatch cover into place and locked it. The roar of the wind was suddenly gone and in its place was the deeper thunder of the bomber's engines. Duke sat in the dusk beneath the bomber, cocooned in his own world now, his own master again. This might be the last flight for a long time and he would make it a good one.

He plugged in on radio communication. "All set, Midge. All set, Ground Control. Beginning checking."

Acknowledgment came from Filene and from Ground Control five hundred miles away at Edwards. Duke went through his checking exercise: he did it thoroughly, as if this were his first time in the plane: he and Matt had told Jane the truth when they had said that a test pilot had to be a cautious man. As he worked the sounds outside faded from his consciousness; he was aware only of the sawing sound of his own breathing in the oxygen mask. From the corner of his eye he could see the oxygen indicator breathing with him: a black circle with two white slits for lips that always reminded him of a blackface Al Jolson silently mouthing "Mammy."

"Five minutes, Colonel." No jokes now: when they were getting down to business, Filene always became serious.

Duke watched the stop watch on the panel in front of him. A minute passed: it was time to prime the jet engine. If there should be a fire warning now, he had already rehearsed in his mind the drill he would have to go through. The warning would get through to Filene, whose decision it would be to drop the US-XP. Duke would blow the canopy and leap for the sides of the bomb bay as the experimental plane would fall away beneath him. It was all very risky, but they had decided it was safer than staying in the falling plane and trying to use the ejection seat once it was away from the bomber. By the time there was enough air room to let fly the ejection seat, the US-XP might have blown itself out of the sky. Several prototypes had gone that way, but so far the US-XP had behaved itself.

The jet engine was rumbling now, its sound puny against that of the bomber's engines. Duke leaned forward, peering at the dials on the instrument panel; he switched on the small light that was necessary because of the dark shadow of the bomber. He could feel the cold getting at him, and he would be glad to be gone.

"Chase plane with you, Colonel. I can see him at four o'clock."

Matt's voice came in over the radio. "On time all the time, chum. Let's get this thing under way."

Duke could not see Matt's aircraft, but it was comforting to know he was around: there was no better chase pilot in the business than Matt. "I'm going upstairs awhile, son. You want to come?"

"Nix on the chatter. Countdown about to begin." That was Ground Control, the guys who never seemed to appreciate that a little levity helped a man up here. They were always ready with the jokes when he was on the ground, when he needed them least, but once they had put him in the air they were all business.

"Teacher's talking, son."

"See you after school, chum."

Countdown was Filene's responsibility. "Okay, Colonel, you're all alone now. Ten—nine—eight"—Duke reached for the data switch, pressed it; glanced again at all the dials—"three—two—one—*zero!*"

The US-XP dropped like a stone spear hurled at the heart of the earth. The sky exploded as an immense burst of white light about it, so bright that Duke was sure that the white plane must be lost in it. He blinked, accustoming his eyes to the glare, saw by the altimeter that he had already dropped a thousand feet. He reached for the switches on the rocket tubes. He felt the kick as they blasted on, but he was used to this by now; the extra G's were something he had learned to live with. But at this fierce acceleration the plane became alive, wanting to yaw if you didn't watch it. The plane was still headed down, but he had it under control now. Then it was time to pull her up, to begin the climb toward the dark purple sky above. He would be already almost halfway back across Nevada and he always aimed to hit his apogee just north of Lake Mead.

"Looks good from here, chum." That was Matt, a mile away on the starboard side. "Take her away!"

Duke drew back on the wheel. The long needle nose of the plane began to quiver; a tremble passed down the length of the plane like a shiver of dread. He felt himself being forced down into his seat, the blood draining down into his stomach; his jaw hung open like that of an idiot screaming in animal terror. He had stopped breathing: the Al Jolson cartoon face stared at him close-mouthed. His eyeballs felt as if they wanted to shoot back into his skull; he was aware of the grayness creeping over him that told him his brain was not getting enough blood. Then the pressure began to ease, his sight suddenly cleared and ahead of him the needle point of the US-XP was steady and pointing upwards. He glanced at the dials in front of him: air speed, Mach needle, altimeter: all working perfectly. Al Jolson began to sing "Mammy" again.

He felt the buffeting as the Mach needle climbed; then she was through the barrier and had smoothed out. Sixty thousand, 65,000, 70,000 and still climbing. There was still slight vibration in the aircraft, but it was no more than a projection of what he himself felt: a tremble of excitement, the quivering that a man feels when he approaches consummation with his one true love. Above him the sky was a color that earth-bound people would never know, a blue-purple that was the colored edge of eternal darkness. The sun was behind him and he could see the stars like inviting diamonds in the dark curtain ahead of him, a curtain that he knew would keep retreating the farther he flew into it. The US-XP was climbing faster now, streaking through the thin unresisting air, but there was no sensation of speed, no dimension at all. Time and space had become one, yet did not exist at all. There was a serenity here that transcended all understanding. He could never explain it to Cleo, but *this* was happiness, and suffering was not necessary.

Experience told him that the plane was climbing at a speed that could, ridiculously, bring him close to stall point. He and the plane, now one, were balanced on a 14-mile-long invisible pole whose fulcrum was the earth. So long as he kept the balance he was safe. He was not afraid. It was almost as if, somewhere between earth and sky, he had passed through a barrier where fear was shucked like an unwelcome weapon at a customs post. He was detached from himself and all the emotions that cloaked him when he was aground. You did not take fear with you into eternity.

Eighty thousand feet: almost the end of the climb. He turned his head and looked out into the brightness that stretched away like an extension of the sun itself. This was not day, it was something far brighter: perhaps *this* was eternity, and not the darkness of legend. In the cockpit the shadows were blacker than one ever knew shadows on earth; he put his gloved hand into shadow and it disappeared completely. There was no reflection, no grayness: everything was black or white, existent or nonexistent. He hated the admission, but if there was a God, this was the light of God.

He was on the edge of reality: the feeling was both uncanny and pleasant. Perception was heightened till it gave the paradoxical feeling of being wide awake in a dream; every experience of every second he had lived had been drawn into this fine core of intelligence. There was no understanding: he *knew,* but he did not understand. He was aware not only with his mind, but with every cell of his body; here in this silent world the mind and the body thought together, came to no conclusion. There were no reflexes, nothing was born out of conditioning, all reference was gone. There had never been any time but now: past and future were encumbrances that had been dropped at the border where fear had been checked. Nobody but he lived or ever had lived.

"Don't hang around up there too long, chum. I know the feeling, but think of me down here in this crate." That was Matt, one of the earthbound in the chase plane, a man who knew the sublime joy of flying at this height but who, today, had to be practical and think of getting them both back to Lake Muroc and the ground.

Matt's voice was the one link with the world, with memory and the past. It was needed: otherwise Duke knew he would have flown on forever. "Okay, son. I'll bring her down."

He eased off, rolled to starboard and saw the world come back into view, into being: he created the world whole with a wave of the plane's stubby wing. California lay below him, flat as a brown beach holding back the dark tide of the Pacific. Somewhere down there were cities, mountains, lakes: they were only blemishes on the long vast beach stretching down the curve of the world. Down there were people, ordinary people, film stars, generals: fame was a message that couldn't be read at this height. Down there was Hollywood, Escape Capital of the World; but it could never manufacture the escapism that one knew up here. Down there was Debbie Fairfax, a girl whose bed could never give him the euphoria that existed for him here in the lonely ocean of the sky.

He turned the aircraft earthwards, reluctantly like a man turning back from a suicide that he had welcomed, that would have offered no pain at all. He turned his head sharply for one last look at the dark oblivion above him; it might be months, even years, before he was flying this high again. Then he was moving down through the gradually diminishing brightness toward Muroc and the convulsions of human nature that were what people called living. He could see the frost melting on the canopy as he got lower: California ran off the map into the Pacific. All at once he did not want to return to earth: *up there* was where he wanted to go! There had been no clouds in the sky, but now a long way south he could see mountains of them building up on the Mexican horizon. He lifted the nose of the plane: he would keep going south, seek the cloudland of long ago, then pull the nose right back and head for the stars.

A mile away in the chase plane Matt saw the nose of the US-XP lift. "No tricks, chum. I'm running out of gas. I've got to put this thing of mine down pretty soon."

"Go on home, son. You're not needed."

Matt at once noticed the slurred speech. "Duke! Check your oxygen indicator!"

"No time for that." Duke sounded annoyed, impatient, like a man being held against his will. "Other things to do. Go home, son, go home."

The US-XP had begun to weave, almost waltz through the sky. Matt felt the sweat break on him as he saw the danger that Duke was heading for. The US-XP was not meant for fancy flying: it could stall at any moment, go into a spin and Duke would be in the ground before he knew where he was. Matt glanced at his altimeter: 28,000. He had to get Duke down to an altitude where he could get oxygen from the atmosphere.

Ground Control came in, sounding like a petulant parent. "What's going on up there? Ground Control to Sitting Bull. Answer!"

"He's in trouble," Matt interrupted, still watching Duke's aircraft anxiously. "Stay off the air and leave him to me. This is urgent. Stay off the air!"

"Go home." Duke's voice was now almost incoherent; he sounded like a tired drunk, a man suddenly weary for a resting place. "Going home. Home."

Matt took the chase plane in as close as he dared to the weaving US-XP. He rode above it, his own aircraft throwing a deep shadow over the experimental plane; he just hoped that Duke would get no ideas about giving the US-XP full throttle because the chase plane would stand no chance of pacing with it. They were well off course now and for a split second he sensed another danger: for all he knew they might be right in the middle of the commercial lanes and at any moment a DC-6 or similar aircraft, one that could not take quick evasive action, might loom up right in their path. But he could not watch out for such a possibility: other than his own, there was only one plane in the sky for him right now.

"Duke, this is Matt! I'm right above you!"

There was no response from the man in the cockpit immediately below. Duke was all alone in the sky, lost in the cloudland that would soon be the blackness of unconsciousness.

Matt looked at his fuel gauge: five minutes' flying at the most. "Duke, I'm running out of gas! I'll never make it home!"

"Home." The word was almost indistinguishable; in less than half a minute Duke would be gone beyond call. Matt could see the helmeted head rolling a little like that of a drunken knight; he wanted to reach out and beat with his fist on the glistening canopy below him. He could feel the sweat pooling in his palms inside his gloves; his breathing was now just a series of quick gasps. He looked at the oxygen indicator, saw the white lips on the black mask opening and shutting like a minstrel gasping for help—

"Duke! Duke! Is Jolson singing?" He was screaming into his mouthpiece now; it seemed like a tight hand over his mouth trying to keep his cry from getting to Duke. "Is Jolson singing? Duke!"

Below him he saw the helmeted head lift for a moment; light gleamed on it, a spark of understanding in an orange eyeball. "Not singing." The words were slurred almost beyond recognition: they rubbed against the ear, understood only because they were the words he *wanted* to hear. "Shut."

"We've got to get him singing! Duke! Follow me down! You hear me, follow me down! We got to get Jolson singing!" It was like shrieking through a thick wall of wool; the hand over his mouth seemed even tighter. He was bathed in sweat now and his throat was tightening up; pretty soon he might not have a voice to continue shouting. "Follow me down!"

He gunned the chase plane and moved ahead of the US-XP, knowing that he was now at the limit of the chase plane's speed. He could feel the buffeting beginning to run back along his plane; she was beginning to be hard to handle. He looked back and down, saw Duke looking up at him, said a prayer, then swung the chase plane over to starboard and down. If Duke didn't follow him down, this was farewell.

"Going down, Duke! Gotta get Jolson singing!"

For a moment the US-XP continued to weave, then slowly the starboard wing tipped. Matt watched anxiously in his mirror. If Duke went too far over, went into a roll, he would never pull it out before his brain was sufficiently cleared for him to be able to control the plane. "Keep right on my tail, Duke! Watch Jolson!"

Matt continued the slow downward curve, turning them so that they were heading back toward Edwards and the safe dry bed of Lake Muroc. He could not hurry the descent for fear that Duke would build up too much speed and go plunging past the chase plane before he had fully recovered consciousness. Away to the west of them Matt saw a big plane climbing out of the smog above Los Angeles, rising like a pterodactyl out of brown swamp mists. He could only hope they were not in its lane. He watched his altimeter as the needle slowly crept down: 18,000, 15,000. He had now cut his power to the minimum, trying to conserve his fuel. If he got home at all it would be on a dry tank.

"How's Jolson?" He talked to Duke all the time, no longer screaming because he was unable to: his voice now was just a hoarse croak. He watched in his mirror, now and again turning his head to check more directly, as the US-XP continued to follow him down. The experimental plane was weaving slightly, but it was following him. He continued to talk, trying desperately to think of things to say, filibustering to save a man from death. He even began to sing "Mammy": his voice cracked against his own ears. He saw the commercial plane from Los Angeles coming up at them on his port wing, and now he was certain they were in its lane. But he was no longer worried about it: if it was going to hit them, it was going to hit them and there was nothing he could do about it. He could take evasive action himself, but Duke would not be able to; Duke was still half-unconscious, still flying by instinct in the gray fog that had enveloped him. And if Matt did peel away to avoid the commercial plane, he would never be able to pick up Duke again, not in time to save him and assuming he missed colliding with the commercial plane.

Out of the corner of his eye he watched the big plane—it looked like a DC-6—coming up toward them. He wondered if the commercial pilot could see them, but there was nothing he could do to warn him: their radios were on different frequencies. There was not time to call Ground Control and have them call Los Angeles Control Center; the planes would meet in the sky before the message was halfway through its circuit. For a moment Matt had a clear picture in his mind of the unsuspecting passengers relaxing in the warm comfort of the airliner; the *Fasten Seat Belts* light had probably just gone off and the passengers were getting out their cigarettes, opening their books, settling down for the long dull haul to Chicago, New York, wherever. Their last moments, like meteors, were rushing through the sky toward them. In a few seconds now life and the cigarettes would be snuffed out together; bodies and books would be shredded, all stories ending in the same tragedy. But there was nothing he could do about it. With unutterable regret, he committed his own life, Duke's and that of the people in the DC-6 to the whim of God. He prayed, but with little hope.

He looked in the mirror again: Duke was still following him.

"Duke, can you hear me?" A mumble answered him. "Duke!" It seemed to him that he no longer had a voice: his throat had closed and the words screamed only in his mind. "Check Jolson! Check your oxygen!"

He waited, and for a moment he thought that Duke had at last passed out completely. Then there was a murmur in his ears, the dazed muttering of a man coming awake. The DC-6 was still climbing toward them, easily recognizable now, heading up the incline of sky as if on a prearranged date to meet them at a given point. Matt knew now that the commercial pilot could not see them: they were above him and against the sun. The three planes swung almost lazily through the air, drawing nearer and nearer to each other: in a moment they would meet, become an exploding black star in the shining daylight sky.

"Duke, check your oxygen!" They were down to 13,000 feet: Duke should not need the oxygen mask now.

"Okay, Matt." Duke's voice was still slurred, but it was now coherent. "The tube pulled loose. Where have we been?"

"Never mind that. Snap out of it! Eight o'clock—bandit! Take action!"

He flipped the chase plane over and away from the path of the still climbing DC-6. He looked back and saw Duke do the same with the US-XP. Both planes plunged down and away from the commercial airliner; it passed above them, no more than two hundred yards away. Matt imagined he saw a flash of faces against the windows, but he couldn't be sure; maybe the passengers were still unaware of how close they had come to death. But the commercial pilot must have seen them, and Matt could guess at the language that must be going on on the flight deck of the DC-6. The pilot would already be on the air to Los Angeles: there would be a report to the CAB tomorrow that two Air Force planes had buzzed a commercial airliner in its own lane. Matt, still a little weak with relief at their narrow escape, shrugged at the thought. He grinned at the anticipation of what the newspapers would make of it if the story got out: Lieutenant Colonel Duke Dalmead, hero of the Berlin airlift episode who had sent two Russian planes crashing to their end when they had tried to buzz him, now accused of buzzing an American airliner. Maybe Duke would make the cover of *Life* again: he would be a national villain for a week.

"How you feeling now, chum?"

"Still a bit woozy, but I'll make it. I thought for a minute there we were going to book a couple of seats in that DC-6."

"I don't think that Joe liked us. We'll probably have the National Guard waiting for us when we land."

"Well anyway, thanks, son. Do we go home now?"

"If we can make it." Matt glanced at his fuel gauge. "I've always wondered what it would be like flying a glider. Looks like I might get a chance to try it. Chaser to Control. We're coming in. I am about to prove it is possible to fly a jet without gas. But in case I'm wrong, better have the emergency equipment standing by."

Ground Control acknowledged, coming in with what sounded like a mixture of relief, impatience and apprehension: it had not relished being told to shut up and get off the air while the previous emergency had been going on. But it cleared its throat and got down to business: "All aircraft in the local flying area—keep clear of Muroc Dry Lake. There is an emergency. Keep clear of Muroc Dry Lake."

Duke was now once more wide awake, fully conscious of what was going on and aware of the risk Matt had taken in staying aloft so long in order to guide him down to a safe altitude. His oxygen tube hung loose, a dead snake, and he tried to remember what might have caused the disconnection. Had it been when he had turned his head for a last look at the darkness of space before he had headed his aircraft down? He had almost died because of the fascination the outer reaches of the sky held for him. And now Matt's life, too, was in danger. Conscience weighed on him with the force of several G's.

Ground Control came on the air again. "Wind is south-southeast. You had better come in on the northern runway."

"You sending someone up to carry me in?" Matt sounded irritable. Duke knew now that Matt was worried. "I'm coming in on the first runway that offers itself."

"What is your approximate position?"

"About eight miles south of the lake bed, I'd guess. I have just gone over to gliders. How are you, chum?"

"I'm okay," Duke said, anxiously watching the chase plane as it slid down through the air. It struck him that he was now flying chase for Matt, but Matt wouldn't want it brought to his notice, not right now. He looked back and saw Lancaster, a rash of buildings on Route 99, the railroad tracks glinting like a trickle of tears. He wondered if Jane had witnessed the near-collision in the air: if she had she would have guessed who were in the two smaller planes. "I'll come in with you."

"Better stay out of the way, Duke. If I fold this thing, I may be all over the runway like a jumble sale. They'd never forgive us if we fouled up that crate you're flying. The last costing on it was four million bucks. You got that sort of money?"

The desert slid by below them: they followed the road in from Lancaster. Duke could see the cactus and sagebrush quite clearly now; the Joshua trees raised imploring arms. The lake bed came up ahead of them. "You're going to make it, Matt. Put your gear down."

"Gear going down. Locked."

"Okay. Good luck, Matt."

Duke could feel the US-XP losing speed. He swung up and went out in a wide turn. He was at the far end of the turn when he saw the chase plane touch down on the end of the runway, bounce a little, then begin to roll, shepherded by the fire truck and ambulance trailing their long trains of dust as they sped down beside the runway. He saw the chase plane roll to a stop, then Matt said, "Thanks, chum. Now it's your turn."

Duke brought the US-XP around and headed in toward the lake. He felt a strange disquiet: not a feeling of fear, nor even of relief that he had escaped death. Death itself did not frighten him; but what lay beyond death now, suddenly and unaccountably, had become something real. Not tangible, but nonetheless real. For years he had denied the myth of The Beyond; but today for a moment he had been outside the gate to The Unknown. Whether they were one and the same, he did not know. But for the first time he began to wonder at the meaning of his own life. It was as if a page had been turned in the wind and for a moment he had glimpsed the word *Truth.*

"THEY HAD A RIGHT TO LIVE"

by Seymour M. Hersh

The Japanese fishermen were cheating in the early-morning hours of September 1, 1983. They had sailed in three boats from Japan into the waters north of Soviet-held Moneron Island thirty-five miles off the southwest coast of Sakhalin Island. All of the waters north of the island were claimed by the Soviets, at least in terms of fishing rights, and the Japanese knew it. But those waters also were the best in Asia for catching squid and shellfish, and the risk was worth it. They had done it many times before, with no problem.

Their profitable and illicit adventure was shattered this day, however, by a few moments of terror. It was an unusually dark morning, with the moon blocked by a thick layer of clouds. The men were busy hauling in their catch, using bright lights to attract the squid, when they felt the whoosh of an aircraft sailing just hundreds of feet above. They could see nothing at first, but the plane's passage was followed almost immediately by a rain of kerosene. They could hear no engine noise, nor did they see any running-lights. The obviously damaged aircraft seemed to be arcing to its left—as if the engines or wing on the left side was damaged. Seconds later they heard what seemed to be the sound of the airliner's engines coughing to life. The pilot seemed to be struggling for control. Almost instantly they could see the aircraft, which had moved to the southwest, burst into flames. They watched as the plane hit the water and exploded.

One of the fishermen was an inveterate diarist, and his kerosene-drenched notes later persuaded American investigators that they finally had some eyewitness evidence about the final resting-place of Korean Air Lines Flight 007. Unfortunately, the fisherman and his notes were not located until months after the shooting-down of Flight 007. By that time, the official U.S. Navy search for the airplane and its voice and flight recorders—the so-called black boxes—had ended. The Japanese fisherman and his colleagues had been too frightened of retribution for fishing in waters vigorously claimed by the Soviets to come forward earlier; they told their story only after being promised anonymity by a senior American Navy officer. The officer kept his word, and his report remains highly classified.

Flight 007, en route to Seoul with a refueling stop at Anchorage, Alaska, had departed New York's John F. Kennedy International Airport a few minutes after midnight local time on August 31, 1983, with 269 people aboard. There was the usual mix of passengers, some of whom had barely caught the flight or had changed plans at the last minute. Twenty-seven-year-old John Oldham, a recent graduate of Columbia Law School, had delayed his flight a day to help a group of visiting Chinese scholars at Columbia find housing on New York's Upper West Side. Oldham, a specialist in Chinese law who had been a Fulbright Fellow, was headed to Peking for a year of study. Mrs. Rebecca Scruton, of Meriden, Connecticut, was en route to what would have been a tearful reunion with her parents in Seoul. It was the first such visit for the twenty-eight-year-old mother of two, whose children were left behind with close friends, since her husband had died of cancer the previous December. Mrs. Scruton, a Sunday school teacher, had been scheduled to make the trip three days earlier, but she had forgotten her passport and had not been allowed to board that flight. She almost missed the departure of Flight 007 on August 31, for her ride to the airport fell through and she was forced to take a limousine at the last minute. Others were on the plane for equally arbitrary reasons. There was a prominent ophthalmologist from Columbia University, Dr. Jong Jin Lim, fifty-one years old, going home with his brother to attend their mother's funeral. Twenty-three-year-old Edith Cruz of Chattanooga, Tennessee, and her uncle, Alfred Cruz, had scheduled a visit with her ailing grandmother in the Philippines; by the time they boarded the airliner, they knew that the grandmother had died, but they had decided to fly to the funeral. Some boarded Flight 007 with the eagerness of typical tourists. Jessie Slaton was one of six women from the Detroit area who were embarking on a two-week sightseeing trip to the Far East. The seventy-five-year-old Slaton, a former common pleas court judge in Detroit, had been the first black secretary hired at Detroit's City Hall and, after attending law school, had worked her way up in a field that black women had not entered before in Detroit.

The flight to Anchorage was uneventful, as such flights invariably were, with the standardized meals and the usual mediocre movie. Only four passengers, an airline freight handler named John Sears and his wife and two children, disembarked at Anchorage International Airport. The Searses were home; for the others, the scheduled one-hour stop at Anchorage was a welcome break in the long trek to South Korea. There was a chance to stretch one's legs and window-shop in the airport transit lounge, Anchorage's largest shopping center. There was a chance, too, to mingle with the passengers of Korean Air Lines Flight 015—also bound for Seoul—a sister flight that originated in Los Angeles and made a refueling stop, along with Flight 007, every morning at Anchorage.

The passenger lists of both aircraft were especially noteworthy this morning because a number of prominent congressmen and senators were en route to Seoul to attend a commemoration of the signing thirty years earlier of the U.S.-South Korean mutual defense treaty. South Korea had emerged as a valued ally in the fight against communism; the six-member official delegation to Seoul represented not only the U.S. Congress but also America's Far Right. The passengers aboard Flight 015 included Republican senators Jesse Helms of North Carolina and Steven D. Symms of Idaho. Representative Larry P. McDonald, a Georgia Democrat and chairman of the John Birch Society, was aboard Flight 007. Senators Symms and Helms looked for their conservative colleague in the transit lounge, but the congressman was not to be found—he had remained, undoubtedly asleep, in the first-class cabin of his aircraft. Senator Helms, affable and courtly, struck up a conversation instead with an Australian couple from Flight 007, Neil and Carol Ann Grenfell, and their two lively daughters, Noelle Ann, five, and Stacey Marie, three. Grenfell was the marketing director for the Eastman Kodak Company in South Korea and was returning after a visit with his wife's parents in Rochester, New York.

Flight 007 had been scheduled to take off at 4:20 A.M. local time, but departure was postponed for forty minutes when it was learned that the prevailing head winds to Seoul would be lighter than usual. An on-time departure would bring the airliner into Kimpo International Airport in Seoul some thirty minutes before the airport and its customs services opened at six the next morning, September 1. (The airplane would cross the international dateline over the Pacific Ocean.) Korean Air, eager to save fuel, like all airlines, routinely delayed departures from Anchorage if the headwinds aloft were not strong.

The delayed departure made it easier for the ground personnel to complete their servicing. As Senator Helms chatted with the Grenfell family, Flight 007 was being tidied up for the next leg. Carpets were vacuumed, ashtrays emptied, and fresh linen was placed on the headrest of each passenger seat. Nearly 38,000 gallons of high-grade kerosene jet fuel was aboard, more than enough to fly the Boeing 747 to Seoul. There would be a new flight crew, led by Captain Chun Byung-in, for the Anchorage-to-Seoul leg of the trip. Captain Chun and his crew, who had flown to Anchorage the day before on a Korean Air cargo plane, were picked up at a nearby hostel eighty minutes before the rescheduled departure and were given a preflight briefing by the airline dispatcher. That briefing covered, as it always did, such routine matters as ramp position, departure time, weather, alternative airports, and details of the computerized flight plan. Three minor cockpit problems had been reported during the New York-to-Anchorage leg of Flight 007: a defect in the copilot's compass system, a damaged map-table spring, and a noise in the copilot's VHF (very high frequency) radio. The ground crew, after checking, reported that the radio system was operating normally and, following usual procedure, deferred repair of the other defects until arrival in Seoul. All else appeared normal, including the plane's weight and balance.

The passengers were summoned back to the airplane, filling two-thirds of the 374 seats. Larry McDonald was one of twelve passengers who had paid $3,588 for a round-trip ticket in the first-class cabin; also in the first-class cabin were six Korean Air crew members, including three captains, who were being ferried—per usual practice—back to Seoul for reassignment. The passengers were a diverse group, including seventy-five South Koreans, sixty-one Americans, twenty-three Taiwanese, twenty-eight Japanese, fifteen Filipinos, twelve Chinese from Hong Kong, ten Canadians, six Thais, and the Grenfells from Australia. Twenty-three were children under twelve.

The flight plan was similar to one flown by Flight 007 every day from Anchorage to Seoul: the airplane would take off on a westerly heading for fifty minutes, about 350 nautical miles,* until it overflew the fishing village of Bethel near the western tip of Alaska. It would then jog 7 degrees to the southwest to pick up an international flight route, known as R-20, the northernmost of five agreed-upon North Pacific (NOPAC) commercial air routes from Anchorage to the Far East, and fly on a direct heading to the Far East. R-20, like all NOPAC corridors, was fifty miles wide, and came within twenty miles of Soviet airspace along the Kamchatka Peninsula and the Kurile Islands. Despite its proximity to the USSR, it is considered by commercial pilots to be the most desirable route from Anchorage to the Far East because the winds there tend to be lighter. Once south of Soviet territory, the airplane would turn farther to the west and head directly across northern Japan to Seoul.

Within ten minutes of Flight 007's departure, however, it began to drift off course. The flight was six miles north of its scheduled course and two hundred miles west of Anchorage when it left Anchorage air traffic control's radar coverage twenty-eight minutes after takeoff. An American Air Force radar station routinely recorded the track of Flight 007 as it overflew the Bethel area thirty minutes later; the airplane was then twelve miles off course—a not-alarming deviation for radar observers. Flight 007 never arrived at R-20, its authorized flight path, but instead flew increasingly to the north of R-20, toward the Soviet Union.

All must have seemed normal, nonetheless, aboard the aircraft. Ninety minutes after takeoff and about seven hundred miles from Anchorage, Korean Air routine called for the stewardesses to change into their native dress: long skirts known as *chima* and flared blouses called *chogori.* Snacks and orange juice and sandwiches were served to tourist passengers (those in first class were provided with more elegant fare, including chicken florentine and zucchini au gratin), and then it would be time once again for another in-flight movie. The off-course airliner was headed directly toward the Kamchatka Peninsula, which, like all coastal areas of Russia, is heavily defended and clearly marked as off-limits on all aviation charts.

In another ninety minutes, as the passengers watched the movie or

---

* Air distances cited herein will be given in nautical miles. The nautical mile is 796 feet longer than the statute mile and is commonly used in air and sea navigation.

dozed, with cabin lights turned off and window shades down, Flight 007 flew into the range of Soviet radar; thirty minutes later it penetrated Soviet airspace north of the major port at Petropavlovsk on the Kamchatka Peninsula. Four interceptors were scrambled by the Soviet Air Defense Force but somehow failed to locate the airliner before it overflew Kamchatka and entered international airspace over the Sea of Okhotsk, the large body of water separating Kamchatka from the Soviet mainland. Flight 007, now more than two hundred miles off course and constantly moving away from R-20, flew over the Sea of Okhotsk for more than an hour, and its crew members continued to make what they thought were appropriate weather and position reports at the usual time to air traffic control officials in Anchorage and Tokyo. Those officials took no notice of the inappropriate weather reports—such reports are routine at best and, with that discrepancy unremarked, there was no reason for those officials to have any concern about the flight, and none did.

Six more Soviet MiG-23 and SU-15 interceptors were ordered into the air as Flight 007 neared Sakhalin Island. This time contact was made by a supersonic Soviet SU-15 interceptor, which closely tracked the airliner for more than twenty minutes. Seven minutes before the end, the copilot of Flight 007 requested permission to climb to 35,000 feet, a normal procedure in a routine flight—aircraft burn less fuel at higher altitude. There still was no sign that the crew members realized how far off course they were; nor was there any evidence that they realized that their airliner was being tracked by Soviet military planes. Flight 007's course, which had not varied since leaving Alaskan airspace, would bring it—if not interrupted—across Sakhalin Island, briefly into international airspace over the Sea of Japan, and then directly over the extensive Soviet military complex at Vladivostok. Five hours and twenty-six minutes after takeoff from Anchorage, at 3:26 A.M. Tokyo time, with Flight 007 only a minute or two from the Sea of Japan, the pilot of the SU-15 was ordered to destroy the aircraft. He fired two missiles, each loaded with seventy pounds of high explosive, and reported to ground control, "The target is destroyed." One heat-seeking missile is believed to have struck the passenger plane's left wing, destroying engines number one and two and triggering a fire. The second missile, which may have been radar-guided, perhaps homed in on the airliner's tail, ripping apart the auxiliary power unit and causing all of the pressurized air in the passenger compartment to rush into the tail. The sudden surge of pressure could have blown apart the airliner's tail structure and ruptured hydraulic, fuel, and electrical lines. Even if the crew could somehow have kept the airliner under control, using the remaining engines on the right side, it would have been only a few moments before the hydraulic fluid would pour out and the aircraft would be impossible to control. It took twelve minutes for Flight 007 to spiral its way to the waters north of Moneron Island and crash. When hit, the airliner was 365 nautical miles off course, to the north and west of its intended location on R-20.

The attack came at a time when passengers would be asleep, or trying to sleep; the last twelve minutes of flight could only have been agonizing. The cabin, whether directly hit or penetrated by missile fragments, would immediately lose air pressure and would begin turning cold; some passengers, still strapped into their seats, may have been killed outright by shrapnel or debris as others watched terror-stricken. Those who suffered the most would be the ones who survived the first moments. The cabin would fog as the drop in air density caused the water vapor in the air to precipitate immediately. Within seconds the airliner's air-conditioning units, reacting to the sudden drop in temperature, would begin pumping heat into the cabin. Many of the passengers, protected by blankets and breathing through oxygen masks, would have survived the initial missile impact—and the descent to the sea—knowing that they were going to their death. The crew members in the cockpit would be equally helpless as they vainly tried to cope with cabin decompression, power failure, and the incipient collapse of many—if not all—of the airplane's systems. Within seconds, the plane began whirling down to the Sea of Japan. It would be almost impossible to think clearly. The crew's report to Tokyo air traffic control, the last known message from Flight 007, was received forty-eight seconds after the missile struck. Not surprisingly, the crew's indistinct message—some experts believe they had put on their oxygen masks before radioing—indicated no immediate awareness that the aircraft had been struck by a military missile, but, as reconstructed by Japanese Ministry of Transportation officials, reported the loss of cabin pressure.* Japanese officials also concluded that the crew members may have further reported that they were going to descend to 10,000 feet—a level at which passengers could survive without oxygen masks.

The crew members' behavior seems to have been amazingly unconcerned throughout the errant flight. Even after their aircraft was struck by a missile, their first thought apparently was of a mechanical malfunction. Similarly, to get as far off course as they did, the crew members must have had to ignore or rationalize many obvious clues that something was wrong. Within ninety minutes of takeoff, for example, Flight 007 had flown out of radio contact with Anchorage air control and was forced to rely on Flight 015, traveling minutes behind on R-20, to relay the required weather data and position reports. Flight 007 crew members would report twice more to Anchorage via Flight 015 without any apparent second thoughts about their radio difficulty and its possible link to the correctness of their course; the problem, they undoubtedly thought, was with the radio equipment. The crew members made no attempt to shield their true position by reporting winds and temperatures that would have been appropriate to R-20. Instead, they accurately forwarded

* The fact that the crew's first radio report dealt with loss of cabin pressure and not the seemingly more crucial damage to the engines on the left side suggests to some crash experts that the airliner was struck by a Soviet radar-guided missile in the tail only, and not in the wing, as widely reported. The fact is that no one outside the Soviet military knows where and how the airliner was hit.

the much-different weather conditions along their errant flight path (while continuing to report as if they were routinely flying along R-20). And finally, in the minutes before being shot down, the copilot filed a routine air traffic control request for clearance to climb from 33,000 to 35,000 feet—a standard fuel-conservation measure. The airliner was overflying Sakhalin Island at the time, with a Soviet interceptor a few miles behind.

Flight 007 was reported within hours by Japanese air control officials as overdue and missing. Anxious family members and friends at Kimpo International Airport in Seoul and around the world endured hours of errant reports, wild rumors, and waiting. It was not until 10:45 A.M. Washington time, more than twenty hours after the shootdown, that a visibly angered Secretary of State George P. Shultz went on national television to announce that a Soviet pilot had shot down the airliner over Sakhalin Island, with the loss of all aboard.

The world joined in the American outrage, and over the next few weeks the destruction of Flight 007 became a symbol of all that was wrong with the political and military leadership of the Soviet Union. The U.S. and Japanese navies would spend September and October in a tense search for the remains of the airliner and its all-important black boxes, whose built-in electronic beepers were designed to operate for thirty days. They were never found.

Senator Jesse Helms, for once representing the view of most in the U.S. Congress, would emotionally tell the Senate upon his return from Seoul of his brief encounter with the young Grenfell daughters in the transit lounge at Anchorage: "If I live to be one thousand, I will never forget those little girls. They played on my lap, giggling and kissing my cheeks. And when they went to get on that plane they waved bye-bye and blew kisses at me. That's why I'll never forget those two little girls. They had a right to live."

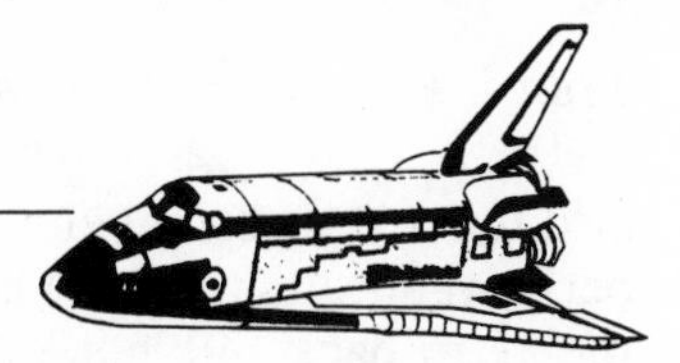

THE RE-ENTRY

by John H. Glenn, Jr.

The three retro-rockets had fired on schedule at five-second intervals. Each one gave me a very solid push, and since I was weightless at the time and they were firing forward, against the direction of the flight, I had the distinct sensation of accelerating back in the direction I had come from. Actually, the rockets were only slowing me down by about 500 feet per second. Both Al Shepard and Gus Grissom had experienced the same sensation when they tested out the retros on their flights, and I was prepared for it. The firing of the rockets caused some motion of the capsule, but since I was using both the automatic and manual control systems together, I maintained the proper attitude during retro-firing and then realigned Friendship 7 for its descent through the atmosphere.

During this phase of the flight, John Glenn's heart was beating at the rate of 96 beats per minute. It had averaged 86 beats per minute during the preceding three hours of flight. As the re-entry phase continued, his pulse increased to 109 beats per minute, and it reached a peak of 134 beats per minute just before the drogue parachute deployed on the final descent and the capsule was going through a period of high oscillations.

Approximately 5 minutes after the retro-rockets fired, I came into radio contact with the tracking station in Texas. I had rather hoped that by this time the people on the ground could tell me to go ahead and jettison the retro-pack. We did not know exactly what effect the retro-pack might have on the even distribution of heat over the shield. It was just possible that it might cause hot spots to break out and damage the shield before we had completed re-entry. Holding onto the pack would also upset the normal chain of events which the capsule was supposed to perform automatically. The wiring was so arranged, for example, that if the retro-pack did not drop, the circuits which were normally set in motion by this event would fail to retract the periscope automatically and close the door behind it to keep out the heat. They would also not be in a position to respond to a special switch which is thrown automatically when the G forces of re-entry reach .05 G, at which time other automatic sequences start for various events involved in the landing maneuver. All of this was supposed to be done automatically, but, for safety reasons, it all hinged on the jettisoning of the retro-pack. If the pack was not jettisoned automatically, I would activate these other functions as well. I was prepared to do all of this, of course, but it was not the way we had planned it; and since any deviation from the standard procedure always leaves a certain amount of room for doubt and suspense, I frankly hoped that we could make a normal descent. I was somewhat concerned, therefore, when the Texas Cap Com sent me the following transmission 17 minutes before I was due to land:

"This is Texas Cap Com, Friendship Seven," he said. "We are recommending that you leave the retro-package on through the entire re-entry. This means that you will have to override the .05 G switch which is expected to occur at 04:43:53. This also means that you will have to manually retract the scope. Do you read?"

"This is Friendship Seven," I said. "What is the reason for this? Do you have any reason? Over."

"Not at this time," the Cap Com answered. "This is the judgment of Cape Flight. . . . Cape Flight will give you the reasons for this action when you are in view."

Some 30 seconds later I came within range of the Control Center at the Cape and heard Al Shepard's voice over the radio.

"Recommend that you go to re-entry attitude and retract the scope manually at this time," Al said.

"Roger," I said. "Retracting scope manually." I reached down for the handle and began to pump the scope in. It came all the way, and the door closed tightly behind it.

"While you are doing that," Al said—and here I finally learned for certain what the problem was—"we are not sure whether or not your landing bag has deployed. We feel it is possible to re-enter with the retro-package on. We see no difficulty at this time in that type of re-entry. Over."

"Roger," I said. "Understand."

"Estimating .05 G at 04:44," Al added.

It was now 04:41, or 4 hours and 41 minutes after launch. In another few minutes, I would be in the middle of the hottest part of my ride. The automatic control system had been acting up again—drifting off center and then kicking itself back into line again—so I was now controlling almost completely by the manual stick. The fuel in the manual system was running low, however—the gauge read that I had only about 15 percent left in the tank. So I switched to fly-by-wire in order to draw on what fuel was left in the automatic system. I was still controlling manually, however, since this was the advantage that the fly-by-wire system provided. I used the manual stick; the nozzles that I activated and the fuel that I expended belonged to the automatic system.

During the final descent through the atmosphere, the blunt nose of the capsule had to be kept pointed so that the heatshield would hit the particles of the atmosphere first. If the capsule were not properly aligned, some of the intense heat could spill over the edge of the shield and flow back along the sides of the capsule, which are not nearly so well protected against the extreme temperatures building up during re-entry. In addition, the capsule might start to oscillate quite a bit as it was buffeted by the atmosphere. That is, it would sway back and forth. This could also let some of the heat impinge on the side of the capsule. As I have said before, it was not the kind of re-entry that we had hoped for. But we had included all of these eventualities in our training, and I was set. It was going to be an interesting few minutes, however.

As we started to heat up on re-entry, I could feel something let go on the blunt end of the capsule behind me. There was a considerable thump, and I felt sure it was the retro-pack breaking away. I made a transmission to Al Shepard to this effect, but he apparently did not hear me. By this time, the capsule was so hot that a barrier of ionization had built up around it and cut off all communications between me and the people on the ground. This was normal, and I had expected it to happen, but it left me more or less alone with my little problem.

Just 24 seconds before John Glenn made this transmission, Al Shepard had started to recommend to Glenn that he jettison the retro-pack as soon as the Gs built up to 1 or 1.5. Glenn did not receive the message, however. The communications black-out had already set in.

I saw one of the three metal straps that hold the retro-pack in place start to flap around loose in front of the window. Then I began to see a bright orange glow building up around the capsule. "A real fireball outside," I said into the microphone. The loose strap burned off at this point and dropped away. Just at that moment I could see big flaming chunks go flying by the window. Some of them were as big as 6 to 8 inches across. I could hear them bump against the capsule behind me before they took off, and I thought that the heatshield might be tearing apart. As it turned out later, these were parts of the retro-pack breaking up. It had not fallen away after all, and the heatshield itself was coming through in perfect shape. This was a bad moment. But I knew that if the worst was really happening it would all be over shortly and there was nothing I could do about it. So I kept on with what I had been doing—trying to keep the capsule under control—and sweated it out.

I knew that if the shield was falling apart, I would feel the heat pulse first at my back, and I waited for it. I kept on controlling the capsule. It was programed to do a slow, steady spin on its roll axis at the rate of 10 degrees per second. The purpose of this maneuver was to equalize the aerodynamic flow around the capsule and to keep it from exceeding the limits that we had estimated were maximum for re-entry. The automatic control system was normally supposed to handle this procedure but I kept control with the manual stick and did it myself. Pieces of flaming material were still flying past the window during this period, and the glow outside was still bright and orange. It lasted for only about a minute, but those few moments ticked off inside the capsule like days on a calendar. I still waited for the heat, and I made several attempts to contact the Control Center and keep them informed.

"Hello, Cape. Friendship Seven. Over. Hello, Cape, Friendship Seven. How do you receive? Over." There was no answer.

Down in the Control Center at this point, the men at the consoles were definitely worried. They were still tracking the capsule's descent on radar and they knew where it was and that it still seemed to be intact. But they were deeply concerned over the fate of the heatshield—and of John Glenn. They knew from previous tests that the temperature of the shield would be about 3,000 degrees Fahrenheit. The temperature of the heat pulse which had built up around the capsule would stand at about 9,500 degrees Fahrenheit—or slightly less than the temperature of the sun itself. The combination of this concern plus the absolute silence in their headsets was almost unbearable. The communications black-out lasted for 4 minutes and 20 seconds. Here, too, the seconds passed "like days on a calendar." Someone behind Commander Shepard's console said, "Keep talking, Al." Shepard spoke once more into the microphone anchored in front of his lips.

"Seven, this is Cape," he said. "How do you read? Over."

This time John Glenn heard the transmission. It was 4 hours, 47 minutes and 11 seconds after launch, with 7 minutes and 45 seconds to go before Glenn's capsule was to hit the water.

"Loud and clear," I said. "How me?"

Al's voice really sounded welcome when it finally came through.

"Roger," Al said, cool as ever. "Reading you loud and clear. How are you doing?"

"Oh, pretty good," I said.

The heat had never come. Instead, the high temperature pulse began to simmer down and the glow gradually disappeared. The Gs built up to a peak of about 8 now, but they were no problem. Al informed me that they had worked out my impact point in the recovery area and that I should be landing within one mile of one of the destroyers.

"My condition is good," I said, "but that was a real fireball, boy."

Twelve seconds after this transmission I reported that the altimeter read 80,000 feet. Nineteen seconds later we were at 55,000 feet. The capsule was rocking and swaying quite a bit at this point, and I was having trouble controlling it. We were almost completely out of fuel in both control systems by now. But, even if I had had sufficient fuel, we were now so far into the thick atmosphere that the control nozzles would not have had much effect on the capsule's movement. I decided to deploy the small drogue chute a few moments before it was due to come out, and damp the oscillations that way. The capsule beat me to it, however. I was just reaching for the switch to override the automatic timer when the drogue chute broke out on its own. I could feel the thud of the mortar which launched it. The window was covered now with a thin layer of melted resin that had streamed back from the heatshield. However, I could still see the drogue open up at 30,000 feet. This was about 9,000 feet higher than where we would normally break it out. The chute held, and the capsule began to settle down into a much smoother descent. The swaying was cut sharply. I had to pump the periscope out by hand since we had interrupted the automatic sequence. At about 20,000 feet, the snorkels opened up to let in outside air. At 10,600 feet, a barometric switch started the landing sequence. Through the periscope and the coated window, I saw a marvelous chain reaction set in. I watched the antenna canister—which housed the chute—detach. It dragged the main chute along behind it, still wrapped up inside its bag. When the shrouds of the chute had stretched out to their full length, the bag peeled off and left the chute, still in a reefed condition, trailing out like a long ribbon straight above me. Then, when the chute was partially full of air and had found its proper position, the reefing lines broke away and the huge orange and white canopy blossomed out, pulsed several times and was steady. I could feel the jolt in the cabin as we slowed. From the indications of the instruments we seemed to be dropping a few feet per second faster than I thought we should. But I studied the chute closely through the periscope and window, and it appeared to be in such perfect shape, with no rips or holes in it, that I decided not to use the reserve chute which was still packed away in the roof of the capsule and available if I needed it. It was a moment of solid satisfaction. As I told Al over the radio—with a real trace of relief and some excitement in my voice, I guess—it was a "beautiful chute." It was a wonderful sight to see that good chute open up.

I was descending now at the rate of 42 feet per second and had 5 minutes and 10 seconds left before impact. I contacted the destroyer *Noa,* which had the code name of "Steelhead," and told the skipper that my condition was good but that it was a little hot inside the capsule. He informed me that he had picked up on his radar the chaff which the main chute had kicked out and that he was heading in my direction. He estimated that it would take him about an hour to get on station.

I started to run down the checklist of landing procedures. I unfastened from my pants leg the plug which connected the biomedical sensors. I removed the blood-pressure equipment from the suit, loosened the chest strap and got it free, unhooked the respiration sensor from my lip mike and stuffed it inside my suit, disconnected the oxygen exhaust hose from the helmet and unstowed the survival pack that I had to the left of my couch and kept it handy in case of an emergency. Al Shepard got on the radio at this point to make sure that my landing-bag light was on green so that it would deploy and take up the shock of landing.

"That's affirmative," I said. "Landing bag is on green."

Then Al came on again to recommend that I remain in the capsule unless I had "an overriding reason for getting out." He knew that the destroyer was only about 6 miles from where I would land and that instead of using helicopters to pick me up as we had planned, I would have to be hoisted aboard by the destroyer. It would be simpler in this case if I stayed shut up inside so we would not take any chance on losing the capsule. We had rehearsed this method of recovery as well as the helicopter method, so I was prepared for either one and I rogered for his message. I kept up a running account now of my approach to the water so that everyone on the network would know my status.

"Friendship Seven," I said, 48 seconds before I hit. "Ready for impact; almost down."

Fifteen seconds later: "Friendship Seven. Getting close. Standing by."

Twenty seconds later: "Here we go."

Ten seconds after that: "Friendship Seven. Impact. Rescue Aids is manual."

I pushed the button which started the flashing light on top of the capsule and the automatic radio signals which would help the recovery force home in on my position.

The capsule hit the ocean with a good solid bump, and went far enough under water to submerge both the periscope and the window. I could hear gurgling sounds almost immediately. After it listed over to the right and then to the left, the capsule righted itself and I could find no traces of any leaks. I undid the seat strap now and the shoulder harness, disconnected my helmet and put up my neck dam so I could not get water inside my suit if I had to get into the ocean. I was sweating profusely and was very uncomfortable. I kept the suit fans going, but they did not help much. The snorkels in the capsule wall were pumping in outside air, but it was extremely humid outside and this did not help to cool me off one bit, either. I thought about removing the lid of the capsule and climbing on out. But I decided against it. I knew that any body movement would only generate more heat and make me even warmer. The thing to do was sit tight, stay motionless and try to keep as cool as possible.

"Steelhead" kept up a running commentary on how she was doing. First, she was 4 minutes away, then she slowed down and was 3 minutes away; then her engines were stopped and she was coming alongside. The capsule window was so clogged now with both resin and sea water that I could not see her. Strangely enough, however, the capsule bobbed around in the water until the periscope was pointing directly at the destroyer, and it kept her in view from then on. I could read her number—841—and I could see so many sailors in white uniforms standing on the deck that I asked the captain if he had anybody down below running the ship. He assured me he did. Then he drifted alongside very slowly until we gently bumped into each other.

Two sailors reached over with a shepherd's hook to snag the capsule, and moments later we were on deck. I started to crawl through the top to avoid blowing the side hatch and jiggling the instruments inside the capsule. I was still so uncomfortably hot, however, that I decided there was no point in going out the hard way. After warning the deck crew to stand clear, and receiving clearance that all of the men were out of the way, I hit the handle which blew the hatch. I got my only wound of the day doing it—two skinned knuckles on my right hand where the plunger snapped back into place after I reached back to hit it. Then I climbed out on deck. I was back with people again.

FOOTPRINTS ON THE MOON

by Gene Gurney

U.S. Highway 1 leading to the Kennedy Space Center was unusually busy on the days preceding July 16, 1969. From all over the United States people had traveled to Florida to watch the launching of Apollo 11. For a lucky few there were seats in a grandstand area some three miles from Launch Pad 39A. But most of the spectators waited along the shoulders of the highway, on the banks of a nearby river—anywhere that they could find viewing space.

When Apollo 11 rose into the sunny Florida sky at 8:32 A.M., the hundreds of thousands of watchers saw the Saturn 5 booster's flaming tail before they heard the roar of its mighty engine because light waves travel faster than sound waves.

"There it goes!" they said. "There goes a rocket to the moon!"

The spectators saw and heard the rocket only briefly, however. Within minutes it had disappeared high over the Atlantic.

Inside the Apollo 11 space capsule were Mission Commander Neil A. Armstrong, a civilian astronaut; Air Force Colonel Edwin A. Aldrin, Jr., Apollo 11's lunar module pilot; and Air Force Lieutenant Colonel Michael Collins, the command module pilot. The three astronauts, all veterans of Project Gemini missions, kept a close watch on the spacecraft's dials and gauges. If Apollo 11 was to be a success, its many complicated systems had to be functioning perfectly prior to each of several major maneuvers leading to a landing on the moon. The go/no-go decisions would be made by flight controllers on the ground after consultation with the Apollo crew. While a no-go decision would rule out a lunar landing, it would not necessarily terminate the Apollo 11 flight. Instead, the astronauts would probably proceed with one of six alternate missions.

Apollo 11 reached its first go/no-go point after ten minutes of flight when the spacecraft was ready to begin orbiting the earth. The decision was go.

Boosted by the third stage of its Saturn 5, Apollo 11 went into a 118-mile-high orbit. After the third stage had shut down the astronauts reported: "Our insertion checklist is complete and we have no abnormalities."

During its second trip around the earth Apollo 11 faced another go/no-go decision: Should the spacecraft head for the moon or remain in earth orbit for a mission similar to Apollo 9's? Again the verdict was go.

High over the mid-Pacific the astronauts restarted the third-stage engine. It burned for 5 minutes and 20 seconds to ram the spacecraft toward the moon at 24,250 miles an hour. When the engine shut down, Commander Armstrong radioed: "Hey, Houston, Apollo 11. This Saturn gave us a magnificent ride." He added: "We have no complaints with any of the three stages on that ride. It was beautiful."

Apollo 11's speed soon slowed from its initial 24,250 miles an hour because of the backward pull of the earth's gravity. Its altitude was increasing rapidly, however, and in quick succession Mission Control had to decide if the astronauts should proceed with three very important maneuvers. They were the separation of the spacecraft from the Saturn third stage, docking with the lunar module in the third stage's forward end, and removal of the LM from the third stage. After checking data on the spacecraft and the Saturn, ground control radioed: "Apollo 11, this is Houston. You're go for separation."

Neil Armstrong answered: "Houston, we're about to sep." And then he reported, "Separation complete."

Communications between Houston and the spacecraft were bad during the next few minutes. When Mission Control was able to contact the astronauts they were reporting: "We are docked." Apollo 11 had backed away from the Saturn third stage, turned around and joined up with the LM.

After making sure that his docking was secure and pressurizing the LM, Commander Armstrong released the four springs that held it to the third stage. "Houston, we have sep," he reported when the maneuver was completed. In four and a half hours of flight the astronauts had successfully accomplished five maneuvers that were vital to the success of the lunar landing mission.

Ground controllers started up the Saturn third-stage engine for the last time to send it past the moon and into a solar orbit. Meanwhile, Apollo 11 continued on its own three-day coast to the moon following a path so accurate that its first scheduled midcourse correction was canceled.

Compared with earlier Apollo crews, the men of Apollo 11 talked very little. "They're the quietest crew in manned space-flight history," remarked one ground controller. The astronauts did radio information of the spacecraft's systems, of course, and occasionally they described what they saw from the spacecraft. From 50,000 miles away Buzz Aldrin reported: "I can see the snow on the mountains in California." When asked if he could see Lower California in northwest Mexico, he replied: "Well, it's got some clouds up and down it."

Because of the problems experienced during earlier flights, Apollo 11's equipment included filters to remove bothersome hydrogen bubbles from the astronauts' drinking water. At the end of the first day of the flight Mike Collins reported: "It's working good so far." And Mission Commander Armstrong announced that the crew was "fit as a fiddle."

As Apollo 11 flew on toward the moon, millions of people all over the world followed its progress. They learned that a midcourse correction on July 17 was a "good burn." On July 18 they actually saw the astronauts enter the docked lunar module to begin preparations for the momentous landing on the moon.

Like previous Apollo flights, Apollo 11 carried a TV camera into space. The astronauts had already sent back views of the command module and the receding earth. Now they trained the camera on the tunnel leading to the LM to show Neil Armstrong removing Apollo 11's docking devices.

"Mike must have done a smooth job in that docking. There isn't a dent or a mark on that probe," observed Buzz Aldrin.

When the tunnel was clear, Aldrin moved the camera into the lunar module. As the LM's hatch opened, an automatic light went on inside the vehicle. "How about that! It's like a refrigerator," Mike Collins said.

For over an hour the astronauts televised the LM cabin for a worldwide audience. They showed viewers the craft's instrument panel and other equipment, and, on the cabin floor, two portable life-support systems and two helmet visors in readiness for the landing on the moon.

Five hours after the conclusion of the telecast, Apollo 11 passed into the moon's sphere of influence. Its speed, which had slowed to 2,990 feet per second, began to increase as the pull of lunar gravity grew stronger. The astronauts were unaware of the change recorded on their instrument panels, however, because they were asleep.

When the time approached for Apollo 11 to pass behind the moon, the astronauts were wide awake and carefully monitoring the spacecraft's dials and gauges. It was a crucial go/no-go point in the lunar mission. Before communications were blocked by the moon, flight controllers had to decide whether Apollo 11 should start up its SPS engine to go into lunar orbit or merely swing around the moon and return to earth. Fifteen minutes before loss of signal, Mission Control radioed the spacecraft: "Eleven, this is Houston. You are go for LOI [lunar orbit insertion]."

"Roger, go for LOI," replied Buzz Aldrin in Apollo 11.

Mission Control finished the transmission with a cheerful: "All your systems are looking good going around the corner and we'll see you on the other side."

Behind the moon Apollo 11's SPS engine burned for the planned 6 minutes and 2 seconds. The thrust, against the line of flight, slowed the craft and allowed it to be captured by the moon's gravity. Apollo 11 had successfully carried out another critical maneuver. Now the spacecraft was in lunar orbit and, if all went well, a lunar landing was approximately 24 hours away.

First, however, the combined spacecraft would complete 12 orbits of the moon. While the astronauts studied the lunar surface, they turned on their TV camera to send pictures to earth that included the track the LM would be following when it came in for a lunar landing. They also fired the command module's SPS engine to improve Apollo 11's orbit.

Before beginning their first rest period in lunar orbit, the astronauts gave the LM a preflight inspection. During the inspection they used the LM's code name for the first time. It was Eagle. An eagle, a symbolic emblem of the United States, was also used on the Apollo 11 insignia in the form of an eagle landing on the moon. The Apollo 11 command module's name was Columbia, another national symbol. "The names are representative of the flight and the nation's hopes," Neil Armstrong explained at a pre-mission press conference.

"Apollo 11, Apollo 11, good morning!" In Houston it was 6 o'clock on the morning of July 20 and Mission Control was awakening the astronauts. If all continued to go well with the flight, it was the day for the historic landing on the moon.

"Oh, my, you guys wake up early," the astronauts replied. But they were as eager as Mission Control to begin the day's activities.

Mission Commander Armstrong and Lunar Module Pilot Aldrin were soon on their way through the tunnel to Eagle to prepare the craft for undocking. Eagle's undocking was another go/no-go point for Apollo 11. Before a decision could be reached, both spacecraft had to be examined by the astronauts who also sent data to the ground for study by flight controllers. Near the end of the twelfth orbit the good news came from Mission Control: "Apollo 11, Houston. We're go for undocking."

Like Apollo 10, Apollo 11 undocked behind the moon where the astronauts were out of contact with Mission Control. When communications were restored, Neil Armstrong announced: "The Eagle has wings."

After remaining close for a few minutes to examine Eagle, Astronaut Mike Collins, all alone now in Columbia, fired his thrusters to gradually move about two miles away. "See you later," he radioed the two astronauts in Eagle as Columbia moved off.

Before the undocked Eagle could proceed toward the lunar surface, Mission Control had to make another go/no-go decision. It involved a crucial burning of the craft's descent engine to drop Eagle into a low lunar orbit. All systems on both spacecraft were looking good, however, and Eagle received the critical go for DOI (descent orbit insertion). The maneuver placed Eagle in an orbit that would take it to within 50,000 feet of the moon's rugged surface.

Mike Collins, who had been keeping a watchful eye on Eagle from Columbia, radioed the first word on the new orbit. "Everything's going just swimmingly," he said. Neil Armstrong and Buzz Aldrin in Eagle were pleased, too, as were flight controllers on the ground. "You're go for powered descent," the latter radioed to Eagle.

Apollo 11 had successfully passed still another important go/no-go point. With a large share of the world's population tensely following their progress, Astronauts Armstrong and Aldrin restarted Eagle's engine for the trail-blazing descent to the lunar surface. Mission Control kept the world informed as Eagle's radar bounced signals off the moon to the craft's computer. "27,000 feet; 21,000 feet and velocity down to

12,000 feet per second; 13,500 and a velocity of 9,000 feet per second; 9,200 feet and dropping at a rate of 129 feet per second," the commentator reported.

When Eagle was less than 200 feet above the moon's surface, the astronauts realized that the craft's automatic landing system was going to bring them down in a crater littered with rocks and boulders. Moreover, a light on Eagle's instrument panel had come on to warn that only 114 seconds of fuel remained. Mission Commander Armstrong had only seconds to decide if he should abort the landing, jettison Eagle's descent stage and use its ascent engine to return to Columbia—or try to maneuver to a safe landing area. He chose to try for a landing.

Quickly taking over control from the automatic system, Armstrong guided Eagle over the Sea of Tranquillity's boulder-strewn landscape looking for a place where he could set the craft down. In addition to avoiding boulders, he had to find a fairly level surface. If Eagle landed at an angle of more than 30 degrees, it would tip over.

With less than a minute's fuel remaining, former test pilot Armstrong found what he was looking for. As he set Eagle down a cloud of dust arose, stirred by the blast of the descent engine. It was a smooth touchdown.

"Houston, Tranquillity Base here," Armstrong radioed. "The Eagle has landed." Eagle had come to rest on the lunar equator, about four miles beyond its targeted landing site.

"We're breathing again," replied Mission Control as the men at the four rows of computer consoles cheered and clapped. Apollo Program Director Samuel C. Phillips spoke for all of them when he said: "In the landing phase of this mission, I was on the edge of my chair."

Mission Control relayed the good news to Mike Collins in Columbia: "He has landed—Tranquillity Base. Eagle is at Tranquillity."

From his 69-mile-high orbit a laconic Astronaut Collins replied: "Yeah, I heard the whole thing." Then he added with enthusiasm: "Fantastic!"

Although they were safely on the surface of the moon, Astronauts Armstrong and Aldrin were not yet ready to go exploring. First they had to prepare Eagle for a quick takeoff if that should become necessary. They did inspect their landing site through Eagle's windows, however. "It looks like a collection of every variety of shapes, angularities, granularities, every variety of rock you could find," they reported. "There doesn't appear to be too much of a general color at all. However, it looks as though some of the rocks and boulders—of which there are quite a few in the near area—it looks as though they're going to have some interesting colors to them."

When they finished checking Eagle, the astronauts were scheduled to begin a four-hour rest period. But they were anxious to leave the spacecraft, and after two hours of work in the lunar module they radioed Houston: "A recommendation at this point is planning an EVA with your concurrence starting about eight o'clock this evening, Houston time. That is about three hours from now."

"We will support it. We're go at that time," Houston answered.

It took another hour to make sure that Eagle's ascent stage would be able to leave the moon. Then Neil Armstrong and Edwin Aldrin began to prepare for the historic moment when they would actually set foot on the lunar surface.

The astronauts were already wearing pressure suits with a special outer layer to protect them from high temperatures and meteoroids. Now, trying to keep out of each other's way in Eagle's small cabin, they put on lunar overshoes, gloves, helmets, and backpacks. Like their suits, the overshoes, gloves, and the two visors of the helmet were designed to protect the astronauts from the hazards of extravehicular activity on the moon. The Apollo backpack, a portable life-support system (PLSS), contained an oxygen supply, water for a cooling system, communications equipment, displays and controls, and a power supply. The 84-pound PLSS was covered by a thermal insulation jacket.

It took longer than they expected for the astronauts to complete EVA preparations, but they were ready to leave Eagle six hours after landing. That was more than five hours ahead of the original schedule.

Mission Commander Neil Armstrong was the first to emerge from Eagle. After crawling through the hatch backward to the front porch, he slowly began to descend a ladder attached to one of the legs of the landing craft. On the way down he pulled a lanyard to expose a camera that televised the rest of his descent.

Perhaps as many as a billion people throughout the world saw Neil Armstrong take the historic first step on the moon. And they heard him say: "That's one small step for man, one giant leap for mankind." It was a truly awe-inspiring moment. For the first time a man was standing on the surface of another celestial body.

Astronaut Armstrong had only a moment to reflect on the significance of the occasion for he had work to do. His reports to Mission Control began at once. "The surface is fine and powdery," he radioed. "I can pick it up loosely with my toe. It does adhere in fine layers like powdered charcoal to the sole and sides of my boots. I only go in a small fraction of an inch, maybe an eighth of an inch. But I can see the footprints of my boots and the treads in the fine sandy particles.

"There seems to be no difficulty in moving around as we suspected," Armstrong continued. "It's even perhaps easier than the simulations at one-sixth g [gravity] that we performed in the simulations on the ground."

The astronaut became so interested in taking pictures of what he saw around him that Mission Control had to remind him several times to gather a "contingency sample." This was material that he was to scoop from the surface with a long-handled tool that had a plastic bag at its end. The filled bag was to be stored in one of his pockets. Then, if an emergency made it necessary for the astronauts to leave suddenly, they would have at least a small sample of the moon's soil and rocks for the earth's scientists.

No emergency arose, however, and after 20 minutes an impatient Buzz Aldrin, who had remained in Eagle while Mission Commander Armstrong determined if the moon's surface was safe, radioed: "Are you ready for me to come out?"

With Armstrong keeping a close watch to make sure that he didn't tear his pressure suit or his backpack, Aldrin descended Eagle's ladder to become the second man to stand on the surface of the moon. "Beautiful, beautiful!" the astronaut exclaimed as he looked around.

While Aldrin accustomed himself to walking on the moon, Armstrong mounted the 7¼-pound TV camera on a tripod and moved it about 40 feet away from Eagle. Then, as earthbound audiences watched, he unveiled a plaque on Eagle's descent stage and read: "Here men from the planet earth first set foot upon the moon, July 1969, A.D. We came in peace for all mankind." The plaque carried the signatures of the President of the United States and the Apollo crew.

As Armstrong spoke, tiny microphones inside his helmet transmitted his words to the communications unit in his backpack which, in turn, sent them to a signal processor in Eagle. Through its own small antenna Eagle beamed a voice signal to the huge dish-shaped antenna at Goldstone, California, a quarter of a million miles away. From there it went to NASA's Goddard Space Flight Center near Washington, D.C., and then to Mission Control in Houston for rebroadcast throughout the world. It also went to Astronaut Mike Collins orbiting 69 miles above the moon in Columbia. Because of his position in relation to Eagle, Collins was in direct radio contact with the moon explorers for only a few minutes during each orbit.

Eagle's transmitter also sent out TV signals from the black-and-white camera that the astronauts had set up on the moon, but those signals were received at Parkes, Australia, rather than Goldstone.

When the two astronauts talked with one another on the moon, they did so by radio, using receivers and transmitters in their backpacks.

The first men on the moon quickly became accustomed to the weak lunar gravity and they learned how to handle the weight of their backpacks. "Got to be careful that you are leaning in the direction you want to go," observed Astronaut Aldrin. Later he had this to say about walking on the moon: "I found that a standard loping technique of one foot in front of the other worked out quite well as we would have expected. One could also jump in more of a kangaroo fashion, two feet at a time. This seemed to work, but without quite the same degree of control of your stability as you moved along. We found that we had to anticipate three to four steps in comparison with the one or two steps that are ahead when you're walking on the earth."

Loping over the lunar surface without any visible effort, Aldrin returned to Eagle and removed a solar wind collector from the craft's external storage area. It was an aluminum-foil screen designed to trap particles streaming in from the sun. Scientists hoped that the screen would enable them to determine the solar wind's composition. Aldrin set it up not far from Eagle.

Although millions of TV viewers on earth were watching the two astronauts on the moon, Mike Collins in the orbiting Columbia was unable to see them. "How's it going?" he asked Mission Control.

"The EVA is going beautifully," Mission Control replied. "I believe they are setting up the flag now. . . . They've got the flag up and you can see the Stars and Stripes on the lunar surface."

Astronaut Armstrong had planted a 3-by-5-foot American flag not far from Eagle. Wire held the flag outstretched in the airless atmosphere of the moon. Planting the flag was merely a symbolic gesture, however. The United States was not laying claim to the moon. The 1967 Space Treaty, to which the United States is a party, opened the moon to exploration by all countries.

After the flag was in place, the astronauts received a message from Mission Control: "The President of the United States is in his office now and would like to say a few words to you."

"That would be an honor," Neil Armstrong replied.

The astronauts were standing in front of their TV camera when the President said: "Neil and Buzz, I am talking to you by telephone from the Oval Room at the White House. And this certainly has to be the most historic telephone call ever made. I just can't tell you how proud we all are of what you—for every American, this has to be the proudest day of our lives. And for people all over the world, I am sure they, too, join with Americans in recognizing what a feat this is. Because of what you have done, the heavens have become a part of man's world. And as you talk to us from the Sea of Tranquillity, it inspires us to double our efforts to bring peace and tranquillity to earth. For one priceless moment, in the whole history of man, all the people on this earth are truly one. One in their pride in what you have done. And one in our prayers that you will return safely to earth."

Neil Armstrong answered for the astronauts. "Thank you, Mr. President," he said. "It's a great honor and privilege for us to be here representing not only the United States but men of peace of all nations. And with interest and a curiosity and a vision for the future. It's an honor for us to be able to participate here today."

Following their talk with the President the busy astronauts resumed their lunar tasks. While Aldrin took pictures and examined Eagle, Armstrong gathered rocks and soil which he placed in a sample-return container. Apollo 11's two "rock boxes" were 19 inches long, 11½ inches wide, and 8 inches high. Each one was hollowed out of a single aluminum block. Armstrong used a long-handled scoop to gather the soil and rocks because it would have been impossible for him to bend down far enough in his pressure suit.

Next, the astronauts removed the Early Apollo Scientific Experiments Package (EASEP) from Eagle's external equipment bay. The EASEP consisted of a very sensitive seismometer and a set of mirrors to reflect back to earth the laser beams that scientists planned to send to the moon. By measuring the length of time it took the laser beams to return to earth, they hoped to measure accurately the distance between the two bodies.

The seismometer, by registering moonquakes, would help scientists determine if the moon had a solid interior, or a molten one like the earth. The astronauts set up the experiments about 30 feet from Eagle.

When Neil Armstrong had been on the moon's surface for an hour and 50 minutes and Buzz Aldrin 20 minutes less than that, Mission Control radioed: "Buzz, this is Houston. You've got about ten minutes left now prior to commencing your EVA termination activities." Aldrin was to reenter Eagle first. Before he went back inside, however, he helped Armstrong gather more lunar samples for the earth's scientists. The astronauts were supposed to note where they found the rocks in the final collection, but there wasn't time to keep a record.

"Neil, Buzz," Mission Control radioed. "Let's press on with getting the close-up camera magazine and closing out the sample-return container. We're running a little low on time." The astronauts' backpacks had enough oxygen for four hours on the moon, but the flight controllers wanted to maintain an adequate safety margin.

After placing the solar wind experiment and some soil samples in a rock box, Aldrin headed up Eagle's ladder with a cheerful: "Adios, amigo." From the spacecraft's hatch he helped Armstrong manipulate a pulley system to raise the two sealed rock boxes which he lifted into the cabin. Twenty minutes later Armstrong joined Aldrin in Eagle. "The hatch is closed and latched," they reported to Mission Control.

The first men to walk on the moon had returned to their spacecraft. They left evidence of their visit behind them, however. The American flag still stood where they had placed it. The seismometer and laser experiments remained, as did 73 microfilmed messages from the world's leaders, and medals and shoulder patches belonging to Virgil Grissom, Roger Chaffee, Edward White, Yuri Gagarin, and Vladimir Komarov, American and Soviet spacemen who had died. There was some lunar litter as well. The astronauts discarded their TV camera, boots, backpacks, and other items they no longer needed. And their footprints remained on the lunar surface to record where they had walked during man's greatest adventure.

REACTIVATING STAR WARS' *ICE FORTRESS*

by Dale Brown

They were in business again.

Navy Commander Richard Seedeck prepared his spacesuit for his upcoming EVA, extravehicular activity—his spacewalk. The forty-two-year-old veteran astronaut, now on his second Shuttle mission, was having the time of his life.

Seedeck had just returned from *Atlantis'* flight deck, where he had been pre-breathing pure oxygen for the past hour. He was now in the airlock, smoothly but quickly putting on his equipment. Jerrod Bates, a civilian defense contractor on board *Atlantis* as an expert advisor and engineer, watched Seedeck put on his suit, marveling at the speed with which he dressed. It always took Bates twice as long to accomplish the same task.

There was nothing like being in space, Seedeck thought, and nothing like being on board the Space Shuttle. No one on board was a passenger—everyone was a crewman, a necessity. Each was busy seventeen hours a day.

And there were fewer "mice and monkey" research flights, too. Like this one. This one was top secret all the way, all heavy-duty military hardware. Even the usual press speculation about the payload was nonexistent—or it had been effectively quashed.

"What are you smiling about, Commander?" Bates finally asked.

"I'm smiling at how good this feels, Bates," Seedeck said, talking through the clear plastic facemask he was wearing. He finished donning the lower torso part of his spacesuit and unbuckled the upper part from a holder in the airlock. Bates reached out to hold the bulky suit for Seedeck to climb into, but that was unnecessary—Seedeck merely let go and weightlessness held the suit exactly where Seedeck had left it.

"I've been doing that for four days now," Bates said through his faceplate. "I forget—nothing falls up here."

"I still do it sometimes," Seedeck admitted. "But I've learned to use it." And he did—Seedeck had his helmet, gloves, his "Snoopy's hat" communication headset and his POS, his portable oxygen system, all floating around the airlock within easy reach.

In one fluid motion, Seedeck held his breath, removed his POS face mask, and slipped into the upper torso part of his suit. If Seedeck started breathing cabin air, he would reintroduce deadly nitrogen into his bloodstream and risk dysbarism, nitrogen narcosis, the "bends"—Bates had also been pre-breathing oxygen for the same reason. Still holding his breath, he attached several umbilicals from the huge life support backpack to his suit and connected the two halves of his suit together, nodding as both he and Bates heard a distinct series of clicks as the unions and interlinks joined.

Bates couldn't believe the brush-cut veteran he was watching. It had been well over two minutes, and Seedeck was still holding his breath and still acting like a kid in a candy store. Seedeck locked on both gloves, put on his "Snoopy's hat" communications headset, locked his helmet in place, and watched the pressure gauge on his chest indicators as the suit pressure gradually increased to 28 kilopascals. When the suit was pressurized and Seedeck had double-checked that there were no leaks, he finally released his breath with a *whoosh.*

"I don't believe it," Bates said as he put on a mid-deck cabin headset to talk to Seedeck. "You went nearly six minutes without breathing."

"You'd be surprised how easy it is after pre-breathing oxygen for an hour," Seedeck said. "Besides, I've done this once or twice before. Check my backpack, please?"

"Sure," Bates said, and double-checked the connections and gauges on Seedeck's suit and gave him a thumbs-up. "It's good."

"Thanks. Clear the airlock. Admiral, this is Seedeck. Preparing to depressurize airlock."

"Copy, Dick," the *Atlantis'* mission commander, Admiral Ben Woods, replied. "Clear any time." Woods repeated the message to Mission Control in Houston five hundred nautical miles below them.

Seedeck turned to the airlock control panel and moved the "AIRLOCK DEPRESS SWITCH" to 5, then to 0, and waited for air to be released outside. Three minutes later, Seedeck was exiting the airlock.

It was a sight he would never get used to—the mind-boggling sight of the Earth spinning above him, the colors, the detail, the sheer size and spectacular beauty of Planet Earth five hundred miles away. *Atlantis* was "parked" right over the North Pole, and Seedeck could see the entire Northern Hemisphere—the continents of North America, Europe, and Asia, as well as the North Arctic region and the Atlantic and Pacific oceans. Clouds swirled around the globe like gentle strokes of a painter's brush, occasionally knotting and pulsing as a storm brewed below. Because of the Shuttle's normal upside-down orientation, Earth would actually be his "sky" during the entire EVA.

Seedeck closed and locked the airlock hatch, clipped a safety line onto a bracket near the hatch and began working his way hand-over-hand along steel handholds to where *Atlantis'* three MMUs, manned maneuvering units, were attached inside the forward bulkhead of the cargo bay. He inspected one of the bulky, contoured devices, then unclipped it from its mounting harness.

Turning around so his backpack was against the MMU, Seedeck

guided himself back against it. He felt his way back with his knees and sides until he heard four distant clicks as the MMU locked itself in place on his backpack.

"MMU in place, *Atlantis.*"

"Copy."

With his safety line still attached, Seedeck made a few test shots from the MMU's thrusters, then unclipped his safety line and moved himself out of the MMU's holder. Pushing gently, he propelled himself away from *Atlantis'* cargo bay and out into space.

"Clear cargo bay, *Atlantis.* Beginning MMU tests."

Seedeck knew that Admiral Woods, who would be watching him from one of the eight cameras installed in the cargo bay and remote manipulator arm, was choking down a protest, but Seedeck had an urge he couldn't ignore and this was his time.

A normal MMU maneuverability test consisted of short distances, short-duration movements, all with a safety tether connected. He was supposed to go up a few feet, stop, do a few side-to-side turns and try some mild pitch-ups, all within a few feet of the airlock hatch and manipulator arm in case of trouble.

Not Seedeck. With his safety line disconnected, Seedeck nudged his thruster controls and performed several loops, barrel rolls, full twists, and lazy-eight maneuvers several meters above the open cargo bay doors.

"MMU maneuvering tests complete," he finally reported as he expertly righted himself above *Atlantis'* cargo bay.

"Very pretty," Woods said. "Too bad NASA isn't broadcasting your performance in prime time."

Seedeck didn't care. There was only one word to describe this feeling —ecstasy. Without a tether line, he was another planetary body in the solar system, orbiting the Sun just like the planets, asteroids, comets, and other satellites around him. He was subject to the same laws, the same divine guiding force as they were.

Seedeck floated for a few moments before bringing his thoughts back to the business at hand. He spotted his objective immediately.

"Inventory in sight, *Atlantis.* Beginning translation."

They weren't allowed to call it anything but "the inventory" on an open radio channel. The *Atlantis* had been parked about six hundred meters away from the huge object, the closest they were allowed to approach it—it would be a short translation, jargon for space-walk, over to it. Seedeck opened a bin in the center of the right side of the cargo bay and extracted the end of a steel cable from its reel mounted on the cargo bay walls, attached the cable to a ring on the left side of his MMU, then maneuvered back into open space and headed for the object floating in the distance.

It was the first time Seedeck had seen it, except of course for photographs and mock-ups. It was a huge steel square, resembling some sort of massive pop-art decoration suspended in space. Each side of the square was a hundred-foot-long, fifteen-foot-square tube. One large rectangular radar antenna, two thousand square feet in area, was mounted on each of two opposite sides of the square, pointing earthward. Mounted on one of the other two sides of the square were two smaller data-transmission dish antennas, one pointing earthward, the other pointing spaceward. On the remaining side was an eighteen-inch diameter cylinder twelve feet long with a large glass eye at one end, also pointing to Earth. Enclosed within heavily armored containers on the four sides of the square were fuel cells, rocket fuel tanks, fuel lines, and other connectors and control units running throughout the steel frame.

Mounted in the center of the square was a huge cylinder, seventy feet in diameter and thirty feet long, armored and covered in shiny aluminum —*Atlantis* had to move its position now and then to keep the brilliant reflection of the sun from ruining its cameras. The spaceward end was closed, but the earthward side had a removable armor cover that revealed five fifteen-foot-diameter tubes, earthlight reflecting around the shining, polished walls inside, all empty.

This was *Ice Fortress.*

In all the articles, presentations, and drawings, it looked like a Rube Goldberg tinker-toy contraption, but out here in position it looked awesome and as mean as hell. The two large radar antennas, Seedeck knew, were target-tracking radars searching for sea- or land-launched intercontinental ballistic missiles. The smaller dish antennas were data-link antennas, one for transmitting steering signals from the platform, the other for receiving target tracking data from surveillance satellites at higher orbits around earth. The large cylinder with the glass eye was an infrared detector and tracker designed to search and follow the exhaust of an ICBM in the boost phase. The radars could track warhead carriers, "busses," in the midphase or even individual reentering warheads as they plunged through the atmosphere, and it could even differentiate between decoy warheads and the real thing.

The large center cylinder was the "projectile" container, which housed the launch tubes for *Ice Fortress'* weapons. The entire station was armored in heat-resistant carbon-carbon steel, and smooth surfaces and critical components like the missile cylinder covers and fuel tanks were also covered in reflective aluminum film. Seedeck had heard rumors about all these strange additions to *Ice Fortress,* but that wasn't his concern.

Seedeck's job today was to make *Ice Fortress* operational for the first time.

The station was almost a military unit unto itself, Seedeck thought as he completed his inspection of *Ice Fortress.* The station received missile-launch detection information from orbiting surveillance satellites that would tell *Ice Fortress* where to look for the missiles. The station could use either its radars or its heat-sensing infrared detectors to locate and track the rockets as they rose through the atmosphere. *Ice Fortress* would then launch its "projectiles" against ICBMs heading toward North America.

Projectiles. Weird name for *Ice Fortress* weapons, Seedeck thought. *Ice Fortress* carried five X-ray laser satellites. The satellites consisted of a main reaction chamber and fifteen lead pulse rods encasing a zinc lasing wire surrounding it, like knitting needles in a ball of yarn. The reaction chamber was, in essence, a twenty kiloton uranium bomb—roughly equal to the destructive power of the first atom bomb that exploded over Hiroshima.

Ice Fortress sensors would track any attacking intercontinental ballistic missiles and eject the X-ray laser satellites toward them. When the satellite approached the missiles, *Ice Fortress* would detonate the nuclear warhead within the satellite. The nuclear explosion would create a massive wave of X-rays that would be focused and concentrated through the pulse rods. The X-ray energy would create an extremely powerful laser burst that would travel down the rods and out in all directions. Any object within a hundred miles of the satellite would be bombarded into oblivion in milliseconds. The explosion, would, of course, destroy the satellite, but the awesome power of the X-ray laser blast would decimate dozens, perhaps hundreds, of ICBMs or warheads at one time—a very potent and, if nothing else, cost-effective device.

Seedeck knew a lot about the X-ray laser satellites that would be used with *Ice Fortress*—the *Atlantis* carried five of them in her cargo bay, and it would be Seedeck's job to load them into the launch cylinder on *Ice Fortress.*

Seedeck now attached the cable to the front of the central launch cylinder and turned back toward *Atlantis.* While Seedeck had been inspecting *Ice Fortress,* Bates had been putting on his own spacesuit and was just emerging from the airlock when Seedeck completed his inspection.

"Seedeck to *Atlantis.* The inventory appears OK. No damage. We'll be ready to proceed at any time."

"Copy," Woods replied.

"This is Bates. I copy." Bates had moved into *Atlantis'* cargo bay and had begun to unlock the canisters containing the partially disassembled *Ice Fortress* satellites. His job would be to remove the mountains of packing material from the satellites, then reassemble the component parts. It would not become an actual nuclear device until reassembly, and it would not even be possible to arm it until it was installed in its launch tube on *Ice Fortress.*

Meanwhile, Seedeck had returned to *Atlantis.* He maneuvered over to the cable reel and activated its motor, tightening the cable. He double-checked the controls. To avoid breaking the cable, a friction clutch device would keep the cable tight during small shifts in distance or motion between *Atlantis* and *Ice Fortress* and an emergency disconnect button would open the pawl on *Ice Fortress* and release the cable. The release could be activated by Bates from the cargo bay, by Seedeck from *Ice Fortress,* or by Woods inside *Atlantis.* Seedeck then attached a plastic saddle onto the cable that rode along it on a Teflon track.

"Guide ready, *Atlantis,*" Seedeck reported. He carefully maneuvered closer above Bates, who was putting the finishing touches on the first X-ray laser satellite. The satellite, its lead-zinc rods folded along its sides, was well over ten feet in diameter and, at least on earth, weighed over a ton; Bates handled the massive object like a beachball.

"Ready," Bates said, and unhooked the remaining strap holding the huge satellite from its stowage cradle in the cargo bay. Using a hydraulic lift on the cradle, Bates raised the cradle a few inches, then suddenly stopped it. The satellite continued to float up out of the cargo bay and right into Seedeck's waiting arms.

Seedeck grabbed a handhold on the satellite and steered it easily toward the saddle. As if he had been doing this procedure all his life, he expertly clamped the cylindrical satellite onto the saddle and steadied it along the cable. Although the satellite was weightless, Seedeck was careful not to forget that the thing still had two thousand pounds' worth of mass to corral—it was hard to get it to stop moving once it got going. He attached a safety line between the saddle and the satellite, and the satellite was secured.

"Heading toward the inventory with number one," Seedeck reported. Despite himself, Bates had to chuckle at the sight. Seedeck had maneuvered over the satellite and had sat down on top of it, as if he were sitting on a huge tom-tom drum. He was gripping the satellite with his boots and knees, riding atop five hundred pounds of high explosives and ninety-eight pounds of uranium. One tiny nudge on his right-hand MMU control, and he and the satellite slid along the two-thousand-foot-long cable toward *Ice Fortress.*

It turned out to be a very efficient way of getting the X-ray laser satellite to the platform. In two minutes, Seedeck and his mount eased their way toward *Ice Fortress,* carefully slowing to a stop with gradual spurts of the MMU's nitrogen-gas thrusters. As Woods and the crew of *Atlantis* watched through telephoto closed-circuit cameras, Seedeck jetted away from the satellite, maneuvered underneath it, unhooked the safety strap and latch, and slid the satellite away from the saddle. Seedeck gave the saddle a push, and it skittered back down the cable to *Atlantis.*

Using a set of utility arms mounted on the MMU, Seedeck guided the satellite toward the open center launcher. With the ease acquired from several days practicing the maneuver in the huge NASA training pool in Texas, Seedeck guided the device straight into the launcher. Once the laser satellite was inserted a few feet into the tube, a pair of fingerlike clips latched onto the satellite and pulled it back into the tube. Seedeck waited until he felt a faint CLICK as the unobtrusive yet frightening device seated itself against the arming plate at the back of the tube.

"Atlantis, this is Seedeck. Confirm number one latched into position."

"Stand by," Woods told him. He relayed the request to Mission Control. The answer came back a few moments later.

"Seedeck, this is *Atlantis.* Control confirms number one in position."

"Roger, *Atlantis.* Returning to Orbiter."

It took Seedeck two minutes to return to *Atlantis'* cargo bay, where Bates had another satellite ready for him. The saddle had slid the two thousand feet all the way back to *Atlantis* with Seedeck's one little push.

"Seedeck is back in the bay, Admiral," Bates reported.

"Copy. Stand by." Woods relayed to Houston that no one was near *Ice Fortress.*

A few minutes later Woods reported: "Control reports full connectivity. The inventory is on-line. Good job, Rich. You're hustling out there."

Seedeck nodded as Bates gave him a thumbs-up. The *Ice Fortress* was now operational. It was America's first strategic defense device, the first of the "Star Wars" weapons—and the first time nuclear weapons had been placed in orbit around the Earth.

"Forty-five minutes from start to finish each," Seedeck said. "Should be done by dinnertime."

"It's my turn to cook," Admiral Woods said. "Thermostabilized beef with barbecue sauce, rehydratable cauliflower with cheese, irradiated green beans with mushrooms. Yum."

"I ordered the quarter-pounder with cheese, Admiral," Seedeck protested. Bates was smiling as he watched the navy commander maneuver the second X-ray laser satellite onto the saddle. Moments later, Seedeck was riding along the cable toward the menacing latticework square in the distance.

"That's the one thing I miss up here," Bates said as he turned back toward unpacking and reassembling the next satellite.

Bates noticed the first light, a bright deep flash of orange that illuminated everything. It got brighter and brighter until it flooded out his eyesight, then turned to bright white. It was as if Seedeck had come back and pushed him in the side, rolling him over, or as if Seedeck had slid the saddle back along the cable and it had come back and hit him in the backpack. Bates wasn't wearing a MMU, but he was secured to the forward bulkhead of *Atlantis* above the airlock hatch by his tether. There was no sound, no trace of anything actually *wrong.* It felt . . . playful, in a way. It was easy to forget you were in space. The work was so easy, everything was so quiet. It felt *playful—*

Bates spun upside down and slammed against the left forward corner of the cargo bay. Some invisible hand held him pinned against the bulkhead. The only sound he heard was a hiss over his headset. He tried to blink away the stars that squeezed across his vision.

He opened his eyes. Seedeck and the second X-ray laser satellite were gone.

"Atlantis, this is Bates . . ." Nothing. Only a hiss. He found it hard to

breathe. The pressure wasn't hurting him, only squeezing him tight—like a strong hug . . .

"Atlantis . . . ?"

"Seedeck. Rich, answer." It was Woods. The hiss had subsided, replaced by Admiral Woods on the command radio.

"Atlantis, this is Bates. What's wrong? What—?"

An even brighter flash of light, a massive globe of red-orange light that seemed to dull even the brilliant glow of the Earth itself. Bates opened his eyes, and a cry forced itself to his lips.

A brilliant shaft of light a dozen feet in diameter appeared from nowhere. It was as if someone had drawn a thick line of light from Earth across to *Ice Fortress.* The silvery surface of *Ice Fortress'* armor seemed to take on the same weird red-orange glow, then the beam of light disappeared.

A split-second later a terrific explosion erupted from the open end of the launch cylinder aboard *Ice Fortress.* A tongue of fire several yards long spit from the earthward side of the station. Sparks and arcs of electricity sputtered from one of the spindly sides, and *Ice Fortress* started a slow, lazy roll backward, sending showers of sparks and debris flying in all directions. Bates ducked as the cable connecting *Atlantis* to the space station snapped back and hit the forward bulkhead of the cargo bay.

Bates' voice was a scream. "Commander Seedeck. Oh, God . . ."

"Mission Control, this is *Atlantis . . ."* Bates heard Admiral Woods' report. "We have lost *Ice Fortress.* Repeat, we have lost *Ice Fortress.* Bright orange light, then massive explosion. One crewman missing."

"This is Bates. What's—?"

"Bates, this is Admiral Woods. Where are you? You all right?"

Bates reached up with his left hand for one of the handholds on the forward bulkhead, found that the pressure was all but gone.

"I fell into the cargo bay. I'm okay—" Just then a sword of pain stabbed into his skull and he cried out into the open communications panel.

"Bates . . . ?"

Bates looked down. The lower part of his left leg was sticking out at a peculiar angle from his body.

"Oh God . . . I think I broke my leg."

"Can you make it to the airlock?"

"Admiral, this is Connors. I can suit up and—"

"Not if you haven't been pre-breathing," Woods told him. "Everyone, make a fast station check, report any damage, then get on the cameras. Find Seedeck. Connors, Matsumo, get a POS and start pre-breathing. Bates, can you make it back to the airlock?"

Bates grabbed the handhold. He expected a tough time hauling himself upright but suddenly found he had to keep from flinging himself up out of the cargo bay in his weightless condition. Slowly, he began to haul himself back toward the airlock hatch.

"Bates, what happened out there?"

"God, it looked like . . . like one of the damn *projectiles* detonated," Bates said as he crawled for the airlock. The X-ray laser satellites had numerous safety devices to prevent an accidental nuclear detonation, but the reaction chamber needed a big explosion to start the atomic chain reaction, and those explosives had no safety devices. Something, some massive burst of energy, had set off the five hundred pounds of high explosives in the satellite's reaction chamber.

Just as he safely reached the airlock, Bates looked back to *Ice Fortress.* It took him a moment to spot it again, several hundred yards from where it had been a few moments before. It was lazily, almost playfully spinning away, its radars and antennae and electronic eyes and spindly arms flopping about as if it was waving goodbye. Occasionally a shower of sparks erupted from its surface. And a trail of debris hovered in its wake, as if it were dropping crumbs on the trail to help find its way back . . .

Commander Richard Seedeck left nothing. Nothing was left of him.

MEXICAN FLIGHT

by Amelia Earhart

There were three factors which determined me to try a flight to Mexico. One, I had a plane in perfect condition for a long distance effort. Two, I had been officially invited by the Mexican Government. (I had never been invited before. I just went to Ireland.) Three, Wiley Post.

I remember telling Wiley Post of my plans. He walked across the room, looked at a globe standing on the table, and asked me what route I intended to use from Mexico City to New York. I told him I planned to fly in as straight a line as possible.

"Are you cutting across the Gulf?" he asked.

I said I was. He measured it with his fingers.

"That's about 700 miles. Almost half an Atlantic. How much time do you lose if you go around by the shore?"

I told him I saved probably one hour, or a little more, by following the straight line.

Wiley said: "Amelia, don't do it. It's too dangerous."

I couldn't believe my ears. Did Wiley Post, the man who had braved every sort of hazard in his stratosphere flying, really regard a simple little flight from Mexico City to New York across the Gulf as too hazardous? If so, I could scarcely wait to be on my way.

On April 19, 1935, NR 965Y (my Vega) and I started from Burbank, California, for Mexico City. Slightly over thirteen hours later we landed at Valbuena Airport, 1,700 miles southward.

From a pilot's standpoint that was an interesting journey. The start made before midnight was lit by a generous moon which gilded the hills gloriously, but by the time I had reached the arid stretches of the Gulf of California there crept up a white haze which made it difficult to tell what was water and what was sand ahead. Only when I could catch a glimpse of the moonlight on the water or see the black shadows of crinkled sand directly below, could I tell which was which. Even the mechanical difficulties which beset the early hours of the flight—chiefly an engine which overheated because of a faulty propeller setting—could not mar the rare loveliness of the night and of the far-flung countryside which slumbered beneath.

Slightly below Mazatlán, on the Mexican coast, a thousand miles or so from the starting point, the chart directed me to turn easterly toward Mexico City, six hundred miles away. Here were ruffles of mountains sloping upward into the high tableland of central Mexico. I was flying by compass and successfully located the towns of Tepic and Guadalajara, and thought perhaps I would escape the fate that had been promised me, that of straying on the final stretch of the journey. But I suddenly realized there was a railroad beneath me which had no business being where it was if I were where I ought to be.

I was flying at an altitude of more than 10,000 feet, with mountains and plains not far below me. I had counted on arriving before one o'clock Mexican time, but when that hour came I realized that, while probably near my destination, my exact location was uncertain.

Just about then an insect, or possibly some infinitesimal speck of dirt, lodged in my eye. In addition to being extremely painful, that minute accident played havoc with my sight. So, with the maps, such as they were, blurred even to my "good eye," which at once went on strike in sympathy with its ailing mate, and having the feeling of being lost anyway, I decided to set down and ask the way.

My landing place was a pasture not unreminiscent of another landing in Ireland, although here the cattle were stolidly indifferent to my arrival while their transAtlantic brethren (sistern?) raised a temperamental ruckus when my roaring motor disturbed their privacy. This field was decorated not with shamrock but by occasional cactus and prickly pear. The near-by village, I found, was named Nopala, which means prickly pear.

No sooner was I down, after brushing the field a couple of times to see if a landing was possible, than cowboys and villagers sprang up miraculously. They were helpful, polite and not at all astonished, even when their visitor turned out to be feminine. My pasture was a dry lake-bed, not overly large, but level and reasonably free from dangerous obstructions. My Spanish does not exist, and none of the vaqueros spoke English. So our negotiations were mostly accomplished with signs and smiles, which sufficed well enough, particularly with a bright dark-skinned boy who established my location on the map, which turned out to be about fifty miles from Mexico City.

After taxiing the ship to the end of the clear space, a couple of the more enthusiastic spectators rode to the middle of my "runway," confident they would be helpful there. To make it quite clear that such a location would be thoroughly unfortunate when my ship charged down on them for the take-off, it was necessary to climb out of the cockpit and plow afoot through the dust for further discussion. Once the point was well established, my friends withdrew to the sidelines and saw to it that the cattle, goats and children were herded to safety.

Actually there was not much difficulty in getting into the air again, and half an hour later I was given a more official welcome at the Capital.

The ensuing days were a kaleidoscope of things done and seen, and hospitable people met. "Fun in Mexico" would be an appropriate title. President Lazaro Cardenas graciously extended official greetings and privileges. We barged through the flower-laden floating gardens of Xochimilco, a bucolic tropic Venice on the fringe of the Capital. We saw the Basque game, jai alai, a fast and furious glorified squash; and a charro fiesta, which is to say a cowboy exhibition, demonstrating that superb horsemanship is the same art the world over, needing, like music, no interpretation.

Unfortunately opportunity lacked to discuss with women, as I would have liked to, their strivings and ambitions. What law and tradition permit them to do outside the home I am uncertain. While I met only sheltered women among the well-to-do, I saw many worn with the hard labor of farm life, and briefly touched a few groups of self-supporting city women workers. I saw enough of the spirit of the new Mexico, however, to want to know more of what reforms the new order holds for its women. I, for one, hope for the day when women will know no restrictions because of sex but will be individuals free to live their lives as men are free—irrespective of the continent or country where they happen to live.

At a concert given in my honor I admired the cowboy regalia worn by the musicians. Forthwith, to my embarrassment (and pleasure!) I found that Secretary of State Portes Gil had ordained that I should have such a one for myself. This outfit is as traditional as the pink coat of the British huntsman or the kilts of the Highlander. Mine, as delivered some days later, is a formal creation of blue and silver, topped by a picturesque sombrero, heavy with corresponding trimmings. How such a colorful costume may be adapted to flying is a sartorial problem I never mastered.

Mine, alas, was a flying visit in both senses of the word. Scarcely had I alighted when the problems of departing pressed upon us.

In Mexico City both the military and civilian airports are excellent. But at the mile-and-a-half altitude their runways, while ample for normal flying, were not as long as my overloaded plane required. So we explored the mud-caked flats which once had been the bottom of Lake Texcoco adjoining the metropolis and there on the lake-bed, aided by Mexican soldiers, who filled a ditch and shaved off hummocks, we contrived a home-made airport with a runway three miles in length.

I have often said the most potent letters in the alphabet of aviation are "w" and "p." In flyers' shorthand "wp" means "weather permitting." It's a wise pilot who prefaces announcement of his plans with that proviso.

For eight days in Mexico City "w" had not "p." Not until one o'clock in the morning of May ninth did I learn definitely that the elements had relented. Over the telephone from the Weather Bureau in New York Mr.

Putnam gave me the final reports as prepared by our old friend Dr. James H. Kimball, dean of record flights.

So I sent word out to the men at the plane to fill the tanks with the 470 gallons of gasoline required, while I curled up for a few hours' sleep. Then at four o'clock, Edmundo Rendon, our able interpreter, drove me to the home-made runway, staked out with flags for my guidance.

Earlier in the day Charles Baughan, a veteran Lockheed pilot who operates a sky-taxi service in Mexico City, had flown my plane from the Pan American hangar over to the level stretches of the lake-bed, whence the take-off was planned. The drums of gasoline already were there, with soldiers, under the direction of Captain Casolando, to guard them and the plane, and to herd people, cows, horses and goats out of harm's way.

Under the direction of Baughan the "gassing up" was accomplished, while Casasolo, Pan American star mechanic, gave my Wasp motor its final check by the light of automobile headlights meagerly supplemented with the dim radiance of a very young moon.

That day I had breakfast in Mexico City and supper in New York—a very early breakfast, to be sure, and a decidedly late supper, for it was 10:30 when I landed at Newark, 2,185 miles to the north.

It was a few minutes past six, Mexican time, when I took off. Although I used perhaps a full mile of the improvised runway the plane got into the air with surprising ease. My Vega was always doing that—surprising me with superb performance. Dire predictions had been made regarding that overload take-off in the rare air of an 8,000 foot altitude. But all I had to do was to keep the plane moving in a straight line and hold it on the ground until we'd built up a speed well over a hundred miles an hour—then it just flew itself into the air.

Slowly I climbed to 10,000 feet, to skim over the mountains that hem in the high central valley where the city lies, separating it from the lands that slope down to the sea. Majestic Popocatepetl raised its snowy head to the south, luminous in the rays of the rising sun. A fairyland of beauty lay below and about me—so lovely as almost to distract a pilot's attention from the task at hand, that of herding a heavy plane out of that great upland saucer and over the mountains that make its rim.

Seen from the air, all countries have characteristics peculiar to themselves. Ireland is recognizable by its green fields, white cottages, and thatched roofs. Like the ubiquitous baseball diamond of the United States, most Mexican towns have their unmistakable bull-ring sitting in the midst of adobe houses and walled gardens. These were vivid in my visual memories of that morning's flight.

Once across the divide, clouds banked continuously below me, stretching down over the Gulf. I saw little but their fleecy contours with the exception of one brief glimpse of a group of oil tanks which I estimated to be close to Tampico. Thence I bore northeasterly in a straight line across the Gulf for New Orleans, a distance of about 700 miles. From New Orleans on, radio communication between my plane and airway stations below was constant. Indeed, our conversations were so continuous I felt as if I were more-or-less sliding home along a neighborly "party line."

All in all, the flight was marked by a delightful precision. Everything worked as it should. Its only exciting moments followed my landing at Newark when the crowd overflowed the field. In due course I was rescued from my plane by husky policemen, one of whom in the ensuing melee took possession of my right arm and another of my left leg. Their plan was to get me to the shelter of a near-by police car, but with the best of intentions their execution lacked co-ordination. For the arm-holder started to go one way while he who clasped my leg set out in the opposite direction. The result provided the victim with a fleeting taste of the tortures of the rack. But, at that, it was fine to be home again.

ON TOP OF THE WORLD

by Sheila Scott

At the airport, we topped off all the fuel tanks once again so as to squeeze in the last pint. Someone else spread anti-icing paste over every protruding bit of the aircraft, while the RAF carefully inspected every rivet. *Mythre* sat solidly down on her main wheels with her tail almost scraping the ground, but her nose was up like a haughty woman surveying her rivals. Her paintwork shone in the sunlight and I could see the smudges of anti-icing paste against the gleaming enamel. Small streaks of green fuel ran over her white wings and mingled among the black oil marks of the tarmac. I looked up at the intertwined flags of Great Britain and the United States on her rudder, and was proud of her. Someone came back with a last-minute check of the weather—no change, so the flight would probably only take sixteen hours to be within range of the other coast for the 3000-mile journey.

Time to get aboard. Everyone lined up and shook my hand wishing me luck—some of their eyes showing that they thought it was more like goodbye—but I knew it was the luck they were wishing me that was needed now more than skill on this journey. My heart was thumping and the unaccustomed heavy layers of clothes made me feel sticky and unwieldy, but at last the long-dreamed-of flight was reality and I was at the beginning of the most exciting adventure I had ever attempted in my life.

I double-checked the time; three watches and the chronograph were in unison to the second. Astro compass and immersion suit were within easy reach, and all remaining loose heavy objects were pulled forward to help the aircraft during her overweight takeoff. I plugged myself into the heart box, recorded the time, and noted that the gauges indicated all was wonderfully normal. We were ready.

Eric climbed up on the wing and somehow lodged himself on top of the black storage box beside me. He carefully supervised my last preflight check of setting the Sperry into its basic direction mode. Once this was done—offset by grid—I could not touch it until I landed on the other side of the Pole. His were simple checks with much at stake, for one simple mathematical mistake here could put me in very inhospitable waters indeed, and would mean almost certain death.

"For heavens sake, turn back if there is anything wrong—anything at all. Don't press on. We shall be here all night," admonished poor Eric. It was obvious that he did not care for this job at all, but knew it was better for him to be here than to leave me to go off alone. He quietly wished me luck, and as the door slammed he vanished off the wing.

"Don't go yet," I wanted to say, but it was too late. The minutes were racing by now, and I would miss the sun in the right position if I did not hurry. *Mythre* groaned and creaked a little in protest as I eased the throttle forward, but her nose was still high as we taxied slowly forward. I murmured, "That's right, no slouching! Let's keep our noses in the air!"

I was aware of the line of men, and the salute, but by now I was hermetically sealed in my lonely little world with *Mythre.* There was only the controller's voice to remind me I could still turn back, but *Mythre* and I now—for *Mythre* had become a person to me, just like my beloved *Myth Too*—would not turn back. Just like Nansen's ship *Fram,* she must go forward. Apart from Goddard's stake, it was not only my life that was being gambled, but also *Myth Too's.* She had been put up as collateral against the expensive *Mythre.*

The wide expanse of concrete looked reassuringly long, and the engines sounded smooth and powerful in the cold air; I smelt the usual slight odor of gasoline and heard it slapping against the steel tanks in the cabin with me. They were steadying, familiar sounds and smells. One quick glance around, as I ran the engines up against the brakes to gain precious extra feet along the runway. The brakes creakingly protested as I released them. Momentarily *Mythre* hesitated before she overcame the inertia and slowly, so heavily moved forward, gaining speed little by little.

The NASA green light gleamed among the multitude of dials—they were interrogating at the moment of takeoff! I could not let go to do the mental acuity test, but one-handedly felt for the "green light off" button, without taking my eyes from the airspeed dial and the runway ahead. Once again, I was not to take off alone after all. It had been merely a teasing remark that I could never escape from them, but the strange thing was that the light invariably flashed when reassurance was most needed.

Lift off at 0113 GMT on 25th June! We were skimming through spiralling smoke from wooden chalets over fir trees and fishing boat masts, slowly headed upward, delicately, imperceptively, turning through a few degrees to get on to track for if the direction indicator gyro precessed, we were lost forever. Then one last glimpse of the wooded land—the last trees I would see for days—before the cloud dipped down, caught us, let us go and teased with its tentacles to envelop us finally in its icy gray heart.

"Watch that speed. Don't climb so fast, the de-icers will do their job," I bullied myself. "Above all hold that heading of three-four-one degrees —you are half a degree out!" Would I be able to hold it for possibly seventeen hours without an autopilot?

At first it had been *Mythre* who was roaring to go and trying to climb up quicker than we should, but now it was I who pushed and coaxed. At six thousand feet, still in cloud, I urged and begged her to keep climbing, but she stubbornly refused more than a foot or two at a time. The wing de-icers were working well, but the antennas on top were probably stacked with ice. Aeons later, at seven thousand feet, I was still cajoling her up at a mere twenty feet a minute, only to fall back to seven thousand feet every time I relaxed at the wheel.

The red stall warning light angrily flickered—*Mythre* gave one drunken lurch—I nearly lost her. It was no good—she was too heavy as yet to climb any higher. Still I had to make nearly ten thousand feet to be able to fly the planned pressure pattern safely and accurately. It was no use turning back, for wherever I went I would find the same problem. Luckily the clouds were thinning into layers and I could keep between them until I lost my enemy, the ice and its excess weight.

The sun peeped into cloud gaps, so it was time to set up the astro compass. My engineers had rigged up a portable sliding bar across the front of the instrument panel so I could move the astro compass across it. Even so, the occasions when I could actually shoot a sun sight were limited, for once the sun was behind the wing it was of no use to me. We had worked out the sun positions as it would be by eye in relation to the aircraft and time of day, but this was really basic and far too slap-happy for real navigation.

At 0238 hours, I managed to get one sun reading, but needed three more at four-minute intervals to start my plot. The sun played fast and loose and quickly hid behind a cloud long before the fourth minute was up. Ten minutes later it was back, and I started all over again. The resultant plot indicated I was two degrees off my desired grid heading, but as I was now flying a different system from our original plans I held my course, using the sun compass as a backing check.

I had raised no one recently on HF, though by switching the frequencies I heard others, sometimes in a strange language. Arctic radio blackout is quite normal, and varies from day to day and at different positions. It is caused by the high magnetic activity in these areas. But now I heard one controller talking to another—possibly Nord again—about GAYTO, and commenting that the aircraft had too little airspeed out of Norway.

"Jeepers, not a woman out there on her own!" came out among some more garbled conversation. I smiled, and as I could not answer him back, said to Buck Tooth and *Mythre,* "Oh, that old argument, and we are not alone. We've got each other. Though I must confess I don't know for sure where we are, and somehow, *Mythre,* you have to curb your drinking until I do."

She was gobbling up fuel. I exercised the propellors to prevent the prop oil from freezing solid, and then leaned the fuel off again. The left engine spat with fury at being robbed of its lifeblood; it needed the fuel, but I hoped the fuel flow gauge was over-reading, as it often did. I was using sixty-five percent power to stay in the air, yet the airspeed was a mere one hundred thirty miles per hour (one hundred thirteen knots)—not even enough to reach Barrow, with this high fuel consumption.

At last I had managed to coax *Mythre* up to the necessary 9500 feet, and hoped we were somewhere in the vicinity of my pressure pattern track. The higher altitude gave the radio more range, and my speaker gurgled with a conversation which clearly included the remark,

"She's heading for Russia!"

I tried to make contact, but no one replied. I reasoned that remark did not necessarily mean me—all aircraft are called "she." Nevertheless, I one-handedly tried to open up a contact chart to see where, according to airspeed and time, I could possibly be heading if I were not on my chosen course. To try to spread a chart the size of a tablecloth in my over-crowded cockpit was quite a feat even with two hands. Was it possible that I was flying in a circle—that I had fallen into the time-honored trap of all Polar venturers, whether they be earthbound on the Cap or in the air? If I were heading for Russia there would have had to have been an enormous wind shift. I looked down, trying to get a clue, but the low sunlight was dazzling over the rolling silver expanse of cloud.

Even though the sun was radiant, I was very cold. I dared not use the aircraft heater, for fear of wasting even a gallon of precious fuel. My electric gloves and socks became hot within seconds, and the smell of burning rubber made me decide not to try again until there was imminent danger of frostbitten extremities. The arrangement of HF radio or heated socks had become too complicated without an autopilot to relieve me, because of all the retuning of stations that had to go with each change. Instead, I pulled on yet another pair of my progressively larger socks. A knitted shawl swaddled my head, and many layers of gloves made my fingers so fat I could hardly turn the knobs. I tried to warm my toes by wiggling them.

But as I warmed up, my arms and legs made themselves known, and began to complain. My fingers were sore where I had cut them trying to get the cabin fuel tank selector on. Because of lack of space, the selector was in a narrow gap behind me among the tank wires, and probably as a result of the sand storms I had flown through in Africa, it had tightened up. Sand seeps into everything, far worse than water. My nails were torn and jagged, and even my jaw ached. I had been clenching my teeth with tension without realizing it.

"Time to loosen up and hold that stick gently," I told myself. "You've only been airborne for seven hours." I hitched a small cushion beneath me to change position slightly, and did some isometric neck and jaw stretching exercises to ease the aches.

I could smell the fruit that someone had put aboard, but where? So much had been loaded forward on the storage box I could not get at anything. The immersion suit lay there, ready to put on quickly should the need arise, though heaven knows how I could stretch my legs far enough to get it on in this overcrowded space. I grinned as I remembered the dress rehearsals with this particular garment at home sitting on a stool, as though I were in the aircraft. It is like a stiff boiler suit with feet, and practically stands up by itself; of course it, too, was designed for men. Somehow one had to get one's head through a tight rubber-banded neck, and one's legs into the lower part, then bend over and pull a zip down the back, and up through one's legs. We had smeared the zip with vaseline to make it easier, but one still had to be a weight lifter as well as an acrobatic contortionist to make it!

Time to try to make contact on the radio again, and this time I tried to tune the radio compass to T.3, the Naval Scientific camp based on a floating ice island two hundred and seventy miles below the Pole (and, unfortunately, two hundred and seventy miles to the port side of my track). Unbelievably, the needles showed interest, but to *starboard,* which meant I had to be flying backwards. It could not be right, so I tried again, and with difficulty read the Morse signal "V.D." That was the Russian scientific team's ice island beacon, and who knows where that is —except almost certainly to the right of my planned flight track over the Pole.

Floating ice islands are used by the Americans and the Russians for scientific purposes in preference to ships which cannot stay for long periods, and cannot get through to the high Arctic. The islands are massive glacier floes which gradually move around the Pole over many years. They are stable enough to build huts on and to install special experimental equipment, and sometimes even to build a rough runway. The life, of course, is incredibly hard for the men stationed there, in spite of supplies flown to them from the Naval Arctic Research Laboratory in Barrow. There have been several American ones, and the Russians still have several today with light aircraft permanently stationed on them.

There are many four-footed beasts on the floes too, and many Arctic tales. A favorite one is of Roscoe, the Arctic fox who stealthily followed the local polar bear to dine off the bear's leftover meals of seal. The bear began to explore, and became too familiar around the huts, so the men had to get rid of him. Lazy foxy Roscoe was left without his easy food supply, but he unwittingly got his revenge on the men by developing a love for insulating cable; everything from telephone wires to electric installations was nibbled. As fast as the men mended one piece of cable, Roscoe chased back to the piece they had just mended, and eagerly devoured the freshest cable. All winter he drove the men mad, and still they could not catch him, until finally another polar bear arrived and Roscoe happily reverted to his old lazy habits. This time the men left the polar bear to his own devices. It was simpler to avoid him than to repair the wires!

Eight hours airborne, and if my preflight plan had been correct I should have been near the Pole, but my airspeed strangely had not improved with less weight. There was something really wrong. As I looked at the outside mirror mounted on the port engine, I seemed to see a piece of fuselage hanging down! Shocked, I looked harder. It was half a wheel. The nose wheel had partly emerged from its casing, and the door was hanging down. There was my loss of airspeed! I recycled the gear mechanism to try to retract it. It worked, except that the amber light signifying "gear up and locked" only blinked at me and then went out again. I tried again and the light only blinked again, but as far as I could see in the mirror the gear was up. Poor *Mythre.* This must have been what had been wrong with her all the time. Maybe the wheel doors had always been slightly ajar; this could account for most of our earlier unsolved problems.

I sadly remembered how often I had murmured, "Are we sure it's not the wheels?" I had had to fly to almost the top of the world to prove it—hundreds of miles from a landing strip or a human being, without even a ship to circle over. It meant serious trouble if the wheel would not stay up. Somehow I had to get more airspeed. Unless a fantastic tail wind appeared—which was highly unlikely, as there was a prevailing headwind in that direction—I would run out of fuel some miles off the Alaskan coast—if it was Alaska I was still heading for.

The ice below was rough, far too rough to land an aircraft safely because of the currents of the ocean below it; but I knew it was much smoother on the Alaskan side, and little aircraft certainly landed there to collect scientific data. Several had force-landed there and escaped. But below me Wally Herbert and his team had crossed by foot over the Pole —it was incredible how they had traversed this ghastly terrain by only their own physical efforts.

No more radio communication was possible and now that the clouds had vanished, the sun was behind me. To have to return to Andoya at this stage could spell equal disaster, as I was no longer sure of my position. I merely knew that whatever my position was, I almost certainly could not stretch the fuel to Alaska either. The very beauty of the scene dispelled gloomy thoughts and euphorically I watched the deeply shadowed, green-streaked, glittering land of ice. I almost felt content, for I was doing what I had chosen to do.

Glistening snow ahead caught my attention. The clouds were dissipating and I saw the ragged surface of shadows caused by roughed-up ice—the pack ice. Now I knew for sure I had left behind Spitzbergen and all its notoriously bad weather; but it was a slender clue for such an expanse of ice. More than five million square miles of it covered this ocean—and I had two thousand of them ahead of me, without a living soul except an occasional polar bear and the seals below the ice.

Navy blue puddles of water oozed up through milky snow, embedded with green rocks and miniature glaciers. If I had been below a high cloud level, I might have found my clue to what lay ahead from the atlas of the sky, from the shades reflected upon it. Open ocean makes black patches on the clouds, but solid ice reflects as gray. Bush pilots in polar regions learn to read many signs from sky reflections. Once a couple of them were forced down off-course with little hope of rescue from the ice without radio communication. One of them thought of flashing the strong torch they had aboard at an angle to the clouds, knowing it might reflect hundreds of miles ahead. It did, and soon a flashing Morse light came back establishing communications, and eventually rescue.

The beastly wheel came down. I recycled it again, but the airspeed continued suspiciously low, indicating the undercarriage doors were not completely shut. Puffy, green-tinged clouds lay to the port of me, and teasingly solid ones built up behind, looking like far-off glaciers, austere and sheer. Clouds? Surely those were mountains! Mirages are frequent in the Arctic regions, but I was wary of this possible manifestation.

Where was I? Had I been flying in circles? Was it St. Joseph Land? No. Those mountains looked 10,000 feet high. Nothing on the charts seemed to fit them and yet they looked suspiciously like the films I had seen of Greenland. That was where I should be if I were making a true track of my pressure pattern path, but the earlier chat overheard on the radio had not indicated that I was following course! I did not know what to believe now. The only station beacon for hundreds of miles up here was Nord in North Greenland, but one radio compass needle pointed to port, and the other to starboard. No recognizable Morse signals. It could not be Greenland.

"GAYTO to any station," I called on the HF frequency. I was currently tuned into the same one on which I had heard voices earlier in the morning, even though earlier they obviously had not received the position reports I had blindly transmitted.

"Nord here, Tango Oscar," most surprisingly replied a deep voice. "Where have you been? The whole world is looking for you!"

"I have been here all the time but nobody answered me." There was nothing else I could say.

"Tango Oscar, where are you?"

What could I answer? I hesitated, and finally honestly replied, "I'm estimating, repeat, estimating, eighty-four North at flight level nine zero, but it is only an estimation. I was unable to pick up Bear Island and Spitzbergen beacons earlier today but now I can see glaciers to port of me."

"That's not surprising, as those island beacons are usually overcome by a stronger Norwegian one. Where do you really think you are now?" said Nord. "Have you got my beacon. Try. . . ."

"I am already tuned to your frequency, but one needle points one way and the other another way! Do you have very high snow-covered mountains—about 10,000 feet with low cloud below them—where you are, Nord?"

"It's all snow here! We have mountains, but clear skies. Its lovely sunshine here! You must come to Nord. There's nowhere else for you to go up here. Everyone is worried about you. Where is your radio compass pointing to now?" That was the trouble: according to the conflicting dials, I could be heading south between Greenland and Iceland, to Siberia or almost anywhere. The normal compass had long since given up its unequal fight against the overpowering northern magnetic forces up here, and the sight of it only made me distrust my direction indicator. It was better not to look!

"I have two and they are pointing in opposite directions," I repeated.

"Are you up there alone? Jesus Christ!"

"Affirmative."

"Then you *must* come to Nord. You will just have to choose one needle to follow and trust it."

Silence, while I decided to trust the port-seeking needle, for the far-off mountains were there too. I made a private deal with the Almighty about my fate, for if it were not Greenland it could be somewhere not very welcoming—or worse, it could be a mirage!

I flew on over low clouds which shadowed the dazzling green ice floes of fantastic colors—a medley of jewels—of emeralds, turquoise and aquamarines laced by glittering silver against jet black shadows. Ahead lay a crown of icebergs and beyond a blanket of snow leading to the blue and white sheer glaciers. This was no mirage. Occasional glints of light, like a hard, sparkling diamond, caught my attention, but it was just the Arctic phenomenon I had noticed earlier. Vainly I chased dark shadows, resembling igloos, and even some graceful Arctic seagulls, but there was nothing to indicate that man had ever been there.

"Where do you think you are now, Sheila? You pronounce it Sheila, don't you?" said the voice from Nord.

There was absolutely no sign of anything like a hut or a puff of smoke, let alone an airfield, yet now there was a strong Morse aural signal from Nord's beacon. I studied the chart again; it could be the other side of the glaciers of this indented coast. Again the NASA green light came on in the strange way that it did when least expected. I gleefully punched all the test buttons. At least somebody would eventually know which land I had ended up in, but to me it was truly "No man's land."

"Nord, I could be at eighty-two North fourteen West. I am going to fly out to sea again and round this mountain range and hope to see you on the other side." I certainly did not want to try to fly over the mountains and get lost, unable to make sufficient height among the glaciers beyond, until I knew exactly where I was. Without roads and rivers, towns or landmarks, and no compass, it could be a hopeless quest among the uncharted glaciers.

"My name is Pierre," continued the heavily-accented voice. I decided the voice sounded French. "And there are twenty-seven men here, all waiting to meet you. You must find us. You must land. It is lovely here, and we will give you food and petrol. We have nine thousand feet of runway."

It must be a good-sized airfield. I looked for a village, thinking he meant twenty-seven men on the field, and that there must be an Eskimo community nearby, as well as the complex of buildings that normally go with such a field. I recalled pictures of runways like tunnels between tall snow banks, and realized that even if I found it, I still had problems, particularly as my wheels could be damaged. There were no skis on my aircraft, nor had I ever made an ice runway landing.

At last I turned the corner, but again it all looked the same. I chased every long dark shadow and looked for a village in the direction that one of the needles was pointing. Nothing for it but to stick to the needle I had chosen, and to follow it toward the mountains. As they got closer I saw a long dark slope—it could be a runway—but where were the houses? Then I saw a tall mast—a beacon? There were a few low huts. It must be Nord. It had to be! It was! I was lost no longer. There among a glittery snow patchwork quilt of brilliant colors was a runway of swept gravel. Huge snow banks on either side of it certainly made it a tunnel. I did not have enough fuel to continue to Alaska, but still there was too much aboard to land with a possible undercarriage problem. I explained that I had to circle to burn up fuel remaining in the tip tanks, particularly as there was a strong crosswind on the runway.

"All right," said Pierre, "as long as you really are going to land here. We are all waiting to meet you."

"I have not got permission to land here. Can you arrange it?"

"That's all right. The Station Manager is expecting you. We are looking forward to seeing you. What color hair do you have? Fly down low, Sheila, all twenty-seven of us want to see you."

"Will do," I said. "I'm blonde, but I am a great age, so don't get excited."

"Oh, we know all about you and what you look like, we already have pictures of you here, but in black and white!"

I descended lower and could see the men waving from snow-covered buildings, some perched on the roof watching the aircraft through binoculars! I circled over magnificent scenery such as I had never imagined.

Pierre informed me that NASA had made contact with them through Thule Air Base and wanted to know how I was physically. I thought they must mean what shape was the aircraft in, as the computers must have passed on data about my low airspeed. I replied that at least one wheel was partly down, but I was burning up the fuel and thought we would get down all right.

"No, no," said Pierre. "They want to know how you yourself are! Are you all right physically? They think you must be exhausted."

"Tell them I am fine, I'm having a cup of coffee at last!"

"They would like you to try radio frequency 17909. Thule Air Base wants to talk to you, to try and link you with Goddard."

I duly changed to that frequency, but could not think how Goddard could possibly talk to me from Maryland on my little radio, even relaying through Thule. Leroy Field, of the U.S. Navy, was now using the ultrastrong naval transmitter in Washington, but today the air was too full of static interruption to make contact. Although I never did reach him, he often heard my airborne reports all round the world, and relayed them to Len Roach, in the Navigation Data department at Goddard. What remarkable people they were; despite all their valuable equipment aboard, and other considerations, their first concern was whether I personally was all right. It was very moving, the deep trust that had grown between these American men, most of whom I had never met, and myself in Britain.

When the aircraft was light enough to land, and after much pumping and pushing, lights showed the landing gear safely down. As I descended to land, banks of *sastrugi*—ridges of hard solid snow caused by wind, up to several feet high—met my startled eyes. It was far from flat snow. Roofs, laden with men, towered above the tunnel of snow banks. A group of blonde-haired, sun burned people dressed in fur-edged parkas waited at the far end. Bearded Morgens Lund, Station Manager, looking like a handsome Viking, welcomed me to Nord with typical Arctic hospitality. No worry with official papers here. Hot coffee and food were waiting. A Land Rover with huge snow tires was ready to drive us to the wooden mess hall hut. Around me lay a jungle, but of sculptured ice, not trees.

There were radio masts and cables instead of trees, and rolls of wire netting to keep the polar bears away. Little puffs of fog rose up from the track in front of us like the pipe smoke of a friendly giant, yet I could clearly see the pink-edged, green icebergs further out. Music streamed from the gaily curtained huts and mingled with the cries of the Husky dogs outside the mess hall.

There was one other guest here—Count Eigel Knuth, an archaeologist who was here to collect his mail and await an airlift home. It could take months to get the lift. He lives quite alone in Peary Land, and is Nord's only neighbor. The nearest so-called civilization is many hundreds of miles away, though there is a village, Danmarkshaun, five hundred and sixty kilometers away, with a grand total of twelve inhabitants to man its radio weather station. No ship or car can ever reach Nord. The occasional Air Force aircraft, which accounts for the beautifully kept runway, is their only means of survival.

Nord is a weather station, built in 1952 with the aid of the USAF, completely staffed by Danes. The Greenlanders, whose land it is, will not take the job, as they say it is too tough! The men here usually remain for two or three years without leave or seeing other people. All are weather scientists or personnel running the station. There were no aviation engineers, but there was plenty of fuel, and the station electrician was eager to help me, if we could somehow make contact with the outside world for advice.

The men regaled me with wonderful stories of how they lived, and how the temperature varied according to who was looking at the thermometer, a pessimist or an optimist. It is a completely dark world twenty-four hours a day from October to March, and the temperature can fall to minus fifty degrees. The storms sometimes become so bad the men cannot even move from one hut to another—a mere stone's throw away—for two or three days at a time. Each hut has a telephone, and every time a man leaves a hut in the winter he must telephone back to say he has arrived safely. One meteorologist walked outside in a gale to take his weather readings and was literally blown away. His body was found thirty miles distant, months later.

Young Helge, a radio operator, grew bored one stormy day, and broke the rules and left his hut to go to his work in the radio hut, a few yards away. He vanished and was missing for two days. It took a whole expedition and chain of men to find him among the huts. He was lucky, for he had stumbled upon the food warehouse door, unlocked, and had enough food for the station for a year. He was a very frozen and thirsty young man, but he was not hungry for a long time. No one ventures from the camp alone, even in the summer, without a rifle; not the least danger are the polar bears, which in spite of their enormous size, are among the quickest animals on earth.

Morgens allotted me a hut. Each hut had about a dozen rooms in it, with a tiny shower room. Clogs and anoraks hung in the entrance. We went then to the radio hut, which was also brightly furnished, with beds and kitchen attached, for the dark days when they could not get back to their own huts. That day messages were pouring in from Thule, as radio reception was fairly good, but not a word from England. We sent off messages home and replied to Goddard that I was determined to go on over the Pole from here, and head for Barrow as soon as I could get the wheel problem patched up. I believed that after a few hours sleep I would be off.

The telex system is an old hand type and the radios are dependent on weather conditions. So telexes took days, not minutes, at Nord, and messages intercrossed and were scrambled together. It was obvious that the answers to my queries from England were not going to be received today. I snuggled under my coverlet to sleep, with sunlight streaming in as though it were midday. I had been awake nearly forty hours without realizing it because of the continuous sunshine. Up here there are no set hours for sleeping in the Arctic summer—you just sleep in the sunlight when you feel like it. No one ever gets sick here either, for there are few disease-causing bacteria. I awoke a few hours later and found no answers had come through. I tried to set up a new grid course and plans on the few charts I had. Nord had not been planned as a possible alternate originally, and I only had charts for Canada and Alaska. I rejected all thoughts of moving along to Canada, or of going down to Thule. As far as I was concerned, it was the North Pole or nothing and somehow I must nurse *Mythre* to Barrow via the Pole. For that there would be no second chance.

Morgens picked me up for breakfast across in the mess hall. Instead of traditional breakfast mail and newspapers, we collected our news from the radio room. There was still no word from England, but Thule's generous Air Force Base Commander planned to fly an aircraft up, with oil and spares, to see if I was all right. I was horrified at the thought of the cost of the huge transport plane, and knew I must prevent that, until I knew for certain that I was really stuck. We sent more messages, and I prepared to wait some more. Were it not for finishing the last leg of the Polar attempt, I would have been content to stay here for months; there were so many new experiences to enjoy, and so much to learn.

Over coffee and delicious Danish pastries, Count Eigel Knuth amused me with tales of his lonely research work and his house—surely one of the most remote habitations on earth. He had discovered evidence of fireplaces and cooking utensils showing that people had lived up here four thousand years ago, and an old boat, proving that people were still here as recently as the fourteenth century, when they appeared to have died out. We discussed the misnomers of Greenland and Iceland, for Greenland is infinitely more icily forbidding.

We returned to the radio station, but no news at all came through. Above me floated a sonde weather balloon, the size of a car; an aviator meeting one of these in the air might well believe it was a U.F.O. Everywhere I looked was dazzling white, full of colored shafts. The brilliance of the scene was painful and it was necessary to wear sunglasses even inside the huts. The horizon was a line of icebergs, as the camp looked straight out over the Arctic Ocean. There was animal life—several birds and many lemmings (a rat-like furry animal), and an occasional seal moving among the navy blue puddles, its throaty voice mingling with the sharp cracks of breaking ice and the muffled creaks of overladen icebergs.

The electrician had finished his normal station duties, and we piled into the truck to drive roughshod over the pebbly, gritty earth tracks among the snow drifts to refuel the lonely *Mythre* at least partly. The hydraulic bottle seemed to be still half full and was not, apparently, the cause of the wheel trouble, but there was a shortage of oil and de-icing fluid. Another day went by, tinkering with the aircraft as though it were a normal day, back home in Oxfordshire. It is always bad to be delayed unexpectedly on the ground during any endurance attempt—one becomes soft again and enjoys the luxury of regular food and of not having to discipline oneself to concentrate solidly on what one is doing. Doubts creep in where there were none before. Again I felt my confidence ebbing away as I fell asleep.

A loud pounding soon woke me up. Draping the downy cover around me, I struggled sleepily to the door for the message. But it only contained advice I had already tried—recycling—and gave further suggestions about oil and hydraulic fluid, none of which we had! I was advised that a new takeoff time would be following; hours of daylike night went by and still no further messages. I quickly became accustomed to the timeless way of life and realized how wonderful it was compared to the rush and bustle back home. I could understand how people at Nord were able to take the hardship—the timelessness outbalanced that, as did the feeling of being out of the rat race, with time to laugh and talk and think.

Later that day an airliner, Lufthansa 650, made contact with the radio station, and asked if I were there. The German captain sent greetings, and said they would like to make a date to meet me to celebrate in Anchorage. We quickly asked them to transmit the weather they were seeing, as long as they were in contact, which would enable me to make my own homemade brand of weather chart. Even though the weather is very different at 35,000 feet, at least I now had an idea of the type and amount of cloud.

Off went another telex to Goddard, this time suggesting replies via airliners overflying Greenland might be quicker. By now we were all hilarious—me probably from the champagne air—and signed the telex, "With love from me and twenty-seven men thousands of miles from nowhere and not even a chart to find our way."

Saturday night was special, and all the men dressed up in their best clothes. Although all I could find was some makeup and I had to make do with straight hair, they treated me as though I were a princess in a ball gown. We toasted each other in beer and schnapps, ate and sang, just like a Saturday night anywhere in the world—except that our night sky was full of sunshine and the view was of icebergs.

The next morning Nord's operators could not keep up with the deluge of telexes that descended on us, mostly addressed to "Santa's Workshop"! The first one gave a takeoff time ten hours before it even got to us. A very formal one from England followed, giving exactly the same information. The outside world did not seem to realize that the earth rotates very slowly on top! We replied to all, as "twenty-seven Danish Santa Clauses and one Mother Christmas"—a name which stuck to me further on, as far as the Goddard Gang was concerned.

More and more telexes poured in, all one day late, one reading "We'll have you in our stocking any time," signed Goddard Gang, and finally another instructing me to revert to "normal test theater," signed "we will be watching, bon voyage." Phil Chapman and the Goddard Gang with Lee Field of the Naval Air Test Center Patuxent were working hard to re-establish communication, as if I were returning from the other side of the moon—and they were equally determined that I should continue over the Pole. There was to be no aborting of this mission, and I was glad that this time I could not escape from them.

The telexes had caught up in time to plan for an eleven-thirty departure later this morning. I hastily rechecked my new grid calculations, with a little sadness, for it was doubtful that I would ever return to Nord again. It's not the sort of place for a weekend visit, however sophisticated your transport may be! I had grown used to the good fellowship of these men, who did not make me feel alone among them, and the clear pollution-free air which had made me feel healthier than I had felt for years. Here life without frills promotes a direct honesty and real friendship straight from the heart, enhanced by the stark beauty surrounding us.

It took hours to fill my inside cabin fuel tanks, for it all had to be done by hand-pump from barrels. I was going to be late for my first interrogation today, and *Nimbus* would find me still on the ground. I knew the satellite had been specially fed with data today to ensure as many position readings as possible over the Pole. Hurriedly collecting thermos flasks of coffee and delicious specially-baked Danish pastries—Nord's culinary speciality—I hugged my bearded friends goodbye, each one of them in turn giving *Mythre* a little caressing pat.

Mythre's head was up in the air again, her tail weighed down by fuel, and once more she looked like a gull ready to soar high into the sky. I knew she must be restrained even though the minutes ticked by toward our planned lift off time, urging me on. Madame Fate would not condone anything forgotten today. I carefully checked and set the direction indicator, very aware that my life was at stake on a single dial, and this, my final check. The telex message had said the weather could not be better, so the only thing now left to chance was the changing wind and its effect on my course. But the fiery ball of orange sun above the horizon would verify my heading on the astro compass.

One last wave before I headed along the grit-covered runway through tunnel banks of snow, with the sound of engines thriving in the sharp cold air—their roar somehow exaggerated by the tranquility of the scenery.

"We have lift off for the Pole," I murmured with relief, as *Mythre* climbed confidently over billowing snow drifts toward sharp peaks of icebergs like soaring glass castles. A firm tug at the undercarriage and amber lights signalled the wheels smoothly up. The first hurdle had been cleared: our wheels were safely tucked away. Smooth air cushioned our wings rather like a springboard, helping us aloft. High cirrus clouds scurried way over to port but ahead the way was clear; the icebergs behind me became pink with distance, backed by glacier shafts of silver reaching to the sky. Below me, the navy blue puddles of Arctic Ocean seeped around emerald ice. Certainly, if this were the gates of heaven and my last glimpse of earth, it would have been the most impressive sight of my life. No words of mine could possibly describe the emotions aroused by the spectacle of this wondrous wilderness of beautiful shapes and colors—the very essence of primeval glory.

The calm air enabled me to return to the more mundane chores in the cabin, like testing the heart tape box, and inspecting the bouquet of wires sprouting out of my tummy. Today would be an important test biomedically, for whatever the outcome it could not fail to be the most exciting challenge of my life—enough to promote any amount of adrenalin, whether in triumph or failure.

Now I had left the most northern piece of land on earth behind me, yet

I would be heading south when I landed, although I was to fly an almost straight line. Imperceptibly, a blue horizon line had developed indicating fog ahead, and the navy blue water had become floating wedding-cakes of ice. In spite of the eternally grinding ice, everything seemed to be silently waiting.

It was as though I had flown straight off the top of the earth to a planet far out in space. Perhaps this remoteness was heightened because I was now totally removed from my normal life in the cooped-up apartment in London with its daily battle of paperwork. My only contact with the earth seemed to be my little green NASA light. I distinctly felt the Space Center's influence; I was very aware of the collective positive thought of the men studying my flight path. I had the unreal feeling that I was two people—one the observer, the other the doer.

Looking around, I found there was one link left with earth. The radio compass was actually giving a back bearing off Nord, and so far indicated I was on course, if my grid calculations were correct. Soon the sun would be in the right position for me to get a sunshot. At 1306 it would be ahead and directly over the North Pole. I tried calling Nord on the radio, and today they answered immediately, loud and clear.

"Operations normal, and a lovely day it is," I reported, but no further reply came back from Nord. Thick clouds appeared from nowhere far ahead. To port, a great mass of damp air nosed forward. I hoped it would not reach as far as the Pole.

I looked back into the cabin and saw that the yellow light for the wheels was out again. Recycle the gear. It flicked on and then off again. Recycle—light on—light off. Recycle and so it went on, with a mere airspeed indication of one hundred and thirty. It was going to be an exhausting trip but at least today there was fuel to spare, providing the head wind was still only ten knots.

At 1415, the time I originally should have been in the vicinity of the Pole, I was scheduled to attempt to call Nord as "November Hotel Kilo Three," the Navy's strong transmitter in Washington, D.C., was attempting to relay HF messages through them today. My dead reckoning told me that the slow speed and half-hour delay on takeoff meant I could only be in the vicinity of about eighty-seven degrees fifty minutes North.

Today we were to try a new plan to solve my communications difficulties, as so often air traffic control could not hear my messages, and yet occasionally I could hear theirs. But invariably the people sending messages to me spoke at such length and so fast, it was impossible to get the gist of the message against the static. This time, we decided that if I deliberately failed all the mental acuity tests, it meant I could hear the radio loud and clear if they would only speak slowly. Now once again nothing answered my call except crackling static from the speaker, and the radio compass had given up the struggle. The famous Arctic blackout again, and my earthly ties had gone!

Gray tentacles of cloud clawed at the wing tips; little rivulets of frosting framed the windshield and slowly crept over it like an army of white ants. Time to put on the heated windshield—a small panel of heated double glass—to make a small clear patch to peer through the frost.

At 9000 feet the temperature was minus 9°C, "warm" enough to be conducive to severe icing. I watched the ice slowly cover the black rubber boots edging the white metal wing, longing to switch the de-icers on immediately, but it was essential to wait a few more minutes. The ice must be allowed to build up so that the pulsating boots could break it cleanly off. If I switched on too early, the boots would be unable to do their job. The HF static aerial, which was strung from the aircraft tail to the far port tip of the wing, turned from copper to a glittering rope of ice, and twanged and quivered like a taut bow. An ugly thud echoed round the cabin as a lump of ice freed itself and hit us underneath. It had probably formed on the loose wheel door. I apprehensively watched the boots pulsate the wing ice, breaking it off in chunks, leaving bare patches of black rubber. As soon as the automatic pulsating stopped, the ice built up at horrifying speed. Time to get down out of this. It seemed to take forever. Below was worse, and the only way out of ice was higher still, but I could no longer climb. I was in the expected Polar inversions near the Pole itself, where the air is much colder down where it meets the permanently super-cooled surface. In my pre-planning I had hoped to escape severe icing here by crossing on a clear day, well out of cloud. But it was too late—the weather had broken at last.

Now I was meeting the ice ogre face to face. Somehow I must get the wheels to stay up, for I needed all the airspeed I could get to fight him off. Recycling had no effect anymore, but the emergency pump for use in an electrical failure still worked. I pumped and pumped with my right hand, hanging on to the stick with my left, trying to hold the aircraft straight and level. The wing leveller could not hold course in the increasing turbulence; it merely levelled the wings every time they dipped. My arm ached until I thought I could not go on. One final hard pull made a reassuring click, and the yellow light gleamed. A tiny bit of comfort for a few minutes in a gray ghostly world.

The HF aerial now whipped and pulled so hard at its restraining nuts that I knew soon it must break. It would not necessarily hurt the tail but the drag would be considerable, and heaven knows how much drag had already built up over my head where the special antennae were. They could be covered with inches, or even feet, of ice! The patter of sound on the windshield now heralded the hail and rain.

Freezing rain is the worst kind of icing to get into, as it flows back over the whole aircraft, wrapping it in a cocoon of ice. Very afraid, I manually switched the boots on and off to make them work quicker—even the defroster did not seem to work. How much could the pressure have changed and caused my altimeter to over-read? How far could I descend, and how much fuel would I waste getting up again if it did not work?

At last I got through the worst of the storm cloud, and *Mythre* stopped bucking. There was silence except for the homely noise of the engines, but the light was still gray and eerie between ragged layers of cloud. Chunks of ice flew off the wings, but sticky little bits remained, like plankton on a whale, riding up and down on the boots. The windshield army of ice crystals slowly retreated. The vibrating HF aerial spat dirty little strands of frozen water.

Now it was bitterly cold in the cabin. I was freezing. Wires festooned me and made me awkward. Three wires sprouted out of my middle to the heart box; another from my ear plug to the panel; wires from both arms and legs to the electrics; another wire to the tape recorder, plus headset, shoulder and lap harness. I had never noticed so much wire before, and, disgruntled, I complained to *Mythre* and Buck Tooth, as there was no one else to groan to.

Perhaps the grayness had imperceptibly lightened—or it could have been the flash of intuition one sometimes finds in the air that told me things were better. Almost immediately the gray mist broke into tattered gaps, to show a great white carpet—a continent of ice. A wide streak like a black river appeared, and the carpet became a smashed-up sea of giant floating, broken china—huge floes of ice unendingly grinding and colliding. A rainbow seemed to dance and glint amid the confusion of ragged ridges which no longer looked motionless. One could almost see the sound of noise and chaos! In fact, the ice moves at the rate of three miles a day—twenty miles in stormy weather—in a crazy ever-circling pattern.

I consulted my air almanac to calculate my sun position ahead of time, for the sun might yet escape through to indicate my true heading. I was now holding a grid course of 022 degrees to make sure I really went to the Pole, and did not curve inward and miss it. Without the sun or radio compass, there was simply no way of knowing where I was truly heading. I had only my watches to roughly tell me how many miles I might have travelled. There is no landmark that signifies the Pole. If one were found, within weeks it would no longer be the Pole. The landmark would lazily drift off over the clockwise currents and around the Pole center. At last the sun thrust its beams through the overcast and I chased it with the shadow bar of the astro compass, but elusively it fled again long before I got my sight. The time was 1530 hours.

"Pole minus twenty minutes and still counting," I said to a lonely sky and to *Nimbus,* the satellite orbiting in clear outer space somewhere above the earthly murk. The North Pole must be very near now if my course had been correct. Doubt tried to creep in, but I pushed it aside. I must believe I was heading for the Pole, come what may when the time was up. This was not the place for doubts. It was too late to change anything.

The outside temperature had incredibly risen to −2°C and it was almost warm again for a while in the cabin. Only the desolate but magnificent sight below was cold and forbidding, yet so strangely compelling. Even if it had meant landing on an ice floe, I would not have missed this scene. The fever of the Arctic caught me, like those before me who had discovered its glories and were to return again and again to its isolation that is like insulation, until it finally claimed them forever. I will never forget it.

The fragments of cloud below the brooding mass parted to frame a tiny perfect hill of snow among the tumbled ice. The time was right for ninety North. I was on top of the world. *Mythre* and I were at the Pole! I was sure I was—it had to be. This was the piece of the Pole that I was going to stake as mine!

The icy slipstream rushed in with a deafening roar and bit my cheeks as I opened the storm window, but the sheer exhilaration of the moment made me uncaring. I unfurled my tiny Union Jack, and found my paper "Snoopy" from my American NASA friends, and stretched a gloved arm through the icy blast to let them go. Both whipped past the window toward the tail, as the icy blast cut into my cheeks and made me gasp with shock.

"We're here—I'm on Top of the World."

MY FIRST SOLO FLIGHT

by Diane Ackerman

Early on a bright, warm day in mid-September, when the sky is the color of Wedgwood blue, broken by a few cumulus puffs and the staccato skywardness of every light airplane owner for miles, I phone the airport. Martin and Tom are both out, so I phone the FBO next.

"How's the wind today?" For a moment, it seems like an odd question to begin a conversation with on a balmy morning in historic Virginia. Although, perhaps it is the perfect question, one a general might have asked his aide before a Saturday morning battle not far from the airport and its nearby strategy of rivers and island hideouts.

"Wind's calm," Mike says. The alternate FBO manager, he's a little more reserved than George and stockier, with a trim mustache and short neatly kept black hair. "Tom doesn't come in on Saturday," he continues. "He'll be out on some golf course, probably . . . and Martin left this morning on a cross-country to Norfolk. He should be back right soon."

"Winds are calm, you say?" It's a question that only a student pilot would repeat with such tentative sincerity.

"Sure are."

"Great. See you in a few minutes."

All I need to hear is that the clear sky is also calm enough for me to do what I've been itching to for so long, take a plane up by myself, without an instructor to cajole or lead the way. Not that I want to stray from the false security of the traffic pattern, where you are always gliding distance from the runway, even though nasty things can happen and often do. Half a mile away, to James River, seems never-never land, the Practice Area five miles away, a spot of myth and rumor. All I want for the time being is to lift the bird up softly, thread by thread, into the invisible weave of the sky, and then cozy it back down again, doing touch-and-goes by myself, somehow to develop a *sense* for the plane that still threatens to lurch away from me at every climb and whose turns I never seem to coordinate just right. Demoralized about landings for so long, I want to persuade myself that I can bring it down to earth, ladderless, without mishap, without losing control, without losing nerve.

The airport is postcard-perfect: royal-blue sky, bright sun, not a leaf trembling on the lush, dark-green perimeter of trees. Cessnas are everywhere, some flying in tandem (a word too sonorous and suggestive for the blunt Latin it comes from: "at length"). An occasional Aztec or

Baron or other low-winged plane appears downwind, scooting in to land, some touching down as fast as my trainer cruises. Two planes in a row jump a bit at the treeline just beyond the end of the runway, where a cleared fairway boils the air whenever there's a crosswind. Today, it's just a little "squirrelly," as the flyers say, but nothing like the treacherous wind shear Poleskie found at Sky Park when we went to Old Rhinebeck.

At eleven-thirty, a green-and-white Cessna 172 enters the pattern: Martin returning with a student who, after 300 hours, is learning to read the sky by IFR. *I got tired of flying into places and being unable to leave because of the weather,* he will tell me later, but at the moment he is landing from an horizon-to-horizon sky, with the earth popping up like a storybook underneath him, and a crosswind giving him an unexpected bit of trouble. A gleaming little silver Ercoupe taxis out to 13, and I can hear its pilot checking his radio, *Williamsburg Unicom, do you hear Ercoupe 715?* With his head poking up through a plexiglass dome, the pilot can see all around him in the squat, tiny trainer, whose rear fuselage points straight back like an Irish setter's tail.

By now, Martin and his student have taxied over to the gas pump, and as Martin gets out, I begin to pester him about letting me go up alone. He makes a melodramatic check of the wind with a finger. He consults both wind socks (one is blowing straight out, the other hanging limp).

"Have you called Flight Service Station for the weather?"

"You're kidding. It's beautiful. Look—blue skies, no birds of prey circling at the end of the runway." I'm amazed to find myself whining.

"Only if you check the Flight Service Station first," he says, fighting back a smile.

"Right." I dial the number printed across the base of the black wall phone, and when a man answers at Patrick Henry International Airport, at Newport News, Virginia, I tell him that I'm a student pilot in Williamsburg, who needs to know the current state of my weather, as well as the forecast. *10,000 broken, 25,000 scattered, visibility unlimited, winds under 10 knots,* he says. Perfect flying weather. Because I'm a student pilot, he translates the forecast from zulu time to what's local. When I hang up, Martin checks the weather report sheet I've filled out in a messy scrawl, then shakes his head.

"The visibility isn't unlimited," he says soberly. "I couldn't see California."

"Could you see your hand in front of your face?" I ask brightly.

"Yes."

"Then you were within legal minimums. Can I fly?"

"Do you know how a plane flies?" he asks.

"I can spell the word *lift.*"

"That's good enough," he says, and adds something else, but I've already grabbed the clipboard and key for 654 and am rushing out the door to start my preflight.

It's only at the plane, which looks suddenly wrong in every way, that I have second thoughts about what I've gotten myself into, and proceed with the longest preflight in history. Everything looks unfamiliar, the cotter pins, the elevator trim, the rusted bolts on the fuselage, the cracked wing tip. But everything is also as it should be, I know. And it's only when I climb aboard and run through my checklist to turn the plane on, enriching the mixture, pushing the carburetor to cold, turning on the master switch, pulling the throttle out all but a quarter inch, and yelling CLEAR PROP! that I realize exactly how nervous I must be. It's no use trying to start the ignition with the key still in my pocket. *Settle down,* a voice whispers from somewhere underneath one of my vertebrae. A long time has passed since Martin first saw me scampering out to preflight the plane, and perhaps that's why he's now taxiing a Cessna 172 around the ramp to park it off my left wing tip, a casual, unobtrusive way of nonetheless seeing what I'm up to. I bring my throttle hand to a nonexistent cap in a mock salute, then taxi past him to the runway I know is being used, or is *active,* as they say. Turning into the wind, at the threshold of 13, I do my run-up, and hear the engine grind and splutter so hoarsely I become seriously worried. That isn't normal. Or is it? Do I play it safe and taxi back for Martin to listen, and risk looking like an idiot when he tells me I'm hearing ghosts, or do I take off a plane I think may be unsafe? After a laughably long run-up, I decide the engine is probably normal; I hadn't listened to it closely before. Then I tell Williamsburg traffic—all of it, anyone eavesdropping on the airways—that I'm a Cessna departing runway 13 and staying in the pattern.

"Watch out for the Pitts," a voice says over the radio, and I laugh back, "I'll do that."

Kiss the world good-bye, I think, and press the throttle against the fire wall, while holding the nose wheel gently off the ground, at just the angle I hope to be climbing out at. Seconds later, I reach airspeed, and the plane follows its nose upward, lifting off in the silkiest, gentlest climb I could wish for. But too soon I am at 400 feet and trying to coordinate nose and wings in a decent turn, as the turn-and-bank ball falls far right. *Jesus, I'm skidding at 400 feet,* I think, and shallow out into a messy, wide arc that takes me a mile toward the river, on a wide downwind. Now my airspeed is too high, and I'm 150 feet above traffic altitude. I cut the power, pull on the carburetor heat, and slow up to 80. Then call the tower, in a husky rush, *Williamsburg tow . . .* no, no tower, it's an uncontrolled field . . . *Williamsburg traffic, Cessna 10654 right downwind for 13, touch and go.* Abeam the numbers and the perfect round run-up bay at the end of 13, I cut the power back to 1,700 rpms, and slow up to 70 mph, adding 20 degrees of flaps. I had meant to add only 10 degrees. The runway seems far away, so I turn straight toward it, adding more flaps and cutting the power, then bringing in more power, as I line up with the center stripe, cutting the power again. Over the trees, the airspeed plunges to 60, and it's in that slower-than-sensible attitude I float in, flaring to a gentle, nose-up landing almost halfway down the runway. But only half remains, and it occurs to me that the electric flaps will take their own sweet time to raise. I won't be able to yank them up or down as I could in the Warrior. I bang the flap switch up, punch the carburetor heat off, palm the throttle clean open, and begin taking off, turning my head as I approach lift-off speed and the end of the runway, to see the last angle of flaps disappearing into the wing.

In the 400 feet between takeoff and first turn, there is a moment of peace, so I check my wristwatch. Only five minutes have passed. How can that be possible? A gust changes my airspeed, and I try to turn more smartly onto a downwind leg, slow to 80, lift the mike to announce my whereabouts. A Cessna Cardinal begins a full conversation with the Unicom operator. When they finish, I lift the mike, try to slow abeam the numbers, begin my descent, and talk at the same time.

"George, is that Cardinal entering the pattern?" I ask with anxious informality.

"Williamsburg Unicom," a voice replies.

Of all the times to remind me that I summoned the demon incorrectly. "Cessna six-five-four," I say, gabbling, "right downwind for one-three. Please advise if that Cardinal is a factor."

"Cardinal is still five miles on approach, six-five-four," Unicom answers. I start to laugh, as no doubt the men inside, watching me through the sun-crazed windows are laughing, and end the conversation: "Six-five-four."

After two more go-rounds, only fifteen minutes have passed. It seems impossible. Though I've mastered the timing right for touch-and-goes—the knack of using up as little of the little runway as possible, and taking off, full throttle, as the flaps are still sliding back up into their housing—my approaches are terrible. Each turn to final, I am all over the sky, lacing it up, rearing through it, bouncing and sliding. It can't be the wind alone making my airspeed so wavery and fitful, all around 70, but not locked onto it. The hands are the flags of the nervous system, and as keyed up as mine is, my hands must be inadvertently trembling, fretting the wheel. Turn to final. Let down 40 degrees of flaps; I feel the plane balloon because I've forgotten to hold its nose down while the flaps go on. Coming over the trees, on a fine, steady descent, I see the runway in front of me, but something is wrong. My hand hasn't moved on the wheel, I'm positive it hasn't, but my airspeed has changed swiftly from 70 to 50. *Jesus,* I whisper, *40 is stalling speed.* Before I have time to correct, the plane lurches into a 45 degree bank to the right, all at once, as if a hand had grabbed the wing tip and yanked it down. I could fall now like a letter opener, on edge, slide a wing deep into the marsh underneath me. My ribs hurt from the tight, loud drumming of my heart, nothing like thought happens, but my foot has already solved the problem, pushing in the opposite rudder pedal, as I level off, force the nose down for speed, and add power to make the runway. Down at last, I hit the flaps-up switch, and taxi to the ramp, still shaking, and decide to stop for the day, while I'm still in one piece. *How could I have messed up that badly? Some solo flight,* I think, as I open the window and let a whoosh of prop-swept air cool me down, and wind my way back toward the FBO trailer and long line of tethered Cessnas. Across the airport, I see Martin and the FBO guys all standing outside the office, applauding with large open-palmed motions, so I can't mistake them. On the radio, and over the loudspeaker, Unicom says, "Nice flying six-five-four." My mouth falls open, and I feel a rush of such intense affection for these flyers who have looked after and protected me, even defended me when necessary, and who encourage me with such generosity. In Ithaca, soloing was an empty climax to months of excruciating trial, degradation, and frustration. The tower was aloof as an Old Testament god, my instructor was unexcited, the FBO boss didn't care. Flying was not something sharably human and delightful, a jump from one energy state to another. It was a taboo-laden ritual by which they defined their seriousness and proved how manly they were, how solid, how in control.

Freeze this moment, I think, *this moment of pure, terse jubilation,* so that you will remember it when you are older, sofa-flying your memories through all the gusty emotions of being young. Not disabled perhaps, but with a quieter, less-visible degeneration of self, when you will need to remember this moment of deep-down, starry, self-amazing thrill.

Martin leaves the others as I taxi back to my stall and try to figure out how to wedge the plane into it. Patiently, he waits until I pivot, gun the engine, and struggle, then finally sweep round, pick up the checklist and turn the engine off, step by step. Together, we drag the plane backward into place and tie its wings and tail. I am grinning so hard you could slide a cassette into my mouth, and he is grinning, too, because he knows that I have just crossed a barrier I'd thought impossible only weeks before. A month ago, I was a groundling. Today I drove to the airport, rented a plane, and took it up by myself. *I did it,* I say with urgent surprise, as we walk back to the trailer. He nods exaggeratedly, eyes wide: positively, absolutely, hats-off, gentlemen.

CHRISTA McAULIFFE: "FIRST TEACHER IN SPACE"

by Robert T. Hohler

Before bed that night, Christa watched the Super Bowl, which helped put her to sleep—the Patriots were flogged, 46–10—and cost her five dollars in a betting pool she and Steve had entered with a group from Concord. Steve watched the game with Scott, Caroline and friends at Disney World while the Corrigans hosted a Super Bowl party of their own. As the Patriots unraveled, the Corrigans quipped that Christa's flight would help New Englanders erase the pain of the loss.

When a reporter asked Betsy if she was worried about Christa's safety, she said she was more worried about flying to Florida from California.

"NASA doesn't compromise at all," Betsy said. "They make sure everything is correct and one hundred percent before they go."

In case it was not 100 percent, workers collected the crew's wallets and personal belongings the next morning and stored them with visas, ready to send them with a seventy-member rapid response team to a country where the shuttle might ditch in an emergency. A one-hundred-member recovery crew lined the emergency landing strip at the space center. A rescue team stood by in Dakar. It was the eighteenth anniversary of the fire that killed three NASA astronauts on a nearby launch pad.

At 6:45 A.M. the *Challenger* crew strode confidently from the Operations and Checkout Building, a banner pinned behind them intended for Jarvis—HAVE A GREAT FLIGHT, GREGO!

"How do you feel, Christa?" photographers shouted.

"I feel great," she said, smiling, waving, finally wearing flight boots.

Jo Ann Jordan, one of her close friends, watched on television.

"I really thought we'd see more apprehension," she said. "I thought, 'Here comes a lady who's a mother, and she's leaving those babies at home.' "

Anne Malavich was not surprised by Christa's determination.

"Someone else with children the age of Christa's might have said, 'Maybe Caroline's too young; maybe I shouldn't do it,' " Malavich said. "But Christa decided this was something she wanted to do and she went right after it. She knew she had a good support system."

Christa was confused by those who would balk at such an opportunity.

"You know, people come up to me all the time and say, 'I really admire what you're doing, but I wouldn't want to do it,' " she had told a reporter. "I can't understand that. If you had a chance, wouldn't you want to do it?"

Now the wind was brisk and the temperature 40 degrees, chilly for Florida, but a full moon shone in a cloudless sky. It seemed another perfect day for a launch. In the white room, a smiling technician greeted Christa in a black mortarboard and tassel. She laughed, slipped into her safety harness and crawled through the circular hatch to the shuttle at 7:36 A.M. Then she waited.

Steve and the children watched with the immediate families of the other crew members at the Launch Control Center, four miles away. The Corrigans, who were not considered immediate family, waited on aluminum bleachers in a nearby VIP viewing area, the top half of *Challenger* visible on the horizon. Ed wore a stadium coat and a Scottish driver's cap, Grace a white coat with a fluffy collar. They looked through a set of giant binoculars and waited, their four other children beside them.

Thousands of people had left, but thousands remained, and the scene at the space center was similar to the sidelines at a Thanksgiving football game in New England. Huddled under blankets in twos and threes, hoods on their heads, scarves around their necks, hot chocolate and coffee in their hands, most of them watched the clock and waited. Others ran in place, shivering. A few, prisoners of their Yankee pride, raised their chins to the wind.

"Just like home," said a coatless Michael Metcalf, the teacher-in-space finalist from Vermont, his nose red from the cold.

Scott's classmates, many wrapped in blankets, waited with their chaperones and a small army of journalists on the edge of a parkway across a swamp from the launch pad. They read, played games and threw rocks into the swamp, hoping to spot an alligator. They waited.

An hour before launch time, the children learned their first lesson in technology's imperfections. Ron McNair spotted a microswitch on the circular hatch that indicated the hatch was not closed. He radioed Scobee, who asked technicians to check it. Using test equipment in the white room, they determined the hatch was closed and that the microswitch must have malfunctioned. But McNair was not convinced and he relayed his doubts to Scobee, who insisted the white-coated technicians open the hatch and check it again, a routine procedure that turned ridiculous.

A quick inspection confirmed the microswitch had failed, but when the technicians tried to close the hatch again, the door handle refused to budge, frozen by a stubborn four-inch bolt. They wrestled with the bolt awhile, then called for a drill and hacksaw. Forty-five minutes later, the tools had yet to arrive, and the angry voices of the restless technicians were audible on NASA's loudspeakers and television network. When the delivery man arrived minutes later, he gave them only a drill, whose battery died before the bolt would budge. They ordered a more powerful drill and, again, a hacksaw.

Meanwhile, the winds kicked harder.

"I'm mad," said Sarah Carley, one of Scott's classmates. "We came down here to see that shuttle take off and if it's not going to take off, I'm going to have a hyper-spaz." A hyper-spaz, she explained, is "when someone goes crazy and takes a fit."

But Scott's best friend, Zachary Fried, waited patiently. Space was his consuming passion, and with the other children he had heard astronaut Vance Brand explain two days earlier that the shuttle was a marvelous machine "when everything works, but only when everything works." Zachary was a serious boy, and he sensed the dangers. He was willing to wait.

The mood was mixed at Concord High, where journalists seemed to equal the twelve hundred students in number. Seated before televisions throughout the building, some of the students wore party hats decorated with pictures of the space shuttle. Some wore T-shirts that said "Concord —Where the Spirit Is High." Others tooted tiny noisemakers or played the military bugle charge on kazoos. A few raised banners that said WE'RE WITH U CHRISTA and TO BOLDLY GO WHERE NO TEACHER HAS GONE BEFORE, paraphrasing the *Star Trek* television theme. The yearbook staff had recently designed a cover for the 1986 edition that featured the space shuttle orbiting the school seal. The theme was "Christa in Space."

But two students walked about the building in protest, toting handmade signs that said I'D RATHER BE LEARNING, complete with "shuttlebuster" logos.

"I'm really getting sick of this," said one of the protesters, Andrew Cagle. "All we hear is Christa this, Christa that."

Andrea Rice, a classmate of Cagle, was more sympathetic. "I pity Mrs. McAuliffe," she said. "She must be, like, losing it."

Actually, Mrs. McAuliffe was sleeping. She had joked for a while with Jarvis about the hatch problems, but after several hours of lying flat on their backs, strapped onto seats that felt like thinly padded, cold steel kitchen chairs, staring at nothing but the middeck lockers, they began to lose the circulation in their legs and their humor as well. Jarvis's legs went to sleep and Christa dozed off altogether.

She awoke when the technicians attacked the titanium bolt with the second drill, which proved as useless as the first. The bolt was so hard that it chewed up the drill bit. Christa listened as they finally removed the bolt with the hacksaw. It was 11:07.

"Isn't this ridiculous?" Grace Corrigan said.

"I would have gotten the hacksaw sooner," said Ed.

"I would have gotten my nail file," said Grace.

The winds had begun gusting to thirty miles an hour—too violent for the shuttle to attempt a landing at the space center in case of an emergency—and the flight soon was postponed another twenty-four hours.

"I guess we'll have to wait another day, but it's getting emotionally grating," Grace said, turning her back on *Challenger.*

Her son Steve and daughter Betsy could stay no longer, and she worried, too, for Christa. The delay was the fourth in six days, the sixth overall, one short of tying the record. The cost to the taxpayers: $200,000.

ANOTHER SHUTTLE CHANCE BOLTS AWAY said the headline in the *Washington Post.*

"It was just not our day," said Robert Seick, the director of shuttle operations.

Indeed, it was so bad that Steve tweaked the technicians by sending them a tool set. And so bad that Christa lost her spirit. After five and a half hours of uneasy confinement, she slouched back to the crew quarters past the same photographers she had waved to in the morning. This time there was no wave, no smile, no bounce to her step. There was a look of deep frustration.

"Her face really struck me," said Mark Beauvais, the school superintendent who knew her well, whose wife had taught with her, whose daughter had babysat for her. "It was a look I'd never seen before. It bothered me."

Christa ate an early dinner with Steve that night at the crew quarters, kissed him good-bye for the last time and called Eileen O'Hara in Concord. She wanted her students to know how she had felt during the long, yawning wait.

"Go borrow a motorcycle helmet," Christa said. "Lie on the floor with your legs up on the bed, and lie there for five hours. You can't read, you can't watch television, you can't have anything loose around. You're strapped down really tightly, with oxygen lines and wires coming out of your suit. You can hardly say anything. Just lie there and you'll know how it feels."

But Christa managed to laugh about the bolt. Here was NASA with a billion-dollar shuttle, the most complex flying machine in the world, and not a tool box to be found. She suggested it might make a bad television comedy. Then she talked about her family. Christa was pleased for her mother that the reception had been a success. She was proud Caroline had been a leader at the party by engaging several other children in games. She was sad Scott had endured intense media pressure, and she was excited about the chance that she would fly in the morning.

"I still can't wait," she said.

Neither could NASA. A record cold front that threatened to destroy central Florida's citrus crop was due to rush in with subfreezing temperatures and Arctic wind-chill factors that would last through the next morning's 9:38 launch time. No shuttle had been launched at a temperature below 51 degrees, but the space agency was about to test *Challenger*'s limits, to take chances it had never before taken. Pressure to meet its schedule was intense, some of it self-imposed, some of it, NASA officials argued, created by the media.

"Yet another costly, red-faces-all-around space shuttle launch delay,"

Dan Rather reported that evening. "This time a bad bolt on a hatch and a bad-weather bolt from the blue are being blamed. What's more, a rescheduled launch for tomorrow doesn't look good, either. Bruce Hall has the latest on today's high-tech low comedy."

The press deserved 98 percent of the blame for the pressure, argued Richard Smith, the director of the Kennedy Space Center. Journalists did not take part in the decision to proceed with the launch, however. Smith did. For the first time in the history of the shuttle program, NASA decided to load the external fuel tank in subfreezing weather.

"We might learn a lot of interesting things," said George Diller, an agency spokesman.

Engineers for Morton Thiokol, the company that manufactured the solid rocket boosters, cautioned that cold temperatures could cause the O rings—the rubber seals between the rocket's sausagelike segments—to lose their resilience and allow explosive gases to leak, an event that could be catastrophic. When NASA officials at the Marshall Space Flight Center downplayed the warning, one of the engineers, Allan McDonald, replied, "If anything happens to this launch, I sure wouldn't want to be the person to stand in front of a board of inquiry to explain."

The engineers were overruled by their superiors, and the giant digital clock continued to tick. Antifreeze was pumped into fluid lines on the launch tower, and the tower itself had grown a thin coat of ice by 10:00 P.M.

"The launch crew is on schedule," reported NASA spokesman James Mizell. "They say it's a miracle because the winds are gusting very hard."

As Monday turned to Tuesday, January 28, the ground crew evacuated the launch pad and began the three-hour process of loading the external tank with a half million gallons of super-cold, highly explosive propellants. Twenty minutes later, the fueling stopped. A computer had detected an electrical problem in the fire detection system, a problem that took two and a half hours to solve. The launch was pushed back to 10:38 A.M.

"We're down several hours," said Hugh Harris, the public affairs chief, "But that doesn't mean we can't catch up some of that time."

As the *Challenger* crew slept, the team at the launch pad grew increasingly wary of the ice. The temperature had dipped to 24 degrees, the wind chill to 10 below zero and, like northern homeowners, the ground crew had kept the water running to prevent the pipes that fed the fire extinguishing system from freezing. Still, a pipe froze, and the cold caused the failure of eleven cameras that NASA had placed in the area to record the lift-off. The launch pad was colder than parts of New Hampshire.

"Some damn Yankee came down here and forgot to shut the door," shouted a shivering reporter into the press center before dawn.

When Christa and the crew woke at 6:20, the full moon spattered silver on the choppy waters of the Atlantic. From her window Christa saw the orbiter glitter in the distance, forty-five flood lamps filtering through the steel launch tower. She showered, pulled on blue jeans, a white crew shirt, her powder-blue sneakers and joined the crew for a light breakfast, her hair still wet. Christa sat at a rectangular table, a centerpiece of roses and American flags before her, Ellison Onizuka to her right, Mike Smith, in his stocking feet, to her left. Bleary-eyed, they smiled when the cooks placed a white-frosted cake on the table. The cake was decorated with their crew emblem, the shuttle *Challenger* and each of their names.

At 7:20, they received their final weather briefing. They were told about the 25-degree temperature, the wind chill in the single digits and the ice at the pad. The day had dawned a pearly white, and it seemed better suited for riding a sleigh than a shuttle, but the winds had begun to weaken and the sky was clear. They were encouraged. None of them knew the dangers of a cold day.

"My kind of weather," Dick Scobee said. "What a great day for flying!"

A few minutes later, Scobee led the crew down the cement ramp past the roped-off throng of photographers, their steamy breath rising in unison. Resnik walked at his side. McNair appeared next, then Smith, who rubbed his hands together.

"Wo-o-o-o-o!" he said, shivering.

Like Resnik, Christa wore yellow gloves. She had rolled up her sleeves because they were too long. Her eyes were bright and the bounce was back in her stride. Christa was going to work. She was going up in space. She was smiling.

"Christa, hey, Christa!" the photographers shouted.

"We're going to go off today," she said hopefully, waving good-bye.

The cold pinched her cheeks as she crossed the catwalk. She saw icicles several feet long on the launch tower, and the giant external tank seemed to groan as its aluminum skin contracted from the chill of the fuel and the air. An unusual number of ground-crew workers huddled in the white room for shelter.

"We *are* going to go off today, aren't we?" Christa wondered aloud.

Scobee jumped around to keep warm, then donned his skullcap, helmet, safety harness and crawled into the orbiter. Smith followed, then Resnik, who hugged one of the technicians before boarding. As McNair inspected the hatch that had grounded them the day before, Johnny Corlew, a quality assurance inspector, gave Christa a gift—a red Rome apple.

Corlew, who had grown up in Indiana, had picked apples for his teachers from the tree in his family's yard. When he learned he had been assigned to the white room for the teacher-in-space mission, he had asked his wife to buy him one at the supermarket for Christa.

"Save it for me," Christa said, smiling, "and I'll eat it when I get back."

At 8:35, she shook Corlew's hand and entered the shuttle. Jarvis and McNair followed, then Corlew closed the hatch, drawing a round of applause from the rest of the ground crew. At last something had gone right.

Launch Control radioed the crew seconds later to test their headsets.

"Let's hope we go today," the controller said to Scobee.

"We'd like to do that," he said.

The temperature in the cabin was 61 degrees, cooler than Christa's apartment at Peachtree Lane.

"Brrrr," the controller said.

"Brrrr is right," said Scobee.

At Disney World, Steve had scraped the frost from the windshield of his rented car, gathered Scott and Caroline and headed to the space center, doubtful they would see a launch, indeed hoping they would see one only if the conditions were perfect. The conditions did not seem perfect.

"Good morning, Christa," the controller said, testing her headset. "Hope we go today."

"Good morning," she said in a teacher's singsong. "Hope so too."

Except for the "loud and clear" of a later radio test, they were her last known words.

At 9:08, a half hour before the original launch time, the countdown stopped unexpectedly. Rocco Petrone, the president of Rockwell Space Transportation Systems, a division of Rockwell International, which built and managed NASA's shuttle fleet, had seen television pictures of the icicles on the launch pad. Concerned that the icicles might snap during the lift-off and damage the tiles that protect the orbiter during reentry, he called the space agency to advise against a launch. NASA dispatched its ice inspection team.

Announcing the delay, launch director Gene Thomas told the crew they sat on "the northernmost pad we've got, and you can probably tell from the icicles out there how far north it is."

Then quickly, reassuringly, he added, "We're going to give you a ride today."

He was right. An hour later NASA managers determined the conditions were safe and ordered the countdown to resume, this time to a launch at 11:38. In the press center, a radio reporter from New Hampshire shouted into his microphone, "We are approaching the moment of truth!" Several rows in front of him, William Broad, the space writer for the *New York Times,* a hood tied snugly under his chin, hunched over his computer keyboard, typing with gloved hands. He thought it a strange day for a launch.

The news sparked a brief celebration in the viewing area, where spectators had waited as if the *Challenger* were an expectant mother. Their cheers might not have died so quickly in the breeze had more people stayed. Monday's delay had prompted thousands more to head home—Steve and Betsy Corrigan, Mike Smith's brother, Greg Jarvis's mother, Christa's college friends, her teaching colleagues from Maryland, her Girl Scout companions, many of her friends from Concord, the governor of New Hampshire and his son, the delegation from China, all but about twenty of the class of 51-L, hundreds who had come to see the teacher's launch, hundreds who had come simply to see a launch. Even at the space center campground, where dozens usually jammed the roofs of Winnebagos to whistle and wave to departing astronauts, only a faithful few remained.

The VIP bleachers were so nearly empty that NASA had bused in Scott McAuliffe's classmates from the parkway. Wearing red, white and blue baseball caps and bundled in every layer of clothing that fit, they stood with Christa's parents, who had left a more secluded viewing area to join the children as a symbol, they said, of Christa's commitment to education. Her sister Lisa and brother Christopher stood there as well. Christopher stirred a cup of cocoa for what seemed like minutes, his eyes fixed on the idle *Challenger.* Nearby, Steve's sister, Melissa, held her three-year-old daughter, Shana.

"Christa's just perfect for this," she said, excitement in her voice, her cheeks pink from the morning chill.

"Mommy," Shana said, "I want to go too."

Barbara Morgan sat a hundred yards away on the windblown roof of a shack next to the press grandstand, preparing to beam her "Mission Watch" program into the nation's classrooms. She dug her hands into the pockets of a light windbreaker, shivering while she waited for someone to bring her a sweater. She had delivered a bon voyage card to the crew two days earlier, and when Monday's launch had been scrubbed, she had reminded everyone, "We have to think about safety, but it's still going to be a wonderful mission."

Now it was 11:29. The final planned hold had ended and the giant digital clock had begun to tick again. The mercury had risen above the freezing point.

On a highway in Daytona, Joanne Brown, who had worn Christa's wedding dress in her own wedding, pulled over to watch the launch. Near Jacksonville, Patricia Mangum, whom Christa had taught to play the guitar, watched from a roadside with Christa's colleagues from her first years of teaching. One of their young daughters looked skyward through the red binoculars Santa had given her. In East Texas, Les Johnson, the chef from Pe-Te's who had introduced Christa to Cajun food, listened to the countdown on his car radio. At Steve's red-brick law offices in Concord, fifteen of his co-workers huddled about a television.

Eileen O'Hara sat surrounded by reporters before a television in the Concord High auditorium where Christa had said good-bye six months earlier. Students blew noisemakers and sounded the charge. Among them were Andy Bart, who intended to ask Christa by satellite how the world looked without boundaries, and Rick St. Hilaire, a space buff who planned to ask her how the toilet worked. O'Hara wore a shuttle pin Christa had given her and assured everyone that "so many thousands of people are checking everything" to ensure a safe launch. A balloon bobbed above her.

At a kindergarten five miles away, Rosemary Martin told her students they were not about to watch a scene from *Star Wars.*

"This is not a fantasy," she said slowly. "It's real, and it's extra special because Christa McAuliffe is just like Mrs. Martin. And Mrs. Martin wishes she could go, too."

At the Walker School, Josh McLeod and Nissa Barker, both six years old, moved closer to the television. They each wore two cardboard boxes covered with aluminum foil—one a space suit, the other a helmet that had holes for their eyes. Nissa wore an airpack she had made from a pink shoebox and had decorated with a yellow sun, a blue Earth and a red moon. She said she wanted to ride the *Challenger* as well.

"I would be a little bit scared," she said, "but mostly excited."

Not since the glories of the moon landings had space lured so many. From the Virgin Islands to an Eskimo village in the Arctic Circle, they waited—two and a half million students and their teachers, among them Christa's colleagues and most of the class of 51-L. They watched at the Sally Ride Elementary School near Houston, the McCall-Donnelly Elementary School in Idaho, the Thomas Johnson Middle School in Maryland. In Framingham, Charlie Sposato's English students continued working through the countdown. They studied *2001: A Space Odyssey.*

In the White House, Nancy Reagan sat before a television, awaiting the launch. The president was busy at work. He was scheduled to deliver his State of the Union address that night, a speech in which he would trumpet the success of the space program as the first private citizen circled the Earth.

Aboard *Challenger,* Christa lay on her back for the third straight hour. She had nothing to read, to see or to do but plenty to consider—her family, her students, the strange road that had taken her there, the unknown ride ahead of her, her mystery vacation with Steve afterward. One thing she did not consider were the first words she would relay back to Earth.

"I don't want to say anything phony or contrived," she had said earlier. "I want my perceptions to be honest. I want them to be just as natural as possible, and if they're very ordinary, well, that's okay. Maybe that's just me."

The visor on her airtight helmet had snapped shut. She was breathing pure oxygen. Beside her sat Greg Jarvis, who looked upon the flight as "the final act of a well-rehearsed play."

As the countdown dipped below three minutes, Mel Myler, the director of the New Hampshire chapter of the National Education Association, moved closer to his young son, who had recently sent Christa a note. The note said, "Thanks for getting me involved in the space program. Love, Jason."

Now they were chanting with dozens of others, "Gimme a *C* . . . gimme an *H* . . . gimme an *R* . . ."

At the Apollo Elementary School, the Sea Missile Motel, the Challenger Lounge, the Moon Hut Restaurant on Astronaut Highway, all along the space coast people stopped what they were doing and turned to the sky. Braced for the cold, reporters by the dozen filed out of the press center to their tables at the outdoor grandstand. Many of them had applied to ride with Mike Smith in September as the first journalist in space. Brian Ballard, the editor of the Concord High newspaper, stood with them, a video recorder in his right hand, a 35mm camera in his left, ready for the triumph that would help him forget the shooting tragedy that still haunted his school. Nearby, Linda Long, who described Christa as a twenty-first-century Cinderella, pulled a video recorder from her camera bag.

"Please, God," she said softly, "take care of Christa and the crew."

"Ninety seconds and counting," said the voice on the loudspeakers. "The 51-L mission ready to go."

Scott's classmates clapped in rhythm. The chaperones focused their cameras and binoculars. A banner behind them said GO CHRISTA!

"Have a good mission," launch director Gene Thomas told the crew.

"Thanks a bunch," Scobee said. "We'll see you when we get back."

At T-minus twenty-five seconds, *Challenger*'s computers ran through their final checks. Sea gulls swirled about the pad. Waves rolled against rocks on the shore. The crew waited. The ride Thomas promised them was about to begin.

The children counted in unison: "Ten, nine, eight . . ."

Christa's sister Lisa stepped back a row to stand with her parents. Grace clutched Lisa's shoulder with her right hand and pressed the fingers of her left into Ed's back. Ed pulled her close, and as he reached for Lisa's hand, he imagined Christa holding hands with Greg Jarvis, her eyes open wide. Christopher removed his teacher-in-space cap for the last time.

With six seconds to go, the main engines started and the shuttle disappeared in a steam cloud that rolled a mile in every direction. A NASA engineer held his breath.

"Bye, Christa," Barbara Morgan said, smiling and waving. "Bye, Christa."

On the roof of the Launch Control Center, Scott and Caroline stood at Steve's side, watching. Steve looked through the lens of his video camera, waiting. Then, at 11:38 A.M., the solid rocket boosters ignited and *Challenger* shook the Earth good-bye.

WEST WITH THE NIGHT

by Beryl Markham

I have seldom dreamed a dream worth dreaming again, or at least none worth recording. Mine are not enigmatic dreams; they are peopled with characters who are plausible and who do plausible things, and I am the most plausible amongst them. All the characters in my dreams have quiet voices like the voice of the man who telephoned me at Elstree one morning in September of nineteen-thirty-six and told me that there was rain and strong head winds over the west of England and over the Irish Sea, and that there were variable winds and clear skies in mid-Atlantic and fog off the coast of Newfoundland.

"If you are still determined to fly the Atlantic this late in the year," the voice said, "the Air Ministry suggests that the weather it is able to forecast for tonight, and for tomorrow morning, will be about the best you can expect."

The voice had a few other things to say, but not many, and then it was gone, and I lay in bed half-suspecting that the telephone call and the man who made it were only parts of the mediocre dream I had been dreaming. I felt that if I closed my eyes the unreal quality of the message would be re-established, and that, when I opened them again, this would be another ordinary day with its usual beginning and its usual routine.

But of course I could not close my eyes, nor my mind, nor my memory. I could lie there for a few moments—remembering how it had begun, and telling myself, with senseless repetition, that by tomorrow morning I should either have flown the Atlantic to America—or I should not have flown it. In either case this was the day I would try.

I could stare up at the ceiling of my bedroom in Aldenham House, which was a ceiling undistinguished as ceilings go, and feel less resolute than anxious, much less brave than foolhardy. I could say to myself, "You needn't do it, of course," knowing at the same time that nothing is so inexorable as a promise to your pride.

I could ask, "Why risk it?" as I have been asked since, and I could answer, "Each to his element." By his nature a sailor must sail, by his nature a flyer must fly. I could compute that I had flown a quarter of a million miles; and I could foresee that, so long as I had a plane and the sky was there, I should go on flying more miles.

There was nothing extraordinary in this. I had learned a craft and had worked hard learning it. My hands had been taught to seek the controls of a plane. Usage had taught them. They were at ease clinging to a stick, as a cobbler's fingers are in repose grasping an awl. No human pursuit achieves dignity until it can be called work, and when you can experience a physical loneliness for the tools of your trade, you see that the other things—the experiments, the irrelevant vocations, the vanities you used to hold—were false to you.

Record flights had actually never interested me very much for myself. There were people who thought that such flights were done for admiration and publicity, and worse. But of all the records—from Louis Blériot's first crossing of the English Channel in nineteen hundred and nine, through and beyond Kingsford Smith's flight from San Francisco to Sydney, Australia—none had been made by amateurs, nor by novices, nor by men or women less than hardened to failure, or less than masters of their trade. None of these was false. They were a company that simple respect and simple ambition made it worth more than an effort to follow.

The Carberrys (of Seramai) were in London and I could remember everything about their dinner party—even the menu. I could remember June Carberry and all her guests, and the man named McCarthy, who lived in Zanzibar, leaning across the table and saying, "J. C., why don't you finance Beryl for a record flight?"

I could lie there staring lazily at the ceiling and recall J. C.'s dry answer: "A number of pilots have flown the North Atlantic, west to east. Only Jim Mollison has done it alone the other way—from Ireland. Nobody has done it alone from England—man or woman. I'd be interested in that, but nothing else. If you want to try it, Burl, I'll back you. I think Edgar Percival could build a plane that would do it, provided you can fly it. Want to chance it?"

"Yes."

I could remember saying that better than I could remember anything—except J. C.'s almost ghoulish grin, and his remark that sealed the agreement: "It's a deal, Burl. I'll furnish the plane and you fly the Atlantic—but, gee, I wouldn't tackle it for a million. Think of all that black water! Think how cold it is!"

And I had thought of both.

I had thought of both for a while, and then there had been other things to think about. I had moved to Elstree, half-hour's flight from the Percival Aircraft Works at Gravesend, and almost daily for three months now I had flown down to the factory in a hired plane and watched the Vega Gull they were making for me. I had watched her birth and watched her growth. I had watched her wings take shape, and seen wood and fabric moulded to her ribs to form her long, sleek belly, and I had seen her engine cradled into her frame, and made fast.

The Gull had a turquoise-blue body and silver wings. Edgar Percival had made her with care, with skill, and with worry—the care of a veteran flyer, the skill of a master designer, and the worry of a friend. Actually the plane was a standard sport model with a range of only six hundred and sixty miles. But she had a special undercarriage built to carry the weight of her extra oil and petrol tanks. The tanks were fixed into the wings, into the centre section, and into the cabin itself. In the cabin they formed a wall around my seat, and each tank had a petcock of its own. The petcocks were important.

"If you open one," said Percival, "without shutting the other first, you may get an airlock. You know the tanks in the cabin have no gauges, so it may be best to let one run completely dry before opening the next. Your motor might go dead in the interval—but she'll start again. She's a De Havilland Gipsy—and Gipsys never stop."

I had talked to Tom. We had spent hours going over the Atlantic chart, and I had realized that the tinker of Molo, now one of England's great pilots, had traded his dreams and had got in return a better thing. Tom had grown older too; he had jettisoned a deadweight of irrelevant hopes and wonders, and had left himself a realistic code that had no room for temporizing or easy sentiment.

"I'm glad you're going to do it, Beryl. It won't be simple. If you can get off the ground in the first place, with such an immense load of fuel, you'll be alone in that plane about a night and a day—mostly night. Doing it east to west, the wind's against you. In September, so is the weather. You won't have a radio. If you misjudge your course only a few degrees, you'll end up in Labrador or in the sea—so don't misjudge anything."

Tom could still grin. He had grinned; he had said: "Anyway, it ought to amuse you to think that your financial backer lives on a farm called 'Place of Death' and your plane is being built at 'Gravesend.' If you were consistent, you'd christen the Gull 'The Flying Tombstone.' "

I hadn't been that consistent. I had watched the building of the plane and I had trained for the flight like an athlete. And now, as I lay in bed, fully awake, I could still hear the quiet voice of the man from the Air Ministry intoning, like the voice of a dispassionate court clerk: ". . . the weather for tonight and tomorrow . . . will be about the best you can expect." I should have liked to discuss the flight once more with Tom before I took off, but he was on a special job up north. I got out of bed and bathed and put on my flying clothes and took some cold chicken packed in a cardboard box and flew over to the military field at Abingdon, where the Vega Gull waited for me under the care of the R.A.F. I remember that the weather was clear and still.

Jim Mollison lent me his watch. He said: "This is not a gift. I wouldn't part with it for anything. It got me across the North Atlantic and the South Atlantic too. Don't lose it—and, for God's sake, don't get it wet. Salt water would ruin the works."

Brian Lewis gave me a life-saving jacket. Brian owned the plane I had been using between Elstree and Gravesend, and he had thought a long time about a farewell gift. What could be more practical than a pneumatic jacket that could be inflated through a rubber tube?

"You could float around in it for days," said Brian. But I had to decide between the life-saver and warm clothes. I couldn't have both, because of their bulk, and I hate the cold, so I left the jacket.

And Jock Cameron, Brian's mechanic, gave me a sprig of heather. If it had been a whole bush of heather, complete with roots growing in an earthen jar, I think I should have taken it, bulky or not. The blessing of Scotland, bestowed by a Scotsman, is not to be dismissed. Nor is the well-wishing of a ground mechanic to be taken lightly, for these men are the pilot's contact with reality.

It is too much that with all those pedestrian centuries behind us we should, in a few decades, have learned to fly; it is too heady a thought, too proud a boast. Only the dirt on a mechanic's hands, the straining vise, the splintered bolt of steel underfoot on the hangar floor—only these and such anxiety as the face of a Jock Cameron can hold for a pilot and his plane before a flight, serve to remind us that, not unlike the heather, we too are earthbound. We fly, but we have not "conquered" the air. Nature presides in all her dignity, permitting us the study and the use of such of her forces as we may understand. It is when we presume to intimacy, having been granted only tolerance, that the harsh stick falls across our impudent knuckles and we rub the pain, staring upward, startled by our ignorance.

"Here is a sprig of heather," said Jock, and I took it and pinned it into a pocket of my flying jacket.

There were press cars parked outside the field at Abingdon, and several press planes and photographers, but the R.A.F. kept everyone away from the grounds except technicians and a few of my friends.

The Carberrys had sailed for New York a month ago to wait for me there. Tom was still out of reach with no knowledge of my decision to leave, but that didn't matter so much, I thought. It didn't matter because Tom was unchanging—neither a fairweather pilot nor a fairweather friend. If for a month, or a year, or two years we sometimes had not seen each other, it still hadn't mattered. Nor did this. Tom would never say, "You should have let me know." He assumed that I had learned all that he had tried to teach me, and for my part, I thought of him, even then, as the merest student must think of his mentor. I could sit in a cabin overcrowded with petrol tanks and set my course for North America, but the knowledge of my hands on the controls would be Tom's knowledge. His words of caution and words of guidance, spoken so long ago, so many times, on bright mornings over the veldt or over a forest, or with a far mountain visible at the tip of our wing, would be spoken again, if I asked.

So it didn't matter, I thought. It was silly to think about.

You can live a lifetime and, at the end of it, know more about other people than you know about yourself. You learn to watch other people, but you never watch yourself because you strive against loneliness. If you read a book, or shuffle a deck of cards, or care for a dog, you are avoiding yourself. The abhorrence of loneliness is as natural as wanting to live at all. If it were otherwise, men would never have bothered to make an alphabet, nor to have fashioned words out of what were only animal sounds, nor to have crossed continents—each man to see what the other looked like.

Being alone in an aeroplane for even so short a time as a night and a day, irrevocably alone, with nothing to observe but your instruments and your own hands in semi-darkness, nothing to contemplate but the size of your small courage, nothing to wonder about but the beliefs, the faces, and the hopes rooted in your mind—such an experience can be as startling as the first awareness of a stranger walking by your side at night. You are the stranger.

It is dark already and I am over the south of Ireland. There are the lights of Cork and the lights are wet; they are drenched in Irish rain, and I am above them and dry. I am above them and the plane roars in a sobbing world, but it imparts no sadness to me. I feel the security of solitude, the exhilaration of escape. So long as I can see the lights and imagine the people walking under them, I feel selfishly triumphant, as if I have eluded care and left even the small sorrow of rain in other hands.

It is a little over an hour now since I left Abingdon. England, Wales, and the Irish Sea are behind me like so much time used up. On a long flight distance and time are the same. But there had been a moment when Time stopped—and Distance too. It was the moment I lifted the blue-and-silver Gull from the aerodrome, the moment the photographers aimed their cameras, the moment I felt the craft refuse its burden and strain toward the earth in sullen rebellion, only to listen at last to the persuasion of stick and elevators, the dogmatic argument of blueprints that said she *had* to fly because the figures proved it.

So she had flown, and once airborne, once she had yielded to the sophistry of a draughtsman's board, she had said, "There: I have lifted the weight. Now, where are we bound?"—and the question had frightened me.

"We are bound for a place thirty-six hundred miles from here—two thousand miles of it unbroken ocean. Most of the way it will be night. We are flying west with the night."

So there behind me is Cork; and ahead of me is Berehaven Lighthouse. It is the last light, standing on the last land. I watch it, counting the frequency of its flashes—so many to the minute. Then I pass it and fly out to sea.

The fear is gone now—not overcome nor reasoned away. It is gone because something else has taken its place; the confidence and the trust, the inherent belief in the security of land underfoot—now this faith is transferred to my plane, because the land has vanished and there is no other tangible thing to fix faith upon. Flight is but momentary escape from the eternal custody of earth.

Rain continues to fall, and outside the cabin it is totally dark. My altimeter says that the Atlantic is two thousand feet below me, my Sperry Artificial Horizon says that I am flying level. I judge my drift at three degrees more than my weather chart suggests, and fly accordingly. I am flying blind. A beam to follow would help. So would a radio—but then, so would clear weather. The voice of the man at the Air Ministry had not promised storm.

I feel the wind rising and the rain falls hard. The smell of petrol in the cabin is so strong and the roar of the plane so loud that my senses are almost deadened. Gradually it becomes unthinkable that existence was ever otherwise.

At ten o'clock P.M. I am flying along the Great Circle Course for Harbour Grace, Newfoundland, into a forty-mile headwind at a speed of one hundred and thirty miles an hour. Because of the weather, I cannot be sure of how many more hours I have to fly, but I think it must be between sixteen and eighteen.

At ten-thirty I am still flying on the large cabin tank of petrol, hoping to use it up and put an end to the liquid swirl that has rocked the plane since my take-off. The tank has no gauge, but written on its side is the assurance: "This tank is good for four hours."

There is nothing ambiguous about such a guaranty. I believe it, but at twenty-five minutes to eleven, my motor coughs and dies, and the Gull is powerless above the sea.

I realize that the heavy drone of the plane has been, until this moment, complete and comforting silence. It is the actual silence following the last splutter of the engine that stuns me. I can't feel any fear; I can't feel anything. I can only observe with a kind of stupid disinterest that my hands are violently active and know that, while they move, I am being hypnotized by the needle of my altimeter.

I suppose that the denial of natural impulse is what is meant by "keeping calm," but impulse has reason in it. If it is night and you are sitting in an aeroplane with a stalled motor, and there are two thousand feet between you and the sea, nothing can be more reasonable than the impulse to pull back your stick in the hope of adding to that two thousand, if only by a little. The thought, the knowledge, the law that tells you that your hope lies not in this, but in a contrary act—the act of directing your impotent craft toward the water—seems a terrifying abandonment, not only of reason, but of sanity. Your mind and your heart reject it. It is your hands—your stranger's hands—that follow with unfeeling precision the letter of the law.

I sit there and watch my hands push forward on the stick and feel the Gull respond and begin its dive to the sea. Of course it is a simple thing; surely the cabin tank has run dry too soon. I need only to turn another petcock . . .

But it is dark in the cabin. It is easy to see the luminous dial of the altimeter and to note that my height is now eleven hundred feet, but it is not easy to see a petcock that is somewhere near the floor of the plane. A hand gropes and reappears with an electric torch, and fingers, moving with agonizing composure, find the petcock and turn it; and I wait.

At three hundred feet the motor is still dead, and I am conscious that the needle of my altimeter seems to whirl like the spoke of a spindle winding up the remaining distance between the plane and the water. There is some lightning, but the quick flash only serves to emphasize the darkness. How high can waves reach—twenty feet, perhaps? Thirty?

It is impossible to avoid the thought that this is the end of my flight, but my reactions are not orthodox; the various incidents of my entire life do not run through my mind like a motion-picture film gone mad. I only feel that all this has happened before—and it has. It has all happened a hundred times in my mind, in my sleep, so that now I am not really caught in terror; I recognize a familiar scene, a familiar story with its climax dulled by too much telling.

I do not know how close to the waves I am when the motor explodes to life again. But the sound is almost meaningless. I see my hand easing back on the stick, and I feel the Gull climb up into the storm, and I see the altimeter whirl like a spindle again, paying out the distance between myself and the sea.

The storm is strong. It is comforting. It is like a friend shaking me and saying, 'Wake up! You were only dreaming.'

But soon I am thinking. By simple calculation I find that my motor had been silent for perhaps an instant more than thirty seconds.

I ought to thank God—and I do, though indirectly. I thank Geoffrey De Havilland who designed the indomitable Gipsy, and who, after all, must have been designed by God in the first place.

A lighted ship—the daybreak—some steep cliffs standing in the sea. The meaning of these will never change for pilots. If one day an ocean can be flown within an hour, if men can build a plane that so masters time, the sight of land will be no less welcome to the steersman of that fantastic craft. He will have cheated laws that the cunning of science has taught him how to cheat, and he will feel his guilt and be eager for the sanctuary of the soil.

I saw the ship and the daybreak, and then I saw the cliffs of Newfoundland wound in ribbons of fog. I felt the elation I had so long imagined, and I felt the happy guilt of having circumvented the stern authority of the weather and the sea. But mine was a minor triumph; my swift Gull was not so swift as to have escaped unnoticed. The night and the storm had caught her and we had flown blind for nineteen hours.

I was tired now, and cold. Ice began to film the glass of the cabin windows and the fog played a magician's game with the land. But the land was there. I could not see it, but I had seen it. I could not afford to believe that it was any land but the land I wanted. I could not afford to believe that my navigation was at fault, because there was no time for doubt.

South to Cape Race, west to Sydney on Cape Breton Island. With my protractor, my map, and my compass, I set my new course, humming the ditty that Tom had taught me: "Variation West—magnetic best. Variation East—magnetic least." A silly rhyme, but it served to placate, for the moment, two warring poles—the magnetic and the true. I flew south and found the lighthouse of Cape Race protruding from the fog like a warning finger. I circled twice and went on over the Gulf of Saint Lawrence.

After a while there would be New Brunswick, and then Maine—and then New York. I could anticipate. I could almost say, "Well, if you stay awake, you'll find it's only a matter of time now"—but there was no question of staying awake. I was tired and I had not moved an inch since that uncertain moment at Abingdon when the Gull had elected to rise with her load and fly, but I could not have closed my eyes. I could sit there in the cabin, walled in glass and petrol tanks, and be grateful for the sun and the light, and the fact that I could see the water under me. They were almost the last waves I had to pass. Four hundred miles of water, but then the land again—Cape Breton. I would stop at Sydney to refuel and go on. It was easy now. It would be like stopping at Kisumu and going on.

Success breeds confidence. But who has a right to confidence except the Gods? I had a following wind, my last tank of petrol was more than three-quarters full, and the world was as bright to me as if it were a new world, never touched. If I had been wiser, I might have known that such moments are, like innocence, short-lived. My engine began to shudder before I saw the land. It died, it spluttered, it started again and limped along. It coughed and spat black exhaust toward the sea.

There are words for everything. There was a word for this—airlock, I thought. This had to be an airlock because there was petrol enough. I thought I might clear it by turning on and turning off all the empty tanks, and so I did that. The handles of the petcocks were sharp little pins of metal, and when I had opened and closed them a dozen times, I saw that my hands were bleeding and that the blood was dropping on my maps and on my clothes, but the effort wasn't any good. I coasted along on a sick and halting engine. The oil pressure and the oil temperature gauges were normal, the magnetos working, and yet I lost altitude slowly while the realization of failure seeped into my heart. If I made the land, I should have been the first to fly the North Atlantic from England, but from my point of view, from a pilot's point of view, a forced landing was failure because New York was my goal. If only I could land and then take off, I would make it still . . . if only, if only . . .

The engine cuts again, and then catches, and each time it spurts to life I climb as high as I can get, and then it splutters and stops and I glide once more toward the water, to rise again and descend again, like a hunting sea bird.

I find the land. Visibility is perfect now and I see land forty or fifty miles ahead. If I am on my course, that will be Cape Breton. Minute after minute goes by. The minutes almost materialize; they pass before my eyes like links in a long slow-moving chain, and each time the engine cuts, I see a broken link in the chain and catch my breath until it passes.

The land is under me. I snatch my map and stare at it to confirm my whereabouts. I am, even at my present crippled speed, only twelve minutes from Sydney Airport, where I can land for repairs and then go on.

The engine cuts once more and I begin to glide, but now I am not worried; she will start again, as she has done, and I will gain altitude and fly into Sydney.

But she doesn't start. This time she's dead as death; the Gull settles earthward and it isn't any earth I know. It is black earth stuck with boulders and I hang above it, on hope and on a motionless propeller. Only I cannot hang above it long. The earth hurries to meet me, I bank, turn, and side-slip to dodge the boulders, my wheels touch, and I feel them submerge. The nose of the plane is engulfed in mud, and I go forward striking my head on the glass of the cabin front, hearing it shatter, feeling blood pour over my face.

I stumble out of the plane and sink to my knees in muck and stand there foolishly staring, not at the lifeless land, but at my watch.

Twenty-one hours and twenty-five minutes.

Atlantic flight. Abingdon, England, to a nameless swamp—nonstop.

A Cape Breton Islander found me—a fisherman trudging over the bog saw the Gull with her tail in the air and her nose buried, and then he saw me floundering in the embracing soil of his native land. I had been wandering for an hour and the black mud had got up to my waist and the blood from the cut in my head had met the mud halfway.

From a distance, the fisherman directed me with his arms and with shouts toward the firm places in the bog, and for another hour I walked on them and came toward him like a citizen of Hades blinded by the sun, but it wasn't the sun; I hadn't slept for forty hours.

He took me to his hut on the edge of the coast and I found that built upon the rocks there was a little cubicle that housed an ancient telephone —put there in case of shipwrecks.

I telephoned to Sydney Airport to say that I was safe and to prevent a needless search being made. On the following morning I did step out of a plane at Floyd Bennett Field and there was a crowd of people still waiting there to greet me, but the plane I stepped from was not the Gull, and for days while I was in New York I kept thinking about that and wishing over and over again that it had been the Gull, until the wish lost its significance, and time moved on, overcoming many things it met on the way.

Acknowledgments

"To the Planet of the Apes" from *The Planet of the Apes* by Pierre Boulle. Copyright © 1963 by Pierre Boulle. Reprinted by permission of Vanguard Press, a Division of Random House, Inc., and Martin Secker & Warburg Limited.

"To Saturn and Back" from *The Martian Way* by Isaac Asimov. Copyright 1952 by the Galaxy Publishing Corporation and 1955 by Isaac Asimov. All rights reserved. Used by permission of Isaac Asimov.

"Leonardo da Vinci: Pioneer in Aviation" from *The Mechanical Investigations of Leonardo da Vinci* by Ivor B. Hart. Copyright © 1963 by the Regents of the University of California.

"Human-Powered Flight Across the English Channel" from *Gossamer Odyssey: The Triumph of Human-Powered Flight* by Morton Grosser and Paul B. MacCready, Jr. Copyright © 1981 by Morton Grosser and Paul B. MacCready, Jr. Reprinted by permission of Houghton Mifflin Company and Julian Bach Literary Agency, Inc.

"Up in the First Balloon" from *Bag of Smoke: The Story of the First Balloon* by John Lonzo Anderson. Copyright 1942 and renewed 1968 by John Lonzo Anderson and Adrienne Adams. Reprinted by permission of Alfred A. Knopf, Inc.

"The Greatest Air Voyage Ever Made" from *Lighter Than Air Flight* by Jack R. Hunt. From *Flying Magazine,* May 1959 issue. Copyright © 1989 DCI. All Rights Reserved. Reprinted by permission of Mrs. Jack R. Hunt and Diamandis Communications Inc.

"Floating on Air" from *Song of the Sky* by Guy Murchie. Copyright © 1954 by Guy Murchie. All rights reserved. Reprinted by permission of Guy Murchie.

"The Last Flight of the R-101" from *The Airmen Who Would Not Die* by John G. Fuller. Copyright © 1979 by John G. Fuller. All rights reserved. Reprinted by permission of International Creative Management.

"The Loss of the 'Shenandoah' " from *Up Ship!* by C. E. Rosendahl. Copyright 1931 by Dodd, Mead and Company, Inc. All rights reserved. Reprinted by permission of Dodd, Mead and Company, Inc.

"The End of the 'Hindenburg' " from *Who Destroyed the "Hindenburg?"* by A. A. Hoehling. Copyright © 1962 by A. A. Hoehling. All rights reserved. Reprinted by permission of A. A. Hoehling.

"The First Flights of Igor I. Sikorsky" from *The Story of the Winged-S: An Autobiography* by Igor I. Sikorsky. Copyright 1938 by Dodd, Mead and Company, Inc. All rights reserved. Reprinted by permission of Dodd, Mead and Company Inc.

"Alcock and Brown Fly the Atlantic" from *Famous First Flights That Challenged History* by Lowell Thomas and Lowell Thomas, Jr. Copyright © 1968 by Lowell Thomas and Lowell Thomas, Jr. All rights reserved. Used by permission of Lowell Thomas, Jr.

"New York to Paris" from *We* by Charles A. Lindbergh. Copyright 1927, © 1955 by Charles A. Lindbergh. Reprinted by permission of Putnam Publishing Group.

"*Columbia* Lands in Germany" from *Oceans, Poles and Airmen* by Richard Montague. Copyright © 1971 by Richard Montague. Reprinted by permission of Random House, Inc.

"First To The North Pole" from *Skyward* by Richard Evelyn Byrd. Copyright 1928 by Richard E. Byrd. All rights reserved. Reprinted by permission of Richard E. Byrd III.

"The Flight of the *Southern Cross*" from *The Flight of the Southern Cross* by C. E. Kingsford-Smith and C. T. P. Ulm. Copyright 1929 by Robert M. McBride Company. Reprinted by permission of Crown Publishers, Inc.

"And Tomorrow" from *Pylon* by William Faulkner. Copyright 1935 and renewed 1963 by William Faulkner. Reprinted by permission of Random House, Inc., and Curtis Brown Ltd, London.

"The Great Sky Duel" from *They Flew the Bendix Race* by Don Dwiggins. Copyright © 1965 by Don Dwiggins. Reprinted by permission of Harper & Row, Publishers, Inc.

"The Wing Walker" from *Guy Gilpatric's Flying Stories* by Guy Gilpatric. Copyright 1946 by Guy Gilpatric. All rights reserved. Reprinted by permission of the publisher, E. P. Dutton, a division of Penguin Books USA, Inc.

"Downing My First Hun" from *Fighting the Flying Circus* by Eddie V. Rickenbacker. Copyright 1919 by Eureka Pictures, Inc., renewed 1947 by Edward V. Rickenbacker. Reprinted by permission of William F. Rickenbacker.

"The Day They Got Richthofen" from *Great Air Battles* by Gene Gurney. Used by permission of Gene Gurney.

"A Most Remarkable Escape" from *Winged Victory* by V. M. Yeates. Copyright © 1934 by Jonathan Cape, Ltd. Reprinted by permission of Jonathan Cape Ltd.

"They Called Him the Indestructible 'Balloon Buster'" by James C. Law. Copyright © March 1955 by Air Force Association. All rights reserved. Reprinted by permission of Air Force Association.

"The Revolutionary 'Spitfire'" from *Fly For Your Life* by Larry Forrester. Copyright © 1956, 1973 by Larry Forrester. Reprinted by permission of Century Hutchinson Publishing Group Limited and David Higham Associates Limited.

"Patrol Over Dunkirk" from *Reach for the Sky: The Story of Douglas Bader, Legless Ace of the Battle of Britain* by Paul Brickhill. Copyright 1954 by Paul Brickhill, renewed 1982. Reprinted by permission of W. W. Norton & Company, Inc., and the Watkins/Loomis Agency, Inc.

"Miracle at Sunset" from *Here Is Your War* by Ernie Pyle. Copyright 1943 by Lester Cowan and renewed 1971 by Holt, Rinehart and Winston. Reprinted by permission of Henry Holt and Company, Inc.

"Mustangs *vs* Messerschmitts" from *Goodbye, Mickey Mouse* by Len Deighton. Copyright © 1982 by Len Deighton. Reprinted by permission of Alfred A. Knopf, Inc., and Century Hutchinson Publishing Group Limited.

"I Flew for the Führer" from *I Flew For the Führer* by Heinz Knöke, translated by John Ewing. Copyright 1953, 1954 by Heinz Knöke. Reprinted by permission of Henry Holt and Company, Inc., and Unwin Hyman Limited.

"The Blond Knight of Germany" from *The Blond Knight of Germany* by Raymond F. Toliver and Trevor J. Constable. Copyright © 1970 by Raymond F. Toliver and Trevor J. Constable. All rights reserved. Reprinted by permission of the authors.

"Back to Bologna" from *Catch-22* by Joseph Heller. Copyright © 1955, 1961 by Joseph Heller. Reprinted by permission of Simon & Schuster, Inc., and A. M. Heath as agent for Joseph Heller. Published in the United Kingdom by Jonathan Cape Ltd.

"Attack on Pearl Harbor" from *Day of Infamy* by Walter Lord. Copyright © 1957 and renewed 1985 by Walter Lord. Reprinted by permission of Henry Holt and Company, Inc., and Sterling Lord Literistic, Inc.

"The Milk Run" from *Tales of the South Pacific* by James A. Michener. Copyright 1946, 1947 by Curtis Publishing Company. Copyright 1947 by James A. Michener, renewed 1974. Reprinted by permission of Macmillan Publishing Company.

"Dropping the Bomb Over Hiroshima" from *Seven Hours to Zero* by Joseph Marx. Copyright © 1965, 1967 by Joseph L. Marx. Reprinted by permission of The Putnam Publishing Group and Curtis Brown Ltd.

"The Rescue" from *The Wild Blue* by Walter J. Boyne and Steven L. Thompson. Copyright © 1986 by Walter J. Boyne and Steven L. Thompson. Used by permission of Crown Publishers, Inc., and Century Hutchinson Publishing Group Limited.

"Fifteen Sams for Geeno" from *Thud Ridge* by Col. Jack Broughton. Copyright © 1969 by Jacksel M. Broughton. Reprinted by permission of Bantam Books, a division of Bantam, Doubleday, Dell Publishing Group, Inc.

"Forced to Eject Over Hanoi" from *Flight of the Intruder* by Stephen Coonts. Copyright © 1986 by the U.S. Naval Institute, Annapolis, Maryland.

"The Elements" from *Wind, Sand and Stars* by Antoine de Saint-Exupéry. Copyright 1939 by Antoine de Saint-Exupéry and renewed 1967 by Lewis Galantière. Reprinted by permission of Harcourt Brace Jovanovich, Inc., and William Heinemann Ltd.

"First Across the Tasman Sea—Alone" from *The Lonely Sea and the Sky* by Francis Chichester. Copyright © 1964 by Francis Chichester. All rights reserved. Reprinted by permission of Francis Chichester Ltd.

"In a Typhoon's Eye" from *I Flew for China* by Royal Leonard. Copyright 1942 by Royal Leonard. Reprinted by permission of Doubleday, a division of Bantam, Doubleday, Dell Publishing Group, Inc.

"Sucked Up In a Thundercloud" by David Lampe, Jr. From *Flying* Magazine, April 1956 issue. Copyright © 1989 DCI. All rights reserved.

"Humility Learned" from *Fate is the Hunter* by Ernest K. Gann. Copyright © 1961 by Ernest K. Gann. Reprinted by permission of Simon & Schuster, Inc., the author, and the author's agent Scott Meredith Literary Agency, Inc., 845 Third Avenue, New York, New York 10022.

"Over the Matterhorn—?" from *The Flying Carpet* by Richard Halliburton. Copyright 1932 by Bobbs-Merrill Co., renewed 1960. Reprinted by permission of Bobbs-Merrill Co., an imprint of Macmillan Publishing Company.

"Clear Ice! The Emperor's Acting Up!" from *The Proving Flight.* Copyright © 1956 by David Beaty. All rights reserved. Used by permission of David Beaty.

"The Crash" from *Alive: The Story of the Andes Survivors.* Copyright © 1974 by Piers Paul Read. Reprinted by permission of Harper & Row, Publishers, Inc., and Aitken & Stone Limited.

"The Flight to East Hampton" from *Flights* by Jim Shepard. Copyright © 1983 by Jim Shepard. Reprinted by permission of Alfred A. Knopf, Inc., and the Liz Darhansoff Agency.

"Hell at 40,000 Feet" from *The Silken Angels: A History of Parachuting* by Martin Caidin. All rights reserved. Copyright © 1963 by Martin Caidin. Reprinted by permission of Martin Caidin.

"Yeager Breaks the Sound Barrier" from *The Right Stuff* by Tom Wolfe. Copyright © 1979 by Tom Wolfe. Reprinted by permission of Farrar, Straus and Giroux, Inc., and Peters Fraser & Dunlop Group Ltd.

"Approach to Chaumont" from *Stranger to the Ground* by Richard Bach. Copyright © 1982 by Alternate Futures, Inc. PSP. All rights reserved. Reprinted by permission of Alternate Futures, Inc. PSP.

"The Experimental Flight of the US-XP" from *The Flight of Chariots* by Jon Cleary. Copyright © 1963 by Jon Cleary. Reproduced by permission of William Morrow and Company, Inc., and Collins Publishers, London.

"They Had a Right to Live" from *The Target Is Destroyed* by Seymour M. Hersh. Copyright © 1986 by Seymour M. Hersh. Reprinted by permission of Random House, Inc., and Peters Fraser & Dunlop Group Ltd.

"The Re-Entry" from *We Seven* by John H. Glenn, Jr. Copyright © 1962 by Simon & Schuster, Inc. Reprinted by permission of Simon & Schuster, Inc.

"Footprints on the Moon" from *Americans to the Moon* by Gene Gurney. Copyright © 1970 by Gene Gurney. Reprinted by permission of Random House, Inc.

"Reactivating Star Wars' *Ice Fortress*" from *Flight of the Old Dog* by Dale Brown. Copyright © 1987 by Dale Brown. All rights reserved. Reprinted by permission of Donald I. Fine, Inc.

"Mexican Flight" from *Last Flight* by Amelia Earhart. Copyright 1937 by Harcourt, Brace and Company, Inc., renewed 1964 by Mrs. George Palmer Putnam. Used by permission of Orion Books.

"On Top of the World" from *On Top of the World* by Sheila Scott. Copyright © 1973 by Sheila Scott. Used by permission of Laurence Pollinger Limited as agent for the Estate of Sheila Scott.

"My First Solo Flight" from *On Extended Wings* by Diane Ackerman. Copyright © 1985 by Diane Ackerman. Reprinted with the permission of Atheneum Publishers, an imprint of the Macmillan Publishing Company, and Diane Ackerman.

"Christa McAuliffe: 'First Teacher in Space' " from *I Touch the Future . . . The Story of Christa McAuliffe* by Robert T. Hohler. Copyright © 1986 by Robert T. Hohler. Reprinted by permission of Random House, Inc.

"West With the Night" from *West With the Night* by Beryl Markham. Copyright © 1983 by Beryl Markham. All rights reserved. Used by permission of North Point Press.